Holy War, Martyrdom, and Terror

Holy War, Martyrdom, and Terror

Christianity, Violence, and the West, ca. 70 C.E. to the Iraq War

Philippe Buc

PENN

UNIVERSITY OF PENNSYLVANIA PRESS

PHILADELPHIA

A volume in the Haney Foundation series, established in 1961 with the generous support of Dr. John Louis Haney

Gedruckt mit Unterstützung der Historisch-Kulturwissenschaftlichen Fakultät der Universität Wien

Faculty of Historical and Cultural Studies

Published by
University of Pennsylvania Press
Philadelphia, Pennsylvania 19104-4112
www.upenn.edu/pennpress

Printed in the United States of America on acid-free paper
10 9 8 7 6 5 4 3 2 1

A Cataloging-in-Publication Record is available from the Library of Congress
ISBN 978-0-8122-4685-8

Contents

Preface

I began writing on this theme—Christianity and violence—at the edge of the desert. The setting was Morocco, 2001–2002. The occasion was an Arabic-language collective volume devoted to the violence and the "religions of the book," where I traced for a local audience some longue durée themes in the Western understanding of coercion.[1] The trigger was an attempt to understand, like many others but as a medievalist, the by then already clear march to war. The medievalist realized, to his surprise, that he could make sense of some of the American president's language. It became clearer, somehow, for instance, when set next to the letters of Pope Gregory VII. The enterprise mushroomed in the direction of a book when I gave a talk in 2004 at the École Française de Rome on "God's Vengeance," attempting to show the advantages of an exploration of First Crusade sources in the light of biblical exegesis. The question then became: What can traits specific to Western Christianity (and transported over time into less religious, "post-Christian" Western cultures) explain about mass violence in the West? As will become clearer to the reader in the course of his or her reading, it is a thought experiment concentrating on religion and ideology as conditions of possibility and leaving aside other factors at play in violence. The essay has also ended up focusing on Western bellicism to the detriment of Western pacifism, which these traits admittedly also help explain.

The bulk of the examination was conducted between 2004 and 2011, while I taught at Stanford University; and also on sabbatical in 2005–2006 at Yale. Some of my teaching fed into the research—in particular a course taught with Amir Weiner titled "Mass Violence in History" and a graduate seminar on secularity, which was accompanied by a small international conference on the topic.

Since I began thinking about this topic, powerfully conceptualized books have appeared focusing on medieval violence, a period central to this essay. Pride of place go to Norman Housley's splendid *Religious Warfare in Europe*

1400–1536 (Oxford: 2002), published as I began my research (a work much more nuanced than this text can ever be), and to several works by Jean Flori. I consulted Jay Rubenstein's elegant *Armies of Heaven* (New York: 2011) too late to benefit fully from it, but there was much convergence between his work on the First Crusade and mine, simply owing to our both being students at Berkeley of the late Gerry Caspary. Among books fundamental for this study should also be mentioned three works devoted to the early modern French wars of religion, all three by Denis Crouzet. To him I owe both concepts and beautiful sources.[2] My debts to Crouzet and Housley, when detailed, would overtax the endnotes. Yet, in almost all cases in which I use primary sources cited or discussed by colleagues, including Crouzet's, I have followed these texts back to their original or critical edition. Some colleagues may find my footnotes not fully up to 2014 standards. There is a dual explanation for this. One, the bibliography is ever-growing. Two, I pretty much stopped consulting an ever-growing historiography in 2009, concentrating on conceptualization and writing. By September 2011, I had moved to the University of Vienna, which did lead to a little more reading in German-language historiography. Duties there, however, prevented greedy assimilation of great masses of materials, for which the Press, ink-spitting squids, and trees will likely be grateful.

Introduction. The Object of This History

> Well, to compare like with like, the majority of our educated class is now suffering from an Abderite epidemic. They are not stage-struck, indeed; that would have been a minor infatuation—to be possessed with other people's verses, not bad ones either, no. But from the beginning of the present excitements—the barbarian war, the Armenian disaster, the succession of victories—you cannot find a man but is writing history; nay, every one you meet is a Thucydides, a Herodotus, a Xenophon. The old saying must be true, and war be the father of all things, seeing what a litter of historians it has now teemed forth at a birth.

Fabula de te narrat—Lucian of Samosata's second-century C.E. fable speaks about us. There was (and is) a war, Heraclitus's "father of all things" (*polemos hapantōn pater*), and many among us scholars took not the sword but the pen. How is the pen wielded for these pages? The historian's intended craft is best delimited, initially at least, through negatives and caveats.

Ambit and Approach: Western Religious Forms and Violence

This essay explores two millennia of Western Christian and post-Christian violence in the West. In "violence" are included holy war, terror and terrorism, and (paradoxically as it may seem at first) martyrdom.[1] By "the West" is meant the cultural areas located in what was, circa 1500, Roman Catholic Europe (plus, an offshoot of the Protestant branch, what became the United States of America). By "post-Christian" is meant not the absence of Christian religion or religiosity but a zone in which, while religious institutions and beliefs no longer seem to organize culture, the inheritance of these institutions and beliefs still shapes culture substantially. The book's intent is not, however, to provide a total narrative that would begin with earliest Christianity and end in the present. It would take too many pages, and it would never be complete enough. Instead, a number of historical moments (for instance, in Chapter 4, the First Crusade, the eve of the American Civil War, and the Stalinist purge of 1937–1938) are mobilized to bring out commonalities and continuities. Even less does this essay aim to explain or understand violence across cultures and time. To scroll back to the beginnings of humanity would make for a very different book, in fact an impossibly huge book.[2] Nor will the essay generalize across historical cultures, as does, for example, Mark Juergensmeyer's stimulating *Terror in the Mind of God*. Influenced by René Girard's dubious but highly popular model, Juergensmeyer proposes that spectacular terror can be explained by an essence shared by all religions. "Public ritual," he writes, "has traditionally been the province of religion, and this is one of the reasons that performance violence comes so naturally to activists from a religious background." Juergensmeyer then cites David C. Rapoport's observation "that the two topics [of religion and terrorism] fit together not only because there is a violent streak within the history of religion, but also because terrorist acts have a symbolic side and in this sense mimic religious rites."[3] But, as Juergensmeyer would be the first to acknowledge, the analysis cannot remain at the level of anthropological universals. One should also politely differ with Schmuel Eisenstadt, who considers that radical religious violence is a common tendency for all religions stemming from the Axial Age (which all have monotheistic or henotheistic leanings). It is likely not by chance that Eisenstadt's best examples stem from the three monotheistic Religions of the Book—Judaism, Christianity, and Islam.[4] It is thus methodologically safer (albeit still risky) to descend to a lesser level of generality. This essay's ambition is thus to sketch out how a fairly systematic set of beliefs and conceptions, Christianity, has left an imprint on violence: in other words, to draw the contours of what is specific to Christian and post-Christian violence, as opposed, for example, to North American Native "mourning" warfare (oriented to honor and reproduction, and whose antithesis was trade) or to a violence enacted in the Aztec cultural world and shaped by Mexica (Aztec or Tenochca) cosmology (oriented to feeding the gods and maintaining the world with blood-sacrifice).[5] Rather than looking for invariants across religions, the essay proposes that Christian monotheism's historical semantics account for quite idiosyncratic forms of violence. It provided the "symbolic matrix" for holy war, martyrdom, and terror, and it "imprinted" itself on successive manifestations of violence.[6]

Islam has been mentioned. This author's lack of expertise makes him shy away from definitive pronouncements on Muslim violence. There is a further ground for caution: since the nineteenth century and in particular G. W. F. Hegel, the intellectual histories and analyses of exalted European movements and of Islam have cross-contaminated one another to the point that Islam (including modern Muslim fundamentalisms), Bolshevism, and the French Revolution have been assimilated to one another, or so tightly compared as to imply some subterranean identity or intimate affinity.[7] Still, tentative suggestions in the conditional or hypothetical mode will appear here and there, given what the two monotheisms share (most obvious may be the cognate of the Christian pair material warfare and spiritual warfare, lesser Jihad and greater Jihad).[8] The study will also leave aside Orthodox Christianity, in part because Byzantium did not know holy war.[9]

This lesser but still high level of generalization—across the whole Christian and post-Christian West—may seem vulnerable to the sort of critique just levied against the Girardian school. There are indeed undeniable and significant differences between—to name just a few political cultures—Civil War England, Revolutionary France, crusader Catholic Europe, New Left 1970s Germany, and America from the seventeenth century onward.[10] Recent scholarship tends to insist on the "diversity" of American Christianity (preferring to speak of "Christianities," plural), but, depending on what it is seeking to explain, an analysis can chose to lump as much as to split. Indeed, next to what distinguishes them, what they have in common should factor in reflections on Western violence.[11] The differences between sects or denominations were generative of internal hostilities within Western Christendom and were hugely important for believers. Yet, in many cases, they were blurred in the process of competition. This was especially the case in America, but not only there.[12]

Second, the discussion has to tread lightly but precisely around the concept of "secularization." By this is not meant what popular usage shares with an important strand of serious scholarship, that is, the fact that formal and informal religious institutions have lost centrality in and influence over culture, society, and politics, and that religion has become increasingly relegated to the private sphere, along with various forms of "separation of Church and State."[13] Rather, it engages a more recent acceptance of the term, in which, paradoxically, the state (and the nation) may have on the surface separated itself from the Church (and the *ecclesia* as a human community) but is its twin and heir, as, for instance, Ernst Kantorowicz argued in the 1950s.[14] Promoted by Karl Löwith and Carl Schmitt, yet implicit in many narratives of long-term historical processes, this other concept of "secularization" posits that religious notions survived into Modernity: they morphed into ideas and ideologies that were stripped of the supernatural and of God, but that retained similar structures. Thus, for instance, Christianity's linear time with its promise of a better world and an improved humankind transmuted itself into the notion of progress. (A possible corollary—and one that has been drawn—is that secularization, given that it preserves the preexisting structures, allows a return of the religious.) In the 1960s, Hans Blumenberg challenged Schmitt and Löwith with a counterthesis: there is not any substantial and hidden continuity between the religious Middle Ages and the Modern Age. Rather, once the Middle Ages had raised some questions, Modernity was forced to take up these self-same questions. But it did so on the basis of its own different epistemology and science. This process, which Blumenberg calls the "re-occupation" of preexisting "positions," produces the illusion of a continuum.[15] How to take sides in this debate? In some complicated middle, as is often the case. It stands to reason that, while Blumenberg may be right for some Modern notions, which are by no means "secularized" premodern ideas, Schmitt and Löwith may be right for others.

When it comes to violence, what then is the nature of the continuities, if any, between the deep Christian past and more Modern cultures? Are we dealing with a continuum of cultural substances, on which religious conceptions gave birth to offspring that have lost references to God and the churches yet kept many of the characteristics of their theological forebears? Or did Modern men and women reinvent—more or less purposefully and consciously—a culture of violence, using materials mined in the half-sunken shafts of the premodern past, in particular its books? Or, in the words of a recent study of the Lutheran moment, are we not dealing, as opposed to a continuity whose definition implies linearity and causality, rather with "the serialization (*Fortsetzung*; also "installment") of discourses, of practices of remembrance, and of recapitulations"?[16] Whichever hypothesis is true, two things stand to reason. First, that the premodern culture of religious violence did not give birth to its Modern offspring without human agency; men and women are not automata but, within the cultures where they dwell, make choices. Second, that innovations—the creation of ideologies of violence using premodern materials—were meaningful only because, at the moment at which these innovations took place, these cultures from which elements of the new were mined had a force of their own.[17] Thus we are not dealing with mutually exclusive mechanisms. The coexistence of continuity and purposeful reinvention is particularly visible for the French Revolution's most radical phase. In 1792–1794, despite an ideology of radical innovation and defiance vis-à-vis Catholicism, the new ideas were meaningful and made sense to contemporaries because they could connect to tropes that were present in France's inherited religious past.

The debate about secularization raises the complicated issue of the relationship between religion and politics in the West. Through different avatars, the *conceptual* distinction between religion and politics belongs to Western history since Early Christianity. But the coexistence of two much more recent concepts, those of "civil religion" (developed relatively recently to analyze a United States where religiousness serves as the backbone of national political identity, but going back to Jean-Jacques Rousseau and before him to Ancient Rome) and of "political religion" (seeking to account for the dynamics of Fascism, Nazism, and Soviet Communism, where a political ideology was made into a set of beliefs and liturgies) suggests the deep interpenetration *in practice* of religion and politics as spheres or dimensions, well into the contemporary era. In their more violent forms, but also as human institutions espousing peace as a value, Modern Western nations are the heirs through secularization of earlier cultic communities.[18] Furthermore, as we shall discuss in Chapter 7, premodern thinkers, even while distinguishing between spheres, long considered it to be religion's duty and right to organize societies and polities or attributed to the religious dimensions duties and rights we now categorize as political.[19] A person could thus perceive a reprehensible "political" behavior in religious matters or allege a transgression of the boundary between politics and religion to the detriment of the latter; but the same person could grant a religious valence to some issues Modernity sees as political.

Third, to Christianity alone should not be attributed the causation of violence. This study does concentrate on the dark side of Western Christianity's imprint. This may lead some among its readership to conclude that this specific religion has been a nefarious factor. However, other cultures have perpetrated massacres and indulged in extreme violence. The Puritans' ruthless warfare in seventeenth-century North America was well matched by Native tribes' terror tactics, involving gruesome mutilations.[20] The thirteenth-century Mongols, in overrunning much of Central Asia, left carefully constructed piles of skulls before conquered towns to intimidate would-be resisters. Furthermore, for the West, if one searches after causality, other factors than Christianity came into play. The brutal slaughter on medieval battlefields of plebeian infantry, without the chance of ransom extended to their aristocratic betters, had nothing to do with belief in God and sanctified warfare.[21] Circa 1900, the

German military was beholden to a culture that privileged results, celebrated will and strength, and had transformed total victory—for Carl von Clauzewitz a means to efficient international politics—into an end in itself. In South-West Africa, with the war of 1904–1907 and its aftermath, quasi-genocidal massacres and lethal deportations were perpetrated on the Herero natives.[22] For the Nazi atrocities, against Daniel Goldhagen's extreme and monocausal emphasis on German antisemitic beliefs, Christopher Browning has under-lined group dynamics and the pressures of war, and has discussed the existence and limits of the choices faced by ordinary Germans charged with the imple-mentation of elements of the "final solution" in occupied Poland.[23] Human beings are influenced by plural institutions; they wear multiple *habitus*; and cultures are never fully integrated. Were the opposite true, men and women would not have any freedom; history would be totally predictable. And it is not.[24] The patterns in Christian and post-Christian violence that this study seeks to highlight had force, sometimes great force, but never obligatory force.

Martin Aurell has inventoried anew those medieval voices, lay as well as clerical, that criticized or refused (which is not quite the same thing) the Cru-sades.[25] They were a minority, but they existed. More fundamentally perhaps, it is important to affirm here forcefully that, if one embarks on the ship of value judgments, one should also see that Christianity has engendered mature human rights and just-war doctrines. It has also brought into being intense commitment to humanitarian action, as Hans-Lukas Kieser has recently shown in the case of American Evangelicals at the beginning of the twentieth century.[26] Furthermore, some among us may appreciate that weapons can be drawn for the sake of justice and to save other human beings from despotism and oppression. This drive and its legitimacy stem from the same tradition. One must concur with Norman Housley's verdict on the European crusades. Housley noticed two seemingly contradictory scholarly positions, one "blam-ing crusading for the quasi-veneration with which war was so often regarded in the Middle Ages," the other underlining that "the constant probing of in-tention and conscience that was generated by this explicit identification of violence with God's will played a significant role in sustaining the ethical di-mension in European warfare." He proposed "that these two viewpoints are equally valid and that crusading helped both to militarize the medieval Church and to sustain an ongoing critique of what warfare was for in a world that was supposedly Christian."[27]

This insight can be extended to beyond the Middle Ages and related to a fundamental theological principle that will be detailed in Chapter 2. The complicated Western Christian dialectic between peace and the sword has not only brought negatives to global politics; the habitual dispositions it has generated are Janus-faced. The form that human rights and just war have taken is genealogically unthinkable without Christianity, just as the form that sanctified warfare and terrorism have taken is genealogically unthinkable without Christianity. This form is unthinkable—and therefore not understandable—if by understanding is meant the ability to apprehend past human action in terms that would not be outlandish to the actors themselves and to their contemporaries. And it is about "form" that we concern ourselves here.

This "form" is a set of constellations or formulas, each of which draws from the same, shared, and limited pool of ideas and practices. Not all these ideas and practices are present in each constellation. But there is a degree of regularity in their expression over time. Given this, the constellations into which they are combined are highly comparable to one another. Thus, this essay adapts to the historical episodes that it mines what Marcel Gauchet posits about the "Jesus Event": the irruption of Jesus in history and its impact "exploited, in a contingent manner, possibilities that were themselves necessarily linked." For Gauchet, elaborating on Max Weber, the actors in history act "within a range of clearly defined possibilities"—possibilities, according to him, produced by the progressive unfolding of the history of religions.[28] Violence, far from being a full invariant and far from being infinitely variable, has shape and form depending on the religions that have molded its actors and their conceptions. With the great French medievalist Marc Bloch and with Michel Foucault, one should of course be wary of "idolizing origins," and of assuming that origins alone can explain historical phenomena often located far from them. But when origins are made present over and over again in a culture, they should be looked at causally. Christianity idolizes origins; in this sense the early Christian centuries were critical. The now plural Christianities are religions of dogma and of books, and these Words and written words, smoothly transmitted or jaggedly rediscovered, did compose serializations or installments (*Fortsetzungen*) that are part of any explanation and, certainly, partial keys for any understanding. The Christian cultural sphere escapes, thus, in part Bloch and Foucault's generally valid critique.[29]

It should be clear by now that these pages will take religion very seriously. When dealing with a topic such as this one, stretching over two millennia, two symmetrical approaches offer themselves. Historians can account for the past of holy war and religious terror with the help of present-day models. They can also consider their own present's sanctified warfare in the light of past understandings and traditions of interpretation. The first approach brings obvious gains, but it may lead to bypassing or downplaying past agents' own understandings of their deeds. These understandings are arguably always a potential factor in action, and thus should be taken into account in any scholarly explanation.[30] The second approach posits, commonsensically, the influence on any given generation of this generation's own cultural past. It too can be tricky, if only because it can lapse into determinism and be blind to breaks, epochal shifts, and "jumps" or "installments" (*Fortsetzungen*). Tracing influences is very different from assessing causation, or—irrelevantly—responsibility and guilt. We are familiar with the argument that the eighteenth-century Enlightenment drove Europe to its twentieth-century totalitarianisms and to the Nazi Holocaust, or with variants that incriminate a number of thinkers along this road, from Rousseau to Nietzsche through Hegel and Marx. We will not join the ranks of those authors in guilt-prone Germany who have made the 1099 Crusade massacre the founding moment of a systematic ideological violence, all the way to the atrocities of the twentieth century.[31] Such accusations are simplistic; they both ignore the multiplicity of the political positions that have been derived from these philosophers' ideas, and forget the role of institutions of all sorts (formal and informal), of circumstances and of conjunctures in the historical process.[32] Some would argue that Christianity per se is "innocent" of violence and that it participates in contemporary violence principally insofar as it underwent over time, and in particular with Modernity, "hybridizations" with other dimensions of culture (including, for instance, market forces and nationalism) and because political religions or civic religions borrowed from and debased Christianities. Such is Jon Pahl's position in *Empire of Sacrifice*, in many ways a reiteration on firmer social-scientific ground and with attention to multiple agency of Eric Voegelin's classic thesis.[33] But one can object that these newer forms cannot be "new"—hybridization entails both difference from its component parts and similarities with them. As long as a focus on premodern Christianity accounts for some of the contemporary hybrids' dynamics, it is heuristically legitimate to explore it in depth.

Thus, in the rush to exonerate ideas from blood-guilt, one should not dismiss them either. Ideas are not mere costumes that historical agents don randomly or tactically, in the chaos of action. Nor should one a priori assume that ideas are simple reflections of institutions, formal or informal, and desires. To refer again to Max Weber: "Not ideas, but material and ideal interests, directly govern men's conduct. Yet very frequently the 'world images' that have been created by ideas have, like switchmen, determined the tracks along which action has been pushed by the dynamics of interest."[34]

But how do ideas and event meet? One may distinguish three not mutually exclusive modalities in which culture impacts, respectively, history during the event, after the event, and before the event. First, preexisting culture and ideas determine an *Erfahrungshorizont*, the cognitive and emotional frame in which historical agents experience and interpret what they do and what happens to them. Second, preexisting culture and ideas often provide formulas legitimizing these deeds once they have been perpetrated. In these two configurations, culture and ideas are not necessarily the cause of these deeds or intimately woven into them at the moment of their happening. Third, though, when historical agents believe in prophecy in any sense of the term, there are moments in which they live or act out the preexisting prophetic script. Prophecy can be straightforwardly Bible-based or the utterance of a philosopher who claims understanding of the logic of History. Such moments are often initiated when the *Erfahrungshorizont* leads a critical mass of historical agents to believe that they stand on the threshold of the realization of the prophecies. As Chapter 2 will develop, it can be the final realization (pure apocalyptic eschatology) or a typological anticipation of this final fulfillment.

Premodern sources, given their paucity, seldom allow the historian to determine whether an event was interpreted after the fact according to a given framework or whether this framework led people to act in the way they did. It is for instance something of a scholarly gamble to propose that eschatological expectations led the first crusaders to Jerusalem and impelled them to act as they did on the road to the holy city's bloody storming in 1099 (rather than propose that the crusaders' experiences led the medieval authors chronicling the expedition right after 1099 to present it as the fulfillment of eschatological prophecies).[35] This is a wager that this book, along with other recent scholarship (notably by Guy Lobrichon, Jean Flori, and Jay Rubenstein), is willing to stake and defend. The hypothesis finds support in a powerful thesis densely grounded in the sources, Denis Crouzet's argument that the French Catholic violent and "panicked" (more on this term in Chapter 3) reaction to sixteenth-century Calvinism should be explained as the acting out of a religious scenario available to them in the Christian tradition. As natural disasters conjoined themselves to the outburst of powerful heresies, as the population read in astrological pamphlets and in the almanacs that deciphered these extraordinary portents that History's final phase had begun, many French Catholics embraced the EndTimes script of John's Revelation along with the Old

Testament prophecies of the cleansing of Babylon and Jerusalem, and turned to holy violence.[36] The Eschaton was a time for the sword; it came also with hope for peace and liberty, for, if this was the last combat, it could open (according to some) an ill-defined millennium or third age of History.[37] End-Times would see the realization of the Christian utopia of unity, unanimity, and uniformity. Historically attested Christian scenarios oscillate between this universalist and homogenizing pole and the ideal of a chosen remnant or elect vanguard that excludes—violently—the majority; other historically attested positions assumed that the End meant a radical refusal of the sword, in imitation of the Apostles. We shall, however, concentrate in these pages on the "dark side" of this force.[38]

The use of eschatological texts as motivators and guides is attested, before the Reformation, with the fifteenth-century Hussite radicals (the so-called Taborites) and, after 1517, all the way to eighteenth-century colonial America, through the English Civil War.[39] Nor is eschatology exclusively premodern or late modern—it still influences culture and politics in the religious fundamentalism of today's United States[40] and is interwoven in some modern violence. Why should it have been otherwise in the (poorer in sources) earlier medieval centuries? Furthermore, if scholars assume that historical agents can take a series of passages from the Bible to legitimize or comprehend, after the fact, their violent actions (the first and second configurations outlined before), why should they not consider that historical agents may be motivated to the deed by such passages (the third configuration)? To allow for cognition and legitimation and not for motivation is to reduce religion's role to a code and not to a force.[41] Consequently, discussion in these pages will distinguish, with Max Weber, "explanation" (*Erklären*) from "understanding" (*Verstehen*), prioritizing the latter. It will flag carefully causal explanations that go beyond the grounds provided by the historical agents, as opposed to these understandings or to elaborations thereof. It will also prioritize "emic" to "etic" explanations of historical phenomena—prefer to take "native" notions as the starting point for analysis of native deeds, behaviors, and ideologies over and above notions exogenous to the culture under analysis.[42] This is not to deny the validity of "explanation" or of "etic" approaches in explanation. It is merely a consequence of this essay's focus.

But is this focus legitimate? Is a history of Western violence that is principally intellectual not bankrupt? Does it not involve a "dehistoricized view of the use of Scripture"?[43] Which results can it actually bring? Scholars have rightly underlined the limits of a focus on ideas and beliefs in analyses of historical processes to the detriment of institutions, circumstances, and the chaos of action. A classic in this genre is Paul Veyne's corrosive argument that "consciousness is not the root of action." Furthermore, monocausal models can yield only a flawed reconstruction.[44] Yet if the historian purposely stops short of producing a full reconstruction, the bracketing out of conjunctural factors combined with the concentration on religion and ideology allows him or her to highlight interesting phenomena. Actual, concrete problems and crises undeniably played a role in religious violence. However, for movements oriented primarily to a utopia, the real—this negative conjuncture—is deciphered and evaluated in the light of this utopia. This vision in turn orients and constrains action.

Furthermore, the utopia, when it has Manichean traits, modifies the classic dynamics of conflict and conflict resolution. In traditional societies, some degree of homeostasis often allows a (if only temporary) return to peace, especially as mediators socially connected to both parties come into play.[45] But this dynamic is inhibited in heavily ideologized situations. Jean-Clément Martin has shown how the French Revolution's violences took physical forms familiar to the Ancien Régime and occurred along fault lines that preexisted 1789. Protestants and Catholics, soldiers and officers, peasants and elites, French regiments versus foreign regiments, clientage group and clientage group, masters and apprentices, or factory owner and workers fought against one another before and after the fall of the Bastille, July 14, 1789. The mechanisms that limited violence and promoted a temporary return to peace failed after 1789 because the participants drew on the absolutist, Manichean ideology of the Revolution. Mediators now could be tarred and feathered as traitors.[46] There was nothing new in this. The sixteenth-century French monarchy had sought to make peace for the sake of the common good between armed Christian confessions; the French Holy League, regrouping Catholic extremists, countered in a bellicose song: "Shall we, then, now have to be neutral between God and the Devil?" In the Ligueurs' eyes, indeed, the so-called "politiques"— monarchists who allegedly prioritized power over faith—were worse than Calvinist heretics.[47] Or, to cite a famous English Revolution pamphlet, *Meroz Cursed*: "The Lord acknowledges no *neuters*. This text *curses* all those who *come not out to helpe* him, as well as those who *come to fight* against him; it is Christ's rule, 'He who is not with Me is against Me' (Matt. 12.30, Luke 11.23)."[48] This Gospel saying undergirded President George W. Bush's uncompromising attitude in the face of the September 11, 2001, attacks. On November 6, he declared, "You are either with us or against us in the fight against terror." Before him, in the Revolutionary Era, Christ's words had animated many colonial Puritan divines.[49] Against us fought the Devil, and the universe was bipartite. There was "the cause of truth, against error and falsehood; the cause of righteousness, against iniquity; the cause of the oppressed against the oppressor; the cause of pure and undefiled religion, against bigotry, superstition, and human inventions. . . . In short . . . the cause of heaven against hell—of the kind parent of the universe against the prince of darkness, and the destroyer of the human race."[50] These were moments when the Manichean strand in Christianity overcame the pacifist strand. Of course, aristocratic honor could work as well against peace-making and contribute to the invalidation of compromises. How could, sneered Brantôme (d. 1614), a veteran of the French wars of religion, "those who profess true nobility, and bear a sword at their side and their honor at its tip" strike alliances, compacts, friendships with their relatives' murderers? How could they have social intercourse with them? Maudlin pardon of offenses at God's command was good for clerics and monks; aristocrats, however, should "die or avenge, and not leave their souls soiled owing to a lack of beautiful resolve and of a fine blow."[51]

Arguably, if historians are looking for "causes," should not the dimension that allows a conjunctural situation to be interpreted as meaningful rather than meaningless, intolerably evil rather than tolerable, worthy of decisive action rather than of sufferance, claim the status of *causa causarum*, "cause of causes"?[52] Or better, since causation is not the issue, of *forma formarum*, the cultural form that forms other forms: to take religion seriously allows us to understand better the contours of violence in the West. Chapter 3 will explore a main reason that one dismisses the beliefs of holy warriors, martyrs, and terrorists as the prime motivator for their deeds. There exists a deeply anchored Western discourse, fueled since its origins by religious polemics, that such people are mad, possessed, or brainwashed. When one cannot relate to an enemy's conceptions, one easily assumes that they are incoherent or are imposed from outside normal human nature.[53] Chapters 2 and 4 will show, by contrast, how an internalist, "emic" approach, which starts from theology, allows historical agents' ideological or religious motivations to make sense and accounts in part for their violence's form and rhythm. The aim here is not to be monocausal; it is merely to recover an important dimension of human action and perception.

Violence, of course, and even more so "terror," are difficult concepts—"unclean concepts" if they are concepts at all. Issues of legitimacy and ethics loom large; such concepts may serve a research and explanation agenda yet are also ideologically negatively loaded.[54] What is the boundary between holy war (in legal understanding, a just war authorized by God) and terror? The matter was simple for Rome, which divided sharply the warfare authorized by constituted magistrates, *bellum*, from banditry, *latrocinium*. Being perhaps more perverse, Western intellectuals have debated for centuries whether state (or societal) coercion and small-group violence are comparable, similar in essence, or radically different. The critique of the established Roman dichotomy appears already in Augustine's *City of God*. The Church Father scaled back any state that would not be beholden to God's justice to the rank of large-scale banditry.[55] In various equations, the boundary, either defended or subverted, appears over and over again. One will think of Sergio Panunzio's comparison of state "force" and revolutionary "violence."[56] One will think of György Lukács's collapse of economics and violence, underlining how "that [false] distinction, like law and violence, order and insurrection, legal and illegal force" obscures "the common foundation in violence of every institution of class societies."[57] One will think of Frantz Fanon's contrast between the violence of the colonized and that of the colonizer, to the moral benefit of the former.[58] The question is raised as well by Walter Benjamin, who like Panunzio and others counterpoises a violence considered legal to a violence condemned not for its being violence but merely for its being extralegal.[59] Benjamin also contrasts "law-preserving" with "law-making" violence, anticipating the more sociological models developed in the 1960s and 1970s by European thinkers (notably Johan Galtung but also members of the Frankfurt school and Herbert Marcuse), that oppose "structural" or "systemic" violence to the violence perpetrated by individuals or groups seeking a new order.[60]

As phenomena, state and insurgent small-group uses of force often look quite similar. Thus, the debate on comparability hinges on verdicts that are ultimately ethical and which, being about ethics, the historian, as historian, cannot adjudicate. Is the suicide bomber substantially similar to the Inquisition? Is the small-group terrorist analogous to Stalinist terror? All the same, while not lapsing into a moralistic assimilation of top-down and bottom-up violence, scholars can delineate historical dynamics that relate institutional violence and violence from the bottom up. We shall explore this in Chapter 5. Over the long stretches of time during which this second, "grassroot" violence was absent, the state and its myths have been de facto its repository. As Natalie Davis has shown for the sixteenth century, popular religious terror borrows again and again its forms from state and religious coercion, and from their mise-en-scènes.[61] Norman Cohn, in his classic *Pursuit of the Millennium*, constructed a subterranean chiliastic movement. It centered on the lands bordering the Rhine, was endowed with a real continuity over time, but flared into the open only episodically. By contrast, Norman Housley has argued that sectarian messianism was impermanent in premodern Europe. It appeared, then disappeared, in brief, often cataclysmic outbursts, without continuity between them. Taking a leaf from Cohn, Housley posits that messianism's real repository was nationalistic messianism. The (usually royal) national institution, because of its eschatological mission, kept alive a potential for anti-institutional eschatological action.[62] Arguably, therefore, the religious violence that messianism often enabled or triggered for small groups was harbored over the centuries in the myths of the polities in which they emerged. The revolutionary Taborites arose in a Bohemia convinced of its national mission within universal Christendom, a conception built up in the century before by Emperor Charles IV (d. 1378).[63]

Yet if Housley's corrective to Cohn's romantic fresco is welcome, it remains to be explained why, despite its ephemeral nature, sectarian messianism kept coming back. Next to the semi-permanent vehicle provided by princely power and proto-nationalism, millenarian violence's core images and ideas were preserved in scripture and canonical Christian hermeneutics. One receptacle, thus, was the tradition afforded by a "virtual library" (something that Cohn was too well read not to perceive).[64]

As will be explained in Chapter 5, the contribution of larger social ensembles to smaller movements is understandable from a theological angle. In the broad Christian and post-Christian world, every terroristic group tends to consider both that it is a small, chosen set of the elect and that it constitutes the vanguard of a larger, more universal (and sometimes fully universal) ensemble or cause. This pairing of exclusivism and universalism owes much to the tension between, on the one hand, a stark theology of election involving the predestination of the few and the damnation of the many and, on the other hand, an inclusive theology of the "broad Church" animated by the desire to embrace and lead all humans out of their mediocrity.[65]

In a by-product of this tension, the ideal of martyrdom central to a state fed (and was fed by) terror waged by and for a vanguard representing a political entity's future. When Gavrilo Princip shot the Austrian archduke in Sarajevo, he was acting in the name of the future South-Slav polity and out of a willingness to die made evident by legends perpetuated by states and foundational to them. Since about 1800, his own Serbian ethnic group had been constructing itself around the legend of the holy warrior and martyr Prince

Lazar, fallen on the battlefield of Kosovo in 1389.[66] Belief in being a "chosen remnant" or "vanguard" also enabled terror against one's own state—in the name of its future. Thus did John Brown understand his bloody mission, in 1859, before he went to the gallows (below, Chapter 4). Brown is representative of a "limit" case. Martyrs, opponents of a polity in their own days and all the way into their own dying moments, could become a symbolic keystones for a later polity, sometimes even of the same polity that had taken their life. Brown, like many an abolitionist, would have broken the Union rather than tolerate slavery. But a few years after having been hung on the gallows, he was alive on the singing lips of Northern soldiers fighting the secessionist Confederacy. By then, in Franny Nudelman's words, he had moved from "having died the state's enemy" to being a "source of collective identity rather than a threat to the state's integrity."[67]

To Forget the Devil, Again

The harshness with which small groups of elect fight polities and the latter's savage repression of the former are not simply questions of survival. Both what political entities and self-styled elect share and what distinguishes them leads them to suspect that something satanic is at play.[68] Indeed, structurally seen, the Devil is the theological principle for both similarity and alterity, for both near-perfect imitation and essential difference. Recognition of this fact can lead the modern scholar to several related (if not always mutually compatible) hypotheses.[69] He or she can posit that human societies need, as systems, to create difference to resolve ambiguities and that this necessary differentiation can be effected through violence. He or she can posit also that there is a systemic necessity that non-difference or ambiguity will engender violently hostile reactions. If the scholar wants to take theology on board, he or she can further gloss that the Devil is the central peg in the native interpretation of these dynamics (be he the principle of difference or the principle of disturbing ambiguity). In this family of hypotheses, Christianity postulates the Devil either because it needs to account for otherness and ambiguity or because it needs to generate otherness and dissolve ambiguity. But a scholar who does not reduce religious ideas to social processes should propose the obverse: The theological postulate of the existence of Satan—ape of God yet total other to God—nurtures an acute attentiveness to otherness and ambiguity and fosters extremely violent reactions to them.[70] To spell out the alternatives, the one in which religion is secondary and the one in which religion is primary: is belief in Satan (and the literal demonizing of other humans) a hypostasis of difference (or of mimesis)? Or is belief in Satan the cause of the manic scrutiny of difference (or of mimesis)?

In Christian and post-Christian cultures (and the monotheistic faiths descended from Abraham), both perceived difference (or deviation) and perceived similarity tend to lead to violence. The former is not acceptable on the eschatological horizon of universalism (all humans should be the same); the latter, on the road to the end of history, is likely a nefarious trick. But polytheistic religions react in less extreme ways. They have mechanisms of accommodation. One is syncretism, which dissolves difference. Another is the assimilation to one another of entities with seemingly similar functions or appearances. The Aztec tutelary god Huitzilopochtli is also the solar-disk god Tonatiuh; the issue of whether the one could be, in a negative sense, the ape of the other does not arise.[71]

For monotheisms, similarity is danger.[72] Thomas Sizgorich has recently explored the boundary-maintenance mechanisms in both late antique Christianities and early Islam(s). [73] They were acutely needed—infinitely more than they would have been in a world cognizant of plural gods and ignorant of Satan. When Rome still worshipped pagan gods, a martyrdom account identified miracle workers who did not belong to true Christianity as mendacious copies of the good. It warned:

> Whenever someone revolts from God he is followed by rebel angels; and demonic ministers assist him with every sort of drug, magician (*magos*), priest (*goēs*), and wizard (*mantis*). And no wonder, for the Apostle says: *Even Satan disguises himself as an angel of light.* So it is not strange if his servants also disguise themselves as servants of righteousness [2 Cor. 11:14–15]. Indeed, even the Antichrist will appear as Christ.[74]

Furthermore, the Devil accounts for the striking flexibility with which historical agents could transfer, in a generation, or within a generation, the identification of the enemy and most of its characteristics from one object to another. In Colonial America, the adversary was, in the 1750s and 1760s, the despotism of Absolutist France (then ruling Quebec) allied with Catholic idolatry and religious tyranny. When the Crown of England sought to tax the North American colonies, it quickly became English tyranny and the Anglican establishment (and Anglicanism's crypto-Catholicism). This might suggest that ideology and theology have a nose of wax and are twisted and adapted to the political hostilities of the moment. Religion seems a convenient set of clothes, put on and off as needs arise. But it is not so. This flexibility was fundamentally Satan's own protean nature. Contemporaries said as much. The Devil tried various tricks, shifted strategies, deployed successive "members" of his body. Circa 1800, having failed to corrupt the North American elect through a false religion, that is, the despotic Roman Church and its ceremonies (that is, Catholicism's profuse sacraments and exuberant liturgy), he could initiate a political plague, Napoleon's tyrannical power. Sanctifying holy war too could be a satanic trick. Having first used the dominion granted along with peace by Emperor Constantine, then the false hope of indulgences peddled by hypocritical friars who pretended to lead the poor life, the Devil turned to the sham promise of sanctification through exterminating warfare for God—such had been Satan's strategy over a millennium, according to the Hussite pacifist Petr Chelčický.[75] It was Satan, then, who was wax-like. In allowing the surface identity of the adversary to change, Christians were honestly consistent with their understanding of that changeling par excellence.

Augustine of Hippo, witnessing the plurality of deviant Christian beliefs that the Roman Empire's conversion had brought into the public arena, had spoken with distaste of "heretics whitened in some way by the Christian name."[76] But this was by no means mere war paint; it was the color of History itself. There was little dishonesty in Augustine's belief that Satan, having tried pagan idolatry and failed, was now using a heretical sect's false martyrs to obtain the same misguided, misdirected worship:

> This dragon saw it, this age-old snake saw it: That the martyrs were
> being honored and the temples deserted. Therefore, since he could not
> make for Christians false gods, his cunning and poisonous vigilance
> made false martyrs. . . . He seeks to blur the distinction between true
> and false martyrs; he wants to snuff out the eye of the heart to prevent
> us from discerning it; he sought against the true martyrs something
> bearing the same appearance.

And Augustine, defiantly, exhorted his flock to employ piety and the Faith to separate what the Devil sought to confuse. But the task was not obvious, since the Enemy used the appearance of persecution to "conjoin false martyrs to true martyrs."[77] It was the same logic and the same tradition—that of the supreme North African authority, the bishop and martyr Cyprian of

Carthage—that had led, a century earlier, the opponents of Augustine's church, the so-called Donatists, to propound very much the same. Cyprian had written that "the Church [should not] succumb and fall to the heretics, light to darkness, faith to perfidy, hope to despair, reason to error, immortality to death, charity to hatred, truth to lie, Christ to Antichrist."[78] Echoing Cyprian's antitheses, from the beginning of their conflict with those they called the Caecilianists, the Donatists considered that the Devil had plotted to create a false church, the best Trojan horse to cast down those Christians whom pagan persecution had failed to sway and whom paganism had failed to retain in slavery to idols. This simulacrum would destroy these true Christians by "joining them to polluted traitors"—those who had yielded and sacrificed or had surrendered the Scriptures to heathen officials during the Great persecution of 303–306. Like their opponent Augustine, the Donatists trusted that the difference was clear. They queried: Who shall "assume that the Church of the martyrs and the conventicles of the traitors are one and the same? No one, for they are so opposed and contrary to each other as is light to darkness, life to death, a holy angel to the Devil, Christ to Antichrist."[79] But as with Augustine, trust in pious, revelatory clarity came with intense principled fears vis-à-vis Satan's grand strategy.

Such fears did not die with Donatism. Gregory VII's Milanese allies, the Patarenes, also considered the established church of Milan to be a satanic simulacrum. "I exhort you," said the future martyr Ariald, "to keep away from any association with false priests, since there should not be any agreement [*conventio*] or participation or association between light and darkness, between the faithful and the infidels, and between Christ and Belial."[80] And in the context of the Hundred Years War, of the Schism of the Church, and soon of the Hussite Revolution, Paris master Jean Gerson (1363–1429) distinguished among fallen knights between "martyrs of God" and "infernal martyrs" (*martyrs d'enfer*). The former were those "men-at-arms who exposed their life for a just cause and the defense of justice and truth, with a right intention"; the latter fought for "an unjust dispute or with a bad intention and perverse works."[81] Yet for some, one of the functions of holy war was to effect the discrimination, within one's own camp, between the truly faithful and hypocrites. It was literally an ordeal, revealing the actual contents of hearts.[82] The revolutionary avant-gardes, proclaimed the West German Rote Armee Fraktion (RAF), had true sight; they would not "believe in the masks worn by their exploiters." Rather, their violent action forced these impersonators to reveal themselves. Specifically, the RAF indicted the West German *Rechtsstaat* (Fr., État de droit; Eng., "constitution-bound state"). The Palestinian Black September action in

Munich had constrained it "to take off its make-up" (*abschminken*) and to reveal itself on History's stage as what it was (*auftreten*), a party in the waging of war against the Third World's liberation movements.[83]

Contexts

The arguments in the next chapters will draw on materials from and scholarship on several historical contexts. This section's main task is to describe, briefly, these moments and epochs (especially the more remote among them) in order to familiarize the nonspecialist reader with them and to signal their import. The specialist will undoubtedly know to skip directly to chapter one. One reason to present these contexts as a timeline, however, has been already mentioned. An epoch's significance can stem from its causative impact on successive generations strung along a continuous timeline, but it can also be the product of the epoch's appropriation by periods located in its future (and at a substantial chronological distance from the epoch, even sometimes quite disconnected from it). The second process becomes most visible from the French Revolution on but did exist before 1789.

The Jewish War

The earliest historical moment the essay shall mobilize is the Jewish revolt against the Roman imperial occupier, 66 to 73 C.E., known from the title of the main historical source recounting it as "the Jewish War." While exacerbated by Roman taxation, by strife over governance in the ethnically mixed cities of greater Syria and Egypt, and by the harsh hand of an illegitimate Herodian dynasty over its fellow Jews, the rebellion was at heart religious.[84] Its principal historian, Flavius Josephus, attributed its onset to a new "philosophy" or teaching, that of Judas the Galilean. Josephus characterized its followers by "a passion for liberty that is almost unconquerable, since they are convinced that God alone is their leader and master." In this pursuit of freedom, added Josephus, they did not fear painful death.[85] This "liberty," however, was not mere political liberty. It meant, to follow a modern scholar, an "eschatological redemption of Israel by God's miraculous intervention," the ability to fulfill "God's will in absolute purity and perfection" in a perfectly cleansed worship centered on Jerusalem.[86] The rebellion's trigger was religious. A great part of the population was ready to rise up owing to the Roman procurator Florus's disregard for the sanctity of the funds kept in the Temple and to other abuses.

The signal of the break with Rome was the captain of the Temple's refusal to allow any non-Jew to send offerings or sacrificial gifts to the Temple; he rejected "even the victim presented for the Romans and for Caesar."[87] And the historical moment's apprehension was religious. Some among the rebels thought they stood at the End of Times, initiating a fight that would be finalized by the Messiah.[88]

Such an apocalyptic and millenarian atmosphere commonly cradled mass religious violence across the centuries, all the way to our present. It is witnessed to by one of the scrolls recovered from the elusive Qumran community's library. This "War Scroll" details how the "sons of light" will wage a series of battles—some lost, some won—against the "sons of darkness." The latter will be led by a nation, the Kittim—which one should probably identify with Rome—"in league with" apostate Jews and assisted by Belial and his devilish minions. They will war until a final victory obtained thanks to God's intervention.[89] Other Qumranic scrolls document that the sectarians were to prepare themselves for "the day of vengeance," love their own, and hate their enemies— but dissimulate this last emotion until the time was ripe.[90] With this community, one sees clearly the puzzling correlation, often verified in Western history all the way to modern-day U.S. Evangelical Fundamentalism and other fundamentalisms,[91] between a small vanguard's ascetic withdrawal from the world and the utopia of a violent purification of the world on the eschatological horizon. And, importantly for debates about agency in the premodern world, the War Scroll assumed that, while angelic hosts and Yahweh Himself would participate in the eschatological struggle, the human elect would fight for Him: "For kingship belongs to the God of Israel; and with the holy ones of His nation He will work wonders." God used Man. Addressing the wicked, the "Rule" exclaimed, "May God hand you over to terror by the hand of all those carrying out acts of vengeance."[92]

The Qumran documents literally demonize the internal enemy within Israel and pair bad Jews with outright heathens, all destined imaginarily to defeat and destruction. De facto, the 66–73 C.E. war against the occupying Roman power was a civil war, pitting rebels against moderates, and rebels among themselves. As will be explained in Chapter 2, the concomitance of foreign and civil war constitutes another common feature of holy wars in the history of the West. In the course of the Jewish War, armed factions contended within Jerusalem, the more extreme carrying out a plan to purge the city from less devout (as they understood it) Jews. It is likely that in their eyes such lukewarm coreligionists were similar to, or identified with Qumran's "offenders against the covenant," expected to be in league with Belial's army. The scriptures provided paradigms for such cleansing of lapsed brethren: Moses' killing the worshippers of the golden calf (Exod. 32.25–29) and Phineas's "zealous" spearing of the Jew whom he saw fornicating with a heathen woman (an incident recounted in Num. 25.1–15, from which may have originated the name "Zealot" attached to one of the righteous bands of the Jewish War).[93]

Civil war could not facilitate resistance against the Romans' siege of the capital city. Their general, Vespasian, was acclaimed as emperor in the course of the conflict and departed from the theater of operations for the western Mediterranean to contend for the imperial office against other ambitious commanders; it was left to his son Titus to storm Jerusalem in 70 C.E. Its temple, the cultic center of Israel, went up in flames. The Jews were slaughtered en masse or sold into slavery or yet preserved temporarily to be victims in the many circus games that the young *imperator* staged in cities throughout the Mediterranean on his way back to his triumph in Rome. The Jewish will to fight was not immediately crushed, however. One of the militant groups, called *sicarii*, or dagger-men, had retreated early on to the fortress of Masada. There, under Roman assault, they committed mass suicide (73 or 74 C.E.). Some *sicarii* stirred up trouble in Egypt but were handed over by more moderate Jews to the Romans. The latter tried to force the revolutionaries—including their children—to recognize publicly the authority of the emperor. In a paradigmatic description of these rebels' martyrdom, Josephus grudgingly expresses his admiration for their constancy:

> Nor was there a person who was not amazed at the endurance and—call it which you will—desperation (ἀπόνοια) or strength of purpose, displayed by these victims. For under every form of torture and laceration of body, devised for the sole object of making them acknowledge Caesar as lord, not one submitted nor was brought to the verge of utterance; but all kept their resolve, triumphant over constraint, meeting the tortures and the fires with bodies that seemed insensible of pain and souls that well nigh exulted in it. But most of all were the spectators struck by the children of tender age, not one of whom could be prevailed upon to call Caesar lord. So far did the strength of courage rise superior to the weakness of their frame.[94]

We shall return to the "desperation," or, in a better translation of the Greek ἀπόνοια (*aponoia*), to the "madness" commonly attributed to terrorists

and martyrs all the way to the twenty-first century.[95] But to keep to the historical narrative, over the centuries, Josephus's *Jewish War* served as the basis for
many Christian renditions of Jerusalem's destruction. God's vengeance on the
Jews for having killed Christ, it also constituted the institutional side of the
epochal turn from the Old Dispensation, governed by Moses' Laws, to the New
Dispensation, the age of the Church and of the Gospel. The Israelites had now
lost both their monarchy and their priesthood. Anachronistically put, they had
forfeited their "manifest destiny." As Bruno of Segni put it in the late eleventh
century, "those who listen to, and treasure God's words, and walk the path of
His commands, cannot in any manner doubt that they shall not one day
obtain revenge on their enemies. But the Jews lost this [privilege of] vengeance since they refused to hear God's words."[96] In popular medieval versions, first surviving from the tenth century, Titus and Vespasian even became
Christian rulers and, as such, exemplars for European princes desirous of
avenging the Lord against heretics or pagans. In the eleventh century, this
model, alongside the biblical narratives of the Israelite conquest of Canaan
and the Maccabean wars against impious Hellenistic rulers, animated the
First Crusade. Along with other factors, it explains the massive massacre of
Muslims (and Jews) that took place at the endpoint of the expedition, Jerusalem, in mid-July 1099.[97]

Scholars have debated whether Jesus was a "Zealot," whether his disciples
participated in the war against Rome, and whether this possible militancy was
obfuscated by the first surviving Christian texts. In this hypothesis, the rebellion's defeat led to a recasting of Jesus' image, with only a few bellicist sayings
surviving the purge.[98] Indeed, it was shortly after the Temple's destruction that
some of Jesus' disciples redacted His sayings and deeds in the three synoptic
Gospels. Jesus of Nazareth, one of many prophets active in the Holy Land
since the Roman conquest, had been put to death about forty years earlier.
Whether the first Christians had been party to the rebellion, Luke, Matthew,
and Mark reported that Jerusalem's destruction had been predicted by Christ
("the anointed" of God) and that it corresponded to His vengeance. Had Pontius Pilatus, the Roman procurator, not washed his hands of the blood of a
man he considered innocent? And had the Jews not accepted that this blood
would fall on their head and their posterity's (Matt. 27.24–25)?

John's Revelation, an apocalypse composed perhaps thirty years after the
three synoptic Gospels, may be chalked up to Jewish Christian milieus close
in spirit to the insurgents of 66–73 C.E. and to the later revolt led by Bar
Kokhba in 132–136. It culminates on cosmic warfare involving angels and

humans in the vein of the Qumranic scrolls, on the earth's cleansing by blood, and on the descent to earth of the new, celestial Jerusalem. Combined with these vaticinations, the Gospel prophecy of Jerusalem's retributive destruction provided a scenario for a holy city's pollution, violent cleansing, and redemption. Along with this apocalypse, pithy sayings such as "I have come not to bring peace but a sword" (Matt. 10.34) or "whomsoever does not have a sword . . . let him buy one" (Luke 22.35–38) contradicted many more irenic sayings of the Lord. This book will explore their fate over time; it will also explain how the contradiction between irenicism and bellicism was dealt with and generated a very peculiar vision of violence's place in History.[99]

Late Antique Martyrdom, the Constantinian Turn, and the Crusading Era

The second dossier is constituted by late antique Christian martyrdom, before and after Emperor Constantine's conversion to Christianity in the first tier of the fourth century. As is well known, a number of Christians accepted death at the hand of Roman persecutors, usually to "profess" or "witness" to their faith (the meaning of the Greek word "martyr") or to refuse, often ostentatiously, to acknowledge the Roman emperor's lordship or divinity. In this, they were not very different from the *sicarii* whose steadfastness Josephus grudgingly admired.[100] Indeed, the martyrs' pagan judges attributed to them the same madness—possession by—as Josephus to the sectarians of 66–73 C.E. Our thesis here is that, from its beginnings, Christian martyrdom, far from being as a general rule pacifist or passive, was often enough bellicose and active.[101] The main source-genre for martyrdom, the "Acts" (Latin, *Acta*) or "Passions" (*Passiones*), distributes into two subclasses: those narratives that scholarly consensus considers authentic and those considered spurious, composed after the fact and often fictional works. The former subclass allows the historian to make cautious statements of fact. The latter, while not affording reconstructions of events, is nevertheless equally important. It produced and transmitted the images and conceptions that informed religious violence for more than a thousand years, well into the early modern era.

As to violence, Constantine's conversion impacted his adoptive religion and its institutions in several dimensions.[102] First, it opened up the possibility to act out in God's name, thus to will to suffer martyrdom, against a heretical ruler (as contrasted with facing off against a pagan one, as had been the mode prior to 312 C.E.). Constantine's immediate successors were favorable to the so-called Arian understanding of the Trinity, which many churchmen, especially in the Western part of the empire, considered heretical. This generated the first of a long series of open conflicts between rulers, who felt themselves responsible for dogma, and ecclesiastics, who also claimed the same duties. These disputes were commemorated in writing. While many late antique and medieval narratives were highly fictional, their audiences embraced them as true and, over the centuries, found in them the trope that a prince's impiety should be met by spiritual warfare. Second, the Constantinian moment also transformed understandings of the relationship between the Church and political authorities. Notably, bishops might now draw on the help of the "secular sword" for the physical coercion of those they thought were heretics.[103] In North Africa, a schism had developed; it opposed two churches that both considered themselves "Catholic."[104] Augustine, bishop of Hippo, faced what his camp called the "faction of Donatus." Heir to conceptions shared by the Hellenized Jew Josephus and the Roman persecutors of pre-Constantinian Christianity, he laid to the door of the (according to him false) martyrs of the rival Christian "Donatist" Church possession by suicidal madness and *furor*.[105] Augustine penned several letters legitimizing the use of force against these "Donatists." To his interlocutors who pointed to past practice—that the Church had never relied on worldly authorities for the enforcement of discipline—Augustine replied that, with the emperors' conversion, a new era had begun. The prophecy that kings would one day come to "understanding" (Ps. 2.10) was now fulfilled; Christian rulers could and should "serve the Lord" (Ps. 2.11) through the "terror of laws" (*legum terror*) designated to compel heretics back into orthodoxy and allow them the liberty to know the Truth.[106] Fatefully, with the twelfth century, when they were taken up and excerpted by Gratian's canon law textbook, the *Decretum*, these texts came to form the base of the mature juridical justification for coercion of heretics.[107] Thus, the Constantinian turn initiated both Christian holy war and terror. We shall see in Chapter 2 how far it built on preexisting potentialities.

Third, the uneasy alliance of Christianity and empire fixated in the faith its preexisting tendency to think in universal, global terms. Augustan ideology, in Ovid's famous phrase, proclaimed that "To other people a land with fixed boundaries has been given; but the City of Rome and the Globe are identical in breadth."[108] Christendom now as a general rule looked systematically to universal expansion and universal values. Thus, it is both as a Christian nation under God and as an empire heir of Rome that the United States—far from alone among Western powers over the last two millennia—believes in its global mission.[109] Fourth and finally, Constantine (r. 306–37) had invoked a symbol of Christ in his military drive to seize Rome from a rival pretender

(312); in his later years, the emperor may have dreamt also of marching under the Redeemer's sign against neighboring Persia—in a Christian holy war. Origins might be insignificant but for the fact that he was for centuries considered exemplary for Christian monarchs. Rulers would long be hailed as "new Constantines," a reference to Christian victory and to their orthodox leadership of Christendom.[110]

The late antique holy war slowly morphed into the high medieval crusade.[111] There exist unmistakable continuities between, on the one hand, Frankish eighth- and ninth-century warfare against pagans, waged under divine protection, and, on the other, the First Crusade of 1096–1100. One dimension in this continuum are the liturgies invoking God's help and the penances that armies undertook before battle.[112] Many of these practices were patterned after Old Testament models, considered to be exemplary for the Christian era. All the same, the Crusades marked a departure from early medieval holy war in that they involved ordinary believers massively, both as combatants and as economic and spiritual supporters. All Christians were supposed to participate, be it with the sword, through donations, prayers, or religious and ethical self-regeneration understood to be a barrier to the defeat of crusader armies.[113] Given the heightened efficiency of communications obtaining in the West from the twelfth century onward, a theology of crusading linking warfare for God's cause with reform of Christian society left lasting imprints on European culture.[114] Preached in November 1095 by Pope Urban II (r. 1088–1099) at Clermont (central France), the First Crusade had taken place in the context, and in part because of, the "eleventh-century Church reform." While this broad-based movement ultimately was captured by the Roman papacy, it sought to reconstruct all of Christian society, and not simply the clergy or the monastic orders.[115] This eleventh-century movement should be more properly spoken of in the plural, for it had several centers—in Lotharingia (and so in the western borderlands of the "German" empire, which normally exercised hegemony over Rome), in France (far less unified than neighboring Salian Germany), in Lombardy (an appendage of the empire), and in papal Rome (initially thanks to the imperial patronage of the reform of the papacy, to free it from exploitation by the local nobility, but on a course of its own during the minority of the future emperor Henry IV). At play, therefore, were (1) the various "peaces of God" or "truces of God," pacts or associations aiming at maintaining order that, from the late tenth century on, sometimes entailed sanctified war under saints' banners against people who ruptured this peace (with telltale provisions exempting bad clergy from the peace's protection and others condemning married clergy or lay control of church appointments);[116] (2) the civil wars in northern Italian cities triggered by groups that sought to force on the clergy avoidance of sex and money (the most famous being the so-called Milanese Pataria);[117] (3) Lotharingian voices complaining about the imperial control of the Church, in particular appointments to ecclesiastical office; (4) polemics between (some) monks and (some) secular clergy over leadership in the Church, the former arguing that ascetic purity placed them above the priesthood and that the latter's ability to confer the sacraments was marred by involvement with sex and money; (5) the papal court from Leo IX (r. 1049–1054) to Urban II, interested in freeing churches from lay domination, simony, and clerical marriage, which starting with Gregory VII (r. 1073–1085) revolted against the German king and which centralized reformist aspirations.[118]

In view of this mix, historians have proposed various explanations of eleventh-century reforms. In older narratives, the Gregorian reform (or revolution), named after Pope Gregory VII, who excommunicated and deposed King Henry IV, has been viewed as a classic power-political event and the first act of the struggle between Church and State over leadership of Christian society. In another explanation, the emergence of a commercial economy led to social changes (including an increased power for priests and their wives) and severe tensions that found an outlet in hatred for clerical marriage and for the sale of sacraments, simony (and also in anti-Semitism and the persecution of heretics). Inspired by Mary Douglas's *Purity and Danger*, this model posits that pressures against the boundaries of the social system homeostatically generate violence against scapegoats invented ad hoc. In a significant variant (which emphasizes activism), pollution concerns served to effect a program of reordering Christendom along well-defined social roles, notably those of priest and knights.[119] Consistent with the politics-centered explanation of the reform movement is the idea that the crusade constituted a safety valve for West European anarchy. Paul Rousset proposed that the failure of peace institutions (which he understood as aimed at peace in the Modern sense of the concept) had motivated the expedition: in calling on the warriors of the West to free Jerusalem from wicked Muslims, Urban II sought to export violence.[120] Along a similar interpretive line, the pope's 1095 call at Clermont was nothing else than an attempt, successful in the short run, to seize leadership over the knightly classes from his enemy Emperor Henry IV (Fulcher of Chartres cues historians in this direction, explaining the obedience of the knighthood to Urban's call as a consequence of his own perfect obedience to God).[121] Having been taught that one could fight righteous wars (defined as the preservation of peace and right order) by the twin influences of Cluny and the sworn peaces of God, Western knighthood was prepared to wage war for Christ outside Europe.[122] It would also be reductionist to imagine that the Peace of God and the Milanese conflict generated a Manichean "with us or against us" dichotomous outlook, opposing friends of reform to their enemies and demonizing the latter, which dichotomy was then projected externally onto Muslims. We shall offer in Chapter 2 another explanation, on the basis of exegetical sources (commentaries on the Bible).[123]

Twelfth- and thirteenth-century preaching institutionalized the linkage between crusade and reform. Into the late Middle Ages and beyond, both religious movements and the ecclesiastical establishment were obsessed by reform.[124] "Re-form," understood as a re-shaping or re-casting of Christian society and of the individual faithful back in the proper, God-willed "form," accompanied and colored conceptions of holy war. This meant that some crusade preaching or even an actual crusade could turn inward, in a more or less violent attempt to reform Christian society at home. An example of the former is the Fourth Crusade preacher Fulk of Neuilly;[125] an example of the latter, the 1251 Shepherds' Crusade (discussed at length in Chapter 5). And holy war as crusade was omnipresent in late medieval culture, even into the sixteenth century. While, after the mid-thirteenth century, Christians failed to launch expeditions that directly aimed at freeing Jerusalem from Muslim rule, they constantly dreamt and talked about it.[126] Intermittent warfare against Islam in Spain and in the eastern Mediterranean, while not crusade according to narrower definitions, still belonged clearly to the same cultural field.[127]

The First Crusade allows one to see the correlation, not obligatory but frequent, between millenarian-eschatological expectations, holy war, and reform.[128] As Ernst Bernheim explained long ago, in a line of argument revived by Richard Landes and after him by Johannes Fried, traces of apocalyptic excitements are necessarily scant, since disappointed expectations of Christ's return led naturally to erasures in the record.[129] But they are unmistakable for the eleventh century.

Another revealing instance of the correlation between reform and holy war is the so-called Hussite Revolution in central European Bohemia and Moravia (which form the bulk of the modern-day Czech Republic).[130] Adherents of Master Jan Hus, martyred in 1415 for his theological positions, the Bohemian Hussites found themselves the target of a series of crusades ordered by the pope and led by Sigismund of Luxemburg, king of Hungary

(r. 1387–1437) and German emperor (r. 1410–1437). The Hussite movement was split into several factions, which sometimes traded blows as much as polemics. We shall highlight here their differences concerning warfare. The more extreme wing consisted of the so-called Taborites. In 1419, Bohemian chiliast radicals established a community of hilltop settlements, nominally five in number, one of which was rebaptized Tabor. What was at first withdrawal from the world in anticipation of cosmic strife turned into armed violence when the signs of the time convinced most Taborites that the militant phase of Sacred History's endgame was at hand. They fanned out into the country, mercilessly killing bad Christians, notably priests sullied by heresy. Reportedly, the Taborite priests preached that "the time of vengeance has come" and that "the simple folk that has gathered on the mountain should march throughout the land and slaughter all the sinners in the whole world."[131] But, as always, Christ did not returned to earth; apocalyptic fervor soon transmuted itself and institutionalized itself. Tabor purged itself of some among its extremists, but it remained an armed camp, indeed an army-centered regime. Under the command of John Žižka (d. 1424) and in alliance with the moderate Hussites, Tabor played a large role in defeating again and again the Catholic crusaders. Tabor would last as a power until the Battle of Lipany (1434), which saw its defeat at the hands of the "centrist" wing of the Hussite movement in coalition with the Catholics. In opposition to Taborite militancy stood equally radical pacifists. Their one surviving voice is Petr Chelčický who, positing disjunctively that the Old and New Testaments stood in radical opposition to one another, correspondingly propounded an absolute prohibition of the sword.[132] In the center were the already mentioned moderates, who controlled Prague, and whose religious leadership drew on the city's university masters. These scholars justified resistance against the impious Catholics but laid down strict conditions to warfare and rejected the Taborites' bloodthirstiness.[133]

Despite these differences on the conduct of war (along with other issues), the Hussites shared a broad platform of demands, encapsulated in the Four Articles of Prague (1420). The articles provided (1) that the laity be allowed to take communion with both bread and wine (since the twelfth century only the clergy were allowed to drink from the consecrated chalice); (2) that the preaching of God's word be free; (3) that all priests should give up excessive property, pomp, and lordship, and lead exemplary lives (a corollary being that communities had the authority to depose unworthy clergy); (4) and that Bohemia be purged of all mortal sins. The extremist wings of the Hussites countered the

Catholic crusade with their own mixture of war and reform. Their under-standing of the Four Articles entailed despoiling from their dominion and possessions lords who did not back the cause of reform. Hussite struggles and success in wrenching from popes and emperors a grudging autonomy an-nounce the Wars of Religion of the early modern era and their outcomes; the pacifist voices among them anticipate the Mennonite Church, the strand of sixteenth-century Anabaptism that survived the confessional conflicts.[134]

The late Middle Ages also saw the emergence of theories and practices of just war waged for a nation endowed with a sacral aura (a "mystical political body," to use the Scholastic term).[135] As such, this just war was often very much holy war, as the Hussite case itself demonstrates, but also (to follow Housley) French and English writings occasioned by the Hundred Years War. Two examples will suffice, on the English side, the *Deeds of Henry V* (*Gesta Henrici quinti*); on the Armagnac French side, a plurality of writings associ-ated with Jeanne d'Arc, the Maid of Orléans.[136] Colette Beaune underlined the precociousness of the belief, shared by the Maid and some members of the Armagnac faction opposed to the English king and his Burgundian allies, that those warriors killed for France on the battlefield should be prayed for in spe-cial ecclesiastical foundations—chantries—both for their salvation and for their memory's posterity.[137]

The Age of the Wars of Religion

By 1800, the belief in the sanctifying virtue of death for the fatherland would become a general feature of European piety. It had taken a theological leap forward during the early modern Wars of Religion.[138] These conflicts' proxi-mate cause, Martin Luther's dissent, built on the reforming drives of late me-dieval Catholicism. But in the absence of compromise and given the support of some German princes, the Lutheran protest became schism. Luther opened the door for other reforming movements. Over the course of the sixteenth century, many of these reforming groups institutionalized themselves into confessions, the main Continental European ones being Lutherans, Calvin-ists, and Anabaptists (all convenient labels that do not, however, correspond to the names the groups assigned to themselves). Besides dogmatic differences, the systematic commemoration of one's martyrs (and the denial of martyr status to members of other confessions) was key for the formation of each group's identity, including Roman Catholicism's.[139] Next to cultivating its martyrs, each confession participated at some time or another in holy war and in violences in the name of God. Even the Baptists or Anabaptists, who emerged into the sixteenth century's second half as a radically pacifist church, briefly but intensely flirted with an equally radical religious violence.[140] The main episode, the Anabaptist takeover of Münster in Westphalia (1533–1535), is famous for the reign of terror imposed by its leadership and for the retaliatory massacres and gruesome tortures that ensued after their defeat. But the Kingdom of Münster was actually not a deviation from some essential Anabaptist pacifism. Rather, as James Stayer has shown, it constituted a theologically logical possibility inherent in the sectarians' principled and extreme rejection of the world.[141] Once one understands this, one can account for the simultaneous existence of the bellicose and the irenic in sixteenth-century Anabaptism that does not relegate Münster to the accidental. Stayer's insight can be extended to other radical ascetic groups. This logic was at play for the Qumran community: world-denying asceticism in this age combined with purge at the Eschaton. And it had allowed the Taborites' sudden passage in 1419 from pacifism to bellicism, a total reversal that provoked hefty critiques by contemporaries. This will be discussed in Chapter 5 and in the epilogue.[142]

The sixteenth century is present in these pages also owing to the German Peasants' Revolt of 1524–25 and the French Wars of Religion. The former (in fact, a set of regional rebellions without real unity) was inspired by early Lutheran ideas but was disavowed by Martin Luther himself. Ultimately defeated by the German princes and lords, the peasants and the townsmen allied to them had penned programs combining socioeconomic and religious aspirations. They wished to return to an idealized customary "old law," which might fend off lords' pressures and the commercial market's impact. This "old law" (as opposed to the then customary lordly customs and laws) they identified with, or they were grounded in, was an egalitarian "God's law" (a position also attested among some fifteenth-century Hussites). Luther reacted with two tracts. The first criticized both the lords for their greed and the peasants for their daring use of the Gospel for material demands and actions that transgressed the Pauline command of submission to earthly powers (Rom. 13.1–7). Then, as the conflict increased and the rebels scored some successes, the Wittenberg reformer lambasted them and called for their merciless repression, unto death if necessary. To the lords, Luther promised martyrdom should they die in the defense of the God-willed order.[143] But while Thomas Müntzer, one of the rebellious groups' leaders, was certainly millenarian-minded and called for the harvesting away of bad Christians, not all the revolts that compose the Peasants' War were dominated by radical eschatology. Some of the programs that can be reconstructed involved a reformation within the framework of the

Holy Roman Empire, with more equality but without the radical destruction of the existing order and its human agents.[144] The year 1525 provides a clear example of the constructive potential of politics inspired by the Bible, through war, yes, but not for all participants through the systematic extermination of the enemy.

France's Wars of Religion, given that they provide much material for analysis, should be presented in more details. Its Protestantism was mainly Calvinist. Jean Calvin guided reformed Geneva in Switzerland, a French-speaking republic right across the border from the Valois kingdom. The Huguenots, as their Catholic enemies came to call the French Calvinists, were repressed sporadically in the latter years of kings François I (Francis I, r. 1515–1547) and his son Henri II (r. 1547–1559). As in neighboring Switzerland in the 1520s and 1530s, in this phase, French Calvinist violence was in the main limited to iconoclasm—the often ostentatious destruction of Catholic religious images and statues.[145] King Henri's accidental death during a tournament opened up a period of major weakness for the Capetian dynasty's Valois branch. He left only underage sons, under the tutelage of his foreign-born wife, Catherine de' Medici. The configuration was ripe for trouble: Aristocratic factions' struggle for the control of the court intersected with religious sectionalism. Catherine and her three sons oscillated between toleration and repression and had to play off the powerful Guise family, which marched under the aegis of militant Catholicism, against an alliance of Calvinist noblemen and princes. Hers may have been a different notion of what it meant to be Catholic and royal, and how a king could bring back the divided kingdom to religious unity.[146]

The French Wars of Religion proper erupted in 1562. They would last into the 1590s, despite peaces that turned out to be no more than temporary truces. The high tide of the bloodshed occurred during one of these seeming lulls: On August 24, 1572, Saint Bartholomew's feast day, urban militias and Catholic noblemen led by the Guises massacred Paris's Huguenots and many Calvinist noblemen who had come to celebrate the wedding of the king's sister to her distant cousin Henri of Navarre. The king, Charles IX (r. 1561–1574), may not have been party to the initial plot but had to jump on the bandwagon.[147] To prove oneself a good Catholic yet to preserve one's leadership constituted the main quandary facing France's last Valois rulers. Or, to put the matter in less instrumental terms, a king's understanding of the principles of good and efficient governance and his sense of what was the essence of Catholicism did not always dovetail.[148] For individual monarchs, and even for the monarchy as an institution, the danger was not small. First, Calvinists, then ultra-Catholics, publicized resistance theories. In their more extreme forms, when intermediary powers (in contemporary parlance, "the magistrate")[149] failed to act against an unjust or impious ruler, the duty devolved upon the individual citizen. As Chapter 5 will detail, this principle of devolution is one of the factors in the similarities, for methods and aspirations in the matter of violence, between the Western State and Western "terroristic" groups. The same notions of a common good to be defended or realized by the force of arms have animated, over the longue durée, the larger, more institutionalized entity and the smaller, less institutionalized ones. Furthering this parallelism was the dialectic characteristic of Western Christian and post-Christian thought between universalism and election. The elect "vanguard" acts in the name of the future global consensus it means to bring about; these spokespersons for a universality often consider themselves to be purer than those outside their group. Thus thought Marx. His proletariat had "a universal character because of its universal sufferings."[150]

Saint Bartholomew's Day produced many martyrs, probably around 10,000 (and, contrary to Huguenot self-image, much apostasy into Catholicism). It was a spectacular event, greeted in Rome with the actions of grace that accompanied victories against the Turks. But two of the more spectacular and debated martyrdoms came during the penultimate phase of the French Wars of Religion.[151] The first was the murder of the Catholic faction's leader; the second, in retaliation, was the suicidal murder by a young Dominican of the ruling monarch.

These two events composed the apex of the monarchy's severest crisis. The rising influence of the ultra-Catholic Henri, duc de Guise, had come to exasperate Charles IX's brother and successor, Henri III (r. 1574–1589). The duke stood behind the Ligue, an alliance of towns dedicated to uprooting Calvinism from France. Along with its aristocratic friends, it had forced the king to swear to its program, the Edict of Union—which included both ecclesiastical-religious and political-institutional measures. Even more humiliating perhaps for Henri III was the "Day of the Barricades" (May 12, 1588), when the Parisian Catholic militias had thwarted the king's attempt to seize control of the capital and had taken prisoner the royal soldiers. In this drama, Henri de Guise had played the leading role, inspiring the rebels whose favorite he was, but also saving the hides of the Swiss guards and of the king himself. Retaliation soon came. On December 23, 1588, the king's bodyguards massacred the duke; the following day his brother Cardinal Louis de Guise was also killed. Popular rumor soon spread that Henri had ordered the bodies cut into pieces and then burnt in the palace's ovens to prevent their being used as relics. The king did not want these two aristocratic champions of militant Catholicism to become martyrs. But they did. In the Ligue's eyes, the two men were the worthy successors in death of their father François de Guise, whom a Calvinist had murdered in 1563. Pamphleteers raged against Henri, accusing him of all vices, including atheism, devil worship, and disorderly sexuality. He was a "scapegoat, woman to several men, and man to all women" ("bouc emissaire, femme de plusieurs hommes, & homme de toutes femmes") and "a ghost of man-woman" ("un phantosme d'homme femme").[152] The king was excommunicated, and some Ligueur pamphlets pushed resistance theory and notions of popular sovereignty very far. Interestingly, they called the monarchist circle around the king's then favorite, the duke of Épernon, "Épernonistes," just as the Church Fathers derived the name of a heretical sect from the name of the heresiarch (so "Marcionites" from Marcion, "Arians" from Arius, and so on). Such would also be a mode of labeling some factions during the French Revolution (for example, "Hébertistes"). The Ligue itself entered into a veritable vertigo of religious exaltation, with the union of all good Catholics against heresy and Machiavellian tyranny conceived of as analogous to mystical communion in the Eucharist that good Catholics defended against Calvinism.

Martyrdom called for vengeance, and vengeance came through God's hand. But this hand could arm a human hand. At least two pamphlets in circulation in Paris in 1588–1589 said as much. A funeral poem (*tumbeau*, Latin *tumulus*) for the two Guises gestured to an effigy or painting meant to excite to both retaliation and commemoration: "To render what they owe to them and to avenge the tyrant's oh so inhumane deed, the people took up arms spontaneously, and will not give them up until the traitor and his minions lose their life. And, to perpetuate such a tragic deed, we have placed here the portrait of these virtuous Peers. . . . Passerby, then, mourn, and also make immortal the deeds, the life, and the death of these princes you see here. They died for Jesus Christ and the public [good], and will live forever."[153] A second broadsheet, in color, showed the two martyrs' effigies on the background of a tapestry representing the instruments of Christ's passion. From the heavens, there rained blood on the two Guises. Between the tapestry and the effigies, there stood Christ on the Cross, a cross firmly planted in the martyrs' space. In an allusion to Revelation 6.9–10, an inscription written in a box at the foot of the Cross explained that their "blood . . . called unceasingly on God's goodness to avenge them and us from such tyrannical deeds."[154]

The graphic parallel with the bloody Christ was culturally embedded. The

Catholic holy warrior Blaise de Montluc had dreamt the night before Henri II's death at the hand of a Protestant nobleman during a tournament that he saw "the king on a throne, the face fully covered with drops of blood, very much, as it seemed to me, how one paints Jesus Christ when the Jews crowned Him with the crown [of thorns]. He held his hands clasped [in prayer]." Montluc had awoken in tears.[155] Within a year after the Guise brothers' demise, a young Dominican, Jacques Clément, knifed the king to death, before being hacked down by the royal bodyguard. The martyr-assassin Clément had executed the ultra-Catholic God's justice (as has been pointed out, he followed to the letter the method, ruse, and gestures provided by an Old Testament model, Judg. 3.15–22).[156] His apologists imagined (or recounted) that he had prepared himself with an ecstatic prayer. The Dominican spoke up in the chilling words of David's Psalm 138 (21–24), preparing himself for death by beseeching the Lord to inspect his motivations, since he "loved with a perfect hatred" Christ's enemies.[157] Hatred of God's enemies was assimilated to a sacrifice. Grimly threatening to the king of France, whom they placed in a typological relationship with the archetypal forerunner of Antichrist, Antiochus Epiphanes, the self-styled Ligueur imitators of the martyr-warriors Maccabees "presented" to God "as a great and pleasing sacrifice the hatred [that we have] for you and our detestation for your behavior."[158] Medieval sermons had explained how love of Christ underwent in the crusader a process of refinement: it transmuted itself into zeal for Christ and thence into hatred for His adversaries.[159] This notion is suggestive both of the aggression inhering in the act of love par excellence—martyrdom—and of the continuum between martyr and holy warrior. It was not uniquely Catholic. On their way to execution, Calvinists sang psalms that called—if one consults the argument that their translator into French, Clément Marot, attached to each of them—for vengeance and also mustered the image of Antiochus.[160]

The Ligueurs did not find problematic the coexistence of Catholic martyrdom and Catholic persecution. One anonymous pamphlet said as much: "The Catholic Christian rejoices in the death of the pagan and of the heretic, since in it God is glorified; and [he rejoices] in the death of the Catholic captain or soldier" who acquires "eternal bliss in Paradise."[161] Another reason advanced for the coexistence of martyrdom and killing for God took a leaf from Saint Augustine's justification of coercive measures against the Donatist heretics. The early Christians, indeed, had accepted martyrdom and had never taken the sword. But this was simply because there were not as of yet, prior to Emperor Constantine's conversion, any Christian magistrates. Christians had been "constrained to go under the yoke, and instead of resisting to willingly offer themselves to martyrdom." But in the post-Constantinian age, Christians now had both the right and the duty to resist. A reversal brought about by a miraculous epochal shift.[162]

Ultra-Catholics resisted for a few years after the conversion to Catholicism of Henri III's heir-designate, the Calvinist Henri de Navarre. And while this Henri IV pacified the kingdom, he too fell to a religious assassin's blade, in 1610. Across the Channel, shortly after this second Henri's murder, the British Isles fell into civil war (1642–1651) and revolution—a revolution that has been seen equally as the first Modern revolution and as the last war of religion (albeit the Gregorian reform can claim one title and the French Revolution the other). The alternatives are owed not simply to different historiographic positions—a tendency to erase the faith of actors such as Oliver Cromwell or a tendency to downplay the social and political dimensions of the conflict. At play are also—as Glenn Burgess excellently puts it—the contemporaries' complicated understanding of religion and politics as dimensions—sometimes distinct, sometimes fused.[163] For Catholics in Ireland, for Scots of various confessions, and for equally religiously diverse English, ecclesiological and dogmatic considerations loomed large in taking sides for or against Parliament, the king, or the Revolutionary Army. The causes of political liberty (or liberties) vis-à-vis the king and of religious liberty (or liberties) were, thus, not always identical, but they were usually intertwined. In the British Isles as well, only a minority advocated tolerance for all confessions.[164]

The sixteenth and seventeenth centuries marked a departure. The ideologies that had animated the medieval crusades against Muslims and pagans or against vulnerable heretics such as the Albigensians remained. But, on the European scale, the Wars of Religion ended on a standoff between the contending Christian confessions, even though, on a more local scale, cities, provinces, and states were lost or won. As in the Hussite crusades, dogmatic differences notwithstanding, early modern Protestant and Catholic parties waged mirror-image war against one another.[165] James Turner Johnson delineated two consequences to this situation of rough symmetry in beliefs and in power. On the one hand, a line of thinkers, culminating in Hugo Grotius (1583–1645) and John Locke (1632–1704), tried to limit and even evacuate religious legitimations for just war. On the other hand, militant believers, Puritans as well as Catholics, reaffirmed God's war and understood their opponents' own justifications and practices as devilish counterfeiting of divinely sanctioned warfare. A single example: in 1562, allegedly, Calvinists wanted to seize

Toulouse, where "they wanted to leave none alive, until the streets be turned into rivers of blood, flowing all the way up to their horses' bridles." This false holy warfare called on the apocalyptic exemplar, Revelation 14; the Catholics countered it with a true Maccabean crusade, which would take the same form, that of a radical purge.[166]

We shall meet the Puritans and other English dissenters from the Anglicanism dominant in the British Isles both within the context of the English Civil War of 1642–51 and in America. In Grotius and Locke's line of thinking, the warring Christian confessions' mirror-image claims to divine authorization neutralized one another. Understandably, like-minded theorists and diplomats relied increasingly on natural law justifications for war and ultimately called into existence contractual and pure reason of state rationales for it. But, in the second alternative that Johnson sketches (which one can call "neo-medieval" insofar as it continued the medieval holy war tradition late into Modernity), the twinship heightened the feeling that Satan, God's ape, was at work. Heretical confessions mimicked orthodoxy's martyrs, heroes, forms of sanctified warfare, and argumentation.

The French Revolution

A nonspecialist may find it odd to place the French Revolution (1789–1799) on a continuum with religious violences, be they medieval or early modern.[167] Yet it did, after all, place religion and cult among its central preoccupations, be it to "dechristianize" France (in the phase where institutional Catholicism was attacked as a pillar of the erstwhile throne) or to create (as Jean-Jacques Rousseau had pleaded) a civic cult that could foster citizenship and unity. Revolutionary language borrowed, sometimes self-consciously, sometimes not, from Catholic and Reformed discourse.[168] This made for conflicts.[169]

Recently, Antoine de Baecque has emphasized the Catholic cultural capital and repertory present in revolutionary thought. He envisages "next to the reference to Classical Antiquity an evident descent from the religious tradition, from the Catholic inheritance."[170] De Baecque is only one in a long line of scholars since the event itself who have perceived that the Revolution's political culture—including its famous climax, the Terror of 1792/3–1794—can be profitably considered as a religious event. To paraphrase Carl Becker, the Philosophes were more medieval than they thought.[171] Some of the revolutionaries, and many analysts and essayists after them—Burke, Michelet, Tocqueville, Gramsci—viewed the Revolution as the latest in many reforms within the Church.[172] It is striking how each generation reinvented this wheel.

Tocqueville wrote that the Revolution had been "a political revolution that operated as a religious revolution does, and took in some way the shape of a religious revolution." It had the scope and methods of the latter genre—including the recourse to preaching and propaganda and the proclamation of abstract principles independent of time and space. "She herself became," argued Tocqueville, "a kind of new religion. It was admittedly an imperfect religion, devoid of God, cult, and any other life; yet it nevertheless—like Islam—flooded the whole earth with its soldiers, apostles, and martyrs."[173] Émile Durkheim's collaborator Albert Mathiez (1874–1932) innocently proclaimed that his thesis—that the French Revolution and its violences were not simply the fruit of a social crisis but, like the Reformation, to be looked at from the angle of "religious fanaticism"—would transform the very understanding of the event.[174]

The most striking analysis of the Revolution as religious phenomenon comes from Edgard Quinet, who saw in the Revolution the triumph of Christianity's "essence":

[Consider] these men who do not believe [in God] but who retain the temper of their belief, extremists in their suspiciousness and in their intolerance in political matters as one was formerly in religious intolerance; [consider] Christianity and Catholicism seemingly banished, yet indwelling at the heart of all things, the one in the spirit of fraternity and equality, the other in the principle of unity and centralization. Understand that ancient religion's very essence actualizing itself in the world at the very moment when the world overthrows its [outward] form.[175]

Quinet's *Le Christianisme et la Révolution française* (1845) anticipates here a whole family of attempts at explaining secularization as the ultimate realization, unbeknown to itself, over the long term, of "Religion" with a capital R, and of its transvaluation into politics. All the same, one should notice how the divine principle that fired religious enthusiasm morphed. To follow Wolfgang Schmale, one of its key idols, next to liberty, was the constitution.[176]

The importance of 1789–1794 both for such reflections and as the originating point for the term "terror" warrants a fairly lengthy contextual exposition.[177] After an initial phase in which France was a constitutional monarchy, the Revolution radicalized itself, in a feedback loop with real or perceived counterrevolutionary threats.[178] In June 1791, Louis XVI tried to escape from

France to join the armies led by French aristocrats positioned in the Rhineland. He also hoped for the help of his fellow Continental monarchs, whom the revolutionary ideas increasingly worried. The failure of Louis' flight led to his quasi-imprisonment. By April 1792, France was at war with Prussia and Austria, and the fortunes of Mars were not always with the *Grande Nation*. Until the end of September 1792, its borderlands were severely threatened. And while, for about six months after that, battlefield successes led to dreams of territorial expansion, from March to August 1793, French armies were in a virtual rout.

Historians sometimes define as the Terror the period that opened in September 1792 with the mob massacres of more than a thousand political prisoners jailed in Paris. Here "Terror" is a scholar's descriptive or analytical category. But "terror" was proclaimed the Republic's policy— "the order of the day"— only in September 1793. Therefore, it is mostly after this date that one can expect contemporary reflections on the idea. The execution of the Jacobin leadership, Maximilien Robespierre, Louis Antoine de Saint-Just, et al., at the end of July 1794, put an official end to it, even if the guillotine still worked against successive leaderships' opponents. From this point on, "terror" and its derivatives became, outside narrow circles, a negative and derogatory word.[179] Any analysis of "terrorism" must take into account this principally negative valence. Since the Directoire, the phenomenon—using violence to rectify society, politics, or religion—has been seldom called "terror" by its perpetrators; a foe's coercion gets so labeled easily.

The Paris September 1792 massacres followed on the heels of the panic that the threats of the general in command of the then militarily ascendant Austro-Prussian alliance had provoked in Paris. The king was accused of conspiracy, proven guilty, and beheaded (November 1792 to January 21, 1793). Robespierre, who two years earlier had written against capital punishment, and his young colleague Saint-Just, also an erstwhile opponent of the ultimate penalty,[180] swayed the Assembly to vote for Louis' death. Another reversal brought about by a miraculous epochal shift? As king, he was, they argued, no longer a citizen but an enemy, an outsider to the social contract. Defeats of the Revolution's army on the battlefield fed despair and paranoia—the idea that the Revolution's inner and foreign enemies had woven a vast conspiracy against the Nation. Until its demise in 1794, the Jacobin faction discovered enemies everywhere in the Assembly and even in its own ranks. The Revolution eliminated in succession several parliamentary groups whom its accelerating leftward course left, relative to it, on the conservative side. In one purge, a faction more radical than the Jacobins was even accused of being the hidden ally of the tepid moderates.

The guillotine was not the sole instrument of terror. Faced from March 1793 on with a massive Catholic and monarchist rebellion in the western province known as the Vendée, the revolutionary leadership ordered its armies to repress the Vendéens with the utmost savagery. Possibly 160,000 men, women, and children were killed, about a quarter of the local population.[181] Bertrand Barère, discoursing on the outside military threat to the Republic (the English-led coalition), put forth that "we will have [external] peace when the interior is pacified." Consequently, he pleaded for "measures leading to the extermination of this rebellious race [the Vendéens], the disappearance of its lairs, the burning down of their forests, the cutting down of their crops." In this same fiery breath, he offered civilization as well as the sword. The Revolution should "fight them as much with workers and pioneers as with soldiers."[182] Barère spared the women, children, and elderly out of *humanité* ("humanity," "humanness," or "humankind"). But in a classic pendulum movement, the orator invoked the same "humanity" to plead for "fire and steel" to cauterize the Vendéen gangrene: "*Humanité* will not complain. To extirpate evil is for its good. To punish the rebels is to do good for the fatherland. Who would plead mercy for parricides?"[183] The taming of the Vendée proceeded like a colonial war. But its promoters discoursed on this colonial war with the classic vocabulary of religious wars.

Historians have bitterly debated the linkage, if any, between the two phenomena, "revolution" and "terror." Was the Terror an accident in the course of the French Revolution, or was there a logic in the Revolution that drove it inexorably to terror? Were contingent factors, such as the foreign invasion, critical, or was it ideology? On a broad canvas, the argument can be made that two waves of military setbacks led to, respectively, the unofficial terror begun in September 1792 and the official policy of September 1793—so that conjuncture's accidents and not ideology caused them. A more fine-grained look at the chronology has led some to counter that fortune had begun to smile again on the French armies before the Assembly voted the Terror—so that ideology and not events determined policy. But this may be to forget the gap between contemporary perceptions of threats and what historians can more objectively reconstruct with the benefit of hindsight. It may also be to underestimate the time lag it takes for an embattled regime to feel substantially secure even after actual victories.

Colonial and Postcolonial America

The senses, plural, in which the French Revolution, its wars civil and foreign, and its Terror can be considered religious phenomena will occupy us throughout. But it is beyond debate that the wars of the other nation that, in the eighteenth century, proclaimed the universality of its ideals, the United States, had a religious component.[184] Grotius, who did not care for religious arguments for military conflict, was known in the colonies. Yet the immigrant Puritans had inherited, via the sectarian struggles of the English Civil War and its preludes, the neo-medieval notion of holy war. Satan animated the New Englanders' Native enemies. Some, but not all, seventeenth-century theologians suspected that he had established his last redoubt in America among the Indians; they would provide the core of his armies—Gog and Magog—in History's final battles. The Indian religion was witchcraft and satanic inversion; during powwows, the Devil "prescribes t[o the Indians] his Law, will and pleasure, declaring to them he [is] the prince of Darkness [and] . . . he persuades them [that] darkness is Light and is good."[185] Facing this satanic enemy, like the Carolingians about a millennium earlier, New England's Protestants fasted to mobilize God's strong helping hand.[186] Or when they hesitated on a course of action, they asked their chaplains to "commend" their "condition to the Lord."[187] While some scholars have found in the early Puritan colonists a relative fairness in dealing with the Indians, respect for property, and greater concern for conversion than interest in holy war, this is not the dominant position in historiography.[188]

The practice did not disappear with the War of Independence.[189] America provides a clear case study in the transfer—with modifications such as democratization or expansion of the contents of the "liberty" for which one would fight—over time of conceptions of sacred violence. Into the nineteenth century, during the Anglo-American War of 1812 and during the Civil War, governors and presidents instituted national fasts.[190] The conflict between the Union and the Confederacy may have been the West's first industrial war, won through factory output and productivity and fought with railroads. But all this Modernity did not exclude a generalized belief, on both sides, that God supported each camp's sense of justice and liberty. The configuration, then, was quite neomedieval: mirror-image holy wars did not engender a generalized suspicion that the Lord of Hosts might not stand squarely behind one's cause. (Such distrust of similarities would carry into the twentieth century's Cold War: since the late nineteenth century, Americans alternated between hope for Russia's conversion to their alloy of Protestantism and democracy and fear that Russia was a satanic "dark double.")[191] On the Civil War's Northern side, the United States had come to be viewed as the particular vehicle of God's Providence for Christendom and the world. This meant that the Union was worth killing and dying for.[192] Into the nineteenth century as well, setbacks on the battlefield, read as God's scourges, ensured the link between moral reform and holy war and, as a result, the participation of noncombatants in the military effort.[193]

Decades of sectional conflicts explain the warring camps' uncompromising mood. But this mood had been prepared as well by the permeation of political culture through the Manichean temper of Evangelical Christianity. Richard Carwardine has made a convincing case for the massive influence of its various denominations on antebellum American politics, beyond what raw church membership statistics would suggest. By the time the United States entered the age of mass democracy, Evangelicals had already developed methods of mass mobilization. Understandably, politicians courted their newspapers and leadership. And electioneering borrowed, intentionally and unintentionally, from the culture of revivals and meetings. The churches' presence ensured that politics would seldom concern itself with value-neutral platforms but rather discoursed on moral visions. Evangelical culture's permeation of this sphere also made for remarkable sharpness and fed either-or mentalities.[194] On the occasion of the (uncharacteristic) antislavery crusader John Brown's trial and execution in 1859, voices in the Southern press (characteristically) understood the differences between parties as unbridgeable opposites:

There is no dispute between Northerners and Southerners; but between conservatives and revolutionists; between Christians and infidels; between law and order men and no-government men; between the friends of private property and socialists and agrarians; between the chaste and the libidinous; between marriage and free love; between those who believe in the past, in history, in human experience, in the Bible, in human nature, and those who, like Greely, and Fourier, Fanny Wright, and Paine, and Thomas Jefferson, and Seaward, foolishly, rashly, and profanely, attempt to bring about a millennium, and to inaugurate a future wholly unlike anything that has preceded it.[195]

George FitzHugh's diagnosis of abolitionism as millenarian and future-oriented was not fundamentally erroneous.[196] Yet large segments of the

Southern religious establishment harbored exceptionalist conceptions that would make peace very difficult after Fort Sumter. Strikingly, both in the North and in the South, once the war began, and all the way to 1865, it was religious periodicals and the clergy, as opposed to their secular counterparts, that expressed the most bellicose and uncompromising sentiments.[197] For the majority of these media, the infidel or heretic was on the other side of the North-South divide.

North and South saw themselves as God's chosen nation,[198] and so processed the ups and downs of military fortunes with the unfalsifiable logic of Providence: any victory was chalked up to the justice of one's cause; any defeat was interpreted as God's chastisement on an elect people that had not yet purified itself or that had momentarily lapsed into vice. Reverses and success alike testified to election. This "faith-based" reality probably contributed enormously to the citizenry's willingness to fight in an increasingly vicious and harrowing conflict.[199]

The colonists and their descendants sometimes massacred the American Indian enemies, including women and children, with a thoroughness that shocked their Native allies. Those Mohegans and Narragansetts who fought alongside Captain John Underhill and witnessed the wholesale slaughter of the Pequots at their stockade in Mystic, Connecticut (May 16, 1637), reportedly "admired the manner of the *English* mens [*sic*] fight." Admiration did not mean some wish to emulate. Rather, it expressed shocked bewilderment and a refusal to accept that this was a proper way of war. The Natives complained, Underhill continues, that "it is naught, it is naught, because it is too furious, and slayes too many men." Prisoners were summarily executed, and surviving women and children sold into slavery. This harshness reproduced that of another holy war, Cromwell's against papist Ireland.[200] At play were Old Testament exemplars.[201] And a predetermined—so all the more determining—belief that there had to be a massive pagan conspiracy against God's elect certainly played a major role in this violence. The witches of Salem admitted under torture that they belonged to a satanic league including an Indian-looking Devil, Natives, and French Canadians, who used a Catholic book of devotions for their sabbaths.[202]

Culturally premodern and American was, also, that famous catalyst of the Civil War: abolitionist John Brown's raid on Harpers Ferry and his trial and execution (discussed in Chapter 4). Abolitionists were not a majority in the North before the war, and violent ones like Brown were quite unrepresentative of general Northern sentiment. For all his oddity, though, and like that other minority, modern religious terrorists, Brown is understandable, in part, through a very old looking-glass. The same can be said of individuals and forces in more recent wars, including the surprising Lieutenant-General William Boykin (discussed Chapters 2 and 5) and his commander-in-chief, President George W. Bush (2001–2008, discussed Chapters 1 and 6), who in 2003 led America into a strategically catastrophic war against Iraq.[203]

Into the twentieth century, the United States took a seldom wavering sense of mission to the battlefield. It was shared by all denominations. Even Catholic editorialists harped on the country's divinely appointed task during the 1898 war against Spain.[204] From the 1812 war with England to World Wars I and II and onward to the Cold War, whose religious component has been recently explicated by David Fogleson, the Christian dimension in America's conflicts cannot be neglected. It is also visible with the European powers that faced off in the years 1914–1918. Seen from the angle of a secularization process defined à la Carl Schmitt, that these European nations were animated by "political" or "civic" religions suggests the continued importance of Christian forms in battlefield violence. The holy nation succeeded to a holy *ecclesia*, an *ecclesia* that, for many centuries, had oscillated between localism and universalism. At the same time, war was rendered meaningful by images of sacrifice, martyrdom, and purification that owed a lot to Christianity.[205]

The Rote Armee Fraktion

A consensus emerged at about the turn of the twentieth century that nations were (and ought to be) integrated by "political religions" rich in rites and symbols and so in the ecstatic togetherness the latter facilitated. As Emilio Gentile has amply documented, citing hundreds of voices, the idea in its analytical and normative dimensions was common to academic thinkers like Émile Durkheim, essayists like Gustave Le Bon, and political agents on the Right and on the Left alike.[206] In a variant of this functionalist model, violence and ecstatic communion in violence made (and should make) the political unit. Ironically, Frantz Fanon, this third-world icon of the revolutionary Left, bought hook, line, and sinker into the idea and rhetoric.

What twentieth-century totalitarianisms owe to religious forms— conscious adaptations and borrowings, including for political liturgies but also eschatological conceptions—is too well known to warrant development here. This essay accordingly will not dip into Nazism or Fascism and do so only in one place for Bolshevism.[207] But Germany is featured with its best-known terrorist group of the 1970s, 1980s and 1990s, the so-called

Baader-Meinhof Gang or Rote Armee Fraktion.[208] The RAF is representative of a vaster galaxy of European left-wing armed militancy—including the French Action Directe and the Italian Brigate Rosse (Red Brigade). Nor was it the sole violent West German group. The Revolutionäre Zellen, for instance, participated in the attacks against a meeting of the Organization of Petroleum Exporting Countries in Vienna and in the hijacking of a French jetliner to Entebbe, Uganda (1976).[209] The RAF's visibility, however, benefited from its first leaders' tragic end and from the availability early on of individual portraits. As a result, worshipped by some as romantic heroes and even martyrs to state oppression, its members have been tarred by others as (in the words of British historian Michael Burleigh) a "ragbag of psychopaths and ideologues who tried to murder Germany into revolution." Ulrike Meinhof—so Burleigh—was a "vehement hysteric," outdone only by "Gudrun Ensslin . . . in psychopathic violence."[210] The RAF activity began with arson in April 1968, but it increased in violence in the early 1970s, with shootings and bombings. After the imprisonment of the leadership in 1972, which was put on trial in 1975–1977, the second generation escalated—with several assassinations, the abduction of the president of the West German Employers' Union, and a hijacking by Palestinian allies. The plane was stormed by German security forces. One day after the assault, Andreas Baader, Gudrun Ensslin, and Jan-Carl Raspe were found dead in their cells (October 18, 1977). President of the Confederation of German Employers'Association Hanns-Martin Schleyer was killed in retaliation. So much for reader-enabling context, already, of course, shot through with interpretation. Now on to analysis.

Chapter 1

The American Way of War Through the Premodern Looking-Glass

Already we hear the roll of the drum, the clangor of the trumpet, and the shout of captains, concentrating and marshalling the hosts.

We come to it at last. The great battle of our time (Gandalf, looking east toward Mordor).

For we are in a desert storm, fighting the Enemy.

A certain way of war is peculiar to the West. By "the West" is meant here the cultural ensembles now located in the territories that recognized Rome's religious primacy before the Reformation, those ensembles that ended up either Protestant or Catholic with the early modern wars of religion. "The West" includes also these regions' offshoots in the United States and elsewhere. By a "way of war" is meant not methods of waging warfare but rather the ideals, ideologies, and conceptions associated with it.[1] The focus is thus on cultural forces insofar as they make warfare meaningful to historical agents and their contemporaries, and insofar as they orient actions.

The aim of this chapter is twofold. First, it presents how American wars, seemingly animated by an idiosyncratic ideology and obviously located on a specific and contingent terrain,[2] are actually peculiarly Western—or more precisely expressed, how much they owe to the imprint of deep-seated Christian notions of freedom, purity, universalism, martyrdom, and History dominant in Western Europe until fairly recently. It may seem illegitimate, especially to readers schooled in New World Protestant diversity, who as such are tendentially more "splitters" than "lumpers," to bunch together under "Western Christianity" the many confessions and denominations that have multiplied since the Reformation.[3] Yet is the distance between them as analytically consequent as the one that separates any of these religious ensembles from Hinduism, Buddhism, or the religion of the Aztecs? Second, this chapter serves as an introduction to these peculiarly Western notions. Later chapters will go into greater depth into their interconnection, and relate them to yet other conceptions, such as vengeance, but the reader will have seen already how these notions tend to be expressed in combination with one another. The combinations or formulas may vary; but the variations play on a limited set of themes.

What then would strike an innocent observer looking from the outside at American warfare as different in terms of ideal types? First, American wars are about the American moral self. For Theodore Roosevelt (1858–1919), to name just one example, conquest in Cuba and the Philippines in 1898 meant both an expansion that would purify the lands and their population, taking them to a higher level, and, for the Americans, a self-purification and conquest of the inner man. This was not a single man's obsession but one characteristic of American political culture in the aftermath of the Civil War of 1861–1865, all the way to World War I.[4] The conflict between North and South itself had been seen as purgative. Horace Bushnell (1802–1876) and the Swiss-born Philip Schaff (1819–1893), a theologian and church historian, concurred in seeing in it (so Schaff) a "baptism of blood [entitling] us to hope for a glorious regeneration" for the nation.[5] This notion of regeneration was shared by both North and South. In a richly documented book, Harry Stout has shown how even in defeat the Confederacy saw in the war a chance for purgation.[6] Of course, spiritual warfare was vastly superior to material war. As a 1863 newspaper explained, God regarded the latter "as far beneath the silent conquest which the Christian gains over his inward foes."[7] But it was also widely agreed that physical war for a just cause could stimulate inner struggles versus vices. This theme—regeneration—can be followed backward into the colonial era: it built on the colonies' deep-seated Protestant tradition. Christianity's missionizing spirit meant that the promised rebirth might encompass more than America. Senator Albert Beveridge, drumming for the annexation of the Philippines, proclaimed his nation as God's "chosen people, henceforth to lead in the regeneration of the world."[8]

Indeed, second, America's wars are the "world's" wars.[9] Already a good half-century before the elder Roosevelt, Secretary of the Navy George Bancroft (1800–1891) could state that the American Revolution had "promised the regeneration of the world."[10] And midway in the century, on the Northern side of the Civil War, Henry Ward Beecher (1813–1887) sermonized in New York that "a battle on the Potomac for our Constitution, as a document of liberty, is the world's battle. We are fighting, not merely for our liberty, but for those ideals that are the seeds and strength of Liberty throughout the earth."[11] This was also a common theme in the initial days of the war. One Northern periodical, the Presbyterian *Banner of the Covenant*, proposed a hymn for a national day of fasting (proclaimed by Abraham Lincoln in August 1861 for the last Thursday in September). As Harry Stout comments, the song "closed with a note of global imperialism": "Unsheathe the gleaming sword, and lead / our loyal armies on, / And smite the rebel bands, until / of traitors there are none. / And then to greater conquests led / By Thine exalted Son. / May we march o'er earth's bloodless fields, / till all the world is won."[12]

The founding fathers' generation already trusted that Providence had instituted the new states and given them the possibility, first among all nations, to express the liberties inherent in natural rights. As such, America was the champion of human dignity, implicitly and sometimes explicitly endowed with a universal mission.[13] Pious America similarly intertwined national and universal, in imagining that righteous bloodshed at home would empower it to global influence. Not uncommonly, ministers predicted that a regenerated Union would spread its missionizing wings over the globe and bring in the nations. This reflex would operate later as well, after 1898 and 1918.[14] As long as fighting to liberate the black slaves could somehow be equated, for instance, with the Italian national struggle against Catholic Austrian rule and the papal states, dreams of an abstract liberty's forthcoming global sway made sense.[15] A half-urban legend dating from 1953 has it that a corporate leader, Charles Wilson, opined that "what was good for the country [America] was good for General Motors and vice-versa." More certain is that, from the Civil War on, and perhaps already from the Revolution on, what was good for America was good for universal humankind.

George W. Bush's speeches on America's Middle East wars are on a continuum with these conceptions. With accents characteristic of the preaching American presidential office, the younger Bush (2001–2008) intoned in his 2004 State of the Union Address that the "cause we serve is right, because it is the cause of all mankind." (The causal connection "because" is noteworthy; universalism implies righteousness.) Two years earlier, on the same occasion, the president had proclaimed that "we have a great opportunity during this time of war to lead the world toward the values that will bring lasting peace."

Third, as explored by Fred Anderson and Andrew Cayton, America's wars are eo ipso wars for "freedom."[16] In his 2002 State of the Union Address, President Bush rhapsodized: "We have known freedom's price. We have shown freedom's power. And in this great conflict [with terrorism], my fellow Americans, we will see freedom's victory."[17] Here again Bush's language is far from exceptional; the theme of freedom is a semiconstant, sounded from the American War of Independence (and even earlier) to the Spanish War of 1898 and beyond, into the Cold War with the Soviet Union.[18] In 1941, during another State of the Union Address read on the eve of a programmed war, Bush's distant predecessor Franklin D. Roosevelt offered the American promise of the "four freedoms," freedom of speech, freedom of worship, freedom from want, freedom from fear. A few years later, as the grand alliance between the United States, Great Britain, and the Soviet Union had dissolved, the incipient Cold War pitted, according to a National Security Council document calling for a military buildup, "the idea of freedom" versus the "idea of slavery under the grim oligarchy of the Kremlin."[19] Over three centuries, the contents of freedom have varied; the invocation of liberty has remained a constant.[20]

A corollary of this third trait follows. American wars being about liberty, "empire," by definition antinomic to freedom, was often denied or recalibrated.[21] To cite a Civil War era poem,[22]

Other flags interpret empire;
Some the pride of rank enshrine;
This alone is Freedom's emblem
Charter of man's right divine.
. . .
Flag of Freedom! flag of glory!
Flag of all Humanity!
Lead the van of marching nations;
Wave! the ensign of the free.

The Methodist *Northern Christian Advocate* conceived in similar terms the intervention in Cuba and the Philippines: "If we go to war with Spain, it will not be for revenge nor for the pride of military power or for the increase of our national territory, but we shall take arms for the freedom of the oppressed, the deliverance of the suffering and in recognition of the claims of humanity upon a strong and prosperous nation."[23] And President Bush expressed as much in his State of the Union Address of 2004: "We have no desire to dominate, no ambitions of empire. . . . [W]e understand our special calling: This great Republic will lead the cause of freedom."[24]

Fourth, American causes are swiftly consecrated by the blood of "martyrs" and "heroes." The near-instantaneous consecration of Private Jessica Lynch, taken prisoner and liberated in the opening weeks of the second American-Iraqi War of 2003 (and initially painted as having fought ferociously to prevent capture), or of football star Pat Tillman, who enlisted out of genuine patriotism in the army rangers and was killed in Afghanistan in April 2004 (but as was found out later by friendly fire and not by the Mujahideen) testify to this cultural need for exemplary figures.[25] Horace Bushnell (1802–1876), reflecting right after the Union victory over the South, could exclaim that "government is now become providential." The same Bushnell found necessary war and its casualties (and the Civil War's had been massive indeed): "Sentiments must be born that are children of thunder; there must be heroes and heroic nationalities, and martyr testimonies."[26] Helmer's 1862 poem eulogized the flag not only as "freedom's emblem" but also as the "banner of the Martyrs slain," calling for vengeance, and depicted the dead soldier "sacred wounds upon his breast . . . [who] sleeps in peace at God's own feet."[27] And their contemporary Oliver Wendell Holmes (1809–1894), in his *Army Hymn*, could invoke "the Lord of Hosts," singing, "Thy Hand hath made our nation free; To die for her is serving Thee."[28]

Fifth, American wars are fought on a peculiar geography, in which inheres a notion of time flowing forward, irreversibly. In the revolutionary era, the disloyal colonists contrasted an Old World of despotism and debauchery with a New World, which, to cite Eric Foner, was to them "the future seat of 'perfect freedom'."[29] A century later, the Methodist *Northern Christian Advocate* said of the 1898 conflict with Spain that, besides being waged for "humanity and liberty," it was fought against an Old World of Latin tyranny and Catholicism.[30] More recently, Secretary of Defense Donald Rumsfeld miffed Germany and France's political elites by calling the two nations "Old Europe," in contrast with other European countries ready to side with the United States in the upcoming war against Saddam Hussein. Rumsfeld himself clarified later that the distinction was "not a matter of . . . age, size, or geographic location," but of the "attitude" and "vision that countries" brought "to the Trans-Atlantic relationship."[31] In 1898, the *Western Christian Advocate*, the leading Methodist paper in Ohio, implored divine action to liberate "unhappy Cuba . . . Spain's helpless victim." Her martyr's blood, the editorialist explained in deliberate echo of Revelation 6, cried to the Lord. "Drive from the shores of this New

World of Thine / This Old World night-bird."[32] Light belonged to the New, blindness and obscurity to the Old. Related to this temporal structure is the intense hope, and often conviction, that the war being fought will be the last in history, or at least open a long era of immense peace.

Sixth, in ideal at least, Old World wars are cruel; American wars merciful. This is a corollary, in the subfield of war and peace, of the general superiority of New over Old. In 1793, an anonymous "citizen," referring to the just begun wars in Europe pitting revolutionary France against neighboring monarchies, had called on fellow Americans to be grateful to God for having spared the country "while the nations of the old world are drenched with blood at the will or the caprice of despotic or ambitious rulers."[33] A contemporary of Thomas Jefferson could intone purple lyrics:

> All former empires rose, the work of guilt, / Of conquest, blood, or usurpation built: / But we, taught wisdom by their woes and crimes, / Fraught with their lore, and born to better times; / Our constitutions form'd on freedom's base, / Which all the blessings of all lands embrace; / embrace humanity's extended cause, / A world of our empire, for a world of our laws.[34]

The same tune was sung by Timothy Dwight in his famous "Columbia": "To conquest and slaughter let Europe aspire; / Whelm nations in blood, and wrap cities in fire; / Thy heroes the rights of mankind shall defend."[35]

Less poetically, John O'Sullivan, when he coined the expression "manifest destiny" in a 1839 article titled "The Great Nation of Futurity," volunteered with fervent certainty that, unlike in the Old World, "our annals describe no scenes of horrible carnage." As Jon Pahl has recently explained, this belief in one's own innocence has been one among several enablers of massive violence in Afghanistan and Iraq after 2001.[36]

The average twenty-first-century citizen of the European Union, a zone with little sympathy for war and its costs,[37] will likely find this all rather odd. Anderson and Cayton have argued that the connection of war, empire, and liberty—for the nation and the world—is a deep-seated characteristic of American political culture. Yet this syndrome is not uniquely American. The cultural traits just outlined have been found, in varying combinations and with differing emphases, in the past of many Western European subcultures and nations. To find occurrences of this common experience, one can backtrack, for instance, to the era of the Crusades. But since the latter constitutes only one moment in the history of the West, in which constellations or formulas linking these notions emerged, other periods will be freely drawn upon.

First, American wars are about the American moral self. This is clearly visible with the Civil War. The opposing side was not only in the wrong politically; it was wrong morally. We have already cited the Southerner FitzHugh's words about Northern libido and free love. And this defect was not envisaged through the lenses of secular ethics.[38] Often enough, it was rank heresy (FitzHugh wrote of "infidels"). The Confederacy might be presented as a God-willed separation from the "contamination" of a religiously deviant North. In this light, war became a struggle for purity.[39] Like an early medieval prelate, Jefferson Davis implored God to give his side victory, peace, and liberty and to "preserve our homes and altars from pollution."[40] To the very end of the war, the *Richmond Daily Dispatch* thundered that "all those who love the Lord Jesus Christ must and will oppose this monster heresy [abolitionism] even onto death."[41] For their part, abolitionists among the Northerners might speak of the fallen soldiers as an expiatory or purificatory libation to cleanse the nation. To cite the memoirs of one among them, "every vestige of the great National Sin, slavery, shall be washed away with their blood."[42] The rhetoric of pollution and purification was as old as late antique Christianity; it was actually not rhetoric but belief.

American wars are about the American moral self? So were many wars of the West. The First Crusade of 1096–1100, and other crusades after it, were penitential expeditions.[43] The initial crusade was intended not only to purge Jerusalem from Muslim filth; as will be discussed in Chapter 4, it would purify also the "army of Christ." In this, the crusade was akin to the second baptism or "red baptism" in blood obtained in martyrdom, the American Civil War's "crimson laver of battle."[44] It was with this understanding that the early twelfth-century Southern French troubadour Marcabru thanked "the Heavenly Lord" for having provided "in His sweetness" a second "washing place, nearby"—just across the Pyrenees mountains, in Muslim Spain, closer at hand than the Holy Land.[45] Evidently, since spiritual warfare was superior to the most righteous of physical struggles, participants in the latter were supposed to remain pure. Not to do so—to consort with loose women on the road to the liberation of Jerusalem—was to invite God's wrath and, as a result, defeat by the Turks.[46] During the American Civil War, letters to the editor and editorials in the *Presbyterian*, a Protestant church periodical devoted to the Northern cause, similarly expressed fears that the Sabbath was not respected in the army; or that there was too much cursing; or that, since civilians were not living morally in this time of war, God prolonged the struggle by way of chastisements.[47] By the time crusading ideology became fully mature, circa 1200, it was generally understood that only a Christendom purified of its vices could triumph over the Muslims. So there existed, as it were, a spiritual home front. Back home, noncombatants fought against the Devil's temptations while crusaders fought against the Devil's human agents. Reform of society and holy war were two sides of the same coin.

It is not surprising, then, that the *Northern Christian Advocate* could pithily title a short paragraph on the war with Spain "First pure, then peaceable."[48] Or that, during the War of Independence, to cite a scholar, "reformation [versus sins] went hand in hand with self-defense."[49] The evil twin of the American Revolution, the French Revolution of 1789, also paired reform and violence. The Revolution was meant to effect the "regeneration" of France. "Regeneration" (also used in Protestant America) was a loan word from the Christian lexicon, where it meant a human being's rebirth from the death of sin into the image of God into which humankind, in the beginning, had been created.[50] The purpose of the Estates General was "to regenerate" the nation.[51] At the 1794 transfer of Jean-Jacques Rousseau's body to the Pantheon, temple to France's great men, Jean-Jacques Cambacérès attributed to the Genevan philosopher France's "salutary regeneration."[52] The Abbé Grégoire wrote a tractate, *The Essay on the Physical, Moral, and Political Regeneration of the Jews*, which extended Christian eschatological hopes for the religious redemption of "Old Israel" to other dimensions of life, as delineated in the title.[53] The Revolutionary's purity was moral. Critics have mocked the stiltedness and rigidity of a good part of the revolutionary leadership, including many Jacobins around Robespierre. But it was not, usually, hypocrisy. The Revolution's methodically violent aspects—to name two, the policy of terror and the battlefield defense of the Fatherland, which turned into a war of expansion that overran much of continental Western Europe—were unthinkable without virtue and served virtue. Between the Crusades and the French Revolution, sixteenth- and seventeenth-century wars of religion also regularly paired sociopolitical reform and purifying warfare. After the Revolution, the Prussia of the German War of Liberation against Napoleon and the European states implicated in World War I commemorated battlefield martyrdoms in part to redeem the nation—as if the nation too, like individuals, could die and be resurrected.[54] All these moments are avatars of a longue durée Western cultural configuration, often invisible to specialists of recent history. They repeat ad nauseam that premodern religious agents did not perpetrate violence to change society in other than religious ways. As we shall see in Chapters 5 and 7, this is not quite right, and it begs the question of what should be categorized as religious and by whom.

All the same, both in the age of the Crusades and in American history, voices—and not always minor voices—could be heard underlining that "regeneration" was so much more important than war that the latter should be disdained, and religious energies turned against fellow Christians—in reality, bad Christians. Alan Heimert has demonstrated this for eighteenth-century America, where many evangelical Calvinists prioritized zeal against heretical "Arminians" over struggles against the Catholic French (during the Seven Years' War) or the religious-political tyranny of the English motherland. Nation and religious denomination did not always reinforce one another.[55] At its most extremes, critiques might call their own country an apostate nation—on the biblical model of an Israel that had finally lost its mantle of election.

Second, America's wars are the "world's" wars. They have universal import, even when as local as the Civil War of 1861–1865 or the War of Independence from Great Britain. Indeed, it is odd to hear the Northern abolitionist clergymen so well studied by Stout exclaim "the present country has seen no such opportunity of blessing the world" or "the world cannot afford to spare us. For the world, freedom lives or dies here and now."[56] That a country can bless the world and that the world cannot spare a country are rather odd and far from commonsensical ideas. (And how did the world acquire a personality and become a subject?[57]) Yet "universalism," the idea of a normative message directed to the world at large, and so potentially to all human beings, is quintessentially Christian. It was born out of the fateful alloy of Rome's sense of its divinely willed imperial destiny—in the words of the Augustan poet Vergil, to take Roman arms and Roman laws to the farthest corners of the globe—and of Christ's command to the apostles to go and preach to all nations (Mark 16.15).[58] Making possible a worldwide religious mission, this universalism also makes possible a world-sized conflict in the service of sacred ideals. (Whether it is actually world-sized, or imagined to be so, is another issue). The First Crusade and a number of crusades after it were meant to impact the whole world. A congeries of apocalyptic scenarios motivated many crusaders, blending straightforward musings on John's Revelation and later prophecies, in particular, the Pseudo-Methodius and the Tiburtine Sibyl (two highly popular myths involving a "Last Emperor") and their reworkings across the early medieval centuries.[59] In a common intersection of these scenarios, once Jerusalem had been taken again, Christ, the Supreme King, would return. The two battles that close John's Revelation involve "the kings of the earth" and "the nations which are over the four quarters of the earth, Gog and Magog." (General Edmund Allenby's successful 1918 campaign, which recovered the Holy Land from the Ottomans, excited similar visions in contemporary American opinion.)[60] But before the last battles take place, the angels (understood as preachers) must first take the Gospel to the ends of the world (Rev. 14.6). The conflict will be total, for, at the End of Times, where many crusaders believed they stood, Antichrist will gather all Christianity's historical enemies into a single, gigantic conspiracy: Jews, idolatrous pagans, tyrants, heretics and false brothers.[61] These minions will all be mowed down, by angels, joined in a variant of the scenario by the saints and Christian elect.

Exterminating angels—missionary angels: the alternation in American ideology and history between interventionism and peaceful influence (conjoined oftentimes with political isolationism) is probably rooted here and deeply so.[62] Medievalists have shown how, far from being in contradiction with one another, crusade and mission constituted an ideological system. In the mid-thirteenth century, Pope Innocent IV (r. 1243–1254) allowed crusade if force was necessary to open the way to Christian preaching,[63] a normative Catholic view not unknown to modern-day Protestant evangelists. Extolling the piety of the American soldier in the first U.S.-Iraq Gulf War, a pastor exclaimed, "The Gospel was spread through our reserve soldiers to the armies of the participating nations, and through those troops to the people of their homelands. This was also the door through which the Gospel went to the Muslim peoples of the world. God used the conflict to start to liberate these countries through the power of the Holy Spirit."[64] And the opening of Iraq to missionary effort was very much on the mind of Franklin Graham and Southern Baptists, who explained in 2003 that "a war for souls" was "under way" in Iraq.[65]

The hymn that the *Banner of the Covenant* proposed in 1861 for the Union's national fast conjoined the purge of inner enemy ("traitors") and world conquest for Christ. So did George Ide (1804–1872), reflecting right after the Civil War on its meaning. The reunited country would march as "one vast phalanx" under God to the spiritual "conquest of the world."[66] This sense of a dual battlefield, domestic and foreign, is axiomatic. The conflict on two fronts is either simultaneous or sequential. As we shall discuss, in the early fifteenth century, Jeanne d'Arc believed her task was first to solve the French civil war by expelling the English from the continent, then to smash the Hussite heretics in Bohemia (modern Czech Republic), then to lead an expedition to conquer back Jerusalem and destroy paganism.[67] This was a common scenario. In the later Middle Ages, it was borne by the legend of the Second Charlemagne and its counter-narratives (since the Second Charlemagne myth tended to be pro-French, pro-German counterparts also developed), related to the prophecies attributed to Joachim of Fiore (d. 1202). In one variant, this last world emperor would conquer England, destroy Rome and Florence, then cross the Mediterranean and be made king of the Greeks, subject to his rule Muslim populations, and "lay down an edict that whosoever would not worship the Crucified would die." He would end up yielding his crown on the Mount of Olives in Jerusalem after having attained universal dominion. Another popular text, Jean de Roquetaillade's *Vademecum*, wove into its own version of EndTimes the extirpation of heresy, avarice, and pride from the clergy.[68] In Iberia, in a very popular prophecy, the mysterious Fray Joan Alamany predicted that a last ruler would lead a crusade of the poor against Muslims, Jews, and Spain's bad Christians, then go on to Jerusalem and institute, after Antichrist's defeat, a thousand years of peace.[69] This scenario involving internal and external enemies had a much older genealogy. For instance, in the middle of the eleventh century, a poet exhorted the German kingdom's nobility to rally behind its young king, tame local enemies (Normans settled in southern Italy and probably the rebellious Lotharingian duke), then go on to vanquish the Saracens (then in control of the Holy Land) plus the "Huns," protect the East from pagans, and conquer the known world.[70]

In the Christian tradition, universalism is regularly balanced with exceptionalism. While the message is universal, a minority, a separate and superior group, bears the message until it can become, toward the End of History, the property of the majority. In conformity with this, recent American wars invoke the notions of the "world" and of an "alliance" or "coalition" of the good nations against evil, led by the United States as its vanguard.[71] The First Crusade involved a congeries of military groups led by greater and smaller princes—prominently French ("Franks") under Hugh of Vermandois, Robert of Normandy, and Stephen of Blois; Provençals under Raymond of Saint-Gilles; south Italian Normans under Bohemund of Taranto and his nephew Tancred; Lotharingians (also "Franks") and Germans under Godfrey of Bouillon.[72] While recognizing the diversity, chroniclers often presented the army as "Franks," the ethnic group that—according to some reports—Urban II's 1095 sermon launching the expedition identified as divinely destined to seize the Holy Land. (It has been recently argued that many crusaders actually saw themselves as "Franks," even if they had another primary ethnic identity.[73])

Christianitas (Christendom) constituted another commonly used collective term for the army fighting against the Muslims, the *exercitus christianus* (the Christian army). The crusading host, suggests Jan van Larhooven, "felt itself a representative of Western Christendom." This was not a mere metonymy. Theology made it possible, just as it made possible for a Baptist sermonizing on the occasion of the November 1863 Thanksgiving ordered by President Abraham Lincoln to state, flatly, that "in this struggle [for liberty] we stand for the world, we represent the world."[74] It is also the imprint of theology, this time eighteenth-century Jansenist Catholic theology, that accounts for the French Revolution's dialectic between two ideals: one that considered that the unanimous consensus of all citizens was necessary and another that posited that the political minority had the clear-sightedness necessary to lead a regenerated France.[75]

For Marxists as well, the Proletariat was both "vanguard" and, on the eschatological horizon of the End of History, universal. It is, in Karl Marx's words, "a social group that is the dissolution of all social groups, a sphere that has a universal character because of its universal sufferings." To gain emancipation, the Proletariat will have to emancipate itself from all other spheres of human society and, in so doing, emancipate them, thereby operating "the complete redemption of humanity."[76] The connection between liberty and universalism here too jumps to the eyes. So does the Judeo-Christian correlation between martyrdom and the march of History.

All the same, there exist more exclusivist conceptions. That the army of 1096–1100 was a metonymy for Christendom may have been true for some First Crusade chroniclers (and the participants they represented). But others— Ekkehard of Aura and Raymond d'Aguilers—toyed with a more radical exclusivism (see Chapter 4). God's army was filled with traitors, and there could not be any simple equation between a visible national group and those predestined to salvation. Nowadays, some equally exclusivist Protestant conceptions assume that, while the Christian message will spread to all corners of the universe, it will be adopted only by a minority of humankind, the rest being destined to damnation. More even, for some evangelicals, America, while vastly better than other states, is by no means identical with an elect nation. The most extreme example may be the Westboro Baptist Church, recently made infamous for picketing the funerals of fallen U.S. soldiers. They died, remonstrate the sectarians, because America is evil and sinful.[77] In these conceptions, medieval and contemporary, the universal is fundamentally an arena in which humans must make their choice for either good or evil, not an all-encompassing group whose majority, it is mercifully hoped, can be saved. Self-styled prophecy scholar Timothy LaHaye's best-selling fictions *Left Behind* (a series that has for part of its readership the status of quasi-scripture) and *Babylon Rising* thus oscillate between a more exclusive and more encompassing vision of redemption. Furthermore, while America is the prime target of Antichrist's forces, its armed forces, FBI, and CIA are unwittingly or wittingly abettors in the creation of the Enemy's worldwide political and religious tyranny.[78]

Third, America's wars are eo ipso wars for "freedom." But American freedom is not just any freedom. This freedom is divinely willed and divinely granted, and is primarily religious, with other dimensions of human life folded in it. To the second President Bush, who otherwise dotted his speeches with coded Christian language—allusions to the Bible—this was explicitly an article of faith:

> I believe in the transformative power of liberty. I believe that if the United States of America does not lose its faith in the power of freedom to transform hopeless societies, that we will see the peace that we all want. I believe in the universality of freedom. I believe there's an Almighty, and I believe a gift of that Almighty to every man, woman and child is freedom.[79]

As Alexis de Tocqueville noted perceptively in 1835, "Americans conflate so completely in their minds Christianity and liberty that it is almost impossible to make them conceive of the one without the other."[80] When the Civil War started, Episcopalian preacher Stephen Higginson Tyng easily paired political and religious freedom: "The enemy to be assailed and vanquished is generally the same. In India and China it finds its embodiment in a Pagan Priestcraft. In Europe it is the despotism of [papal] Rome. In America it is met in the system of African slavery."[81]

Since the eighteenth century, and into our own century, American discourse had regularly associated freedom of access to the Truth that liberates from enslaving sin with the availability of democracy and other social and political liberties. Midway through the French and Indian War (1754–1763), a Thanksgiving Day sermon speculated that God had "revealed His purpose," to gradually operate "a most signal revolution in the civil and religious state of things in this world."[82] In this conviction of coupled political and religious transformations, Jonathan Mayhew was just one among many in his generation. Here again former President Bush's words belong to a long tradition of pulpit rhetoric and genuine conviction. Furthermore, already in the late eighteenth century this liberation concerned a vaster world, envisaged in the light of the eschatological struggle:

> Behold, then, this hero of America [the "hero of civil and religious liberty"], wielding the standard of civil and religious liberty over these United States!—Follow him, in his strides, across the Atlantic!—See him, with his spear already in the heart of the beast!—See tyranny, civil and ecclesiastical, bleeding in every pore!—See the votaries of the tyrants; of the beasts; of the false prophets, and serpents of the earth, ranged in battle array, to withstand the progress and dominion of him, who hath commission to break down the usurpations of tyranny;—to let the *prisoner out of the prison-house*; and to set the vassal in bondage free from his chains;—to level the mountains—to raise the valleys, and to prepare an highway for the Lord [Jesus Christ].[83]

In American thought, the pairing of deviant religion and political oppression is common. But it is not exclusively American. Before the French Revolution's course quashed the liberal clergy that had helped it take off in 1789, these men of the cloth could hope that the spread of French democracy throughout Europe and beyond would open humanity's eyes to the true religion—Catholicism. Embracing our institutions, nations would embrace our faith. The End of History had come. God was "readying Himself to hand over the reign of universal liberty . . . in the last days of human generations." Salvation would "come out of our Fatherland and communicate itself to all of humankind, just as formerly it came out of Judea" with the First Coming of Christ. "God's intention" was "to call France to be liberty's cradle for humankind"; it would become "the center for the joining of all people to the Gospel's sanctity," and Paris, "the free universe's capital." The "religion of the French" would spread "along with the spirit of liberty to all the lands that will receive our laws."[84] So Catholic clergyman Antoine-Adrien Lamourette. But, as said above, seven hundred years earlier, West European warriors had believed that, grouped around the Franks or even identifying with them, they would bring by the sword freedom from heathen oppression to the Eastern Christians and unify the world for Christ. The apocalypticism of freedom and French election were evident facts for revolutionaries, including, of course, Robespierre. "Providence Eternal called you [the French], alone since the world's origin, to reestablish on earth the reign of justice and freedom," he intoned.[85] One almost hears an echo of the visionary revelation Saint Andrew made to a crusader in 1098 (and the expedition too was expected to inaugurate an earthy era of liberty and justice): "God elected you among all nations just as the good grain is separated from the chaff, for in merits and grace you are ahead of all those who came before you and shall come after you, just as gold's price is ahead of silver's."[86] The revolutionary bishop just cited, Lamourette, assumed that religious errors maintained themselves "only through their unity with the political systems to which the nations are subjected," that is, with despotisms. Thus, a precondition of Christ's return consisted in the destruction by liberty of all tyrannies.[87] But, after 1792, Republican anticlericalism ensured that pundits on both sides, revolutionary and counterrevolutionary, paired not democracy with Catholicism but Catholicism with despotic monarchy. Lamourette was guillotined in early 1794.

The predisposition to alloy tyranny and persecution, evil kings and pagans or heretics, and thus, contrariwise, political liberty and religious freedom antedated the two eighteenth-century revolutions, American and French.[88] The enabling context for the First Crusade was a movement of reform whose motto was *libertas ecclesiae*, freedom for the Church. Cardinal Humbert of Moyenmoutier (d. 1061), one of the first Rome-based reformers, wrote indignantly that the clergy was enslaved through simony (the buying of sacraments and church offices), even though clerics "should be more free than all human beings, insofar as their share in the [heavenly] inheritance is God Himself."[89] In 1068, after a monk had undergone an ordeal by fire to prove that the bishop of Florence had bought his office, the clergy wrote Pope Alexander II (r. 1061–1073) and beseeched him to "take arms against the enemies of Peter the Apostle, form his battalions, enter holy wars . . . and free us from captivity by fighting against the simoniacs." These were images of spiritual warfare for *libertas*.[90] The enabling fantasy of this reform movement was the just mentioned conspiracy of Antichrist and his minions. The pope who transformed the reform movement into the first European revolution, Gregory VII, penned a letter stating flatly that royal power was an invention of sinful men and of the devil: "Who does not know that kings and princes derive their origin from men ignorant of God who raised themselves above their fellows by pride, plunder, treachery, murder—in short, by every kind of crime—at the instigation of the Devil, the prince of this world?"[91]

But this freedom was (as is well known) not the freedom to chose evil, to the contrary. Since at least the reign of Constantine's sons, *libertas* often meant "freedom from heresy" or sin.[92] Nor (as is also well known) was late antique and medieval *libertas* the philosopher's "negative freedom," that is, freedom from external constraints, especially freedom to do anything one desires. Since early Christianity, freedom has been linked with service to God. In the Roman legal process of manumission, the former slave, now a freedman (*libertus*) or freedwoman, remained the dependent of and in debt of service (*obsequium*) to the former master (*dominus*). The Lord Christ (Dominus Christus), having liberated humanity from slavery to sin and from bondage to Old Testament Law, was now the patron-like figure to Whom the redeemed species was bound in a form of honorable obedience.[93]

Fourth, American wars generate "martyrs" and "heroes," whose generous blood quickly consecrates the causes for which it is shed. George W. Bush concluded his victory speech on May 1, 2003 with biblical accents, linking freedom and martyrdom. About the fallen American soldiers, he said, "Their final act on this Earth was to fight a great evil and bring liberty to others." To the surviving military men and women, he added, "Wherever you go, you carry a message of hope, a message that is ancient and ever new. In the words of the prophet Isaiah [49.9], To the captives, come out; and to those in darkness, be free"—a prognostication announcing liberty, political liberty evidently, but, for the born-again president, also the chance offered to the liberated populations to find liberty from sin and liberty to believe the Truth.[94] Other scholars have recently subsumed "martyrdom" under the label of sacrifice and explored the mechanisms by which this notion, in the United States, makes violence self-evident and meaningful: sacrificing oneself allows one to sacrifice others. While not excluding this mechanism, this essay remains at the level of theological forms.[95]

Martyrdom at war does, of course, antedate Christian America. Already with the Crusades, and possibly before in the ninth century, it was possible to die a martyr with weapons in hand. One could be a martyr to defend a written or unwritten constitution, the principles and norms regulating a polity. Martin Luther, the catalyst of the sixteenth-century Protestant Reformation, offered the crown of martyrdom to those German lords who might die on the battlefield fighting "on the side of authority (*oberheyt*)" the massive 1524–1525 popular uprisings known as the Peasants' War. And not die fighting with an arm tied behind their back: Luther exhorted the noblemen to "smite, execute and stab, secretly and openly, remembering that nothing can be more poisonous, hurtful or devilish than a rebellious man." Luther, who rejected warfare for the Christian faith, legitimized it and with it martyrdom, for the protection of the God-willed earthly order.[96]

Martyrdom and even holy war were especially authorized for liberty. Over the centuries, one adduced biblical examples, mostly from the Old Testament, to this effect. Regicide Jacques Clément had not feared "to die to put the Church and the [French] people into liberty."[97] Such was the position expressed by the Holy League's printing mill. This "Sainte Ligue," an ultra-Catholic alliance of townsmen, whose backbone consisted in anti-Calvinist religious confraternities, had turned against the king of France, Henri III. The monarch had proven himself too tepid in fighting against Calvinist heretics. In the Ligue's book, "liberty" was simultaneously freedom from heresy and freedom from despotic rule. For it, one had to be ready to die.

Martyrdom could be vindictive, in the sense that one offered oneself to death with the assumption that God, or History, or the human agents of History, would take vengeance (and in some scripts, as we shall see in Chapter 4, move History forward). Robespierre, the leader of the Jacobin faction associated with the guillotine and the Terror, in a single breath proclaimed himself willing to be a martyr and called for the destruction of the Revolution's enemies:

> Strike; we await your blows. How easily a few hundred assassins can thrust a murderous sword in the heart of the good man whose only defense lies in his virtues and in the watchfulness of the people and of Providence. But, on the other hand, take stock of the depth of your criminal nature and of the punishments that the enormousness of your perfidies will draw upon itself. Expect the people's judgment and that of Providence: You will escape neither the one nor the other. O French, friends of equality, rely on us to take care to use the little life that Providence grants us to fight against the enemies surrounding us. We swear in the daggers reddened by the blood of the Revolution's martyrs (and since then sharpened against us) to exterminate to the last the criminals who would steal from us happiness and freedom.[98]

During the French Revolution, as in the Middle Ages of the Crusades or the early modern Europe of the wars of religion, martyrdom justified terror; the willingness to die legitimized massive shedding of blood. Conversely, the quest for order or liberty called for martyrdom. For, finally, Christianity transported and vulgarized the old Roman conception that unjust death, when avenged, lead to constitutional transformations.[99]

Fifth, American wars muster the terms "New" and "Old." America is

"New," radically "new" in two theological senses. First, the newness of the Gospel as opposed to the Old Law; second, the newness of the *novissimum*, the very last. We meet here the two caesuras that give rhythm to the Christian theology of History. The first is carried by the Christ-Event (Incarnation, Passion, Resurrection); the second divides this world from the onset of the next, whether it be millennium of peace or the Last Judgment. As will be developed in Chapter 2, the opposition between Old and New is culturally overdetermined by Christian theology's complementary, often dialectical, pairs consisting in the New and Old Testaments, the time of grace and the time of the (Mosaic) Law, the era of mercy and the era of vengeance, the age of unavoidable sin and the age of redeemed humankind. This temporality is normative: The New is better than the Old. This temporality is irreversible: History itself sides with the New against the Old.[100]

To be placed at EndTimes meant to be living in a very special state, for the terminal zone within the New Era, the threshold to the eternal Kingdom, was charged with a special valence. As the Ohio Methodist journal put it in its 1898 prayer to God, "Build Thou within these boundless Western seas, / As Thou hast built throughout four hundred years, / In answer to Thy people's prayers and tears / Time's last, best empire—Thine and Liberty's."[101] Or during the Civil War, a pamphlet tellingly titled "Palingenesy: National Regeneration" explained that America, tested by war and brought to proper governance, would "stand" through the last and "better era" of the world. "Our political structure—the House of Liberty and Law and Love—shall abide," so it affirmed, "till its glory of arch and spire and dome shall blend with the amethyst and chrysolite and sapphire of the New Jerusalem" (cf. Rev. 21.11–21).[102] The idea of the last empire was Jewish and Christian, developed around the visions interpreted by the prophet Daniel. King Nabuchodonosor of Babylon had dreamed of a statue, with a golden head, breast and arms of silver, stomach and thighs of brass, legs of iron, and feet of iron mixed with clay (Dan. 2.31–33). But later in the dream a great stone had broken off from a mountain, destroyed the statue, and filled the whole world (2.34–35). Daniel interpreted the dream; it signified four successive world empires and their supersession by a kingdom willed by God, which would "stand into eternity." On the basis of this prophecy, Christian theologians wove the model of a succession of empires over History's course—a very popular model in the Middle Ages but also in more "modern" early America. There, Bishop George Berkeley's highly popular "Verses on the Prospect of Planting Arts and Learning in America" rehashed a cultural evidence: "Westward thye course of Empire takes its way,

/ The first four acts already past, / a fifth shall close the drama with the day; / Time's noblest offspring the last." On the New Continent, circa 1800, many equated the growth of Daniel's stone with the expansion of American republicanism; its diffusion of liberty was the precondition or the companion for the Gospel's spread.[103] Kingdom would follow kingdom, until the End. The last kingdom emerging out of the stone was God's Kingdom, the "New Jerusalem" studded with precious stones invoked by the 1864 *Palingenesy*. Interpreters differed as to whether the Kingdom would already exist in this age or only after Christ's return in glory or after the Last Judgment. Each Christian polity, and many European states that evolved out of Christian kingdoms, has at one point or another believed that it was "the Last Kingdom," after which History would stop. Thus wars perceived as major are often also thought to be the war to end all wars.[104] These religious conceptions translated themselves into more secular lexica. Maximilien Robespierre's fond belief was that "to reach the peaceful kingdom of constitutional laws, we must finish liberty's war against tyranny."[105] In 1992, three years after the end of the Cold War, pundit Francis Fukuyama proclaimed "The End of History."[106]

Daniel's final kingdom was—in one aspect at least—a gentler empire, a different empire. The rule of Christ contrasted with Roman rule, explained Augustine of Hippo in *On God's Polity* (*The City of God*), as counsel (political deliberation) to domination (top-down, arbitrary rule). Or, in the words of Juan Ginés de Sepúlveda's 1544 justification of Christian intervention against the idolatrous, despotic, cannibalistic Mesoamerican states, since "the evangelical New Law is more perfect and more gentle than the Old Law of Moses (because the latter was a law of fear, and the former is a law of grace, gentleness, and charity), wars should now be waged with mercy and clemency." George W. Bush assumed his foreordained war against Saddam Hussein's Iraq would be both just and gentler: "If war is forced upon us, we will fight in a just cause and by just means, sparing, in every way we can, the innocent." In the same breath, however, the president warned that "we will fight with the full force and might of the United States military."[107]

While the second Bush was not promising extermination to the enemies of an America that considered itself fundamentally peace seeking, his pairing of mildness and strength constituted a derivate product of an age-old Theology of History. If the age opened by Christ is fundamentally an age of mercy, toward its end, toward the moments prophesized in John's Revelation, it can become cruel again (when it does not turn radically pacifistic). Listen to the Yale Puritan Jonathan Edwards: "The saints in heaven may and will hate the damned;

they may therefore delight in seeking just revenge for their injuries to them." In the present world, though, "we ought not to desire revenge on our fellow creatures . . . because we ought not to hate them." This is a time when "love ought to prevail." "But when those reasons of love cease, and our enemies become the proper objects of our hatred, then we may delight to see just revenge executed upon them." At the End, the saints will "rejoice in God's vengeance upon their carnal enemies."[108] This is about heavenly judgment, not about human agency. But, more than once in the history of Christianity, "the saints go marching in," carrying a sword for Christ: the crusaders, of course, but also the Hussite revolutionaries in 1419, the radical Anabaptists in 1534–35, Cromwell's men during the English Revolution, John Brown at Harpers Ferry—and before Captain Brown, Jonathan Edward's own disciples.[109] The End is not a point but a phase, a phase devoted to vengeance. The radical superiority of the future over the past makes possible radical measures, the last purge before Christ returns, or, in a Godless secular version, before History ends.

The American propensity to identify America's own history (or its perceived turning points) with the Bible's epochal transformation from Old to New, or with the promised millennium of Revelation (21–22) or with the destiny of the Last Empire belonged squarely in the Western tradition. But because of the eschatological horizon's acute presence in the New World, American religious culture gave this tradition a particularly intense twist. "Free people," trusted George W. Bush on the eve of the second Iraq War of 2003, "will set the course of history." Not so pious a Christian, Thomas Paine still exclaimed at the end of *Common Sense* that "we have it in our power to begin the world over again" and that "the birthday of a new world is at hand."[110] The people of the New Alliance were endowed with true sight and spiritual senses. Paine could thus state—meaningfully for his audiences—that "our style and manner of thinking have undergone a revolution more extraordinary than the political revolution of the country. We see with other eyes, we hear with other ears; and think with other thoughts, than those we formerly used. We can look back on our own prejudices as if they had been the prejudices of other people."[111] Paine's faith in the progressive march of History, where the New supersedes the Old, pushed to its logical extreme a Christian potentiality: God judged History and revealed His judgment at EndTime; the future became the judge of the present; and those who can understand the future—God's will—are judges alongside it. At its logical extreme, exemplified by Hermann Melville's novel *White-Jacket* (1850), this conception annihilated the exemplarity of the past.

In *White-Jacket*, the ship in which the action and the meditations take place, the *Neversink*, serves as a metonymy for America. Through it, Melville expresses hopes and ideals for what the nation should be, conjoined with cynicism and critiques vis-à-vis what it is.[112] In an attack on the navy's traditional punishment by flogging, Melville ups the ante by drawing on American exceptionalism and the widely shared theology of history that underlay it. America is to look to the "prospective precedents of the Future in preference to those of the Past." The Past, more sharply put, "is the text-book of tyrants; the Future is the Bible of the Free." In embracing the latter, Americans, "the peculiar, chosen people . . . the Israel of our time" in the dimension of politics, will lead, an "advance-guard" for great things. Just as religious pagans have submitted to Israel of Old, so will the "political pagans" (understand, Old World despotisms?) to this predestined race.[113]

Melville was here in harmony with the inventor of the expression "manifest destiny." O'Sullivan had labeled his country "the nation of futurity." The same vision of norms emanating from the eschatological future as opposed to tradition served both the novelist's laudable progressive political goals and O'Sullivan's perhaps less palatable imperialist and annexionist dreams. The future as source of "prospective precedents" also animated revolutionary Marxism—in the light of Soviet history not too palatable either. But at least one sympathetic and perspicacious analyst had perceived, in the moment, the aporia's subtle quality. For Maurice Merleau-Ponty, Bolshevism was coherent:

> The revolutionary judges what exists in the name of what does not yet exist, but which he regards as more real. The act of revolution presents itself both as the creation of History and as the truth of History in relation to its total meaning. . . . Bourgeois justice adopts the past as its precedent; revolutionary justice adopts the future. It judges in the name of the Truth that the Revolution is about to make true.[114]

Merleau-Ponty wrote in the late 1940s, in an attempt to account for the attitude, a decade earlier, of Bolsheviks during the trials (1937–1938) that eliminated much of Lenin's old companions and other opponents, real or imagined, of Stalin's dictatorial rule, including Nikolai Bukharin (about whom more in Chapter 4). He provided an exegesis of the peculiar ethics that, according to him, governed decision in epochs or moments of radical uncertainty. This analysis covered the twinned political alternatives available to individual French during the Nazi occupation of France—armed resistance to Germany or collaboration with Germany (including joining the fascist French *Milice* and fighting against resistors alongside German soldiers and police). In a revolutionary moment, choices have to be made, and those who choose to risk choice have to choose in the light of a fervently hoped-for future.

To conclude, two remarks that depart from the historian's domain and lapse into that of ethics. First, for nonpacifist politics, the call to the future as judge and norm makes for a morality of involvement, which one may consider, with Merleau-Ponty, as more ethical than cautious passivity. Second, that "empire" is supposed to be different does influence the way actual empires are run; that there is concern for "the world" means global action; that one utters concerns for "liberty" may limit power politics. Without American idealism at war, no Nazi defeat. Without the American sense of mission, no intervention in Bosnia or Kosovo to stop genocide. And this theology of History so present in the West is not only a theology of war. It is also, and inextricably so, a theology of peace. Peace, for Augustine, is inextricably tied to justice. With the Western way of war have grown the Western institutions of peace and justice, for which, it may be hoped, the West will still go to war. We now turn to exegesis, to better understand the Christian dialectic between war and peace.

Chapter 2

Christian Exegesis and Violence

> One can indeed mock Marcion's God, Who knows neither how to
> get angry nor how to avenge.
> —Tertullian, *Against Marcion*, 5.4.14

> No religion was ever more fertile in crimes than Christianity. From
> Abel's murder to the torture of [Jean] Calas [1762], there is not any
> line of its history that is not bloody.
> —Diderot, *Salon de 1762*, §42

> We should always limit ourselves to the following historical truth:
> The Muslims' lawgiver was a powerful and terrifying man, who es-
> tablished his dogmas by his courage and by his weapons; yet his reli-
> gion became merciful and tolerant. Christianity's divine founder
> lived in humility and peace, and preached forgiveness of offenses;
> but owing to our furious madness, his holy and sweet religion be-
> came the most intolerant and most barbarous of all.
> —Voltaire, *Essai sur les mœurs*, chap. vii

Violence and the Grammar of Exegesis

With characteristic wickedness, the anticlerical philosopher Voltaire toyed
with a paradox. While Muhammad's Islam, founded by the sword, quickly
had become peaceful, Christianity, initially a religion of peace, was presently
a cause for unrivalled fanaticism and war. Voltaire's eighteenth-century wit
dovetails with the current mainstream conception of Christianity: a religion
that was, is, and ought to be fundamentally irenistic and in which violence

was, is, and must be a radical perversion. To account for it, an outside force, process, or event has often been blamed. To list the main villains in this sorry plot, Emperor Constantine's conversion to the Faith (first third of the fourth century), the acculturation to a warlike worldview forced by Rome's barbarian invaders (between the fifth and the tenth centuries), feudalism (anytime between the ninth and the twelfth centuries), or state building (anytime). For Carl Erdmann, writing in 1935, the turning point came toward the year 1000, when the Church gave up its initial irenistic ethos, which it had actually strengthened during the early Middle Ages to parry the barbarian emphasis on feud and vengeance.[1] James Russell proposed recently an early acculturation of Christianity to these very "Germanic" feuding values. Jonathan Riley-Smith suggested that the feudal ideal of fidelity, projected onto the Lord Christ, fed during the 1090s enthusiasm for the crusade. Jean Flori also at one point spoke of the "substitution of warrior and feudal values for primitive Christianity's pacifist values."[2]

But is Christianity actually straightforwardly pacifistic? And was it so in Christianity's origins? Words can deceive. By "pacific," the Middle Ages could mean a "peacemaker," usually through the sword.[3] By "tolerance," the Early Church meant effectively "bearing with" and "suffering through" either (when the Church was an illegal organization) persecution or (when a church was in a majority position or held power) heretical dissent, paganism, or the presence of Jews. This is by no means tantamount to a principled acceptance of pacifism or religious difference.[4] "Tolerance" was related to martyrdom, insofar as it meant to be tormented, deeply, by the existence of these vicious opponents.

The earliest Christian community wrestled with the issue of violence; it may even have been, in whole or in part, physically militant. Some scholars, a minority, consider that some among the apostles, and possibly Jesus himself, may have been Zealots—related to the broad family of Jewish revolutionary groups that rose up in 66–73 C.E. against Rome and against bad fellow believers.[5] Might not Simon Peter, who took the sword to defend his master when soldiers came to arrest Him and sliced off with his sword the ear of the high priest's servant (Mark 14.47; Matt. 26.51–54; John 18.10–11, Luke 22.49–51), have belonged to one of these militant and often millenarian factions? Or was the Gospel, with Jesus' rebuke to Peter ("Put back your sword in its scabbard"), merely teaching the distance that ought to exist between His disciples and the violence of the sectarians?[6] First-century Christianity, let alone the Christianity of Jesus at the time of His death, is hard to reconstruct on the basis of the Synoptic Gospels, Mark, Luke, and Matthew. They were all composed after the great Jewish revolt of 66–73 C.E. And, with the exception of a few ambiguous sayings (and of Jesus' cleansing of the Temple from moneychangers), they all rejected violence. Almost half a century ago, S. G. F. Brandon proposed that, after the defeat of the Jewish rebellion, the evangelists censured the earlier militant tradition and erased most traces of zealot sympathies. Rare Christic sayings such as "I have not come to bring peace, but a sword" (Matt. 10.34) represent leftovers from the earlier bellicist position.[7] (Used as fragments, these isolated texts legitimate modern-day Christian terrorists, such as the apocalyptic group "The Covenant, Sword and Arm of the Lord," founded in 1971 and dismantled in 1985.[8])

Brandon's theory is unfalsifiable (insofar as he can allocate any irenic element to the post-Jewish War rewriting and any bellicose fragment to the original temper of Christianity); therefore its truth-value cannot be adjudicated. Still, it is worth exploring Scripture in this general direction. Might not the Gospels constitute an exoteric corpus, whose esoteric but bellicose counterpart we have lost, with the exception of John's bloody and vengeful Revelation? The case of the Essenes might suggest as much. Posterity first encountered this ascetic Jewish sect from descriptions in Josephus, Philo, and Pliny the Elder; since the first half of the twentieth century, the Dead Sea Scrolls discovered near Qumran have offered insights into what Essenes read, copied, and wrote.[9] In 68 C.E., the Romans destroyed the Qumran settlement; very likely the group had joined the rebellion. Qumranian manuscripts have been found in Masada, where the Zealots took their final stand against Rome and committed mass suicide (73 or 74 C.E.). The community is thus present at two violent bookends of the Jewish War.[10] And the Essenes' own writings indicate that the strongly regulated, purity-oriented sect practiced dissimulation.[11] It waited to join angelic hosts for the final war that would annihilate Satan, his supernatural minions, the idolatrous pagan empire, and collaborationist Jews. It would be fought at the End of Times:

> Then the sword of God shall hasten to the time of judgment and all the children of His truth shall awaken to put an end to [the children of] wickedness, and all the children of guilt shall be no more. . . . The eternal gates shall open to bring out the weapons of war, and they shall be mighty from one end of the world to the other. . . . But there is no escape for the creatures of guilt, they shall be trampled down to destruction with no rem[nant].[12]

The sectarians were ordered to hate wicked men and evil forces with a perfect hatred but also to dissimulate this hostile emotion until the Last Days. Exoterically, the Essenes were peaceful ascetics; esoterically, they were holy warriors bidding their time, or rather, God's time.[13] This configuration would appear again with some Melchiorite Anabaptist groups of the 1520s and 1530s. For this broad family of radical reformed Christians inspired by the chiliast prophet Melchior Hoffmann, the question was not whether, but when to draw the sword, and (after the Münster Kingdom's destruction in 1535) whether to turn clandestine.[14]

Ultimately, though, important as they may be in their own right, the exact stances toward armed violence animating the earliest Christians and the Essenes are irrelevant to the present inquiry. So is in its own way the exact identity of the historical agents who contaminated the putative initial irenicism. More importantly for us, the scholarly debate over origins raises the question of violence's inscription in time—in the temporality governed by God, Sacred History (or as the Germans call it, *Heilsgeschichte*, a History divinely oriented to salvation and damnation). For the Qumran community, time was bipartite, divided into two stretches, one devoted to peace, the other to war. As we shall see, some Christian conceptions of Sacred History developed this notion and made it tripartite, with a bellicose Old Testament era, a pacifist time of the Church opened by Christ's First Advent on earth, and a brief EndTime—the Eschaton—where warfare would return.

The second debate (that of contamination by political forces) is also substantially important yet ultimately not central to this inquiry. However, it motivates the exploration of a contrarian, and intellectualist, position (which will be developed first, before discussing the bipartition of Sacred History). Do there not exist within Christian theology structural forces that, with some autonomy vis-à-vis conjuncture, can produce violence and make it legitimate? A decade ago, Schmuel Eisenstadt proposed that violent fundamentalisms and radical-utopian revolutions worldwide are historically related to the heresies that the great axial religions systemically engender.[15] This thesis refines and extends to a global scope a classic paradigm in the historical sociology of Christianity. Scholars and intellectuals have posited a connection between heresies and revolutions and proposed models relating constitutional forms to forms of Christianity (revolutions' contemporaries often drew such a connection themselves, usually disapprovingly).[16] Eric Voegelin drew a parallel between what he identified as "Gnosticism"—a hatred of the world conjoined to a belief in its possible transformation—and the twentieth century's violent political religions. As far as I see, he did not propose a continuity over time between the Gnostics, a branch of the polymorphous early Christian movement, and Fascism, Bolshevism, and Nazism, but such a transhistorical tradition has been implied by some among his readers.[17] Yet a *heretical* continuum is not necessary. To see, with Eisenstadt and (perhaps) Voegelin, in heresy the matrix of Christian religious violence would still be to locate this bellicism's origins outside Christianity's core. Consider that Eisenstadt himself, and following him Marcel Gauchet, have posited that axial religions systemically produce heresies.[18] If it is so, the violence attributed to heresy is very much a product of the inner dynamics of *orthodoxy*. Christian theology was shaped by vivid controversies between different wings within the Christian movement and, as a result, is for many issues the dialectical synthesis of plural heresies. In the case of violence, we are dealing with a dialectic between bellicism and irenicism, which is usually in favor of the latter (but this essay will focus more on the former, in an approach meant to be heuristically contrarian).[19] Pure pacifism and radical religious violence are, thus, potentialities that can always be rediscovered in the folia of orthodoxy's key texts (it entails excising the complementary and opposite factor). The Christian tradition has conceived heresy in precisely these terms. A heresy is a partial truth, yet false owing to its incompleteness. Joseph Cardinal Ratzinger, the recently abdicated pope (r. 2005–2013 as Benedict XVI), began a fierce critique of left-wing liberation theology (a Catholic movement that sometimes legitimized armed resistance against oppressors) with what may seem a sharp concession:

An analysis of the phenomenon of liberation theology reveals that it constitutes a fundamental threat to the faith of the Church. At the same time it must be borne in mind that no error could persist unless it contained a grain [Ger., *Kern*, meaning also "core"] of truth. Indeed, an error is all the more dangerous, the greater that grain of truth is, for then the temptation it exerts is all the greater. Furthermore, the error concerned would not have been able to wrench that piece of the truth to its own use if that truth had been adequately lived and witnessed to in its proper place (in the faith of the Church). So, in denouncing error and pointing to dangers in liberation theology, we must always be ready to ask what truth is latent in the error and how it can be given its rightful place, how it can be released from error's monopoly.[20]

Ratzinger's concession is in fact a reiteration of a deeply held and long-established Catholic belief in dialectics. The more seductive errors are so enticing precisely because they are one component of the whole truth, but not the whole truth.

With the third century and Origen of Alexandria (ca. 185–ca. 254), the dialectic that conditioned over the longue durée the relationship between irenicism and bellicism emerged in mature form to historical light. Origen faced Gnostic and Marcionite Christians who rejected the authority of the Jewish Bible. One of their principal arguments against the Old Testament was its being saturated with violence.[21] A good God could not be responsible for a world filled with evil and for scriptures that authorized war. But since Jesus' own authority was founded on Judaism and since Marcion's dualist solution (to attribute the this-worldly situation, and the two scriptural bodies, to two antagonistic gods) was unacceptable to many strict monotheists, other strands in the Christian movement found necessary to defend the Jewish sacred texts. Yet the Old Testament's bellicose nature remained embarrassing.[22] Origen's solution was allegory. Anything that was shocking in the Old Testament was not to be read literally, but contained a "mysterium," a higher, spiritual sense; it was to be interpreted allegorically. Thus, most, if not all, Old Testament events and institutions ("shadows," "types," or "figures") prefigured New Testament realities ("truths," "realities," "sacraments," or "antitypes"). The first group constituted the "letter" (also called *historia*); the second contained this letter's "spiritual" or "mystical" sense.[23] The spiritual senses were plural. Later Scholasticism usually listed sometimes two, and more often three mystical meanings: moral or tropological (dealing with vices and virtues); ecclesiological or allegorical in the restricted usage of the term (dealing with Christ and His Church); and anagogical (dealing with transcendental matters such as the Trinity or Heaven and Hell).[24] Over time, and massively by the seventh century, the "realities" anticipated by Old Testament types came to include Church institutions and events in the Age of the Church.[25] Thanks to typology and allegory, violence was spiritualized. To cite Origen's *Homilies on Joshua*: "Unless these carnal wars (*bella*) were meant as types of spiritual warfare, the books of Jewish histories would never have been handed down by the Apostles to be read in the churches by the disciples of Christ, Who came to teach peace."[26] So transposed, Old Testament conflicts became "wars of the Spirit;" and Christians, especially martyrs (but also, later, monks, and other perfects), could see themselves as "spiritual warriors," members of a "spiritual army."[27] The apostle Paul's Letter to the Ephesians, chapter 6, 11–17, provided a key authority for this transformation:

Put you on the armor of God, that you may be able to stand against the deceits of the devil. For our wrestling is not against flesh and blood; but against principalities and powers, against the rulers of the world of this darkness, against the spirits of wickedness in the high places. Therefore, take unto you the armor of God, that you may be able to resist in the evil day, and to stand in all things perfect. Stand therefore, having your loins girt about with truth and having on the breastplate of justice. And your feet shod with the preparation of the gospel of peace (*pax*). In all things taking the shield of faith, wherewith you may be able to extinguish all the fiery darts of the most wicked one. And take unto you the helmet of salvation and the sword of the Spirit (which is the word of God).[28]

Saint Jerome (d. 420) commented:

The Apostle seems to be telling us with other words the following: O Ephesians, what you read about the combats of Israel against the pagan nations seems to mean the flesh and the blood, for example, of the Egyptians, Moabites, Ammonites, Idumaeans, and other nations. But if you want to truly know, reckon that "all these things happened to them in figures." They were written for our sake, for us, in the direction of whom the ends of time are coursing forth [cf. 1 Cor. 10.11].[29]

Some American divines would adopt the idea. Henry Boynton Smith, addressing a Phi Beta Kappa audience in 1853, claimed that the battles of earlier American History had a spiritual message. These struggles had a meaning "in which they ignorantly [*sic!*] fought for us."[30] The sixteenth-century Reformation had not put an end to typology; Calvinists, in particular, including Puritans, employed it, and its honest use lasted in America well beyond the eighteenth century.[31]

Thus, for the Church Fathers, and for much of the Christian tradition after them, the Old Testament wars signified spiritual warfare—against vices and heresies—in the New Age of Christ, the Age of the Church. As with Qumran, time, God's time, was divided into two stretches, respectively devoted to war and to peace, vengeance and forgiveness. As the twelfth-century canonist Gratian later commented, "the one begins with terror, . . . the other with the sweetness of clemency and mercy."[32]

But, for several reasons, allegory did not fully evacuate war from the age opened by Origen's Christ of peace. We shall list five reasons summarily, then detail the last four, along with their intertwined consequences, before turning to an analysis of the First Crusade in the light of exegesis and to a comparison between the eleventh-century Gregorian Revolution (of which the Crusade was an integral part) and the French Revolution. First, as Gerard Caspary showed in a foundational book, because, in Christian eyes, spiritual warfare was more intense than material battles. Anything signified by Old Testament types was reality pure. In dying, martyrs killed spiritually their persecutors and passive pagan audiences, sending them to eternal torments.[33] Because of allegory, there existed still a real, really real war. Spiritual combat could be graphic and described with (to us) troubling relish. Jerome's contemporary Prudentius, in his *Psychomachy*, depicted the single combats of virtues against vices, personified, crowned by the savage and bloody mauling of the latter—spiritual warfare with all the arousing colors of gladiatorial cruelty. For instance, "Faith" tore Heresy to pieces and scattered its shredded fragments as fodder to various animals.[34]

Second, and perhaps more important, war was placed at the heart of what Caspary calls the "grammar of exegesis." Caspary demonstrated how the relationship between letter and spirit, critical for Christian biblical interpretation, was, from at least Origen, on interwoven with military images. Two swords were featured in an enigmatic pericope (Luke 22.36–38). Jesus had ordered the disciples to buy swords; they answered, "Behold, there are two swords"; He concluded, "It is enough." For the late antique and early medieval Fathers, the two swords signified a series of binary pairs: the Old and the New Testaments; Moses' Law and Christ's grace; war (*bellum*) and peace (*pax*); justice (*justitia*, or vengeance, retribution, *vindicta*) and mercy (*misericordia*); the letter and the spirit; *regnum* (kingship) and *sacerdotium* (priesthood); and, later, State and Church. The letter killed, the spirit vivified. But the Christian appropriation of the Hebrew Bible was itself an act of symbolic violence. Just as Judas Maccabeus had killed the Greek Appolonius, taken his sword, and fought wielding it day after day, so Christian preachers "took the *historia* of the Divine Law from the carnal people," the Jews, and, interpreting it in the light of the Holy Spirit and the apostolic tradition, fought with it against paganism's errors.[35] Reflections on exegesis called into being reflections on violence and History, and vice versa.[36]

Arguably, without Origen's grammar of exegesis, Cardinal Ratzinger's dialectics on liberation theology would not exist. For indeed, third (and relatedly), the nature of the relationship between Old and New became dialectical. Something of the first age's violence was preserved in the second. Since Christ's mission on earth would be complete only with His Second Coming (the Parousia), some of the Old Testament types, including vengeful retribution (*justitia, ultio, vindicta, vindicatio*), had not been evacuated in an age of the Church governed by merciful peace (*misericordia, clementia, mansuetudo, pietas*).[37] There were still, by God's will, kings and princes, to whom the sword had been entrusted "to vindicate against evils" (Rom. 13).

Fourth, the Qumran scrolls' vision of a war at the End of Times is paralleled in Christianity by the bloody apocalyptic conflicts depicted in John's Revelation (and alluded to in the so-called "little apocalypses," Matt. 24–25, Luke 21, and Mark 13). While some Christian groups, practicing disjunctive typology, also evacuated violence from EndTimes, and even made passive martyrdom the key scenario of the Last Days, others did not see it so.[38] At the Eschaton, Christ will return at the head of an army—but is this host composed only of angels or does it include fighting humans (Rev. 19.15–21)? The first option tended to make all elect suffering, passive martyrs; the second, holy warriors and agents of the great purge. God will destroy the impious and make their blood flow in abundance. Prior to this, or simultaneously with this, will take place the great harvest, announced also by Gospel parables, which separating the elect from the foreknown to damnation (Rev. 14.14–20), will make the latter's blood flow in gigantic abundance, "up to the horses' bridles." Here too the question of human agency is at play. No matter who executes this scenario, in this third age, crowned by the Last Judgment, there will take place a return to the vengeance and justice that had characterized the Old Dispensation.[39]

But, fifth, EndTimes did not generate violence only within its own temporal confines. Royal justice was not simply a remnant of Old Testament coercion; it was also, in Martin Luther's expression, a forerunner (*vorlaufft*) of Hell, understand, of God's eschatological vengeful Judgment. Or in the earlier words of Hervé de Bourg-Dieu (d. 1150), an obscure medieval exegete of Paul's Letter to the Romans, active sometime after 1120: "The secular prince is God's minister in order to execute vengeance (*ultio*) in His stead in this meantime (*interim*) and to prefigure (*praefigurare*) His Judgment."[40] An exegetical scheme that developed between the fourth century and the Carolingian era also placed sanctified violence with an eschatological tinge before the Eschaton itself. Saint Jerome (d. 420) posited that Old Testament prophecies or types could point simultaneously to the mission of Christ and to the End. Here Jerome extended an earlier exegetical principle, which held that a prophecy (for example, of massacres and cannibalism within Jerusalem besieged) was realized, first, partly (*partim*) in the Old Testament age itself (in this example, with the Babylonians), but then again and more fully (*plenius*) at or around the time of Christ (in this example, Titus and Vespasian's siege of the Jewish capital).[41] Jerome was not alone. For his younger contemporary Augustine (and also for some modern Protestant commentators), Christ's tearful words over Jerusalem announced a partial catastrophe, its fall to the Romans, but also, fully, the war at the End of Times.[42] And starting at least with ninth-century Carolingian exegesis, prophecies and types admitted, next to "fuller," "true," or "perfect" accomplishments at EndTimes, "partial" ones in the Church's own present. The heterodox Cistercian Joachim of Fiore (d. 1202), conversely, used this logic for the millennium of peace, in which the saints would reign, announced by Revelation: The prophecy applied "in part" to the Church after the Passion, but "according to plenitude" at the Eschaton, "from the Beast and Pseudoprophet's destruction."[43] There existed thus a plurality within History of such "partile accomplishments," to use the much later expression of the New England preacher William Adams (1679):

> If it be granted that they [prophecies] do respect *a signal dispensation* of God to the Jews in the *last* times, yet that hinders not that there is many a *like dispensation* of God in accomplishing these promises under the Gospel. Prophetical Scripture is often fulfilled. And though there be in special one grand accomplishment of Scripture [sic] Prophesies and promises; yet there are also many Specimens, beginnings of fulfilling them, partile accomplishments, like dispensations of Gods [sic] providence, wherein those prophesies and promises are fulfilled in their measure and degree.[44]

Importantly for the history of the Crusades, it was understood that "the Great Day" of Judgment, in the much later words of John Wesley, "was typified by the destruction of Jerusalem."[45]

One vector of the transmission of the Hieronymian notion may have been Francis Bacon (1561–1626), who explained in 1605 that "Prophecies, being of the nature of their Author, with whom a thousand years are but as one day" can be "therefore not fulfilled punctually, at once, but have springing and germinant accomplishments throughout many ages, though the height or fullness of them may refer to some one age." He too was received in the colonies, as attested by a 1773 Harvard College sermon that spoke of double and multiple fulfillments: "partly fulfilled," "more fully accomplished," and of the "full and absolute completion" in "the time of the restitution of all things."[46]

Thus, from Late Antiquity on, types could be accomplished both within the era of the Church, in the exegetes' own present, and at the Eschaton, with a "full" or "true" (meaning, fully real) realization. Such partile fulfillments could themselves be types for EndTimes. The final eschatological violence thus reintroduced, from the future backward, bellicose shadows into the Church's normatively peaceful present.[47] This is a form of eschatology that is not properly speaking millenarian, but modes of behavior and forms of meaning were energized and in part determined by the radioactive potency of the Eschaton.

What are the consequences of this exegetical grammar for the longue durée of violence in the West? They emerge from a closer examination of points two to five.

From their beginnings, Christian hermeneutics were interwoven with military images (the second complicating factor), and they are still. Violence, spiritual, remains an important presence at the very heart of contemporary Christian imagery and symbols.[48] Innocently, as befits a Minnesotan, a Minneapolis Catholic mother explained that "I am raising little soldiers for the kingdom of God."[49] An American radio evangelist could recently build a whole sermon around a rhetorical query—Is the Church an army or a hospital—in answering that it is both. Spiritually, it fights and it heals.[50] An evangelical station could, in February 2005, broadcast an uplifting song, whose refrain was "For we are in a Desert Storm, fighting the Enemy." As is well known, "Desert Storm" was the name that the American army had given to its 1990–1991 push against Iraq. The lyrics, likely composed in 1990, also referred to Ephesians 6: "Stand, stand, stand! Be strong, be strong in the Lord and His mighty power; Fight versus the Devil's schemes."[51] A century earlier, Union soldiers in the American Civil War had adopted as battle song a dirge based on these same verses. They had originated at a quite civilian funeral, in peacetime:

Stand up, stand up for Jesus!
Stand in His strength alone;
The arm of flesh will fail you,
Ye dare not trust your own:
Put on the Gospel armor,
Each piece put on with prayer;
Where duty calls, or danger,
Be never wanting there.[52]

Institutions devoted to the good also refer to spiritual militancy—one need only mention such groups as the Salvation Army, the Legionaries of Christ, and the Legion of Mary. The capital of images and values embedded in spiritual warfare will either remain spiritual, especially in traditions emphasizing the absolute antithesis between letter and spirit, and animate Appleby's "militant peacemakers," or be reinvested into material warfare, as we shall discuss below, and as Adolf von Harnack hypothesized a century ago in his *Militia Christi*.[53]

Through the "grammar of exegesis," the primary opposition between the bellicist Old Law and the pacifist New Law is miniaturized within the New Era itself (it will also be miniaturized in the Last Age)—the third factor.[54] In the Christian *ecclesia*, rectifying violence and justice are delegated to kings or warriors, evangelical suffering to priests. This caste-like specialization is a division of labor, as the *Life of Saint Boniface*, "apostle" of Germany and Frisia, shows.[55] When Boniface and his companions, on a journey to convert the borderlands of the Carolingian realm, realized that armed pagans were about to assail them, the saint's lay servants took their own weapons "to defend the saints (and later martyrs)." But Boniface, citing the Gospel precept to render good for evil, forbade combat to them and exhorted his other companions, the clerics, to constancy, announcing that they would "be able to reign with Christ into Eternity." In so doing, Boniface offered to his lay servants a chance to suffer like clerics. The whole group was slaughtered. The victors, however, in the first act of a providential retribution, quarreled over the booty, all the way to an internecine brawl that left dead a majority of the raiders. The second act in retribution followed. God "wanted to take vengeance of His enemies, and with the zeal of His customary mercy (*misericordiae zelum*), to punish the blood that His saints had shed." Simultaneously, God was realizing His ancient anger against Frisian idolatry. Christian warriors executed this *ultio*. Their crushing victory convinced the pagan survivors of the truth of the message that the saints had been preaching. They converted massively. Good for them: "broken by miseries in this present, and enlightened by the lightning of the Faith, they avoided eternal torments."

The martyrdom of Boniface's troop of clergy and the vengeance executed by Christian warriors (*bellatores*) were thus not pure opposites but complementary. Origen had argued that Christians rendered a more potent military service to rulers than the soldiers who killed—seemingly—other men. Through prayer, Christians could vanquish the demons who stirred up wars, inspired the violation of pacts, and disturbed peace. They fought as priests with bloodless hands, "putting on the whole armor of God." Since Christ's First Coming, and as long as this world would last, two legitimate forms of resistance to aggression and crime would coexist: one waged by pagans in the form of just war, the other conducted by Christians through prayer. Augustine adapted Origen's dichotomy to a Christianized empire, portraying how those Christians who fought with prayer against the "invisible enemies" and those who "labored against visible barbarians" rendered one another a reciprocal service. As Caspary emphasizes, the coexistence of these two warfares was a consequence of the third factor, the dialectics between Old and New Dispensations, insofar as the former lingered within the latter.[56] The division of labor between clerics (physically noncombatants but spiritual warriors) and laymen (who were allowed to shed blood) transposed within Christendom the early Christian distinction between prayerful Christians and pagan warriors.[57] In the Modern era, it survived with the Quakers, who refused to fight but were willing to see others fight in the causes they deemed just, as we shall see when discussing John Brown.[58]

There are, of course, as often is the case in scholarship, alternate explanations for the Christian copresence of bellicism and irenicism. J. Scott Appleby assumes an initial common ground in all archaic religions structured by Rudolf Otto's numinous. He combines this notion with René Girard's concept of mimetic violence between similar and neighboring human ensembles—in which religion both perpetuates and limits violence. In this archaic state, the numinous, in its essence ambiguous (both good and evil, both positive and destructive) fosters equally the disposition to violence and the disposition to its overcoming, and equally haloes both. Appleby further suggests—meeting here the lines of Girardian apologetics for Christianity's exceptionality as *the* one religion that, through the Cross, escapes the logic of violence—that the great universal religions have channeled through hermeneutics the numinous away from the pole of violence and toward peacemaking. Still, in these religions (among which Appleby counts Christianity, Islam, and Judaism, plus Buddhism) the most intensely committed and sincere believers are either "extremists," holy warriors who employ "violence as a privileged means of purifying the community" and who are bent on annihilating the religious other, or "militant peace-makers" actively devoted to justice within their community and to coexistence with other human ensembles, including religious ones. These restrict "the war against oppressors and injustice to noncoercive means" and resist "efforts to legitimize" material violence "on religious grounds."[59] One can debate Appleby's optimistic historical scheme (grounded in the assumption that all archaic religions, be they attested to or forever lost to the historian, obeyed Otto's scheme, thus that the great religions constitute departures); one can also simply say that Christianity's basic dialectics account equally well for, if not better than, the numinous's alleged "ambivalence" for the concurrent existence of "extremists" and "militant peace-makers."

Out of this third factor come many a paradox. The troubadour Marcabru began a song calling for a crusade into Muslim Spain with the words *Pax in nomine Domini*, "Peace in the name of the Lord." Similarly, the poem "You who love with true love" proclaimed, "Now has come the day of peace." Marcabru may have meant that holy war leads to a righteous peace, including, through martyrdom, to the peace that transcends all, in Heaven.[60] At least Dante thought so. His fallen relative Cacciaguida, whom the poet-seer meets in Paradise, explains to him, *Venni dal martiro a questa pace* (I came from martyrdom unto this peace).[61]

Fundamentally, the dialectic entailed that both righteous war and justified peace were goods. The God of the Old Testament, most visible under the Ancient Dispensation, is the Lord of Hosts; the Christ of the New Testament and of the Age of the Church is the prophesied Prince of Peace (Isa. 9.6). Since They are one and the same divine nature, the One God is simultaneously God of war and of peace. Toward the middle of the twelfth century, a liturgical drama, the *Play of Antichrist*, staged this paradox and oxymoron through the lips of an uncomprehending personification of polytheistic paganism, *Gentilitas*. At her entry onstage, Heathenism declares:

All should honor
The gods' immortality,
And everywhere one should show fearful respect
To their plurality.
Those who say that God is one
Are stupid and, in truth, dumb,
And they contradict insolently
The age-old custom.

For if we say that He is one,
He who presides over all things,
We admit that He is subjected
To opposites and contradictions.

For on the one hand He would
   foster the good of peace
With clemency and mercy;
On the other He would summon wars
   and their disorders
With ferocity and cruelty.[62]

Synagogue, *Synagoga*, the personification of Judaism, next comes onstage, to asseverate as an evidence mocking Christianity that a god who dies cannot save humankind from death.[63] The play's presuppositions are clear: just as the Jews are blind to the paradox of the Cross, central to Christian dogma, pagans cannot grasp the mystery of a single God Who governs opposites, the most shocking example being the coexistence in His dispensation of war and peace, generous mercy and implacable vengeance. It is important to underscore what may seem banal. War for Christians may be a good, insofar as it avenges, rectifies, purges, and purifies. But unlike in Aztec culture—which celebrates war to the exclusion of peace and even glories in fratricidal conflict—peace is a good as well, if it is a peace that is identical with justice. Famously, Augustine had identified *pax* with *ordo* and *iustitia*. True peace entailed right hierarchical relationships in this world, with the other world, and within our inner individual world between the passions.[64] In mimesis of this oxymoronic God, the medieval ruler conjoined in himself *bellum* and *pax*. Accordingly, the ninth-century court poet Sedulius Scottus addressed King Charles the Bald (r. 840–877) in a panegyric poem in these terms: "You love the lilies of peace, mixed with the rose gardens of war; for this reason you shine, white and red."[65]

   The Play of Antichrist's Synagoga opposed "ferocity and cruelty" to "clemency and mercy." The pair vengeance-mercy and the condemnations of excessive justice as cruelty and of excessive clemency as weakness (so paradoxically cruel) became a commonplace in European discourse. Just as the Old Law and the New Law coinhered, *vindicta* and *misericordia* were coinherent. To cite Nicolas of Lyra (d. ca. 1349, perhaps the most influential late medieval exegete): "Mercy without justice is tantamount to pusillanimity, and justice without mercy is tantamount to cruelty. These vices destroy the king and the kingdom. But mercy stimulated by justice, and justice tempered by mercy protect the king and the kingdom."[66] Justice generated fear in the subjects, and mercy, love. The Jacobin leader Robespierre agreed. There were, he lectured, "two shoals, weakness and temerity, shallow moderation (*modérantisme*) and excess [of fervor]." The balance between justice and mercy was not easy to strike, he recognized: "Who will trace the dividing line between all these contrary excesses?" Robespierre's answer was not un-Christian (had Augustine not written "is then charity not light?"), if à la mode of the Enlightenment: "Love for the fatherland and for truth." It was quite Christian, in fact: Augustine considered that what enabled one to evaluate a scriptural passage as either literal or allegorical was its conformity to love for God and one's neighbor, to dogmatic truth, and to morality.[67]

The binary pair justice-mercy (and its equivalents) generated oxymorons, positively normative, for instance, *saevitia misericors* to characterize the firm, painful correction meted out by God as doctor with His curative blade: "Where there is terror, there is salvation. . . . Oh merciful cruelty!" exclaimed Augustine of Hippo. More incisively, Jerome spoke of a "clement cruelty," when slaughtering spiritually "without any mercy" heresies.[68] In discussing the incomprehensible mechanisms of predestination, the same Augustine spoke of God "mercifully pardoning, justly avenging, and just the same avenging mercifully and pardoning with justice."[69] The binary also produced negatively-normed paradoxical expressions, such as "une sensibilité cruelle," meaning, a weak-kneed extension of mercy to the traitors that, de facto favoring tyranny, ultimately led to more bloodshed.[70] Saint-Just echoed Robespierre, condemning "cruel clemency" (*une clémence cruelle*), which could potentially "lead to the State's destruction."[71] Oxymoronic formulas circulated between the leadership and the Parisian street. A Sans-culotte section pleaded, "For the love of humankind, be inhuman; thus a skilled and helpful surgeon, to save a patient's body, cuts off with his cruel and benefic blade a gangrened member."[72]

The dialectic was not acceptable to all Christians. In the early twelfth century, one finds, for instance, Sigebert of Gembloux protesting that Paschal II's (r. 1099–1118) call to holy war (*bellum Dei*) against Emperor Henry IV's partisans, which the pope presented as a sacrifice pleasing to God, was an unacceptable lapse into Old Testament mores. In Sigebert's opinion, "the Apostolic [pope], who mandated this sacrifice, war, to his son [Count] Robert, wanted to return to the zeal of Phineas; wanted to do what Moses did to consecrate the Levites' hands in the blood of their brothers."[73] But how consistently Sigebert would have refused Old Testament exemplarity in all matters is unclear.

It is only with the early modern era that one can speak of a continuous and strong current of pacifism, based on the antithesis between the two testaments.[74] Sébastien Castellion (d. 1563), a ferocious opponent of persecution, volunteered that "the Old Testament sword is nothing but a figure of the sword of God's spirit," and complained: "Shall we confuse the symbol with the reality symbolized?"[75] George Fox, the Quaker leader, lambasted the bellicose Fifth Monarchy Men. They would, he said, kill the Whore of Babylon outside them. But, in fact, he countered, "the whore was alive in them" and had not been burnt by God's spiritual fire.[76] During the American Civil War, a horrified Republican theologian, Charles Hodge, complained that his fellow Northerners had "become so demoralized or demented by passion, as to maintain that it would be just to visit the South with the fate of the Canaanites [Israel's enemies, vowed to total annihilation, see Deut. 7.1–5 and 20.10–18]." Indeed, such was sometimes the abolitionists' rant.[77] And indeed, biblical warfare fed abuses of the law of war. When he burnt down Darien, Georgia, in June 1863, Colonel James Montgomery explained to a subordinate that "the Southerners must be made to feel that this was a real war, and that they were to be swept away by the hand of God like the Jews of old."[78] The pacifist current here represented by Hodge, though, had a strong cluster of late medieval "antecedents."

A fairly systematic line of argument ran from John Wyclif (d. 1384) through some Hussites (notably Petr Chelčický), all the way to many Anabaptist groups; it propounded what has been called "disjunctive typology."[79] As opposed to "connective typology," which considers that Old Testament institutions can be literally replicated in the postincarnational era, disjunctive typology denies literal exemplarity to the Old Dispensation.[80] True to Origen and Jerome, Wyclif and Chelčický rejected the sword of war and coercion. Both men considered that the theological argument for war in the New Era had been inspired by the Devil and Antichrist. It was the Enemy, said Wyclif, who starting from "a truth," "that under the Old Law it was lawful for men to fight, authorized by God," went on to deduce from this correct premise that "since it is the same God now as then, why should men not fight now?" Wyclif added that, if a war was for God, the three Scholastic requirements for just war—just cause (to avenge God's injuries), legitimate authorization (by God), and right disposition (for God and one's neighbor)—could never be met. The God of peace would never authorize warfare for Himself; and right disposition under the New Law was to "love our enemies, and make them our friends." Besides, earthly princes, the only figures besides God who could authorize just wars, were *comynly proude*, "usually prideful" (and so likely to be unjustifiably bellicose) and "lacking in the intelligence" (*witte*) to ordain when men should fight a just war.[81] As for Chelčický, he openly claimed that connective typological arguments justifying the Hussite war to purify Bohemian religion corresponded to the last temptation through which Satan sought to corrupt God's Church.[82]

In their own time, Wycliffites were branded with the stigma of heresy. These early minority voices endearing to the ethicist are enlightening for the historian, for they highlight by contrast the characteristics of the dominant position. But, like radical violence, the expression of pacifist ideas does not need to have been generated by a single heretical movement that traversed the centuries. Precisely the dialectic between war and peace, which was constitutive of orthodoxy, preserved within itself the twin virtualities, for pure peace without war, and for pure war without peace.[83] For this reason, it is methodologically safer to speak of antecedents rather than of ancestors.

Fourth, EndTimes would be an age for *justitia* (synonymous with *vindicta*, vengeance or vindication, and *ultio*, revenge), following the Church's age in which mercy predominantly ruled. Ashkenazi Judaism preserved, or more likely found again, Qumran's grim map of History: just as a vengeful God had liberated Israel from Egypt with the ten plagues and the destruction of Pharaoh's army, so would He free His people again with violence at the End of History.[84] On the Christian side, Cyprian of Carthage rejected vengeance here and now, but announced that Christ, Whose First Advent had taken place "in humility" and Who had remained silent before Pilatus "at the passion," would return "in power" at His second Advent and would speak out "at [His] vengeance."[85] In the third phase of what Caspary, in his seminar teaching, called the triad *tunc-nunc-tunc* (back then-now-then at the End) and correlated to the triad justice-mercy-justice, the Old Dispensation's vindictive retribution would return. Its letter would be activated anew. The militant Münster Anabaptist theologian Bernhard Rothmann propounded that "the Scripture that belongs to the Third Age is none other than the one of the First;" consequently, at EndTimes (in which Rothman believed he was), the Old Testament should no longer be allegorized. To cite him, one must "not make any spiritual interpretation or figurative exegesis (*figurlick vthlegen*)" of it. This pertains in particular to the biblical sword, which becomes material again; the Anabaptist brethren must "arm" themselves "for battle, not only with the humble weapons of the apostles to suffer, but also with the lordly armor of [King] David to avenge."[86] In this manner, Rothman transposed Ephesians 6 into a ternary temporal structure and limited its pacifist ambit. He performed the same operation on the Gospel sword pericopes. When one was aware of the distinction between Sacred History's two phases after Christ's First Advent—the "time of suffering" (*tydt des lydens*) and the "time of vengeance" (or "of restitution")—one understood that "the sword that the apostles had to buy and leave in its sheath until the Time [of Restitution] will not remain glued there forever." Rothmann explained:

[Christ] ordered His apostles that he who had two tunics should sell one and buy with it a sword [Luke. 22.36]. But when Peter wanted to use his, He had him put it back in its sheath. Yet [He did] not [order Peter to] throw it away, because the Scripture of suffering must first be fulfilled (*veruult*) before the sword can be used in the Christians' protective and avenging hand. But now that it has elapsed, all those who took up the sword against God must go to the sword.[87]

Rothmann may have belonged to a marginal sect, but his conceptions were not so alien to the mainstream. A polished twelfth-century courtier and scholar, John of Salisbury, could—in passing, during a discussion of whether it was allowed for the Church to have recourse to force against a schismatic antipope—allude to the difference between "the present" and EndTimes. It was proper for the Church to "restrain its hands [from conflict], since Peter's sword, which out of a carnal affect thirsted for blood, is for the present time (*ad praesens*) hidden in its scabbard; and since the disciples, who were hastening to eradicate the cockle, have been ordered to wait for the harvesting angels."[88] In a small but significant number of historical moments, a plurality of Christians, having observed the prophesized signs of the End listed in the evangelical "little apocalypses" (natural catastrophes, wars, and the emergence of false prophets, heretics, and witches), convinced themselves that the time had come and took up the sword on God's side to harvest without mercy, since the age of mercy was over. A militant Anabaptist confessed that, after the Tribulation (cf. Matt. 24.21), "those of the just who still survive will come together from all parts of the world and slay all the surviving ungodly," one thousand apiece; "such a design is given by God to His people."[89] The sudden conviction that one has stepped into the Eschaton explains the speed with which sword-refusing Christians can turn to radical bellicism, as happened with the Taborite Hussites in 1419.[90] The radical preacher Václav Koranda then proclaimed: "Brothers, the Lord's vineyard has begun to flourish, but he-goats are coming now who wish to eat the grapes; the time has come when wandering around with the staff (*huol*) is over; now we march with weapon (*branj*) in hand" (Koranda's contrast between "staff" and "weapon" was duplicated in the debates between irenic and bellicose Anabaptists a century later, labeled

"Stäbler" and "Schwertler," those of the staff and those of the sword).⁹¹ The hour had come to exchange the peaceful pilgrim's garb for that of the warrior of the Lord. A century later, some Anabaptists thought the same. "A Christian can indeed have a sword," professed Hans Hut (d. 1527), "as long as he allows it to remain in the sheath until the Lord tells him to draw it." After a period of dispersal and testing, the Lord would finally gather the saints "and come to them with His Parousia. At that time the saints would punish the others, the sinners who had not repented." Hut's scenario entailed as well a reckoning for the governing orders: "The priests who had preached falsely would have to give an account of their teaching, and the powerful of their government."⁹² The revolutionary instant, insofar as it is a prophetic Event, can reject everything that came before it, and live a total inversion of values without heavy afterthoughts.

Christians expected such a sudden jump into a radical future. According to a spy, John Rogers, a Fifth Monarchy man, stated in plain words that "very shortly" EndTimes would come to pass and "that they [the Fifth Monarchy Men] are the saints that must shortly injoy and possesse the glory of the earth, and all men being either saints or devills, whosoever is not of their mind are devills, and they the saints."⁹³ The Fifth Monarchy's name derived from this loose group's conviction that the four world empires prophesized in the book of Daniel had come and gone. Under Christ's monarchy, His saints would cleanse the earth. In one scenario, they would take over England, then cross over to the Continent to take the (Spanish) Netherlands and France all the way to the capital of Antichrist, Papist Rome—a Calvinist version of the late medieval last crusade of Jeanne d'Arc, which involved, after the resolution of a civil war, an expedition against the heretic Hussites, and finally the conquest of Jerusalem. The deduction that EndTimes was a time for the sword was, however, not obligatory; the Fifth Monarchists' contemporaries, the Diggers, refused the death penalty.⁹⁴

But men and women also agonized, and scrutinized. How could one know that it was the End?⁹⁵ Then as now, one beseeched and wondered: "Come on time, o Jesus, and take us away; come on time, o Jesus, could this be the day?"⁹⁶ The chiliast Hussites of 1419–1420 wrote a letter to convince their brethren that the times had come. There were signs (many of them from the "small apocalypse" of Matt. 24.3–44) for "this hard, terrible, and dangerous time," known as the time "of the greatest wrath." These signs were biblical. The End announced itself by wars, by seductions, by heresies, "by conflicts, by many scandals, by the spread of evil, by many oppressions, by destruction, by abomination in the holy places—that is, sins, idols . . . and other disorders abominable to God, by torments, by imprisonments and primarily by the killing of God's elect."[97]

The Hussite chiliast letter bemoaned that many considered "that it is not necessary to carry on a regular fight with a physical sword against evils and abominations, against errors and heresy."[98] These "many" may have been brethren true to Wyclif's line or to the Waldensian refusal to bear arms. Or this position may have been owed to another disagreement among people who agreed that the End had come: would God alone with His angels fight the last war? Or would humans join in on His side? Some Puritans in the English Civil War's New Model Army wondered. One of them reported in 1647 that there was "a scruple amonge the Saints, how farre they should use the sworde." We shall discuss this later, but the alternative was not new.[99] Already in the second century B.C.E., Jewish apocalyptic thought provided for the two options. In the one, men would fight to establish the Kingdom; in the other, represented by the book of Daniel (2.45, 9.25, 11.33–34), God would destroy by Himself the fourth and last world empire, without the help of human hands.[100] In 1419–1420, for the so-called Taborite communities gathered in refuge cities in southern Bohemia, human cooperation with the returned Christ was the order of the day. It would be fiery and merciless, as the following articles show (the Taborite leadership apparently debated them with the Prague masters, who disapprovingly annotated them):[101]

First, that right now, in this very year, 1420, there will occur and is occurring the consummation of the age, that is, the extermination of all evil men.

This is an error.

Furthermore, that right now are the days of vengeance and the year of retribution, in which all of the world's sinners and opponents of God's law, will perish and must perish (to the extent that none shall survive), by fire and by the sword and by the seven EndTime calamities described in Eccl. 39[.33–36; cf. Is. 66.16]. . . .

This is an error.

Furthermore, that now, in the present time of vengeance there is no time for grace and forgiveness as far as God is concerned, and therefore one should show no mercy in deeds to bad humans and opponents of Christ's law . . .

This is an error.

Furthermore, that now, in the present time of vengeance, one should not imitate and follow Christ in showing meekness, clemency and mercy to the opponents of Christ's law, but [imitate and follow Him] only in zeal, fury, cruelty and just retribution . . .

This is an error.

Furthermore, that in this time of vengeance any faithful [Christian] is cursed, if he forbids his sword from shedding the blood of the opponents of Christ's law, in their own persons, physically. Rather, each faithful must wash his hands in the blood of Christ's enemies . . .

This is an error, and tyrannical cruelty.

Furthermore, that in the time of this vengeance every priest of Christ is allowed to, and must, by *lex communis* [common law?], fight in person, strike, wound and kill with the material sword or other instruments of war sinners . . .

. . .

Furthermore, that only those faithful who have gathered on the aforesaid mountaintops are that body, to which (wherever it may be) the eagles will gather [Matt. 24.28], and that they are the armies sent by God throughout the world to execute all the calamities of the aforesaid vengeance, and to inflict vengeance on the nations, their cities, their villages and fortresses. And that they are those who will judge at the [Last] Judgment every nation (*lingua*) that resists them.

The eagles, the Venerable Bede explained in his *Commentary on Revelation*, signified the saints. They were the birds called to the apocalyptic banquet to satiate themselves on the flesh of the horsemen who had ridden to battle in the army of the beast and of the kings of the earth, against the returning Christ.[102] Cannibalism? We shall come back later to the chains of associations afforded by this act of allegorical anthropophagy in particular and to apocalyptic symbolism in general. The semantic fields that they compose allow one to understand the meanings that Christians attached to holy war's violence.

Fifth, sacred violence "of the End" did not need the Eschaton. Typology allowed it to be present in the Age of the Church. The war at the End of Times admitted of types in a non-apocalyptic present. As will be more fully discussed in the final chapter, in the later twelfth century, one poet understood the 1096–1100 First Crusade in this light: announced by types and prophecies, it was itself a type for the Final War. Initially late antique and early medieval, this logic did not disappear with Luther and Calvin. Not with great sophistication, but in conformity with theological understandings, the Colonial militia captain Edward Johnson explained that America was the place where God would create a "New Heaven and a new earth," and exclaimed, "Then judge all you . . . whether these poore New England People, be not the forerunners of Christs army."[103] These soldiers of Christ, as Johnson liked to call the Pilgrims, were "forerunners of Christ's Army" in very concrete ways. Johnson penned an account of the gruesome 1637 Fort Mystic massacre. When the native Pequots killed two Christians, mocked a Colonist attempt to get redress, and blasphemed the Lord, they became the target of a war of extermination.[104] More sympathetically perhaps, one of Cardinal Ratzinger's neo-Marxist targets, the liberation theologian Gustavo Guttiérrez, used the notion of partial fulfillment to criticize those among his learned peers who dismissed Old Testament political history and who through a disjunctive typology favored a conservative, quietist Catholicism:

> It is a matter of partial fulfillment [of biblical types] through liberating historical events, which are in turn new promises marking the road toward total fulfillment. Christ does not "spiritualize" the eschatological promises; He gives them meaning and fulfillment today . . .; but at the same time He opens new perspectives by catapulting History forward, forward towards total reconciliation. The hidden sense [of Scripture] is not the "spiritual" one, which devalues and even eliminates temporal and earthly realities as obstacles; rather, it is the sense of a fullness which takes on and transforms historical reality. Moreover, it is only in the temporal, earthly, historical event that we can open up to the future of complete fulfillment.[105]

We shall discuss in Chapter 7 how this logic of fulfillments "fabricated" a specific Christian History.

War on Multiple Fronts: The Senses of Scripture and the Crusade

The conflicts that theology allowed back into the present were never simply material or one-dimensional. For if exegesis, as it were, sublimated war, this was not a simple chemical process; nor did this alchemy target just one member of the pair war and peace. Peace can also be allegorized. Augustine read spiritually the Gospel precept to turn the other cheek: it commands not to pursue warfare or vengeance with a cruel spirit but rather to do so out of love (in the twelfth century, this exegesis was excerpted into the authoritative compendium of ecclesiastical law, Gratian's *Decretum*).[106] As for complexity, several senses can be active simultaneously. A conflict can be both moral and allegorical. Sara Lipton's focused study of the thirteenth-century *Bibles Moralisées* has thus richly shown how, in this source genre, which combines sets of texts and illustrations, war versus demons is isomorphic with war versus religious deviance, including—and this was the century that saw the burning of the "heretical" Jewish Talmud—contemporary Judaism.[107] One can have (and one had already by circa 400) the combination of violence against unbelievers and heretics with the militant disciplining of the flesh.[108] One can have a material struggle authorized by a parallel spiritual struggle. Thus, explained a late sixth-century Catholic bishop and historian, when the orthodox Frankish king Clovis marched against the "heretic host" of the Arian Visigoths ruling southern France and Spain, he did so under the patronage of the dead saint Hilary of Poitiers, who had "so often done battle" against the Arians "for the faith."[109] One can also have a warfare that is all at once material and spiritual. Such was, as shall be developed shortly, the First Crusade in the eyes of its chroniclers and no doubt of many of its participants. Bohemund of Taranto exhorted his standard-bearer to charge against the Muslim foe: "Know for sure that this is not a carnal but a spiritual war (*bellum carnale non est sed spirituale*). Consequently, be an athlete of Christ, and a strong one. Go in peace (*vade in pace*); may the Lord be with you always."[110] Bohemund's call uses a formula that echoes but reconciles the Ephesian antithesis between fleshy and demonic enemies; musters for the knight of Christ the persona of the monk as *athleta Dei*; and, unsurprisingly (given the dialectic between war and true peace), speaks of *pax* in the midst of battle.

Scriptural logic also explains some odd High Medieval images. A fresco in the Templar church of San Bevignate in Perugia (Italy) depicts, on a lower register, the knights fighting Muslims (who have the dragon as armorial) and, on the superior register, the knights, cowled, facing a lion. The Rule of the Templars forbade all hunt, with the exception of this specific animal. Likely it signified—both there and in the Perugia iconography—the Devil. The knights fought on two levels and against two enemies, material and spiritual. The Cistercian Bernard of Clairvaux, in his *Praise of the New Knighthood*, said as much. The Templar was "a fearless knight, safe on every side, who vests his soul with the armor of faith [cf. Eph. 6] just as his body with iron; thus protected with these two armaments, he fears neither demon nor man."[111]

Another iconographic program has elicited puzzlement. In thirteenth-century Bible Moralisées, which serially pair an image and literal explanation of a scriptural passage with its mystical explanation and the latter's illustration, one can find crusader knights. Reiner Haussherr opined that, since these knights were understood allegorically, they were not references to contemporary holy wars. Christoph Maier demonstrated the contrary. The reading of a crusading scene as allegory indicates the spiritual significance of crusading, a warfare that is far from simply material.[112]

Thus, warfare can be all at once literal, moral, and allegorical. In a crusade, Christendom struggles simultaneously against physical enemies outside, against vices inside the human being and against vicious men inside Christendom—for instance, resident Jews, false brethren (*falsi fratres,* see Gal. 2.4), bad clergy, perverts, and heretics—and against the demons.[113] To cite Gilbert of Tournai's late thirteenth-century sermon. "Not only the infernal and material enemies (*hostes infernales vel materiales*) are beaten with this sign [of the cross], but also carnal passions (*affectus carnales*)."[114] This understanding was incorporated in the metalogic of exegesis. A Carolingian biblical commentator viewed biblical commentary itself as a battle through the senses of scriptures. Christ "fights with three battle-groups (*ordines*), that is . . . with a partitioned teaching: historical, allegorical, and tropological."[115] "Know for sure that this is not a carnal but a spiritual war. Consequently, be an athlete of Christ, and a strong one. Go in peace; may the Lord be with you always."[116] The words the anonymous *Deeds of the Franks and Other Pilgrims to Jerusalem* attribute to Bohemond of Taranto gesture to Ephesians 6, "our wrestling is not against flesh and blood; but against principalities and powers." Ephesians 6, as already said, was a key scriptural passage for the sublimation of warfare. It participated in the appropriation of warfare's prestige by the ascetic and clerical *militia Christi,* the army of Christ. The monks and priests were the true "athletes of Christ" and "knights of Christ."[117] In referring to Ephesians 6, the *Gesta* imparted that the Crusade was spiritual warfare and that behind the events' letter, *historia,* stood a *mysterium.* The historian, taking this cue, can read accordingly, recovering something of the web of meanings that chroniclers, their readers, and (likely) the actual actors of the First Crusade perceived. The reconstruction passes through the quarrying of patristic (meaning, produced by the men whom Late Antiquity and the Early Middle Ages recognized as authoritative "Fathers of the Church") and Carolingian biblical commentaries, guided by another web, that of these exegetical works' mesh of cross-references. The pages that follow will thus begin by retracing interpretations and usages of Ephesians 6. They will then turn to the exegetical "virtual library" available to reformers and crusaders in the eleventh century. Subsequently, they will shuttle between the First Crusade chronicles and exegesis.

The history of Ephesians 6 is that of the progressive (but never complete) subversion of the dichotomy "spiritual war" against demonic powers—"material war" versus "flesh and blood." Jerome had listed the spiritual evils that the demons inspired to human carnality; they included, nestled between sins of aversion and excesses of the belly, "heresies."[118] In this Father's view, did the Christian struggle merely against unorthodox beliefs or also against heretics, actual men and women? Late Antiquity's practice affirms the latter alternative;[119] but exegetically and normatively, it is first attested in Haymo of Auxerre's stunning mid-ninth-century commentary on the Pauline Epistles and in a sermon that he culled from it.

For Haymo, victory against the demons, obtained through prayer, fasting, good works and virtue, will result in victory against evil humans:

> It is against those [demons], then, that we should fight rather than against men composed of flesh and blood, since it is these demons who suggest to men whichever evil these men plot against us. And if we overcome those who are the leaders of this army [*militia*], by whose instigation the vices of our flesh rage against us, we shall be able to overcome all their servants, by the grace of God, just as when one overthrows an army's leader, the army is easily put to flight.[120]

How did the princes of darkness relate to flesh-and-blood armies, and who manned these evil militias? Haymo had an answer:

> One may further query wherefrom Paul drew it to call demons and malignant spirits princes and powers and regents of these darknesses, understand [by darknesses,] infidel human beings, who ignore God and are sinners. . . . One can answer that he drew this from the Book of Daniel, where one can read [concerning two angels] "the princes of the Greeks and the princes of the Persians" [Dan. 10.13 and 10.19–21]; and from Ezechiel's book, where the prince of Tyre is told [Ez. 28.12], "You were the seal of likeness in God's paradise," and other things that are said there concerning him and the princes of other nations, to wit, of the Egyptians, Assyrians and Idumeans. For one understands by these princes, that is, by the demons, those set over these pagan nations.

Indeed, just as to each faithful has been delegated a guardian angel, so the pagans have bad angels who rule them by God's permission. And just as Michael was placed over the Jewish and the Christian people . . . , so the nations that dwell in infidelity have evil princes. Let us state it at a higher level. Filled by God's grace, the Apostle learned through the Holy Spirit that just as the Israelites' good kings signified the Lord Jesus and the princes who belong to the Church, for example, such as David . . . and many others, and just as the people of Israel signified the people of the believers [in Christ] who are the real Israelites, so the evil kings and princes with their nations who fought against God's people—as were the kings of the Ismaelites, the Assyrians, Idumeans and Philistines—signified the demons, who rule over the pagans and heretics, who permanently assail God's Church.[121]

A ninth-century churchman would have had in mind a conflict between good princes and pagan invaders—the Vikings and Saracens who plagued Latin Christendom. They (along with Jerome's heretics) were the material enemy, subjects and physical members of their dark angelic princes, the spiritual enemy. The liturgical blueprints for the consecration of kings, elaborated in the same century, spoke of "enemies visible and invisible," whom the new ruler was tasked to combat. The same text mustered the terms of Ephesians 6 and beseeched God to bestow upon the king "the helm of Your protection and Your shield, which cannot be overcome." The Lord's anointed would thus inflict "terror upon the infidels" and bring "peace" to "those who fight for [or serve, *militantes*]" God.[122] In Haymo's commentary and in the anointing formula, purely spiritual warfare and its spiritual targets were still foregrounded; but in a sermon heavily drawing from his commentary, Haymo went one step further. The Devil ambushed humans in three ways: through evil inspirations, through vices and delights, and "through his agents, for example through heretics, false brethren, and pagans." Christians were to "manfully struggle against them all." These agents were the "flesh and blood" in Ephesians 6. Christians were not to fight "only"—*solummodo*, an adverb Haymo tellingly injected in Paul's sentence—against these humans but also against their demonic princes.[123] By the mid-ninth century, thus, warfare according to the mystical senses had spiritualized physical war against pagans; it was to be waged both against evil angels and the evil men they ruled.

Haymo's subversion of the Pauline dichotomy is not a hapax. His contemporary, Hincmar, the powerful archbishop of Reims (d. 882), a king-maker and prolific writer, addressed panegyrically the West Frankish kingdom's ruler, Louis the Stammerer (r. 877–879):

> You do not take so much delight in chasing after woodland beasts in the hunt, than in fighting against pleasures of the flesh and against the enemies of God and His Church, both corporal and spiritual. And indeed as the Lord says through the Apostle: "The flesh lusts against the spirit, and the spirit against the flesh" (Gal. 5.17). And: "Our fight is not against flesh and blood, but against evil spiritual powers" (Eph. 6).[124]

The polarity between flesh and spirit has, in this address to the king, shifted locations. The hunt—lascivious fighting against beasts—is carnal; it is opposed to another fighting, which is spiritual. This positive fighting encompasses the traditional ascetic warfare against the flesh, the struggles against heresy, and the warring against the Church's corporal enemies. The latter, one must assume, included the pagans.

Such was the conception of (some at least among) the crusaders and their chroniclers. The duke of Brabant left in 1197 on a journey to Jerusalem to "overcome Saracens both visible and invisible."[125] Such was also, much more recently, the worldview of Lieutenant-General William Boykin of the U.S. armed forces, as uncovered by William Arkin's investigative journalism (*Los Angeles Times*, October 17, 2003). Then deputy undersecretary for intelligence, Boykin lectured between January 2002 and June 2003 to several Protestant churches and groups.[126] He showed his audiences slides of Osama bin Laden, Saddam Hussein, and the North Korean dictator Kim Jong-Il, and queried rhetorically whether these were the enemy. He answered his own question: the true enemy was a spiritual one, "the power of darkness," "a guy named Satan." On a slide, probably depicting this Satan, Boykin had marked "principalities of darkness," a clear reference if needed to Ephesians 6. Concluding his speech, the lieutenant-general said that the United States was "in a spiritual battle" and that he was recruiting a spiritual army.[127] George Bush had also employed the image of a "spiritual shield," another reference to Ephesians 6 (the "shield of faith").[128] This army is unlikely to have been fully immaterial; America's material battlefield enemies (bin Laden, Hussein, and potentially Kim) were not going to be spared physical assault just because the enemy was the Devil. At least in his Toronto and Salt Lake City speeches, Boykin identified radical Muslims with a "demonic presence" that had to be fought.[129] His "real" meant, as for Haymo, the principal and transcendental, but Satan and his angels were not the only adversary. Not that he need have read Haymo. Closer to him was, for instance, the nineteenth-century *People's New Testament*, which stated that "the real enemies are evil spiritual powers," but not exclusively so, since, according to the same commentary, Satan "uses for his dominion not only evil spirits, but wicked men."[130] The present epoch, Boykin intimated, was special. Just as God had raised Esther to be queen and save her people, the Jews in Persia, in a moment of crisis, so had George Bush become president "for such a time as this" (Est. 4.14).[131] This is vintage typology, and perhaps eschatology as well. For what might have been, to Boykin and his audience, "a time like this?"[132] The book of Esther tells of a massive massacre of the Jews' enemies. Widely diffused among evangelicals is the belief that intense warfare constitutes (as stated in the Gospels' "little apocalypses")—a potential sign of the End. And, for some religious pundits, the captains marshaling the hosts of evil are, literally, possessed. So John Wesley White, expounding a collage of Gospel and Revelation verses:

"You will hear of wars and rumors of wars. . . . Nations will rise against nation, and kingdom against kingdom." So Jesus replied to His disciples' question: "What will be the sign of your coming at the end of the age?" (Matt. 24.3, 6, 7). . . . Jesus enlarged on how human warmongering would escalate into worldwide war incited by the "spirits of demons performing miraculous signs," driving blindly the heads of state "of the whole world, to gather them for the battle on the great day of God Almighty . . . to the place that in Hebrew is called Armageddon."[133]

Boykin's trio shown with slide mug shots corresponded likely to White's "demonized rulers" with "minds drugged and bewitched by Satan."

The born-again Protestant Boykin may or may not pardon the present writer for comparing him, for his usage of Ephesians 6, to a medieval Catholic. Furthermore, the fighting "spiritual army" he wanted to raise has medieval antecedents as well.

The mid-ninth-century compilation owed to Hrabanus Maurus (d. 856), Haymo's contemporary, provides an obvious guide to what a "spiritual army" was and to what its tasks were. An obvious guide, because, drawing on the Fathers, it covered much of the Bible; obvious also, because much of Hrabanus's labor was extremely well propagated; and obvious, finally, because it passed, usually with scant modifications, in the ultimately authoritative *Ordinary Gloss*, which began to be compiled around 1100. Hrabanus did have his own opinions, which he inserted alongside long excerpts from Isidore, Augustine, Jerome, Bede, and Gregory the Great. His personal touch appears most conspicuously in the commentary on the first two books of the Maccabees—no exegete before him had commented on them. Recounting the struggles of righteous Jews, led by members of the Maccabean family (most eminently Mattathias and Judas), against Alexander the Great's impious and idolatrous successors, their generals, and collaborationist Jews, these biblical narratives, starting with the tenth century, enjoyed great popularity; they provided the Christian aristocracy with a sanctifying model when it fought pagans.[134]

As his patristic predecessors, Hrabanus spiritualized Old Testament warfare. The good Jews were *milites Christi* (an expression found already circa 200, with Tertullian), typologically identified with preachers and ecclesiastical prelates; their weapons became "spiritual swords" wielded to "avenge" the Church's public disorders. They should be willing to suffer martyrdom; preachers should "not fear to place themselves as a sacrifice, and to hand themselves over [to death] for the salvation of their people";[135] as commanded in the Gospel, they should love their enemies. Old Testament depictions of slaughter were only types of the killing of vices.[136]

But how spectacular these mystical massacres and with what realism and relish did Hrabanus gloss them! The storming of a fortified place, Bosor, typified the destruction by "the Holy Spirit's sword" of all the power inhering in heretical strongholds; plunder became the seizure of the scriptural passages the sect had usurped. Burning the city translated into the anathema thrown on the heretical creed.[137] Another city's temple was set afire, with all the citizens herded in it, signifying how "our Savior burns down with the fire of a just vengeance all the heretics and persecutors' plots and their error, and all those who have faith in this [error]."[138]

The righteous Jews' plural enemy—the impious King Antiochus's minions, pagan Greeks, and apostate or collaborationist Jews—was transmuted in "the [modern] Jew, the pagan, the heretic, the schismatic, or any hypocrite or wicked person."[139] Hrabanus speaks of "three orders of persecutors" (*tres ordines persecutorum*), pagans, heretics, and false Christians.[140] Contrariwise, "heretics and pagans" who deny Christ's divinity are "soldiers of the Devil" (*milites diaboli*), prefigured by Pontius Pilatus's staff, which had tortured the Lord.[141] Comparatively speaking, Hrabanus did not frequently mention tyrants, but they appear as protectors of the wicked.[142] Sent by "the mystical Antiochus, that is, Antichrist," the *potentatus istius mundi* (power of this world) backs persecution against the Christian religion; it aims at "taking the people of the faithful captive through error or kill it through blasphemy."[143] Earthly power and its agents try to lure down to the plain of earthly desires and worldly delights the holy doctors placed in the mountains.[144] False security allows vices to develop. The "power of this world" protects the nations physically and allows them to enjoy the "pleasures of the flesh."[145] In one rare passage, Hrabanus alludes to the fate of earthly power at EndTimes. The *potentatus istius mundi* confides "more in the power of kingship (*potentia regni*) than in God's might" and so oppresses the doctors of the Church and the faithful people. But things will take a different course, for, as Daniel 2[.31–45] predicts, the stone will destroy the statue symbolizing the world's empires, with its horizontal layers, from head to toe, of gold, silver, brass, and iron mixed with mud, "and the kingdom shall be given to the saints as a people."[146]

Hrabanus's *milites Christi* were forceful reformers. Their task was to cleanse the Church from vice and heresy. Judas Maccabeus's reconquest of Jerusalem from the idolaters was a purge:

> Appropriately, the Scriptures say that Judas [Maccabeus] placed in battle-order his men so that they would fight against those who were in the citadel until they purified the holy places. This is because our Redeemer ordains through His preachers that His soldiers fight vehemently against those who live in pride's citadel (that is, humans raised high by an inflated spirit), or against malignant spirits swollen through pride, until they purge the elect's hearts from every blot of iniquity.

One notices here the classic tropological back-and-forth between purgation and self-purgation. Hrabanus went on:

> And they chose priests without stain, whose will was in God's law, and they cleansed the holy places, because they ejected from ecclesiastical office those men who had the leprosy of error or the stain of wicked deeds, and they chose men of good will, tested in virtue, to administer the Word, so that the Holy Church's assemblies may be estranged from every erroneous thought.

The exegesis had turned to the purge of the clergy; it was followed by war against heresy, including in clerical ranks:

Even more, it is asserted that <u>he took away polluted stones into an [im]</u> <u>pure place</u>, because heretics who refuse to be made precious stones through living an orthodox faith and sane doctrine are struck with anathema and thrown out, and it is made evident to all that they were reprobates. <u>And he considered what he would do with the altar of the</u> <u>burnt sacrifices, which had been desecrated</u>, etc. The altar of burnt sacrifices is the pure faith, pure doctrine, and clean way of life of Christ's ministers. But this altar was desecrated by heretical depravity or the monstrosity of wicked deeds, so it was now <u>to be destroyed</u>, understand, deposed from the priestly dignity, lest by chance Holy Church be shamed for having crooked and vicious teachers, seduced by the Devil's cunning.[147]

Thus, mystically read, the purge of Jerusalem targeted heretics, but also bad clergy. Such was the fantasy of the thirteenth-century Maccabean romances, where Judas slew a lecherous high priest (in one manuscript dressed as a Christian bishop, miter in head).[148] And in the High Middle Ages, a standard initial type illuminating the First Book of Maccabees was Mattathias slaying a renegade Jew—companion in conspiracy to hypocritical clergy were apostates and traitors.[149] Jean d'Abbeville, in a sermon possibly of 1217, explained how God "has allowed the captivity of the earthly Jerusalem in order to signify" the captivity of its spiritual counterpart, the Church, at the hand of "eunuchs," "bastards," "Moabites," and "Ammonites," figures of bad ecclesiastics in Jean's own time, who pursued sex, the exploitation of the poor, and secular sciences. And if this spiritual captivity were to cease, "the captivity which signifies it [the Muslim possession of Jerusalem] would also cease." This logic linked crusade and reform.[150]

Hrabanus did not envisage the reforming tasks typified by the Maccabees with a quiet heart. Like Bede, he felt urgency. While not a chiliast, Hrabanus positioned himself "in the very last age of the world, in which . . . the knights of Christ most intensely wage spiritual warfare."[151] Reform was all the more urgent as the Eschaton neared. Hrabanus's commentary on the "little apocalypse" in Matthew's Gospel is worth citing:

And according to the spiritual senses, <u>when we shall see standing up the</u> <u>abomination of desolation where it should not be</u>, that is, when we shall see heresies and vices reign among those who seemed to be consecrated to the divine mysteries; when we shall become aware that men acting against equity, speaking lies, "men of blood and deceit" whom "God hates" [Ps. 5.7] disturbing the peace among the faithful; then whomsoever stands firm in Judea (understand, in the true faith's confession), and not serve terrestrial things or weak works. The more we see many people following the wide and serpentine roads of vices, the more we should climb up towards the summit of virtues.[152]

Thus, in these commentaries, a sense of the acceleration of Sacred History went hand in hand with a program of purge, targeting vices, heretics, tyrannical auxiliaries of depravity, false brethren, modern Jews, and impure clergy. This "Satanic universalism" constituted the counterpoint of the Church's universal mission.[153] In the eleventh-century conjuncture, heightened apocalyptic expectations fed reformist drives, and resistance to these drives confirmed to some that Antichrist was at work. One such was the bishop of Florence, observing the state of the empire and the coexistence of two popes. As a consequence, the exegetical utopia descended with physical violence upon earth.[154] In conformity with it, purification would take place on two fronts: reform within Christendom and holy war outside it.

The First Crusade was the external facet of the great ecclesiastical eleventh-century Church reform, which attacked delinquent priests and kings, propounded penance, and fought against the heresies of clerical marriage and simony (the sale of the sacraments). True to the tradition just explored, the reformers, placed on the threshold to EndTimes, considered that they faced a universal plot combining in a single, simultaneous assault all of the demonic members of Antichrist, who from Christianity's beginning, had assaulted the Church one by one—Jews, tyrants, heretics, and false Christians. This fear, also typical of terrorist groups and of modern conspiracy theorists (one will think of the *Protocols of the Elders of Zion* and the idea of a universal plot linking Jewish bankers and Bolsheviks),[155] accounts for the reformers' course of action. Holy war ended up being fought against enemies within Christendom as much as against enemies outside.[156] As in Hrabanus's exegesis of Judas's recapture of Jerusalem, holy war against filthy pagans and purge of the domestic clergy (and its lay allies) combined. Gregory VII offered remission of sins (by which he possibly meant exemption from penance for sins committed) on plural battlefields. Remission would benefit warriors willing to die in fighting the Turks or Christian schismatics. It would benefit laity who helped expel from their church a perjured and adulterous provost, an obstacle to reform.[157] In several letters to leaders of this movement, the pope used Ephesians 6, exhorting them to strength in the spiritual struggle versus demonic powers. Several were about muscular reform in Milan; one called to resist the "conspiracy of kings and heretics;" another comforted the living martyr Liprand (a priest facially mutilated by reform's enemies).[158] Shortly after Robert II, count of Flanders (d. 1111), having participated in the 1099 capture of Jerusalem, arrived back in his land, another pope, Paschal II, promised to him the very same rewards that Urban II had proposed to the crusaders—"remission of sins." One may wonder whether Robert's just-concluded expedition to the Holy Land had not sufficed! If, "having returned from Jerusalem," Robert conducted holy war versus Liège and Cambrai "with acts of just knighthood," he would "go to the Jerusalem in Heaven." Liège and Cambrai were two bishoprics faithful to Rome's arch-opponent, the "tyrant" Emperor Henry IV.[159] Already in the 1070s and 1080s, the civil war pitting Henry against his German enemies, allied with the papacy, often took the color of sacred warfare, and this on both sides.[160] The protection afforded by the lay *potentatus* to wicked clergy—from the northern Italian civil strife of the 1060s and 1070s to the wars fought against partisans of Henry IV from the mid-1070s onward— recalled the universal conspiracy in Hrabanus's Maccabean commentaries. One should not be surprised by Carl Erdmann's remark: Gregory's "usage of 'the military service of Christ' was sometimes literal, sometimes metaphorical [Ger., *in übertragenen Sinn*, "figurative"]; and, occasionally, the meaning was left unclear. . . . This wavering between literal and metaphorical meanings characterizes the expressions drawn from military life" in the pope's letters.[161] In this epoch at the edge of the Eschaton, warfare straddled all senses of Scripture.[162]

Farther from northern Italy, and earlier (from the very late tenth century on), more "grassroot" events breathed the spirit of related utopias. While partial, the congruence between exegesis and the programs of the various "peaces" proclaimed in southern France and northern Spain is striking. As Amy Remensnyder demonstrated, a number of these sworn pacts combined a limitation and redirection of warfare with provisions disciplining the clergy. This was not a random juxtaposition, for these decrees stemmed from the same Augustinian understanding of peace as right order and from a sense of pollution that had to be rectified.[163] At Le Puy (994), it was decreed that clerics were not to bear weapons and could not accept gifts or money in exchange for the sacraments. Two decades later, the Council of Poitiers provided that "priests or deacons who have women in their house shall lose their clerical order."[164] The Council of Reims (1049) presided by Pope Leo IX mandated the protection of the poor and clergy; prohibited usury, the clerical bearing of arms, and lay possession of ecclesiastical office and properties; regulated lay marriage; forbade compensation "for burial, or baptism, or for the [holy] host or for a visit to the sick," and the buying or selling of "the sacred orders or ecclesiastical offices or altars;" and called for prelates to be elected by clergy and people (that is, they should not be appointed by lay aristocrats).[165] The elusive Adhémar de Chabannes, a man involved both in the Peace of God and in apocalyptic expectations, sermonized about the opposition "between the congregation of Christians who truly believe in the Faith, and the congregation of Jews, pagans, Saracens, and all heretics," identifying the Catholic faith with "the salvation of the whole Christian empire and the destruction and confusion of the Jews, the Saracens, the pagans, the heretics, Antichrist, and the Devil."[166] The universal conspiracy Hrabanus (among others) had envisaged was alive and well in Aquitaine, a thousand years after Christ's Passion.

As for the external front of the war against all evils—the crusade—it too is illuminated by exegesis. It is now agreed that the First Crusade was not some things. It was not a safety valve for anarchistic military families, short on land for younger sons. It was not a cynical papal ploy to take over the leadership of the warrior aristocracy by bypassing the kings with whom the reform popes were in conflict. It was not merely a remarkable reconciliation of the warrior's bloodstained way of life with monastic purity.

The apocalyptic atmosphere allowed two seemingly opposite processes, a literalization or historicization of Old Testament prophecies and a spiritual surcharge to current, literal events. First, as has been noticed for the chronicler Robert the Monk of Reims, passages understood up until then allegorically or anagogically were treated literally.[167] Second, the crusaders' historical travails were read in the light of the spirit—so of exegesis's mystical senses. The journey that brought Christ's army to Jerusalem's walls in July 1099 had been long and arduous. Hunger and thirst had been the crusaders' constant companions. They were, mystically seen, the hunger and thirst for justice of the blessed (Beatitudes, Matt. 5.6). It was the thirst of those who, having left a city, would find the true Jerusalem of Psalm 106.5.[168] In 1589, hunger and thirst for justice explained—so his partisans—Jacques Clément's righteous assassination of the wicked king Henri III, and one can deduce from the chronicles that it motivated crusader violence five centuries earlier.[169] For hunger and thirst looked, apocalyptically, forward to the EndTimes victory against Antichrist, when the saints would be satiated thanks to the execution of justice.[170] The elect were the birds who in John's vision were called to devour the flesh of the soldiers in Antichrist's army. The eighth-century English monk Bede had commented,

> [John] calls the saints, who live their lives in Heaven, "birds." . . . Come ye, gather for God's great banquet, so that you may eat the flesh of kings (and so on). Come ye, he says, you who hunger and first for justice, to the festive meal of the future kingdom, where you will be satiated by divine justice's light after the madness of the proud has been repressed. . . . And all the birds were sated with their flesh. If now "the just man will rejoice when he sees vengeance" (Ps. 57.11), all the more when the Judge will be present and they will be one spirit with Him. . . . Tyconius explains this banquet as follows: "The Church eats at all times the flesh of its enemies while it is being eaten by them; but it shall be sated at the Resurrection, avenged from their carnal deeds."[171]

This was the "satiety of sight," *satietas visionis*, that the saints would enjoy, according to Isaiah 66, watching the horrific torments of the reprobate in Hell, and so appreciating all the more their own bliss in the contemplation of God.[172] Tertullian, in his *On the Spectacles*, had imagined the *spectacula* of EndTimes. He wrote of a double joy—at the Lord's Second Coming followed by the New Jerusalem's descent and at the punishment of the wicked, especially the Christians' persecutors. With characteristic mordancy, the Carthaginian added that there was one spectacle of which he would never have enough: the torments of Christ's tormentors.[173] The elect's eyes would finally be sated—so commented the late eleventh-century bishop Bruno of Segni, a partisan of Gregory VII and Urban II—when the blood of the wicked would rise up to the horses' bridles in the great final harvest.[174]

The First Crusade's harvest was indeed massive and sublime. In his conviction that a demonic enemy animated his flesh-and-blood Muslim adversaries, Lieutenant General Boykin would have been at home in July 1099, before the walls of Jerusalem. Ten to twenty years later, Baldric of Dol recounted (or imagined) a sermon preached prior to the storming of the Holy City. It is so rich that it should be cited at length:

> Before the assault against the city, bishops and priests dressed in sacerdotal vestments addressed the people. One, placed in a high place, began in the following words: "Hear, brothers and lords. Even though you know (having heard them already many times) everything which we are

presently going to tell you, nevertheless it is most beautiful and sweet and pleasurable to speak at length about our Lord God. And you must always listen, and understand with effects."[175]

At this point, the sermon echoed an earlier sermon in Baldric's chronicle, the words placed in Urban II's mouth at Clermont, 1095. As the pope launched the expedition, he had cued his audience: "What shall we say, brothers? Hear and understand." The full weight of this expression was developed in the web of scriptural passages centered on Matthew 13.9–17. There, Christ explains why He speaks in parables. The apostles can understand mysteries to which others are blind and deaf: "To you is given the mysteries (*mysteria*) of the Kingdom of Heaven; but to them it is not given." Exegetes since Bede had used the scriptural expression "Let him who has ears to listen, listen" (*Qui habet aures audiendi, audiat*) to point that a sentence was not evident (*planum*), but rather *mysticum*, and that, consequently, one needed to prepare oneself to understand it.[176] Urban, therefore, was about to issue a deep typological message. Ancient Israel, the Jews of the Old Dispensation, conquerors of the Holy Land, announced the Franks' expedition: "The sons of Israel . . . in their crossing the Red Sea prefigured you; with their weapons, they acquired that land under Jesus' guidance; expelled from it the Jebusites and other indigenous people; and cultivated the terrestrial Jerusalem as a figure of (*instar*) the celestial Jerusalem."[177]

The anonymous preacher developed Urban's typology:

Christ redeemed you, and God instituted Christendom (*Christianismum*) in this city which is before you. It is from it that the mystery of Christianity (*sacramentum Christianitatis*) emanated all the way to us. We came from our countries in order to pray here and kiss the tomb of our God. This city which you see is the cause of all our labors. But it is nevertheless a figure of (*instar est*) the celestial Jerusalem; it is a type (*forma*) of that city to which we aspire. See with what wicked persistence these vile, stupid, and alien men contest it [Jerusalem] against us? See with what obtuseness they contend against us over what is not theirs by right and what ought [to] be ours? Furthermore, you know with what boldness they pollute God's sanctuary, and with how many pollutions they subjected the holy city. Truly, if you are willing to consider the matter rightly and properly, this Jerusalem, which you see, to which you came, in whose presence you are, both prefigures and stretches toward (*et praefigurat et praetendit*) that other city, the celestial [Jerusalem].

What was the lesson for warfare? That it was double-pronged: one prong, physical (yet no less spiritual) aimed at the visible Jerusalem defended by Egyptian troops; the other, spiritual, targeted the Muslims' demonic masters (*magistri*) and lords (*domini*). The two struggles were linked, since the "visible enemies" were the *membra*, members (another manuscript proposes *umbra*, shadows, a variant not out of place for exegesis) of the "invisible enemies":

> Behold, visible enemies contend for the former [this earthly Jerusalem] against us; further, invisible enemies besiege the paths leading to the latter [the celestial Jerusalem]. Against them a spiritual conflict takes place. And it is more burdensome to wrestle "against evil spiritual entities among the celestial powers," than against the "flesh and blood" which we see. Those men who growl in this smaller city are the members (*membra*, variant; *umbra*) of those [powers], and are inferior and less apt at war than their masters.

The conclusion was clear. It inverted Haymo's prioritizing of prayer over weapons. A knight of Christ who could not conquer visible enemies would fail to overcome spiritual enemies:

> Thus if these men who are almost nothing could vanquish us and take away from us the city which we see, what do you think their lords can do when their serfs dare do such things? For sure, if we are lazy and if these malefic outsiders expel us from our dwelling, we should fear that that heavenly city will be shut to us and taken away from us. If, fearing some kind of death, we do not rise up against these insipid, effeminate, and toothless dogs who are not even able to bark, we shall be fully unfit for war and inefficient in the spiritual struggles.

The sermon climaxed on a harangue:

> O followers (*familia*) of Christ, wake up, then, wake up, ye battle-trained knights and lightly armed footmen, and seize with resolve this city, our commonwealth (*res publica*)! . . . Act, therefore, adjust your weapons, and co-helpers of God, assail this city with constancy. Let it be

beautiful for you to die in this region, you for whom Christ died in this city. Begin the combat; He, your guide, will give reinforcements in war and rewards for good deeds and glorious actions!"

Baldric's text raises a question. How could the knights of Christ harm the Muslims' demonic lords and masters? Here reconstruction must be tentative since the answer involves putting together one biblical commentary chosen among several and another chronicler than Baldric. The crusaders could harm demons, it seems, not only through prayer and purity but by slaughtering Muslims mercilessly. Raymond d'Aguilers famously summarized the massacre: "in the temple and forecourt of Solomon, one rode in blood to one's knees, and up to the horses' bridles."[178] With these words, he gestured to Revelation 14, where the angels harvested the Lord's vineyard and the blood of the wicked surged out. What the crusaders were supposed to perceive through the vision of such an abundance of gore may be provided by Bede's commentary on this passage: "The blood oozed out from the winepress all the way up to the horses' bridles. Vengeance oozed up all the way to those who rule the nations (*rectores populorum*). Indeed, in the very last combat (*novissimum certamen*) the vengeance for the saints' blood which was shed will ooze all the way to the Devil and his angels."[179] This was the very last combat in History, *novissimum certamen*, or a type for it; the slaughter of Muslims was so massive that, through the volume of the blood of the slain, Christ's soldiers succeeded in reaching and harming the demoniac horsemen, *rectores populorum*. As shall be argued in the final chapter, far from being exegetical dressing on events, a narrative ornament crafted after the fact, the gory image was what the massacre's actors perceived. A historian who accepts that medieval men and women believed they saw Christ in the Eucharist, or believed in the saints' miracles, should be ready to assume crusaders' eyes beheld what was, literally, a vision.

The French Revolution and the First Crusade

Monarchists and conspirers are only foreigners, or better put, enemies. Is this terrifying war that liberty has to bear against tyranny not of one piece? Are not the internal enemies the allies of the enemies outside [France]?[180]

Similar constellations combining spiritual with material warfare and joining sanctified war outside to reform inside emerged after the Christian Middle

Ages. One expressed itself during the French Revolution, that transformative upheaval that, despite its symbolic status as the midwife of Modernity, Ernst Bloch labeled the "Christian event *par excellence.*"[181] And Bloch was far from the only or first analyst to have considered it in this mode. As Paul Vialla-neix demonstrated, from the very beginning of the Revolution, most learned commentators would have agreed with Pierre-Simon Ballanche's later (1818) opinion that "the matters which relate to the existence of society are religious matters before being political matters."[182] For Edmund Burke, in 1791, the year 1789 constituted Europe's "last revolution of doctrine and theoretick dogma," an analogon to the Protestant Reformation that had "divided [Europe] into two great factions." The struggle between the camps that had just formed could only be be a "religious war," prophesized the Englishman.[183] Mutatis mutandis, Michelet, Tocqueville, Quinet, and at the beginning of the follow-ing century, Gramsci and the Durkheimian Mathiez, agreed.[184] The analysis sometime used conceptions drawn from religious culture. Edgard Quinet saw the Revolution as a sort of palingenesis;[185] Jules Michelet proposed that "the Revolution is nothing but the belated reaction of Justice . . . against the reli-gion of Grace,"[186] a formula related to the triadic pattern in which vengeance, characteristic of the Old Testament, returns at the End of times after the in-between Age of mercy. And indeed there was a strong millenarian component in the Revolution's political culture.[187] In the wake of this distinguished tradi-tion, the pages that follow will compare notions present in 1789–1794 with those of the eleventh century.

Just as the eleventh-century ecclesiastical reform and crusade, conducted on all the fronts generated by the senses of Scripture, the revolutionary strug-gle was multifaceted. It was a war with outside powers (now foreign monar-chies, Austria, Prussia, and England, back then Muslims); it was a civil war (now against monarchists and de facto allies pretending to be revolutionaries, in the eleventh century against false brethren and heretics); it was a moment in which, as with the reforming clergy, opponents of bloodshed and of the death penalty for dissidents came to embrace them as the ultimate solution; it was a rebellion against tyranny and for liberty (as the Gregorian uprising ver-sus lay, including royal, domination of the Church); it was a war against vices and for social virtues (as the ecclesiastical reformers had struggled against mis-guided sexuality and the sale of the sacraments for money or service). Maxim-ilien Robespierre, who had received his schooling in Oratorian and Jesuit institutions, said as much:

This is a war where man faces man, Frenchman Frenchman, brother
brother, combined to the war between prince and nation; it is a civil war
combined with foreign war . . . It is the war of nobility against equality,
of privileges against the common nature [of human beings], of all vices
against public morality, of all tyrannies against all liberties and the safety
of all individuals.[188]

The Jacobin clubs agreed. One addressed the Convention: "Inside [France]
you unmask and punish conspirators . . . outside, you direct our armies from
victory to victory." So did some soldiers, such as these hussars who exhorted
the lawmakers to "keep at their work against the internal enemy" while they
themselves "persecuted the external one" and vowed to take to the foreign
despots "iron, fire, terror and death."[189]

One does not usually think of the modern French as paragons of virtue,
but the Revolution's war against vices should not surprise. Robespierre and his
ilk, though not believing in Satan, belonged to the tradition represented by
Jerome, who had catalogued in his commentary on Ephesians 6 what the devilish principalities distilled into human carnality: "fornication, impurity, debauchery, idolatry, enmities, conflicts, rivalries, brawls, dissensions, heresies,
traps, drunkenness, and gluttonous eating."[190] Revolutionary discourse commonly conjoined material and spiritual warfare.[191] Sermonized Robespierre:
"All the vices fight for them [the tyrants]; the Republic has only the virtues as
her own. Virtues are simple, bashful, poor, often unlearned, sometimes unpol-
ished. . . . Vices are surrounded by all possible treasures, armed with all of
debauchery's allurements and with all the baits of perfidy; all the dangerous
talents, trained in crime, escort them."[192]

His younger colleague Louis-Antoine Saint-Just assumed that, in order to
divide Paris, "foreign powers" (*l'étranger*) would "spread there immorality, and
sow there a new fanaticism, doubtlessly that of vices and of the love for mad
pleasures (*jouissances insensées*)." Lesser voices agreed: "Liberty cannot reign
where vices reign."[193] Catholic heresiology assumed that all religious deviances
were essentially one, even when their teachings diverged (they were little foxes
with tails tied together, see Judg. 15.4); Saint-Just considered that antagonistic
"factions," moderates and radicals, that "seemed to fight against one another"
"met at night to synchronize their assaults of daytime."[194] The hatred of "faction" stemmed both from Roman political discourse and from the ancient
Christian idolatry of unanimity and universality (paradoxically conjoined

with notions of election and vanguard).[195] And as in Catholic heresiology, one tended to name the factions by the name of their founder or leader. Brissotins, Hébertistes, Dantonistes, or Rolandistes (next to Girondins, Feuillants, and Enragés) succeeded Arians, Nestorians, Apollinarians, or Jansenists.

Was Robespierre madly paranoid? Was Revolutionary France collectively paranoid? The next chapter will deal with this issue. Robespierre certainly believed in a universal conspiracy, unfolding over time like Antichrist's world-historical plot. By 1792, Robespierre, to cite Carol Blum's fine book,

> had explained the basic conceptual framework of the Terror: in the be-ginning, he said, "the nation divided into two parties, the royalists and the defenders of the people's cause." After destroying the royalists, how-ever, the so-called patriots divided "into . . . two classes: the bad citizens and the men of good faith." This antithetical pattern marked Robespi-erre's discourse until Thermidor. Each purification left France still di-vided between the pure citizens and the wicked ones, the latter ever disguising themselves under new masks.[196]

There was a logic to this process, and it was quasi-Satanic. The seeming success of the good against one type of persecutor led the Devil to assume a new shape and redouble his efforts. One should never lower one's guard, Ber-trand Barère thundered, in the face of such an enemy: "Good citizens have the task not to fall asleep in the comfort of victories, and to strike terror into the soul of conspirators, who seem to multiply themselves the more our arms are victorious."[197]

In the revolutionary era, warfare also meant reform. Terror marched with virtue, a famous pairing that also entailed that the violent purgation and re-generation of France was unthinkable without a reconstruction of the French individual self—especially that of the revolutionary leaders. "*Mœurs* had to be regenerated," for otherwise the State would be only "errors, pride, passions, factions, ambition, cupidity," and these "vices [would] necessarily lead back to tyranny."[198] Envoys from Paris paired political and moral purgation: "It should not be enough for you to have expelled from your midst men whom the Fa-therland considers suspect; you must, further, extirpate from all hearts the seed of those passions which are noxious to the public good."[199] The sense that France's enemy was one yet protean in its works, now striking in the guise of a French moderate, now in that of a French extremist, now from the inside, now from the outside, now with tyranny's swords and bayonets, now by sowing vices in the body politic—the polymorph essence of counterrevolutionary perversity would have been at home in the age of the Crusades and ecclesiastical reform.

If inner enemies, including not only "suspects" but also vices, worked mysteriously in concert with foreign powers, conversely, success against the one could impact the other. In this optic, for some revolutionaries, foreign war could seem a fortunate boon. It would allow "regeneration in blood."[200] As will be discussed in Chapter 6, the solution proposed in 1793–1794, the *Terreur*, was indebted both to political philosophy (Montesquieu) and to age-old Christian conceptions of liberation through coercion.

By the time of the Terreur, the French revolutionaries inveighed against a league of "enemies from the outside" and "enemies from the inside." The foreign and civil wars were coessential. The king could not be a citizen; as king, he was outside the social contract and had to be treated like a foreign enemy. He was to be judged as such, according not to the civil law but to the *jus gentium* that governed relationships among foreign powers. Such had been the ultra-Catholic radicals' understanding of the excommunicate king Henri III de Valois: being a beast, he could be killed. But Saint-Just generalized it: "Every king is a rebel and a usurper."[201] Symmetrically (as legislated on May 26, 1794), when captured on the battlefield, soldiers in the service of foreign tyrants who opposed the Revolution would be meted out the death penalty like conspiratorial French monarchists or other *factieux*. The erstwhile rules of war, which, since at least 1648, had spared from slaughter captive enemy combatants, were thus superseded.[202]

But we are not dealing with the "birth of warfare as we know it," as the subtitle and thesis of a recent work put it:

The late eighteenth and early nineteenth centuries saw fundamental changes in the Western attitude toward war and the start of a recurrent historical pattern, of which events since 1989 provide only the most recent, if also a particularly clear, example. In this pattern, the dream of perpetual peace and the nightmare of total war have been bound together in complex and disturbing ways, each sustaining the other. On the one hand, a large and sustained current of public opinion has continued to see war as a fundamentally barbaric phenomenon that should soon disappear from a civilized world. On the other hand, there has been a recurrent and powerful tendency to characterize the conflicts that do arise as apocalyptic struggles that must be fought until the complete destruction of the enemy and that might have a purifying, even redemptive, effect on the participants.[203]

Just cited, David Bell's book is a compellingly good one. Total war and total peace have indeed remained with the West since the French Revolution, with their apocalyptic tonality. Their complex interweaving is a fundamental cultural fact. But the thesis should be qualified. If, on the short run, from the 1648 Peace of Westphalia to the French Revolution, the culture of war seems to have undergone a sea change, a step backward by a few centuries dispels this impression. If one turns to the Wars of Religion, or even sideways beyond Europe to the English colonies in North America, one sees at least as much resurgence as innovation. The universalism that Bell considers a root cause of the Revolutionary soldiers' radicalism was old Christian; the togetherness of "perpetual peace and the nightmare of total war" stemmed from this religion's fundamental dialectic.

To come to the conclusion of this comparison between two epochs in Western History, the anti-monarchist exaltation of "liberty" belonged, alongside regeneration, virtue, and righteous violence, to the core of Jacobin ideology. Liberty, alongside purification and holy war, had formed a similar constellation around 1095. *Libertas ecclesiae* meant the immunity of the Church, its property, offices, and office holders, from the domination of the laity.[204] Reformers branded those laymen who persisted in exercising traditional rights *tyranni*, tyrants. The most visible tyrants of all were the princes and kings who favored the sale of offices and sacraments—the heresy of simony—and did not act against married clergy. So tyranny was connected to moral turpitude and heresy; heresy and paganism were fellow travelers; and paganism went hand in hand with tyranny. In the following centuries, political liberty, religious purity, and holy war came together. In its fabulous oddity, a myth of origins floated to public opinion in 1500 brings this home: the Swiss confederation, settlers who had immigrated to the Alps from Sweden, defeated in 387 with "knightly deed" a pagan tyrant named Eugenius. As a reward, they received their famous liberty.[205] The commonplace that medieval revolts never aimed at the institution of kingship but at incumbent kings is true. But in their polemics, eleventh-century reformers came very close to eighteenth-century revolutionaries, as when Gregory VII dismissed kingship as an institution invented by "men ignorant of God . . . who dared to seek domination over their equals, meaning, human beings, at the Devil's instigation."[206] The three decades between 1070 and 1100 constitute a historical moment conjoining three rare extremisms—an ecclesiastical purge, a holy war, and an attack on the foundations of kingship. While not often paralleled, this moment obeyed an inner cultural logic: the linkage of the three was embedded in the conceptions of the Devil's works and of the ways in which God's elect had to counter them. In this sense, one can agree with Eugen Rosenstock-Huessy, who in 1931 proposed that this moment should be seen to have been the "first [European] revolution."[207]

It is only, then, out of ignorance of the very longue durée of Catholic culture that one can dismiss its contributions to Revolutionary culture. Frank Tallett's otherwise fine article on "Robespierre and Religion" does so:

> Although the language that Robespierre adopted when talking of his God was drawn eclectically from the stock of vocabulary used by Christians since the early seventeenth century, there was nothing that was Christian left in his narrow vision of an implacable and unforgiving deity, who presided over a Manichaean universe divided between upholders and opponents of the Revolution.[208]

But as this chapter has sought to explain, orthodox Christianity had transported within itself, from its very beginning, the Manichean formula, balancing it with more irenic counterformulas. The War of the Last Days is the moment when this formula expresses itself without compensation. Manicheism then becomes very Christian. "Implacable and unforgiving"—these epithets fit precisely the work of God and His elect in visions of the End.

Chapter 3

Madness, Martyrdom, and Terror

> Au nom de quoi affirmerait-on que des individus correspondant à la
> moyenne de leur groupe, disposant dans les actes de la vie courante
> de tous leurs moyens intellectuels et physiques, et manifestant occa-
> sionnellement une conduite significative et approuvée, devraient être
> traités comme des anormaux?
> —Claude Lévi-Strauss, "Introduction à l'œuvre de Marcel Mauss"

Popular opinion, journalistic punditry, and some scholarship attribute to terrorists in general, and recently and in particular to the 2001 jihadists, madness
and mental imbalance. Whether this characterization is right or wrong—and
there are serious grounds to deem it misguided—it is worth reconstructing
this propensity's history.[1] For one is dealing here with a deep-seated cultural
image, whose distinctive features are well rooted in the past. As we shall see,
the mad terrorist (and its phenomenological twin, the suicidal martyr) appears
as a character in the first century C.E. It travels all the way to the Middle East's
al-Qaeda, and slightly before it to the European, and secular, German Baader-
Meinhof Gang. Yet since the modern version of this discourse was markedly
reshaped by the Enlightenment, it is in the eighteenth century that this chapter begins, before it turns back to late antique origins.[2]

The Longue Durée of Madness Across the Enlightenment Divide

Ever happy to have a good whip with which to flog religion and the clergy, Voltaire devoted a long article of his *Dictionnaire philosophique* to "fanaticism."[3]

These pages embraced in the same scorn and irony mass violence such as the medieval crusading movement or the early modern Saint Bartholomew's Day Massacre and individual figures such as François Ravaillac, the assassin of Henri IV of France (1610) or Jacques Clément, the Dominican who knifed Henri III to death (1589).⁴ For Voltaire, fanatics were delusional personalities who did not stop at their dreams but acted upon them murderously. "We understand by fanaticism a dark and bloody religious madness," he wrote, contagious like a disease and which spreads through the influence exerted by "fiery men with a strong imagination" to "men with less imagination." The leader's influence was, as it were, elemental: "His eyes are aflame, and this fire communicates itself; his tone [of voice], his gestures, shake down the nerves of his audience." The generic fanatic was characterized by "rage" and "fury" (*fureur*). The philosopher compared him or her to an "énergumène." The word, two centuries earlier (in its Latin form of *energuminus*), would have denoted exclusively a person vigorously (with *energeia*) possessed by the Devil. In the eighteenth century, it was beginning to mean also a person violently agitated with enthusiasm or anger, yet without supernatural agency. Voltaire—in this the heir of ancient Stoicism—stated that the spread of a philosophical spirit would inoculate minds.⁵ But he also considered that there was not any remedy for fanaticism once people had been seized by it:

> Once fanaticism has attacked a brain like gangrene, the disease is almost beyond cure. I saw spasmodic men and women (*convulsionnaires*) who, speaking of the miracles of the Holy [Deacon François de] Pâris [d. 1727], got progressively more heated: Their eyes took flame, their whole body trembled, fury distorted their faces, and they would have killed any one who disagreed with them. Indeed, I saw them, these *convulsionnaires*, I saw them stretch their limbs and froth at the mouth. They shouted, "There must be blood." ⁶

The dominant sectors of enlightened European opinion (with precocity in England, intensely disrupted by sectarian prophets during its seventeenth century) shared in a marked distaste for the preceding centuries' holy warfare and religious terrorism.⁷ This repugnancy allowed Voltaire to tar ecstatic saintliness by associating it with sectarian fury, in the service of his critique of theistic religion. Both fanaticism and ecstasy were diseases; both had nothing to do with God's presence. Be it to kill or to heal and transmit divine prophecies, there was not any such thing as a divine mission (the philosopher listed some of the favorite premodern biblical authorities for tyrannicide, including Ahod or Ehud, assassin of Eglon [1 Judg. 3.15–21]; Judith, who beheaded Holofernes [Jth. 13.6–21]; and Samuel, who did not spare fat King Agag [1 Sam. 15.32–36]). Nor, of course, was the Devil at work. All the same, Voltaire's antireligious critique preserved the rhetoric and vocabulary stemming from partisan early modern and medieval religious attacks against opposing sects' acts of regicide and from the discourse on witchcraft (since the thirteenth century, men and especially women exhibiting paranormal abilities were either considered as holy or suspected of being witches or demoniacs, or both). The watchwords in this premodern lexicon that Voltaire preserved were "fury," "possession," and fascinating "influence," along with "fire" and "darkness."[8] His *Dictionnaire* article is, therefore, a good point of entry into premodern notions of religious terrorism, both in their medical dimension (destined to last into our twenty-first century) and in their supernatural dimension (destined to disappear from the scholarly and journalistic mainstream).

The *convulsionnaires*, men and women convinced of the deceased François de Paris' holiness and divinely granted powers to heal, were a cause célèbre in Voltaire's century.[9] They sought cures from disease and diabolical influence and also, positively, to be indwelled by the Holy Spirit. The ecstatic devotees' claims were polemical since the holy man, a Jansenist, was not so holy for the other faction in French Catholicism, led by the Jesuits. The dossier of the *convulsionnaires* provided nascent eighteenth-century psychiatry (*aliénisme*), and its more mature nineteenth-century daughter, with materials to discuss hysteria, nymphomania, and masochism.[10] Medicalization was not always confessionally innocent. In the last years of the sixteenth century, Marthe Brossier, allegedly possessed, was examined by physicians, who concluded that there was not any demon in her and that she was a fraud.[11] Devout Catholics often took offense at any such denial of possession, whether it targeted a specific case only or attacked the principle in general (Calvinists did not believe in exorcism so tended to be skeptical of what it was supposed to cure).[12]

In the appropriation by the medical profession of a phenomenon initially located within the purview of theologians,[13] rhetoric and prejudices remained, but the hierarchy of causes was transformed. Causality was relocated exclusively within the human subject's physiology and material makeup. Formerly, violently agitated men and women's religious opinions had interested theologians. They served as touchstone of orthodoxy, therefore of potential sanctity (or its opposite), and were messages either vouched for by God or crafted by the deceitful Devil. Thus, in this earlier system, beliefs belonged to the causal nexus. With professional medicalization, analyses demoted the religious words uttered by the deranged; and their contents became irrelevant for the cures that the alienists envisaged.

One can illustrate the transformation that took place across the late early modern era with the historiographic fate of Jacques Clément. Voltaire's list of fanatics included this young Dominican, a partisan of the ultra-Catholic Holy League in control of Paris between 1588 and 1594. Clément, having knifed to death the reviled Henri III, was butchered on the spot by the dying king's guards (August 1, 1589).[14] Mid-nineteenth century, the great German historian Leopold von Ranke painted Clément in fully secular colors. The Dominican novice was an impressionable weakling:

> if fanatical beliefs can easily serve to lead men and make them cling together, they seize with their full force only those individuals who are extraordinarily receptive to them. There lived in those days in Paris a young Dominican by the name of Jacques Clément, who had just received the priestly orders, whom members of his age-group and his friends mocked more than respected. He was weak (*schwach*) of body and a simpleton (*einfältig*), but it is precisely on such natures that a fanatical doctrine often operates the most irresistible effects.[15]

The German Ranke seems to have known the royalist Étienne Pasquier's 1589 attack against the Catholic League's canonization of Clément as a martyr (or a very similar critique or set of critiques). Ranke used, secularized, similar descriptive terms (youth, simplicity, physical disability) and kept the French argument's structure (such personalities are par excellence disposed to fanaticism). Countering Ligueur eulogies, Pasquier had written:

> [Clément's apologists] say that he was young, simple, infirm, and a monk, qualities indeed proper to becoming the instrument of a diabolical calling (*vocation*)! For his youth, simplicity, infirmity, and monkishness, even his very fasts, rendered him capable of being easily seduced by Satan.[16]

Clearly, there raged a hefty polemic around Clément. On the side of the Holy League (Sainte Ligue), an apologist, possibly the fiery Jean Boucher, felt compelled to mention that there were some "who chalk up this [knife] blow to despair, and say that he [Jacques Clément] was impelled by some evil spirit."[17] Such was the debate: was the Dominican angelic or demonic? The other debate, whether a person was naturally insane or the prey of supernatural forces, had barely begun in the sixteenth century, around the question of witches' ability to harm.

Begun, or begun anew? In the Greco-Roman world, around the time of Christ, there circulated several conceptions of madness, some quite materialistic, some involving divine or daemonic entities, some combining medical lore and belief in supernatural action.[18] Lucian of Samosata, a Skeptic Philosopher and satirist, provides a picturesque example of the second approach. In Abdera (northern Greece), an epidemic of fever was accompanied, as it were, by a cultural epidemic. All affected by the medical condition simultaneously fell to "a fit of tragedizing, spouting iambichs, and roaring out most furiously, particularly the Andromeda of Euripides, and the speech of Perseus, which they recited in most lamentable accents." Lucian attributed this mass poetic logorrhea to a professional performance of the tragedy earlier during the summer and in excessively hot weather. It "had such an effect over the spectators, that several of them, as soon as they rose up from it, fell insensibly into the tragedizing vein; the Andromeda naturally occurring in their memories, and Perseus, with his Medusa, still hovering round them." Colder weather cured them all.[19] According to ancient medical lore, such phenomena stemmed from an imbalance of humors (the fluids making up the human being), most often from an excess of black bile, so from *melancholia*. "What we [Roman] call fury (*furor*), they [the Greeks] call melancholy, as if no other thing than black bile could disturb the mind," nuanced Cicero in his *Tusculan Disputations*.[20] Burnt yellow bile (also called unnatural black bile), others explained, resulted in furious *mania*.[21] By the Middle Ages, melancholia and mania tended to be interchangeable and viewed as related.[22]

Although the surviving record does not permit the historian to measure frequency, during Antiquity, the supernatural explanation of madness may have been more in vogue than its medical counterpart. Since Homer, the warrior's insane rage and the prophet's ravings could be attributed to the entry into the individual of supernatural forces.[23] Cicero's *furor*, fury, was, in fact, an umbrella term for madness and the most common in Roman law discussions of mental disorders. It had initially designated possession;[24] probably already in archaic times, and certainly by the golden age of imperial legislation, it entailed that the man seized by fury, the *furiosus*, could not perform any action at law.[25] Blindness and disabling rage—but also their opposite (which sometimes accompanied cecity), supernatural foresight—stemmed from *furor*.[26]

Seers "vaticinate through fury," said Cicero in his *On Divination*. He explained that "there is in minds a power to predict, divinely injected and enclosed from the outside in them. And when it flames out with greater intensity, it is called fury, since the mind (*spiritus*) is drawn out from the body by a divine force and inflamed (*concitatur*)." This separation allowed the human being's more divine part, the *spiritus*, to be more open to supernatural truth.[27]

Possession took place, thus, with both negative and positive results. The Greeks employed the term *daemon* to designate the superior entity responsible for it, irrespective of its malice or goodwill (*daemon* would take only with the Christianization of the Roman Empire the univocal and purely evil meaning of "demon"). Rome's emperors had an inner *daemon*—their "genius," the upper, supernatural part of their soul. *Daemones* were active in high political tragedies or revolutions. The fall of the praetorian prefect Cleander in 190 C.E. was provoked by a circus riot, which allegedly "a tall maiden of grim aspect" led. She, because of the outcome, was thought to have been a *daimona*.[28] Politics and supernatural madness were also at play in the explanation of the Jewish rebellion, which occupied a good quarter of all Roman legions between 66 and 73 C.E. and which has become a set piece of scholarly discussions of religious fanaticism and terrorism.[29] Its analysis is complicated by the difficult position of our principal informant, Flavius Josephus.

Flavius Josephus was a traitor, or more kindly seen, a collaborationist who (like the first rabbis) sought to preserve his people from savage repression, yet also to be in the good graces of the victors.[30] He was an upper-class Jew, of royal blood, from a Pharisian priestly family. But Josephus ended up bearing the cognomen of Rome's new imperial dynasty, the Flavians, indicating either that he had been adopted into it or, more likely, that he had been freed from a prisoner of war's slave status by one of its members, Vespasian.[31] His *Jewish War* thus juggled three somewhat divergent constraints: exalting the Flavian commanders, Vespasian and his son Titus, who had suppressed the Jewish revolt of 66–73 C.E.; accounting for this revolt; and not incriminating and demeaning overly his own people.[32] Captured in Galilee by Vespasian during the first phase of the Roman general's expedition, Josephus (by his own allegation) had recognized prophetically his victor's imperial destiny. One of the *Jewish War*'s frameworks is, thus, Yahweh's will that Rome conquer the rebellion, owing to the Jews' sins and the Flavians' divine election. One can patch from Josephus himself that the Jewish uprising was fairly widespread and broadly based, and that it involved not only political and social gripes but also an intense religious hostility against the heathen Romans. This last component

Josephus hesitated to put too much to the fore, especially when it came to the extremist groups known as *sicarii* (dagger-men) and Zealots. The latter seem to have been animated by apocalyptic, messianic hopes.[33] Had the Romans convinced themselves that all of Judaism was motivated by such beliefs, the repression would have been severe, and the Jew Josephus's position as a courtier would have been quite uneasy.[34] Yet Josephus had to account for the revolt, and it was known to the Romans (witness Tacitus) that it had a religious component.[35] The solution, found probably more through hesitations of the quill than led by a premeditated plan, was to leave Zealots and *sicarii* in the narrative; attribute to them a maximum of the disorder (as was probably the fact); and instead of harping on the contents of their eschatological hopes (attested to in the Qumran scrolls), rather challenge their claim to be the heirs of Phineas of Numbers 25 and of the Maccabees, zealous for God. With this in mind, Josephus painted the leaders of the various and contending radical factions—John of Giscala, Eleazar ben Ananias, Eleazar ben Simon, Eleazar ben Jair of Masada fame (and his relative Menahem) Simon bar Gioras, and their troops—as men demented.

Josephus's description had to employ terms intelligible to his Greco-Roman audience. The key Greek words here are *mania* (μανία, frenzy), *ánoia* (ἄνοια unreason, lack of *nous*), and *aponoia* (ἀπόνοια, desperation, folly). The leadership of revolts against Rome prior to 66 C.E. the Jewish historian characterized as "deceivers and impostors." These men "perpetrated innovations and revolutions, and under the guise of divine inspiration (*proskhēmati theiasmou*), persuaded the masses to act as if possessed" (another translation yields "to abandon themselves to divine powers," *daimonan to plēthos epeithon*).[36] In so charging the sectarians, though, Josephus left enough information to allow Ernest Renan (1823–1892) to draw the conclusion that the turncoat did not wish the Flavians to draw, that is, that "those 'sacred diseases' that ancient medicine confessed itself powerless to cure seemed to have become the normal temper of the Jewish people."[37] In other words, that the Jews were collectively possessed. And Renan, as if drawn by the rhetorical field of Antiquity linking possession to rage and anger, went on to speak of a Jewish incapacity to have a "civil society parallel to religious society," noting Israel's "permanent rage against Tyre and hatred for Edom, Moab and Ammon." Incidentally, and interestingly for current debates about "fanaticism" in the Muslim world, Renan compared this to Islam's inability to separate church from state.[38]

Madness made for blindness, a disability Josephus often associates with *aponoia* and *ánoia*. There was blindness in the wrong-headedness of the war against Rome, which the Zealots conceived of as a war of obligation, that is, a war mandated by divine law (both Josephus and the founder of the first rabbinical academy in Yavneh disagreed).[39] Madness was contagious, and furious slaughter inspired more. Recounting factional struggle within besieged Jerusalem, Josephus depicts men trampling on the bodies of the dead and inspired to more cruelty, as "the frenzy inhaled from the corpses at their feet increased their savagery."[40]

Josephus's understanding of resistance to Rome as madness is mirrored in slightly later sources presenting Christianity and its martyrs. This new religion's ultimate victory means that the historical record is richer in sympathetic, in-house Christian renditions than in Greco-Roman pagan opinions. But a few of the latter survived. Stoic emperor Marcus Aurelius considered Christian martyrs the opposite of the Stoic *apatheia*; the sage, unlike the sectarian, was *atragodos*; he avoided the tragic posture—by which the emperor likely meant ostentatious opposition to power and (this is a hypothesis) excessive passion or madness. Epictetus saw in the Christians an example to shame the sage into fearlessness before tyrants. Here religious frenzy paradoxically made for control of at least one passion. If Galileans, Epictetus wrote, so transformed by "mania" (*hupo manias*) or "habit" (*hupo etous*), can resist fear when they face a tyrant, all the more should philosophers, with their reason.[41]

The Christian side did also make madness and fury a central theme in the authentic Acts (*Acta*) and Passions (*Passiones*) of the martyrs. The Acts in particular were either based on the written proceedings of Roman tribunals the Christian hagiographers had access to, or they were composed in imitation or allusion to this bureaucratic genre. They thus preserve or replicate the tone and structure of official legal actions against the sect. In this source genre, Rome's magistrates interrogate Christians who refused to sacrifice to or for the emperor, or boldly proclaimed themselves followers of Christ, or attacked idols, or rejected the legions' sacred symbols or rites. The pagan officials quite frequently charge them with madness (*amentia, dementia, insania, phrenoblabeia, mania, mōria*), and if so, often exhort them to desist from folly (become *sobrius* or *sōphrōn*, σώφρων).[42] In a variant, the magistrates repeatedly advise their charges to "change their mind," literally to "convert" (*metanoēson*), a word familiar from the New Testament's exhortations (Acts 8.22; Rev. 2.16 and 3.3).[43] The accusation is usually countered with a denial and a demonstration of poise, *constantia*, sometimes accompanied by "free speech" (*parrēsia*) that propounds the Truth.[44] For instance, in 298, having thrown to the ground his belt, sword, and staff on the anniversary of the ruling tetrarchs, the centurion

Marcellus was sent under escort to the representative of the praetorian prefect, Agricolanus, with a report of his deeds. The magistrate queried: "What fury possessed you . . . to throw down the symbols of your military oath and to say the things you did?"

Marcellus replied: "No madness possesses [is there in] those who fear the Lord."[45] The martyr announces his (or her) immunity from possession, an understandable claim for devotees of a Christ whose seal of baptism protects from demons. All the more as, since at least Tertullian (d. ca. 220) and Cyprian of Carthage (d. 258), apologists claimed for the Church the ability to expel demons. Tertullian ironized; it was a service rendered to humanity and to the emperor by those very men the Romans called "enemies of the human race."[46] In early hagiography, martyrs sometimes claimed another sort of possession, a positive and protective one: it is Christ or the Holy Spirit Who fights or suffers in them.[47] Jesus Himself was possessed by the Spirit, explained one Phileas to the Roman magistrate: "He was a man similar to us, but the divine Spirit was in Him, and in the Spirit He performed miracles, signs and prodigies."[48]

Both camps, pagan and Christian, believed in possession, by good and bad powers. The physics were identical. To cite the late fourth-century author Prudentius, demons "devour in the manner of wolves the innards that they capture, suffocate the minds, and embroil themselves within the senses." As Peter Brown explained three decades ago, late antique Christian culture proposed the solution. The saint cured the possessed by means of a spiritual appropriation of Roman judicial torture. His "power coerces, tortures, burns, puts in chains," wrote, circa 400, the Spaniard Prudentius.[49] Such had been also, about 150 years earlier, Cyprian's portrait of the Christian exorcism's power over "false gods." It was, here and now, a tribunal: tortured by spiritual whips, feeling divine scourges and blows, the demons confessed "with cries and moans" not the authority of some earthly judge, but the Last Judgment (*uenturum iudicium*).[50] And just as, in some Passions, it was Christ who suffered within the martyr, so it was the Devil who was tortured in the possessed.[51]

Early hagiography took this mirroring of true and false powers to a polemical extreme. The magistrate accused, erroneously, the martyrs of madness and possession; in several authentic Acts or Passions, it was this self-same pagan main character, who faced with Christian resistance, *constantia*, and mental fortitude, abandoned himself to (or was seized by) fury.[52] While this aspect would be hypertrophied in later, post-Constantinian hagiography (as the discussion of Prudentius shortly below will show), it was already quite present in the sources composed during the persecutions. In the Donatist *Passion of Maxima, Donatilla and Secunda*, Donatilla retorts to the proconsul Anulinus: "Still the demon stands firm in you. You are being put to the test by it but you will not be able to put others to the test."[53] In the *Acts of Marian and James*, it is the "bloody and blind" presiding magistrate who is indwelled by *furor, crudelitatis insania* (mad drive to cruelty), and *ferox amentia* (ferocious dementia).[54] Here the Christian authors shared in the earlier Greek philosophical tradition, and paralleled the Suetonian critique of bad emperors. Suetonius's near contemporary Josephus, who attributed fury to the revolutionaries, also tarred with *mania* the Roman tyrant Gaius Caligula.[55]

Christians, in so perceiving the prosecuting magistrate, may have been subverting the legal process. Blindness, the reader shall recall, comes with fury and is the sensorial manifestation of mental disability (just as, on the other hand, "no darkness can impede the vision of a soul that is free").[56] Given that demented persons were incapacitated at law, it may be that the hagiographers intimated that furious magistrates' decisions were *eo ipso* invalid. The juridical notion of will may also have been in play. Martyrs go "willingly" to their death, but the demented magistrate is deprived of the will (*voluntas*) that authorizes legal actions.[57] Indeed, often enough the martyr drove his judge to folly. Tazelita's free speech "wounded" the interrogating proconsul "by a spiritual sword;" he descended into mad violence: his "fury burst into flame, and, groaning"—like a demon struck by God's Word—"he beat Christ's martyr with very heavy blows."[58]

Martyrs and False Christian Martyrs

At a hard-to-define point before his death in 337, Emperor Constantine converted. But—as we shall see with Prudentius—Christian triumph did not lead to the waning of Passions and Acts depicting mad pagan persecutors. Nor did it engender the disappearance of the Greco-Roman reading of martyrdom and violent rebellion as madness that Josephus and pagan magistrates had favored (all the more as Josephus, translated into Latin, provided Christians with a favorite history of the punishment God had meted on the Jews for the "deicide," the judicial murder of Christ). The fourth- and early fifth-century conflict between two Christian churches in North Africa known as the Donatist schism perpetuated the need to invalidate the opposite side's religious heroism (or, less cynically seen, to make sense of it). The ultimate victors, who as such came to monopolize the name of Catholics (but whom their adversaries labeled "Caecilianists"), had called on the imperial secular sword to coerce their opponents ("the party of Donatus") to what they considered orthodoxy. The move was problematic, since the pre-Constantinian churches, especially in North Africa, had based their identity on resistance to the armed power of Rome—on being persecuted. Furthermore, better rooted in the North African tradition and countryside, the so-called Donatists could boast not only the martyrs produced by the fourth-century struggle and the intervention of the now Christian army but also pre-Constantinian martyrs. Criticized by Emperor Constantine for madly seeking martyrdom's blessings, the Donatists were not, however, solely on the receiving end of the sword. They had the sword in hand as well, in particular with armed groups known as the Circumcelliones. Therefore, because the struggle between the two churches in North Africa had led to reciprocal bloodshed, each side could point to its opponent's violence. The Donatists generated their own Passions, which staged in traditional fashion the madness plaguing the persecuting Catholics or the soldiers mustered in the service of Catholicism.[59] And both sides, Donatists and Caecilianists, had inherited from Cyprian of Carthage a notion of spiritual coercion, meted both to demons (and pagans) through exorcism or martyrdom and to heretics through excommunication. As we saw with Tazelita, such spiritual warfare could be materialized.[60]

In several tracts and letters, Augustine, bishop of Hippo, brought together the case against the Donatists and for the "Catholics." First, his own church could use force legitimately, terrifying and coercing (*terrendo et cohercendo*) the opposite side for its own good, to preserve it from damnation and bring it back to unity.[61] Second, it was not violent death that made one a martyr but the cause for which one died. The Donatists might well argue that they were martyrs because the emperor persecuted them "and seek from human beings the glory of martyrdom, which they cannot acquire from the Lord." But what mattered was the cause behind coercion; their prosecution was for the sake of the sacraments and the Church's unity.[62] Third, the Donatist martyrs were mad (*furiosi*) and possessed by self-destruction. Here Augustine turned to a theme broached by his opponents' favorite Church Father, the North African Cyprian of Carthage. Cyprian had proposed that "lack of patience . . . creates heretics in the Church, and pushes them, on the Jews' pattern, to rebellion and to hostile and furious hatred against Christ's peace and charity."[63] These false martyrs were actually *homines desperati*, who (as Augustine described them) burned themselves, drowned themselves, or threw themselves from cliffs. To characterize their temper, the bishop of Hippo spoke of *rabies, dementia, furor* (a semantic field his Donatist opponents also used against Augustine's own "Caecilianists").[64] These people would have rejected the Devil's suggestion to commit suicide under the guise of martyrdom "had they borne in their heart Christ the teacher," Who rejected on the Temple's pinnacle Satan's tempting proposal, that He should throw Himself into the void (Matt. 4).[65] Instead, the Donatist false martyrs "have given a place within themselves to the Devil." There are, thus, only two roads for them: they either perish like the flock of pigs that threw itself to its death over a cliff (Matt. 17), or (which is better) the Church draws them back to its bosom. There, they are as if exorcized and liberated from the demon.[66] Augustine compared the Church's gentle coercion to a father's dealings with his undisciplined son and to a doctor's dealing with a "frenetic in fury" (*furens phreneticus*).[67] It was precisely because the Donatists were inhabited by suicidal fury and because they dragged others into suicide (literally, or spiritually by drawing them to heresy) that coercion was necessary. Here Augustine operated a calculus: better use force against a few madmen than allow a greater group to perish.[68] Some among the schismatics, he argued, were ready to kill themselves so that the others would not be liberated from error. They also "terrorized the piety of the [Catholic] liberators" by instilling in the latter the fear of causing these deaths.[69] The bishop's discourse did not focus on killing and did not mention, let alone relish, blood. It soberly bemoaned "the countless mass" of people who would "be damned for eternity and tortured in everlasting fires" if, in order to spare a small number of "desperate men" from martyring themselves in (material) fire, the Church renounced the use of liberating coercion.[70] Such calculus, while chilling, is not unethical; Augustine's was based on different priorities than those of our enlightened Modernity. It is also in terms of ethics that one should consider Jean-Paul Marat's willingness to weigh the death of a few hundred counterrevolutionaries against the survival of hundreds of thousands of patriots. Over and over again, he proposed variants of this principle, for instance, in August 1790: "To shed a few drops of impure blood so as to avoid to spill buckets of pure blood is to be humane and just." And in another variant, Marat explained that this was a "simple calculus mandated by wisdom and philosophy." For the French Revolutionary, too, not striking against the dangerous minority was "false pity."[71]

Thanks to Augustine and others, thus, Roman coercion of madmen and resistors survived Rome's Christianization. There survived also, as one sees with Augustine's Spanish contemporary, Prudentius (d. after 405), the trope of the mad tyrant who deserves resistance. Prudentius's *Hymn on Lawrence* (Laurentius) plays, like many hagiographic texts or sources informed by exegesis, on the disjunction between appearances and reality.[72] The greedy prefect of the city of Rome, "servant of a mad leader," convokes Lawrence. He wants to confiscate the great wealth that rumor attributes to the city's churches. Lawrence will trick the magistrate by volunteering to him the Church's true wealth, by which the saint means (but he does not at first disclose this identity) the poor—beggars, cripples, and others, who depend on material riches. While the prefect, like all persecutors, is fundamentally insane (*furebat feruidus iudex auaro spiritu*),[73] he manages during his initial meeting with the saint to pretend moderation:

> You are wont to complain that we rage more than is just when we cut into pieces, with a cruelty beyond words, Christian bodies. But there is in me no flaming (*fervens*) anger and excessively violent impulses (*atrociores motus*); I shall request from you sweetly and calmly something that you should willingly agree to.[74]

This aspect of the Passion's plot is paralleled elsewhere in Prudentius. In the hymn devoted to Romanus, Asclepiades, who had contained his anger while the saint sermonized him, "finally vomited the violence of his hidden fury." And after a miracle that terrified him, this persecutor could not "control his rudderless mind's violence" (*nec uim domare mentis effrenae potest*).[75] Likewise, once Lawrence produces the promised wealth—and these horribly crippled men and women clamor loudly for alms before the prefect's seat—the pagan's quiet outward demeanor lapses, revealing his true nature: he "was horrified and stupefied, and turning to Lawrence, threatened him with convulsive eyes." Far from what we know from late antique statuary, the huge eyes, turned towards heaven, in clear, knowing sight, of the inspired philosopher or emperor! We are here rather in presence of the phenomenology of the maddened zealot according to Cyprian of Carthage ("threatening expression, savage in mien, a pallid face, with trembling lips, gnashing teeth, raging words, unbridled abuses, plus hands ready to violent massacres, and even when deprived of a sword, armed with the hate of a mind in fury").[76]

Prudentius paints the raging magistrate in the same colors that he deploys for the possessed in the hymn devoted to Eulalia. Under exorcism, "the man in fury, filled by his Enemy, is forced to stand; he exudes frothy saliva, rolls bloody eyes."[77] Lawrence's explanation of what is true wealth (along with true honor and true beauty), as opposed to fictive monetary wealth, angers the prefect even more. *Furens*, he calls Lawrence's pedagogical ploy "a comedy" of whose joke he is the butt. "We are being played with in extraordinary ways through this *figura*," the prefect exclaims. In these telling terms, the magistrate is refusing the Christian spiritual reading that reveals the Truth beyond appearances and is reducing it to a metaphoric figure of speech meant to deceive and mock.[78]

And indeed, throughout his "Hymn on Lawrence," Prudentius harps on the opposition between seeming and real, including through sensorial divergences. The pagans, blind, do not see Lawrence's illuminated face. The smell of Lawrence's burnt flesh is stinking fumes (*nidor*) to the pagans, sweet (*nectar*) to the elect; it "affected with a vengeful horror (*horror vindex*) the noses [of the former]" and "pleasured and soothed [the noses of the latter]" (cf. 2 Cor. 2.15–16).[79] The antinomy, playing on sameness and difference, is familiar: what is terrifying to the opposite side is a blessing to one's own side. By nature, the reprobate will perceive as terror what is sweetness to the just. This structure was fated to last over the longue durée of Western writing. It made sense of the wicked's inability to perceive the justice of a cause, to move from letter to spirit, to distinguish between a martyr and an impostor, between a holy warrior and a terrorist, between a holy entity and a profane one. The lilies of the Nation France smelled good to the good and bad to the bad.[80] And a violence that was from the standpoint of phenomenology identical for the two opposite sides (including the plunder of churches) was "zeal" when perpetrated by the "pious" reformist Patarenes, "fury" when perpetrated by their "impious" simoniac enemies. The one was for Christ, the other for Satan.[81]

These notions of possession, good and bad, passed, if one may use a medical image, into the cultural bloodstream. Pope Gregory the Great's *Commentary on the Book of Job*, one of the most read biblical primers of the Early and High Middle Ages, maintained the connection between anger and madness present in early hagiography:

Anger makes one lose the light of Truth . . . because when anger instills in the mind the darkness of confusion, God hides the light-ray of His knowledge. . . . Therefore, when anger takes away tranquility from a mind (*mens*), this mind closes itself to the indwelling of the Holy Spirit, and with Its departure the intellective soul (*animus*) is left empty, is soon led to open madness, and is shattered from the deepest layer of its thoughts all the way to its surface.

Gregory (d. 604) also described in graphic details the symptoms of this anger, in no way dissimilar from the possessed's behavior insofar as both the possessed (*arreptitii*) and angry men are "not conscious of their actions."[82]

The positive counterpart was transmitted as well and refined. When the late antique or early medieval saint acted violently against tyranny, paganism, but also heresy, he or she could be understood as indwelled by the Holy Spirit. Although it was far from an omnipresent theme, the High Middle Ages sometimes described the holy warrior as possessed, by God. According to thirteenth-century sermons, crusaders experienced Christ's Passion through a penitential opening up of their heart to Him. Love and zeal fruitfully—in the view of pious contemporaries—combined.[83] Later commentators would not be so sure about the Crusades' value. Thus the earl of Shaftesbury in 1707 happily commented that "the Crusades, the rescuing of Holy Lands, and such devout Gallantry" (which he placed on a par with Knight-Errantry) "are in less request than formerly." He categorized these religious wars within the genus "enthusiasm," alongside love and "panic" fear.[84]

Shaftesbury meant to relegate the religious passions of his own age to an archaic past—to the Middle Ages. He was not fully off the mark as to origins, for indeed the High Middle Ages witnessed the first mass movements in European history. Religious in essence, they stimulated contemporaries' explanatory abilities.[85] Circa 1266, the Franciscan polymath Roger Bacon (d. ca. 1292) developed on the basis of his optics a theory of influence through voice and sight (the latter he named "fascination").[86] Any object emitted *species*—material images that multiplied themselves in the space between the object and any creature that would perceive it. So did any person endowed with a bad complexion, for example, a leper. If such a person, furthermore, malignantly "thinks forcefully to infect another, desires it vehemently, turns his intention to it with assurance, and believes vehemently that he can cause harm," he is likely to have a proportionally strong effect.[87] Bacon did not detail these mechanisms for the sake of pure knowledge. Antichrist, a fine user of all wisdoms, in his enterprise of world domination, would doubtless use these techniques to seduce not simply individuals but entire cities and kingdoms into subjection, or make them war against one another. He was endowed, after all, with "a great desire to harm conjoined to the most steady intention and an intense confidence." Antichrist's minions, the Saracens and Mongols, with their knowledge of astrology, so in possession of the science that determined human complexions, were likely to select agents who would wreak havoc within Christendom by fascinating its people. They would also, Bacon feared, use fascination to create conflicts among Christian princes. Something like this had already taken place earlier in the century when secret agents had fascinated children into following them. These hapless youth ended up being sold in Muslim lands (Bacon was referring here to the so-called Children's Crusade of 1212).[88] He himself had witnessed a second such mass seduction (the Shepherds' Crusade of 1251):

> A master shepherd put in motion all of Germany and France, and a multitude of people followed him; he ingratiated himself with the whole common laity to the confusion of the Church and with contempt for the clergy. And he told Lady Blanche [the regent of France] that he would go to her son [the crusading King Louis IX] beyond the sea. With such words he deceived this most wise among women. Let wise men not doubt that these [leaders] were the envoys of Mongols or Saracens, and that they possessed some objects (*opera*)[89] with which they fascinated the plebe. And I saw with my own eyes [their leader] carrying openly in his hand something as if it had been a sacred object (as when a person transports relics). He was going barefoot, surrounded by a multitude of armed men which was so spread out in the fields that he could be seen by all who came this way, with that thing that he carried in hand with great ostentation.[90]

Late medieval mass movements such as the flagellants, a "race without a head," sometimes engaged in murderous anticlerical violence, could also be attributed to changes in complexion wrought on a human collective by the stars' influence.[91]

Medieval science proposed new explanations for religious exaltation; medieval hagiography perpetuated its own models. The thirteenth-century *Golden Legend*, one of the most widely reproduced books of the Middle Ages, delivered to the age of the wars of religion the twinned but opposed strands developed in late Antiquity. The Roman interpretation of rebellion as madness and the pre-Constantinian understanding of persecution as furious folly, along with the correlated steadfastness of magistrate or martyr, informed sixteenth-century perceptions of violence suffered for God and inflicted for God.[92] For example, illustrating in painting, circa 1438, this primer's version of the martyrdom of Cosmas and Damian, Fra Angelico counterpoised the saints, kneeling quietly and hieratically, with a constancy and poise denoting indwelling by God, to the magistrate Lysias, seating in a twisted posture, with two devils slapping him.[93] In the same *Golden Legend*, Saint Catherine confronts the pagan emperor Maxentius with an equation of persecuting fury and illegitimate rule: "Caesar, I adjure you not to allow fury to conquer you; a wise man's mind (*spiritus*) should not be the toy of a dire disorder; has not the poet said, 'Should the mind govern you, you are a king; if it is the body, you are a slave'?"[94] Circulating in the 1570s, a French version of the apocryphal Fourth book of Maccabees explained that Éleazar and the Maccabean children could endure all their sufferings and tortures because, touched by grace and "aflame with ardor," their "reason dominated and mastered" their "affects" (*l'affection*). On the other hand, tyrants—men who held the wrong faith and so oppressed the saints—did not.[95] As in Hrotsvith of Gandersheim's Saxon plays and poems, Jesuit counterreformation drama featured confrontations between a saint and an oriental despot, who lost all control over his passions (including sexual desires) and, therefore, ability to rule.[96] A common outcome was the tyrant's suicide, motivated by doubt, or a palace revolution against him.[97]

The fifteenth century gave birth to the witch craze. Thus, another legacy of the Middle Ages to the early modern era was acute concerns about the "discernment of spirits," meaning, whether a man or woman exhibiting the physical symptoms of sanctity was actually a holy person or rather a witch or demoniac.[98] Over time, as we shall see, the recourse to medical examinations in order to discriminate would allow the collapse of the two categories into a single, secular ensemble of the mad. As Brad Gregory and David El Kenz have emphasized, observers on both sides of the confessional divide agreed on the presence of a supernatural force at the execution of a heretic, an indwelling that explained the victim's steadfastness. A later age would see in this constancy the fruit of autohypnosis (so self-possession, as it were); the sixteenth-century question was only whether steadfastness's agent was Holy Spirit or Satan.[99] Protestant and Catholic polemics opposed true martyrs to the Devil's martyrs and drew directly on Augustine's writings against the Donatists. One sees this inheritance at work, for instance, in a sermon preached in 1563, for the funeral of François de Lorraine, leader of the ultra-Catholic faction, assassinated by a Calvinist. It featured a contrast between this true martyr and the suicidal death of the heretical fanatics, prey of the Devil.[100]

As we have seen, discussion over discernment was particularly heated around the martyr-assassin Jacques Clément. In reaction to Henri III's assassination and to the ultra-Catholic rebellion, royalists tarred the Ligue with fury and madness. We can do no better than follow Denis Crouzet here.[101] The rebellious Ligue's plans were not inspired "from above," but "from Hell's furies and Spanish furies."[102] While the murdered king's designated successor, his cousin Henri IV of Navarre, a convert from Calvinism, besieged Ligueur Paris, royalist pamphleteers turned to Stoic models to criticize the ultra-Catholic rebels. France was in chaos and unreason. God had abandoned the Parisian Ligueurs, an "insensate people," to their "souls' unbridled passions and affects"; they were the prey of frenzy (*phrenesie*).[103] The Stoic vision encompassed much more than a reflection on *pathos*; the key argument consisted in the homologies between the rule of the king and the rule of reason and between rebellion against the monarchy and turbulence of the animal affects against the rational mind.[104] But as in late Antiquity, the Stoic construct framed a Christian discourse. The other side was tarred with the by now familiar characteristics. The Ligue's leadership, besides plotting treasons and barricades and using false information, "made maniacal preachers froth at the mouth and bray."[105] An anonymous "gentilhomme serviteur du Roi" contrasted, negatively, the Ligueurs' self-destructive annihilation of France with Samson's suicide (Judg. 16). You "seek to do the same that Samson did when he brought low the great temple's two pillars in which the Allophiles were gathered, thus making them perish and destroying in this manner the enemy nation; you in perishing and unraveling yourselves seek to ruin totally and bring down your own commonwealth's foundations."[106] The contrast brought into play one of the Bible's most disputed authorities for holy violence. Further, it echoed Augustine's polemics against the Donatist martyrdoms. A Parisian panegyric also characterized the Ligue's violence as a contagious and delusional "popular sickness": "This mania kills the people, who believe themselves to be quite healthy;" it is "a frenzy (*frenaisie*) that throws them over a cliff like the runaway horse that believes to be free, an invisible torture that torments them while they believe that they are tormenting the king, a fury that tortures [itself] by itself."[107] The image of suicidal pseudo-martyrdom (over a cliff) was Augustinian; the idea of self-torment stemmed from the trope of the magistrate who fell into fury and sometimes death in the process of torturing the saint (to cite a vision granted to Saint Agatha, "even though the mad consul afflicts you with torments, you affect him even more by your responses").[108] Against the lower orders, who "easily allowed themselves to be carried away to impetuosity and furors that like waves swelled in their hearts," stood (as Crouzet explains) the impassible astral ruler, who, through his very impassibility, would save them. The Parisian royalists' proposed remedy was clemency—Henri IV's program for reconciliation.[109]

Germany provided model fanatics to both Catholics and mainstream

Protestants. The 1524–1525 Peasants' War, followed by the 1533–1535 Anabaptist uprising in Münster, with their attendant chiliast violences, became poster children for collective madness.[110] The Calvinist Friedrich Spanheim called the peasants *fanatici et seditiosi isti homines* (these fanatical and seditious people).[111] The Anabaptists' antinomian deportments as they lay besieged in Münster occasioned prudish depictions of collective folly: "We should rather pass under silence than offend chaste ears [by describing] with which an unbridled libidinous fury they rushed into the female sex; and how with less temperance and more eagerness for intercourse than any beast; with which insatiably they paid their dues to most shameful embraces; and with which monstrous ardor for pleasure they flared up."[112] Sexual frenzy was paired to blood frenzy. Another Münsterite, Knipperdolling, did not spare one of his lovers, one Dreierschenia, accused of favoring defections out of the city. He grabbed the executioner's sword and beheaded her. Allegedly, Knipperdolling "excused his *furor* by proclaiming that he had been stirred by [God] the Father's inspiration, and that his hands had been moved and impelled to avenge this crime [Dreierschenia's] by His signal and decision, against his own opinion."[113] But, equally attested, the sectarians' constancy was a problem. The Anabaptists' strength of character vis-à-vis torments, said Spanheim, made some observers misidentify them; to these impressionable sympathizers, the sectarians seemed "to be pitied rather than to be considered evil," and "their pertinacy was attributed to courageous steadfastness."[114] Hostile observers thus attributed to the sectarians both a remarkable Stoic-grade impassibility and a differently astonishing lack of self-control. These men and women had been taught by the examples of old, but hostile observers also expected disorderly conduct, which they also saw. In the sixteenth century, the contradiction was resolved by the presence of the Devil: "It is certain that Satan grants strength and constancy to those whom he holds netted by his snares." One did not feel any contradiction when zealots on one's own side combined a heart aflame and a tranquil spirit.[115] As we shall shortly discuss, circa 1900, Jean-Martin Charcot's school resolved the tension: *apatheia* and zeal constituted alternative and non-mutually exclusive symptoms of a single pathology, hysteria.

In the sixteenth century, these physics of the spirits were not employed solely for suffering martyrs. As sometimes in the Middle Ages, Catholic holy warriors were also "as if eaten up and devoured internally from their innards all the way to their bones' marrow." Their soul was so much "occupied" that they no longer "followed the dictates and proposals of human reason"; rather, their divine zeal weakened "carnal prudence" and transformed their mind. Denis Crouzet has abundantly documented how it was a commonplace that sixteenth-century crusaders were possessed by the Holy Ghost.[116] The divine spirit allowed them to overcome, as in the first centuries' Acts and Passions, pagan philosophy and false reason.

The century of Voltaire, with which this chapter began, subverted the opposition between good possession and bad possession. The subversion was not only medical. Denis Diderot, in his essay on the sacred art exposed in Paris in 1761, perceived in all the figures, saintly and persecuting, the selfsame madness:

> Fanaticism and its mute atrocity govern all the faces in the painting depicting *Saint Victor* [by Deshays]. One sees it in the old praetor who interrogates [the saint], and in this [pagan] pontiff who holds and sharpens a knife; and in the saint whose glances reveal his mental alienation, and in the soldiers who having seized him, maintain him. [As many characters,] as many heads quasi-thunderstruck (*étonnées*).[117]

For John Locke, discussing the same sort of beings ("Men, in whom Melancholy has mixed with Devotion"), only the logical light of reason ("the Evidence of the truth of any Proposition") could distinguish between "Delusions of Satan, and the Inspirations of the Holy Ghost," since the former "can transform himself into an Angel of Light."[118]

Yet Enlightenment critique, although it put on the same plane martyrs and persecutors, pagan and Christian fanaticism, and although, with Locke and others, it proposed itself as the efficient discriminator, did not put an end to Christian tropes. The new creed of enlightened reason merely projected these figures onto all religious enthusiasts. So, in the moment when culturally Catholic Revolutionary France embraced martyrdom, it also turned to the related Christian discourse linking tyranny and madness. Witness Jean-Paul Marat's caricature of the Legislative Assembly's demeanor. It could have been composed by Gregory I or by Cyprian of Carthage, the observer of sectarian envy and zeal.

> To see them agitated like madmen fit to be bound when the stake is to prevent the laying down of some right for the people; to see them leap from their seats, tromp, grit their teeth, run against one another,

threaten one another by gestures; to hear them bark at one another, quarrel, insult one another, shame one another, emit furious howls and give themselves over to all of rage's excesses—how would one not recognize in these alleged representatives of the people factious men, whom their material interests divide, and who doggedly fight over power?[119]

"Factious" and "factions," let it be said in passing, belonged to the early Christian discourse on heresy, in which those who splintered the Church were often depicted as mad.[120] Marat claimed for himself, however, the positive enthusiasm of the warlike saint, trumpeting his "courage aflame to battle for such a beautiful cause," and his fearlessness "as long as I was in the arena." "I unmasked traitors," he went on, "and I defended your cause with the holy zeal of a martyr for liberty."[121] Dechristianizing revolutionaries were bent on uprooting "fanaticism." They did so with "reason" but also with "zeal."[122]

Religious America both benefited from Enlightenment critique and deployed the image of fanatical madness in its own conflicts. On the one hand, its medical profession shared the diagnostics of its transatlantic counterparts on enthusiasm (as one sees in one of the very first issues of the later *Journal of Psychiatry*, which advocated staying away from new sects' meetings, given the dangers of contagion through word and sight).[123] And, on the other hand, radicals, notably enemies of slavery, were perceived as latter-day Puritan fanatics and new Cromwells or as "monomaniacs." In the case of John Brown, captured at Harpers Ferry as he attempted to trigger a slave rebellion (1859), the Virginian magistrates had to ascertain whether he was *compos mentis*, a legal requirement all the more pressing given the widespread understanding that white abolitionism was madness.[124] Brown, for his part, considered any proslavery man to be equally deranged, as the following dialogue shows:

A Bystander: To free them [the slaves, you] would sacrifice the life of every man in this community.
Brown: I do not think so.
Bystander: I know it. I think you are fanatical.
Brown: And I think you are fanatical. "Whom the gods would destroy they first make mad."
And you are mad.[125]

There was the hint of a threat in Brown's retort. While he cited a pagan poet on the tactic of the gods, plural, a good Protestant would easily have deciphered the martyrological undertone: fanatical fury was a mark of damnation, certainly in the other world, and oftentimes in this one. Brown "still" belonged to the culture of religious wars. "Still," but as Ernst Bloch underlines, "not all people belong to the same now."[126]

Group Madness: Explanations, Worries, and Hopes for Usability

Fanaticism splintered, but holy zeal united, sacramentally. This positive emotion transformed a congeries of individuals into a holy body, as Catholic communion with the Eucharist assembled the faithful into the single bread that was Christ. Unsurprisingly, therefore, Late Modern quests for national or social unity turned to this earlier tradition in its affective dimensions. In this specific pursuit, associated with the emergent discipline of sociology, the negative valence associated with sharing in an extreme emotionality took a back seat.[127] But negativity was at the forefront of another new discipline, clinical psychiatry. Thus, in sum, circa 1900, the new, vanguard milieus of psychiatry and sociology diffused and vulgarized in widening circles across professions and disciplines scientific notions of exaltation and folly. They built on trends begun within the sixteenth-century critique of enthusiasm. In particular, they refashioned the initially negative notions of contagion of madness. To these we now turn.

*   *   *

It is unclear when one first began to theorize phenomena of collective or group madness and the mechanisms of contamination and influence. Be it as it may, the two issues, collective and contagion, were squarely present in the Enlightenment. One can cite Voltaire's discussion of Islam's founder Muhammad:

Once Mahomet came to know well his countrymen's character (their ignorance, their gullible nature, their propensity to enthusiasm), he understood he could raise himself up to be a prophet. . . . One must think that like every enthusiast Mahomet was impacted violently by his own ideas; first doled them out in good faith; strengthened them with daydreams; deceived himself while deceiving others; and, finally, supported a doctrine that he considered to be good with necessary tricks (*fourberies*).[128]

Voltaire evoked self-deception or self-hypnosis—a notion that would become key for twentieth-century political religions' understanding of the leader's role in mass mobilization—but did so only summarily. His reflections on influence, here and in the *Dictionnaire Philosophique*, show the influence of Roger Bacon's theories, elaborated circa 1260 in the worrisome shadow of Antichrist, or of models cognate to them.

These models likely were mediated through England. A good century before Voltaire, the Anglican Méric Casaubon polemicized against inspired fanaticism, Puritan and Catholic. As every so often, the combat against contemporary heresies was fought on the battlefield of past deviations. Casaubon drew on Byzantine heresiology's polemical depictions of the fourth-century Messalian sect. Messalian initiates were fed stories of angels and devils and prepared by "the wild and stern countenance of his Instructors, and all their ghostly crew, and by some mysticall wayes, practiced at this day among the Jesuits in some places." Such techniques, Casaubon opined, would be "enough to crack the brains of them that were not extraordinarily sound."[129] Bridging exalted late antique heretics and the Counter-Reformation's Catholic Society of Jesus, Casaubon's discussion of spiritual manipulations would not be out of place in Cold War fantasies of Communist brainwashing. As for contagion, the same Casaubon wondered whether it could take place and answered in the affirmative. He did not foreground direct devilish operation. Rather, it was likely "that naturall Ecstasies and Enthusiasms such as proceed from naturall causes merely, should be contagious: though not contagious in the same manner as the Plague, or the Pox is."[130] One case of "epidemical disease or distemper" that he mentioned, without explaining the mechanism of propagation, was the flagellants, a penitential movement that had spread in 1260 through Italy and central Europe, and that had known remakes with the Black Death of 1348–1351.[131] Another was Lucian of Samosata's already discussed portrayal of an epidemic of fever and tragedy declamation in Abdera.[132]

England during and after the Civil Wars had good reasons to dislike religious exaltation but also good reasons not to make it a ground for persecution. Equally interested in demoting into the sphere of nature seeming supernatural possessions, Anthony Ashley Cooper, earl of Shaftesbury (1671–1713), in his *Letter Concerning Enthusiasm* (1707), stepped closer to an analysis of contagion:

> We may with good reason call every Passion *Pannick* which is rais'd in a Multitude, and conve'd by Aspect, or as it were by Contact or Sympathy. Thus popular Fury may be call'd *Pannick*, when the Rage of the People,

as we have sometimes known, has put them beyond themselves; especially where Religion has had to do. And in this stage their very Looks are infectious. The Fury flies from Face to Face: and the Disease is no sooner seen than caught. Those who in a better Situation of Mind have beheld a Multitude under the power of this Passion, have own'd that they saw in the Countenances of Men something more ghastly and terrible than at other times is express'd on the most passionate occasions. Such force has Society in ill, as well as in good Passions: and so much stronger any affection for being *social* and *communicative*. THUS, my Lord, there are many *Pannicks* in Mankind, besides merely that of fear. And thus is Religion also *Pannick*; when Enthusiasm of any kind gets up; as oft, on melancholy occasions,[133] it will do.[134]

Shaftesbury likely understood contagion's mechanics in similar ways to Roger Bacon; his "aspect" translated the Latin *aspectus*, a cognate of the medieval *species*, and meant a gaze or glances, emitted or received.[135] He proposed to heal such diseases not by exorcism but by "humour"—a reference to the humoral conceptions that underlay mirth and sadness. They were curable, and not by persecution, but remained problematically antisocial.

To this negative verdict, a positive dimension was added when the emergent social sciences seized the notion of fascination and autodeception. This took place at the turn of the twentieth century. And soon enough, to cite Robert Nye, "the authoritarian political tradition . . . utilized insights gleaned from social thought and social science."[136] This was notably true of Gustave Le Bon's studies in social psychology. This highly influential polymath (1841–1931) befriended, read, and consulted Parisian alienists, including men from the school that had studied the last *convulsionnaires*, in particular, the great Jean-Martin Charcot himself (1825–1893).[137] The social sciences, reciprocally, harvested earlier historical or philosophical narratives and essays, along with the notions of human action implicit or explicit in these. Le Bon's *Psychologie des foules* (*Psychology of the Crowd*), a much read and widely translated book, proposed that it was crowds "that have furnished the torrents of blood requisite for the triumph of every belief." Being suggestible, *les foules* were capable of the worst excesses in cruelty or massacre and of the most altruistic self-sacrifices— in Le Bon's own terms massacre and martyrdom.[138] In his *History of England*, noticing (as one narrative had it) that the conquerors of Jerusalem in 1099 had suddenly passed from murderous "fury" to tearful devotion, David Hume had marveled about this very copresence of slaughter and self-sacrifice: "So

inconsistent is human nature with itself! and so easily does the most effemi-
nate superstition ally, both with the most heroic courage and with the fiercest
barbarity." Others had echoed him, with sex thrown in. Thus Charles Mac-
Kay's *Extraordinary Popular Delusions*, highlighting the "unbounded licen-
tiousness" with which "the courtezan with the red cross on her shoulders plied
her shameless trade with sensual pilgrims, without scruple on either side," allowing "the sounds of lewd revelry and the voice of prayer" to rise "at the same
instant from the tents." The Franks of 1099 had been mad, a position characteristic of the Enlightenment's disapproving discourse on the Crusades, a
philosophic critique that also highlighted the duality between murderous fury
(plus sometimes debauchery) and piety or mercy.[139] Le Bon's model accounted
for this seeming contradiction and transposed it to later, and apparently secular, violence. Crowds' energies, according to Le Bon, were religious in essence,
even when they thought themselves political: "The convictions of crowds assume those characteristics of blind submission, fierce intolerance, and the
need of violent propaganda which are inherent in religious sentiment, and it
is for this reason that it may be said that all their beliefs have religious form."[140]
Le Bon drew his examples from the familiar fundus of fanatical moments—
the Crusades, the Inquisition, the Reformation, Saint Bartholomew's Day, the
Jacobin "Reign of Terror" of 1793.[141] The same logic governed, for example,
the September massacres and those of Saint Bartholomew's Day. It was an
"openness to suggestion, credulity, mobility, the exaggeration of the sentiments good or bad, the manifestation of certain forms of morality, etc."

But a crowd was not self-moving. Appropriate leadership was necessary
for a human group's effective operation as a religious movement, regardless of
whether its ideals and aims were religious *stricto sensu*. A leader would incul-
cate the shared passion to unite men, give them direction, and enable radical
action. To convince others through a process tantamount to hypnosis or seduction, the leader (not unlike Voltaire's Muhammad) had to convince himself of his mission—in the terms of contemporary psychiatry, autohypnosis.[142]
Whether or not Le Bon was the sole fountainhead of the idea (which is unlikely),[143] it became widely accepted in the earlier part of the twentieth century: masses were mobilized by political faiths, by leaders who both
manipulated and believed. The Fascist cadres both manipulated the masses to
instill belief and believed themselves in this same belief. Dubious if supreme
praise: Adolf Hitler plagiarized Le Bon in *Mein Kampf* and modeled his own
Germanic prophetic leadership according to the French recipes.[144] One must
agree with Alberto Toscano that this desire to cultivate the affects for the social

good was in tension with a negative understanding of enthusiasm as fanaticism. The tension still endures.[145]

Le Bon's sense that a form of trance was necessary for group formation and cohesion was also central to Émile Durkheim's thought. With Durkheim's *Elementary Forms of the Religious Life*, however, the normative aspect of the analysis receded very much into the background. Le Bon still departed from, so left apparent, transparent traces of Enlightenment disapproval for group emotions, insofar as he began his analysis with the paradox that a crowd could be stirred to martyrdom as much as to massacre. But Le Bon proposed to use collective folly, regardless of its surface valence, for political ends that served the common good. Similarly, Durkheim granted the same positive efficiency to, on the one hand, joyful and, on the surface, positive emotions and, on the other hand, apparently less commendable ones. Both group festive revelry and the anger shared during a criminal trial generated the "collective effervescence" that maintained and re-created the social group. The two French thinkers minimized the theological or ideological contents, and prioritized action and emotion. Le Bon's prophet had to simplify ideas and make them into images in order to fascinate crowds. To be effective, arguments had to be sewn together by some sort of primitive associative logic.[146] Myth and dogma's truth-value were irrelevant; and in myth and dogma per se, there did not inhere the function of a religion or quasi-religious movement. For Durkheim, it was not the message or dogma that mattered; it was the ritual generative of collective effervescence and these inarticulate group emotions.

Without quite saying so, Durkheim was intimating that collective folly constituted the collective. The identification of religion to group irrationality, inherent in Shaftesbury's veiled identification of "panique" and religion, but now given a clear creative role, braided into political conceptions a positive counterpart to the Enlightenment's negative discourse. To the Left, it was shared by Georges Sorel, a reader of Le Bon, and by Ernst Bloch.[147] In the religious sphere, William James accepted the verdict of the *aliénistes*, but disconnected the question of origins from the issue of value and validity. All paranormal sensitivity was at heart pathological. But psychophysiological abnormality and real inspiration were not antithetical. For James, imbalance was part and parcel of the makeup of key religious figures: great "religious leaders have been subject to abnormal psychological visitations. Invariably they have been creatures of exalted emotional sensibility. Often they have led a discordant inner life, and had melancholy during a part of their career."[148]

The positive appreciation did not displace the critique; the Western

European discourse remained dual. For, indeed, others drew from Charcot's medical psychiatry negative appreciations that dovetailed with the Enlightenment dislike for enthusiasm. Charcot and his school had embarked upon the retrospective psychological analysis of individual figures from the past (a move that, as shall be explained shortly, others, doctors or historians, extended to "psychopathologies" of collective events such as revolutions). Charcot is famous for having turned the old but vague notion of hysteria into a clinical concept, defined by a series of symptoms.[149] His "grande attaque hystérique" consisted in a set of four potential phases that could occur in sequence or be each present predominantly to the exclusion of the other three, or with these other three being present in a highly attenuated form. What is critical for the present discussion—the genealogy of the idea of the mad terrorist—was his notion of "médecine rétrospective" (retrospective medicine). Charcot identified purported demoniac possession and ecstatic deportment (so, possession by God) as, respectively, phases two (the "grands mouvements," ample bodily motions) and three ("attitudes passionnelles," impassioned attitudes) in the hysterical sequence. The first set's wild contortions (as we have seen them described by the Fathers from Cyprian of Carthage on) and the second set's indifference to the world, withdrawal, and erotic fantasies of fusion with God (the martyr's constancy or the saint's meditative other-worldliness) were hysterical symptoms. The prepsychiatric past had been unable to fathom this. Like a number of his *aliéniste* predecessors, Charcot used as a key dossier the Convulsionnaires de Saint-Médard. They were for him a group of contagion-prone hysterics. With his collaborator Paul Richer, a doctor and sculptor, he published a *Les démoniaques dans l'art* (*The Demoniacs in Art*): iconographic and statuary representations of demonic possession from the fifth to the eighteenth century documented the deep past of hysteria. The radically anticlerical Désiré-Magloire Bourneville, a close associate of Charcot, went even farther in this "retrospective medicine," the medical analysis of the past. He directed a nine-volume series titled "La Bibliothèque diabolique" (The Diabolical Library). Bourneville's collection was scientific insofar as the volumes reproduced early modern religious sources, sometimes publishing them for the first time; it was also scientific as Bourneville understood science insofar as descriptions of possession or ecstasies were read between the lines and reinterpreted as hysteria or neurosis. One author in the Bibliothèque discussed the case of a Norman woman, Françoise Fontaine. She labored, adjudicated this Vicomte de Moray, under hysteroepilepsy, probably provoked by a rape. His dismissal of Satan illustrates the remanence of exegetical categories (or at least of the exegetical lexicon) in the social sciences: the presence of the Devil "is impossible to accept according to the letter, and one should carefully disengage from it [the narrative] its spirit."[150]

The psychoanalysis of the past spread well beyond Charcot's Salpêtrière Hospital. Drawing on Charcot's writings and on the *Bibliothèque diabolique*, for instance, the Polish doctor Wladyslaw Szumowski painted the Middle Ages into a veritable factory for the irrational. Invaded by the supernatural, with countless stories of miracles, enchantments, and Satan, medieval Europe all too easily fell into bouts of "panic fear of hell or in religious ecstasy, and over time became an excellent terrain for the development of psychopathological states and in particular of characterized hysteria." The verdict, loud and clear, was that "the whole Christian society (also its Jewish counterpart, but much less Islam) was from top to bottom electrically charged with hysterical tendencies."[151] The Children's Crusade and the flagellant movements were thus collective psychoses.[152] Szumowski explained contagion by an endogenous vulnerability, owing to superstition and its myths, to suggestion and autosuggestion. In particular, when exorcisms occurred, there could develop, owing to these native dispositions, veritable epidemics of witchcraft.[153]

In the second half of the twentieth century, hybrids of the systems elaborated circa 1900 entered professional history writing. Some interpretations of medieval violence combined the Durkheimian functionalist tradition and psychopathology. In a theory developed in the late 1960s and 1970s, Lester Little posited an "ethical lag, stretching from the time of the commercial revolution . . . in the eleventh century, until the mid-thirteenth century, when the friar-theologians formulated a definitive theological justification for the urban, commercial life." For two centuries, medieval theologians stuck to "old ethics" ("old" insofar as it had been elaborated successively in downtrodden, first rural, then feudal contexts); they failed to make meaningful and acceptable to Christians, and especially merchants, the rapid transformations Europe was experiencing in moving from a gift economy to a profit economy.[154] Christians, clergy and laity, consequently "projected" onto the Jews their own fears, guilt, and dissatisfaction. There was, first of all, in ritual murder accusations a Christian projection of guilt for the pogroms they had perpetrated owing to such accusations; there was, more fundamentally, a projection of guilt over Christian calculating profit making. "The Jews functioned as a scapegoat for Christian failure to adapt successfully [their religion] to the profit economy."[155] In a more recent variant, it has been proposed that medieval European violence against the Jews initially originated in the inability of the Christian population to believe in the irrational and novel dogma of the Eucharistic real presence and from the projection onto the Jewish minority of this sinful religious doubt.[156]

The historiography of the European Middle Ages also mustered the notions of paranoia and hysteria. Mid-century, Norman Cohn's famous *Pursuit of the Millennium* (first edition of 1957, tellingly titled in French *Les fanatiques de l'Apocalypse*) had seen in often violent medieval movements (and in modern counterparts including Nazism and Bolshevism) the materialization in action of "a collective paranoid fanaticism."[157] To cite the book's conclusion,

> The megalomaniac view of oneself as the Elect, wholly good, abominably persecuted yet assured of ultimate triumph; the attribution of gigantic and demonic powers to the adversary; the refusal to accept the ineluctable limitations and imperfections of human existence, such as transience, dissension, conflict, fallibility whether intellectual or moral; the obsession with inerrable prophecies—these attitudes are symptoms which together constitute the unmistakable syndrome of paranoia.[158]

Cohn was not alone in singing this tune. In 1969, for Norman Zacour, the Children's Crusade of 1212 was "a sort of mass hysteria," the kind of "mass psychosis that might develop when religious enthusiasm ran riot." Zacour employed the classic early modern terms of "enthusiasm" and, with that era's religious moralists, spoke of "free rein" given to "passions." In his *The First Crusade and the Idea of Crusading* (1986), the great British expert Jonathan Riley-Smith presented the popular component in the crusade as "hysteria" whipped up by "demagogues" on the basis of eschatological expectations. While this very un-Anglo-Catholic malady affected only a minority, and from the lower classes to boot, it still struck no less than Godfrey of Bouillon's chaplain. This Abbot Baldwin was one among many who "either in hysteria or to deceive, had branded or tattooed crosses on their bodies."[159] Like Riley-Smith himself when dealing with apocalyptic symptoms, the upper clergy tried to limit the impact of the prophetic extremists, "showing a proper pastoral concern to play down manifestations of hysteria, although it cannot be said that they were any more successful in this regard than churchmen usually are."[160] Still, in the early 1990s, a professional historian of the Middle Ages could follow, if cautiously, in the footsteps of Charcot and Szumowski, in her analysis of the "unscrupulous adventurers" who in a millenarian atmosphere manipulated lower-class masses. She did warn that the sources, penned by opponents of these movements, were problematic. But she wagered that she could still, next to cynical motivations, detect in the behaviors of these men a pathological component. Why not? All charismatic leaders "regardless of time and space" are either "psychotics whose systematized chronic disease is accompanied by various hallucinations; paranoid personalities with a hypertrophied Ego and megalomania, flawed judgment and lack of social adaptation, who can have phases of delirium; egocentric, instable and aggressive psychopathologies; [or] individuals with a complex psychosis or neurosis, with a strong hysterical component."[161] As for mystics' "apathy"—a sad transmutation of the noble Stoic *apatheia* (which made control of passions into absence of passions) and of the martyrs' fiery passionlessness—the psychiatric tradition was kept alive with Rudolph Bell's famously flawed study of 1985, *Holy Anorexia*.[162]

The notion of collective pathology was not only applied to the dark Middle Ages. It was used to explain the infamous Mystic Fort Massacre of 1637: the Pequot War's violence externalized problems internal to the Puritan colonies. The Puritans felt that communities were rife with sin and scandalously divided. In a 1996 book, Alfred Cave lists half a dozen historians from the 1970s and 1980s who explained the slaughter in this psychologizing vein. Gary Nash's position epitomized it:

> The Puritan leaders talked morbidly about God's anger at seeing His chosen people subvert the City on a Hill. In this sense, the Puritan determination to destroy the Pequots and the violence manifested at Mystic Fort can be partially understood in terms of the self doubt and guilt that Puritans could expiate only by exterminating so many of "Satan's Agents." Dead Pequots were offered to God as atonement for Puritan failings.[163]

Psychopathology, individual or collective, was much used right after World War II to explain Nazi terror and genocide (famously with Theodor Adorno's model of the "authoritarian personality").[164] It also inhabits a few recent analyses of the French Terror. Thus, in the conclusion of an otherwise excellent 1999 book, Alain Gérard volunteered that the Jacobins were individuals who sought to overcome a personal failure or a stain: "All of them, it seems, are loners, who have broken up with their families" and (the diagnosis here is paranoia) "who believe themselves encircled by legions of enemies." "Their love for others . . . seems to be primarily founded on self-hatred." Put together into a group, they compose a utopian communal grouping (*phalanstère*) which, "without fathers or women," is "only made up of brothers who refuse to accept their homosexuality, a world of the undifferentiated and of the unique, watched over by the teary eye of Big Brother."[165] The Jacobin's willingness to die becomes suicidal propensity and his abnegation, self-hatred.[166] Another much less scholarly interpretation of Revolutionary violence posits a generalized misadaptation of political society to an acceleration of history. During the Revolution, there was yet "no secular sacred, no civic nationalism" that would have eased the transition to a nationalism conjoined with popular sovereignty. Fatal absence! The gap engendered a collective "Modernity psychosis" and "paranoia," the projection onto others, in France and outside, of the society's own primitive aggressions.[167] Not unlike in Little's model for medieval anti-Semitism, the absence of the sacred canopy provided by a (here political) religion explains radical, generalized violence.

In the case of the French Revolution, too, recent psychopathological interpretations had been prepared by the wide circles around Charcot.[168] Raymond Clauzel's series, *Études humaines: Fanatiques*, devoted its first volume to Robespierre. Published in 1912, it sought to define the "psychopolitical characteristics of fanatics who lead human beings: demagogues, tyrants, theocrats," a whole cabinet of curiosities that included Calvin, Philip II of Spain, and Oliver Cromwell. Robespierre stemmed from a broken family, was withdrawn, friendless, could have become a "monster or a saint" (translate, a terrorist or a mystic), and drifted to the former.[169] In another example, Doctors Augustin Cabanès and Lucien Nass devoted two volumes, titled *The Revolutionary Neurosis*, to explaining how "the social body" was prone to diseases, most commonly those which, caused by catastrophic events, "impact the mental being and belong to psychopathology" and make modern societies lapse back into archaic and characteristically medieval instincts—"cruelty, sadism, vandalism, involuntary abdications of the self." Fear led to the creation of fetishes; in 1789–1794, "society, terroristic and terrorized, was obsessed by a true religious insanity."[170] "Collective madness" took hold of these populations, and they could find release in "the most violent debauchery (*stupre*)." Indeed, the conjunction of "sexual pleasure-seeking (*volupté*)" and "cruelty" characterized both any revolution and any great mass movement (the good doctors listed the Leper Plot of 1321, the Sicilian Vespers, the Saint-Bartholomew's Day Massacre, the September 1792 massacres, the Armenian genocide, and the pogroms against Algerian Jews). As Le Bon had posited, it also instilled in populations a "contagious" and "epidemic" collective "passion for suicide" (the common offspring of social neurosis), which Nass and Cabanès identified, in essence, with the suicidal mysticism inherent in all religions (including atheistic belief systems).[171] This position—that terrorists are fundamentally people who desire suicide—has been resurrected for Muslims by Ariel Merari since the 1980s and by Adam Lankford much more recently.[172] Gender historians will appreciate lengthy chapters that *The Revolutionary Neurosis* devotes to sex and violence and to the feminine essence, more prone to debauchery and mystical madness than its male counterpart. The long shadow of medieval debates about women's propensities to mystical sanctity and demoniac possession extended itself all the way to a French medical rationalism that saw in the Middle Ages the epitome of archaic fanaticism.[173]

Last but not least, Le Bon, whom all these practitioners of "retrospective medicine" read, provided his own history, *The French Revolution and the Psychology of Revolutions*. It took up the tradition developed by Burke, Michelet, and others, of interpreting the 1789 phenomenon as a religious upheaval. In something of a circular reasoning, Le Bon attributed the fanaticism of revolutions to the need for psyches to "re-aggregate themselves" after a massive crisis. The most potent means to form new aggregated selves was provided by a "strong belief" that would reorient the whole understanding of the individual: "Thus are shaped the personalities that one can observe in periods of great crises, notably the crusades, the Reformation, the [French] Revolution."[174] A society disrupted by great change seeks a new sacred canopy in a religion, be it with or without an explicit God, and in the process produces violence.

Thus, by the twentieth century's first two decades, the positive, or seemingly value-neutral, sociological explanation of inspired group dynamics (Le Bon, Durkheim, and others)[175] and the negative analyses of violent or mystical figures and movements from the past (derived in France from Charcot) stood side by side, authorizing our own era's commonplace that terrorists and suicide-martyrs are fit to be tied. Psychoanalyzing the original French "Terror" may be innocent enough. It is safely in the past. The method becomes dangerous when applied to present-day terrorist groups. The latter call for policies grounded in reliable assessments. Yet enthusiasts are still being put on the couch. An articulate if cautious scholarly representative, Jerrold Post, submits that "political terrorists are driven to commit acts of violence as a consequence of psychological forces." Post does admit that individual terrorists do not in general have any "major psycho-pathology" but backtracks to contend that "mechanisms [of externalization and splitting characteristic of "borderline or narcissistic personalities"] are found with extremely high frequency in the population of terrorists, and contribute significantly to the uniformity of terrorists' rhetorical style and their special psycho-logic." The "psycho-logic" is a special logic that terrorists construct; it serves "to rationalize acts they are psychologically compelled to commit."[176] In this model, ideological discourse is a hypostasis of imbalance.

Owing to limited competencies, and to the agenda of this essay, bounded as it is by Western Christianity and post-Christianity, the case of the anti-American Muslim jihadists will not be discussed. It suffices to summarize Marc Sageman's fine critique of Post and others. On the basis of his study of the empirical data available on individuals and of his review of the theories of psychopathology deployed to explain their deeds, Sageman submits that contemporary Muslim holy warriors may be even more balanced than the average and have in their immense majority enjoyed a happy life. Jihadis are "surprisingly normal in terms of mental health."[177] They are not using radical religion to paper over deep personality wounds. Sageman notes that one has often pointed to terrorists' belief in conspiracy theories as a sign of psychological imbalance. But, as he counters, this is common to many nonterrorists[178] and, one should add, an understandable feature of Christian and post-Christian belief systems (to which jihadist creeds are historically related).

While focusing on radical Muslim violence, Sageman, in passing, critiques psychopathological models that purport to account for recent European terrorism. In his wake, but with a focus on ideology, let us turn to the dossier of a secular West German group of the 1970s, the Rote Armee Fraktion (RAF, also known as the Baader-Meinhof Gang). A violent byproduct of the leftist student movements of the 1960s, the RAF formed in 1970. Ideologically, it saw itself as the German branch of a worldwide armed struggle against an equally worldwide imperialist and capitalist oppression whose center was colonialist America. Its actions, which led to more than thirty deaths, including several assassinations, dragged on until the late 1990s. The section that follows limits itself to a discussion of the so-called first generation, whose leadership died in prison in 1977.

The Baader-Meinhof Gang, a Mad Bunch?

In her popular 1977 study, Jillian Becker dubbed the RAF members "Hitler's Children." The "children" were young men and women in rebellion against their parents, whom they believed were tainted by having participated in the Nazi regime of 1934–1945. But these children, despite their rejection, were their parents' children, therefore, in actuality Hitler's children. As such, the Baader-Meinhof Gang replicated this older German generation's Nazism in its violence, in its willingness to dehumanize the enemy, and (last but not least for Becker) in its anti-Semitism.[179] In Becker's *Hitler's Children*, Gudrun Ensslin makes her first appearance "shrilly" crying that one cannot have a discussion with "'the generation of Auchwitz' . . . and reaching a pitch of hysteria and weeping uncontrollably." Emotions "overwhelmed the hysterical blonde." Perhaps, suggests the author, she was in tears because of what she desired and had not yet allowed herself, "the extreme and violent act," killing. Also in Becker's narrative, the casual, self-evident, clichéed comparison surfaces. Ensslin's "fervor" was of the kind "with which old religious wars, crusades, and persecutions had been fired with" and also, when she was still a baby, "the Nazi movement."[180] In the same 1970s, other observers attributed the RAF's violence, and in particular (but not only) its attacks against Jewish targets, to psychopathology. This stance was not only characteristic of popular opinion; many scholars were beholden to it.[181] After Ulrike Meinhof's death by hanging (likely a suicide), the West German authorities mandated a secret autopsy. Her brain was removed and tested by a neuropathologist; it was then transmitted to a psychiatrist for further examination. The two professors in charge compared the data thus obtained with that available for an early twentieth-century serial murderer, Ernst Wagner. Like the female harpies of Cabanès and Nass's *The Revolutionary Neurosis*, the women members of the RAF were often characterized as hysterics (in the German case, the readily available contraceptives and free lifestyle allegedly maddened them with repressed desire for children). This characterization surfaced in serious studies as well as in the press, with expressions such as "missionary zeal" and "emotional instincts." "Women can unfortunately be very fanatical," mourned *Die Welt*. Official documents considered that the group's women were in their majority "lesbian or bisexual" (*lesbisch bzw. bi-sexuell veranlagt*). The same sources explained that Ensslin and Meinhof were *gleichgeschlechtlich veranlagt*—had homosexual tendencies.[182] In less physically trenchant studies, the childhood and adult lives of the group's members were analyzed, with a strong bias in favor of disruption and malfunction.[183] Intergenerational conflict, allegedly, stemmed from postwar Germany's denial and repression of the Nazi past. The younger set desired to break with it and differentiate itself. Yet, in this process, it may have been inhabited by the fear of having internalized part of the older generation's experience. This made, psychologically, for an acute need to distinguish the "us" from the "them," in Manichean fashion.[184]

Yet Becker's and related theses are empirically invalidated. The family adults in the RAF members' growing year were far from being always unrepentant former Nazis. To the contrary, Ulrike Meinhof, Gudrun Ensslin, and Andreas Baader's parents were more on their left-wing offspring's side than not.[185] And, hamstringing theses arguing for psychopathology, sociological studies have evidenced that the members of the Rote Armee Fraktion did not labor under mental illnesses any more than the average citizen of the German Federal Republic.[186] Their distrust of institutions as guardians of freedom, their view of the state as lacking in legitimacy, their wide feeling of not being represented, their readiness to have recourse to illegal, even violent action to change society, were shared by a broader segment of left-wing sixteen- to thirty-five-year olds.[187] Shall one say that a huge sector of the West German population in the 1970s was affected by a collective disease? Shall one accept the existence of a generational conflict between, on the one hand, youths, and on the other, parents who had lived the Nazi era and had not come clean? And that the children rejected these parents who were (in a normal process of maturation) necessary as figures for identity formation? Ironically, the RAF also psychoanalyzed its opponents, both individuals and collectives. Wrote Meinhof: "Whomsoever imagines the illegal organization of armed resistance on the model of the Freikorp [right-wing militias of the early Weimar era] and Feme [Vehme, a secret premodern group devoted to striking down unpunished criminals], desires himself pogroms. The psychological mechanisms that produce such projections have been analyzed in connection to fascism in Horkheimer and Adorno's *The Authoritarian Personality* (*Die Autoritäre Persönlichkeit*) and in Reich's *Mass psychology of Fascism* (*Die Massenpsychologie des Faschismus*). A coercive revolutionary character is a contradiction in itself." And Bernward Vesper, Ensslin's erstwhile companion, explained circa 1968 how a sick society reacted to treatment by violence:

> Every psychoanalyst is familiar [with] that phase in which the patient attacks him—when in the course of the treatment he comes close to the critical complex. The same occurs with those who force the sick society to confess to its own sickness. They are doomed to be condemned.[188]

But this mirroring of state and chosen remnant discourse is not mere irony; in the grand sectarian tradition begun with the first Acts of the Martyrs, the RAF logically considered that the opponent was mad and that, like a demoniac, it raged with paroxysmic intensity when the exorcist's forceful and enlightening action brought it to the threshold of sanity.

If one considers that the West German terrorists' violence is "unthinkable" or beyond understanding, it is logical to favor the idea that they were the prey of psychological pathologies. Otherwise put, deeds that we cannot relate to are chalked up to madness.[189] But an analysis of the RAF's deeds that seeks understanding—that tries to enter in the perpetrators' heads by taking seriously their words—leads to alternate conclusions. It has long been a commonplace that Western atheist utopias are positioned on a genealogical continuum with Christian ones.[190] If—in a maneuver that may seem artificial but is heuristically fruitful—one reinscribes the RAF's godless ideology within the figures of thought of Christianity, these deeds become "thinkable" again.[191]

What does this heuristic desecularization yield? The RAF, like the Christian matrix, propounded liberty as emancipation from the law, held a progressive vision of History, and felt a radical opposition between (to cite Ulrich Matz) an "until now repressed good (their Utopia) and an absolute, still triumphant evil (the situation)." Like many a monotheistic sect, the RAF proclaimed its radical dogma's absolute authority, founded on selective aggregations from received scriptural authorities; it valued disputes concerning dogma and its purity; and it claimed simultaneously universalism and election.[192] Like many a sect, and like, for example, Cyprian or the Donatist martyr acts, it employed a Manichean language of either/or.[193] The RAF pursued ideals recognizably related to those of West German democracy, all ultimately going back to the Enlightenment. In this sense, terrorism was not culturally exogenous to German society. The proximity in values between the terrorists and the state lent an intensity and harshness to the struggle opposing them that might have been absent in a less intestine conflict. Both parties hurled at one another charges of Nazism, as Christian sects or confessions that accused one another of paganism or judaizing.[194] That polemics between ideological neighbors are so shrill and can turn violent is understandable on the background of the longue durée of Western culture, across secularization. For many centuries, heretics, so theological neighbors, had been more feared than pagans, and radical, even exterminating measures against them were more acceptable. During the early modern Wars of Religion, and visibly already with the fourth-century Donatist controversy, the opposing Christian sect's evil consisted in great part in its satanic ability to mimic the good. Outwardly almost the same, so all the more seductive, heretical "synagogues of Satan" were the hardest opponent imaginable.[195]

Like its demonized American opponents, the RAF considered that the Vietnam War was part of "a World War of a new kind."[196] The conflict was global and involved several "actors" (the RAF spoke of *Charaktermasken*): the head of the beast, the United States; its military agent in the Middle East, Israel; and the pseudodemocratic but in essence fascistic West German state.[197] Not unlike Christian moralists, the RAF thought in terms of a home front, where the issue was vice, in linkage to a foreign front of warfare and economic oppression. An "offensive against the human psyche" in Germany went hand in hand with the exploitation of the Third World.[198] Like Augustine, who spoke of the shackles of custom in which the Donatist rank and file were held, the RAF considered that the West German workers had been blinded. Ensslin wrote from prison in 1972 that the alienated proletariat lived in the "dog's kennel of morality, so of corruption," in the belief that freedom was having left the exploitative eighty-hour work week and hard bread, analphabetism, and child labor, for the forty-hour week, decent eating and drinking, a TV acquired on one's own salary, perhaps a car and vacations, and the illusion of buying of one's own free will the *Bild Zeitung*.[199] Another proclamation made the same diagnosis:

> With the introduction of the 8–hour workday—condition for the increase in labor intensity—the system has mastered to its own interest all the free time of people. They have added to their physical exploitation in the workplace the exploitation of their feelings and thoughts, desires and utopias, so [added] to the despotism of the capitalists in the workplace the despotism of the capitalists through mass consumption and mass media in all spheres of life.

This freedom was false freedom.[200] Violence was necessary to return the Proletariat to clear-sightedness. The RAF saw modern society as a "system" (long a term of abuse, since at least the Nazi era) and as a "total [and in its jargon it suggested totalitarian] complex of blinding (*totaler Verblendungszusammenhang*)," an expression borrowed from Theodor Adorno.[201] The solution could only, then, be radical. Only a visible victory could turn around such blind people. The RAF members' diagnosis was that they were "dealing here with a quite complicated process of consciousness-fashioning;" given the German worker's alienated comfort in a capitalistic society, the revolutionary could not wait (as orthodox Marxism prescribes) for the "approval of the masses." A bourgeois superego had built itself into the Proletariat's head. This superego had first to be brought down, by violence: "Only a praxis, in the sense of an unmediated experience, can pry open this fateful structure of consciousness."[202] The identification of the enemy as "system" is shared by right-wing terrorists, such as Timothy McVeigh, the American Christian supremacist who bombed the Oklahoma City Federal Building.[203] The blindness of the masses was also far from new. When the early New England observers found it necessary to explain why the Native Americans did not convert to Christianity despite its evident superiority, they had recourse to the idea that their priests kept them in "blindnesse." Only the elimination of this elite would change things.[204] It was an old Christian idea as well that humankind faced an evil that dissimulated itself. Thomas Müntzer, a leader of the peasants in revolt in 1524–1525, writing to the princes to convince them to take up the sword and radically reform the Church, spoke of a "mask" that had to be removed by force "from the world."[205] Müntzer's Calvinist contemporaries agreed; so did, later, Maximilien Robespierre, who also used the notion of "masque."[206] Violence revealed hypocrisy; it also remedied blindness. As we shall develop in Chapter 6, Augustine, in his famous letter to Count Boniface, justified the use of force against the Donatists for their own good. He recounted how God had coerced to conversion the erstwhile persecutor Paul by striking him blind. The journey to spiritual sight passed through trauma.[207]

Unsurprisingly, the question of the RAF's anti-Semitism leads one back to the same ensemble, to deep structures in Western Christian culture. Becker's bestseller opens on a famous episode, meant to prove the psychopathological continuity between the Nazis and the Baader-Meinhof Gang. In June 1976, Palestinian terrorists, along with Brigitte Kuhlmann and Wilfried Böse, two German members of the Revolutionäre Zellen (Revolutionary Cells), a group close to the RAF, hijacked a French jetliner to the Ugandan airport of Entebbe.[208] The Germans helped sort out Jews and Israelis from non-Jews. Kuhlmann and Böse were not subliminally—as Becker would have it—reproducing the parental Nazism they so emphatically rejected.[209] Neither were their RAF colleagues. In prison, the RAF leadership compared its situation to Auschwitz. But it had drawn on these analogies before capture. Vietnam was on a par with the Holocaust and legitimized bombs against the United State forces based in Germany (May 1972), killing four GIs. To cite the manifesto, the Germans "have not forgotten Auschwitz, Dresden and Hamburg . . . they know that bomb attacks against the mass murderers of Vietnam are justified."[210] If those men and women Becker dubbed "Hitler's children" reproduced anything, it was not Nazi anti-Semitism, but older structures, ancient Christian equations.

For the Christian Middle Ages, the Jews of the New Dispensation had failed, sinfully, to draw the lessons of Christ's judicial murder and so had lost the dignity of "True Israel." Having rejected their Savior, Jews in the New Era could not draw on the aura of the Old Testament Israel of the Covenant and the prophets. The Gentiles were now the "True Israel" in the spirit. Similarly, in the eyes of too many within the New German Left, modern Israelis, in not having learned from the Holocaust and in having objectively allied themselves with American imperialism, had cleft themselves asunder by an unbridgeable divide from the victims of Fascism. Bommi Baumann documented this notion: "Today, the Zionist re-enact on a daily basis in the Occupied Territories, in the refugee camps, in Israeli jails the 1938 Night of Crystal. The Jews, expelled by Fascism, have become themselves Fascists, who in collaboration with American Capitalism want to eradicate the Palestinians."[211] From the wider circle around the RAF came a question: "When will you finally begin the organized struggle against the Golden Calf, Israel?"[212] Dieter Kunzelmann's reference was to Moses' bloody cleansing, on the road to the Promised Land, of those Jews who had fallen back into idolatry (Exod. 32).[213] There had been hardly any tenderness in premodern Christian circles for the Jewish victims of another providential purge, Titus and Vespasian's conquest of Jerusalem. This "Ancient Israel" had been displaced by the New Christian Israel, "True Israel," many of whose members were "Gentiles," that is, had come from Israel's pagan enemies. Only one part of Old Israel would convert to Christianity in the very last days, the rest going to fry eternally in Hell. As we saw in Chapter 2 with the Christian interpretation of the story of Maccabees, contemporary Jews foreknown to damnation, who composed one of the several wings of Antichrist's conspiracy, were prefigured by Hellenistic pagans and apostates or collaborationist Jews who had sided with Antiochus, not by the righteous Jews who had resisted idolatry, unto death. In the RAF's Theology of History, one surmises a similar inversion: the Israeli children of the righteous martyrs of the Nazi Holocaust had forfeited their birthright by converting to the dark side. They had lapsed from anti-Fascism into Fascism. Is it too much to suspect that, in their own understanding, the left-wing German children of Nazi forebears, like the New Dispensation Gentiles, had inherited this lost mantle?[214]

This last suggestion is speculation. A firm conclusion is, rather, that an internalist, "emic" approach to terrorism recovers the coherence of ideologies, just as a fine-grained knowledge of medieval theology provides an understanding of the First Crusaders.[215] Evidently, the internalist approach should not lead to monocausality. It has its limits. It does not explain why these, as opposed to those, West Germans sixteen to twenty-five joined the RAF or a cognate group like the Revolutionary Cells, and why they remained committed to the group. It does not explain why many West Germans did not join in terrorist action, even though many, stemming from the same milieu and the same cultural tradition, did share many of the Gang's ideas. For this, the microconjuncture—the existing human networks and their evolution—and pure chance are likely responsible. But the approach allows one to dismiss the presumption of madness and understand as coherent the discourse the terrorists tried to live.[216] The former is important for policy-making, insofar as it suggests that the solution to terror is not some vast campaign of psychiatry (anyway impractical); the latter is simply, it should be hoped, good history.

Chapter 4

Martyrdom in the West:
Vengeance, Purge, Salvation, and History

As explained in Chapter 2, deep structures within Christian theology make agents operating within Western political cultures likely to link together ideas of external war, of purification of the self and of society (or the church), and of liberty. This linkage, or, more cautiously put, this likelihood of a correlation, is itself enabled by a specific notion of History in which vengeance and retribution play a pivotal role. It is as yet another element in this semi-system that these pages will consider martyrdom. Like so many actions with a religious charge, martyrdom has a strong bend toward repetitiveness; it is strongly patterned. As such, it has sometimes been considered, heuristically, as a "ritual"— as patterned symbolic action par excellence—or examined, without too much reflectivity, through this conceptual lens. Its "ritual" nature might explain indeed its long-lastingness as a form of religious and postreligious violence in European and American culture. Considered in a related manner, martyrdom was a form of self-sacrifice; it could thus (so recently Jon Pahl, positing a transformation with Modernity when Christianity entered in hybridization with other forces) engender more violence; the willingness to forfeit one's life called for more sacrifice—in this model, the readiness to sacrifice others. Yet notwithstanding the seductiveness of these approaches, this chapter will instead insist on the importance of theology and ideology—so of "emic" or "native" understandings of this practice, and thus stay with "martyrdom" as opposed to "sacrifice." Furthermore, it questions the difference between premodern and modern martyrdom posited by some scholars of religion.[1]

Martyrdom was a practice oriented to the future—as against, as is sometimes argued, exclusively to the past. Indeed, the notion of an orientation to the past becomes problematic once one takes into account a Christian view of

History directed by, and toward, retribution (a view that persisted in the political religion of Marxism, which we shall approach with reference to the trial of Nikolai Bukharin). History was shaped by God's vengeance, including vengeance for the blood shed by His very own—the martyrs. As we saw, on a first level, the harsh vindictive dispensation of the Old Testament and its Law had been replaced through Christ's priestly sacrifice on the Cross by an age of mercy. On a second level, though, it was also by vengeance that humankind had been propelled into this New Testament age, and this age would end in the vengeful retribution announced by John's Revelation. For, first, Christ's martyrdom was an act of injustice that called for justice—*iustitia, vindicta,* or (in the lexicon of Roman judicial processes) *vindicatio.* The Cross and the first apostles' persecution had brought about the so-called "Vengeance of the Savior," which had annihilated Jerusalem's temple and, with it, the Jewish priesthood and kingship.[2] Christians had made theirs the Jewish notion that election entailed travails and that any injustice committed against Israel would result ultimately in the guilty party's destruction. But the "New Israel" or "True Israel" (*verus Israel*), Christendom, had usurped the mantle of the chosen people and transferred onto the Jews (the "Israel of Old," *vetus Israel*) the role of perpetrator of injustice. In the late eleventh century, it was articulated explicitly that the Jews had lost the privilege of being avenged by God (*haec autem ultionem perdiderunt Iudaei*);[3] it now belonged to the New Israel. To this appropriation, Christians may have conjoined a Roman conception. In Roman historical thinking, the development of institutions was sometimes the product of *vindicationes,* retributions for judicial abuses. Most famous is the case of Verginia. Her father was forced to kill her to preserve her chastity, consecrating with her blood the wicked magistrate to the infernal gods. Verginia's sacrifice caused the second plebeian secession and the legislation of constitutional powers for the plebs (Livy, *Ab urbe condita,* 3.44–55).[4] Similarly, in early Christian theology, martyrdom moved History forward. The first martyrdom of all, Christ's, had resulted in the disappearance of Jewish institutions. And toward History's End, the accumulation of martyrdoms would propel Time into its last phase. In John's bloodthirsty Revelation, martyrs joined their brethren to cry out to God: "How long, o Lord, shall you not judge and revenge our blood on those men who dwell on the earth" (Rev. 6:10)? This clamor is an interrogation about Time and the course of History. The holy dead have to wait until their number was full, when all those foreordained to be killed will have joined their ranks. Then the End will begin.

A first agenda of the pages that follow is, therefore, to document the permanence of this theology of retribution, well into the American nineteenth century and beyond. It is certainly not an agenda historical agents would always have been in sympathy with. Would a radical Protestant have been comfortable with an insistence on his or her cultural debt to the Catholic Middle Ages? How far would even a sophisticated bolshevik intellectual have agreed that religious forms still molded her or his being? The issue may also seem puzzling to scholars devoted to the present and the near past. Indeed, it is very much a medievalist's agenda. When considering the more recent Western cultures of violence, the historian of the European Middle Ages can recognize within them vast ideological slabs that have traveled (or jumped) toward our present from his or her period of professional expertise. This has already been evidenced for the cases of the French Revolution (Chapter 2) and of the Rote Armee Fraktion (Chapter 3). This justifies the choice to order this chapter's exposé with a beginning in Modernity and an end in the Middle Ages. A second agenda is to highlight the notion, embedded in this theology of retribution, that martyrdom moves History forward.[5] A third is to explore the relationship between martyrdom and purge—purge of the wicked by the elect but also purgation of the elect themselves (either definitive, through elimination, when black sheep are hidden among the seemingly uniformly clean vanguard, or purgative of lingering sins within those predestined crusaders).[6] Selected with a view to bridging medieval and Modern and to problematizing the nature of the caesura when it comes to violence,[7] three dossiers form the main documentary basis for this reflection: that of the radical abolitionist John Brown, hanged in 1859; that of the Bolshevik Nikolai Bukharin, shot in 1938 as the lead victim in the so-called "Moscow show trials"; and a set of figures in a chronicle of the First Crusade (1096–1100), the "*Liber*" composed by Raymond d'Aguilers. One could multiply the case studies (the Introduction has already detailed, for instance, the double-barreled martyrdom of the Guise brothers and their avenger Jacques Clément, to which this book shall return in Chapter 7). These would, of course, open other dimensions in the relation between martyrdom and a sacralized History driven by violence. They would not, it is hoped, invalidate the insights produced by this tripolar comparison.

John Brown: "To purge this land with blood"

On October 16, 1859, a small band of men, nineteen strong, led by a self-proclaimed captain, John Brown, sneaked into Harpers Ferry, Virginia, the meeting place of two rivers and the site of an armory and an arsenal.[8] Brown quickly secured the two buildings. His aim was to begin a large-scale slave rebellion[9] and arm the blacks with Harpers Ferry's military supplies. Yet not only did the slaves not rise up and join him, but Brown soon found himself besieged by federal troops. In the final assault that led to his capture, he was severely wounded. Two of his sons lay dead next to him, along with eight other raiders. He and four other captured men were quickly tried by the State of Virginia. On December 2, Brown was hanged from the gallows. Between his capture, October 18, 1859, and his execution, the raid at Harpers Ferry inflamed public opinion.[10] Historians, including those (the majority) who consider John Brown unrepresentative of abolitionism, agree that the raid and Brown's hanging further polarized the North and the South, and so contributed to the American Civil War.[11] In a sense, Brown's own belief that martyrdom caused History to move forward was not erroneous. His abolitionist audience understood his death on the gallows as a call to action; what often with them had been merely inflammatory words became after December 1859 much more ready to concretize itself into fiery deeds. Belief in causation made for causation.

John Brown's last days, at least as he envisaged them, proceeded along a classic martyr narrative plotline. We have the confrontation with the magistrate, in clipped dialogic form. We have the friendly jailer, who should be among the enemy but whose kindness betrays the truth of the martyr's position and hints at his and others' conversion. We have communications with the outside world, allowing the martyr to define his or her position, publicize it, and interpret his or her fate. We have, next to the martyr's verbal engagement with the opponent, his or her refusal to compromise and a ringing denunciation of heresy.

Historians have underscored the role of public opinion and interpretation in the making of a martyr.[12] They are not wrong. Brown's enemies and partisans vied with one another to locate him out of or within martyrdom. Sympathizers colored him in sometimes divergent hues, depending on how much they considered his violent action might impact the cause of abolitionism or the Republican Party, so close to the 1860 presidential elections. There exists many an example of the total construction of a martyr, even to the point of inventing fully the person. This was more the rule than exception in the early Middle Ages, when religious institutions needed to put an identity and a story onto miracle-working human remains.[13] Closer to us is the case of Horst Wessel (1900–1930), the victim of a criminal revenge killing more at home in the shadowy demimonde of pimps and prostitutes than under the Third Reich's glorious sun, but whom the propagandist Goebbels transmogrified into the ultimate heroic Nazi German youth.[14] We shall return to this construction by an "audience" of Captain Brown's last months at those points where, being consistent with Brown's own "self-shaping" as a martyr, it illuminates the theology that inspired him to action and that underlay his own pronouncements.[15]

Indeed, Captain Brown plotted actively his course toward martyrdom. Self-immolation for the God-willed cause of freedom stood on a continuum with his earlier deeds and thoughts. One year before the raid, he mused on sinful America with apocalyptic images: "Indeed; I tremble for my Country, when I reflect; that God is Just; and that his Justice; will not sleep forever &c. &c. Nature is mo[u]rning for its murdered, and afflicted Children. Hung be the Heavens in Scarlet." At this point, he already saw himself as another "Samson" (the Jew who had, in killing himself, annihilated the Philistines idolaters) and a future "reaper."[16] Obviously, it is risky to mine Brown's statements after his capture with a view to unearthing preexistent motivations for the raid. But one cannot say that Brown decided on martyrdom only after having been captured—as an *ex post evento* rationalization of his forcible passive position as prisoner. In other words, Brown the "terrorist" (if it may be allowed to call him so) is of one piece with Brown the martyr; his willingness to die consistent with his willingness to kill.[17] As will be explored in Chapter 5, the conviction that one is in the right against the legal order, to the point of seizing arms for redress, is at the heart of the Western right of and duty of resistance and has always put terrorists on a problematic continuum with the resistors whom this political tradition so much admires.[18] Brown considered that the righteous minority that he represented could take up arms against any institution, including the state, that did not uphold justice. In fact, for his apologists, given the existence of the Supreme Judge, "minority" and "majority" were both relative and absolute concepts. One well-wisher stated "Our good FATHER is on your side, and this places you in the majority." Wendell Phillips (d. 1884) made explicit the paradox: "In God's world there are no majorities, no minorities; one [man], on God's side is a majority." According to Brown's friend, such was "the ground of morals."[19] The paradox was not uniquely American; the French Revolutionaries, with Robespierre, conceived of a "general will" borne in some moments by a de facto minority.[20]

Brown was a militant abolitionist, raised in a strict Congregationalist family in which the Puritan sense of sinfulness, election, and punitive justice was strong.[21] In jail, he was uncompromising. He refused the spiritual succor of Southern clergymen. "My knees will not bend in prayer with them," he explained, "while their hands are stained with the blood of souls."[22] To him, they were not ministers of the Gospel, only fakes who either owned slaves or advocated slavery.[23] These false brothers corresponded to the *traditores*, the apostates and heretics of pre-Constantinian martyrdom narratives.

Even words of Christian meekness were of one piece with vengeful brimstone. Brown pardoned the Virginians for hanging him, paraphrasing Christ at His crucifixion (Luke 23:34): "I forgive them, and may God forgive them, for they know not what they do."[24] But what kind of a forgiveness was this? Did Brown anticipate that God would forgive? Puritan mercy was ultimately grim. It called for one to love, not hate sinners—not hate, that is, until the other world had come and the sinners roasted in Hell. Then, as Saint Jerome had taught, and as Jonathan Edwards reiterated in 1758, it would be fine to hate, since "grounds of love will cease."[25] At least in the passage here alluded to, Edwards rejected this-worldly violent activism. But others could draw a different conclusion. When one felt either that the very End of Times was at hand or that one lived an epoch that was a type of the End, one could lapse into the role of God's executioners. "May God forgive them, for they know not what they do": for medieval interpreters, the Jews did not know that they were slaying their own Messiah and that in so doing were condemning Jerusalem, along with the Jewish kingdom and priesthood, to annihilation at the hands of Titus and Vespasian's Romans. John Wesley (1703–1791), like his Catholic forebears, spoke of the "suspension of vengeance even for the impenitent" lasting forty years between the Crucifixion and the destruction of the Second Temple.[26] The *Geneva Study Bible*, discussing the immediately following episode, Luke 23.39 (the two robbers), which was traditionally linked to this prayer, commented that Christ expressed there "that He hath both the power of life to save the believers and [the power] of death to [take] revenge [on] the rebellious."[27] The prayer for forgiveness was a call for the crucifiers to choose the right camp or be damned like the bad thief.[28] Like in medieval exegesis, in the Protestant tradition transferred to New England, mercy did not always mean the absence of retribution.

Well into the nineteenth century, then, there survived the medieval notions that peace was not nonviolence and that figures who were defined—or who self-defined—as figures of peace could approve and even foster the righteous use of weapons. One sees this when one juxtaposes to Brown's own statements certain positive reactions to his action. William Lloyd Garrison, the pacifist abolitionist, applauded Brown's raids. Use of material arms for liberty represented a progression from use of arms for despotism to the ideal endpoint of pure pacifism. Here Garrison was in the ideological position of a medieval cleric, who, forbidden by his orders to bear arms, would still have exhorted a crusader to his killing labors.[29] His understanding dovetailed with that of a Rhodes Island Quaker lady, who exchanged two letters with the imprisoned Brown. While the Friends refused weapons, they could still see Brown as a "deliverer," legitimated by God's own destruction in the Red Sea of Pharaoh's Egyptians in pursuit of the enslaved Hebrews. Brown answered with a reasoning his Quaker correspondent probably disagreed with yet whose elements she likely understood: he reminded her that Christ Himself had armed Peter. So had he, Brown, been providentially vested with a sword. But he went on to state that God had now taken this weapon from him and that he was now wielding in each hand the "sword of the spirit."[30]

Such a conception spanned the two roles, that of the holy warrior, girded with a material sword in God's service, and that of the martyr with his spiritual sword, who consecrated his mission by preaching on his way to the gallows. Said Brown in another letter: "Christ, the great captain of liberty as well as of salvation . . . saw fit to take from me a sword of steel . . . but He has put another [sword] in my hand ('the sword of the Spirit'), and I pray God to make me a faithful soldier, wherever He may send me, no less on the scaffold than when surrounded by my warmest sympathizers.[31]

God had used Brown as His instrument on the battlefield and now intended to use him in another way—as a witness to the truth of abolitionism, as a martyr.[32] The ability to combine warfare and preaching granted a potent aura to holy violence; at least one Anabaptist, who in 1537 went all the way to martyrdom, revered the memory of the revolutionary leader Thomas Müntzer as one "who grasped the inner Word so well, in the sense that he wielded the outer sword with the inner Word."[33]

Next to sermons and speeches, Brown's captivity generated an outpouring of letters from sympathizers. A number of these correspondents volunteered their understanding of the impending hanging. One finds there a large spectrum of related conceptions of martyrdom, from the straightforward and unabashed call for immediate divine retribution on the sinful South to the hope that martyrdom would bloodlessly convert the South to slave liberation—but sometimes with the expressed fear that it would not happen in a peaceful way and that God's rectifying violence lurked right around the corner.[34]

These letters show how present, even in the mid-nineteenth century, something akin to medieval conceptions was—and, therefore, how medieval conceptions can shed light on the place of violence in American political culture. At least two letter writers sought from Brown a lock of his hair—a form of Protestant relic.[35] Many asked him for the privilege of a written answer, only a few words even, which evidently would also serve as a memento.[36]

One writer, a self-styled Covenanter from New Alexandria, Pennsylvania, saw in the trial an occasion for the "guilty nation" to repent. Brown's profession of faith in abolition would, it was hoped, "purge" the United States.[37] But, for the letter's author, the trial constituted also a "warfare," sent by God. Moving to the register of spiritual battles materialized, he referred to the Old Testament exemplar of death-doling martyrdom: "What matter if it be from a scaffold, Samson-like you will slay more Philistines in your death, than you ever did or could by a long life; and I pray God that in your dying agony, you may have the gratification of feeling the pillars of Dagon's Temple crumbling in your grasp."[38] In this reference to the Samson of Judges 29 (a model Brown himself called on before and after Harpers Ferry),[39] the letter's author may have meant to stay within pure spiritual warfare, without suggesting material bloodshed. One cannot quite tell. But at the very least, the Covenanter expected that martyrdom would give an irresistible impulse to History, and propel it in the right direction.

Another well-wisher also developed notions of spiritual warfare in relation to the providential course of History. This self-described "Old School Presbyterian" expressed his agreement with the Quaker belief that "Christ's kingdom *will be* peace." Going on, he counterpoised to this peaceful future the bellicose nature of the present age: "but *now* Christ told his disciples, He that hath a sword, let him take it. Therefore, I cannot say I think you exceeded your commission, and I rejoice that a *man* has been found worthy to suffer for Christ." The Gospel pericope was followed by a reference to Revelation 6.10. Once martyred (the Presbyterian went on), Brown would be led straight to Christ and "join the souls under the altar, crying, How long before your blood be avenged on the earth?"[40]

Not all correspondents approved, however. And the disapproval took classical forms. One reverend expressed astonishment that Brown could have assumed that he could free the slaves "without wading in blood." He went on:

The time has not come. It is not the right way, and it will never be. It is right to pray, "O Lord, how long?" but not to run before and take the avenging sword into your own hands.[41] . . . It becomes you prayerfully to inquire how far you will be answerable at the bar of God for the blood which was shed at Harper's [*sic*] Ferry, and for the fate of those who are to die with you. I judge you not; but there is One that judgeth, with Whom is mercy and plentiful forgiveness to all who truly repent and savingly believe in Him Whose blood cleanseth from all sin.[42]

Counterpoised to the militant captain was a Lord who had shed His own blood, a God of mercy Who would judge this bloodied affair. But Reverend Humphrey's God, interestingly, was also (as the reference to Rev. 6.10 indicates) the One Who would avenge at the End of History (furthermore, the letter left unclear whether then humans could take up the sword). Yet "the time has not come."

Brown agreed with his well-wishers. He too knew that in his martyrdom would inhere the vengeance characteristic of holy war. In a letter dated November 8, 1859, Brown informed his wife and children that he was ready to "seal my testimony for God and humanity with my blood." He added that he was "besides, quite cheerful, having (as I trust) 'the peace of God, which passeth all understanding' [Phil. 4.7] to rule in my heart."[43] Peace, but not the pacifist's peace, one should underline. Commenting these Pauline words on peace, the nonconformist exegete Matthew Henry (1662–1714) placed them— as Paul himself had—in the context of Judgment's imminence: God "will take vengeance on your enemies, and reward your patience."[44] Brown indeed felt close to the End, and this feeling allowed him to conjoin vengeance and martyrdom. He had rejoiced a year before Harpers Ferry that he had allowed himself a little bit more life on this earth in order to be a "reaper in the great harvest."[45] In Henry's Philippians 4.7, "peace" was synonymous with reconciliation with God, entailed hope for Paradise, and had as its absolute precondition the performance of one's "duty."[46] Brown pushed the apocalyptic note away from irenicism. His "duty" consisted in God's "cause" of abolition; his "peace," far from excluding violence, called for grim reaping.[47]

On his way to the gallows, Brown passed on to his followers a last, now famous note: "I John Brown am now quite certain that the crimes of this guilty land will never be purged away, but with blood." America, like the biblical Holy Land, and so many other holy lands throughout the course of European history, needed God's ineffable violence.[48] Thomas Müntzer had consoled imprisoned "brethren" in Sangerhausen, in one breath reminding them that Christ had shed his blood to redeem them and announcing "that the time had now come for a great shedding of blood would cover the hardened earth owing to its lack of faith."[49] The tandem of martyrdom and vengeful justice would move History forward. For Brown and some others, then, his death would bring retribution. The erstwhile nonresister leader William Garrison exclaimed: "Whether the weapons used in the struggle against despotism have been spiritual or carnal, the verdict has been this: Glory to those who die in Freedom's cause! . . . manglers of martyrs' earthly frame . . . Vengeance is behind, and Justice is to come!"[50] God—but also History—would judge. Brown's partisan Wendell Phillips "appeal[ed] . . . to the American people fifty years hence" after progress would have done its work. The current position of the abolitionist vanguard, "a small band," would by then have been embraced by the majority.[51] Wendell Phillips ended his speech on his belief that Brown's death moved "the future":

> Hope! there is hope everywhere. It is only the universal History:
> Right forever on the scaffold, Wrong forever on the throne
> But that scaffold sways the future, and behind the dim unknown
> Standeth God within the shadow, keeping watch above His own.[52]

The God of justice and vengeance, judge at the End of History, points toward the divinized historical process of the twentieth century so eloquently denounced in 1951 by Albert Camus, and to another trial and perhaps martyrdom, that of Nikolai Bukharin.[53]

Nikolai Bukharin: "Return into the Soviet Union"

During the night of March 15, 1938, Nikolai Bukharin, along with seventeen other Bolsheviks, was shot. These men (and three others who were spared capital punishment) had been on public trial since March 2, 1938, and in prison since 1937. Bukharin was allegedly the leader of the plot now being prosecuted, which allied a Trotskyite left wing to his own right wing within the Communist Party. In conjunction with nationalists and foreign, especially Fascist powers, he had long plotted against the Revolution and even considered assassinating Lenin, then Stalin,[54] a universal conspiracy, as it were, paralleling those feared by the eleventh-century reformers and by Robespierre's Jacobins. And as in the Western European discourse, some of the conspirers had fallen into madness, hypnotized. The public defender for three among the accused (Kazakov, Pletnev, and Levin), alleged that former NKVD chief Genrikh Yagoda had seduced them "with his evil, piercing glance." The picture was dramatic: "I can imagine that this fatal, piercing glance crushed their consciousness, paralyzed their will, killed their feelings," he said. "Reason, when shaken, Comrade Judges, often does not bear up under its own weight and goes mad, and a free man is broken." As was traditional, these deviants were both suicidal and assassins: "The moment Yagoda broke them, the moment they gave their consent, they became moral corpses, they killed themselves" in an act of "moral suicide" which anticipated their "murder of others."[55]

Mad or not, they were shot. The executions formed the crest of a wave of purges that aimed first and foremost at the ruling Communist Party. On the one hand, the purges had been engineered by Stalin to get rid of the old bolshevik guard, those veterans of 1917 and companions of Lenin whose prestige could still challenge his own. On the other hand, they fed (as recently explored by Jochen Hellbeck) on almost two decades of a bolshevik culture of purification—the purification of the party but also of the individual self.[56]

The trials concluded on the final pronouncements of the accused—pleas and confessions, for whose extraction various coercive techniques were used.[57] That Bukharin was coerced, however, and severely so, does not invalidate the approach here taken. Early modern martyrs, equally imperfect human beings, could break down under pressure, either temporarily or definitively.[58] Bukharin, in his mixture of concessions and defiance in the sight of death, parallels Jan of Leyden, king of Münster, in the months prior to his gruesome execution (about whom more in Chapter 7).

Immediately after the executions, the proceedings were publicized and printed in many languages, complete with these "Last Words."[59] Among them, Bukharin's eloquent final speech, delivered on March 12, soon fascinated Western intelligentsias. Most of the twenty-one men, while fully recognizing their crimes, had pleaded not to be executed, often asking for a chance to cleanse themselves of their "sins" or "dirt" through work for the Soviet Union.[60] At least in the official English translation of the proceedings, the lexicon of penance jumps to the eyes: "to expiate," "to atone," "to redeem." One among the accused, Vladimir Ivanovich Ivanov, expressed most vividly why he still wanted to live despite his incommensurable guilt: "I shall accept the most severe sentence, but I find it inexpressibly hard to die when I have [not] at last cleared myself of this filth, of this abomination." Consequently, to have time for this purgative labor, he asked for mercy.[61] Not so Bukharin, at least not before the tribunal. He refuted many individual charges, such as plots to kill Lenin or Stalin or the existence of an actual conspiracy joining Left to Right deviationists in which he would have been the hinge. But he accepted the accusation in its broad strokes. He had indeed betrayed the Soviet Union. Yet he now realized, he said, that he had been on the wrong side of History's march forward. In prison, he had meditated on his own past, and wondered, "If you die, what are you dying for?" The need to die for something explained his repentance; the something he would die for—that is, the Revolution— explained his willingness to accept a death verdict. Others tried in March 1938 shared the fear of a vacuum in death.[62] Grigori Fedorovich Grinko's only wish was to "die not as an enemy taken prisoner by the Soviet Government, but as a citizen of the U.S.S.R." Repentance, he hoped, brought him back into the "fatherland" he had gravely betrayed.[63] Similarly, Akmal Ikramov did not want to die "as an enemy of the people." He hoped that it would be known that "even if in the last hour of his life . . . he abandoned the position [of treachery and enmity] and died an honest citizen."[64] They were eager to be reincorporated through purgation, if necessary in and through death. They wanted to participate in the positive march of History forward. Bukharin shared in this desire, even if his wish was challenged by the prosecution and by some of his fellow accused. Isaac Zelensky bitterly shoved him back among the ranks of the damned: "You, Bukharin, want to come out of it unblemished. But you will not succeed. You will go down in History with us, branded with the shameful stigma (klejmo) that marks the forehead of all of us."[65]

"In reality everything is clear. World History is a World Court of judgment."[66] Uttered toward the end of Bukharin's "Last Words," this sentence, famous since 1938, quoted Hegel's Die Weltgeschichte ist das Weltgericht. In encapsulated form, it alluded to a complex vision of History shared by many Marxists. The individual mattered not. His or her political choices, innocent or not, were validated or invalidated by the direction of historical developments. Here, too, Bukharin the intellectual was in lockstep with his fellow conspirators, who often attributed the sudden revelation of their errors to their awareness of communist successes.[67] Bukharin had genuinely chosen and genuinely been proved wrong. In arguing for his sincerity while recognizing Soviet achievements under Stalin's new course, he preserved both his authenticity as a revolutionary and the revolutionary rightness of the Communist Party.

Two of the most interesting minds of the mid-century, Ernst Bloch and Maurice Merleau-Ponty, powerfully argued for the sincerity of Bukharin's speech. Bukharin, wrote Bloch, had fought against Stalin's political line but, in the end, had come to see its success. The confession had not been extirpated by force or drugs; it was a genuine revolutionary position. Bukharin—as he himself stated—had finally realized that his was a divided self, torn between criminal instincts and praise for socialist realization.[68] Ernst Bloch understood Bukharin's confession to be the end of his metaphysical isolation:

> It is along with the death that follows—and Bukharin has not begged for his life—the return [*Rückkehr*, a word suggestive of conversion, *Bekehrung*] in the Soviet Union. "What are you dying for?"—for the Soviet Union, and for a last profession of faith to it. Seen from the endpoint of an individual life, the Soviet Union is the otherworld of Communist atheists. Bukharin has made this clear . . . to all those who still understand believers.[69]

Merleau-Ponty also zoomed in on the paradoxical authenticity of the situation: "The Moscow trials only make sense between revolutionaries, that is to say between men who are convinced that they are *making history* and who consequently already see the present as past and those who hesitate as traitors."[70]

Were Bloch and Merleau-Ponty in any sense right in believing in the sincerity of Bukharin's statements on the grounds of their ideological consistency? Was Bukharin actually of a single mind, and did he speak to the revolutionary future with a steady voice? In the late 1980s, Bukharin's political "Testament" was published. He had dictated it on the eve of his arrest—so at the very beginning of March 1937—to his second wife and soon to be widow, Anna Larina, making her learn it carefully by heart.[71] Anya, as he called her, committed it to her memory by means of periodic rewritings. This document, titled "To a Future Generation of Leaders of the [Communist] Party," reinforced existing doubts concerning the trustworthiness of the published "Last Words." In a second phase, in 1993, surfaced from the Soviet Archives Bukharin's 1937 letter to Stalin (dated December 10, 1937), an anguished and fawning plea whose verbal meanderings and prayer to be spared the firing squad's painful bullets, the public humiliation of a trial, and perhaps even the death penalty sat uneasily with the stoic, self-sacrificing voice of March 12, 1938.[72] Had a weakling's feeble will been broken and Bukharin been forced to read a script right before his death?

Where, then, is Burkharin's true voice? A classic interpretation had suggested itself in the 1970s: The "Last Words" were a facade; the true political Bukharin spoke in the Political Testament. But by March 1938 already, observers had intimated that the trial should be read between the lines. In 1965, introducing a new edition of the official Soviet proceedings, Robert Tucker could explain that Bukharin had accepted to go on trial in the hope that it would convict Stalin. He wanted "to dramatize by his own self-immolation in the show trial what Stalin was doing to Bolshevism" and to "transform the trial into an anti-trial."[73] Following this line of interpretation, the "Last Words" were a message to future generations. Bukharin's quip, "the confession of the accused is a principle of medieval jurisprudence" (and so unnecessary here) gestured toward the medieval Inquisition, an institution present to the mind of observers of Russia owing to the figure of the Great Inquisitor in Dostoyevski's *Brothers Karamazov*.[74] The Hegelian sentence, *Die Weltgeschichte ist das Weltgericht*, could be read as an appeal to the further course of History against the trial itself.[75] And, indeed, this was a classic move for medieval and early modern martyrs, which we have seen still operative with John Brown in the mid-nineteenth century: an appeal to the God Who governs History and Who at the End of History will judge each and all. The "Testament" after all stated that time would rectify Bukharin's reputation: "I am certain," he dictated to Anna, "that sooner or later the filter of History will inevitably wash the filth from my head." The Party would one day "vindicate" him and "reinstate" him into its ranks.[76]

But it is unlikely that Bukharin spoke his "Last Words" in code. After all, Stalin, who was not stupid, would have seen through cyphers and could have censored this and other suspicious phrases. Editing could also have denied Bukharin his tragic grandeur, all the more as we now know from recently discovered archival documents that the Soviet dictator and prosecuting team did tamper with the publication of Bukharin's "Last Words."[77] It is striking how little they saw fit to edit out or in. Bukharin's message was acceptable to both the victim and the perpetrator of the purge. Did Stalin, then, consider with Bukharin that Bukharin was redeemable in death? If he did not think so personally, he expected Soviet public opinion to accept this idea.[78]

We should not expect absolute consistency in Bukharin. He was tired, afraid for his family, and concerned for his posterity. He himself diagnosed that he labored under split consciousness. This diagnosis came easily to Bolsheviks,[79] among the accused or among the general population, as we now know from personal diaries, so well explored by Jochen Hellbeck. Ivanov, for instance, explained that "like duplicity (*dvurushnichestvo*), defeatism literally became part and parcel of the psychology of everyone of us"; that "there were many moments when my heart was torn by repentance, and the thought throbbed insistently in my mind to go and tell about the organization of the Rights, but I did not do so"; and finally that he "now experience[d] a dual feeling with regard to the sentence."[80] The coexistence of Political Testament, letter to Stalin, and Last Words, with their conflicted contents, refracts the range of Bukharin's very human hesitations. He hesitated until the very last hours. On March 13, 1938, right after his Last Words, he penned a letter to the Presidium of the Supreme Soviet of the USSR, which has recently been discovered, pleading for his life, promising to work for the Soviet Union and proclaimed himself a new man.[81] But hesitations made cultural sense. Like others among the accused, Bukharin explained his "double-dealing." His codefendants had accounted for "duplicity" and "phariseeism" (*dvurušničestva* and *farisejstva*, Ikramov's expressions) through partial blindness, the fear of being exposed (Ivanov), the "inertia of many years of stubborn and underground struggle against the Soviet government" (Bessonov), or full blindness and *libido dominandi* (Rakovsky).[82] This blindness, explained one of the accused, Rakovsky, in a statement worthy of a medieval heretic's recantation, had allowed the conspirators to delude themselves that they belonged to a vanguard of elects: "We considered ourselves to be people sent by providence (*providenie*); we consoled ourselves with the thought that we would be summoned (*pozovut*), that we were needed": and we failed to see "the entire development of the Soviet Union," social, economic, and cultural.[83] Duplicity went hand in hand with the inner struggles of a split consciousness. Ivanov told of his tortured experience of the October 1917 Revolution. It had combined in these revolutionary heydays "both joy and fear: joy, together with the victorious masses, and fear at the menace of exposure." "As time went on," he pursued, "I came more and more to resemble a man who had been flung into the water with a weight tied to his feet, a man who passionately desires to reach the shore, while the weight steadily drags him to the bottom."[84] The apostle Paul would have readily quipped that two laws struggled within the man Ivanov (cf. Rom. 7.21–23). Like his coaccused, Bukharin had been taught by the bolshevik culture of confession before the Party and of diary-keeping to interrogate the self and monitor inner struggles between the "old" (bourgeois or reactionary) and the "new."[85] He probably oscillated between hatred for Stalin and acceptance of a History in which Stalin rode the white horse of Providence, a History that called for his, Bukharin's, death.[86] No matter what, the "Last Words" and "Political Testament" agreed on two remarkable points. They both considered that there was such a thing as martyrdom for the right course of History. The "Testament" ended on a neomartyr image, red-colored: "Know, comrades, that the banner you bear in a triumphant march toward Communism contains a drop of my blood, too!"[87] And they both accepted the idea of proletarian terror. The NKVD, the Soviet political police, was bankrupt, but not the ideas of coercion, terrorism, and purge that animated it and had animated its predecessor, the Cheka. To cite the "Testament":

I am leaving life. I bow my head, but not before the proletarian scythe, which is properly merciless but also chaste. I am helpless, instead, before an infernal machine that seems to use medieval methods, yet possesses gigantic power, fabricates organized slander, acts boldly and confidently.

Dzerzhinsky is no more; the wonderful traditions of the Cheka have gradually receded into the past, those traditions by which the revolutionary idea governed all its actions, justified cruelty towards enemies, safeguarded the state against any counter-revolution.[88]

Bukharin, the old Bolshevik, shared an understanding that had been the Cheka's own. "Everything is allowed to us" had stated the organization's periodical, *The Red Sword*, in 1919. And it explained on which grounds it took this liberty, in the name of liberty: "Our humanity is absolute. . . . We are the first in the world who have drawn the sword not with the aim to enslave and oppress, but in the name of freedom."[89] Bukharin did not have any problem with the "proletarian scythe" as it had been wielded in the first decade of the Russian Revolution. "Mercilessness" or "cruelty" was not a problem as long as it was clean—a notion that may have echoed Robespierre's famous formula pairing terror and virtue.[90] In the "Testament," Bukharin avowed that he would have been willing to "bow his head" before the blade of a pure institution of proletarian purgation. In his "Last Words," he resigned himself to being killed by an institution that was not yet pure.

Odd as it may be, Bukharin's positions illuminate the medieval past of martyrdom. In 1937–1938, the old Bolshevik must have at some point—a point of equilibrium between resistance to Stalin and utter self-sacrifice for the Party—imagined himself as both sinful and yet soon to be redeemed, as a martyr in the making in need of being cleansed. We now turn to the third dossier, from the First Crusade. The tragedy of 1937–38 highlights a strikingly analogous configuration among the eleventh century "soldiers of Christ": they were both God's reapers at the Eschaton and themselves the object of a purge.

Martyr Figures and Figures of the Purge in Raymond d'Aguilers

And the armies that are in Heaven followed Him [Rev. 19.14] . . . By the armies which John saw following Christ . . . understand the saints who will be born at World's End and fight against Antichrist.[91]

Raymond d'Aguilers is arguably the most interesting chronicler of the First Crusade.[92] In his interpretation of the expedition, composed in or very shortly after 1100, the crusaders' travails allowed both martyrdom and purge. Jean Flori has counted in Raymond's *Liber* eight mentions of crusading casualties acquiring martyrdom or direct entry into Paradise.[93] There seems to have existed a generalized if hazy understanding that even people who died by drowning or of hunger were, or could be martyrs, exciting God's vengeance.[94] Along with the saints already reigning in Heaven, these sanctified dead joined the living on the battlefield at critical junctures ("various saints, Christ's knights, in truth accompanied us").[95] In a later chapter, it will be explained how killing and dying for the right cause were both bathed in the splendor of God's sublime justice.

As we shall see, the papal legate Adhémar of Le Puy, deceased shortly after the key battle fought outside Antioch (June 1098), was assimilated to those warriors who fell arms in hand and, like them, was believed by some to labor as a ghost or saint for the expedition's success. Next to this interpenetration of Heaven and Earth in combat, Raymond's *Liber* is characterized by a ferocious, leveling theology, conjoined to a sense that the Crusade is the holy war that will end all wars—the last act in Sacred History.[96] The poor and a handful of lesser clergy constituted the vanguard of Christ's army. They obtained visions that instructed the crusaders how to gain God's grace and that edicted liturgies, often penitential, meant to secure from God victory in battle against the Muslims. These visions also criticized the institutional leadership, lay princes, and upper clergy (including Bishop Adhémar).[97] The poor, "children of God," pushed the expedition forward, forcing the princes to abandon the fortresses and cities seized on the march, because occupying them and squabbling over them delayed the arrival into Jerusalem. They even threatened to elect their own leader.[98] The prince who came closest, despite his failings, to siding with these radicals and their prophets, the Provençal Raymond of Saint-Gilles, exhibited very odd behavior. He refused to be considered a candidate to kingship in Jerusalem, following the clerical position that "it is wrong to elect a king where the Lord suffered and was crowned," because the king might become corrupt and because Daniel's prophecy announces that "when the Holy of Holies shall have come, unction will cease."[99]

On the one hand, the crusaders were the purest of the pure. But, on the other hand, they were most in need of purgation. Saint Andrew, in a vision, told the crusaders:

Don't you know why God led you here? And how much He loves you, and how He elected you particularly? He made you come here to avenge His spurning and that of His people. He loves you so much that the saints already placed in the repose [of Paradise], knowing in advance the grace [allotted to you] by divine disposition, want to be in the flesh and fight alongside you. God elected you among all nations just as the good grain is separated from the chaff [cf. Matt. 13], for in merits and grace you are ahead of all those who came before you and shall come after you, just as the price of gold is ahead of that of silver.[100]

Andrew the apostle knew what a vanguard was, along with Maximilien Robespierre, who proclaimed that his group, the Montagne, was "pure" and "sublime"; "conspirers do not belong to the Montagne."[101] However, all the crusaders were not among the elect. Just as the Jacobins would eliminate the more tepid Danton and his faction from the Montagne, so God's army was in need of a purge. There were among it "unrighteous men," destined to "return to him who refused to hold on to justice [Satan]."[102] Another vision was triggered by Peter Bartholomew's wish to see Christ as the Crucified (He had up until then appeared only as a standing man). The Lord complied, transforming Himself accordingly, then explained the meaning of His five, blood-saturated wounds.[103] They represented participants in His Passion as well as five kinds of crusaders. The first kind, akin to Christ, does not fear weapons; they are the active fighters in the army. Explicitly, they can become martyrs: "when such men die, they are taken together to God's right hand, where I sat after My resurrection and My ascent to Heaven." The second, akin to the apostles, are reserve forces. The third supplies the fighters and is compared to those who complained of the injustice meted to Christ. The fourth stay neutral in war; they are like the crucifiers. The fifth run away and dissuade others from fighting, like the Jews and Pilatus. After this self-exegesis, Christ offered to reveal the identity of the "traitors" (*proditores*), "doubters" or "unbelievers" (*increduli*, like the hated Jews)—the last two ranks—through a miracle. Once the army was arrayed for combat and the hallowed battle cry "God help us" shouted thrice, the Lord would make visible the five groups. Further interrogated about what was to be done with the doubters, Christ answered chillingly: "Show no mercy; kill them; they are My betrayers, brothers of Judas Iscariot. Give their worldly goods to the first rank proportionately to their need; and by this act you will find the right way [to Jerusalem] which you so far have circumvented."[104] This sanguinary command to purge was fittingly borne by a vision of Christ in His aspect as the bloody Crucified, an image calling for vengeance.[105] Christ went on, among other orders, to command extreme caution toward enemies who converted to Christianity[106] and toward crusaders who had apostasized and then returned to the fold. Raymond's Lord was not a Lord of mercy.

For Raymond d'Aguilers, thus, purge accompanied martyrdom and God's war. Was this radical voice idiosyncratic? Not so, or not fully so. Those monastic chroniclers who redacted the crusade story at a decade or so in temporal distance from the 1099 capture of Jerusalem are unlikely to have preserved extreme opinions like those Raymond conveys.[107] The German Ekkehard of Aura, present in the Holy Land in 1101—where he consulted a little book (*libellus*) on the events he had not lived through—struck, though, a note in tune with Raymond's melody.[108] Ekkehard began his narrative by detailing the numerous miracles that mobilized every status in society. Yet with success came a satanic reaction (as predicted by Matt. 24.24, and following him, by the Pseudo-Methodius's scenario of EndTimes):

> By these and other similar portents, the whole creation was inflamed to [join into] the army of the Creator. And so the Enemy . . . did not delay to sow his cockle over this good seed, to raise up false prophets, and to mix into the armies of the Lord false brethren and loose women under the guise of religion. Thus Christ's flocks were so sullied by the hypocrisy and the lies of others, and by others' nefarious pollutions, that as the good pastor prophesized, even the elect were led into error [cf. Matt. 24.24].[109]

Ekkehard echoed a concern also present in Raymond d'Aguilers. Writing after 1102, perhaps in 1105, the German advised that one should query the seducers about the details of their participation in the expedition and force them to penance.

The "leaders of the army that was *truly* of the Lord" (*vere dominicae militiae duces*), that is, Godfrey and other princes, managed to reach Jerusalem. On the way, the winnowing had "thrown out the chaff from the threshingfloor of the Lord," and "the good grains (*grana triticea*) [did] perdure owing to their natural heaviness and solidity."[110] Like Raymond, Ekkehard wrote within an eschatological framework.[111] The epoch at the End of Times that produced martyrdom also necessitated a purge. As in later conceptions, it would begin "at the sanctuary." To cite the Jacobin Garnier de Saintes, "If we are purging [the National Assembly], it is to have the right to purge France. We shall not allow any heterogeneous body within the Republic . . . We want to trim this great tree of its dead branches."[112] Augustine had depicted how on this "thresh-ing-floor" would be "segregated" the chaff "for eternal fire," that is, "all those destined to damnation." Thus, the group of the "purged" could "stand to the right [of Christ], without fear that any among the evil would mingle with it."[113] Isidore of Seville had rejoindered that "many among those who now seem to be elect and holy may perish on Judgment Day, for as the Prophet Amos [7.4] says, 'The Lord will summon a trial by fire, and the Abyss will devour much, and eat part of [God's] House'."[114]

The association of purge, crusade, and martyrdom was transported across the centuries by at least two media. One was the various romanced versions of the biblical story of the Maccabees, a medieval favorite. Manuscript illustra-tors seem to have been especially fond of representing Mattathias killing an idolatrous Jew at the altar (1 Macc. 2.23–24).[115] And the narrative itself pre-sented next to the Old Testament warrior-martyrs' death for God the same's slaughter of lukewarm Jews and Hellenized pagans. The other medium con-sisted in sermons on the Cross and the crusade. They allied a discourse on the rewards of bellicose martyrdom to social criticism. One of the earliest, from the pen of Jacques de Vitry, a member of the reformist galaxy associated with the Paris schools at the turn of the thirteenth century. Jacques took as his theme verses from Revelation, which led him to comment on a passage in Ezechiel announcing the angelic mass massacre of all those who were not marked with God's sign:

They were told to begin at the sanctuary [Ez. 9.6], which means with the priests, because, as the Book of Wisdom says, the mighty are might-ily tormented and on the highly placed the harshest judgment falls.[116]

For Jacques de Vitry, those who did not side with Christ were de facto against Christ:

The dragon swept the third part of the stars [Rev. 12.4]. The first part defends the faith with the word like the doctors against the heretics; the second part defends the faith with the sword like the soldiers of Christ;

the third part defends neither with the word nor with the sword and they are the Devil's part.[117]

And, indeed, over the next hundred years or so, two popular crusades—the so-called Shepherds' Crusades of 1251 and 1320–1321—turned revolutionary, attacking nobles, royal representatives, and the clergy, turning even—forsooth—against university professors.[118] "To begin at the sanctuary": All the way into the modern era, there existed the idea that the purge was to start with the elect—elect status groups or elect nation. The Fifth Monarchist Christofer Syms, for instance, queried rhetorically, "Must not judgement begin at the house of God? If this *British Northern* nation bee the people chosen of *God* to accomplish the last wonders of the world, to clens the church of heresy, schism, atheism, and hypocrisy, . . . was it not necessary the nation itself be first purged?"[119] In the words of another seventeenth-century radical from the same sect, William Aspinwall (d. 1662), "The Church is God's furnace," in which its rightful rulers "should . . . be . . . thoroughly purged and refined from their drosse and tyn."[120] We have already explored in Chapter 2 the parallels, as to this moral warfare front, between the French Revolution and the First Crusade.

To return to this crusade, the Manichean notion of the radical purge was compensated by a strange mechanism. We mean to explore here the odd case of papal legate Bishop Adhémar of Le Puy. This member of the expedition leadership had doubted the veracity of the visions received by the prophetic group of poor crusaders and lesser clergy.[121] In particular, Adhémar had considered fraudulent the revelations that had led to the discovery of a powerful relic, the holy lance. To this prelate, neither the messenger nor the object seemed authentic.[122] A victory-bringing object that worked battlefield miracles, the holy lance was the symbolic keystone of the whole bundle of messages—radical and egalitarian in tenor—the group conveyed to the army and its leadership. Soon after the elevation of this relic, the crusaders won a great triumph before Antioch, and Adhémar, "a man beloved of God and men," died, "dear in every way to all."[123]

But this general appreciation was not quite justified. Adhémar soon appeared to Peter Bartholomew, the peasant visionary, to tell him he had just completed a tour in Hell.[124] The bishop confessed that his head and face had been severely burned because of his doubts concerning the lance.[125] Adhémar, however, also announced that, like the martyrs of the crusade, he would contribute to the march toward Jerusalem: "I shall be far more useful in death than in life if they [the crusaders] are willing to keep the laws of God. I and all my departed brothers shall live with them, and I shall appear and offer better counsel than I did in life."[126] He did indeed, exhorting a priest who was sick because he was a doubter and, when the army marched toward Jerusalem, dictating the proper victory-bringing penance.[127] Not only this, but he was seen in Jerusalem when it was stormed, leading "the way over the walls [and] urging the knights and people to follow him."[128] Adhémar of Le Puy was, literally, the first man to enter the Promised Land.

The strange case of Bishop Adhémar, flawed yet perfected saint, companion of the fighting saints and glorified dead, inspires two comments. It has struck some observers that the West did not commemorate as martyr any dead among the First Crusaders, even if contemporary chroniclers spoke of martyrs and identified some by name.[129] The doubts Raymond d'Aguilers reveals about the inner worth of leaders and followers in the expedition, Ekkehard's sense that Satan blurred the purity of the ranks, and their shared sense that death on the crusade could be part of a winnowing or threshing constitute a partial explanation for this fact. Who was ultimately to say what a death in the Holy Land meant before God?[130] Even Raymond had had a moment of doubt about the lance; even Peter Bartholomew had initially doubted concerning Andrew's mandate to find this relic (which explained his partial burns during the ordeal he had undergone to prove its authenticity).[131] But, second, the winnowing and threshing did not mean necessarily the rejection of the lukewarm. Contrary to this historian's expectations, even the black-and-white Manichean scheme of the First Crusade made room for religious gray. There were human beings who stood between betrayal and holiness and whom death and repentance could purge back into the ranks of the elect.[132] Adhémar the bishop converted in Hell—a privilege probably denied to the Muslim dead. And so Adhémar, posthumously, worked toward the great day—the "new day" proclaimed with the conquest of Jerusalem on July 15, 1099, the "day" that "emptied out all paganism."[133] Here, too, Bukharin, in his trust that "the banner you bear in a triumphant march toward Communism contains a drop of my blood" was the heir of the medieval culture of martyrdom.

*   *   *

The following thoughts do not constitute so much a strict conclusion to this chapter as a set of reflections. The parallels between the three episodes are striking. They testify to the force, beyond medieval Catholicism, and even in a post-Christian culture, of connections between notions of History in its eschatological dimensions, purity, violence, elite vanguard, martyrdom, and vengeance. To this complex of likely cultural fellow travelers we should add liberty and universalism (about which more in Chapter 6). To make for the longue durée permanence of this form, confrontational martyrdom, a number of forces must have been at play. Obviously, there worked in the favor of continuity a first belief—widely shared in western European cultures and in those ensembles deeply influenced by it, and broadly transmitted by narratives, art, and monuments—in the potency of this manner of death. Martyrdom constituted the ideal way for an individual to die for a cause, and it was believed to move God to action, and to propel History forward. But it takes two to tango. As Brad Gregory demonstrated, martyrdom was also maintained by the willingness of elites to prosecute dissent publicly and through the channels of law (as opposed to simply repressing dissent swiftly or quietly).[134] For after all, the would-be martyrs' adversaries usually knew only too well that, in doling death, they were dealing a potent card to the other side. Still, they often had to dole and deal. In the Western legal tradition, normatively, a criminal could be destroyed only after a fairly conducted trial . This second belief, in the primacy of the law and due process, meant that, even though prosecuting magistrates tended to realize that public judicial debate afforded a would-be martyr a chance to publicize his or her oppositional belief, and so open the door to further troubles, they—more often than not—took the risk of open trials.[135]

Continuities are striking, but so are differences. They are visible on the background of the first Christian centuries' martyrdoms, to which Raymond d'Aguilers is closer than Brown or Bukharin. Early Christian martyrs found death at the hands of opponents who were full outsiders: the pagan magistrates and their pagan minions. Thus, these willing victims stood against, and different from, what can literally be called an out-group.[136] Sometimes, as in the *Passion of Polycarp* or the *Passion of Perpetua and Felicitas*, they announced the destruction, spiritual or physical, of their persecutors. The spectacle of Hell would ultimately answer the spectacles of the Roman arena. Tertullian delighted at the prospect of watching "the magistrates who persecuted the Lord's name melting in aggressive flames more savage than those with which they savaged Christians."[137] On the other hand, Bukharin was condemned by his own Bolsheviks and claimed membership in the Party, embracing it and its mission. Martyrs were privy to God's will and the course of Sacred History and, in deference to this knowledge, accepted death. They did not, however, usually confess to major lapses against the Church, unlike Bukharin against the Party (even if both Bishop Adhémar and Peter Bartholomew, plus the chronicler Raymond himself, admitted to doubts about the most important relic of the poor pilgrims). John Brown was executed at the order of fellow Americans. He denied, vociferously, this fellowship in citizenship yet still affirmed it *sub specie aeternitatis*. Brown engaged his Southern opponents in dialogue, leaving open the door of their conversion to antislavery. He was confident that the historical horizon would see the triumph of his abolitionist faith throughout America—if only after violent, bloody travails. While Brown and his friends rejected the legitimacy of a state that defended slavery (as is well known, a position embraced by many abolitionists who were ready to break up the Union rather than allow slave power's extension), they still hoped for its reform as a global entity.[138] Bukharin believed in the Party and the State, the USSR, that tried him; if there had been an alienation, it was his, owing to double-consciousness. The last sentence of his "Testament" proclaimed the hope that he still contributed to the march of History and a poignant desire to belong. By contrast, there is not much of an indication in the authentic martyr acts—composed before Emperor Constantine embraced Christianity during the fourth century's first half—that the victims or their hagiographers expected Rome's conversion, in whole or in substantial part.[139] Some martyrs protested that they did not have to sacrifice to the idols because they prayed for the empire or the emperor.[140] But a common answer to the imperial magistrate's demand that the accused identify themselves, "I am a Christian," proclaimed alienation vis-à-vis Roman citizenship.[141] Already encountered in Chapter 3, the fourth-century poet and hagiographer Prudentius will illustrate a new configuration, made more likely after the imperial embrace of Christianity, in relation to the martyr's alterity. His hymn on the passion of Saint Lawrence begins in these words: "The age-old mother of pagan shrines, Rome, now consecrated to Christ, conquers under Lawrence's guidance, and triumphs over barbarian rites."[142]

Converted by the martyrs' "not bloodless struggles," Rome, which has subjugated all nations, now will yoke also the "monstrous idols." Lawrence, tortured on the grill, announces Constantine and Theodosius I, and in the midst of his pain, prays for the conversion of Rome, "the city of Romulus." The imperial capital will become itself the agent of the orb's Christianization. Thus, Lawrence, at the moment of his death radically different from his Roman tormentors, is still, when one considers him from the standpoint of a providential future, a Roman: his martyrdom is sacramentally both cause and prophecy of Rome's Christianization and its universal Christian mission. Still, we are not dealing with a straight line from Prudentius to Bukharin, perhaps not with a line at all. Raymond d'Aguilers gives little sense of an interest in the conversion or redemption of an identifiable totality. Perhaps he was thinking of "the Franks" or "Christendom," but we hear hardly anything about the latter as a widely embracing ensemble. He mistrusted apostates from Islam to Christianity and Christian apostates who wanted to return to their original faith.[143] He thought that the Dalmatian pagans encountered on the road had an either/or choice: having learned the strength of God's soldiers and their willingness to suffer (*patientia*), they would either convert at the realization of the strength of Christ's army or be the objects of God's merciless doom.[144] He welcomed back a lightly toasted Bishop Adhémar into the ranks of the pure but did not look forward to a totalizing group of the saved. For Raymond, if there was a totality, it was the totality of Christ and in Christ, now, on this day that had "emptied out all paganism" with the bloody purge of the Holy City.[145] His was not an optimistic, open universality comprising all or most or even many human beings. Such was not his concern.[146] Closer to us, Timothy La-Haye's best-selling apocalyptic novels (and the wider genre they belong to) also oscillate between salvation for the few and for the many.[147] In the culture of the Christian and post-Christian West, when it comes to martyrdom, there coexist, thus, two radically opposed configurations. The one is inclusive and universalistic, the other, exclusive and sectarian. The former is more easily reconciled with nationalism and various forms of manifest destiny; the latter can dovetail with terroristic identities. These are, of course, pure forms, since sectarian elitism can merge with the ideology of the vanguard and so rejoin universalism.

Chapter 5

Twins: National Holy War and Sectarian Terror

How long shall one call the despots' fury justice, and the people's
justice barbarity or rebellion?
—Maximilien Robespierre, February 5, 1794

to bring to a common denominator revolutionary violence and
bourgeois violence, [this] won't do.
—Rote Armee Fraktion, "Das Konzept Stadtguerilla"

Holy war and terror belong together. They do not simply do so phenomeno-
logically—that is, inasmuch as they have in common observable practices and
beliefs, as Bruce Lincoln remarked a decade ago, putting face to face Osama
bin Laden and George W. Bush's speeches—but also genealogically.[1] There is
a commonality in the willingness to use force against heathens and religious
dissenters, enemies outside and enemies inside. Since the establishment of
the absolutist state—especially in its nation-state variant, which considered
that internecine conflicts were in essence illegitimate, and imposed this view
successfully—European thought has distinguished sharply between foreign
and civil warfare. But this distinction had been hardly rock-hard in the preceding centuries and has been periodically subverted, for instance, during the
French Revolution. And have we not seen very recently the United States of
America treat some of its nationals as "enemy combatants" and subject foreign
soldiers to its law courts? First, before the triumph of sovereignty came to be
understood as the monopoly of the means of violence, Christian universalism
blurred the boundaries between polities; furthermore, aristocrats of all ranks,

cities, and even peasant communities claimed a right to feud for justice within and across borders, including against their own lords.[2] Second, theologically seen, the inner enemy, heretic or false brethren, was on a continuum with the pagan outsider: "The whole body of the Devil consists in all the aforementioned figures (*personae*), that is, the Jews, the heretics, false Christians, and pagans."[3] In the domains of exemplary punishment and conversion, the notion of salutary fear applied to both insiders and outsiders. To cite Augustine again, *Ubi terror, ibi salus*.[4] Theologians did find coercion against heathens more debatable than against heretics, but, when they accepted the former, the arguments (and so the measures) proposed for the latter tended to apply.[5]

A single polity could, thus, both exercise terror and wage sanctified warfare. But holy war and terror are braided together in another manner, as terror meted out by two different agents—the state and the "terrorist(s)." We shall develop in this chapter this second comparison and submit that the violence of the polity (be it inward or outward directed) and the violence of terrorist groups mirror one another owing to historical reasons, more precisely owing to conceptions of the polity and to the notion of the duties and rights of ruler and people. Since the Gregorian Revolution, and with the twelfth-century Scholastic elaborations that came in its wake, it was sometimes voiced that the prince's coercive duties, along with the sword that the *princeps* or magistrate "does not bear in vain" (Rom. 13.1–7), could devolve upon lesser figures, including the commons as a collective, even onto the lone individual Christian.[6] Allegedly, during the first urban revolution of medieval Europe, the Patarene leader Ariald reminded the Milanese commoners (the *multitudo civitatis*) that Christians bore the sword for no other reason than the defense of the Faith and called on his audience to employ it. Given that Milan's clergy in its majority was tainted by simony, the Pataria claimed for nonclergy (monks, and, in a restricted way, laymen) the right-duty to preach; parallel to this, the ordinary laity as a group was to take up armed coercion.[7] The peace decreed in Cologne in 1083 placed in the power of "the counts, officials, and powerful" just as much as of "the whole people in common" the task to execute "vengeance" against those who would infringe the "holy peace"; implicitly, a failure of the nobles would have led to action by the commons.[8] The sixteenth-century wars of religion would systematize the discussion. In the mid-sixteenth century, radical Calvinist Christopher Goodman would write that "a portion of the sword of justice" was committed to "the whole multitude."[9] The sixteenth century would also see popular justice ape the ceremonial forms by which royal magistrates normally meted out punishment.[10] The rectifying violence of the Christian state thus has a twin in the violence of the smaller groups that take on themselves the duty to defend the religious common good.

In the devolution of the right and duty to coerce, two theological principles were at work. The first was collective responsibility vis-à-vis injustice. Any man who did not intervene even though he could was passively an accomplice. Building on the early twelfth-century *Gloss on the Psalms* (itself a composite of Augustine and Cassiodorus's commentaries), Peter the Chanter and his circle explained that the Jewish commoners should have acted to prevent Christ's crucifixion, a judicial travesty, and therefore were collectively guilty of deicide. They could have intervened effectively, given that the "princes" (the Jewish religious leadership) feared the plebe owing to its numbers. (On the basis of the same gloss on Ps. 81, this position was also staked out in the pages of Gratian's authoritative legal compendium, the *Decretum*.) Peter debated whether it made sense for a lone individual from the commons, as opposed to a person with status (for instance, a bishop or another undefined member of the elite), to initiate a rebellion against injustice. But he also underlined the higher force of justice over and above the established hierarchy of offices. The example of Phineas (Num. 25.6–8), a private individual, showed that "for the most atrocious cases, all must rise up together, I do not say to avenge, but either to resist or to accuse." The Chanter proposed here a right of resistance (in high medieval practice the privilege of the higher nobility), not the devolution of the magistrate's judicial sword legitimized by Paul's Romans 13.[11] Yet this came very close. "Devolution," it should be said at this point, may actually not be a perfect term, as it implies a one-way process, rights and duties traveling from top to bottom. The movement was not always unidirectional, from princely prerogatives to small group or popular rights. In his justification of the Spanish kings' sixteenth-century conquests in the New World, Juan Ginés de Sepúlveda mustered biblical passages and interpretations that had been used in the twelfth century to argue for the popular right-duty of intervention against injustice.[12]

The second theological principle derived from the concept of mystical body (*corpus mysticum*). In his classic *The King's Two Bodies*, Ernst Kantorowicz showed half a century ago how there took place in the thirteenth century a transfer of notions from the Church, a *corpus* whose head was Christ, to "political mystical bodies," elect Christian nations whose head was the consecrated king. The scheme of the mystical body not only constitutes a way station toward a secular nation-state still inhabited by religious forms, but, as Kantorowicz's book demonstrates, also contains two divergent potentialities, one toward absolutism (the perpetuity of the polity concentrated in the royal office) and one toward parliamentarianism (in which the corporation of the realm ended up claiming against its royal head this same perpetuity).[13] It too could lead to a participation of the body in violent rectification, even against the head.

The Crusader-King Louis IX and the Pastoureaux

One can see the devolution process at work with Louis IX's Seventh Crusade to Egypt (1248–1254), and (chronologically and causally embedded in the expedition) with the so-called Shepherds' Crusade of 1251, a popular movement triggered by the French king's defeat, meant to rescue him from captivity. In this tragic moment, the sacrality of holy war, inclusive of martyrdom, came to encompass the king-centered polity, France.[14] Merit and agency were positioned throughout the collective body, both at its top and at its bottom. A knight's report of Louis IX's speech before the French landing off Damietta in June 1249 suggests as much. The king (r. 1226–1270) harangued the men on his ship:

> My friends and vassals, if we remain undivided in charity, we shall be unconquered. . . . Let us disembark on these shores, however strongly they are guarded. I am not the king of France; I am not the Holy Church: it is surely you all (*vos utique omnes*) who are the king, and you who are the Holy Church. I am just but one sole man (*non sum nisi unus solus homo*) whose life, when God wills it, will be snuffed out like any other man's (*unius alterius hominis*). For us, every outcome is a safe one: if we are defeated, we fly forth as martyrs; if we are victorious, the glory of the Lord will be proclaimed and that of all France—indeed of Christendom—will be enhanced."[15]

On the backdrop of holy war and in the perspective of potential martyrdom, a king of France, head of the political body, proclaimed the collective monarchy of his "*gent*" (as Louis called his people in the vernacular).[16] For victory or for defeat, the people, being the mystical body of the realm, were the real France and the real vehicle of national and religious glory. This was a compact collective: the king had opened up his exhortation with a mention of how *caritas* bound together the group, as taught by contemporary eucharistic lore.[17] From the same mid-century years survives an account of the Battle of Bouvines (1214), according to which Louis' grandfather Philip Augustus had said to his magnates and knights, handing them his crown, "Behold, I want you all to be kings, and in truth you are kings, since 'king' derives from 'ruling,' and were it not for you, I would not be able to rule alone my kingdom." The story, likely mythical, also had a eucharistic framework; and the battle was seen as holy, fought against an excommunicate king, Otto IV.[18]

Louis IX's France was also an elect vanguard: It was nestled within Christendom, and stood for it as a whole, as *pars pro toto*, in a classic combination of elect particularism and universalism.[19] On his way to the Mediterranean harbors, the king, afraid that intestine West European conflicts would harm France in his absence, had beseeched the pope with a tearful entreaty: "Guard France, [guard] France as the apple of your eye; for on its state depend your prosperity and that of all of Christendom."[20] Louis' trope of France's crusading mission *for* Christ and Christendom also worked in the negative, as when Jeanne d'Arc famously reminded Philip, duke of Burgundy, that "all those who wage war *against* the holy kingdom of France, wage war against King Jesus, King of Heaven and of all the world, my rightful and sovereign Lord."[21]

Were Louis' words convincing to his audience? The administrative and religious reforms that he had initiated since the earlier 1240s in preparation for the expedition to Egypt may have authenticated them. Crusade and reform: as explained in Chapter 2, any crusade was supposed to be accompanied by a reformation of the self and of the polity.[22] This correlation between external holy war, reform, and purge of society (if necessary all the way to civil war) and purgation of the self appears periodically throughout the history of the West, through the French Revolution and all the way to the twentieth century's bloody utopias. In its thirteenth-century version, the fight against evil took place on all fronts: on the spiritual and material battlefield against pagans; in the domestic trenches versus heresy, false brethren, bad clergy, and Jews; in the moral arena, collective or individual, of the struggle against vices. A similar alloy of anti-Semitism, critique of the clergy, and hope for the destruction of Islam animated the Catalans and Aragonese.[23] Historians have applauded the holy king for his reforms of justice and administration; less understandable are Louis' rabid anti-Semitism, his order to burn the Talmud, and the financing of the expedition through exactions against Jewish possessions. On the very eve of his departure for Egypt, he had "captured" Jewish goods to finance the expedition.[24] He had also, in a now lost ordinance, ordered "Jews to desist from usuries, blasphemies, sortileges and [magical] characters, and" commanded that "the Talmud and other books in which one finds blasphemies be burnt." Jews who did not obey would be expelled and transgressors punished according to the law (*legitime*).[25] Unpalatable they may be to us, yet all these measures formed a coherent whole. They were of one piece in the king's religiosity; they were of one piece thanks to the interplay of the several senses of scripture, literal, moral, and allegorical.

In April 1250, Louis was captured on the Nile with a substantial part of what had survived of his army. In terms of religious dynamics, crusading culture—by the thirteenth century, Western European culture at large—knew that defeat at war stemmed from sin in the army and at home. Innocent IV wrote to the king's mother, Blanche of Castile, explaining that God's anger, and, consequently, Louis' captivity, could not be imputed to the defects or negligence of the king, who had devoted himself to the cause, but was "possibly" the fruit of "some transgressions on the part of the people" (*aliqua forte peccata populi*).[26] Sin was often sexual but could be social. Answering defeat, the king, who had reformed his judicial and domanial administration and enforced proper religious behavior in the kingdom to prepare for his departure in 1246, would on his return from the Holy Land work with even greater energy to improve both royal governance and Christian piety, expelling prostitutes, regulating taverns, forbidding games, and prosecuting the Jews.[27] Yet there did not exist full unanimity as to what right order exactly was, as some contemporary explanations for the failure readily betray. The English chronicler Matthew Paris attributed the king's defeat to excessive crusading taxation (as God vindicated what was right);[28] the troubadour Austorc d'Aurillac incriminated the avarice of the clergy from the pope down and sputtered against "false clerics in whom faithlessness holds sway."[29]

Who would correct these vices, cause of defeat? Louis himself had asserted that the people were France and the Holy Church. If this statement represents something that commoners could also think, the odd movement of the Shepherds (*Pastoureaux* or *pastores*) becomes quite understandable, including in its violence.[30] Formed as a relief army to succor the imprisoned king (and indeed, according to Matthew Paris, some among the shepherds after the movement's forcible break-up received the cross from the proper authorities and went off to the Holy Land to join Louis),[31] the Shepherds' Crusade received the approval of Blanche as regent of France. The queen mother may have recalled then how, in 1227, the commons of Paris had saved her and her son from a baronial plot. Louis, at least, recalled well this event and recounted it to his companion Jean de Joinville.[32] But the queenly mandate hallowed a movement that quickly turned violent (in any crusade, there existed a potential for a turn against established authorities). Uniformly hostile chroniclers painted the shepherds of 1251 into a raving mob that had been deceived by impostors endowed with powers of fascination. We have seen how Roger Bacon explained scientifically this ability to madden a whole crowd. For several contemporary authors, the *pastores*' chiefs were crypto-Muslims and secret agents of Louis' enemy, the sultan. In a gesture redolent of the wicked pact between the Muslims and Ganelon in the *Song of Roland*, the sultan had showered their leader, known to historians as the Master of Hungary ("a master who knew magical arts") with gold and silver and "kissed him on the mouth as a sign of great love" to seal the conspiracy.[33] Letters from the sultan in Arabic and Chaldean script were found among the belongings of one of the Master's associates.[34] Thus, this mob was one element in a global conspiracy of religious and moral deviants. Malcolm Barber aptly comments that, for the clergy, the movement was "a kind of reverse-image of the crusade, in that it was in reality a Moslem plot to conquer France."[35] It comprised, in the words of the *Chronicle of Metz*, "thieves, outlaws, apostates, pagans, heretics and prostitutes." Roger Bacon, as we saw, proposed that they might be in league not only with Saracens but also with Mongols.[36] The *pastores* organized themselves into an army, in battalions, and carried before them banners "painted with images of the vision" of the Virgin that had authorized their crusade.[37] Despite the sources' hostility to the movement, one can reconstruct its religiosity. Mary, painted on their banners, was a Virgin of Peace but also a Virgin of War for the sake of Peace, and a figure of reconquest and reconsecration to Christianity of pagan sites.[38]

It was not the first time that, owing to the failings of lords and princes, a popular army had fought in France under the emblem of the Virgin. As Jehangir Malegam has recently explored, in the 1180s, a vision of Mary led to the formation of a *pacis fraternitas* in the Auvergne. Like the *pastores*, this sworn association of commoners devoted to peace making ended up fighting local powers and, after initial successes, was suppressed in blood. Historians know them as the *Capuciati* or "encapuchonnés," the cowled ones, from the white hood worn by members, which bore a medallion of the Virgin. The region had been infested by mercenaries, and the "peace brotherhood" moved against them. The fraternity's statutes provided, according to a hostile chronicler from Laon, that the *Capuciati* "would not swear false oaths, not curse indecently" by the bodily parts below the belt (literally, "navel") of God, His Mother, or any of the saints. Decency was mandated in demeanor and clothing: "No one who plays games of chance or any game of dice shall enter into this peace fraternity; he shall not have any noble vestment" nor "a knife with a pointed end," nor shall he "visit taverns."[39] Luckily for the historian, Geoffroy of Vigeois put down his pen in 1183, before the destruction of the movement, so we are left with a monastic chronicler who was, on principle, hostile to popular upstarts but was neutral to the *Capuciati.* Geoffroy even reports that Christ "deigned show some miraculous marks (*signa*) on the bodies" of some treacherously slaughtered members "to honor His Mother."[40] Also marked in their flesh with the cross had been some of the pilgrim-warriors who had died on the road to Jerusalem in 1096–1100.[41]

But the 1251 shepherds did not fight under Mary alone. Matthew Paris attributed to them another standard, depicting a lamb holding a banner. On this banner there was a cross. "The lamb" signified here, reported the monk, "humility and innocence," while the "banner with the cross was a sign of victory."[42] This was the Lamb of Revelation and of the Last Judgment, which (if one trusts Matthew's words) suggests an apocalyptic component to the movement.

It was not only the patronages of Mary and of the apocalyptic lamb that inserted the shepherds in the traditional culture of holy war. Even though lacking priestly status, the *pastores'* leaders released couples from marriage vows, complain some chroniclers.[43] But was this not because marriage could be an obstacle to the crusading vow? Contemporary sources also bemoan that the leaders married together celibate male and female pilgrims. But was this not possibly to protect the purity of the expedition by providing a legitimate channel to sexual impulses? As Conor Kostick has shown, such had been the policy on the First Crusade. To cite but one proof-text, before the conquest of Antioch, Saint Peter berated the first crusaders for committing, among other transgressions, "many adulteries, even though it pleases God that you all should take wives."[44]

The *pastores* attacked the clergy, including the mendicants. Matthew Paris painted how

> when their supreme leader preached, surrounded on all sides with armed men, he condemned and reproached all orders (with the exception of their sect), and especially the Preachers and Friars Minor, calling them wanton wanderers (*girivagos*) and hypocrites. He asserted that the monks of the Order of Cîteaux were most greedy lovers of flocks and of lands. As for the black monks, they were gluttonous and prideful;

canons, half-worldly and devourers of meat; the bishops and their officials hunted only after money, and overflowed with all sorts of vices. Finally, he preached about the Roman Curia disgraceful things, [so disgraceful] that one cannot repeat them, to the point that they [the Romans] seemed to be openly heretics and schismatics.[45]

But was this not in part because ecclesiastics were considered responsible for the crusade's dismal failure? Like Austorc d'Aurillac, the *pastores* blamed Louis' 1250 defeat on the clergy in general, and more pointedly on the priests and mendicant friars who had preached the Seventh Crusade. Matthew Paris's many entries on the crusade refract popular hostility to a papacy and its agents, who used the crusade as a pretext to soak up the faithful's money by guile or impositions.[46] Salimbene of Parma reported that the friars' involvement in promoting a crusade in which the king had been defeated made them an especial object of rancor.[47] The friars had also preached, concurrently and on the pope's behalf, a crusade against the interests of Emperor Frederick II of Hohenstaufen (r. 1212–1250) in Germany. For many years before 1250, public opinion had considered that Innocent IV's hostility to the German emperor was hamstringing the crusading efforts in the Holy Land.[48] Austorc d'Aurillac even wished "that the Emperor would have taken the cross, that the empire would still belong to his son" and, more tellingly, desired a very special alliance: "that the French *gent* would hold to him [Frederick] against the false clergy, among which Faithlessness reigns, who killed Prowess and Chivalry, and all courtliness, and worry little about others' hurt as long as they can wallow and rest in pleasure."[49]

The shepherds may have oscillated between a desire to purge the clergy and a desire to reform it radically. Like the impeccably orthodox crusade preacher Jacques de Vitry or like those first crusaders represented by Raymond d'Aguilers, they may have considered that Christian society had to be purified "beginning at the sanctuary (Ez. 9.6)."[50] Possibly the shepherds used violence against the clergy only when the latter refused to convert to the way of life that befitted their ecclesiastical calling. They despoiled the Dominicans of Tours of the wealth that, given their vows of poverty, they should not have owned. Wrote a Franciscan, "they deprived them of the victuals and goods that Christian piety had handed over to them"; furthermore, they "dragged some without the habit of their order behind themselves as if captives" and (according to another source) flogged them "through the middle of the city in the sight of all," probably to inflict on them public penance (hence the absence of habit).

They then considered killing these friars outside the city, possibly because they resisted.[51] In Bourges, the *pastores* went after the Jews, plundering them and burning their books.[52]

Some of this violence was popular, in the sense that, since about around 1200, some preachers of the crusade had propounded that only members of the lowest populace, the poor, were pure of sin. How could one conquer without Christ? And Christ (so preached Alan of Lille, d. 1202) neither dwelled in the prelates owing to simony, nor in the knights owing to rapines, nor in the burghers owing to usury, nor in the merchants owing to their lies, nor in the plebe owing to theft. Only the poor of Christ could conquer the Kingdom.[53] Popular in this elective sense, then, but also in a cultural sense: Much of the shepherds' violence did not stem from a "popular" culture insulated from the culture of the ruling classes. First, the movement may have drawn from the Joachite prophecies produced during these very years. Had not *On the Prophet Jeremiah*, dating to circa 1243/1248, envisaged a wicked coalition between the Roman Empire, the Saracens, the heretics, a pseudo-pope and a "king with an impudent face"? Did not this Joachite tradition envisage a last world ruler who would coercively renew a depraved church? In this increasingly influential prophetic tradition, there were fantasies of bad, tyrannical rulers in church and state but also of a crowned reformer.[54] Like the hostile chronicler of Metz and Matthew Paris, the shepherds likely believed in a universal conspiracy, but with inverted actors: treasonous elites, bad clergy, and Jews, all in league with the Muslims. The shepherds may have been sensitive to the innuendos and accusations against the papacy. In having persecuted Frederick II, Innocent IV (r. 1243–1254) was Islam's objective ally. Was he or was he not that Joachite pseudopope?

More to our subject (but relatedly), the shepherds' violence consisted in a mimesis of the king's own measures. Prior to his departure, Louis IX had sought to reform the kingdom; he had also brushed against the pope and the clergy and rebuked them. As to the Jews, he had despoiled the hapless minority and sent the Talmud to the pyre. Louis' hatred for the Jews was public knowledge.[55] Possibly it was known that the pope had tried to limit the burnings; possibly it was known that allegedly the Jews in a daily prayer cursed three times "Church ministers, kings, and all others who are in enmity with the Jews," a prayer that also asked God for the destruction of the *regnum nequicie* (kingdom of evil). Recent scholarship has demonstrated that this was not only a fantasy: animated by their own eschatological calendar, which made possible the Messiah's return for circa 1240, some northern European Jews awaited with glee God's vengeance against the Christians and had even greeted Mongol victories with hopeful joy.[56] The papal legate, later legate and preacher for Louis' crusade, Cardinal Eudes de Châteauroux, had vigorously countered the pope's order of toleration and, in 1248, went on to burn the Talmud.[57] Thus, the *pastores* fought for the king's order, as they understood it.[58] William Chester Jordan has stated that "the Pastoureaux are substantive proof that the lower levels of society equated or could be convinced to equate their social and political well-being with the king's welfare."[59] No wonder, if the king had sent through his reforms the signal that the people were, collectively, the king of France and Holy Church. This all the more as the shepherds knew that Louis was the Mamluks' prisoner; and all the more as the Church's head, the pope, shamefully squabbled with Emperor Frederick II of Hohenstaufen and proved himself to be a bad, possibly even false, pastor. No wonder, if public opinion understood that the king's reforms were intimately intertwined with the crusading effort. And no wonder, finally, that (as Jordan underscores) substantial aspects of the shepherds' violence owed much to the royal spirit of reform.[60]

A Holy Warrior, the *Pastourelle* Jeanne d'Arc

The career of the patriotic Maid, Jeanne d'Arc, burned at the stake by the Anglo-Burgundians in Rouen (May 30, 1431), also intersects the themes of devolution, crusade, and reform. It was short lived, yet several clusters of sources—chronicles friendly or hostile, letters, the records of her trial and the process in rehabilitation (1450; 1455–1456)—allow the historian to triangulate her. This young woman had in common several traits with the *pastoureaux* (albeit with different priorities and intensities): her humble origins, her desire to purify the kingdom, and her focus on the crusade. Like the armed bands of 1251, the shepherdess had received a divine mandate to help a French monarch in distress. Her king was the beleaguered Dauphin Charles VII (r. 1422–1461), hemmed in a small corner of the kingdom by his English rival for the French throne, Henry VI (r. 1422–1471), and by the House of Burgundy, allied to the insular power.[61] In a classic study, Paul Alphandéry affirmed, using the typical French interrogative-positive mode:

> Is she not a *pastorella*, a poor child, this Jeanne d'Arc who wants to effect the coronation in Reims of the King of France, an elect king, king of the Last Days, and after that fight and vanquish the Turk, the apocalyptic

enemy who holds the Earthly Jerusalem? . . . The universal mission that Jeanne d'Arc proclaims demonstrates the force of the popular tradition of the crusade.[62]

Indeed, and the comparison can be pushed farther. Like the shepherds, Jeanne fought under Christ and Mary's patronage and carried a banner or banners related to the vision that had authorized her mission. Singular or plural, the banner seems to have combined the lilies of France with either Christ the Judge or Christ wielder of the orb, or a Virgin in majesty. This Christ, considers Colette Beaune, was the apocalyptic Judge of EndTimes.[63] Her confessor Pasquerel recalled "her banner, on which was painted a likeness of our Savior seated in judgment in heaven's clouds; and there was also there depicted an angel; he held in his hands a fleur-de-lys (*flos lilii*), which the likeness [of Christ] blessed." The lilies were, of course, Mary's flower; they were also the emblem of royal France, perhaps in Jeanne's understanding the Last Kingdom.[64]

Crusade—in essence, a universalist Christian dream—and nationalism also relate Jeanne to her contemporaries, the Hussites. These mostly Bohemian and Moravian reformers were "elects" with the mission to be better than all but also to convert all others. They were the "faithful Czechs" and a holy nation, *sancta natio*, because, in Ferdinand Seibt's words, they were "true to the religious, universally Christian task."[65] However, the Hussites came quickly to understand in a nefarious light the relationship between holy Bohemia and its king—first in his later years Wenzel IV (r. 1378–1419), then his half-brother Emperor Sigismund (r. 1419–1437). "Not to obey an evil prince is to obey God," intoned the popular Prague preacher Jan Želivský.[66] The Hussites shed monarchical sentiment and, facing a series of imperial crusades, progressively put on the back burner the universalism that initially had accompanied their nationalism.[67] The configuration was different with Jeanne. Christine de Pizan reported the Maid's program as follows: first, she would cast down the English, who had made French blood cry out to God (a reference to the classic Rev. 6); second, she would restore harmony in Christendom and, taking in the erstwhile English foe, lead a united army against the heretics; and third, she would destroy the Muslims.[68] Norman Housley has downplayed the crusading aspect of Jeanne's action, but Beaune has successfully defended it, noting in particular that the utopian and millenarian atmosphere present circa 1429 had to disappear in the trial held in 1455–1456 to rehabilitate the Maid: "Owing to their concern to prove the truth of Jeanne's prophecies, the royal theologians [of the rehabilitation trial] could only set aside a crusade that had never taken place."[69] In the late 1420s, the atmosphere was indeed apocalyptic. The very year of Jeanne's appearance, a Franciscan soon associated with her, Brother Richard, had preached eleven sermons in Paris and Boulogne and organized a bonfire of vanities. He had been in the Holy Land and there had met crowds of Jews who were flocking to Babylon in the erroneous belief that the Messiah had been born. This migration indicated the arrival of Antichrist.[70] The End was, therefore, in sight, and everything had to be righted, including social and political relationships.

As so often in the later Middle Ages, peace was a precondition to the last, apocalyptic crusade.[71] In the 1390s, for instance, one Robert le Mennot had sought to reconcile France and England, with the two kings going on a crusade against the Ottoman Turks.[72] Jeanne's famous Letter to the English, adjuring them to leave France to its rightful king, assured them that, if they made peace on her terms, they might "still join her company, in which the French will do the fairest deed that has ever been done for Christianity."[73] That "fairest deed" was—evidently—the war to end all wars, the last crusade.

But peace was also peace according to all senses of Scriptures. In devotional practice and moral action, Jeanne's spirituality was a spirituality of regeneration.[74] Like contemporary mystics, but also like the Hussites, Jeanne favored frequent Communion.[75] Her enemies reported she had taken the Eucharist one day three times and another day, twice.[76] The Hussite soldiers before Vyšehrad (1420) also listened to sermons and took a double dose of Eucharist before battle.[77] Other measures of purification that Jeanne took harked back to the First Crusade.[78] As also provided for by the Hussite Taborite commander Jan Žižka's military ordinance of 1423,[79] Jeanne chased away camp followers from her army (going as far one day as beating several such "women of ill fame" (*femmes diffamés*) and, in another instance, breaking her sword in the doing). Camp followers hampered diligent male service to the king. But more, as her confessor Pasquerel explained, she knew that God would punish the French for such fornications with defeat.[80] Like Žižka, she hated blasphemy and punished it.[81] Preventive measures accompanied these punitive gestures. She organized before Orléans collective prayers to Mary by her troops' clergy and pushed the soldiers to confession, lest they die in sin.[82] After the storming of a fort, she threatened to remove from her company any who would not confess and render graces to God for victory.[83] One witness in the rehabilitation trial, a canon of Saint-Aignan, Orléans, volunteered that she had converted to a better life some very dissolute men-at-arms.[84] Jeanne was rumored to detect married clergy.[85] She was known to be generous in alms and had reportedly said that she had been "sent to the poor and needy for their consolation."[86] Correspondingly, she also refused to eat food that had been plundered, even when the necessary victuals could not be had otherwise.[87] She "detested greatly the game of dice." As Malcolm Vale puts it, her army "was like a revivalist meeting in motion."[88]

The sources are difficult to weigh against bias, but Jeanne's moral concerns dovetail with those of her alleged confessor Brother Richard, of this man's putative spiritual master, Vincent Ferrer, and of their contemporary Bernardino of Siena.[89] To cite a treatise attributed to Jean Gerson and dating from right after Orléans, the *De mirabili victoria cuiusdam puellae*, the Maid had given four public "warnings of civil and religious order" bearing on the king, the princes of blood, the army, the churchmen and the people, all calling for "the same end: to bring one to live in righteousness, in pi[e]ty towards God, in justice towards other people, in sobriety, which is in virtue and temperance toward oneself."[90]

Jeanne would have taken the French and the English to fight the Hussites, according to Christine de Pizan and to a "Letter to the Hussites" attributed to the Maid.[91] But, unsurprisingly, since they were Christians as well and breathed the same rarified air of EndTimes, her would-be heretical adversaries too conjoined war, peace, and reform. This ideological configuration is encapsulated in the opinion of Jakoubek of Stříbro (or "of Mies") "on how to pacify the realm," which antedated the imperial and papal crusade against Bohemia. In the light of the breakdown of "peace with God" (and not yet of political peace with the Holy Roman Empire and its Czech Catholic allies), the Prague master called for the destruction of "the heresy of simony, adultery, fornication, concubinage, excess in temporal goods and secular lordship on the part of the clergy"; wanted the laity to be led into its proper calling; and opined that one should abandon "all customs that had been evidently introduced in the Christian people against Christ's Law."[92]

Yet, as in the case of the shepherds of 1251, the opposing side smelled a rat. In the Last Days, all Christians believed, there would arise many false prophets, who would mimic the Truth in order better to deceive.[93] All agreed on this, Hussites and Catholics, English, Burgundians, and Armagnac. There were many grounds on which Jeanne could be a false prophet, a witch even. One was related to warfare. Debates over Jeanne as warrior take us to the structural contradictions inherent in Christian political culture on the subject of violence. In Jeanne's case, it was doubted whether, under the New Law, which was spiritual in nature, a person could receive a mandate from God to realize the material prosperity of a kingdom.[94] It was also doubted whether such a prophet could prove his (in this case, her) mission through works of war. Did not the Letter to the English threaten "should they not obey, I shall have them all killed"?[95]

As Deborah Fraioli has shown, this issue was debated from the very beginning of Jeanne's entry onto the public scene, when she first approached Charles's court in 1429.[96] It also featured in her 1431 trial and condemnation. The articles of accusation, while concentrating on heresy and witchcraft, underlined her extremism at war:

> The said Jeanne, as long as she was with Charles, dissuaded with all her strength Charles and his people to apply themselves in any way in the direction of peace tractations or an arbitral sentence with the enemies. She always incited them to killing and to the shedding of human blood, arguing that peace could not be had but at lance's point and sword point. She said she had been appointed by God for this reason, because otherwise the king's enemies would not give up what they occupied in the kingdom. And to wage war against them in this way was one of the greatest good—so she said—that could occur for Christendom.[97]

Bloodthirstiness featured even more centrally in the English and Burgundian propaganda that followed and justified her execution. The pacifist strand in Christian theology (and probably also fatigue with war after decades of devastation on the French soil) expressed itself in this polemical context. Some of the advices (*opiniones*) given for the Maid's rehabilitation in 1455–1456 had to face the issue. Thus the lawyer Paul Pontanus had to invalidate the following proposition: "It seems to be proven [that she was sent by the Devil] by the reason given for her mission, that is, to make flare up the torches of war, and consequently, to make human blood flow, which the devils greatly desire. . . . Indeed, the perfect who assert that they are inspired by the Author of Light must not involve themselves in carnal wars, but busy themselves with spiritual warfare," as Gratian's *Decretum* had it.[98] Such was also, *mutatis mutandis*, the critique that the Hussite pacifist Chelčický levied against his bellicist brethren of Tabor: the last temptation of the Devil consisted in convincing Christians that the sword could be taken up for God's cause, on the model of Old Testament wars. And in a less radical fashion, the Hussite masters of the University of Prague considered material warfare, grounded in the Old Law, to be the less secure and more dangerous road to peace. Polemically, they juxtaposed in lists of damnable positions Taborite eucharistic heresies with Taborite willingness to shed blood.[99]

There are indications, though, that Jeanne, like Jan Žižka, fought, fought hard, and fought often without mercy. As one would expect, the more eloquent data come from enemies of the Valois cause. The anonymous chronicler known as the Bourgeois de Paris reported the sermon preached by the chief inquisitor at Rouen on May 30, 1431, in Jeanne's presence, recounting her crimes. Jeanne had gone "to the King of France. She had told him that she had come to him by God's command, that she would make him the greatest lord in the world, that it was ordered that all who disobeyed her should be killed without mercy."[100] The sermon underlined her severity, brutality, and blood-thirstiness, along with her superstitions and witchcraft: "In several places she had men and women killed, both in battle and in deliberate revenge, for she had anyone who did not obey her letters killed immediately without pity whenever she could."[101] She had, "ever since" leaving her parents, "been a murderer of Christian people, full of blood and fire, till at last she was burned."[102] This was the official Anglo-Burgundian line. Henry VI told Pierre Cauchon, the bishop presiding at the trial, that Jeanne had "committed and caused much murders."[103] The trial proceeding called her "rebellious (*sedici-osa*), a disturber of peace and an impediment to peace, a war-mongerer, cruelly thirsting for human blood and inciting to its shedding."[104] In her abjuration, Jeanne was forced to confess as much. She admitted that she was "cruelly avid for the shedding of human blood" ("desirant crueusement effusion de sang humain") and "was avid for strife."[105] Among particulars, she had ordered the beheading of the Burgundian captain Franquet d'Arras as "murderer, thief (*larron*) and traitor"; and Guichart Bouren had been drawn and quartered because he had refused to hand over Soissons.[106] Besieging towns, she allegedly offered stark alternatives (verbally or in letters). The pro-Burgundian Bourgeois de Paris reported that Jeanne threatened the Parisians: "By Jesus, surrender to us fast, for if you do not surrender before nightfall, we shall enter by force whether you like it or not, and you will all be put to death, mercilessly." The Maid had promised her men that the town would be put to plunder and those Parisians who resisted put to the sword or burnt in their houses.[107] The topic of blood shed by the visionary was a delicate one, as Jacques Gelu's careful retort shows:

> Even though she practiced weapons, she never called for cruelty, but was merciful to all those who fled to her lord the king and wanted to

abandon the enemy. She does not thirst for human blood, but offers to the enemies a peaceful exit to return to their own lands, and to the rebels [she offers] regress to their homes through a good obedience [to Charles] having received from the king indulgence and pardon. It is of course true that when having being asked to do what they should, they refuse to do it, she tries to accomplish [through warfare] what she was sent for, that is, to subjugate the enemies and put the rebellious necks under the yoke. Such indeed is the way of the common law (*juris communi*), in harmony with reason.[108]

Jeanne's banner was actually a flag of mercy, according to the rehabilitation trial. The Franciscan Elie de Bourdeilles testified that she "sedulously tried to avoid massacres of human beings, and it is for this reason, as she herself asserted, that she carried the banner on which was written 'Jesus Maria,' to avoid killing anyone. And she never killed anyone."[109] Other witnesses attested to Jeanne's care for the English as Christians (she made sure that wounded or dying poor soldiers received confession).[110]

But, despite Jeanne's defenders, there was some degree of accuracy in the Anglo-Burgundian accusations. The emblems of Christ or Mary were polysemic, since the Virgin was a figure of both war and peace and Christ the King of both vengeance and mercy (further, as we have seen, war and peace, being in a dialectical relationship, did not exclude one another). Jeanne's possibly contradictory practice—an oscillation between harshness and mercy—may not have been determined by the messiness of war alone.

The Old Testament authority Jeanne quoted (we have her authentic words) in proposing surrender to Anglo-Burgundian towns also authorized massacre if the proposal was refused.[111] Jan Žižka conducted war on the same scriptural basis, Deuteronomy 20, first demanding a peaceful surrender, then moving to slaughter men (sparing women and children) if the doors were not opened to him. Before Prachatice in November 1420, he offered to spare bodies and goods if the citizens opened the gates and allowed his troops to enter peacefully with Hussite priests and the Eucharist. Upon meeting an insulting refusal, the Hussite captain "raised his voice" and said, "I swear today to God that should I acquire" the city "by force, I shall allow none to live, but order that you all, as many as you are, be slaughtered." And indeed having stormed it, while women and children were spared, the men were either slaughtered on the spot or lumped together in a sacristy and burned in it. Here Žižka combined the Deuteronomic norm with the Maccabean example, the stormings of

Bosor and Carnaïm (1 Macc. 5.28 and 44). In the first city, the males were put to the sword; in the latter, having found refuge in the temple, the population was given over to the flames. When Žižka warred, the Old Testament models overrode chivalric courtliness.[112] Even without the deuteronomic sponsorship, the Maid could be at times "without pity." As much transpires in the *Chronique* that one of her closest associates, Perceval de Cagny, penned in 1436.[113] In one instance, Jeanne denied surrender to the enemies manning the Bastille of Saint-Lo, before Orléans: "Those in this fortress desired to surrender to her. She refused to take them to be ransomed; said she would take them against their will; and intensified her assault. And immediately the fortress was taken, and almost all of them killed."[114] Animated by a program of reform, conducting her war for France as a protocrusade, the Maid was dangerously relentless. How dangerous, in fact, was she?

Otherwise put, how far was the shepherdess Jeanne from the shepherds of 1251 or from the Hussites who ended up warring against their kings? Again, Perceval de Cagny gives a glimpse into her close entourage's opinions. After the Reims coronation, which Charles VII owed to the Maid, the king had proven himself tepid in reconquering his kingdom. Jeanne had disagreed, wanting to attack Paris, and the disagreement had led to her departure from Charles without taking formal leave. The king lacked fighting spirit.[115] Biting, if still respectful, comments against royal leadership suggest that the prophetess, like the 1251 Master of Hungary, might have turned against the Valois and his entourage had they persisted in not following her advice. This advice was bellicose. Like many a good Augustinian, like her near contemporary the Hussite Jakoubek of Stříbro, Jeanne considered that there existed such a thing as a "false peace."[116]

So how could saner heads, or holier heads, plead for a true peace? The archbishop of Reims' disdainful reaction to Jeanne's capture shows that she had become a liability for the peace party at court. The Maid had "raised herself up in pride"; she "did not want to trust advice, and did everything as it pleased her." He likely agreed with the Rouen verdict that she was an "impediment to peace."[117] One should also mention the dispute Jeanne got into with another visionary, Catherine de la Rochelle. Catherine was inclined to "journey to the Duke of Burgundy to strike peace"; against this diplomatic approach, the Maid retorted that peace would be won "only at lance's point."[118] There were even moments of veiled disdain for the king. In a letter to the people of Reims, Jeanne expressed doubt as to the prospects of the Burgundian truce and a very grudging willingness to uphold it: "If I keep them, it will only be to preserve the king's honor."[119] For Charles VII, then, it may have been a good thing that the Maid was burnt before turning against him, like a mad shepherd.

Peace, War, and the Commoner in the Hussite Revolution

Starting a decade before Jeanne d'Arc's short career, the Hussites had also flirted very seriously with antimonarchical sentiments. Their revolution involved a devolution, to groups well below the king, of the right-duty of resistance and rectification of the *ecclesia*. This process demands explanation; so does the rather sudden transition from pacifism to bellicism. This section will explore these intertwined issues.

The Hussites' violence has long been problematic to historians, especially those with sympathies for their ecclesiology and reformist ideals, considered as harbingers of the Protestant age. To the Czech scholar Amedeo Molnár scholarship owes the concept of a "First Reformation." This epoch spans the twelfth to sixteenth centuries, from the Waldensians and Hussites to the early modern radicals and takes in the bellicose Taborites and the Münster Anabaptists.[120] As conceptualized, these "First Reformers" kept to the scriptures and took the Gospel as a model for the Christian life; they were motivated by a stark eschatology that made them see the world as radically opposed to the true Church. To some, this category has seemed debatable. True to his convictions, the Mennonite scholar Murray Wagner (from whom this summary of Molnár's position is borrowed) had no doubts: "when the category of 'First Reformers' includes both absolute pacifists and apocalyptic warriors, the typology breaks down." Yet Wagner went on to open up the road for a refutation to his own objection: "Consistency [within this category that encompasses both irenists and bellicists] can only be found from a theological assumption that the same eschatological expectation can be expressed either through courage under suffering or, by ideological inversion, through courage to risk revolution."[121]

Accidentally or not, Wagner placed his finger on the issue's vital pulse. We are not dealing here with some wild in essence "numinous" à la Rudolf Otto, vacillating between a destructive and a creative face; we are in a Christian context.[122] Indeed, as James Stayer demonstrated, it is imperative to take into account such a "theological assumption." A theology that rejected the world (*saeculum*) was a determining factor for the Anabaptist groups, allowing both outcomes, bellicose and pacifist, purification of the world or separation from the world. Its modern-age relative is the well-known oscillation in American political culture between the poles of interventionism and isolationism. One is not here imposing "consistency" through theology as if this consistency had not been, from the beginning, present in a culture that was religious through and through. The theological copresence of bellicism and irenicism also means that one cannot too hastily see in the former (bellicism) the "inversion" of the latter (irenicism) and its companion (passive martyrdom), as if irenicism were somehow (historically or normatively) prior to the bellicism. To follow James Stayer, when a Christian considers the world to be hopelessly sullied, he or she can draw two consistent if mutually opposite conclusions: on the one hand, the one drawn by Tabor and Münster and, on the other, that of the Hussite pacifist wing and the disciples of Michael Sattler, Menno Simons, and other nonbellicose Anabaptists.[123] "Courage to risk revolution" did not, then, constitute an "inversion" of suffering; it was an option that enjoyed, structurally, a standing theologically equivalent with suffering.[124] We have already mentioned the Essenes of the Qumran scrolls as the first Abrahamic example for this position: convinced of the impurity of everyone but themselves, severely ascetic, and secretly waiting to take up the sword alongside God's angels against Belial's Kittim.

For the Taborites (as for many others) a religious understanding of good and evil, and of History (one can even say, a theological understanding of the same), was primary. But if the scholar accepts this premise, he or she still has to explain—and given the premise, understand in theological terms—how and why in 1419–1420 one wing of the Hussite movement crossed the divide from pacifism to bellicism.[125] It is beyond dispute that this crossing to violence was enabled and shaped by conjuncture. Sigismund of Luxemburg's crusade and his unwillingness to compromise or even strategize led many Hussites to despair.[126] Yet, as H. Howard Kaminsky underscored, in the face of force, the sectarian Taborites did have the option to withdraw or bend. Not only was it an option, but it would have been mandated by the irenic strand of theology and also by learned just war theory. They did not. Sociopolitical conjuncture, then, cannot have been the major determinant.[127] Without dismissing the impact of circumstances and the importance of context's noncultural dimensions, the historian must envisage how religious discourse itself could both smoothly evolve and radically switch from irenicism to bellicism, this without being a crass instrument that bent and bowed to fit needs and times.

Bohemian reformist religious discourse did evolve, a transmutation enabled by the exegetical tradition itself. There is a real continuum between the early and the late 1410s when it comes to imagined holy violence and its counterpart, "peace." Bohemian pacifism was a spiritual pacifism and, therefore, came alloyed with spiritual warfare. And spiritual warfare could include actual physical measures for a spiritual reform of clergy and laity, Church and society. For the Hussites as well as for Jeanne d'Arc, reality was not always what it seemed; something apparently good could be in actuality "false." There was, thus (as we have seen with the Maid), "false peace," just as there were (in the thought-world of late medieval nationalism) "false Frenchmen" or (preceding it, in ecclesiastical reformist conceptions) "false brethren." The belief in the presence among one's coreligionists or fellow-citizens of "traitors" may be a constant of fundamentalisms.[128]

The Hussite reform was about true and false peace. Jakoubek, whose notion of "peace with God" and its moral and institutional contents we have already mentioned, countered critiques of the Hussite push for Communion under both species (since the twelfth century, the Catholic laity had been allowed only the consecrated bread and excluded from the wine chalice). Opponents seem to have inveighed that this demand created disputes and disturbed "charity." Jakoubek retorted that the chalice works "for the elect's salvation and God's good pleasure" and that "it pacifies and increases charity" (the virtue that ties human beings together and to God). What the chalice "occasionally disturbed" was "a faked peace in riches, delights, secular glory and worldly alliance." Jakoubek went on: "The Savior said that the peace of evil men should be broken; 'I did not come to bring peace but a sword'. Indeed, the Gospel's Truth concerning communion under both species, just like other Truths, separates the elect from the reprobate, through their unequal lives and unequal wills."[129]

A Truth functioned like an ordeal: it forced people to take sides, for their salvation or damnation, and revealed who was with whom.[130] Elsewhere, in his 1417 *De quibusdam punctis* (antedating the Hussite wars), Jakoubek detailed the two peaces—calling them "unions"—with much more militant accents:

There are two sorts of unity or union. There is indeed a sort of union of evil men and hypocrites to transgress the Law of the Gospels. Christ came to destroy this union and its peace, and [brought] a sword to cut through it. . . . But a holy union in Christ consists in a holy observance of His evangelical Law. . . . And in order to establish this union in cities and communities, evangelical priests must *ex officio* destroy all mortal sins by their preaching the Gospel.[131]

Like Jakoubek, his mentor Jan Hus meant to disrupt the false peace. His attitude suggests how pacifism could become, through spiritual warfare, materialized. Hus was willing to become a martyr—the prototype of the spiritual warrior. He broadcast this readiness in a remarkable sermon in which he confronted his own excommunication and the accusations that he was a heretic. This envisaged martyrdom was bellicose: Hus linked readiness to suffer with the Old Testament's bloodiest internecine purge. The alternatives before him, he explained to his Bohemian audience, were indeed either the free preaching of the Truth or—and he was ready for it—forced exile or death in prison. But in the sermon's finale, Hus struck a far less passive note: "[Hus] exclaimed loudly in the vulgar tongue to the people, provoking it insofar as he could: 'Truly, just as under the Old Law God ordered through Moses that whomsoever wanted to defend God's Law should gird himself with the sword and be ready, it is necessary that we so gird ourselves and defend God's Law'."[132]

The passage of the biblical book of Exodus that Hus adduced, and applied to the people of Prague generically, is famous.[133] Having received the Law on Mount Sinai, Moses found the Israelites lapsed back into Egyptian idolatry. They were worshipping the Golden Calf. He called out: "If anyone is on the Lord's side, let him join with me," buckle up his sword, and slaughter "his brother, friend and neighbor." The tribe of Levi answered the prophet's call and slaughtered about three thousand among the recreants (Exod. 32.26–28). Moses exclaimed: "Today you consecrated your hands to the Lord" (and he rewarded the Levite tribe with the hereditary priesthood). The so-called *Ordinary Gloss* filled in: "Consecrated, in executing this vengeance out of zeal for the Lord."[134]

Did Hus mean physical violence, or was he rather calling his audience to gird itself with the spiritual sword—meaning, for spiritual warfare—without military action? Purely spiritual warfare was what, in the 1420s, in the face of the Catholic crusade, Jakoubek of Stříbro and Nicholas (Mikuláš) of Pelhřimov advised as the "more secure" road, reserving for the constituted powers of Romans 13 the peril-prone application of just war. This was as well the stance of the ultra-pacifist Chelčický, who considered every violence and coercion to be devilish and pagan in origin and nature. Yet it is likely that Hus hovered in his sermon between letter and spirit, on the—since the First Crusade well-traveled—continuum between the two warfares. One can parenthetically leave emic logic and its principled dichotomy and observe that, practically speaking, there cannot quite be a clear chasm between physical coercion and moral rebuke and that, to fight spiritual vice in a collective, one must act physically, on the sociopolitical plane.

Jan Hus's analogies pointed in this direction. He had borrowed from Wyclif the solution to bad clergy's refusal to reform itself, its coercion by lay lords. Wyclif (and Hus following him) had adduced a troubling biblical exemplar. Forty-two years after the Lord's Ascension, Titus and Vespasian had punished the Jewish priests—as had been pleasing to God, by despoiling them of their goods and even killing them. On this basis, God would allow secular lords to inflict an identical penalty on "modern-day" (*moderni*) delinquent clergy.[135] This argument from ancient to modern was a dangerous one, given that Vespasian and Titus were types for the crusaders. And being themselves typologically linked with the Maccabees, they were understandably types for the violent purification of the Church. Bad clergy, also argued Hus following Wyclif, could "destroy the *regnum*" and, thus, kings had a duty "to resist" them, starting with the duty of fraternal correction common to "kings, princes and all temporal lords."[136] Radical reform was a spiritual crusade.

When the reforming priesthood failed, explained Jakoubek in his *De quibusdam punctis*, the laity was to take up the task. Jakoubek did not in this text lay the duty of correction on individuals, nor on the king, but on urban officials, the members of the city council (*scabini*, échevins):

When they [the reformers] cannot effect this through the Word, the échevins must do it by the power God conceded to them, destroying all disorders and sins, that is fornications, adulteries, usury, greed. They must throw down and root out all other things that have been introduced against Jesus Christ's Gospel, so that the Lord God and Christ may be their Lord and that they may be His people, and that He may dwell with them into eternity, giving them His peace.[137]

Thus, before the conflict with Wenzel of Luxemburg and his half-brother Sigismund had exploded into the open, Jakoubek effortlessly laid upon urban officials the task to purify Prague, the capital city of the Luxemburger dynasty. Jakoubek would by 1420 move away from radicalism and become the main figure among the Prague masters interested in finding a middle course between the Catholic Crusade and the Taborite holy war. He admitted then that his earlier pronouncements had fed bellicism and radicalism.[138] Perhaps they had inspired the following:

Whosoever does not defend Truth, is a traitor to Truth. . . . Just as a priest has the duty (*debitor est*) to preach freely the Truth that he heard from God, so the layman has the duty to defend faithfully the Truth that he heard from the priests (demonstrated in the Sacred Scriptures). Should he not do so, he would betray Truth. It is for this reason that Ambrose said quite aptly that sometimes a people can be raised up to punish perverted men's sins. Indeed, just as the clergy can judge and condemn the pope should he err from the faith, so perhaps can the people do the same vis-à-vis its superiors who would try to destroy the Christian faith. . . . True and just warriors must also take stock of that strongest of men, Mattathias the Maccabee.[139]

In 1420 and 1421, the moderate Prague university men literally danced around the question of the commons' right of resistance and the related issue of the authority to purify the *ecclesia*. The Catholic crusade forced them to allow armed force, and consider that it could be wielded by lesser figures or groups below the higher aristocracy; the gruesome exactions of the Taborites and other chiliasts led them to place barriers to devolution. All their learned pronouncements and responses were far from consistent. Or rather, rules left open exceptions, which themselves were hedged with cautionary qualifiers. In 1420, masters Jakoubek of Stříbro and Křišťan (Christian) of Prachatice were tasked to answer several questions. One was "Should secular lords be sluggish to the point that they refuse to defend the Truth with the sword that they have received [as magistrates, cf. Rom. 13], can and should the believing communities that are under them defend it [the Truth] with the material sword, that is, by killing its adversaries physically"? The masters' rescript strongly and at length took position. The sword of Romans 13 had been given to princes; the apostles had preached patience to believing communities; and just war involved its authorization by a constituted power, not by individuals. Yet it conceded "that the secular lords can resist God and His law to such an extent that God could by Himself take [legitimate] power (*potestas*) away from them, and it would be licit for communities (*communitates*) stirred up by Him for this task to defend the evangelical Truth actually (*realiter*) and not figuratively (*fantastice*)." This armed defense, "however," was to take place "always preserving the right order [of just war] in conformity with Christ's Law, and not in the absence of a divine inspiration or a secure revelation or proof." The masters continued warning against an easy belief that God had deprived lords of their *potestas* and against any hasty popular assumption of this duty, especially if their lords' defects were not evident, not notorious, and not "manifestly beyond correction." They ended their discussion with a reminder that this was a perilous road, the safer road being the traditional road of patience and spiritual combat.[140] In another rescript, Jakoubek also danced, stating preference for pure spiritual warfare; conceding that "higher secular powers" were "allowed to wage war" on the authority of Romans 13, "yet incur in so doing a great peril to their souls"; forbidding the "subject people . . . to usurp, against [established] order and against a lord, that sword from the higher powers," unless it had "an authentic and special revelation."[141]

In practice, the communities had seized the sword, as anticipated by Jakoubek's own peace-time appeal to the city councilors' duties. After the crusading army's first defeat before Prague (1420), "the Lord Mayor (*magister civium*), consuls, échevins and the whole *communitas* of the city of Prague" directed a letter at their opponents. It reasserted that "the faithful in the Kingdom of Bohemia stand, and with God's help propose to stand either through death or through life" to defend the Four Articles. Concerning the purification of Bohemian society and especially its church, the letter further affirmed that it should be performed "properly and reasonably" by those to whom it pertained. The authors shared the moderate university masters' subtle touch; their text, indeed, added, "Every faithful servant of Christ and true son of his mother the Church is held to persecute in himself and in others each of these vices and all of them singly; and hate them and detest them as the Devil himself, preserving nevertheless in all matters the order and status in which he was called."

"Order and status"—one must assume that only clergy and officials would discipline clergy; the individual ordinary laymen might have had limited prerogatives, like exhortation. All the same, the authors—the officials of Prague as representatives of the civic community—claimed for themselves the sword of Romans 13 against "anyone attacking us on the account of this and seeking to divert us, against God," from the Four Articles (identified with the "Truth of the Gospel"). He would be resisted "as a tyrant and a most cruel antichrist all the way to the end" with "the power of the secular arm bestowed upon us."[142]

In Tabor, the apocalyptic and chiliast atmosphere obviated this scholastic need for and disposition to balance. The Taborites expected the ultimate destruction of royal power at EndTimes and the assumption of its punitive role by the saints: "In that second advent of Christ, before the Day of Judgment, kings, princes, and all ecclesiastical prelates will cease to exist. And there will not be in the Kingdom thus restored any tribute or tax-collector, because God's sons will trample underfoot the necks of kings, and all kingdoms under heaven will be given to them . . . . And thus the elect will no longer suffer persecution, but will render retribution."[143] Experienced reality is often messier than theological positions, but, in the Hussite century, the rebels lived the devolution of the duty to rectify the Church through the sword. The hymn "Arise, Great City of Prague" rang forth: "Whoever is a friend of the Law of God / Will overcome the cruel Holofernes," like Judith, a private Jewish widow who had beheaded the Chaldean general.[144] Pavel Soukup underscored how the persona of the *miles christi* allowed a democratization of these tasks: mass knighting on the battlefield became "one of the rituals of holy war warranting to Hussites the status of Knights of Christ."[145] It enlisted a plurality in the task of reform. The Taborite captain Jan Roháč of Dubá wrote to Lord Oldřich Rožmberk that it was "proper for every Christian knight (*keždy křesľansk rytiř*) to put on his belt (*pés*) and sword (*meč*) and do his best in order to spread the Truth of God and to praise the holy writings so that the knaves of Antichrist (*neřédy Antikristovy*) might be destroyed."[146]

And destroy Antichrist's minions the Taborites did. On account of the Four Articles, they "hate[d] all bad Christians"[147] and moved against them, living out biblical scenarios. The moderate Hussite Lawrence of Březová, horrified, criticized their exterminatory warfare, but one must lend credence to his chronicle's description. The Taborites mustered some of the scriptural passages that the more eschatologically minded First Crusade chroniclers had employed:

A priest holding high on a raised staff a wooden monstrance containing Christ's venerable sacrament always preceded them. And these priests and other clergy incited these armed vassals and toga-wearing rustics to fight festively, saying that God would deliver to them every place that their feet trampled [cf. Josh. 1.3]. It is indeed written in the Psalm. . . . The meek shall inherit the earth and take delight in the multitude of peace [Matt. 5.5]. These priests labeled "meek" their peasant brethren who were more cruel than all the wild beasts of the forests, these people who killed men mercilessly and joyfully, as if they [their victims] had been dogs. They asserted that they were following God's will in removing them from the earth, and that they were angels of God and true knights of Christ sent to avenge the insults done to Christ and the holy martyrs [cf. Rev. 6.10]. And in this way one separates the chaff from the wheat with a winnowing fork, and throw[s] it out of the threshing floor, and destroy[s] the chaff from this floor [Luke 3.17, Matt. 3.12], understand, Christ's Church. Furthermore, if any among their brethren was killed by their enemies, they immediately buried him with joy in any place, and stated that he had died for the cause of God and would enter Heaven without any purgatorial time after this earthly life (they deny the existence of Purgatory), and would return imminently with Christ to judge with other brethren the enemies of God's law, and to purge His threshing floor.[148]

Familiar are the motifs of the harvest and the threshing floor; the merciless slaughter; the idea that the dead brethren will return along with the saints and fight for the living. The parallels between texts produced by two different historical moments—the First Crusade and the Taborite holy war—cannot be explained as clichés or *topoi* imposed on the chroniclers by a literary tradition (as can be the case in descriptions of heresies). They demonstrate that scripture itself animated the warriors of EndTimes. Moderate Hussites and Catholics painted the Taborites as false holy warriors, mimicking perversely the awesome practice of washing one's hands in the blood of the ungodly. This does not entail, though, that some radicals did not actually do so. For that earlier apocalyptic moment, the First Crusade, an Armenian source reported— approvingly—that in 1099 the patriarch of Jerusalem had ridden through the street of the stormed city, slaughtering, and then had washed his hands in the Church of the Holy Sepulcher, reciting "May the Just rejoice in the Lord, contemplating the vengeance whose minister he is; he shall wash his hands stained with the sinner's blood" (cf. Ps. 57.11).[149] And Pope Paschal II (r. 1099–1118), in a letter composed in 1100, beseeched God that hands "that He had consecrated with the blood of His enemies would" remain "unstained to the end."[150]

As Tabor's military might declined and its eschatology became less urgent, its bishop Mikulas of Pelhřimov stepped back into predominantly spiritual warfare. Yet he did not dismiss entirely material warfare waged in the light of the Spirit. God's elected share "waged war throughout its life . . . since [the saints] have renounced every loyalty to the world, the flesh, and their bodies."[151] As Kaminsky explains, the fundamental struggle with Antichrist was conducted through the preaching of the pure, but this warfare did not preclude a lesser material warfare, problematic as it was to Mikulas.[152] Thus, the trajectory of Hussite violence traversed three territories. In the 1410s, combat had been purely spiritual, to the exclusion of the material sword but holding it in potentiality; in 1419–1420, it had become quite physical but waged in the light of the spirit; in the 1430s, it had turned primarily spiritual again but allowed, if reluctantly, the sword.

Sanctified Minority Violence from the Reformation to the Present: Of Legality and Legitimacy

The three evidentiary clusters just discussed demonstrate, first, how the royal duty of defense and regeneration of the realm might devolve upon *communitates* (as the Hussite debates put it) or even individuals. These duties might even devolve to the people against the king. Second, debates around Jeanne, and also in Bohemia between bellicist Taborites, conservative Prague university masters, and pacifists like Petr Chelčický, show how the simultaneous holiness of peace and of war—which we have seen exemplarily presented in the *Ludus de Antechristo*—generated constant and unsolvable tensions. They were fruitful. The oxymoronic duty to shed blood yet not to shed blood, discussed in Chapter 2, and the duty to reform, even against the king, were arguably among the most long-lasting gifts of late medieval Christianity to modern European political culture. We now follow them, briefly, into centuries closer to the present—briefly, because that part of the narrative is well known.

Devolution was a position available to all sides during the Wars of Religion—including the English Civil War, whose motivators combined constitutional issues and piety. Theories of resistance circulated between Protestants and Catholics.[153] The Ligueur justification of tyrannicide, likely influenced by second-generation radical Calvinist discussions, grounded itself on the notion of individual responsibility before God.[154] Right after Henri de Valois' assassination, a Ligueur pamphleteer posited that tyrannical kings were effectively savage beasts, "noxious" and "devoid of reason." Such men were de jure not princes; they became "declared public enemies, and as such and in consequence"; the pamphlet went on: "they are placed as a prey to anyone who wishes to, dares to, and can, kill them." The last Valois king of France's alleged anti-Catholic tyranny constituted a case of extreme necessity. In such circumstances, "everyman is *gendarme*," a man-at-arm (in fifteenth-century French usage synonymous with knight).[155] Jacques Clément's individual regicide, hence, was fully justified. Among the Ligueurs, the model of the commons' revolt under Maccabean leadership, in refusal of the idolatrous Antiochus's authority animated resistance to Henri. A tract possibly owed to Jean Boucher presented the one "who fights for God's honor and for Catholic religion" as immune to sin in killing or in being killed and as a magistrate. This holy warrior, "protector and defender of Catholic Christians," argued the author, did "not have the power to bear arms without a good and just cause, all the more as he is a minister of God for the punishment of malefactors, and for the praise and security of good men." More even, resistance allowed the "little people" to present to God "as a great and pleasing sacrifice" their hatred for the devious king.[156] Like the medieval crusade, religiously grounded rebellion allowed everyman to accumulate credit with Heaven.

In the British Isles, against a king, Charles I, suspected of crypto-Catholicism, and against his partisan Bishop John Maxwell (author of a *Sacrosanct Majesty of Kings*), Samuel Rutherford's *Lex, Rex* (1644) presented the Scottish Presbyterian position as follows:

> If the king refuses to reform religion, the inferior judges and assembly of godly pastors and other church officers may reform; if the king will not . . . do his duty in purging the House of the Lord, may not Eli[j]ah and the people do their duty and cast out Baal's priests [3 Kings 18]? Reformation of religion is a personal act that belongeth to all, even to any one private person according to his place.[157]

Here was brought in action the individual duty to resist, expounded about a century earlier by Calvinists such as John Knox, Christopher Goodman, and John Ponet. Covenanted individually with God, the Christian, if he or she did not oppose blasphemy, risked God's wrath in this world and damnation in the other. Therefore, even an individual had to rise up against religious tyranny. This was, to cite Knox, "required of the whole people, and of everie man in his vocation" as a member of this whole.[158] In 1649, five years after Rutherford's treatise (and referring to its position), the Puritan divine John Goodwin justified a fortiori a (purged) Parliament's duty and right to condemn Charles through necessity and exception. Duty, on the neglect of authorities, "devolves (as it were) of course, unto those who are not Magistrates; yea by way of duty and necessity unto such, who have opportunity and means to perform it." The "generality of the people" and even individuals ("every man in his order and place") were "to interpose and act in an extraordinary way, as *viz.* by executing Justice and Judgement in their land, upon the default of those, who bear the sword in vain [Rom. 13.4, that is, inferior and superior magistrates], and therefore expose the land unto a curse."[159]

Goodwin and Rutherford's colonial contemporary, Edward Johnson, reported with approval (or invented) the same sort of authorization applying to everyman. The New England Pequots, on top of the alleged murder of two traders, "had blasphemed the Lord." A reverend in Hartford, Connecticut, had told the militia raised to punish these natives that "you need not question your authority to execute those whom God, the righteous judge of all the world, hath condemned for blaspheming his sacred Majesty, and murthering his Servants: every common Souldier among you is now installed a Magistrate."[160] As in Tabor, God's cause allowed the most extreme devolution of the sword.

But God's cause allowed also the constitution of new political entities. In the absence or failure of established institutions, devolution could lead to the creation of a new magistracy to defend what was right. This, submitted representatives of the English New Model Army, had taken place in Scotland with the 1638 Covenant—"contractually" and "by consent." The Presbyterian Scots had had to "associate in covenant" because "they had no visible form either of Parliament or King to countenance them" in the defense of "principles of right and freedom" (Charles I had tried to impose on the Scottish churches a more pompous liturgy smacking of Roman Catholicism). The English army men, likewise, argued that the representatives, could join "together to insist upon the settlement of those freedoms which they have purchased with their blood out of the hands of the common enemy, which God hath subdued by them."[161]

New political creations, even though brought into existence by an active minority, derived their legitimacy from their resistance to evil, justified in the light of future History. The December 1648 purge, which eliminated from Parliament a majority of its members—those who still recognized Charles I as king and would have refused to try him for treason—was justified as the action of a virtuous minority.[162] After Charles's execution, Goodwin reflected that the "Generality of the Nation" disagreed and hated the regicides but that future generations would embrace what had seemed "new and strange." He mused: "Every succeeding age hath an opportunity of being wiser than the former.[163] This orientation to a future to which one grants a normative valence and this idea of missionizing by the elect would be systematized by the French Revolution.

Devolution had been refused by Martin Luther. He was here arguably faithful to Paul's quiescence. The apostle seems to have redacted his call for Christian obedience to the prince, Romans 13.1–7, in the expectation that the end would soon come and make the this-worldly order bygone history. Apocalyptically minded like Paul, Luther grounded in eschatology his justification of authorities' repression of the German peasants. His ferocious reaction to the rebellions of 1524–1525 made place for a crown of martyrdom acquired by dying while committing atrocities for the sake of civic order. "Stab, knock, strangle them at will, and if you die, you are blessed; no better death could you ever attain"—Friedrich Engels's paraphrase simplifies but is true to the drift of Luther's *Against the robbing and murderous hordes of peasants* (1525), an exhortation to the German princes to massacre and execute by all means possible the devilish rebels.[164] Luther envisaged no mean reward:

> Thus, anyone who is killed fighting on the side of authority [*oberheyt*] may be a true martyr in God's eyes, if he fights with the kind of conscience that has just been described, for he walks in God's Word and in obedience [to Him]. Conversely, anyone who perishes on the peasants' side is an eternal firebrand in hell, for he bears the sword against God's Word and against obedience [to Him], and is a member of the Devil.[165]

Luther did require due Christian process. The German princes and lords were exhorted, as a first step, to pray to God for help against the Devil because they were fighting not "only against flesh and blood" but also against Satan, best met with prayer. Notice here the adverbial "not only" (*nicht alleyne*), already met in a crusading Catholic reading of Ephesians 6 and in Haymo of Auxerre.[166] Next, they were to offer terms to the peasants. Finally, if this did not work, they would take up the avenging sword entrusted to them by God.

That Luther wanted the princes to try to strike up peace before striking off heads may indicate that he was not 100 percent certain that the hour belonged to the sword alone. He left room for mercy toward those "poor" who had been led astray by the rebels.[167] But the pamphlet's ending is indicative of Luther's mindset. It was apocalyptic. As we have seen with other Christian groups, EndTimes mandated unforgiveness: "If anyone thinks this too hard, let him consider that rebellion is intolerable and that the destruction of the world is to be expected any hour."[168] So close to the End, and probably already at the End, there could be "no time for sleeping, no place for indulgence or mercy. It is the time of the sword and wrath (*des Schwerds und Zorns Zeyt*), not the time for grace (*der Gnaden Zeyt*)."[169] This was a wondrous time in which a prince could earn his paradise by shedding blood more easily than other men gained theirs by praying. Death, then, if it came to the lords, would be "in the service of love, to save your neighbor from hell and the devil's hands."[170]

This call to holy war did not escape criticism. Soon Luther found himself forced to pen an apology for his bloodthirsty pamphlet, which he titled *The Open Letter on the Harsh Book*. But characteristically stiff-necked, he retracted little. One could not be merciful where God wanted vengeance. Yes, indeed, the Church as Kingdom of God was what one would now call a "pacifist" sphere. But the other realm—which, for Luther, was not necessarily un-Christian—was "peace making." As in the Carolingian age, peace making was violent:

> The Scripture's passages which speak of mercy apply to the Kingdom of God and to Christians, not to the kingdom of the world, for it is a Christian's duty not only to be merciful, but also to endure every kind of suffering—robbery, arson, murder, devil, and hell. It goes without saying that he is not to strike, kill, or take revenge on anyone. But the kingdom of the world, which is nothing else but the servant of God's wrath upon the wicked and is a real precursor of hell and everlasting death, should not be merciful, but strict, severe, and wrathful in fulfilling its work and duty.[171]

The two violent eras that, in late antique and medieval theology, bracket the ordinary, meek time of the Church legitimated for the Luther of 1525 the prince's coercive, merciless power. Lutheran princely wrath, while it took exemplars from the harsh Old Dispensation, was also a forerunner (*vorlaufft*) of hell, that is, of God's EndTimes vengeful Judgment.[172] As against Thomas Müntzer or the Münster Anabaptists, Luther rejected the sword's devolution and called instead for pitiless coercion. Paradoxically, each side derived its position from Sacred History's ruthless End: Müntzer and the Münsterites to allow the commons' fighting and killing; Luther to explain the princes and nobles' duty to suppress disobedience and their chance for martyrdom's crown. We shall not spend ink to evaluate the verdict of J. N. Figgis: "Luther . . . refuses to make that sharp distinction of sacred and secular so characteristic of the Latin world; and paves the way for the exalted theory of the State entertained by Hegel and his followers"; he is, thus, the "spiritual ancestor of the high theory of the State."[173] Nor even the less categorical yet similar opinion of Ernst Troeltsch's *The Social Teachings of the Christian Churches*.[174] In fact, Luther (when facing Charles V) and the Lutherans did develop a theory of resistance to persecuting magistrates based on the private law right to repel force with force.[175] But the point of the preceding paragraphs is to underscore how a shared outlook on History's course fed both princely and popular understandings of violence, the violence of magistrates who represented the human community and the violence of commoners who constituted an elect vanguard.

*   *   *

The French Revolution inherited, probably via Jansenism, what stands behind this paradox: the dialectic pairing of two beliefs, the one, in the necessity of a unanimous consensus, the other, in the existence of a minority endowed with quasi-prophetic clear-sightedness. The "general will" could, thus, mysteriously be borne by the few.[176] Robespierre expressed the minority's positive influence with an optimism and irenicism quite acceptable to today's democrats:

> Being not any party's property, the majority cannot be permanent. Since it is the commonwealth's property, and that of Reason Eternal, it renews itself with each public deliberation. When the assembly recognizes an error (as it sometimes happens), the minority becomes the majority. The General Will is not formed in shadowy parleys, nor around ministers' tables. The minority has everywhere an eternal right: To make Truth's voice be heard (or what it considers to be Truth's voice.[177]

But in Paris' streets, the clear-sightedness of a minority expressed itself with a butchering aggressiveness. After the September 1792 mass slaughter of counterrevolutionaries (including priests) in their Paris jails, newspapers could both express distaste for the atrocities yet present them as rightful and useful.[178] To cite Danton, "No human power was in the position to stop the excesses of the nation's vengeance."[179] The Parisian mobs, which conceived of themselves as the people in its universality, claimed sovereignty with these September massacres. They had the duty to "avenge" the Revolution. Arguably, they reacted to the National Assembly's perceived default in sovereignty, its inability or unwillingness to protect the Revolution and punish its enemies.[180]

Popular violence for justice could, thus, be seen as simultaneously illegal and legitimate. The 1792 formula was far from new, as two examples will suggest. The 1391 Valencia pogroms and forced conversions of Jews were perpetrated by mobs against the king's express prohibition and in subversion of his special rights vis-à-vis "his" Jews. Popular violence also accomplished what he himself, as God's representative, was duty bound to execute. The transgression was legitimized by numerous miracles pointing to divine authorization. A recent study detects at play in 1391 two forms of sovereignty face to face, the sovereignty of law and the sovereignty of miracle.[181]

Closer to the French Revolution, during the Wars of Religion, the same dynamic was at play. In 1562–1563, Calvinists took short-lived control of a few cities. Mobs cleansed churches of Catholic relics and holy images. Because this was violence from below, absent any magistrate, the reformed leadership in Lyon felt it necessary to pen a justification:

> as concerns the [destruction of the] images, they [the Catholics] also know well in conscience that it was done without our knowledge, and that one cannot prevent the people from doing this, moved (*esmeu*) by the ardent zeal it has for God's veritable service. He, in His just judgment, excited it [the people] to do this, just as one reads in many places in the Bible that such acts happened several times, by an extraordinary call [of God, *vocation*], praised and made exemplary for the execution of His will.[182]

Calvin's successor in Geneva, the leading theologian involved in Condé's revolt of 1562, Theodor Beza (Théodore de Bèze) could therefore both state that popular iconoclasm was against all law, including God's, therefore reprehensible, yet see in it the working out of Providence, so a higher legitimacy. "The deed is in itself according to God's will," he wrote, "[God] Who condemns idols and idolatries, and . . . it seems to me that in such a general thing ["une chose si generalle," meaning, a collective action or a matter touching the generality of human beings] there is some secret counsel of God, Who maybe wants by this means to shame greater men through lesser ones." Beza abstained, therefore, from condemnation and sought instead to moderate this sort of impulsiveness. In his *Ecclesiatical History*, the same Beza recounted how the Prince de Condé had sought to prevent iconoclastic disorders in Orléans. Even though he and the Admiral de Coligny ran about beating their zealous brethren with sticks and swords, it availed them nothing. Ready to shoot a man who was trying to throw down a religious image, Condé was begged by this iconoclast: "My lord, be patient; wait until I have toppled down this idol, and the let me die if it so pleases you." This forced Condé to let the purification of Orléans proceed all the way, since "this deed was more God's deed than human." Elsewhere Beza opposed inspired popular zeal to mere "men": "The impetuosity of the people (*des peuples*) against the images was so great that it was impossible for men to resist it." And with "men" he implicitly gestured at the Prince de Condé, initially angered at disorderly violence for religion's sake![183] We shall meet in Chapter 7's discussion of the sublime Raymond d'Aguilers' analogous understanding of popular action against princely will.

"The people" can legitimately but illegally usurp princely violence; the street—sans-culottes and others close to the Parisian *commune insurrectionnelle*—

can act in the stead of the Assembly. So can a terror group in the name of the Proletariat. The revolutionary, according to the Rote Armee Fraktion's 1970s manifestos, is endowed with the consciousness of "its historical mission to be a vanguard" and also with a "humanity" (*Menschlichkeit*) conditioned by his or her awareness to be fighting against an oppressive system (*Herrschaftssystem*).[184] Yet the West German terroristic vanguard expressed some degree of scorn for, or at least despair about, ordinary "humanity," including the proletarian masses.[185] The RAF considered that, given the apathy induced by material prosperity (a bourgeois superego built in the workers' heads), it could not wait for "the approval of the masses" but had to bring them to a new consciousness through combat.[186] The RAF's dismissal of the Proletariat, and its de facto usurpation of the role Marxist theory attributed to the workers (that of a revolutionary motor of History), was, it has been argued, grounded in the philosophical idealism that György Lukács (an author whom the RAF read) had reinjected in traditional Marxism. While ideally the Proletariat was the Subject of History, it was de facto prisoner of "false consciousness."[187] We are familiar with this configuration. Christians sometimes separated radically the not-so-visible ensemble of the elect, with which they identified themselves, from the wider visible Church, while believing that they struggled for it. They saved the *ecclesia* despite itself. Visible too with the RAF (as discussed in Chapter 3) is a dynamic observed with the shepherds of 1251. The antagonism between the entity managing the vaster human group—the state—and its terroristic opponent was sharpened not only by ideological differences but also by shared values. These values the state had betrayed.[188]

Even in a nation chosen by God or History, a bellicose minority can be in the right as against a blind majority. And this too constitutes a transgressive intervention of God in History (or of History's future into History's present). Lecturing to the Good Shepherd Church in Sandy, Oregon (June 21, 2003), Lieutenant-General William Boykin commented on the disputed Gore-Bush presidential election of 2000: "The majority of Americans did not vote for" George W. Bush. Rather, it was a miracle. He was "in the White House today because of a miracle. You think about how he got in the White House."[189] Trumping legality, the miracle occurred in an urgent eschatological framework: "God put him there for a time like this"—the combat against the Devil and his human agents revealed by September 11, 2001. And thus, Bush's election by a (one must assume in its critical core, righteous) minority had universal ambit. Boykin expanded: "God put him there to lead not only this nation but to lead the world in such a time like this."[190] The general's fundamentalist audience did not protest against this implicit disdain for democratic process; whatever its belief in the legitimacy of majority voting in general, it was trumped by the miracle and the exception. But the framework was still an equation between America and Christendom. At the same church, the general emoted both that other countries "have lost their morals, but this is a Christian nation" and that America is "a godly nation."[191] Another service at which Boykin spoke, and which mentioned the election miracle, had opened with a pledge of allegiance to the U.S. flag. This oath was tellingly phrased: "I pledge allegiance to the Christian Flag, and to the Savior for Whose kingdom it stands. One brotherhood, uniting all Christians in service and in love." The congregation then pledged allegiance to the Bible.

The disregard for the majority also meant that, for Boykin the patriot, and for his Oklahoma audience, some fellow Americans did not belong. America was a chosen nation, but not all its citizens were predestined to salvation, for example, eight soldiers who featured in the same speech. Boykin recalled the ill-fated 1979 airborne expedition, launched under Jimmy Carter to free the Americans held hostage in Tehran. In Egypt, before boarding the helicopters, he had led a prayer, beseeching the Lord to protect "by Your might and power and Your grace" the soldiers from their foe. Eight men had not partaken. They died in the collision between a helicopter and a C 130 refueling plane that forced the expedition to abort. Those forty-five other soldiers, however, who had prayed along, were preserved from the ball of fire, untouched "except for a few singed eyebrows and some singed hair."[192] Boykin's remarkable position complexifies any neat equation between a nation and the ensemble of the elect. His stance is located on a jagged spectrum whose one extreme is constituted by the far more exacting schemes of the Essenes in the War Scroll or of Raymond d'Aguilers and his circle. America is not the ensemble of the saved, but it harbors nestled into itself the core of the forces for good. This complexity characterizes also Timothy LaHaye's highly popular *Left Behind* and *Babylon Rising* series. How many "false brothers"; how many men and women so deeply entangled in error that their salvation seems well nigh hopeless! LaHaye's "Christian" (meaning, predestined and evangelical) heroes—a thin minority of (mostly) Americans—do face, and turn against, national figures and institutions, including the CIA and the FBI.[193] In these groups' imagination, the latter are, knowingly or unknowingly, part of a gigantic conspiracy, led by Antichrist, to uproot religious and political liberty. For liberty, one should be ready to die but also to coerce and to kill. The paradoxical relationship between freedom and constraint constitutes the theme of the next chapter.

Chapter 6

Liberty and Coercion

It is more noble . . . to fight at length for Holy Church's freedom (*libertas*) than to lie under a wretched and diabolical servitude (*servitus*). Indeed, the wretched—understand, the Devil's members—fight in order to be oppressed in wretched servitude to him; contrariwise, Christ's members fight in order to lead these same wretched persons back to Christian liberty.

—Pope Gregory VII (1081)

We shall hammer out peace
Between God and us, [hammer it out]
On Him with strong blows
As long as He shall avenge us
From the accursed Snake
Who quickly will fall into rage
Forbidden to enter the center.
Then shall we be put back into freedom.

—Artus Désiré (1561)

One must wage a long war against all pretensions; and since self-interest in human beings cannot be vanquished, it is only through the sword that a people's liberty can be founded.

—Louis Antoine Léon de Saint-Just (1794)

To his fellow prelates, fiery Pope Gregory VII presented two alternative combats, fundamentally asymmetrical insofar as one led to liberty and the other to bondage. Just as zealous as the pope, the French Ligueur preacher Artus Désiré sketched resounding images: a forge hammering peace into existence, with God the Avenger as anvil; an allusion to Eden and Paradise as a charmed circle from which Satan is excluded; and the Christian dream of return to liberty. For both Catholics, freedom would come about through holy warfare. A few centuries later, Saint-Just, to posterity known as the "exterminating angel," did not propose any other solution. For his associate Maximilien Robespierre, both "corruption" and patriotism used violence. "Terror" was indeed, as Montesquieu had it, "the spring-coil of despotic government." But in the present revolutionary emergency, the revolutionaries were right "to tame through terror the enemies of liberty." This was legitimate, since this terror was paired with "virtue," just as in the Middle Ages fear was paired with love.[1]

Libertas, to Die for and to Kill for

For much of Western history, liberty has been a common component in the constellation of conceptions that envelope violent episodes. One fought to put oneself, or others, or one's nation, or the Church, into freedom. Yet discussions of "freedom" were also usually accompanied by a discourse on coercion. Human beings should be compelled to liberty, either more softly through persuasion or (as Gregory VII's word choice suggests) through force. What liberty was in essence and how coercion was conceived allowed the pairing of the two to be less of a glaring contradiction and more of a coherent formula.

What was liberty? First of all, it was liberty from sin and from its consequences, including eternal death, a liberty obtained thanks to Christ's sacrifice of Himself on the Cross. Conversely, the Augustinian position, adopted by countless preachers, held that, when human beings were—in the words of an Episcopalian toward the end of the American Civil War—"servants to sin, unwilling to govern themselves," they became "incapable of governing others, and . . . yielded themselves the slaves of despotic power in some form."[2] Or in the words of Gregory of Tours (the same author who exhorted Catholic Frankish kings to wage war, materially, against the Arian heretics whom Saint Hilary had fought dogmatically), rulers, who "earlier, in chains, served the root of evils," were now to fight a civil war within their souls against vices and "serve freely" their "head," Christ.[3] This "liberty," *libertas* in Latin, did not correspond to negative freedom, the freedom from all constraints.[4] Irenaeus, in the last quarter of the second century, explained how the Word of God's liberation of humankind actually entailed that "the decrees of liberty were amplified and the subjection owed to the [heavenly] King augmented." Freed from sin and death, one owed to one's liberator not to lapse; rather, one was to honor Him and obey the Ten Commandments. These Old Testament mandates had not been abolished "but fulfilled and amplified and dilated in us." There was, thus, "as it were, a greater operation of liberty, and a fuller (*plenius*) subjection and affection rooted in us towards our Liberator."[5] Gerd Tellenbach, in his classic *Libertas: Kirche und Weltordnung im Zeitalter des Investiturstreites*, showed long ago how this conception dominated the Middle Ages: true freedom was service to Christ.[6]

Consistent with the fundamental belief in the systemic presence of deceitful, diabolical simulacra of the good, there existed both a true and a false freedom. Theodore de Bèze (Beza), Calvin's successor, bemoaned toleration as a "diabolical liberty." It had "filled Polonia and Transylvania with so many plagues of opinion." "Liberty of conscience," if one understood by it that "every man may worship God after what manner he will himself," was a "diabolical opinion," a tolerance or sufferance for spiritual suicide.[7] On such grounds, Oliver Cromwell shoved back into the throats of his Irish Catholic opponents during the siege of Waterford (1649) their plea for "liberty of conscience." If they meant by it "a liberty to exercise the Mass," they were cannon fodder.[8] A good century later, observing the different courses of the two great eighteenth-century Western revolutions, the American and the French, and convinced of his country's providential and exceptional bond to freedom, Timothy Dwight stated his obvious preference. The French experiment had been marred first by the Terror in the name of *liberté*, then by various dictatorships in the name of the people: "The liberty of Infidels was not the liberty of New England; [and] . . . France, instead of being free, merely changed through a series of tyrannies."[9]

Libertas meant the disappearance of those constraints that blocked the road to the Good, a Good that one would be subsequently bound to serve. Hence the perhaps odd usage, in the late antique and early medieval Latin church, of *libertas* to mean freedom from heresy and adherence to orthodox dogma. This definition becomes less puzzling when one considers its antecedents. In the age of the persecutions, it had meant freedom from having to sacrifice to the polluted pagan gods. Said Tertullian, polemicizing against the Gnostics, Valentinians, and other "opponents of martyrdom," "martyrdom frees . . . from idolatry."[10] This was the liberty that the Jewish rebels of 66–73 C.E had fought for, and the early Christians followed in this tradition.[11] After Constantine's conversion, and especially after Theodosius I's prohibition of public temple worship (388–91), the problem shifted from paganism to heresy. Understandably, the Roman papacy and its allies frequently used the expression "freedom of the apostolic faith" to mean the exclusive validity of dogma approved by the pope and protected by the emperor, with its freedom from sullying religious deviance. And deviance there was, since the fourth-century emperors' preference for Christianity had brought into the open dogmatic debates and amplified them. The first controversy to flare up in public opposed two factions of the North African church, over the status of clergy who, during the Great Persecution of 303–306, had handed over the Scriptures to the pagan persecutors. Both sides ended up appealing to Constantine, and imperial involvement (reluctant at first) generated debates over coercion, which we shall return to. The second controversy concerned the divinity of the second person of the Trinity (the Word, which had become flesh in Christ) between so-called "Arians" (the followers of the priest Arius) and "Nicenes" (who held to a version of the decisions of the 325 Council of Nicaea). The influential Nicene bishop Hilary of Poitiers (ca. 315–367) told the Arian-leaning emperor Constantius II (r. 337–361) that Catholic bishops sought the "freedom of the Faith from contamination by the Arian sect" (*a contagione Arriani nominis*). By this, Hilary meant that the orthodox should not be subjected to heretical dogma. A century later, Pope Leo I (r. 440–461) demanded of emperor Theodosius II (r. 408–450) "to give freedom to the Faith that he ought to defend, which [freedom] . . . no force and no earthly terror will be able to take away." And in an address to emperor Marcian (r. 450–457), Leo equated the "freedom of the apostolic faith" with being "purified from the contagion of the diabolic dogma" of Monophysitism (the idea that in Christ the human and the divine had been fused into a single nature, *physis*). This return to dogmatic security was the "peace of the whole church."[12]

Over time, the definition of heresy, and therefore that of freedom, varied. An interesting example is provided by the Episcopal Church, in the context of the American constitutional dogma of the separation of Church and State. Unlike most U.S. Christian denominations, the Episcopal Church long remained reluctant to drum for the Civil War. The 1862 convention's opening sermon called on participants to pray "for her freedom from the introduction in her Councils of any worldly or secular subject that might dim her beauty and lessen her influence in the world." "Liberty" was invoked in its ancient sense of freedom from a heresy, but, refreshingly, this heresy was the "Puritan" militant entanglement in politics—the holy war that other Northern churches ferociously promoted from the pulpit and in their periodicals. Into 1864,

Northern Episcopalians and their *American Quarterly Church Review* pleaded for a reform that would start from a conversion of human hearts and move outward to institutions; lambasted radicals on both sides; and sternly criticized Northern abolitionists as "Infidels" and "Puritans," children of Oliver Cromwell and imitators of the French Revolution, who would "try to exterminate" perceived "moral and social evils."[13]

The Good was often materialized in an institution. Precisely because they fostered the religious welfare, bishoprics, monasteries, and other ecclesiastical entities claimed the right to be served. As recently elucidated by Jehangir Malegam, conversion from sin and reform meant the sundering of chains binding to evil custom and evil institutions and attachment to good spiritual bodies through bonds (*vincula*) as substantial as the ones just broken.[14] As such, the latter, positive institutions were to receive freedoms, plural (often synonymous with privileges, immunities, exemptions, or exceptions from rules or laws).

For freedom(s) so deservedly claimed, and for the freedom to speak out for such freedom(s), one had the duty to risk one's life. The First Crusade, fought to free the holy sites from Muslim filth and domination, including from the dues and humiliations that the heathen rulers of Jerusalem reportedly imposed on Christian pilgrims, entailed martyrdom. Analogously, in the following century, Thomas Becket, archbishop of Canterbury, stood ready to be killed for the *causa ecclesiae*, "the Church's cause." By this expression, Thomas's friends and hagiographers understood the freedoms of the Church, a bundle of rights limiting the authority of the Plantagenet kings, a bundle in which the archbishop included the obedience of English bishops to the papacy.[15] This notion countered a recent assertion of royal power in the Anglo-Norman realm. With the Constitutions of Clarendon, Henry II (r. 1154–1189) had sought, in particular, to allow the king to screen appeals to the pope; to settle whether possessions litigated over were in essence secular or the product of charitable gifts to the Church (thus the case would go either to lay or ecclesiastical courts); and to prevent churchmen from leaving the kingdom without royal consent. Henry also wanted the Church to defrock criminous clerks after a guilty verdict rendered by a secular court of law. In the polemics of the conflict, the expression *causa ecclesiae* paralleled *causa Dei*, "the cause of God" for which crusaders willingly died. Thomas, reported one author, had felt the weight of his duty the night before the Northampton assembly of October 11–12, 1162. Henry had threatened him with beheading or imprisonment: "As he himself explained later . . . his whole body trembled; he feared less death than chains, lest he would lose the freedom to speak for the Church's cause." One can understand why Henry would have wanted to silence Thomas. A cleric's speech was supposed to be free and biting, on the thundering model of Paul's First letter to the Corinthians, written, commented Tertullian "with bile . . . bombastic, indignant, contemptuous, comminatory, and arousing hatred." Tertullian, the fiery Carthaginian jurist, appreciated the apostle's tone: "How public and free his reproach, how drawn out the blade of the spiritual sword (*machaera spiritualis*)!"[16] The king knew his prelate's Tertullian-like personality. For the sake of fortitude, a pious man advised the archbishop to celebrate the Eucharist in honor of Saint Stephen right before going to the court. Thomas complied; and he challenged his king, spectacularly entering the royal assembly with a cross held in both hands. By this gesture, he conveyed his defiant willingness to suffer like Stephen, the first martyr.

Medieval Christian *libertas* thus had both a transcendental dimension and specific, sometimes institutional, contents.[17] This conjunction survived into the modern age. For American colonist preachers of the French and Indian Wars era, "liberty" denoted national independence, or constitutional rights, or spiritual freedom, or all these simultaneously.[18] They were to be fought for, necessarily with virtue;[19] even more, they were founded on martyrdom. The colonial "fathers"—so explained evangelist Samuel Finley in 1757— had "purchased this godly heritage [of liberty and pure Christian religion] for us at the price of great labour, and much blood."[20]

Freedom called for martyrdom; it also called for holy war to put humans "into freedom," in Artus Désiré's expression. There was no opposition between the two. During the Third Crusade (1189–1191), Becket's successor to the See of Canterbury led a contingent of crusading knights to the siege of Acre, behind a banner representing the martyr.[21] The First Crusade was waged to avenge Christ and "vindicate" back for Christendom lands lost to Muslims, including their holy keystone, Jerusalem, and Jerusalem's own holiest keystone, the Church of the Holy Sepulcher. *Vindicare* straddled the semantic realms of vengeance, recuperation, and liberation. Jerusalem's freedom was all at once freedom for its churches from Muslim domination, freedom for its liturgy from being sullied by heathen rites, and freedom for pilgrims from being overtaxed and blasphemously mishandled when entering the city. As discussed in Chapter 2, for many in the eleventh century and after, the bellicose work of crusading liberation of the holy places went hand in hand with ecclesiastical reform.[22] Then as now, different freedoms could be piled up and seen as a single complex. During the eleventh century, reform had often meant on the ground that ecclesiastical institutions should possess their lands in full property. Robert II of Flanders (d. IIII) linked his forthcoming "journey to Jerusalem to liberate God's church, which savage pagan nations had so long trampled underfoot," to a donation, through which he meant to propitiate God's help for this labor. Count Robert had obtained the land, formerly granted as a fief, back from its current holders, "free (*liberum*) from every due (*exactiones*)"; he donated it on the Lord's altar "similarly free, to be" the canons' "perpetual allodial possession" (meaning, in full ownership).[23] And on his return from the Holy Land, in 1101, proudly adorned with the epithet of *hierosolymitanus*, the count carried on a small work of reform. He gave to Saint-Donatian of Bruges some freedoms. He wanted, he explained, to "exalt through the grant of liberty" the churches constructed by his ancestors and to "preserve them from now on under the protection of peace, so that, after this puny earthly dwelling shall have dissolved itself, I may obtain an eternal mansion in Heaven, where are the highest peace and perpetual liberty." This was the same Robert who, at Pope Paschal II's behest, would soon attack, in a *bellum Dei*, the city of Cambrai, loyal to the excommunicate and simoniac king Henry IV.[24] There were, for Robert and many others circa 1100 and afterward, two ways to put God's church into freedom. One was reform; the other was the sword. Both allowed the enjoyment of "perpetual liberty"—from sins and from demonic onslaughts.

Liberation from error might necessitate the freedom to preach. Christians waged war for the liberty to missionize others into liberty, in the Near East or on the Slav frontiers or at home. A chronicler recounted disapprovingly how some Hussites had fallen into extremism. Initially, the movement wanted "freedom to preach and . . . communion [under both species, bread and wine] for the people" (1414). In 1419, it came to "heavy conflicts and wars . . . under the pretext of freeing Christ's Truth, and in particular [of allowing] communion with the chalice." The moderate Hussite chronicler Lawrence of Březová condemned the horrors perpetrated by men "who said they had taken up weapons for the liberty of God's law against all the servants of Antichrist."[25] In matters of freedom, the Catholic side agreed with the radical militants. Its crusading liturgy hoped to propitiate God for His help, in order "that all adversities and errors may be destroyed, and that Your Church may serve You in secure liberty (*secura libertas*)."[26]

Free Will, Good Will, Coerced Will

One fought for one's freedom; one also fought to compel others to freedom.[27] The dominant Christian position has long been that entry into the Faith should not be coerced.[28] Right before Constantine's conversion, Lactantius proposed, for instance, to debate religious matters with pagan priests, "using words (*uerba*) rather than blows (*uerbera*)," so as to ensure that conviction would be an "act of the will" (*uoluntas, acte uoluntarie*).[29] It was the dominant position, but was never the only one. Mid-fourth century, ca. 343–350, Firmicus Maternus exhorted Constantine's sons, emperors Constantius II and Constans, to destroy the cult of idols in the empire. Pagan diehards, he wrote, "fight back, craving their own [self-] destruction with headfirst cupidity." But God has entrusted the ruler with the highest authority to cure them: "It is better that you free unwilling people, than to grant destruction [damnation] to people who seek it." Drastic force was called for; Firmicus drew on an old precedent, the Roman consuls' suppression of the indecent Bacchanalian rites in the second century B.C.E., with "avenging swords" (*uindices gladii*) and the death penalty (*animaduersio*); he also adduced Old Testament laws and examples. That only one manuscript survives, and that no one cited the work, suggests that his position was not too popular, at least in the earlier centuries.[30] In the main, the churches were much more willing to constrain heretics than pagans. Relatedly, in the High and Later Middle Ages, and beyond, crusade versus heretics was more urgent than crusade versus pagans. Mid-thirteenth century, the canonist Henry of Susa (Hostiensis) would privilege the *crux cismarina* (taking of the cross on this side of the sea) against schismatics, "in order to preserve the unity of the Church" (*pro unitate ecclesie conservanda*), over the *crux transmarina* (overseas cross) against Muslims to recover the Holy Land.[31] Entry into the Faith was one thing; apostasy or deviation from it was another. This willingness was visible even prior to Constantine's momentous adoption of Christianity, in the age when the increasingly intolerant Roman state harshly prosecuted the monotheistic sectarians. That North African hardly prone to compromise, Tertullian, had staked circa 200 C.E. that "those who deny the good should not be pleasantly persuaded until after they have submitted. Heretics should be compelled to do allegiance, not enticed. Induration should be conquered, not persuaded."[32] Tertullian's words suggest that it did not take the conversion of the Later Roman Empire, a state prone to religious coercion, for Christianity to be infected with a taste for force in matters of belief and cult. After the emperors' embrace of Christianity, Augustine rejected the forced conversion of pagans, but, when it came to religious dissenters (as we have seen with Chapter 3's elucidation of the trope of madness), he reasoned as Firmicus: the Donatists could not be allowed spiritual suicide. Wrote the good bishop, discussing the *circumcelliones*, roving bands of armed schismatics: they could only be cured "by being bound by the chains of the [secular] laws (*legum uincula*) as if phrenetics."[33] Compulsion through fear of the laws, simply put, would lead to salvation (of course, if God's grace also intervened). *Ubi terror, ibi salus* (where there is terror, there is salvation), wrote Augustine, *O saevitia misericors* (O merciful cruelty), anticipating the famous Jacobine "terror, salutary terror."[34]

The Church was, thus, more ready to coerce to the true Faith heretics or schismatics than pagans. The normal rules of war might be laid aside against the former. Glossing the Deuteronomic passages devoted to war, the authoritative Dominican commentary produced under the direction of Hugh of Saint-Cher in the 1230s bemoaned that Moses' "moral precept" not to cut down fruit-bearing trees to make siege machines was "ill observed today." But the *Postilla* went on to add that there was a dispensation to this rule, "when there existed necessity, as when the Church fought against heretics or schismatics." To cut down all trees could "coerce them faster to desist [from error], and return to the Faith and the unity of the Church."[35] The Dominican team compiled its commentary right in the wake of the Albigensian Crusade (1209–1229); and Hugh, as cardinal, would later preach crusades against the Hohenstaufen princes.

Yet concerning both heretics and pagans, the Church's position was not simple; as often, several voices coexisted.[36] According to Thomas Aquinas, if a person agreed with another not out of his or her spontaneous will, but compelled by fear of suffering some evil, this "concord" was not a true peace.[37] This position may have been fuelled by doubts as to the immediate efficacy of forced conversions. In the Albigensian Crusade's aftermath, the Council of Toulouse (1229) provided that heretics who became Catholics out of fear of death (as opposed to spontaneously, *sponte*) should undergo penitential imprisonment, taking precautions that they could not corrupt others in the prison. Unlike those who had spontaneously returned to the fold (and so had been condemned to a much lighter penance), they were not to be trusted.[38] But practical considerations were not alone at play. High Scholasticism's doubts on coercion were in harmony with contemporary theories of peace making, which, from the tenth century on at least, insisted that defeated parties should ideally come to surrender "willingly" (*voluntarie*)—whatever that meant.[39] The criterion of will was taken up in thirteenth-century ecclesiastical law:

> It is contrary to Christian religion to compel anyone who has always been reluctant and has thoroughly spoken out against [conversion] to receive Christianity and remain a Christian. For this reason, it is not absurd that other [interpreters] distinguish between unwilling and unwilling, coerced and coerced. There is [on the one hand] the man who is violently drawn into Christianity by terrors and tortures, and, lest he incurs harm, receives the sacrament of baptism. And [there is on the other hand] another man, such as the one who comes to baptism insincerely and takes on the seal of Christianity. The latter man, since he is willing [to convert] conditionally even if not absolutely willing, should be coerced to observe the Christian Faith.[40]

A fine, fine distinction! As we shall see, the Devil was in the details. There was indeed "coerced" and "coerced." Where did acceptable coercion end, and where did unacceptable coercion begin? Before turning to this quandary, however, we must examine two other logics, which pleaded in favor of compulsion. One logic involved the belief that the will could be reformed;[41] the other logic operated from the point of view of absolute justice, which mandated the acknowledgment of the Word's power on the eschatological horizon. From this standpoint, coercion was good. The ultimately wicked provided a limit case. In the Gospels, the demons, willy-nilly, acknowledged loudly and painfully the authority of the Lord, Whose presence tortured them (see, for example, Mark 5.6–7). In hell, explained Counter-Reformation scholastic Francisco Suárez (1548–1617), the damned are forced to render an outward cult to God. Against their will, they bow to Him, recognizing His Lordship:

> [Question:] *Does there inhere religion in the damned?* [Answer:] . . . Even though the damned are coerced (*coguntur*) to bend a knee to Him (according to this passage of the Letter to the Philippians, 2.10, "Every knee should bow [to Christ], of those that are in heaven, on earth, or in Hell," as many interpret it), nevertheless they do not do this out of virtue, but out of necessity, because, whether they want it or not, they are coerced (*coguntur*) to recognize Christ as God and Lord. [When] the damned show Him signs of reverence, it is only because of a wicked

intention, or because God coerces them through the ministry of His holy angels and makes this a necessity.[42]

Suárez did not discuss whether the damned's outward display of subjection might not lead to the instillment of inner faith, so to a change of will, a theme to which we shall return. Given where these reprobates were—in Hell—one must assume that this was no longer within the realm of the possible. Furthermore, the Spaniard's inquiry addressed a specific early modern context. The sixteenth and seventeenth centuries were acutely concerned with the issue of outward forms of respect rendered to a heretical prince (sometimes within ceremonials that were confessionally marked). In the wake of the Reformation, which had produced Catholic aristocrats under Protestant princes and vice versa, Suárez and others now distinguished between, on the one hand, religious worship, which was fundamentally interior yet involved external display (while not absolutely needing it), and, on the other hand, political reverence, which was outward and could be without internal conviction.[43] In the following century, both Thomas Hobbes and Baruch Spinoza would propound that the State could demand outward religious obedience expressed in public ceremonial forms and leave private conscience intact.[44]

A second logic, just alluded to, pleaded in favor of force in matters of faith. Suárez's medieval forebears had envisaged a positive effect of outward compulsion on the will. It could be reformed. Trust in the efficacy of compulsion inspired the Inquisition. The Dominican and Franciscan friars who staffed inquisitorial missions did send to the stake obdurate heretics. But they did so less often than the man in the street now believes. The inquisitors favored what Bernard Gui presented as a "spiritual" destruction (conversion "from heresy to the Catholic Faith") over physical annihilation through the secular arm and the pyre.[45] To make heretics convert, the friars used a variety of penalties, ranging from pilgrimages to distant sites to the wearing of demeaning clothing marked with yellow crosses and long-term imprisonment on meager fare.[46]

All these penalties that came short of the stake were penitential. Christine Caldwell Ames has recently shown how the Dominican Inquisition's coercion of heretics was of one piece with the friars' own self-understanding and their conception of the Christian community. Christendom was a society composed of different grades of penitents. The Dominicans, like all monks, mourned their own sins and coerced flesh and will. An elect group, they led other groups in doing the same, including the most sinful of all, the heretics.[47]

In conformity with this understanding, the ultimate coercive act at the End of Times, the Last Judgment, would mean the purgation of all, differentially. So the massive thirteenth-century Dominican primer on the Bible, the *Postilla* directed by Hugh of Saint-Cher:

> In the First Advent, [Christ] came with dew; in the second, He will come in fire. The first advent was an advent of grace and pardon; the second will be an advent of vengeance and punishment [*pœna*, meaning also torture]. And further, He <u>shall come in fire</u>, because fire will precede Him, and will set aflame His enemies around Him, and will <u>purge</u>, understand, the elect.[48]

Circa 1108, Guibert of Nogent did not understand the grand apocalyptic event of his own times much differently. The crusaders were wielding twin fires. The first, loving "spiritual teachings," consumed "sins among the gentiles" and "incorporate[d] into the Christian Faith" those pagans destined to salvation. The second, the fire of war, burnt the reprobates as if straw and wasted them away in a just and vengeful massacre.[49]

As with Suárez's discussion of Hell—this extreme realm in supernatural geography—the Dominican *Postilla* and Guibert constitute a limit case—at the endpoint of temporality. But within time, too, the will could be purged and transformed. Thomas Aquinas, who expressed doubts about the quality of coerced peace pacts, was consistent in holding that "coercion and violence are contrary to the will." But he also affirmed that compulsion had its use for those humans who were prone to vice and beyond persuasion (as opposed to those virtuous people whose will was in harmony with God's own will and with the law). Law restrained "by force and fear" the wicked-willed from perpetrating evil against others. It had a second effect: it worked on them to the point that, over time, they became habituated to doing good and did good willingly. The "discipline of the law" was, thus, a form of training that modified the will.[50]

The Dominican is not cited here because he is famous but because he is representative. Aquinas followed a line inaugurated by Augustine, who had been heavily excerpted by twelfth-century canon law, the law of the Church.[51] Facing the Donatist madness, the bishop of Hippo had come to abandon, circa 405, his earlier rejection of force.[52] His adversaries were so tied up in the bonds of custom, which hampered their will, that they could not see the light and return to the fold. Coercion, wrote Augustine, had been effective on diverse populations. There were, first, those who had refused to learn the

Catholic Truth, but a "goad of terror"—the fear of loss of temporal possessions to confiscation—made them explore this Truth, which they would never had done had they been materially secure. There were, second, those who had already known the Truth (as they now confessed), but who had been up until this point held back by custom (*consuetudo*), that is, by the bonds that tied them comfortably to their heretical communities. Coerced, they now rejoiced: "Thanks be to God, Who ruptured our fetters (*vincula*), and transferred us into the bond of peace (*pacis vinculum*)." False rumors had "terrified," third, others away from entering the Church, rumors that they "could not have known to be false, unless" they entered it; and they would not have entered it without compulsion.[53] Some Donatists, fourth, convinced by Catholic arguments from reason and Scripture, had wanted to rejoin the Church, but they had feared, reported Augustine, "the violent enmities of spiritually damned human beings." Good fear would counter these bad fears: "When salvific teachings are conjoined to useful terror, as a result, not only does the light of Truth expel the blindness of error, but also the force of fear ruptures the chains of evil custom (*consuetudo*)."[54]

Augustine's position became canonical. Pope Gregory VII, among many others, believed in the need to forcefully break bonds that chained humans onto the road to damnation. The pontiff invited bishop-elect Adalbert of Acqui to struggle alongside him against clerical incontinence and "Simon Magus" (the personification of the selling and buying of holy things) "with the shield of Faith and the helm of salvation" (cf. Eph. 6.16–17). The new prelate was to help spiritually the Patarene Erlembald (d. 1075), this "most strong knight of Christ," who led the struggle in Milan against the simoniac and married clergy. By so doing, Adalbert would offer the "hand of freedom" to people "bound by the chains of death" (*uincti catenis mortis*). In a written letter at the same time, Gregory exhorted Adalbert's neighbor, the bishop of Pavia, to the same task and called Erlembald's mission "God's war" (*bellum Dei*).[55] A few years earlier, the monk Peter had shown, as it were, the light concerning simony to the Florentine clergy by undergoing a trial by fire. With it, "Christ gave his people from the fire's midst a verdict [against simony] clearer than fair weather, brighter than the sun, more open than any word and more certain than any sight."[56] The ordeal's flaming rage enlightened. So did the burning of heretics at the pyre. For one participant at the Council of Constance (1414–1418), the wondrously pungent stench emitted on the pyre by the crackling flesh of the false martyrs Jan Hus and Jerome of Prague sealed as one among several miracles the healing of the Great Schism.[57] A century later, early modern Calvinists practiced iconoclasm as a terrifying enlightenment. The spectacular destruction of Catholic idols, unmet by any divine vengeance, was to provoke a change of heart. Papist ceremonialism was a "folly" that had to be parodied, defied, and cured through iconoclastic violence.[58]

The physics of conversion led from fear to love, or rather, with more complexity, they began with *timor pœnae*, fear of punishment—which was sometimes a fear of future tortures in Hell, but more proximately, the "fear to suffer some evil, . . . some illness . . . , or damage, or bereavement, or the loss of some dear one, or exile, or condemnation, or prison, or some tribulation"— and ended on a "chaste fear" (*timor castus*; cf. Ps. 18.10) that was conjoined to love for God.[59] This transit mechanism was related to the chemistry whereby love for God precipitated itself into zeal for God and into hatred towards His enemies, a staple of the French Wars of Religion also present in the medieval crusading era.[60] Right before Henri III's assassination, the Parisian Ligueurs had defied the impious king, presenting to God "as a great and pleasing sacrifice the hatred we have for you and our abhorrence for your misdeeds." And soon enough, Jacques Clément had perpetrated regicide. God, it was said, had made the young man enter ecstasy and recite this militant Psalm (138.21–22): "Have I not hated them, Lord, those who hated You, and have I not shriveled in sadness against Your enemies? I have hated them with perfect hatred."[61] Clément's deed was an act of "charity": he had put his life on the line for his own. This love was a "Christian force, which hungers and thirsts for justice . . . through which the Apostles were killed by the sword."[62] Mid-thirteenth century Cardinal Eudes de Châteauroux explained this process of sublimation to the crusaders:

> Conversion thus happens through love. And when someone converts to the Lord through love, he renounces the world (*mundus*) and everything that is of the world, so that he may not love them. And when his love of God grows, so that it becomes zeal, or when his love is turned into zeal, then this renouncement [is turned] into tedium, so that he cannot stand this world any more and he casts it off altogether. This happened to saint Paul who was converted to God through love. This love was converted into ardor and zeal and turned his fondness [for the world] into hatred, so that he cast off everything that was of the world.[63]

The Dominican's logic provides us with an emic point of entry into the duality of Christian asceticism. Love of God, being refusal of the world, leads either to total rejection of involvement in the world or to radical purification of the world.

Augustine, during the years in which he busied himself with the North African schism, had developed a theory of the two fears, in particular in his *Concerning Grace in the New Testament*.[64] The first fear, "fear of punishment," *timor pœnae*, belonged essentially to the Old Law; the second, "chaste fear," *timor castus*, to the New Law. Christ's First Advent had effected the transit from one era to the other and from one fear to the other. But, within this present age of the New Law, the opposition between Old and New was miniaturized and reproduced. When offered conversion (or less momentously, ethical betterment), the human being was invited to travel, individually, from fear of punishment, gendered Old, to chaste fear, gendered New. Augustine elsewhere invoked the example of Saul-Paul, initially a persecutor of Christians. On the road to Damascus, Saul, "who saw nothing [of the Truth] with his open eyes," had been thrown down and blinded corporally. God had so smitten him that he "who had raged in the blindness of infidelity would be pushed to desire light in his heart." Following this divine intervention, the persecutor had been compelled to seek healing, physical and spiritual, from his Christian enemies and had converted. Commented Augustine: "A great fear forced [him] into love (*caritas*)" so that "his love, made more perfect, expelled fear." The bishop of Hippo invoked this apostolic exemplar to justify coercing the Donatists.[65]

The two fears, *timor pœnae* and *timor castus*, were connoted sociopolitically. Terminologically, this is brought home by Peter Lombard, who in his *Sentences* (late twelfth century) considered that *timor castus* was synonymous with *timor amicalis*, fear for friendship (*amicitia*, since Aristotle the basis for free human associations, including the polity).[66] As Augustine had explained, what the human being feared at this second, better stage was the loss of association with God, Whom the convert now loved.[67] But more to our point, the whole thrust of the Augustinian argument on the two fears and two loves involved the loaded status opposition between slave and free. Conversion (or simply ethical betterment) was a movement from slavery to freedom. The Old Law, a law of fear (symbolized by Ishmael, Abraham's son by the slave woman Hagar) constrained into fearful slavery to itself humans who would otherwise have been slaves to sin. As Gratian summarized it, "the Ancient people were forced to observe the law by fear of punishments."[68] The New Law of grace (symbolized by Isaac, Abraham's son by the free woman Sarah) was different. Had not Paul explained that, with Christ's lawgiving, humankind "did not receive anew, in fear, the spirit of servitude" (Rom. 8.15)? Indeed, another sort of fear befitted "those who live by Faith, are heirs to the New Testament, and have been called into freedom."[69] As Tellenbach and others have taught medievalists, this freedom also bound to service, if to a quite different service. There were, thus, two fears and two servitudes, but the higher servitude paradoxically encompassed freedom, since "those whom a chaste fear subjects to Christ are truly free."[70] Righteous coercion, hence, led to liberty and was therefore not antithetical to it.

Coercion and liberty thus stood in a paradoxical relationship; constraint was both acceptable and unacceptable. Christianity both had experienced Roman persecution and believed in the need to discipline its own (a tension that lasted well into the age of divided religious confessions, the sixteenth century of Reformations and Catholic Counter-Reformation). Augustine's Sarah and Hagar interacted hostilely, signifying respectively, the righteous persecution inflicted on dissenters and the dissenters' illegitimate resistance to the righteous. Sarah, the free woman, figure of the True Church and of the Celestial Jerusalem persecuted the servant woman Hagar, "or rather Hagar by her pride persecuted more Sarah than Sarah persecuted Hagar by coercing her."[71] By the turn of the fourth to the fifth century, when Augustine wrote his influential tractates and letters, the Roman state was squarely on his Church's side, and it loaned its coercive powers against the Donatists. Augustine denied the equivalence between his side's violence and that of the schismatic resistors. His position became so canonical that even a rebel against magistrates and kings— the radical Hussite preacher Jan Želivský, who led the Defenestration of Prague in 1419—employed it. He listed a series of classic couples, including heretics and Christians, and then went on to apply the antithesis to justify rebellion: "the faithful community does not persecute the magistrates and councilors (*iudices et iurati*), but the magistrates and councilors persecute the faithful Christians."[72]

The paradoxical tension between coercion and liberty was eased at the level of system (but not at the level of particular cases) by the haziness of boundaries. Where did coercion exactly begin and end? As in modern American contract law, the boundaries between forced and free agreement were fluid and, for any episode involving constraint, a potential object for controversies.

Controversies there were. The Teutonic Knights and the Polish-Lithuanian Crown engaged in hefty polemics at the Council of Constance (1414–1418).[73] Andreas Didaci de Escobar, bishop of Ciudad Rodrigo (Spain), defended the

Teutonic Knights' military enterprises against Poland and its pagan allies. To justify the Order's harsh measures against the heathens, the bishop drew on Augustine's exegesis of Paul's violent conversion on the road to Damascus, as transmitted by Gratian's *Decretum*:

> The lords of the Sacred Order of Prussia were not attacking them [the pagans], rebuking them, and striking them with blows in order to directly coerce them to the Christian Faith, but in order that they might give up the blindness [existing] in their mind and voluntarily (*voluntarie*) submit their necks to Christ, receive His baptism, and freely abandon Christ Jesus' lands which they occupied. . . . This is not coercing to the Faith, but this is illuminating their minds' obscurity [*tenebrae* also means blindness] by means of the scourge of tribulations, and this is keeping them away from sin through the fear of Hell, as Augustine says commenting Psalm 127, "When a human being restrains itself from sin out of fear of Hell, there arises a custom to do what is just; what used to be hard begins to be loved; fear begins to be excluded from charity; and there follows a chaste fear, which lasts into eternity."[74]

Also on the Teutonic side, Johannes Falkenberg vociferously attacked the Polish spokesman, Paul Wladimir, for having proposed that the Baltic pagans were not to be coerced to Christianity. Falkenberg granted that "it is true in itself (*absolute*) that one cannot coerce infidels to the Faith, and that they should not be coerced, since the will is not subjected to coercion, and since Faith is fully in the will of the believer." But he went on to counter that "it is an intolerable error that 'the infidels should be left to [their] free will (*liberum arbitrium*)'." Free will, *liberum arbitrium*, had to be guided, pagans sins had to be expurgated and atoned, and the Faith had to be explained to them. If they were reluctant to listen, their will had to be coerced.[75]

For the Teutonic Knights' defender Didaci de Escobar, the Order's dealings with the pagans both were and were not coercion:

> One understands in the following way what is said, that no one should be coerced to the Faith.[76] One manner [of coercion] is direct, as if one were to say, "Unless you become a Christian, I shall kill you!." But if it is said, "I do not want to provide you from my goods, because you are an infidel; I do not want to interact with you, because you are a Jew; I do not want to rent you my house or buy or sell anything with you; or I do

not want any longer that you hold and manage my house or property, because you are an infidel—this is not to coerce directly to the Faith. In fact, it is to minister salvation to the infidel, and lead him to the road of rectitude and justice, so that a penalty opens up the eyes that sin had closed.[77]

But the Spaniard's application of the distinction was—at least to modern eyes—spurious and, in its expression, messy: "We do not do this directly, nor do we coerce anyone to the Faith through threats and blows or fear which could affect a steadfast man (*quo potest cadere in constantem*), but we only coerce the infidels through arms, blows, deaths (*mortes*), and prison."

These violences were the "indirect" by-product of wars waged to recuperate goods and lands taken away by the heathens or conducted to avenge and wipe out their blasphemies against God (idolatry and statements such as "God has a body").[78] Torture, according to the canonists, did not produce immediately a valid, "free" confession, but once the confession was repeated at some distance from torture, it became an expression of "spontaneous will." Analogously, violence produced indirectly and mediately a valid conversion.[79]

As had the early medieval popes in their conception of the "freedom of the Roman Church," the Teutonic Knights' partisans claimed to liberate from or prevent religious contagion; legitimate instruments and antidotes were war and compulsion. At the century's end, contagion would be one of the motivations for expelling the Jews from Christian Spain.[80] To preserve one's freedom, one could even launch what is now called a "preemptive war." Cardinal Pierre d'Ailly opposed on principle the dispossession of pagans who wanted "to live in peace and under the laws of nature." But if one feared "that infidels in the end lead the faithful to perdition" because "they refuse to live without affront to the Creator and drag Christians into error" (in particular, through their crimes against nature), attacking them was not in essence the offensive warfare frowned upon by just-war theory.[81] The Dominican Johannes Falkenberg opined that the Emperor could force infidels, even peaceful pagans, back into his dominion, since by essence they would harm Christians. This was justified on plural grounds. One was that peaceful pagans "blaspheme Christ's name all day long." Another was "the danger to the Church that one fears will come from them in the future" (*propter periculum, quod ab eis timetur ecclesie futurum*).[82] Another university master active in the polemics agreed that present facts and history taught that the "Saracens" (Baltic pagans were "Saracens of the West") were enemies who, while peaceful right now, would strike at the first occasion.[83]

The Teutonic Knights failed to convince the council. But the early modern law of war, all the way to World War II, received a principle that the Knights had appealed to: preemptive strike. To the horror of liberal American commentators and many Western Europeans, it was resurrected by George W. Bush for his attack against Iraq in 2003. Saddam Hussein allegedly hoarded weapons of mass destruction that threatened America. But one should note how fears of moral and religious contagion can be interwoven with such considerations of raw power and also make one consider "preemptive strike." During the long nineteenth century, all the way to the end of World War I, the United States justified its bellicose expansionism through a mixture of geopolitical fears, sense of "manifest destiny" on the continent, and anxieties concerning the corrupting influence of despotic or Catholic European foothold on the New Continent. Territorial proximity—even very remote—raised the specter of contamination. They were triggered by the English interest in Oregon;[84] circa 1843, the American willingness to take over Texas was motivated, from some quarters, by a fear of British imperialism. For President James K. Polk (1845–1849), Britain was hostile to "the expansion of free principles." Whatever these "free principles" exactly were, they were threatened by the "contaminating proximity of monarchies," as Representative Lewis C. Levin opined, concerning the Oregon question. The *American Review* saw in further British designs, this time on California, a barrier to "the progress of republican liberty."[85] As is the case for all wars, this ideology was not shared by all, and alone did not suffice to engender wars. But the protection and fostering of liberty contributed to war and threat of war. In the Texas question, a congressman declared that Providence had "given to the American people a great and important mission—and this mission they were destined to fulfil [*sic*]—to spread the blessings of Christian liberty and laws from one end to the other of this immense continent." It would end up "burning with patriotic love of country, and enjoying all the blessings of civil and religious liberty."[86]

The boundary between heavier and lighter blows, or between direct and indirect coercion to the Faith, is hazy; hazy also is to what one can or should constrain a heretic or a pagan. English Separatists and radical Puritans both preserved coercion and rejected it, a reconciliation of compulsion and free will that studies by Stephen Brachlow and before him by David Little have mapped out. To cite Brachlow, Separatist leader John Robinson (1575–1625), famous for his mentoring of the American Pilgrim Fathers, acknowledged "that although the civil sword should not (nor could) compel a human conscience in religious matters, it could (and should!) root out idolatry and compel individuals to that place where their conscience could be freely persuaded by the sword of Christ's Spirit to choose the way of Faith." For godly magistrates, to cite Robinson directly, it was "not unlawful . . . by some penalty or other, to provoke their subjects universally unto hearing for their instruction, and conversion." He added that, if this teaching failed to move these men and women "to offer themselves . . . unto the Church," the magistrates could "inflict upon them," understand, go after them with punishments.[87] Another English Separatist, Henry Barrow (d. 1593), in a sharp 1588 debate with one Doctor Some, saw matters in much the same way. He denied to the prince and the power of the sword the ability to "make any [man or woman] a member of the church," while saying that he could "compel al[l] his subjectes to the hearinge of Godde's Word, punishing the deriders and contemners of the same."[88] Doctor Some had proposed, citing Augustine, to combine "to teach" and "to punish"; Barrow retorted that the Anglicans had to teach first through the Word to convince their opponents, before trying punishment. Doctor Some had further proposed, also on the basis of Augustine, that people could be "compelled to the trueth against their willes" (since God's power "maketh those [men] willing, though they be compelled against their willes"). Barrow countered that Augustine had merely said that the Donatists should be forced to listen to preaching and that Doctor Some could not twist the Church Father's position to argue that dissenters should be coerced to partake in the Anglican sacraments.[89] Barrow was being consistent, since, for him, liturgy could not effect conversion; only the Word could.[90] The paradox was well expressed by William Perkins (1558–1602). The Word alone could change the will, but to make one hear the Word, some compulsion could be necessary:

> True it is, the will cannot be compelled; and true it is likewise, that the Magistrate doth not compell any to beleeve: for when a man doth beleeve, and from his heart imbrace true religion, he doth it willingly. Notwithstanding meanes are to be used to make them willing, that are unwilling, and the meanes is to compell them to come to our assemblies, to heare the word, and to learne the grounds for true religion.[91]

The paradoxical montage that Separatists and Left-Wing Puritans expressed was not in its basic structure new. It was, *mutatis mutandis*, the Augustinian position, which had allowed Bishop Didaci de Escobar two centuries earlier to deny forced conversion while pleading for compulsion: "salvific teachings" should be "conjoined to useful terror."[92] It placed limits on the prince's potestative abilities, while asking of him the creation of a constraining framework that would allow religious teaching to take human beings freely into liberty. From the thirteenth century on, under royal authority, Jews and Muslims had been coerced to listen to Christian sermons.[93]

There were two eschatological hopes at play. The first was a Christianization of the world at EndTimes (the renitent going to fry, of course). The distaste for coercion expressed itself with a second eschatological expectation. The Presbyterian Thomas Cartwright (1535–1603) identified the State magistrate with a positive, God-willed coercive order. But in one version of Calvinism, the Church was ideally a realm of freedom, free will, and consensus. In its progressive actualization of this ideal, it was served (so God had ordained) by the state's coercion. Having this coercive role as its fundamental function, however, the state would ultimately wane and disappear as it realized its task.[94] The principle of compulsion for the sake of spiritual liberation (classically identified as the freedom to choose well) was conjoined to attributing—in the light of History—a clear second-rank status to the coercive institution. Maurice Merleau-Ponty noticed the same hope in the earlier Marx, a waning of the inevitable terror on the horizon of the proletariat's ultimate victory, a vision opposed by the later Hegel, for whom war and force, waged by the state, alone will create humanity.[95] In a related tradition, equally rooted in medieval theology, freedom—here, freedom from fear—also came with the State. For Thomas Hobbes, the (servile) fear of all against all in the prepolitical chaos of nature transmuted itself, through the political pact, into a filial fear intertwined with love directed at the Sovereign. Such was (as recently elucidated by Andreas Bähr) the very Augustinian physics of emotions inspired by the quasi-divine state entity, that poster boy for secularized Modernity, the Leviathan.[96]

Medieval and early modern coercion aimed to enlighten into a free acceptance of religious Truth, that is, into Freedom Itself. But enlightening into freedom through forceful means is by no means only medieval or early modern. An earlier chapter discussed the Rote Armee Fraktion's rationale for its violent actions: it sought to free the Germans—in particular, the alienated Proletariat—from a *Verblendungszusammenhang* and "false consciousness." One of its manifestos summarized it well: "The bombs [that we use] against the repressive [state] apparatus, we also chuck into the consciousness of the masses."[97] An author the group read, Frantz Fanon, described how anticolonial violence not only constituted the new postcolonial nation, created a shared consciousness, but also "enlightened" and made impossible tyranny.[98] As we shall now see, during the French Revolution, Reason's philosophical light was also paired with liberating coercion.

The Searing Light of the Enlightenment

> Whoever refuses to obey the general will shall be constrained to do so by the entire body [politic]; which means nothing other than that he shall be forced to be free.[99]

If the French Revolution was the child of the Enlightenment (a genealogy historians debate), it was a shocking offspring. But then, despite Voltaire and the *Encyclopédie*, the men and women of 1789 did not necessarily associate with the Enlightenment what we now attach to it—tolerance and peace. Or it may have been, simply, that the new developed in the chrysalis of the old (a historian's metaphor interestingly indebted to theology). Drumming the Revolution's victory, in November 1793, Jean-Baptiste Carrier told the Comité de Salut Public that "prejudices and fanaticism were crumbling down under reason's irresistible force" (*préjugés et fanatisme, tout croule aujourd'hui devant la force irrésistible de la raison*)—a program the present Western world in its majority would approve of—but Carrier pursued in the same breath, unacceptably to the same, that "philosophy's flaming torch sheds light on everything and burns its enemies" (*le flambeau de la philosophie éclaire tout, brûle ses ennemis*). The second part of Carrier's formula sits ill-poised next to the first part's proclamation of the sweeping away of fanaticism.[100] The same Comité exhorted its representatives to the Nation's army on France's northern borders to "take to the traitors light and the sword." This was a revealing and aggressively hot torch, which animated its bearers with "flaming zeal," a "zeal" that should be transported "wherever mission called."[101] How far then was the light of the Enlightenment from the fire of the stake? Guibert of Nogent had paired the fire of "spiritual teachings" and the destructive fire of crusading purge. Facing a perceived emergency, Robespierre deployed a similar dyad: "One must smother the Republic's internal and external enemies, or perish with it. In this situation, the first axiom of your policy must be that one leads the people through reason, and the people's enemies through terror."[102] Guibert and Robespierre paired; others, like Carrier, blended. In his *Hymn on Lawrence*, Prudentius had sung that "the fire that Eternal God is . . . both fills the just and burns the guilty."[103] Here was a fire singly of zeal and of vengeance (a word that the more radical revolutionaries readily uttered). It had long been at home in Catholic France. Placed in a memorial chapel for the two murdered Guise brothers in Lyon, between two pyramids (one for each man), "there was a flaming and burning heart, a hieroglyph for the zeal, the love, and the burning affection that these princes had for the Fatherland"; it also "signified the conflagration and general combustion that their having been massacred [in Blois by the king's guards] would bring against the enemies of God's House . . . or the perpetual desire which ought to burn in Catholic souls to raise up their ashes through a just and legitimate vengeance."[104]

The pairing of reason and terror or constraint was a Christian classic. Augustine had commented: thus "the rampart of a hard custom is not only conquered with human terrors, but the Faith and the mind's understanding is also instructed by divine authorities and reasonings."[105] In pushing for the emancipation of France's Jews in the early years of the Revolution, the Abbé Grégoire—a cleric—echoed the discourse initiated by Augustine. Legislation, proposed the Abbé, would compel the Jews to become citizens; "reason" would "recover its rights."[106] But the question since at least the bishop of Hippo had been what to prioritize of terror and reason. Another issue was how much violence should be done to custom. Raised over and over again in the Middle Ages when conversion from paganism was envisaged, the question had a translation in the French Revolution. In discussing how to coax the populations' adhesion to the new order, exchanges between representatives of the Parisian center to the provinces and the governing central organs reproduced—*mutatis mutandis*—the medieval debates over compulsion in matters of religion. After having demanded from the clergy a loyalty oath to the reorganization of the Catholic Church in France (late 1790 to early 1791), the National Assembly embarked on an active policy of "dechristianization" that peaked during the second half of 1793.[107] Paris' envoys in the provinces pursued it with different degrees of ardor and extremism. At its most radical, dechristianization could involve plundering churches, confiscating and melting down ornaments, mocking the Catholic liturgy in theatrical parodies, and forcing priests to marry. It was, as perceived by the soldiers often charged with these operations, a struggle against "fanaticism," the old Christian name for paganism and mad heresy that the Enlightenment had turned against Christianity. The lexicon of righteous zeal now served the Revolution. One committed army lieutenant even recycled the Gospel parable of the tares (Matt. 13:24–30): "You have destroyed many bad weeds . . . but many remain that hamper our agriculture from bearing fruit."[108]

But Paris was divided. Robespierre and the Jacobin leadership preferred tolerance for Christianity, so as to fend off accusations that the Revolution was tantamount to atheism.[109] Individual envoys to the French provinces reacted to the controversies in the capital. Antoine-Joseph Lanot (1757–1807), a militant representative of the Comité de Sureté Générale in the northern Massif Central—whose brother Jean-Baptiste, a constitutionalist priest, had joined the campaign of dechristianization—argued for the need to continue "the war of reason against religious opinions" and "superstition."[110] He retraced how "the kingdom of ignorance had been invaded" by freedom's friends but added that "all its inhabitants were not yet amalgamated in feelings with the victors." Education and some sweetness were now called for: "Terror made them submit, but instruction must conquer them." Yet for Lanot the Convention's recent decree on freedom of worship had thrown a regrettable wrench into this process. Many priests had participated in revolutionary iconoclasm and "massively rushed to the people's altar to sacrifice and immolate on it their old existence." Now they were returning to their old habits. Lanot called for coherent, unified measures across France (*la plus grande harmonie de pensées et d'actions*) to enable a "new revolution" continuing the pre-decree policy: "It is only identical motions and instructions and a uniform system of persuasion and terror that will allow us to recreate natural man and annihilate the old man" shaped by Old Régime education. The alternative, disorder in policy, would nurture in each and every citizen (*l'homme public*) "fanaticism" and the "memory of his old habits." While Lanot was calling for some sweet persuasion, then, his main theme remained terror and coercion.[111]

André Jambon Saint-André (1749–1813) too drew on the register of warfare, reason, and superstition. The "reign of reason was advancing with giant steps," and the people wanted "no other guide than morality, no other priesthood than its own magistrates." The Revolutionaries respected the Deity more than those opponents who accused them of atheism and who bloodied the Vendée, "sacrificing . . . wretched victims of [your] error." Jambon Saint-André's side rendered a superior cult: "the practice of social virtues," "duty," and duty's best vector, "the holy and burning love of the Fatherland." But Jambon Saint-André ultimately rang a different bell than Lanot. He recognized that, despite the ultimate horizon of civic and patriotic perfection, the Convention should take into account "timorous consciences"—he spoke these contemptuous words to the face of his devout Catholic audience. You are allowed, he explained, to keep "the objects of your worship," whatever they may be (and Lanot piled on more contempt, unrolling a laundry list that encompassed Islam and the Tibetan cult). Freedom of conscience and of worship were granted, if within bounds, "in places earmarked for its gatherings; [yet] outside these nothing should impact the gaze but the cult of the Fatherland and the beloved symbols of freedom." What was to motivate the Convention's "sweet condescension"? A very Augustinian understanding of the "empire" of "an age-old habit, a theological education. The Convention is "aware," explained the envoy, "that a weak and sensitive heart is in need of support; you believe that you can still find it in the old prejudices that your fathers inspired in you; the Convention does not want to break it within your hands."[112]

The ancient theological matrix underlying these two discourses is obvious. There is the familiar antithesis between "new" (the Revolution) and "old" (habits, "old man"). There are the bellicose metaphors of the "kingdom" (*règne*) on the march against fanaticism, which, in the Christian lexicon, denoted militant paganism and heresy. There is the opposition between uncontrolled emotions and a regulating reason. To cite Jambon Saint-André's invective against the Chouans, "barbaric human beings! Your God is your passions; ours is Justice." Both he and Lanot proposed a mix of compulsion and persuasion on the road to the Kingdom but in different proportions. Augustine of Hippo had defined this very same equilibrium in dealing with the Donatist heretics: "Were they to be terrified and not instructed, it would be considered an impious domination. Conversely, were they to be instructed and not terrified, hardened by an old habit [*uetustate consuetudinis obdurati*] they would be moved to take up the road of salvation with greater laziness." In the same letter, the bishop explained that one had to tolerate, not despair about," the "weakness" of people who feared their former brethren's enmity "until they become strong."[113] For more than a millennium after Augustine, clergymen had debated about the right dosage of fear and teaching regarding heretics and pagans.[114] The revolutionary representatives continued this discussion. Lanot wanted more coercion—and coercion systematically applied in the tradition of the Catholic imperative of unity and uniformity. Jambon Saint-André, a former Calvinist clergyman from the French southwest, called for more persuasion. His sensitivity to human weakness, minus perhaps his contempt, may have been informed by the premodern debates. Augustine, vis-à-vis North African pagans, and Pope Gregory I (r. 590–604), with respect to recently converted Anglo-Saxons, had argued for tolerance of lingering superstition, with the understanding that time would do its work. Initially, lukewarm converts would progressively change their habits and become sincere believers. Gregory called for the reconsecration of pagan shrines to Christian cult, as opposed to their destruction, so that "this nation [the Angles] would converge with great familiarity to the places to which it was accustomed [to come]." The slaughter of oxen in sacrifice would cease but be transformed in food served at happy "religious banquets" taking place on saints' days or the anniversaries of the temples' conversion: "This way, while they keep something of their outward joys, they may be able to give their assent more easily to interior joys." The logic was one of progressive accommodation: "Hardened minds" could not at one stroke give up everything, and the road to Christianity could be traveled only "by steps and not by leaps." Had not precisely for this reason Ancient Israel's God converted to His own use the sacrifices that formerly honored in Egypt the Devil?[115] Gregory I also proposed that one could bribe with tax exemptions the Jews of Sicily to convert to Christianity; the first generation might be insincere, but its offspring, raised in the Faith, would be genuine believers.[116] But as we have developed at length, Augustine, when dealing with heretics, presented the other side of the coin, which found Lanot's favor: namely, a Latin word one may translate by force, might, or violence, was necessary to shatter enslaving custom (what Lanot and Jambon Saint-André called "habits," *habitude*). "We rejoice," wrote the Church Father, "when the teachings of salvation (*doctrina salutaris*) are joined to a useful terror, so that both the light of Truth may dispel the darkness of error and the might of fear (*uis timoris*) may break off the shackles (*uincula*) of evil habit (*consuetudo*)." In Augustine's understanding, God had foreordained the conversion of Roman imperial power to Christianity precisely to this end. It was the jump into another phase of Sacred History that permitted, ultimately, coercion for liberty.[117]

Conversely, "terror" was a means to historical progress and purification. The road to enlightenment and perfect liberty passed through travails and compulsion. In a famous essay deeply indebted to the profound but difficult musings of Ernst Bloch, Michael Walzer analyzed the biblical book of Exodus as the paradigmatic story of human liberation from bondage, where freedom was acquired not so much by God's grace as through persistent human effort. Struggles, setbacks, and lapses there were, indicative, suggested Walzer, of a realistic apprehension of agency.[118] But the Israelites' exit (*exodos*) from Egypt and their entry into the Promised Land were less due to the Jews' free will and agency than to God's prophet Moses' persistent goading. *Pace* Walzer, to escape Egyptian slavery, God's chosen people needed Moses the slave driver. Three further points deserve elaboration.

First, the story of Exodus was by no means monopolized by "progressive" revolutionaries. The ultra-Catholic Ligue—"black revolutionaries" or "reactionaries" so to say—used it as well, for instance, for the "day of the barricades" when Paris rebelled against its king, too accommodating toward Calvinists.[119]

Second, on the basis of the same biblical narrative, theologians repeated again and again that "the ancient people" had to be fed milk and be disciplined like children; they could not yet take in solid food, unlike the chosen people of the New Alliance. But the grammar of exegesis allowed a transposition of this lesson within the *ecclesia*. The New Dispensation miniaturized within its own hierarchies the contrast between itself and the Old Dispensation. In the age of the Church, the laity, typified by the Old Testament's Jews, needed pedagogy and coercion. The clergy's relation to the laity is analogous to the New People's relation to the Jews; as such, clerics are spared the rod (unless delinquent and behaving like laypeople). The Western notion of an elite leading a much less clear-sighted flock is thus embedded in a notion of sacred history. This vanguard (the part of an army, which, on the march, reaches the encampment faster, leading the rest) is closer to the future than the mass of the people, just as the New Alliance in comparison to the Old Alliance.

Third, the vanguard sacrificed itself on the march. Moses never reached the Promised Land; he merely beheld it from the heights of Mount Nebo. He was not the only Jew not to enter it. In forty years of meandering in the desert, the older Israelites almost all perished. Edgard Quinet's superb reflections on revolution and religion constitute a sophisticated theoretical counterpart to Lanot's not fully articulated position. In a chapter tellingly titled "French Terrorism and Hebrew Terrorism," Quinet explains that Moses wanted to make a tabula rasa of Israel's experience of slavery in Egypt. He decided to "regenerate" his people by forcing the Jews to give up idolatry through "forty years of terror" in the desert, purposefully delaying entry into the Promised Land; "after that he strove to remake this people's tradition and education."[120] This notion also found its way into Communism. "The present generation," wrote Marx, "resembles the Jews whom Moses led through the wilderness. It must not only conquer a new world, it must also perish in order to make room for the people who will be equal to a new world."[121]

Marx illustrated his belief in historical epochs and caesuras with the Old

Testament. The affinity was not superficial. For Catholic theology, Moses' inability to enter the Promised Land symbolized the intrinsic limits of the Old Law and its ceremonies (epitomized by circumcision), which ended with Christ's baptism. *Ex negativo*, thus, it symbolized the passage from one era to another.

*   *   *

In the very longue durée, the idea that some religious coercion was desirable disappeared, as far as America is concerned, from the mainstream only in the late eighteenth century, with the disestablishment of the official churches.[122] It had faltered in Europe sometime in the seventeenth and eighteenth century (the ruler could impose outward conformity but not inner beliefs). Yet it returned on the Continent in godless variants with twentieth-century political religions, which sought not only to govern behavior but also inner convictions.[123] Along with the related notions of vanguard, it was transported by colonialism and anticolonialism to the so-called Third World. The socialist founder of the Ba'ath Party, Michel 'Aflaq, born in Damascus in a Greek Orthodox Christian family and educated in Paris, justified revolutionary warfare and terror with the classic Christian idols of love, unity, enlightenment, administered by a clear-sighted vanguard. There had to be first civil war, he explained:

> Our faith calls upon us to announce a division in the nation, because the nation . . . will not recapture that ideal unity which is today a matter of principle until it divides on itself. However, in this struggle we retain our love for all. When we are cruel to others, we know that our cruelty is in order to bring them back to their true selves, of which they are ignorant. Their potential will, which has not been clarified yet, is with us, even when their swords are drawn against us.[124]

Secularized, Christian liberty also journeyed east. Nonsecular, and non-Christian, a key ideologue of the Egyptian Muslim Brotherhood, was Sayyid Qutb (hung in 1966). "Islamic Jihaad," defined Qutb, was the "defense of man against all those elements which limit his freedom . . . beliefs and concepts, as well as of political systems, based on economic, racial or class distinctions." So understood, Islam manifested its "true character . . . a universal proclamation of the freedom of man from servitude to other men, the establishment of God and His Lordship throughout the world, the end of man's arrogance and self-ishness, and the implementation of the rule of the Divine Sharia'ah in human affairs."[125] For this father of Political Islam, as for his Christian cousins, sub-mission to God was humanity's true liberty.

Yet ideas of coercion for the good did not reappear only in political religions. As we saw, without reference to God but with precise conceptions concerning how belief functioned, the French mused about coercion's role in the instilling of a revolutionary faith. In contemporary democracies, exceptional situations can still command transgression. Witness the American Paul Nitze, who, in an early Cold War National Security Council document (NSC 68) attacked the Bolshevik regime and its tyranny but slid in a small caveat: "Compulsion is the negation of freedom, except when it is used to enforce the rights common to all."[126] Elastically defined, human rights demand recourse to coercive arms. This modern ideal is derived from high medieval and early modern Scholasticism, which allowed military intervention whenever a foreign governing class perpetrated abuses against the law of nature. Of course, there will be massive disagreements about the contents of any law standing, as natural law did, above positive law. Famously, Juan Ginés de Sepúlveda justified the Spanish conquests in the New World by the crimes against nature that heathen societies perpetrated. A modern citizen of the West is likely not to side with Sepúlveda in seeing in polygamy or idolatry legitimate reasons to topple foreign rulers. But will he or she not agree with Sepúlveda when it comes to mass cannibalism and human sacrifice—or similar horrors?[127] Here is a bridge, in the dimension of international ethics, between premodern and Modern; the distinction between the two epochs constitutes the core focus of the next and last chapter.

Chapter 7

The Subject of History and the Making of History

Strike, barons, do not slacken! . . . God has sent us to make the true judgment.

—*Chanson de Roland,* laisse 248

Insofar as "future" signifies for us the productibility of History . . .
[Da Zukunft für uns die Machbarkeit der Geschichte bedeutet . . .]
—Langhans and Teufel, *Klau mich*

History, as it is now proceeding, is devoid of meaning. We must immediately and concretely begin the armed struggle.
[Die Geschichte, so wie es jetzt läuft, hat keinen Sinn. Wir müssen sofort konkret mit dem bewaffneten Kampf anfangen.]
—Baumann, "Tupamaros Westberlin," in *Wie alles anfing,* 65

Modernity

How modern is Modern violence? Scholars specializing in twentieth-century terror or in the French Revolution's *Terreur* routinely posit a difference between premodern and Modern violence. Let us start with an example, the revolutionary martyrdoms of 1789–94, which owed much to the confluence of classical Roman and Christian exemplars. Antoine de Baecque, in an essay focusing with high sensitivity on the Catholic discourse's influence, can still assert in passing that the revolutionary martyr's corpse is glorious, contrary to the Christian tradition, which considers the body despicable.[1] Another scholar, Alphonse Jourdan, hammers in a much more categorical opposition:

> more and more heroes took the form of martyrs. But a republican martyr was not the same as a Christian one. His tireless energy made him different. The republican was a ferocious defender of the new and entirely secular faith, and he was required not only to know how to suffer and die, but to carry on the armed fight until exhaustion. . . . The Christian martyr was entirely passive, his eyes on heaven alone, indifferent to his fellow citizens. The revolutionary martyr, by contrast, worked for the public good, for humanity and for this life, to bring about liberty, equality and fraternity for the happiness of all. And this brought him much nearer to the heroes of antiquity than to the saints of Catholicism, even though, like the latter, he stood for a new faith, gave up his life for his beliefs, and obstinately spurned the most awful dangers.[2]

Medievalists and historians of early Christianity will smile at the martyr's putative indifference to others and to the common good, at his or her entire passivity, and at his or her lack of "tireless energy." The heroism and willfulness portrayed in the earliest Passions and Acts should put this erroneous contrast to rest. The martyr's activism traverses the Christian centuries. Closer to the great Revolution, Milton's Christian heroes, rather than suffering in patience, actively defied evil. The poet of the English Revolution cared more about victory than about agony.[3]

De Baeque's light faux pas and Jourdan's antitheses concerning death and dying do not constitute a hapax in scholarship. One finds it also with a scholar who devoted much work to the transition between premodernity and Modernity, Reinhart Koselleck. Koselleck conceptualizes the monuments dedicated to soldiers fallen on the battlefield, a memorial practice that emerged throughout western Europe around the time of the French Revolution, as a "political cult of the battle dead," men who died for the "political salvation of the whole people." According to him, "posterity" (the active and organized remembering by humans in this world) became, around 1800, the warrantor of memory, replacing the liturgical commemoration, *memoria*, the recitation within the Christian Mass of the names of the dead deemed destined to eternal bliss. A major transformation: "the promise of eternity is relocated within time"; it is now the political community that is in charge of the "salvation" of the individual soldier's soul, meaning, his perpetual commemoration. Koselleck adds that "what is new with the political cult of the dead in Early Modernity is that it is the violent death [of the fallen] that legitimizes the unit for political action (*Handlungseinheit*)."[4]

Undeniably, what Albert Camus eloquently attacked in his 1951 critique of Communist terror did take place in late Modernity: History replaced God. The cult of this new idol, elaborates Camus, subverted the prior ethical balance between ends and means in favor of the former. Dissimulation, a disregard for self-sacrifice, and an absence of love would from then on characterize terror.[5] Eric Voegelin had diagnosed the same from his 1938 Cambridge exile: "the mandate of God" has become "synonymous with intramundane formulae such as 'the mandate of History,' 'historical imperative,' 'the mandate of blood'."[6] Then, as Koselleck has it, "the promise of eternity" was "relocated within time." In many European lands, the *ecclesia*, as community of the faithful, morphed into the national community. Yet three nuances are in order. First, as Koselleck would be the first to recognize, both the pair religion-politics, and the related (but not equivalent) pair church-state, are not dichotomous. Nor does the Church care only about "religion" in its restricted, Modern sense. Second, the premodern commemoration of martyrs (and generally of saints) also "legitimized" sociopolitical groupings and also aimed at a collective salvation. Third, as ever so often, what seems Modern is not unprecedented, and boundary stones can be moved backward along the historical timeline. The "political cult" of the fallen did not appear first in the eighteenth century. Jeanne d'Arc requested that chantries be established, in which stipendiary clergy would pray for the salvation of the war dead— "for those who had died at war for the defense of the Kingdom (*pro defensione regni*)."[7] They had fought for France. Should this not be categorized as "political salvation"? John Foxe's *Book of Martyrs*, in its several editions over the turn of the sixteenth and seventeenth centuries, both hallowed English Protestantism and crowned England as the nation coterminous with pure Christianity. It welded together holy deaths with the failure of the Gunpowder Plot and the wrecking of the Spanish Armada.[8]

In sketching differences between premodern and Modern violence, scholars mobilize classic master narratives. As just discussed, Koselleck posits a major transformation in the later eighteenth century, in conformity with his school's axiom that an epochal shift took place then, with the so-called *Sattelzeit*. Others zoom in on a transformed relationship of political action and legitimacy to "Truth" (understood as the objective realities that a culture believes exist). Yet others articulate difference around one or several among three interrelated cultural dimensions: the attitude to change, the nature of the political sphere, and conceptions of agency. Let us first deal with the question of Truth, before turning to change, the political, and agency.

According to one line of analysis, terrorism in a religious universe stems from a radical critique couched in the terms of the established religion; secular Modernity's terrorism is an attack in the name of Truth on a state that, since Thomas Hobbes, derives its legitimacy solely from its ability to dispense well-being and peace. *Authoritas non Veritas facit legem* (It is authority not Truth that grounds the law), wrote Hobbes, to explain that only the sovereign magistrates, not moral philosophers, were entitled to interpret the natural law. The "Truth" (*veritas*) that this formula aimed at was religious Truth (or claims thereto).[9] In the legal positivism nowadays dominant in Western democracies, this zone of *veritas* on which the law can no longer be grounded has been extended to encompass all facts and norms. The Modern State cannot anchor its legitimacy in a "Truth," an entity transcendent to it, be it God, the Good, Nature, or a miracle—the situation that Carl Schmitt deplored in his *Political Theology*.[10] To paraphrase two German scholars, Günter Rohrmoser and Jörg Fröhlich: Now based on compact and contract, the contemporary state is fairly helpless when its legality is assailed "in the name of a higher and different legitimacy." It cannot avoid being denounced as an avatar of "structural violence." It can be envisaged as a monstrous political "system," a shell preserving and masking a vast system of hidden coercions, economic and spiritual, which drug off, enslave, and alienate human beings.[11] Otherwise put, because the contemporary State has denied itself a grounding in some Truth, it invites radical critique and rejection from quarters that claim access to such a Truth.

Yet in what sense is this Modern configuration fundamentally different from the premodern one? First, one should not misconceive the fit between premodern polities and the universe of images, notions, beliefs, and practices that we call religion. The sacral canopy that (we are told) stabilized archaic political systems was never fully impermeable. It is correct to say that these older polities could call on the transcendental and on absolutes, and recreate after a crisis Hobbes's *veritas*: the trajectory of the French monarchy in the two decades that concluded the Wars of Religion shows as much.[12] But what a crisis for the preceding half-century! Comparatively, the pathogenesis of Modernity (the European collective madness allegedly generated by the rapid transformations in industry and politics) has lasted, thus far, only a short half century, the century of genocidal Nazism and Communisms, with lulls. Why should these years, 1917–1953, weigh more than an equal length of time five centuries ago? Simply because our times are more important given that they are closer to us? Second, the premodern European sacred canopy also systemically generated crises, precisely because it was a Christian canopy, thus bound to criticize the world. Even before the so-called crisis of Church and State that Gregory VII set into motion in the late eleventh century, out of the religious realm came, regularly, critiques of the this-worldly order. Most were critiques of incumbents, meaning, individual rulers of Church and State. But there occurred also, if much less frequently, attacks on the institutions' very principle of existence. Power was both of God and of the Devil.[13]

Another model explaining Modernity's violence also posits a fraught relationship to Truth, this time not on the part of contemporary democratic states but on the part of democracy's enemies. In his otherwise profound book *Fanaticism*, Alberto Toscano states that "twentieth-century fanaticism . . . unlike the religious fanaticisms diagnosed by the Enlightenment . . . is not a fanaticism of certainty"; it always suspects. And this instability makes for its violence. Toscano builds here on French philosopher Alain Badiou's *The Century*, to the effect that "we are in the realm of suspicion when a formal criterion is lacking to distinguish the real from semblance." Toscano comments: "this explains the autophobic, and autophagic, character of Modern militancy, since suspicion dictates that whatever conviction seems most real, there too we are to look for treachery and falsity."[14] Indeed, the 1938 Moscow trials are rife with such anxieties, both on the part of the winners (who expected traitors deep within the revolution's ranks) and on the part of the victims (who doubted the coherence of their revolutionary self). And, indeed, the Rote Armee Fraktion believed that fascistic imperialism always wore the optimal "character-masks," be they "Nixon and Brandt, Moshe Dayan or Genscher, Golda Meir or McGovern," a "gallery of character-masks" into which imperialism also press-ganged the "governments of Third-World countries."[15]

But here, too, a lack of in-depth knowledge of earlier centuries weakens the argument's comparative leg. Satan's ability to create false churches (discussed, for example, by both sides in the Donatist controversy), to raise up witches almost indistinguishable from saints, and to sow cockles within the very ranks of the elect (as assumed by Raymond d'Aguilers and Ekkehard of Aura for the First Crusade) also indicates the absence of a "formal criterion . . . to distinguish the real from semblance." If secular Modernity's axiomatic "Cartesian" doubt and lack of belief in Truth is pathogenic, the Christian axiomatic belief in the Devil and his wiles was systemically generative of doubt. Satan had been a deceiver from the beginning, and Antichrist would be a deceiver at EndTimes. Power was, as a result, either of God or of the Adversary.[16] Two among Raymond d'Aguilers's heroes, Bishop Adhémar and Peter Bartholomew, plus the chronicler Raymond himself, had their moments of doubt about the Holy Lance—overcome in the prelate's case only in hell. Of course, we could psychoanalyze—as Toscano psychoanalyzes "Modern militancy"—Raymond and Peter, who literally dreamt the extermination of hardened doubters within the crusaders' ranks. This approach would involve positing a double projection of their doubts, first onto these weak brethren, then onto outsiders, the *infideles*, literally, "those lacking in faith." In this line of analysis, Raymond and Peter's clear desire to slaughter Muslims would derive from this projection. But we have discussed the limits of similar approaches, in particular for anti-Semitism, in the chapter devoted to madness. The point here is rather that the Badiou-Toscano analysis of the specificity of Modern fanatical violence is unconvincing.[17]

Equally simplifying are positions that assume sharp transformations in the Western attitudes to change, in the nature of the political, and in notions of agency.[18] First, Modern violence is said to be oriented to the future and to aim at a radical transformation of the sociopolitical order; its premodern counterpart was oriented to the past and, correspondingly, was conservative. It sought merely the restoration of a bygone golden age. Second, the goal of premodern religious violence was allegedly religious reform and not political construction. Third, for Modernity, Man is the Subject of History, meaning, he or she understands himself (or herself) self-consciously to be the agent of change. To cite Karl Marx, "History is nothing but the activity of Man pursuing his aims."[19] But—so the received understanding—for the earlier age, an all-powerful God was the Subject of History, and the human being's deeds were not free. In what follows, several scholarly utterances will serve as a basis for a critical discussion of these axioms. As every so often, a more correct position is likely to be found in a compromise; in these pages, however, the similarities between premodern and Modern will be sketched out uncompromisingly. To other scholars I leave the glories and pleasures of compromise.

Charles Townshend's *Terrorism: A Very Short Introduction* recognizes the commonality in language between, on the one hand, Enlightenment-era revolutionary *Terreur* and, on the other hand, crusades and millenarian holy war. The book reflects aptly on the culturally bound limits of the dichotomy sacred-secular, Church and State. But it wobbles when discussing the dominant conception, whereby premodern religious terror is unconcerned with change and Modern terror assumes the possibility of change:

> The practitioners of religious violence do not appear to be working on this assumption [that it will create change]. The Assassins, for instance, *although they were concerned with social change—the lapse of society from earlier standards of religious observance*—were not concerned to convert people by direct action. Rather, they were testifying before God, a bilateral relationship which actually excluded the rest of the world.[20]

Experts will tell us whether such was indeed the fact for this medieval Shi'a Muslim sect, but this does not represent at all Christian martyrdom and terror. Martyrdom was hardly ever bilateral, involving only the saint and God; it addressed a community (either the nonbelieving audience or the Christian's own, or both). As detailed in the conclusion to Chapter 4, there existed two nonexclusive genres of martyrs. One sought to convert outsiders; the other was more concerned with the in-group. In dying in public, the martyr of the first type presented the unbelieving audience with a choice: to side with true Christianity or to remain in error and endure eternal death.[21] In the alternative genre, the martyrs sought to orient their community's behavior; in one Passion, the death speech called for the return of apostates and heretics to the fold, for women's chastity, for the clergy's unity and concord without squabbles, and for the plebe's respect for its priests.[22]

Townshend does qualify himself; the premodern religious terrorist does have some desire to transform his or her environment. Schmuel Eisenstadt is more categorical: in their scope, the transformations that the Modern fanatic wants to effect are without premodern equivalent. Eisenstadt locates the key difference between, on the one hand, the premodern period's proto-fundamentalist movements and, on the other, the Modern fundamentalist movements in the latter's "strong emphasis on the reconstruction, through political means and action, of state, society, and the individual alike." This action takes place in the political arena.[23] In an authoritative encyclopedic entry, Gerd van der Heuvel also posits a break in outlook, which he locates with the French Terror. The novelty in the Revolutionaries' justification of violence based on natural law, when compared to the older tyrannicide theories that allowed a king's execution, is that it is not only the ruler who will be overthrown, "but the whole sphere of state, politics and society will be remodeled in the sense of the radical and universalistic philosophy of the Enlightenment . . . with the help of terror through the intimidation or annihilation of the political opponent."[24]

As Townshend, criticized above for a trifle, cogently remarks, our dominant twentieth-century dichotomous categories (Church-State and religion-politics) are not adequate for an apprehension of God-driven violence. And as this essay has argued, recent secular violence is more understandable if one heuristically translates its ideology back into religious terms. Thus, on the one hand, scholars specializing on the present risk misapprehending earlier violence for God; and on the other, they do not always see how the understanding of this earlier form of violence can serve the analysis of its present counterpart. The inadequacy can be demonstrated with examples drawn from the medieval crusades and from the French wars of religion.

The thirteenth-century *Song of the Albigensian Crusade*, depicting the seizure of the Cathar fortress of Termes and "how Jesus Christ manifested His power there," juxtaposes to this victory the county of Toulouse's reform, including the end of usury and tolls, the dismissal of mercenaries, the restitution of rights and possessions to clergy, and the penance in food and dress imposed on the count and his vassals.[25] As we saw, in the same century, Jean d'Abbeville considered that the captivity of the earthly Jerusalem signified that of the Church, enslaved to the vices of some clergy and the exploitation of the poor. The remedy for the former necessitated the suppression of the latter; holy war was *eo ipso* linked to war versus social vices, thus to a program of regeneration.[26] As Jonathan Riley-Smith puts it, in the Crusades, "sacred violence always stemmed from the conviction that Christ's wishes for mankind were associated with a political system or a course of political events in this world."[27] The stunning twelfth-century poem *Fides cum idololatria*, for example, called for absolute equality between rich and poor.[28]

Like the eleventh-century papal revolution, the fifteenth-century Hussites blended demands from the two spheres we now distinguish as "religious" and "sociopolitical." Note, for instance, the fourth of the Four Articles of Prague: "We stand for the purgation of, and cessation from all public mortal sins, by each in his own person; and for the cleansing of the Bohemian realm and nation from false and evil slander; and in this connection, for the common good of our land."[29]

The Hussites did not deem it incongruous to pair moral and ecclesiastical reforms with sociopolitical rectification. And the more radical Taborites soon tried to impose in Prague very specific social measures, whose tenor František Šmahel rightly compares to their captain Jan Žižka's ordinances for the army.[30] At moments at least, Hussites promised war and coercion to those who would not buy into this program. The Diet of Čáslav (Csaslau) proclaimed that those "persons or communities" who did "not wish to unite with" the agreement just reached, and with the Four Articles of Prague, plus a governmental structure of twenty "governors" for the administration, establishment, and due process of the Bohemian kingdom, would be coerced to do so and considered as enemies.[31] Slightly more to the West, all sides in the Hundred Years War—English, Armagnac, or Burgundians—hardly ever envisaged any peace without expressing a vision, even if in shorthand, of the restructuring of society and politics.[32]

One century later, Calvinists and Catholics regularly commingled concerns that Modern thinking would parse out as either religious or political. A song attributed to the Ligueur preacher Jean Boucher will illustrate this for the Catholic side. It would be abominable to give up the Ligue, to have commerce with heretics, to make peace with pagans, to have an heretical king, to tolerate the sale of (ecclesiastical) benefices and the sale of (royal) offices, to see connections rather than right triumph in matters of justice, to allow criminals to be immune from punishment, to permit new taxes and the "corruption of all estates." Fundamentally, for the author, passivity was damnable; tolerance was an unacceptably perverse peace with ultimate evil. It meant to be "neutral between God and the Devil." The song's refrain rang a spirited call to martyrdom: *Sus, sus, faites-moy donc mourir! Il n'est que de mourir martyr* (Come on, come on! [If this is so,] then make me die! Nothing is better than to die a martyr).[33] Boucher called for martyrdom for a program combining Church and State reform. His was not a lone voice in and around 1589–1590. In this paroxistic crisis moment, the ultra-Catholic Holy League commemorated its Guise martyrs and its righteous assassin Jacques Clément and summoned to action in words that straddled the two realms. The Ligue's fight versus the king and his *politique* loyalists aimed at upholding "God's honor" but was also waged for France's "defense" and "peace."[34] The poem attached to a memorial portrait of the two murdered Guise brothers paired Church and common good: "They died for Jesus Christ and the public, and will live forever."[35] One year later, Ligueurs proclaimed that their martyr, the tyrannicide Clément had killed King Henri III "not fearing to die in order to put the Church and the people in [a state of] liberty."[36] A few years earlier, a pamphlet had summoned good Catholics to action pell-mell for "the preservation of God's honor" and of the Faith's integrity versus heresies; for "the defense, protection, and fostering of" the kingdom; and, finally, for the "general and common quietude of all the good and loyal subjects, servants of God and the king." Far from being a pacifist call, this text queried whether it was not fitting "to avenge the cruelest indignities and the most scandalous cruelties that one ever heard about in this kingdom? For so many and so horrible blasphemies, sacrileges, pollutions, murders, plunders, thefts, banditries, sackings, rapes and deflowering of virgins devoted to God's service, and so many other inhumane deeds they perpetrated?" The horizon of action was retribution. The pamphlet concluded on the familiar reference to Revelation 6: "See that the blood of the just and innocent, killed and martyred, clamors before God in a loud voice."[37]

The Calvinist camp, too, conflated demands for religious and sociopolitical regeneration, sealed in blood. A Lyon text of 1563 both reaffirmed Tertullian's dictum that the martyrs' blood was the Church's seed (*pépinière*) and called for reform. It set its sights against archiepiscopal corruption, "idolatries and persecutions" (but not those directed at Anabaptists and blasphemers, who were to be punished), Catholic "pomps" and "excesses," the farming out of justice, and the sale of offices. It called for a return to the selection for office of "the better men, God-fearing and greed-hating." The ordinances of the kings of old, but also Scripture, commanded as much.[38]

The 1563 Lyon text grounded its demand for virtuous magistrates on past royal ordinances and on the Bible—Moses' appointment of "able men, such as they fear God, in whom there is truth, and that hate avarice" to be district magistrates and judges for lesser cases (Exod. 18.13–26). In this passage, one should note, Jethro, Moses' relative, had suggested that the prophet-legislator concentrate on cultic and moral matters, matters of God. This shows that, while biblical culture recognized a distinction between spheres, it also considered that such "political" issues as justice were mandated and supervised (more or less directly) by "religion." Such was the thrust of the Old Testament's first five books, the Pentateuch. They legislated cult, morality, and justice, and even proposed several models of political organization. The *synagoga* was, thus, a church and a polity. So was, for most Christian groups, the Christian *ecclesia* that the synagogue had prefigured. The main issue that divided churches and exegetes was to define exactly what had been abolished with the Incarnation, what remained binding under the New Dispensation, and what could be imitated without sin (and indeed be useful). One will recall, for example, how the Anabaptists could argue that the permission of "sword, and war and government in the Old Testament" had been annulled with Christ's First Coming.[39] The Dominican Thomas Aquinas, by the sixteenth century the most authoritative doctor of the Catholic Church, is representative not of the solutions adopted—there were several—but of the framework of the debate.

According to Aquinas's discussion in the *Summa Theologiae* (II.I. q. 99, a. 4), the Old Law contained three kinds of precepts: moral (specifying principles contained in their generality in the Natural Law); ceremonial (governing worship and humans' relation to God); and judicial (determining justice among human beings). Aquinas (like most other Christians) considered that the ceremonial precepts had lapsed with the Incarnation of God's Word; they had served their typological role as "foreshadowings of Christ to come." The judicial precepts contained determinations of the people's relation to its rulers; of dealings between co-citizens within the community (for instance, buying, selling, judging, punishing); of relations with foreigners including war and hospitality; and of domestic issues such as marriage, children, servants (ST II.I. q. 104, a. 4). God had laid them down to order the "state of that people" (the Jews), which was ordained to Christ. Insofar as the nascent Church had taken in the Gentiles alongside those Jews who recognized their Savior, this *status* changed (ST II.I. q. 104, a. 3); in the New Dispensation, the judicial precepts were, therefore, no longer mandatory. On this point, Aquinas may have known the very similar argument in Origen's *Against Celsus*: after Christ's advent, the widening of the *ecclesia* to the Gentiles, conjoined to the existence of a Roman empire, called for, and made possible, pacifism. Conversely, under the Old Dispensation, pacifism (and the rejection of all forms of judicial coercion) would have meant the destruction of the Jewish *politeia*.[40] But, continued Aquinas, it is not a sin for Christians to retain an Old Testament judicial precept (as long as they do not do so in order to observe the Old Law, which would constitute "judaizing," a heresy). It can be adopted by a Christian polity where and when this state's circumstances (as they bear on this precept) are similar to those in which the Jews found themselves in the Old Alliance.

The details in Aquinas' position do not matter, even if it should be underlined that Jean Calvin (and the Calvinists) shared its tripartition and its flexible position concerning the adoption in the New Age of Old Testament judicial precepts.[41] The point here is rather the widespread presence across Christian sects, confessions, and denominations, of conceptions in which religious institutions and norms were responsible for the common good, however conceived. In conformity with this concern, premodern religious violence aimed at a reconstruction of the bonds that mattered for the common good of the *ecclesia*, the ensemble of believing human beings. Thus, if one can grant that medieval and early modern violence did not aim at producing an entirely novel state of things, it is inappropriate to say that it was essentially "religious" (according the Modern, laicizing definition of religion, which denies to it any social and political dimension).

The Subject of History

Paradoxically, agency—the third dimension in the face-off between Modernity and premodernity—provides a case where a clichéed, superficial acquaintance with theology weakens the historian's apprehension of premodern mentalities and, even more, leads him or her astray. When it comes to agency, the boundaries between premodern and Modern are far from clear. They are not clear in the farther past; neither are they clear closer to our times. The United States preserved and still preserves many traits of archaic Europe, including a double Subject of History, Man and God. In the 1770s, God might be History's prime mover, but the revolutionary struggle was one among His chosen means. In a poem that took as its departure point the founding of Zion—in the New Age, the rebellious colonies—a reverend called for human action:

> Let not my theme by any be abus'd,
> Tho' Zion's founded, means must yet be us'd.
> When foes with spears rush on us like a flood,
> Curs'd be the man who keeps his sword from blood. [Jer. 48.10][42]

Jeremiah 48.10, incidentally, had been Pope Gregory VII's favorite prophetic verse. Conversely, in current American novelizations of EndTimes struggle, the tension between human agency and God's iron-clad dispensation remains. In the highly popular *Left Behind* series, the resistors against Antichrist, determined to assassinate him, say to themselves that they "must guard against trying to help God, as it were, fulfill His promises."[43]

If the matter is not too clear so close to us, what then about the farther past? The medieval man or woman, it has often been posited, was unable to conceive himself or herself as the Subject of History.[44] One can well understand this idea. What else might expressions such as "God willing" (*Deo volente*) or "with God's help" (*Deo adiuvante*) mean? In a theological culture that often assumes predestination, and the priority of God's will, how much freedom could "Man" have? Or in the terms of this essay's focus, how can "Man" be the Subject of violence? To answer this question, an obvious method is to scroll back through time, looking for a genealogy of the conception of Man as agent.

For many historians and sociologists, the sixteenth and seventeenth centuries constitute the threshold to Modernity. Thus, it makes sense to begin one's inspection there, with the confessional conflicts and the English Revolution. Denis Crouzet's reconstruction of the French Wars of Religion marks a notable methodological advance vis-à-vis the 1970s and 1980s generation of the French Annales school, insofar as it takes religion, and so religious forces and causes, very seriously. Crouzet has recovered, rather than human ambition or frustrations expressed through, or cloaked in, religious forms, human beings honestly and sincerely living out religious scenarios scripted in holy writ and astrological prophecies.[45] There is, however, an implicit methodological tension between this highly attenuated agency and what Crouzet also documents and underscores (in discussing, in particular, the doctrine of dissimulation): the sophistication of high political figures in planning either rebellion or murderous repression. Right after the Saint-Bartholomew's Day Massacre, the Jesuit subprior of the Paris Collège de Clermont reported to the Abbot of Saint-Gall that "Everyone is unanimous in praising the king's providence and magnanimity; after having (so to speak) fattened like cattle the heretics, with his benevolence and tolerance, he suddenly had his soldiers slit their throats."[46] Arnaud Sorbin, the king's court preacher, sang the same tune: Charles IX knew perfectly how to prudently hide things that could serve God and his people. One could only admire "his outward coldness [masking] the fire that filled his heart." And, indeed, in a form of reverse Machiavellianism, pious early modern princes knew how to dissimulate a religious agenda and cloak it with power-political pretexts.[47] While France's sixteenth-century holy warriors "lived" scriptures, they were also self-consciously agents and demanded human agency. So much is conveyed in a Huguenot call to arms, composed in early spring 1562 after Duke François de Guise had massacred three dozen Calvinists in Vassy:

> I: This divine Providence / Which governs through Its power / the world and all its citizens / Uses many means. In all these things that one sees It do, / It takes help and ministers / In some human instruments. / Thus the humans who worship It / Quite in vain implore Its succors / When they want not to employ their own hands.
>
> II: Vows, wishes, clamors, / Desires, saintly prayers, / And even faith itself cannot always / Obtain from God what one wishes: / It is often enough necessary / If we want to complete our designs / To add to them our efforts . . .
>
> III . . . / It is a very vain thing / Than [this:] an idle man who rests / On the succor of his vain hope / And who does not embrace and use / The means that God gives him / To perform His will / . . .

IV . . . / We moan and clamor in vain / cry to God, joined hands to
Heaven / And shed tears as effeminates [do]: / The wicked will perform
their massacres / And God will not send to beat them back / A squadron
of armed angels [cf. Matt. 26.53]. . . .
V: But if leaving aside vain tears / We grab in hand strong weapons, /
And if we place more hope / In God than in our human powers, / He
will arm us with His grace / To repel far away the bold / Who would
dare assail us, / And to ensure the Church / With such a long-lasting
respite / That this respite will never falter.[48]

It would be tempting to chalk up this notion of human providence, thus
of human agency—one that Calvinist ministers took to the America of the
War of Independence—to the modernity of the early modern confessional
wars.[49] But two considerations militate against this. First, the arguments in
this putatively Modern call to action are couched in religious language and
argued for theologically. Christian conceptions allowed a space for the human
subject. On the eve of the English Civil War (1642–1651), future regicide John
Cook (executed in 1660) penned a rambling pamphlet ramblingly titled *Monarchy, no creature of Gods making, &c, wherein it is proved by Scripture and
reason, that monarchicall government is against the minde of God, and that the
execution of the late king was one of the fattest sacrifice that ever Queen Iustice
had.* Cook considered (with the help of Isaiah and Revelation) that he was
witnessing in his own present a "righteous war" led by God against evil. He
cautioned that it was a war where the good were duty bound to actually fight:
"It is an error in any to hold that the power of Anti-Christ must not be destroyed by the materiall sword, and [this error is] maintained by such only as
turne all Scriptures into allegories." For this reason, he approved of the Polish
gentry, who, during the reading of the Creed, "stand up," to indicate that they
will "fight for their religion against all opposers."[50] Other Puritans (but not
all)[51] also favored direct human action. During the Putney debates of 1647,
another regicide, William Goffe, argued that the destruction of Antichrist in
religious matters had to be accompanied with great transformations in political matters because the "mistery [*sic*] of iniquity" is "interwoven and intwisted
in the interests of States." This work of reform would be effected by Jesus
Christ with a "company of Saints . . . such as are chosen and called and faithful [cf. Rev. 17.14]." Goffe, who after the Cromwellian episode escaped to the
American colonies, averred that "itt is a scruple among the Saints, how farre
they should use the sworde," but pointed to past episodes, in which "God hath

made use of them in that worke."[52] And in the circle of the imprisoned Fifth Monarchist John Rogers, according to a spy's report sent to Cromwell's secretary John Thurloe, it was said "that we did not live in an age to expect miracles; that Babylon cannot be destroyed, nor the saint [Rogers] at Windsor be released, by only faith and prayer; but you must be of courage, and make use of material instruments, and proceed by force; per example (said he) if this house of Lambeth were to be pulled down, you must make use of materials, and not expect it will ever fall by faith or prayer."[53] Contemporaneously, across the Atlantic in Puritan New England, John Cotton, commenting on Revelation 11.15, told his congregants that "they being the Kingdom of Christ, they were bound to goe out against all people, to subdue all such as are weaker than they." It was not dematerialized spiritual warfare, or not merely that: a decade later Cotton expressed to Oliver Cromwell (whose combats were not solely allegorical or moral, far from it) his satisfaction that the English Lord Protector had fought the Lord's battles.[54]

Such opinions had been common in the previous century, on the reformed side of the religious wars. Radical reformer Thomas Müntzer, like Cook after him, lambasted those who argued that the sword was fully allegorical: "our scribes . . . say in their godless, stolen way that the Antichrist will be destroyed without a hand being lifted." To the contrary, "the elect did not win the promised land with the sword alone, but rather through the power of God. Nevertheless, the sword was the means, just as for us eating and drinking are the means for sustaining life." Müntzer's *Sermon to the Princes* ironized, "do not offer us any stale posturing about how the power of God should do it without your application of the sword." Was it given to rust in the scabbard?[55] A decade later Anabaptist theologian Bernhard Rothmann mobilized the Münsterites to action in these words:

> There are some who think that God Himself will come with His angels from heaven to take revenge on the godless. They wait confidently for it. No, dear brother. He will come, that is true. But the vengeance must first be carried out by God's servants who will, as is right, render retribution on the godless and unrighteous, as God has ordered them. God will be with His people; He will give them iron horns and bronze claws against their enemies. Indeed, shortly, we, who are in alliance with the Lord, must be His instruments to attack the godless on the Day which the Lord has prepared.[56]

That human agency was argued for theologically may in itself not be the strongest objection to the putative linkage between Modernity and the emergence of Man as the Subject of History. After all, the new has to emerge from the old and must speak its language in order to explain and assert itself. Michael Walzer underscored the extent of human agency in Puritan thought but chalked this to Modernity, even though the textbook for this activism was the biblical story of Exodus.[57] Thus—second consideration—it may be a more potent argument to point out that this Modern activism was not unprecedented. Scrolling back further in time, one finds apologies for agency a century earlier, with the already discussed Jeanne d'Arc. In early 1429, the Valois pretender to the French throne, Charles VII, and his court were puzzled by the sudden appearance of this young woman. She claimed to have been sent by God to free the realm from the English. Modern secularist history offers an easy explanation for this surprising entry onstage of "the Maid." She arrived on the scene after a century of war, in which more often than not the English royal line descended from Philip the Fair's daughter Isabella had trounced loyalists to the rival dynasty descended from Philip's brother Charles de Valois. The Hundred Years War was accompanied by the usual sorry train of exactions, murders, and rapes, savaging the civilian population. This long-term crisis had called into existence prophets and visionaries before the Maid.[58]

To us, therefore, Joan is explainable. But she was not so clear to her contemporaries. They wondered whether this female holy warrior was not in fact a fraud. In Poitiers worried theologians in Charles's entourage interrogated her. Did God need a human agent to save France? "You assert that a voice told you, God willed to deliver the people of France. . . . But if God wills to deliver them, it is not necessary to have soldiers." Jeanne answered: "By God's name, men-at-arms (*gens d'armes*) will do battle and God will grant victory."[59] The Dominican Guillaume Aymeri was satisfied by her answer, but others, likely, were not. The notion of divine agency was braided with a disbelief that stemmed from the pacifist component in the Christian dialectic between war and peace. Could God warrant by granting her an exploit at war that Joan was sent by Him? Could the relief of the siege of Orléans, 120 kilometers south of Paris, which the Maid asserted would demonstrate her divine mission, be a proper sign? To those who argued that the Lord could act by Himself to save France, Jacques Gelu (d. 1432) retorted that it was forbidden to tempt Him. Humans should not ask God for a miracle when they can work by themselves. Of course, if God intervenes, Gelu explained, humans must cooperate with

Him, because, in the words of the Pauline First Letter to the Corinthians, 3.9, "we are God's co-helpers [*Dei . . . coadjutores sumus*]." This, he explained in the course of his treatise, meant full and intelligent human military measures for a God-willed just war.[60]

Gelu did not hurriedly invent these ideas, then cull authorities in the sacred scriptures because he was pressed by the need to legitimate Joan's intervention on the side of the Dauphin Charles de Valois. By the thirteenth century, biblical exegesis had developed the notion that a ruler would be tempting God if that ruler relied exclusively on Him, and did not take measures dictated by human prudence or foresight (*providentia*). Such was, in particular, the mantra of the scriptural commentator most read in the Late Middle Ages, the Franciscan Nicolas of Lyra, a friend of the Valois dynasty and partisan of strong royal power. The king had to exercise his providence, plan, and build an army and strongholds in preparation for war.[61]

As often, texts produced around the First Crusade bring home these notions with their full, bloodiest import.[62] They take us back three centuries before Bishop Gelu. Chapter 2 analyzed a sermon that Baldric of Dol reported (or imagined), as having been preached right before the 1099 assault against Jerusalem's walls. It concluded with a ringing call: "Act then, put on with confidence your weapons, and assail with confidence this city, you helpers of God [*coadjutores Dei*]."[63] The sermon refracts here what must have been a commonplace. Baldric, indeed, a nonparticipant in the crusade, shared with the participant Raymond d'Aguilers this understanding of agency. The final battle of the First Crusade was fought after the conquest of Jerusalem, near Ascalon (August 12, 1099), against a Fatimid Egyptian army. As Jay Rubenstein has shown, the apocalyptic charge was still high. The Christians called Cairo, the Fatimids' capital, "Babylon," since early Christian exegesis the city of Antichrist. Recounting the crusaders' mood prior to combat, Raymond d'Aguilers drew on the same Pauline passage: "We wanted Him [God] to be our defender in our cause, and [we wanted] to be His helpers in His cause" ("in nostra parte defensorem et in sua adiutores illi esse voluimus").[64] The early medieval legend of the Last Emperor, likely well known to crusaders, gave implicitly a role to the Christian holy warrior as Subject of History. A Christian army would open up the Last Days, and it would not be merciful.[65]

Contained in a manuscript variant of Raymond's *Liber*, a long sermon, addressed to the knights of Christ, which celebrated with gruesome glee and anti-Semitism the Jerusalem massacres of July 15–18, 1099, picked up the same theme. It reminded its crusading audience that God could have realized His vengeance against the Muslims by summoning more than twelve legions of angels. The reference is the same as in the 1562 Calvinist call to arms: Matt. 26.53, Jesus' rebuke to Peter for having taken up the sword in His defense ("Thinkest thou that I cannot ask my Father, and that He will give me at once more than twelve legions of angels?"). But God, the preacher goes on, "in order to honor you, decided to accomplish through you [the crusading army] what He refused to accomplish through" angelic might.[66]

A few decades later, Bernard of Clairvaux explained theologically the notion of cooperation with the Lord: "God generously founded merits for the human being, where He established that, through Him and with Him, good people can worthily perform good works." Humans are joined together to the divine will through consent and free will. This explanation brought to Bernard's quill pen military images: "God uses angels and humans of good will as if His co-fighters and co-helpers, whom He will reward with great generosity once victory has been achieved."[67] Perhaps not an unsurprising transition on the part of the most notable partisan of the Templars, that synthesis of monks and knights, spiritual warfare and physical warfare.

The idea of cooperation with God in holy war become a commonplace by the thirteenth century, as Jacques de Vitry's crusade preaching shows: "You must note carefully that, although God could liberate His land by Himself with one word, He wants to honour His servants and wants to have companions in its liberation, giving you the chance to save your souls, which He redeemed and for which He spilled His blood, and which therefore He does not like to lose."[68]

The militant *Passion of Raynald of Châtillon, prince of Antioch* (ca. 1187/89) took the notion to a stunning extreme. Raynald, whose disregard for truces had triggered Saladin's attack on the kingdom of Jerusalem and the defeat of crusader forces at Hattin (1187) was beheaded by the Muslim leader himself. Peter of Blois concluded his hagiographic text with a justification of conversion by the sword, the alloy of crusading and mission:

Even though with a will turned to evil they [the heathen] disparage the service owed to God, one must force them to serve the Living God, willy-nilly. I consider that this sort of coercion is most pleasing to God insofar as it procures the salvation of human beings. Let us promote God's will as much as we are able; indeed, "we are God's helpers." Thus just as we pray that God's Kingdom may come, so let us strive in action (*actualiter*) that His empire may spread; that the heathen may submit to

Him under an iron rod; and that those who do not want willingly to enter may be dragged by violence to the Kingdom. About this violence the Lord speaks through the Prophet [Ez. 20.33 and 40], saying: "I shall reign over you with a strong hand and an outstretched arm, and in My fury; and I shall bring you into the bonds of My alliance."[69]

The Pauline expression, "helpers" or "co-helpers of God," had initially applied to the field of missionary work; one should not be surprised of its extension to holy war and crusade. Benjamin Kedar has shown how, contrary to our presumptions, crusade and mission were not opposed. Witness how, in the Pseudo-Turpin *History of Roland*, in an episode also depicted in the Charlemagne window of Chartres Cathedral, Roland jousts with the Saracen giant Farragut or Ferracutus; during a truce the paladin preaches to his Muslim counterpart, step by step (it is a *disputatio*), the difficult points of Christianity; and then kills him as a testimony to the veracity of his sermon.[70]

At the same time, if Man could be, in a way, the Subject of History, History was still God's History. The crusade was precisely a God-sent moment in which, simultaneously, God's will and God's choice of elects realized themselves on earth and in History. It meant a sorting out of elect and non-elect among the crusaders on the threshing floor of tribulations. To put the argument in more provocative terms, human agency appeared when God's cause was at stake, therefore, in particular, when Christians fought in holy war for the *causa Dei*. In Providential History's epochal moments, it was men who performed holy vengeance, by God's grace. This was the paradoxical avenue He chose to grant merit, on extraordinary occasions, to His in principle powerless creature.[71] Homilies on the exaltation of the Holy Cross said as much. Emperor Heraclius was graced with the recovery through war of the True Cross, the victory-bringing relic par excellence, because it had allowed itself to be captured at war, for its own and for the Christian ruler's exaltation. In this line of thought, the Cistercian Henry de Marcy mused over the defeat of Hattin and the loss of the Holy Cross to Saladin:

These events did not take place because Muhammad could do them, but because Christ willed them. He wanted to give Christians an occasion to be zealous for their Lord's glory, to avenge an injury done to the Father, and to vindicate their inheritance. Behold, indeed, this is the time acceptable [to the Lord], when those who have been positively tested will be displayed, when the Lord will test who is His: who is His faithful;

and who is unfaithful; who are the false sons; and who are His [true] sons.[72]

The Cross's captivity in 1187 was but one of a chain of felicitous rebounds, made of losses and glorious recoveries—by Helena, Heraclius, Charlemagne, and the first crusaders. In specific moments of Sacred History, God and pre-modern man were co-agents. Unpleasant as it may be to us, this human agency took place in two fields, mission and holy war. Comparably, in the Modern era, the divine did not efface itself behind Man. Marx—who insisted that History was Man's work—could still write of History as the judge, and of the Proletariat as its executioner.[73]

God's sovereign will manifested itself in miraculous exceptions to His ordinary dispensation. It showed itself when He allowed crusaders to do His work, even though humans, no matter how exalted socially, were in principle, powerless compared to History's divine Subject; it showed itself (as we saw in Chapter 5) when He allowed ordinary Christians to execute His plans despite the existence of the magistrate of Paul's Letter to the Romans 13. When depicted, this second form of rupture, like the first, involved the sublime.[74]

The Sublime

> In this earthly Jerusalem there flow rivers of blood, since the nation of
>   error perishes!
>   O Jerusalem!
> And the Temple's pavement is made bloody with the blood of the dying.
>   O Jerusalem!
> They are handed over to hellfire; we are blessed and rejoice, since the
>   evildoers are perishing.
>   O Jerusalem!
> The invader has been proven guilty, and the expelled Jew mourns be-
>   cause Christ, God holds it.
>   O Jerusalem!
> Glory to the cave whence came the lion resurrected, awakened by God![75]

This gruesome chant immediately follows the crusade sermon, which we just discussed, that stated that God had chosen to use the crusaders rather than His angelic hosts. Its aesthetics of death and gore take us to a second facet that theology can illuminate, terror and beauty in sacred violence—or otherwise put, the sublime.

The First Crusade's Sublime

With the ethical asymmetry that characterized western European culture until at least the Enlightenment, horror in the sublime mode carried different valences, depending on whether its source was the crusaders or their enemies. This asymmetry makes sense given medieval mentalities in general—according to which, for example, it is right to ambush the enemy, but an ambush by the enemy is treasonable. But further, this asymmetry was theologically driven. As recently explored by Jay Rubenstein, most First Crusade chronicles report that the starving Christian army committed acts of cannibalism just after (or during) the conquest of Ma'arrat al-Nu'man in Syria.[76] The sublime, it shall be argued here, was at play for at least one direct observer. For him, cannibalism was not a planned tactic, unlike—if we trust Adhémar de Chabannes (d. 1034)—during the Norman Roger of Tosny's campaign in Spain circa 1020. The Norman lord had faked cannibalism on executed Saracen prisoners; the "monstrous" tale, broadcast, had made Spanish Muslims "lose spirit," "demand peace from the Countess of Barcelona Ermesende," and promise "to pay a yearly tribute." The chronicler Adhémar sounded almost amused.[77] Not so Fulcher of Chartres circa 1104. Fulcher, although not an eyewitness, recounts the Ma'arrat episode only with "great horror" (*dicere perhorreo*).[78]

But a chronicler could understand horror as Providential. Raymond d'Aguilers, unlike Fulcher an eyewitness, reports two effects of this incident. First, it threw into despair some crusaders among the Franks, who left the expedition (*iter*). Second, the Muslims came to view the Franks as "stubborn and bloodthirsty" and assumed that cannibalism and "other extremely bloodthirsty practices . . . existed among us." Tellingly, Raymond adds, "God had given fear of us to all heathens, but we did not know it." This fear was, precisely, awe, as a fuller citation allows us to see:

> Meanwhile there was such a great famine in the army that the [common] people ate with great avidity many Saracen bodies, which were already rotting, and which had lain in the swamps of that city for two weeks and more. These deeds terrified (*terrebant*) many, both men from our nation and outsiders. Because of them, quite many among ours turned back, having lost hope of getting help for our journey from the

Frankish nation. However the Saracens and the Turks said: "Who can resist this nation which is so stubborn and bloodthirsty that it could not be forced away from the yearlong siege of Antioch by famine or the sword or any dangers, and now feeds itself on human flesh"? The pagans were saying that among us existed these practices and other extremely bloodthirsty ones [carried out] against them. For God had given fear (*timor*) of us to all the pagan nations, but we did not know this.[79]

First, cannibalism struck divine fear into the Muslims, a terror all the more divine as it was not planned by the crusaders. Second, it purged the Christian army of lukewarm elements, this very same group of "cowardly men, useless for war, who abandoned us," which d'Aguilers excoriates as apostates in the preface to his *Liber* and which is vowed to destruction in the vision of Christ's five wounds discussed in Chapter 4.[80] While one should agree with Jay Rubenstein that many chroniclers (such as Fulcher) felt uncomfortable with crusader anthropophagy, Raymond d'Aguilers had few qualms about it. Willed by God, it served His dual purpose, to purge the Holy Land of "paganism" and to purify Christ's army.[81] The incident was framed by two miracles. The first, one of the many visions granted to Peter Bartholomew, berated crusader vices in the light of earlier divine favors granted at Antioch, ordered "justice" in the army, and announced God's merciful delivery of Ma'arrat to the Christian army. To transmit this message, Andrew and Peter appeared to Peter Bartholomew, initially in the humble clothes in which they had been martyred; then they revealed their martyrs' beauty. "Terrified" (*perterritus*), the visionary broke into sweat.[82] In Ma'arrat, cannibalism was accompanied by another act of transgression, which constituted a further miracle. The march to Jerusalem had been plagued by delays occasioned by disputes among the princes for the possession of cities and strongholds, in particular Antioch. The same conflicts surfaced over Ma'arrat. The commoners, enraged, in order to force the march forward toward Jerusalem, tore down the city's walls. They did so despite the explicit opposition of princes and bishops; they did so with superhuman strength, a starving man being able to throw at a distance from the walls stones "that three or four teams of oxen could hardly have dragged." At this point, Raymond of Saint-Gilles (according to his chaplain Raymond d'Aguilers) understood that there was something divine at work given that the poor could not be stopped. He followed their wishes.[83]

The historian's natural explanation will be that cannibalism was the material consequence of terrible conditions for a huge army far away from provisioning. But it was also, viewed theologically, an awful element in an awesome cycle of election, sin, travails, and divine redemption, a cycle that culminated in victory and massacre in Jerusalem on July 15–18, 1099.

Asymmetrically, the sublime meaningfulness of horror was denied to the opposite, Muslim side. Marching to Jerusalem, in a lived narrative of sieges and hunger, crusaders had in their heads the Vengeance of the Savior, a family of legends based on Flavius Josephus's *Jewish Wars* and diffused in the West since at least about 900 C.E. In this story, an act of cannibalism constituted the symbolic capstone for Ancient Israel's defeat in 70 C.E. at the hands of Titus.[84] The Jews' own sacred History, built of cycles of election, failure, and redemption, had been terminated definitively by the deicide. Its punishment had been the harsh Roman siege of Jerusalem, culminating in the destruction of the Temple. Famine had so taxed the city's defenders that a Jewish woman had roasted her newborn child, then shared the flesh with the starving soldiers who had followed the alluring smell.[85] The deed did not hold any positive charge, to the contrary. In the Vengeance of the Savior textual tradition, the awe elicited by the vanquished's cannibalism was not an awe of election, but an awe of wrathful damnation. And circa 1099, who were the Jews, murderers of the Incarnate God, if not a type for the enemy, the Muslims now occupying the terrestrial Jerusalem and defacing His images? Raymond had referred to the Vengeance before his account of the Ma'arrat cannibalism: a supernatural vision had exhorted the crusaders, hemmed in Antioch between a still Muslim citadel and Kerbogha's relief army, to combat, lest they be trapped in the city "for so long that they would eat one another." But the message had reassured them of election: "Know of sure that the days have come, which the Lord promised Blessed Mary and His Apostles, that He would raise up the kingdom of the Christians, and throw down and trample under feet the kingdom of the pagans." No, the army of Christ would not be eaten; it would eat. Raymond d'Aguilers likely understood the popular crusaders in the light of Revelation. They were the birds (or perhaps a type for the birds) that the angel calls to the "great supper of the Lord" and that find satiation by devouring "the flesh of the kings and the flesh of tribunes and the flesh of mighty men and the flesh of horses and of them who sit on them, and the flesh of all freemen and bondsmen and the flesh of small and great" (cf. Rev. 19:17–21).[86] Horror was positive for the elect, damning for the foreknown. One will remember how the roasting of Lawrence on the grill "affected with a vengeful horror" pagan nostrils but "pleasured and soothed" their Christian counterparts.[87]

It was also asymmetrically that the chroniclers envisaged massacre. Old

Testament vaticinations described very much the same forms of mass killing for Babylon and Jerusalem but with different valences. The former, a good purge, avenged the heathens' misdeeds against the elect; the latter, a scourging willed by God, purified His people but did not grant any rewards, to the contrary, to the evil perpetrators. The slaughter in Jerusalem in July 1099 constituted even more than cannibalism a sign of God's awesome presence. Its descriptions and tone have left modern interpreters doubtful that the massacre was as intense as contemporary chroniclers depicted it.[88] Norman Housley has wondered "why the crusaders themselves so crudely exulted in what they had done," and proposed, tentatively, that they were conscious of the expectations of the Christians back in Europe, who expected "radical dispossession of the polluters." Thus "it was best to claim that this had occurred in order to secure the continuing military support that was necessary."[89] Military historian John France has accepted that the massacre was massive but chalked up this intensity not to religious zeal but to the enormous stress of a long expedition, dense in travails and reversals. Compared with other eleventh-century war atrocities, the 1099 slaughter in Jerusalem was not exceptional.[90] Yet another scholar—Kaspar Elm, who has come closer, if it is proper to put it so, to the truth of the matter—has proposed that chroniclers chose to exaggerate the massacre because this war was God's war. Consequently, they painted it using the awesome colors of the "literary tradition" composed of Old Testament, Flavius Josephus's *Jewish Wars*, and other quasi-scriptural sources. Writes Elm: "They wanted to make manifest the theological relevance . . . of the event and to see it in the light of the Holy Writ."[91] But these explanations do not convince. First, given Elm's hypothesis, as Benjamin Kedar has suggested, why not go one step further and assume that the crusaders themselves acted out the theological script?[92]

Crusaders "crudely exulted" not simply in the folia of the chronicles but in fact. They exulted in massacre because this was what the Psalms and the prophetic books of the Bible mandated holy warriors. Five hundred years later, a Jesuit would similarly shudder in horror and pleasure at the bloody purge of the Calvinists during the Parisian Saint Bartholomew's night. It was a *horrenda tragedia*, on which one should not linger too much. But all the same, this Joachim Opser S.J., later prince-abbot of Saint-Gall (1577–1594), described what had not only "ravished in marvel the Christian world" but even more taken it "to the summits of joy": "Immense massacre! My soul shuddered (*horruit*) at the sight of this river saturated with the naked corpses of the killed and with shamefully wounded bodies."[93] Catholic rapture and contortions from the age of Michangelo da Caravaggio, but present in the pre-Baroque Middle Ages! Finally, *pace* John France, Jerusalem 1099 was not the ordinary sack of an ordinary city.[94] How to account for the ways in which the crusaders killed (sometimes simply, sometimes with tortures)? Was stoning people the quickest, most efficient way to massacre?[95] How to explain why the crusaders slaughtered women and children, sometimes by dashing the little ones' skulls against the walls?[96] How to account for the absence of any mention of rape in the Christian sources, this until the twelfth-century *Chanson d'Antioche*? There, the rape of "the beautiful pagan women" is perpetrated by the grotesque, savage, and plebeian Tafurs. With disapproval: the poet comments that "it bore heavily on Jesus, Paradise's King."[97]

In Jerusalem, sexual violence was avoided. It was likely frowned upon during the whole expedition. According to Fulcher of Chartres, after the victory against Kerbogha before Antioch, during the Turkish camp's plunder, the crusaders "killed the women whom they found in the tents." Fulcher later redacted this passage anew, to clarify that "as to the women whom they found in their tents, the Franks did no other evil than pierce their bellies through with lances" (a likely adaptation of Phineas's zeal in Num. 25, where the priest spears the heathen "harlot" through the womb).[98] As for Jerusalem, letters preserved in the Cairo Geniza indicate positively that the crusaders, while they burnt the Jews in a synagogue, did not rape Jewish women ("unlike others" do, meaning the Muslims, possibly in the Egyptian Fatimid reconquest of Jerusalem from the Turks in August 1098 after a forty-day siege).[99] One should underline here how religious considerations—the refusal of sexual pollution— overrode the normal male warrior drives. In the words of a much earlier, Visigothic source: "Behold, judgment by combat is at hand, and it would be pleasing that a person fornicates?" (*libet animam fornicari?*).[100]

Rape was eliminated from the script, but other cruel biblical types not so. The same Jewish letters confirm Raymond d'Aguilers: the crusaders tortured some of their prisoners—not the most efficient way to massacre.[101] A good portion of the Christian army was living a biblical scenario of retribution. The brutal killing of children, skulls smashed against a wall or stone, was scriptural. The models both refer to Babylon; they are Isaiah 13.16 (depicting the Medes' sack of the Chaldean capital), "their infants will be smashed," and Psalm 136.9, "Blessed be he who will take your little ones [Babylon's] and smash them against a stone." *Pace* Martin Aurell, Albert of Aachen, who underlines the immensity of the bloodshed and this gruesome treatment of children, did not disapprove. Plainly, the crusaders "were piercing through with the sword's point women who had fled into the turreted palaces and dwellings; seizing by the soles of their feet from their mothers' laps or their cradles infants who were still suckling and dashing them against the walls or lintels of the doors and breaking their necks." A final massacre involved stoning, also not the most efficient way to kill.[102] A poem celebrating the 1087 Pisan expedition against Muslim Mahdia in North Africa described the same methods of purging.[103] Another poem, hard to date but given its accents possibly penned after the First Crusade, breathes the same foul air. It called for deluded paganism to convert—but the convincing was performed by God's work at war, realized by "blessedly cruel" swords. As in the chiliast imagination of Raymond d'Aguilers's circle, the endpoint of the conquest (performed by "the rich in union with the poor") was social equality: "The last will be the first, and the first last; they may have had unequal callings, but will have an equal reward, . . . There will not be here greater over inferior, poor compared to rich; one will not oppose another, and there will be no place for shame."[104] Coincidentally (?), the vengeance involved skull-smashing:

As the Prophet testifies,
You wretched daughter of Babylon,
Blessed is he, who smashes your
Small ones against the stone.
Now, capital of Chaldea
You render retribution for your age-old crimes.[105]

This form of killing also guided some centuries later the 1572 Saint Bartholomew's Day Massacre. The Parisian Catholics lived Isaiah's prophecy against pagan Babylon—in their present, against the heretical Calvinists. The transposition was unproblematic. The prophet's words were stamped by their mystical interpretation. Jerome had commented on Isaiah 13.17–18:

[And I shall arouse against them the Medes, who neither seek silver nor desire gold, but who will kill their little ones with arrows and shall not spare those who draw milk at the womb] . . . May God give us the power to desire neither the silver and the gold of eloquence and secular wisdom, but let us kill with spiritual arrows (that is with the testimonies of the Scriptures) the sins of heretics and of all those who have been deceived. And let those fed by error's milk be slaughtered without any mercy, and let them die by a clement cruelty. And let us not have mercy on anyone's infancy, and let us be worthy of the following Beatitude, "Blessed be he who will take hold of his little ones and dash them against the rock" [cf. Ps. 136.9].[106]

The Church Father's exegesis had not defanged literal violence. In Paris, inflamed to zeal by God, the ultra-Catholics performed the letter in the spirit. It was a "cruel day," a "day of wrath and fury" (Isa. 13.9) perpetrated by a "war militia" of "strong men," God's "sanctified ones," who "rejoice in his glory" (Isa. 13.3–4), when houses are pillaged, wives raped (this form of violence French holy warriors avoided), and infants dashed to pieces before their parents' eyes, even those still suckling, or still in the womb (Isa. 13.16, 18). Everyone found [in the street] shall be slain, and any who would help them will fall to the sword (Isa.13.15). Testimonies belonging to plural source-genres attest in particular to the butchering of infants and children as well as pregnant women.[107] One Strasbourg citizen testified in Calvinist Heidelberg to the following:

> On Thursday, he saw a woman, greatly beautiful—she seemed a countess. She was being stripped naked on the Pont des Moulins [the Pont-aux-Meuniers, going from the Quai de la Mégisserie]. She was beautifully dressed and richly adorned with precious arm [bracelets] and necklaces, and in such an advanced state of pregnancy that one saw her fruit stirring in her body. They first ripped her clothes away, then threw her down, pulled her hair out and larded her through with blows, even though she was begging them pitifully to at least take her child alive out of her, then to do with her as they pleased (*ires geffallens*). Then they threw her in the water, and as she fell backward in it, one could still see the child wiggle in her body.[108]

The biblical references, far from being literary coloring, actually indicate that many protagonists wished for a massive massacre (and perpetrated one as far as it was possible). The chronicler and crusade participant Peter Tudebode cued through Scripture his readership on the ambit of the slaying: "Who ever saw, or heard of, such massacres of pagan people? And their number is unknown to all, with the exception of God" ("Tales occisiones de paganorum gente quis unquam vidit nec audivit? Numerum quorum nemo scivit, nisi solus Deus").[109] These words echo Isaiah 66.08, "Quis audivit umquam tale, et quis vidit huic simile?"[110] One is here amid the very last chapter of Isaiah's prophecy, announcing Jerusalem's miraculous restoration, the conversion of the Gentiles, and divine vengeance ("God giving retribution to His enemies," Isa. 66.6). Tudebode's pointer should be taken seriously. Far from cueing for disbelief, his words signaled the realization by Zion's true sons of the Eschaton's great purge. As announced by Isaiah, it would leave the land strewn with corpses. And so, indeed, was Jerusalem in July 1099.

Raymond d'Aguilers's famous description of the slaughter also incorporates what to a Modern can look like critical distance. Was the massacre "hardly credible"?[111]

> But what we have said thus far is small and limited. However let us come to the Temple of Solomon, where the pagans used to sing their rites and ceremonies. And what was done there? If we tell the truth, we shall go beyond what is credible (*Si verum dicimus, fidem excedimus*). Let it then suffice to say only that in the temple and forecourt of Solomon, one rode in blood to one's knees, and up to the horses' bridles.[112]

This last image is, as is well known, a citation of Revelation 14.20. What, thus, "suffice[d] to say" in approximating the massacre's amplitude was to cite John's gory vision. Revelation 14.20, being a vision, expressed in images a higher reality, which human words were unable to encompass.[113] For Raymond d'Aguilers, Tudebode, and the *Gesta*, the description of the massacres was a figure of speech, as Joseph-François Michaud understood to a point: "These statements . . . are evidently a hyperbole, and demonstrate that the Latin historians exaggerated matters which they should have hidden."[114]

Commenting the same biblical text around the time of the crusade, the Gregorian Bruno of Segni agreed: "Grammarians call this mode of speech a hyperbole." But what exactly was medieval Christian hyperbole? For Seneca, the incredible provides a path to the credible ("incredibilia adfirmat, ut ad credibilia perueniat") through hyperbole. This figure of rhetoric leads to the truth (*verum*, the word used by Raymond) through falsehood ("in hoc omnis hyperbole extenditur, ut ad uerum mendacio ueniat"). According to the ancient grammarian Quintilian's definition, hyperbole "consists in a proper excess of the truth (*est haec decens ueri superiectio*)." It is proper when dealing with something extraordinary. "When the thing of which we speak transgresses the bounds of nature (*cum res ipsa de qua loquendum est naturalem modum excedit*)," the writer is "allowed to speak in an ampler style (*amplius dicere*), because it is not possible to express how great this thing is (*quia dici quantum est non potest*), and discourse (*oratio*) is more efficient when it goes beyond [something] than when it stops short of it."[115] Augustine, closing his commentary on John, asserted the same principle as Quintilian, underlining that the person who uses hyperbole to point to a truth has no "wish to deceive."[116] The principle passed into Isidore of Seville's influential *Etymologies*.[117] And it stayed in the stream of biblical commentaries: Alcuin picked it up; so did a commentary attributed to Bede;[118] it passed into the authoritative biblical commentary for the High and Late Middle Ages, the twelfth-century *Ordinary Gloss*.[119] Hrabanus also mentioned hyperbole in his commentary on the Second book of Maccabees, an apocryphal work of great importance for early medieval holy wars insofar as the *milites christi* had an antetype in the Jewish fighters against Seleucid paganism.[120]

This medieval notion of the sublime explains why, reportedly, the crusaders expressed their joy in songs, not through speeches: "Their mind offered to the victorious and triumphant God actions of grace, which they could not unfold (*explicare*) in words."[121] Michaud, who suggested that the depictions were hyperbolic, was his enlightened age's spokesman in considering that "imagination turns its back with fright (*effroi*) from these scenes of desolation." But medieval hyperbole guided medieval imagination to focus eagerly on such gruesome landscapes, as indicators of God's presence. In sum, a careful appreciation of Raymond's choice of words shows that (1) the massacre occurred; (2) it was much greater than words could describe (hence, the recourse to a vision); and (3) it was so intense and so beyond description precisely because God's hand was at work. It is not too far-fetched, then, to imagine with Guy Lobrichon how some crusaders lived the assault: as they breached the walls of Jerusalem, the trumpets that the army sounded must have been the trumpets announcing the End of History and the opening of Heaven's Gates.[122]

Hyperbolic symbolism also explains a striking feature of Raymond d'Aguilers's chronicle. The *Liber* mentions, as far as I see, beauty or delectable sight in only four moments, which all have to do with death. Two such moments relate to the death, en masse, of Turkish enemies—horses and riders falling down a cliff or mutilated bodies rolling in a bloodied river.[123] A third moment of beauty was the terrifying transformation in Ma'arrat of Andrew and Peter from abjectly dressed martyrs into shining saints. The fourth moment of beauty relates to the glorious death of two crusaders, one of whom appears to the other in ghostly splendor. Right before his death in battle, Anselm of Ribemont had a vision of the deceased Engelrand de Saint Pol.

The former asked the latter "how he had acquired his beauty, which was intense" ("de pulchritudine eius quę nimia erat, unde accidisset ei"). By way of answer, Engelrand showed his heavenly mansion to Anselm and announced to him that he would inhabit an even more beautiful one. The following day, Anselm was martyred.[124] This relation to aesthetics—which found progeny, for instance, in eighteenth-century evangelical feelings of delight and beauty at the apprehension of God's justice—differs markedly from that of the lay chronicler of the mid-thirteenth-century Seventh Crusade, Jean de Joinville.[125] Joinville takes clear delight in describing the ship of his relative, the count of Jaffa, arriving alongside the king's nave. It "seemed to fly owing to the rowers who forced hard at the oars; and to hear the sound produced by the streaming banners and by the din of the kettledrums, drums, and Saracen horns that were in his galley, it seemed as if lightning was falling from the sky." The knight Joinville, who displays delicate appreciation for his Muslim enemies, was sensitive to beauty. Influenced by the culture of courtly romances, he saw it everywhere: in the Mamluk soldiers' glistening armor on the shore off Damietta; or in a cloth thrown overboard burning softly on a night sea; or (in the same scene) in the agile nakedness of Louis' young queen.[126] But Raymond d'Aguilers's splendor crystalized itself only on the mysteries of God at war. Habitually sensitive to courtly beauty, Marcabru agreed with Raymond. In his tellingly titled song "Peace in the Name of the Lord," the troubadour promised ultimate splendor to those who would go to the "washing place," the war cleansing all sins in Spain: "And their beauty will be—do you know what it will be, the beauty of those who will go to the washing place? Greater than the beauty of the morning star. Only, we must avenge God for the wrong they [the Muslims] are doing to Him here, and over there near Damascus."[127]

In Raymond d'Aguilers's *Liber*, the sublime and human agency come together. In an exceptional Event—which for the chiliast chronicler was uniquely final—the crusaders both experienced the sublime irruption of the transcendental into the phenomenal and experienced being full agents moving Sacred History forward, cohelpers of God. One should go one step beyond Elm's suggestions and propose, in the line of Crouzet, that, in 1099, the "literary tradition" did not simply inform the chroniclers.[128] If the "specific kind of war" that occurred in 1096–1100 determined the verbal excesses of the chronicles, it more likely than not also stamped the actual and factual violent deeds of the Christian warriors,[129] through the reproduction of holy exemplars. Evidently, not all wars, not even all crusades, were so perceived and prosecuted.

But this was how some among the first crusaders lived the sacred violence of July 15, 1099, the storming of Jerusalem.

But how "Christian" was this mode of perceiving and acting? Are we not dealing with an "anthropological universal" when it comes to violence for the gods? Such is Kaspar Elm's position, invoking René Girard, Walter Burkert, and Mary Douglas, and bemoaning "the simultaneity of bloodlust and enthusiastic devotion for God, the shocking proximity between *violence and the sacred* and the conception of a fearsome God bent on lordship and vengeance."[130] Cultural nuances are in order. The year 1099 cannot have been the first time in European history where horror met the numinous, and a useful point of comparison is provided by one of pagan Antiquity's most unpleasant texts. Likely penned for Emperor Titus (r. 79–81), or perhaps for his brother and successor Domitian (r. 81–91), Martial's *De spectaculis Liber* (*Book on the Spectacles*) is a chain of panegyric poems celebrating the ruler's power and divinity (*numen*). Its argument has been reconstructed by Kathleen Coleman in a now classic article.[131] Each poem recounts a performance in Rome's Coliseum (Martial, as it were, thus represents representations). Some of these reenact, sometimes with a surprising departure from the received plotline, often with sophisticated mechanical props, old legends from Greek mythology. Other vignettes involve animals performing extraordinary feats or facing off with humans. Yet others celebrate some gladiatorial combat or a massive reconstitution of naval battles from the Greco-Roman past (for which it was necessary to bring water into the Coliseum). Overwhelmingly dominant themes are coercion, violence, or submission. A woman impersonating Pasiphae (the lustful mother of the minotaur) is sexually penetrated by a bull (and probably dies in the process); a pregnant sow is speared and gives birth; a bandit is mauled by a bear, like Prometheus by the eagle appointed by Zeus to punish him; and so on. Having fought a bull, an elephant prostrates itself before the emperor; a hind hunted by dogs obtains asylum by going to Caesar and the hounds miraculously desist.

These displays simultaneously taxed belief and induced belief. The *On the Spectacles* uses five times the Latin verb *credere*, to "give credence" or "credit to," to "prove," to "believe." To cite the relevant sections:

> - You must believe (*credite*) that Pasiphae did couple with the bull of Dicte: we have seen it happen, the age-old myth has been vindicated [has received proof, "accepit prisca fabula fidem"].

- Who denies that Bacchus was brought forth by his mother's death? A deity was delivered by that means, you must believe it (*credite*): [for] so was born a beast.
   - Respectful and suppliant, the elephant that was recently so formidable to a bull worships you, Caesar. It does not do this on command, nor on instruction from any trainer: believe me (*crede mihi*), it too feels the presence of our god.
   - You don't believe (*non credis*) [that there was land where there is now water]? Watch (*specta*)!
   - In recognizing her prince [the doe] carried off this reward [immunity]. Caesar possesses a divine aura (*numen*): sacred (*sacra*) is, sacred his power (*potestas*). Believe it (*credite*), [since] beasts have not learnt how to lie.[132]

The representations, argued Martial, lent credence to the emperor's "sacred power" and divinity (*numen*). They lent credence as well to legends, staged with cruel gore. *Credere*, in the original sense, meant belief that gods existed—belief with a proof, the best proof being visual, a tangible manifestation.[133] But the emperor was also the person who, as giver of these technologically sophisticated spectacles, made the legends credible. Martial seems to want that this induced credence should resonate with and feed credence in the ruler's numinous nature. And in this scheme, violence, unbelievable in what it reveals to astonished eyes, should induce belief.

The pagan Martial shared this last assumption with the Christian authors who used hyperbole to recount the 1099 Jerusalem massacre. The difference is that the panegyrist is pleading for the presence of the numinous in the arena and in the emperor and, as a panegyrist, likely does not have to believe himself (nor does his audience believe him if it is cognizant of the genre's logic). On the other hand, the chroniclers of 1099 had just sincerely witnessed the manifestation of God's hand in History.

A Christian author (or ruler) did not need to instill faith in the equivalent of ancient Greek legends (*prisca fabula*), the Old Testament. The irruption of the sublime in 1099 was a unique Event, unlike the Roman games, which year after year sought to confirm both the emperor's divinity and the empire's manifest destiny. And the sublime in 1099—for Raymond d'Aguilers and similarly minded participants—manifested the election of a chosen remnant, not of a wide polity. Over time, this would change; eschatology, strident and apocalyptic in 1099, attenuated itself; the purge of Jerusalem became the founding moment of a messianic earthly kingdom meant to last into a now rescheduled Last Age, the kingdom of Jerusalem.[134] We shall return to this process, but want at this point to turn to the purgative virtues of God-willed violence.

Sublime, Horror, Merciless Purge, Terror

Scenarios of the End reveal and explain the logic of violence within more normal temporality. The twelfth-century Cistercian monk Aelred of Rielvaux (ca. 1110–1167) portrayed the contrasted fate of the elect and wicked at the Last Judgment, when Christ would appear in glory:

> For sure, fire will precede Him, and will set aflame His enemies. How they shall then tremble! how they shall quiver! how they shall want to hide yet will fail to do so! Then, for sure, instead of a sweet smell they will emit a stench [cf. 2 Cor. 2.15–16], instead of the girdle [they will wear] a rope, instead of curly hair baldness, and instead of the pectoral filet [carry] a hairshirt.

Among the reprobates would be many clergy finally forced to wear the vestments of penance. They would have realized their error—as the repentant Bolsheviks of the Moscow Trials—but—just as for the majority of the 1938 accused—it would be too late to obtain pardon. A first lesson of this sermon is that, at EndTimes, wrathful justice is so dominant that mercy becomes unthinkable. All those destined to damnation would behold a Christ showing a different face than to the good, and hear Him sounding a different timbre than would the good:

> Whether they [the wicked] want it or not, they will see Jesus on this day. Yet it will be a terrifying (*terribilis*) [Jesus], Who will thunder terrifyingly: "Depart from Me, accursed ones, into the eternal fire, which was prepared for the Devil and his angels" [Matt. 25.41]. But you, who are now building up in your soul Bethlehem, and transcend the world's allurements, its riches, and false honors . . . just as you will see His face, charming, similarly you will hear His voice, most sweetly saying: "Come, ye, blessed ones of My Father, receive the kingdom readied [for you] since the world's beginning" [Matt. 25.48].[135]

Another lesson of EndTimes is that horror does not only tame (or purge) corrupt humans. It works also on the good. The highlight of the spectacle at

History's End, Satan's punishment, will be purgative for those elect still alive at the moment of Christ's Second Coming. This had been common lore since Isidore's *Sentences*:

At the Last Judgment, the impious will be all the more harshly punished by a spiritual pain insofar as they will see that the elect have deserved glorious blessedness. The Devil will be thrown down [into the pit], and all will watch. Then in the sight of all the good, angels and men, he will be led away into the eternal fire with those who sided with him. While the Devil will be taken away to his damnation, many elect, still in the body when the Lord comes to the Last Judgment, will be struck by fear (*metus*) seeing that such a sentence punishes the impious. And these [living] elect will be purged [of their sins] by this terror (*terror*). Indeed, should there remain in their body any sin, they will be purged through that very fear [awakened in them] by the sight of the Devil's damnation. Whence Job [41.16] says, "When he will be led away, the angels will fear, and terrified will be purged."

Going on, Isidore, like Raymond d'Aguilers, considered that the apocalyptic moment would unmask false brethren. Thus, it combined the purgation of the truly good and the purge away from their ranks of hypocrites, including people who performed miracles and exorcisms in the Lord's name: "Many of those who now seem to be elect and saintly could perish in the day of the Judgment, as the prophet says, 'The Lord will call a trial by fire (*iudicium ad ignem*), and the abyss will devour much, and eat a part of the household'" (cf. Amos 7.4).[136]

Within time, in those numinous moments where God's hand shows itself, the same duality of blindness and true sight can operate. Recall how, when Lawrence was being grilled—a moment of horror in itself—the saint's burnt flesh smelled sweet to the elect but stank for the pagans, affecting them "with a vengeful horror."[137] The *horror uindex* pointed to the sublime vengeance that would come at the End of History, but the blind pagans could not understand the spirit behind the event. They stayed at the level of bare fear. Early modern Puritans sometimes conceived their holy violence similarly. Describing the Pequots burning en masse within Fort Mystic's besieged stockade (May 1637), William Bradford wrote that "horrible was the stink and stench thereof; but the victory seemed a sweet sacrifice."[138] One of the captains, Mason, marveled at the Indians' quasi-suicidal panic: "such a dreadful Terror did the ALMIGHTY let fall upon their Spirits, that they would fly from us into the very Flames, where many of them perished."[139] To their eighteenth-century Calvinist successors also, sermonizing during the French and Indian Wars or the American Revolution, "distempered Eyes" and "blind and guilty minds" could not apprehend God's justice, which, while "dreadful," was righteous delight and beauty to the elect. It afforded "so much terror to the wicked," but pleased "all holy beings" just as much as His mercy.[140] Hence, it is wrong-headed to suggest that two other captains involved in the Mystic massacre had bad consciences.[141] Just as at the Last Judgment, there was not any place for mercy when one executed God's vengeance. Philip Vincent wrote that "severe justice" replaced "pity." John Underhill described the emotions inspired by the scene: "Great and doleful was the bloody sight to the view of young soeldiers that never had beene in warre, to see so many soules lie gasping on the ground, so thicke in some places, that you could hardly passe along. It may be demanded, Why are you so furious (as some have said)[;] should not Christians have more mercy and compassion?"

Underhill referred his imaginary questioner to Old Testament war, mandating extermination, sometimes including women and children, for any people who had "growne to such a height of blood, and sinne against God and man." Outside this framework, mercy was of course normal: "If God had not fitted the hearts of men for this service, it would have bred in them a commiseration toward them: but every' [*sic*] man being bereaved of pitty fell upon the worke without compassion."[142] Underhill and Vincent had read their classics. Commenting on the grim precepts of Deuteronomy, which command to kill even relatives, even one's bosom wife, and even one's best friend if they should attempt to lead one to idolatry, Calvin explained that Scripture was conveying there that God wants in cases where one should "avenge His glory" the pious to overcome the strongest natural feelings; they should "trample underfoot natural affections" when His honor is at stake.[143] As in the Old Testament, the outcome was providential: the Pequots' country "was fully subdued and fallen into the hands of the English."[144] The horrifying dashing of little children's heads against the stone and the spearing through of pregnant women were prophesied; they were not meant to evoke pity. Calvin again: "However much it seems a cruel thing when he [David] desires that the small children, still tender and innocent, be shattered and broken against stones, yet it is nothing but the praise for a just judgment, since he does not speak out of his own impetus, and rather takes the words from God's mouth."[145] Stephen Marshall, in 1642, employed this horrifying image to plead for rigor against the monarchists.[146] Milton would a few years later turn the accusation of pity against the Presbyterians, who wanted to spare the king.[147] The Calvinist position was not only Calvinist. The Jacobins too understood quite well that, out of love for humankind, one had sometimes to forget human feelings. Thus reflected Robespierre over the pitiable Louis Capet; his death was necessary to found the Republic.[148]

Pity, therefore, when expressed at a key moment in History, was by definition erroneous or, to use the charged medieval adjective that survived the Middle Ages, "false." The revolutionary French Convention's representatives bewailed that selective mercy had hindered the reconquest of Toulon, a key harbor town, from the royalists. With a quill oozing pathos, Fouché, Albitte, Sébastien de Laporte, and Collot d'Herbois lamented: "Ah! . . . If eternal justice were not slowed down along its terrible course by exceptions, which, to spare tears to some individuals, lead to the shedding of flows of blood!"[149] Such miscalculations in revolutionary economy were a frequent target for the radical revolutionary Jean-Paul Marat. Marat propounded—like Augustine in his own way—the blood sacrifice of the few for the sake of the many. It made sense. We have already cited his reasoning: "to sacrifice six hundred heads in order to save three million three hundred thousand is a very simple calculus mandated by wisdom and philosophy."[150] This was "humanity"; the reverse— as he had proclaimed already in 1789—was "fausse humanité."[151] Among many similar statements calling for reasoned blood, Marat reminded his readership that popular judicial killings (exécutions populaires) at the Revolution's very beginnings had tamed into "spontaneous submission" the clergy and the aristocracy and made possible the Declaration of the Rights of Man. But a "false zeal" on the part of the Fatherland's soldiers and a "false pity" on the part of uncorrupt citizens had hindered the consistent application of this economical violence. Now—he wrote in July 1792—one had to return to these "exécutions populaires" and shed blood, alas in much greater buckets, à grands flots.[152]

Yet the revolutionary culture was not only so refreshingly calculating and rational. As has been recently discussed by Antoine de Baecque, it enlisted, sometimes unconsciously, sometimes consciously, the sublime and its terrifying face—la gloire et l'effroi. De Baecque cites a panegyric for one Geffroy, a man who had been involved in preventing an assassination attempt on Collot d'Herbois and had been lightly wounded in the process. It is remarkable for its neo-Catholic evocation of EndTimes:

What a day of dread for the depraved is that on which, legislators, you have recalled man to his original dignity, to another life, that day on which you have engaged the very Divinity in the cause of liberty. What a day of terror for the corrupt is that on which the martyrs raise themselves by the thousands to make a rampart of their bodies facing the blows of assassins. . . . It will be sublime, our regeneration, it will consume the old man to form the new man; it will annihilate the kings and the priests. Instead it will offer a God, virtue, the law; it will present a great fatherland of thinking, free, happy beings. Yes! a people which recognizes the Supreme Being, which is ready to sacrifice absolutely everything for the law, is a virtuous people, and a virtuous people never perishes: it has a right to the immortality of the soul.[153]

The paean recycled images from the Last Judgment and the resurrection of the dead. It drew on the Christian holy war fantasy that the saints and dead crusaders would rise up to fight against the Devil's armies.[154] It linked causally the willingness to die with immortality. It spoke of a new day and of regeneration. In the many proclamations concerning the assassination attempt and the live martyr Geffroy delivered between May and June 1794, the leitmotiv was "vengeance."[155] Without direct signals from the Jacobin leadership, the local patriotic societies sang with an avalanche of neo-Catholic accents. Or was there not cuing? Paris had given the green light insofar as, ending a phase of official "dechristianization," it had proclaimed with its Cult of the Supreme Being war against atheism.

La Fabrique de l'Histoire: The Generation of History Through Eschatological Violence

As discussed in Chapter 2, typology did not link in a simple one-on-one relationship a type to a single antetype, a person or event in the Old Dispensation to a single accomplishment in the New Dispensation. The scheme present in the fourth century with Jerome allowed a type to have plural antetypes all the way to the Eschaton. This had consequences for conceptions of the historical process. Plural, partial accomplishments of a type became nodes of sacral temporality placed on the axis of History's last age opened up by Christ's First Coming. Anticipated by biblical types and prophecies, these momentous Events (or momentous characters) also pointed forward: they were themselves types and prophecies of a total fulfillment at the End of Times.

This development was not immediate. Early patristic theology had not envisaged a historical process, if by this expression is meant a march forward of History driven by multiple events. Most radically, to avoid both the identification of the Christianized Roman Empire to the community of the elect, and the obverse denigration of all earthly polities as satanic, Augustine of Hippo had rejected the idea that the history of worldly institutions might have providential meaning. For him, while all events were, of course, governed by God, hardly any event revealed, let alone expressed, God's plan.[156] A rival model, developed by Eusebius of Caesarea and Augustine's own protégé Orosius, posited that the fate of kingdoms deployed and displayed God's will in an intelligible fashion. This conception triumphed in the sub-Roman "barbarian" Western kingdoms and in Byzantium. The Orosian model allowed any *regnum* to hope that, if virtuous, it might be a New Israel, a New Holy Land and chosen nation. However, it too did not foster a scheme in which History moved forward through progressive steps. The succession of kingdoms called to the mantle of empire, the *translatio regni*, would have been equally at home in a cyclical scheme of history, if not for the fact that this series ultimately ended on the Church or Christ's Kingdom. For instance, there was nothing progressive in the transfer of governance from Franks to Saxons, as envisaged by imperial historiography in the tenth century.[157] It was only starting with the twelfth century that clerics multiplied the events in the Church's past that they viewed as significant turning points,[158] as (partial or total) fulfillments of prophecies, notably those of the trumpets, plagues, or seals of Revelation.[159] The events were not impersonal—human figures personified them, often attached to the angels of the apocalyptic vision.

Some (not all) high and late medieval commentaries on John's Revelation began to incorporate some of Christendom's great conflicts as way stations toward the apocalyptic war to end all wars. While the intermediaries are not clear, the logical endpoint of this development was a History fully invested by transcendental meaning and driven at every moment by violence and retribution. In the eighteenth century, a novel notion of enlightened "revolution" that transformed History met the bloodshed of the French Revolution. In the nineteenth century, the concept of violence as motor blossomed with the Hegelian "cunning of reason" scheme.[160] But how did an event impose itself as a motor of History? And what kind of event had a chance of being allotted this role? This process cannot be reconstructed with full certitude; for this reason, the considerations that follow are highly tentative. We shall, first, look at how the exegetical logic summarized at the beginning of this section contributed to the transformation of an event into an "Event," with a capital E. We shall, second and briefly, look at the First Crusade as an Event in medieval exegesis and literature. We shall, third and finally, propose that the apocalyptic charge of some events made them more likely to become Events.

As we have seen, for the Church Fathers, Old and New Testament prophecies of Jerusalem's downfall announced two events, a partial realization at the hands of the Roman imperial armies in 70 C.E. and the full apocalyptic destruction of the earthly city at the End of times.[161] This exegetical chain of prophecies had all the more weight as Christ had joined His voice to the lamentable chorus: in the so-called "little apocalypses" of the synoptic Gospels, He wept over Jerusalem. It is likely that many among the first crusaders believed or suspected that they were realizing fully this second and ultimate "Vengeance of the Savior."[162] But the End did not come (even if, as Guy Lobrichon and Jay Rubenstein have shown, the expectation took more than a decade to disappear).[163] Yet the expectations had been so huge they could not fully be erased. The *Chanson d'Antioche* suggests how the apocalyptic charge metamorphosed itself.

Sometime after 1099, perhaps around the time the Third Crusade was preached in the wake of Saladin's 1187 victory at Hattin, perhaps only in the first half of the thirteenth century, perhaps much earlier,[164] the *Chanson d'Antioche*, an anonymous Old French epic narration of the First Crusade, placed the First Crusade in the typological-prophetic framework, without however making it "the war to end all wars."[165] From his cross, the good thief had asked Christ whether He would take vengeance on the Jews. Answering, the Lord had predicted a double retribution. The first, realized by Titus and Vespasian, would take place forty years after His death, when the Roman soldiers stormed Jerusalem's walls. The second was more general but more remote: in a thousand years, the pagans would be wiped out by a people not yet born, the Frankish First Crusaders whose deeds the poet was recounting.[166] Likely, the poet mustered and adapted here Haymo of Auxerre's commentary on Isaiah 63 (or a related theological scheme). Haymo had explained that, on the Cross, Christ had had in his heart "the day of vengeance." It was a double day. First would occur the Roman retribution against the deicide Jews, second, "the punishment of the demons, of the reprobate Jews, of all the infidels, and the rewarding of the just."[167] One sees here at work within the *Chanson d'Antioche* a process of stratification.[168] Losing the status it had had for many participants—the status of the last apocalyptic war—the 1096–1100 expedition was eschatologically demoted. Yet it was not secularized. Rather, it became a lesser fulfillment of the initial prophecy and an example for the future—on a par with Titus and Vespasian's Vengeance of the Savior." Thus, it was fine exegetical logic for the *Chanson* to propose that "our Lord was avenged from them [Pilatus and Jewish leaders], and He will be avenged again." The *Chanson* exhorted its baronial audience to join in another crusade: "Who goes off to avenge Him will receive a good reward: he will wear a crown in the heavenly paradise."[169] One's duty was "to take up the cross for Christ, and go avenge Him from Antechrist's lineage, which neither believes in Him, nor serves Him, nor loves Him, nor has a taste for Him."[170] The poet saw in the First Crusade a type for the expedition it was recruiting for; 1096–1100 also constituted an antetype to the vengeance of 70 C.E.

The *Chanson*'s rendering of the First Crusade owed its recruiting exemplarity precisely to its being the recounting of a type of the full and ultimate—and therefore simultaneously material and spiritual—final struggle. The enemies that the new wave of crusaders would face were "Antechrist's lineage."[171] The familial image implicit in "lineage" should be taken seriously. The Muslims were the "bastard sons" (literally, the *adulterini filii*, born of the misalliance with the slave Hagar). The Jews were the legitimate children (through Sarah) who had lost their inheritance by killing their father. As for the crusaders, they were, Christ had announced, His adoptive progeny: "they will serve me as if I had engendered them . . .; they will all be my sons."[172]

One cannot quite date the *Chanson*. But as Jay Rubenstein's research shows, the process that it makes visible seems to have been underway in the twelfth century's first decades—although, interestingly not immediately so.[173] The expedition of 1096–1100, thus, made eschatological sense in the light of exegesis. In turn, in the course of the twelfth century and beyond, the expedition came to be incorporated into exegesis, including exegesis of the Eschaton.[174] Gerhoh of Reichersberg, musing on guardian angels and the protective virtues of the Cross, provided a précis of the conquest, drawing on Robert the Monk and Raymond d'Aguilers.[175] In those high and late medieval commentaries on John's Revelation that interpreted the seals and trumpets as prophecies of historical events, the First Crusade became a major way station toward the End. The German Franciscan Alexander "Minorita" incorporated chronicles of the First Crusade in his explanation of Rev. 17–19, centering the material on Godfrey and his brother Baldwin, the first rulers of Frankish Jerusalem. He did the same for Revelation 20–21, locating there the events of the Second to Fifth Crusades (1145 to 1221). For Alexander, the predictions of all chapters of John's vision had now been accomplished.[176] This rambling commentary

was picked up, simplified, and popularized by a fellow Franciscan, Pierre Auriol or Aureol (d. 1322). Auriol summarized in detail the First Crusade proper
and the reign of Baldwin, second Christian ruler of Jerusalem (1100–1118). The
sixth angel of Revelation was Gregory VII; the seventh angel was Alexius (who
had moved Urban to preach the crusade). The fifth vision covered the times
from the recuperation of Jerusalem to Antichrist and Judgment Day, a period
that included Hattin, the rise of the Franciscans and Dominicans, Frederick
II, and the Mongols.[177] And while the even more popular Nicolas of Lyra
(d. ca. 1348/9) did not find cogent his predecessors' injection of rather recent
events into John's prophecies, he reproduced their interpretation.[178]

Next to its reception into exegesis, the First Crusade also percolated into
literature. Noticing the disappointment of First Crusade eschatological expectations, which he places in 1100, the great French expert Jean Flori has ele-
gantly written that "the First Crusade does not engender the Time of the End;
it engenders the crusades."[179] The statement is true, first, insofar as the Holy
Land, once conquered, had to be rescued again and again. The statement is
true, second, in terms of literary production. The statement is true, third, insofar as the First Crusade became a model for other expeditions, in a prosaic
sense, of course, but also with varying degrees of typological charge. One sees
this with the "Complainte d'outremer," the Lament for the Overseas Holy
Land, which the often mercenary poet Rutebeuf sang circa 1270 in order to
muster Frenchmen for a new crusading expedition:

> See now the time has come when God comes to seek you, / His arms
> stretched out, stained with His blood / Through which He will extin-
> guish the fire / both of Hell and Purgatory /.
> Start anew a new history (*reconmenciez novele estoire*) / Serve God with
> an entire heart. / For God shows you the path / Of His land and of His
> steps / . . . / For this reason you should have the understanding / To vin-
> dicate and defend / The Promised Land.[180]

Only through participation could a Frenchman prepare himself for his individual judgment after death.

Was this *novele estoire* a new "history," a new episode in a serialized war (as
the *Estoire de Eracles*, the crusade chronicle beginning with the reign of Emperor Heraclius)? Was the expression "secular" and, if yes, in which way? Or
did Rutebeuf's expression instead come closer to meanings present during the
First Crusade and its aftermath—*historia* as prophecies literally realized and

filled with spiritual truth? One finds this acceptation of the term with two chroniclers, Ekkehard of Aura and Guibert of Nogent. The first recounted Christmas 1099 in the Holy Land: Christians from all over the Orient had streamed together to celebrate the Nativity in Jerusalem, and many bishops were consecrated there. The scenes called to the German monk's mind the joyful and celebratory verses of Isaiah 60, which proclaimed the glory of Jerusalem, the streaming to it and conversion of the Gentiles, and the destruction of the enemy. Ekkehard gushed forth: "The prophecies that had been so far mystical [have] turned into visible histories" ("versis in hystorias visibiles eatenus mysticis prophetiis").[181]

Like Ekkehard, Guibert expressed the tangible crusade events as "historical." Right after his description of the Ascalon victory against "Babylon," in a movement analyzed fully by Rubenstein, Guibert tried to find in the twelfth chapter of Zachary's prophecy what could be on the same harmonics (consonum) as their deeds. In the course of this exegesis fitting crusade events with Old Testament prophecy, he came to comment on the vast contingents that the Fatimids had gathered in Ascalon: "Once Jerusalem shall have been relieved, 'all the earthly kingdoms will gather against her' (Zach. 12.3). This [verse] was not put forward to be deciphered (subintelligendum) as allegory, but to be stared at with spiritual eyes (supernis oculis) as history newly narrated (historia noviter relata)."[182]

Here, circa 1108, historia did not have its more common meaning. It was not the biblical letter (usually from the Old Testament), which was to be read through the mystical senses, to unveil a hidden truth.[183] "History" was itself to be apprehended directly in the light of the spirit, supernis oculis. Consequently, Guibert the exegete limited his own quill's vagaries through the historialis veritas, the truth of historia. In the interrogative mode, he developed a little further his position: "But wither does the freedom to allegorize run out with protruding words, when the truth of historia constrains us, lest we be seen wandering about to and fro through [various] interpretations (opiniones)"?[184] A few years later, against the Jews, Guibert would treat similarly Isaiah 62–64: the prophet referred directly to Christ's Passion; he "did not wander to and fro in prophetic riddles; but he described in the historical mode (historialiter)."[185] Guibert closed his disquisition on Zacharias by gesturing to the "material Jerusalem" now in crusader hands, seposito omni misterio, disregarding any veiled meaning. In the apocalyptic moment that, for Guibert, the First Crusade had been and was still, the truth or reality of things was not allegory, it was the plainly and literally realized prophecy, historia. But this "history" was charged with the Spirit.

So what did Rutebeuf mean by *novele estoire*? From the eschatological lexicon, the poet kept the words "new," but this new did not mean "the last." He did compose, after all, two laments concerning overseas, titling the second, "The New Lament for Outremer." Furthermore, in Rutebeuf's literary production, the semantic field of *estoire* straddled our "history of events" and our "story" (with *conte*, "tale," as a synonym). It was, thus, not identical with the one Ekkehard and Guibert had deployed in the aftermath of Jerusalem's conquest. Yet it was not unrelated. After all, Rutebeuf's poem fictionalized an advent of Christ—His return at the End of Times, preceded by the bloodied instruments of His redeeming Passion. This advent implicitly called for vengeance and explicitly on French knights to reenact the deeds of the first crusaders (Rutebeuf named Godfrey, Bohemund, and Tancred)—to "start again" a "new history." These forebears had gained Paradise through travails and martyrdom.[186] There were, thus, in Rutebeuf's vocabulary the as it were feeble radioactive traces of the First Crusade's vengeful aura and of its transformation, as in the *Chanson d'Antioche*, into a type. The *novele histoire* was to be a literal reiteration, charged with Providential meaning, of the First Crusade's deeds.

As the list of Events for Pierre Auriol and others shows, Sacred History was, in the main, a History of holy wars—spiritual conflicts with heresies or physical yet also mystical warfare against pagans, heretics, and false brothers. It was also, in part, a History that included demoted apocalyptic moments. It may be that events that had been seen in their own times as apocalyptic could transmute themselves into special nodes within Sacred History's course *precisely* because of their apocalyptic charge. The hypothesis is impossible to prove, and it would be excessive to posit that each Event featured in (to stay with this example) Auriol's interpretation of Revelation was generated by this mechanism. But the hypothesis is strengthened by two odd details, one from the eleventh century and one from the sixteenth.

Charlemagne's deeds were a favorite candidate for placement among the trumpets and seals. A decade before the First Crusade's departure, in 1084, Bishop Benzo of Alba had made Charlemagne (d. 814) a type for his own emperor, Henry IV. Benzo addressed Henry as the last world emperor announced by the Sibylline prophecies, destined to journey to the Holy Land and its shrines and to be "be crowned in Solomon's city."[187] In a fictional address, Benzo made Charlemagne harangue Henry. The Frankish emperor began by calling his successor "Caesar, my image" (*imago*).[188] Then he pointed out the sacrament (*misterium*) that linked them. It included gifts by the Byzantine emperor in 1082—relics of Christ's Passion (bits of His shroud, cross, and crown of thorns). Benzo calls them "signs that figured," "figuralia signa". They had been foreshadowed by the presents (also *signa*) once brought to Charlemagne from Jerusalem, including the keys to the Holy Sepulcher and a banner. The newer relics would ensure Henry's victories and his role as "standard-bearer of the Christian religion in that task"—the recovery of the holy sites (as often, the correspondence is also an exhortation not to demerit and not to transgress divine and human laws).[189] By the eleventh century, Charlemagne was haloed with mythical deeds; his figure constituted a type for later kings; and his legendary exploits foreshadowed these monarchs' hoped-for pious exploits, including the expedition to end all expeditions, to Jerusalem.[190]

Speculatively put, the figure of Charlemagne gained an aura from the polarization on him as a potential emperor of the Last Days—both in Benzo's century and earlier. Charlemagne could present Henry as Last World Emperor because the eleventh century had placed Charlemagne in this role, as hinted by a number of converging sources, especially Otto III's opening of Charlemagne's Aachen grave at Pentecost 1000—an apocalyptic date if any.[191] One historian has gone as far as saying that, in the eleventh century, Charlemagne's empire "prefigured" the reign of the Last Emperor.[192] This eschatological charge may have already have been present during Charlemagne's own reign. He was crowned emperor on a highly charged day, Christmas of 6000 in the year-count according to the Septuaginta translation of the Bible (December 25, 800), which was still current in Francia alongside the newer Anno Domini computation.[193]

The same mechanism was at work after the fall of the Anabaptist kingdom of Münster to the allied Lutheran and Catholic forces led by the city's bishop (June 1535). Anton Corvinus, a Lutheran pastor, was allowed to debate with some imprisoned leaders. He would a few months later, in January 1536, witness these men's savage torture and death. The bloodthirsty Catholic executioners' joy, he quipped, would have been greater only if their victims had been Lutherans. In this moment, the constancy of Jan of Leyden (Jan Beuckelszoon), the Münster chiliasts' defeated king, impressed him. But, ultimately, no wonder! the Devil had given his man strength.[194] Earlier, in prison, "the Preacher" and "the King" (so did Corvinus's contemporary report call himself and Jan) had entered in a necessarily unequal theological dialogue over the latter's "errors," in this asymmetry comparable to Bukharin's 1938 trial. The King was in prison, probably already weakened by torture; the Preacher represented authority. Against the Lutheran position that Christ had allowed only a spiritual kingdom, King Jan stood firm. It was for the previous "age of suffering," and only for it, that scriptural authorities demonstrated a pure spiritual nature for the Kingdom. But the prophets and John's Revelation announced a material kingdom (*leiblich Reich*) "in the age of glory and splendor, which Christ and His people" would enjoy. Here Jan followed the partition of times that the Münsterite theologian Rothmann had delineated. Rothmann had warned that one was not to "confuse the Time of Suffering [when the sword is forbidden] and the Time of Restitution," which involves vengeance with the sword; and he had underlined that this discrimination constituted "the highest skill in matter of Scriptures, to know how to distinguish between times."[195] The king conceded that his defeat had taught him a lesson: Münster could not have been that final material Kingdom. Furthermore, he had realized in prison that his initial belief that "our Kingdom would last until the arrival of Christ (*zukunfft Christi*)" was an error. Yet, yet, it still belonged to Sacred History. For Jan concluded: "And it is of this [final] Kingdom that our Kingdom of Münster became a figure (*bild*), for as you know, God shows (*anzeigt*, prefigures) and intimated many things through figures."[196]

The king, however, was unable to maintain long this still positive interpretation. A few months later, in his final, signed confession, Jan conceded definitely. He used a negative semantic field reserved for Old Testament ceremonial observances that had been superseded with Christ's First Advent: "the Kingdom launched in Münster was only a vain and dead figure (*eitel tod bilde*); thus, given its abuses, it necessarily had had to go to ruin."[197] It prefigured nothing.

In his first concession, therefore, just as the *Chanson d'Antioche* had reinterpreted the initially apocalyptic First Crusade, King Jan had relocated and historicized (as it were) his Münster realm. It was not part of History's endgame or seamlessly on a temporal continuum with it, lasting (to cite the King again) "until the *zukunfft Christi*." Jan of Leyden had demoted it to a type for the eschatological Jerusalem on earth. But, unlike in the case of the First Crusade, commemorated by the elites of the West and which, in conformity with the *Chanson*'s position, entered commentaries on John's Revelation as a way station of Sacred History, the upstart Jan, soon gruesomely tortured with red-hot tongues and executed, was unable to impose his typology. The Kingdom of Münster lapsed from being a partial fulfillment and real type of the eschatological Kingdom into a "vain and dead figure."

*   *   *

As is often the case, Hegel's model impressed the Modern Age because it articulated authoritatively an emergent commonplace, shared by many others. Across the Atlantic, Protestant America also believed in a History moved forward by conflict. For example, a 1853 article tellingly titled "Laws of Progress" proposed that military storms and convulsions might be "necessary to purify the mental and moral atmosphere, and fit men for universal equality and Christianity." A few years later, an entry in the same *Presbyterian Quarterly Review* presented the course of History as governed by a "law of conflict" with an opposing power that was "morally evil." Common were, around the time of the Civil War, statements to the effect that wars are God-willed and open up new eras.[198] It was not simply, as Orosius and his tradition wanted, that God determined and ordained every event. More, violent episodes were examples and types, which propelled History forward. Even in a culture as future-oriented as America, typology and its language "redeemed" past struggles. Henry Boynton Smith, lecturing to a Yale audience in 1853, explained that "battles fought in the material [sphere] are renewed in the spiritual sphere. They end not with the defeat or victory of the hour. They come up again with a wider scope, and under a wider sky." The role of History was "to call up the spirits from the realm of the shadowy past, to make their conflicts live again in the mind of the present, that we may see in a rarer atmosphere the elements and the meaning of the struggles in which they ignorantly fought for us." Understand, the wars of Israel against the pagan nations had been fought, "in figure," for modern Christians, who lived in the world's last age. Smith extended this exegetical scheme to all of History's battles prior to his American present. The lexicon and conception remained heavily indebted to Christian hermeneutics. The terms "material," "spiritual," "to renew," "shadowy" all belonged to exegetical language. The New Dispensation saw renewals of the old miracles, the latter being shadows of the former, and took them to a higher level. "Re*new*ing" something material spiritually expresses precisely the typological relationship between the material Old and the spiritual *New* Testaments. That earlier struggles were "ignorantly fought for us" is an axiom in this relationship. Smith's formula here repeated Jerome's understanding that the Old Testament wars had taken place to convey a spiritual message. The obverse of this former quasi-Jewish ignorance, the ability to "see" the "meaning" inherent in the conflicts of "the shadowy past," characterized the exegete's craft.[199]

Postface: No Future to That Past?

As explained in the Introduction, this essay does not assert that Christianity alone accounts for the forms that violence has taken in the West. Neither does Christianity alone explain how violence has had meaning and how it has been meaningful in this cultural ensemble. In a typical laboratory experiment, albeit one conducted with pen and paper, these pages have sought to isolate one factor among many—this religious tradition's character traits—and relate it to these forms, meanings, and meaningfulness. Building on Gerard Caspary's insights, they have underlined in particular how violence in the West was related to a series of ancient paradoxical pairings (and the tensions they generated): Old and New, letter and spirit, war and peace, election and universalism, coercion and liberty.

One main thesis of this book has been that some cultural forms have come to our present from the far past. It should be reasserted here that transmission did not proceed only along continua but also through reinventions and (more to this later) "installments."

Reinventions

As Chapter 3 detailed in the long wake of Nye and other researchers, around the turn of the twentieth century, scholars, pundits, and politicians of all stripes scouted religion for recipes to realize social engineering dreams. Some sought to recreate cohesion through rituals and liturgies.[1] Others, or the same, wished to summon quasi-religious energies and myths in the service of reaction or revolution. Pyotr Lavrovich Lavrov, a sympathizer of the terroristic Russian Narodnaya Volya (People's Will), clamored for "martyrs whose legend" would be "far greater than their real worth and their contribution to the [revolutionary] work."[2] Georges Sorel found in the Christian myths of martyrdom and of crusade a model for the modern-age myth that the Proletariat needed, the general strike. Massive change, he wrote, would come about not through the power of reason but through warlike images "able to evoke instinctively all the feelings that correspond to the various facets of the war waged by socialism against modern society." According to Sorel, the French Revolution had not operated much differently. It had enshrined modern innovations in France not through reason or thanks to progress, but through "the epic of the wars that filled the French soul with an enthusiasm akin to the one provoked by religions." Such aggregates of images, explained Sorel, were unfalsifiable, therefore eminently potent. In the first centuries, it had been the figure of the messianic David that had allowed the Jews to fight Rome. This figure, more than rabbinical learning, had preserved Judaism after the destruction of Jerusalem.[3] For the ideologue Sorel, enthusiastic religion—ersatz or authentic—did not mean stupidity. People who put ideology first could be quite shrewd in its pursuit.[4] Perceptively, he noted that the American sectarians of his own days dreamt up "apocalyptic myths" comparable to that of the general strike yet all the same were quite able to act efficiently in the world and be eminently practical.[5]

In the nineteenth and twentieth centuries, ideologies of violence were, therefore, shaped as much by the conscious and willed reinvention or reappropriation of crusade and martyrdom as by deep cultural continuities. Continuities were at work in another manner, insofar as they made self-evident to their audiences proposals such as Sorel's. The darling of the radical anticolonialist left, Frantz Fanon, and his narcissistic impresario, Jean-Paul Sartre, benefited also from the intelligibility that embeddedness in a traditional language affords even to scandalous innovation.[6] In his preface to Fanon's *Les damnés de la terre* (*The Wretched of the Earth*), the Left Bank guru piled up laden images: "one must remain terrified, or become terrible"; "violence's son," the colonized revolutionary "at every instant draws from violence his humanity"; the rebels' "fraternal love" in overcoming tribal divisions "is the obverse of the hate that they have for you [colonialists]"; the revolutionary knows that "this new man begins his life as a human being from its end; he holds himself for potentially dead (*un mort en puissance*)." In drawing from the repertory of Christian holy war, martyrdom, and terror—mediated by the Jacobin tradition as in the last sentence cited—Sartre rivaled with Fanon, the author whom he was prefacing.[7] Fanon himself painted the first phase of the colonized's insurrection in familiar colors:

> This disinherited people, which was wont to live in the narrow circle of [internecine tribal] struggles and rivalries, will proceed in a solemn

atmosphere to the grooming (*toilette*) and the cleansing (*purification*) of
the nation's local face. In a real collective ecstasy (*extase collective*), enemy
families decide to erase and forget everything. . . . The assumption (*as-
somption*) of the nation makes consciousness progress. National unity is
first [made in] the group's unity, in old quarrels' disappearance and the
final annihilation of reluctances. At this same moment, purification will
take in the few natives whose deeds and collaboration with the occupier
dishonored the country. On the other hand, traitors and those who sold
themselves will be judged and punished. . . . A constant effusion reigns
in the villages, a spectacular generosity, a disarming goodness, a constantly reasserted will to die for the "cause." All of this is evocative of, all
at once, a confraternity, a church, a mystique.[8]

A first substratum for Fanon's vocabulary is Durkheimian sociology (which
with Émile Durkheim himself was static, but which Fanon here dynamizes
into a political process). One will recognize Durkheim's famous equation of
"church" and "society," transposed to the nation; his formula that "collective
effervescence" in shared rituals makes this church-society; Durkheim's obsession with "unity"; and Durkheim's notion of impurities that rites have to expiate. Behind Durkheim, however, stands an older, neo-Catholic substratum.
One recognizes notions familiar from the ultra-Catholic Sainte Ligue's paean
to violence: union in zeal and mystical exaltation in killing and being killed.[9]

Leninists will be reassured. Fanon was orthodox on at least one point:
after the first enthusing and enthused phase comes the obligatory organization. Exaltation and the ecstasy of martyrdom alone would not allow a successful revolution. But this realism does not mean, in Fanon's book, the end to
eucharistic discourse. The newly born decolonizing nation is everywhere, like
Christ's consecrated body after Communion: "Wherever they burst out, the
plural peasant rebellions born in the countryside testify of the ubiquitous presence and general density of the nation. Each colonized who takes up arms is a
piece of the nation, [a nation] from now on alive." Ideas of purification, effervescence, creation of national consciousness through communion in violence did not stay in Fanon's book; they passed into at least one Palestinian
Fatah pamphlet.[10] Members of the Rote Armee Fraktion read *The Wretched of
the Earth*. And so did many others.[11]

The thesis that some cultural forms have come to our present from the far
past may provoke a question: What can one predict about the future of this
past? If it is legitimate for the historian to draw connections between past and

present, is he or she forbidden to look forward and sketch history into the future? Cautiously, the pages that follow speculate.

Holy war, martyrdom, and terror will occur again, in nonobvious places and at surprising moments.

Place

In the West, the location of holy violence has often migrated, as a product of holiness's own transmigrations. Sacred topography—theorized starting in the 1960s by Jonathan Z. Smith and so eloquently analyzed more recently by Sabine MacCormack and by Norman Housley—was both geographically mobile and reversible in valence.[12]

Mobility

Especially after Jerusalem's seventh-century fall to the Muslims, spiritual Jerusalems dotted the landscape; Babylon, the Devil's city, could translate itself in space. The chronicler Ekkehard of Aura could thus state as a matter of fact that, occupied by the Saracens, Jerusalem "served Babylon, which is now the capital of the Kingdom of Egypt [that is, Cairo]."[13] Jerusalem also could be translated. Charlemagne's courtier Alcuin told the king that he ruled over a heavenly Jerusalem, "a city of eternal peace constructed through Christ's precious blood . . . whose live stones are bound together by the glue of charity."[14] Here the Carolingian *ecclesia-regnum* took the sacred city's form; elsewhere a town rich in relics could be vested in the same. In the aftermath of the conflagration that engulfed in March 1071 strife-torn Milan, including its cathedral church, the chronicler Arnulf grieved aloud: "Oh temple, by none in the world equaled! And oh city, in whose comparison other cities were vile! Heu, heu, the prophetic lamentations seem to have been almost transferred (*translata*) into you."[15] As a general rule, prior to the eleventh century and its crusade, every monastery or church could be seen, allegorically, as a "Jerusalem."

The Crusades rematerialized the Holy City in the Holy Land. Consequently, some scholars have proposed a reverse process: that with the capture of the last Catholic outposts in the Near East, the Latin West re-spiritualized Jerusalem. Defeats, from Hattin (1187) to the fall of Acre (1291), brought back the early medieval allegories; the material city was translated, as in the seventh century, to Western ecclesiastical institutions. In establishing the urban Feast of Corpus Christi (1264), the Church made explicitly every town into a

Jerusalem. Yet this transposition did not mean (as this same scholarship has postulated for the crusading movement) the end of holy purge. Cleansing violence too was translated. Precisely because cities were Jerusalems, one fought hard, and one executed justice harshly, to make them pure. So with Prague in the early fifteenth century; so with Paris between circa 1560 and circa 1590; so with Florence circa 1500—the Florence of Savonarola and his successors. And this process of translation of Jerusalem as a locus for cleansing warfare antedated Hattin and Acre; it had actually begun immediately after the First Crusade—toward the home front of the conflict between the pope and the emperor and toward pagan Slav areas.[16]

Reversibility

Late medieval Prague oscillated between being Babylon and Jerusalem. Within the Bohemian capital city's boundaries, the fourteenth-century reformer Jan Milíč of Kroměříž (Jan Militsch von Kremsier) had converted (literally) a former brothel known as Venice and its female inmates into a convent called "Jerusalem." His disciple Matthias of Janov understood this transformation as a metonymy of Prague's own conversion into a Jerusalem—at least as long as Milíč's reformist influence lasted:

> [He] entered the metropolis of Prague, capital city of the Empire, then greatly soiled with vices and (if one sees properly) a spiritual Babylon. He manfully attacked the Dragon whom people spiritually worshiped as a god, and the great prostitute, ancient mother of fornications, as well as the scarlet beast whom the purple-clad whore ruled. . . . Through Milíč's merits and travails this Sodom returned to its ancient dignity, and now Prague has been transformed spiritually from Babylon into Jerusalem, rich in every word of Christ and salvific teaching.[17]

Emperor Charles IV of Luxemburg—a ruler who, too, wanted to make his Bohemian capital into a Jerusalem—had helped Milíč. Yet this did not prevent the radical preacher from suspecting that the ruler might be the Great Antichrist.[18] A good generation later, Prague became ambiguous again, and Charles's son Sigismund suffered the same fate. The Hussite song "Arise, Great City of Prague" exhorted its citizens to "rise up against the king of Babylon [Emperor Sigismund], who threatens the New Jerusalem, Prague." Victory against this lesser antichrist would mean the end of the spread of "error" into Holy Church.[19] But once Prague had turned, in the eyes of the Taborites, tepid, it became Babylon again. It was as such to "be destroyed and burnt by the faithful" in this "year of vengeance." In May 1420, the Taborites entered Prague, with the intention of purifying it and transferring their own holy city there.[20] The Hussite moderates countered through the quill of Jan Příbram that the Taborites "lied in naming her Babylon"; the city was, in fact, Jerusalem, "metropolis in Israel, a holy city, the mother of truth . . . which had taught those fake prophets to know the truth and had fostered and brought them up in every capacity besides falsehood" ("matrem civitatem in Israel, civitatem sanctam, matremque veritatis . . . que huiusmodi pseudo somniatores veritatem noscere docuit, et in omni ingenio preter falsum fovit et educavit"). They could argue for the city's Jerusalemite identity by pointing to its successful resistance before the royal fortress of Vyšehrad against "40 princes and an army mustered from so many kingdoms," its miraculous battlefield victory in which eighteen barons had been killed, and finally the capture of the castle itself.[21]

Paris shifted identity as well. Besieged by Henri III and his ally and heir-apparent Henri de Navarre, the city devoted to the ultra-Catholic Guise family—"this noble and virtuous house of [our] French Maccabees"—was for the Ligueurs analogous to Jerusalem besieged by Antiochus.[22] For Paris' ultra-Catholic theologians, the potential destruction of the French capital paralleled the destruction of Jerusalem, which had been the cause of the annihilation of "the Jewish faith, ceremonies, and sacrifices." With Paris would "doubtlessly perish the holy faith and Catholic apostolic Roman religion, true path of our Lord Jesus Christ."[23]

Reversibility, But Also Polysemy

A city could pass from being Jerusalem to being Babylon and back. And it could be both Jerusalem and Babylon, simultaneously. Jerusalem, too, suffered violence; it was flagellated and purged for its own good and transformation. For the Catholics of the 1572 Saint-Bartholomew's Day Massacre, Paris, *mala parte*, was the Babylon of Isaiah 13 and Ezechiel 50–51, sinful and to be purged of Calvinists. But positively seen, the French capital was also Jerusalem, a covenanted city vowed in the opening of the same prophet's vaticinations to violent purgation, but ultimately to spiritual and political reform (Isa. 1).

In a third example, Florence, election went with constitutional revolution and moral purgation. "Blessed will you be, Florence, for you soon will become that Jerusalem on-high" (*superna*), exclaimed the prophet Savonarola—the precondition being compassion toward the poor and care for the common good. With Christ as king, Florence would then be "a city of God and not of

Florence"; from it could begin the reform (and conquest) of all Italy and other nations, all the way to the conversion of Turks and infidels.[24]

Time

Sometime after 1422, an anonymous enemy of the Taborites marveled at the swift passage from pacifist passivity to violence. He commented the deadly Prague defenestration of anti-Hussite city councilors (July 30, 1419): "See how quickly the Wycliffites' mendacity was revealed. Hardly eight days had passed since they announced to the king from Mount Tabor that they would rather be killed by others than kill others themselves; and now the opposite was so suddenly made evident."[25] Already a few years earlier, in February 1420, Jakoubek of Stříbro had questioned a fellow magister: "Did you not earlier preach against killing, and how come now the matter has turned into its opposite?"[26] So often did such reversals happen that Max Weber, with some distaste, generalized and explained:

> In the real world, admittedly, we repeatedly see the proponent of "ethics of conviction" [such as the one espoused in the Sermon on the Mount] suddenly turning into a chiliastic prophet. Those who have been preaching "love against force" (*Liebe gegen Gewalt*) one minute, for example, issue a call to force the next; they call for one *last* act of force to create the situation in which *all* violence will have been destroyed for ever— just like our military leaders who said to the soldiers before every attack that this would be the last, that it would bring victory and then peace.

Weber chalked these reversals to the passion inherent in absolutist ethics: "The man who espouses an ethic of conviction cannot bear the ethical irrationality of the world."[27] There is indeed a drive in ascetic spirituality (which normally entails withdrawal and quiescence) to turn to the world and reform it, enter in the domain of politics. But—as we have seen with the Hussite Koranda and others—these sudden reversals were understandable to contemporaries.[28] The Taborites were honest; the anonymous chronicler should have been able to account for their sudden passage from passive martyrdom in Truth's service to active purgation of the realm. He chose not to since he disagreed with the Taborites' perception of the hour and believed they were Devil-inspired hypocrites.[29] In the understanding shared by all Western

Christians, one could pass brutally from one age to another, without warning, without feeling a contradiction. A slow evolution leading to full transformation (or the later Hegelian "cunning of reason") was not the only process in God's playbook. The Event, typologically or prophetically anticipated, also belonged to it—the passages from Old to New and from Now to Then—it was God's favorite method.[30]

Next to the social-scientific explanation of such surprising reversals, therefore, is a cultural enabler of the same. Our understanding of actors' understandings should be part of any reconstruction. Historians can explain the swiftness with which American clergymen began beating the drums of war in 1861 or 1898 or the relative speed with which Saint-Just and Robespierre switched from opposition to capital punishment to advocacy of the king's execution to the Terror. Only through Louis XVI's execution could the République be founded. The Convention had to adopt and regulate violence to survive.[31] But in both cases understandings of History, Christian or post-Christian, made the radical switch culturally possible and understandable to the historical agents. As long as time can be conceived of as heterogeneous, humans will surprise themselves and suddenly recognize that a moment is the moment for the Event.[32]

In the future of this Western past, therefore, martyrdom, terror, and holy war are likely to occur and likely to surprise both observers and agents. As long as the West is culturally post-Christian, fights to the death and deaths for the cause will suddenly erupt, at unexpected times and in unexpected places. If one wants to inhibit them, understanding, alongside the knowledge that sociological approaches have generated, will be key. All the same, if one must predict, the force of the dialectic between war and peace should continue to maintain, as a norm, just war as a value. Contended, disputed, but present.[33]

Abbreviations

AA	Moorhead, James H. *American Apocalypse: Yankee Protestants and the Civil War, 1860–1869.* New Haven, Conn.: 1978.
AN	Stout, Harry S. *Upon the Altar of the Nation: A Moral History of the American Civil War.* New York: 2006.
CCCM	Corpus Christianorum Continuatio Medievalis.
CCSL	Corpus Christianorum Series Latina.
Crouzet, DesR	Crouzet, Denis. *Dieu en ses royaumes: Une histoire des guerres de religion.* Paris: 2008.
Crouzet, GdD	Crouzet, Denis. *Les guerriers de Dieu.* 2 vols. Paris: 1990.
Crouzet, NStB	Crouzet, Denis. *La Nuit de la Saint Barthélemy, un rêve perdu de la Renaissance.* Paris: 1994.
CSEL	Corpus Scriptorum Ecclesiasticorum Latinorum.
JB	*John Brown,* ed. Richard Warch and Jonathan F. Fanton. Englewood Cliffs, N.J.: 1973.
Kaminsky, HHR	Kaminsky, H. Howard. *A History of the Hussite Revolution.* Berkeley, Calif.: 1967.
Lawrence, HH	Lawrence of Březová, *Historia Hussitica,* ed. Jaroslav Goll, 327–534. Fontes Rerum Bohemicarum 5. Prague: 1893. Tr. Josef Bujnoch, *Die Hussiten: Die Chronik des Laurentius von Březová 1414–1421.* Graz: 1988.
Liber	*Le "Liber de Raymond d'Aguilers,* ed. John Hugh Hill and Laurita L. Hill. Documents Relatifs à l'Histoire des Croisades 9. Paris: 1969. Tr. J. H. Hill and L. L. Hill, *Raymond d'Aguilers: Historia Francorum Qui Ceperunt Iherusalem.* Memoirs of the American Philosophical Society 71. Philadelphia: 1968.

Mansi	Mansi, Johannes Dominicus et al., eds. *Sacrorum conciliorum nova et amplissima collectio.* 53 vols. Rev. ed. Paris: 1901–1927.
MGH	Monumenta Germaniae Historica
RACdSP	*Recueil des actes du comité de salut public*, ed. François-Alphonse Aulard. 16 vols. Paris: 1889–1904.
RAF	*Rote Armee Fraktion: Texte und Materialen zur Geschichte der RAF*, ed. Martin Hoffmann. Berlin: 1997.
RHGF	Bouquet, Dom Martin, Léopold Delisle, et al., eds., *Recueil des historiens des Gaules et de la France.* 24 vols. Rev. ed. Paris: 1869–1904.
Sanborn	Brown, John. *The Life and Letters of John Brown, Liberator of Kansas, and Martyr of Virginia*, ed. Frederick B. Sanborn. 2nd ed. Boston: 1891.
SC	Sources Chrétiennes
Šmahel, HR	Šmahel, František. *Die hussitische Revolution.* Ger. tr., 3 vols. MGH Schriften 43:1–3. Stuttgart: 2002.
Tisset	*Procès de condamnation de Jeanne d'Arc*, ed. Pierre Tisset. 3 vols. Paris: 1960–1971.
Tuveson, RN	Tuveson, Ernest Lee. *Redeemer Nation: The Idea of America's Millennial Role.* Chicago: 1968.
Weise, *Traktate*	Weise, Erich, ed. *Die Staatsschriften des Deutschen Ordens in Preussen im 15. Jahrhundert.* Vol.1, *Die Traktate vor dem Konstanzer Konzil 1414–1418 über das Recht des Deutschen Ordens am Lande Preussen.* Göttingen: 1970.

Notes

PREFACE

1. Philippe Buc, "Violence and Terror in the Western Christian Cultural Sphere: An Overview" (in Arabic), in *Religions and Violence*, ed. Abdelkebir Ismaili el-Alaoui (Rabat: 2002), 123-45.

2. Denis Crouzet, *Les guerriers de Dieu*, 2 vols. (Paris: 1990) [henceforth GdD], *La Nuit de la Saint Barthélemy, un rêve perdu de la Renaissance* (Paris: 1994) [henceforth NStB], and *Dieu en ses royaumes: Une histoire des guerres de religion* (Paris: 2008) [henceforth DesR].

INTRODUCTION: THE OBJECT OF THIS HISTORY

Epigraph: Lucian of Samosata, "The Way to Write History," tr. Fowler and Fowler, III; *Lucian [Works]*, ed. Harmon, 6.4-5.

1. Debates on the concept of "holy war" and "religious war" now rage in the German-speaking academic world; see for a recent polemical introduction, Holzem, "Gott und Gewalt."

2. See, however, P. Walker, "Bioarchaeological Perspective," Gat, *War in Human Civilization*.

3. Juergensmeyer, *Terror in the Mind of God*, 127-28; Elm, "Eroberung Jerusalems," discussed Chapter 7 at nn31-92, 130-34. For a cursory critique of the Girardian scheme, see Buc, "Religion, Coercion," 156-58; for a constructive discussion, see Denton-Borhaug, *U.S. War-Culture*, 149-52, building on Chilton, *Abraham's Curse*, 139-62.

4. Eisenstadt, *Fundamentalism, Sectarianism, and Revolution.*

5. For an orientation, see Anderson and Cayton, *Dominion of War*, 1-5, 23-29, 433-36; also White, *Middle Ground*, ch. 1. Comparison with Mexica warfare in Buc, *L'empreinte du Moyen Age*, 2-24, drawing on Soustelle, *Vie quotidienne des Aztèques*; Conrad and Demarest, *Religion and Empire*; Clendinnen, *Aztecs*; and Carrasco, *City of Sacrifice*. Against religion as determinant, see Hassig, "Aztec and Spanish Conquest," 91-93; idem, *Time, History and Belief*; rejoinder: Gillespie, "Blaming Moteuczoma."

6. See, among others, Assmann, *Price of Monotheism*, 22-23; German original *Mosaische Unterscheidung*, 37. The notion of an "imprint" or "symbolic matrix" that impacts a culture's *longue durée* comes from Claude Lefort's "Introduction" to Quinet, *La révolution*, 20: "[Quinet] conceived of symbolic matrices . . . that preserve themselves [identically] as events take place, even more, impress upon these events their characteristics." Unless otherwise noted, throughout this book, all translations are mine.

7. Toscano, *Fanaticism*, esp. chs. 4 & 6 (references to earlier scholarship, 155n11).

8. For which, see Hillenbrand, *Crusades: Islamic Perspectives*, 162; and Christie, "Religious Campaign," 69. See in general Cook, *Understanding Jihad*; and Bonner, *Jihad*, with bibliography. For the family resemblance, see Sizgorich, *Violence and Belief*—my thanks to Jehangir Malegam for this reference—and Appleby, "History in the Fundamentalist Imagination."

9. See the state of the field in Treadgold, "Byzantium, the Reluctant Warrior"; recent literature, discussion and nuances in Stephenson, "Religious Services" (bibliography at 40n2).

10. In this sense, I side with Cohn's interest in continuity over centuries in his *Pursuit of the Millennium* (1st ed.), xiii–xv. The subtitle of the second edition (New York: 1961) is telling: *Revolutionary Messianism in Medieval and Reformation Europe and Its Bearing on Modern Totalitarian Movements*. For the continuum between utopian Europe and America, see Eisenstadt, *Fundamentalism*, 83: the fundamentalist, Jacobine orientations of the early colonies were transformed "through their institutionalization in more pluralistic settings" yet remain "a continual component in the American political scene." Note, however, that by "continuities" I myself do not mean a constant "continuum"; see below n16 and the Postface.

11. For "diversity," see, e.g., the first section in *American Christianities*, ed. Brekus and Gilpin.

12. See, e.g., Krakau, "Response [to John H. Moorhead]," 166, for the "jumbling," among others, of pre- and postmillennial notions of History across American denominations. Also Bloch, *Visionary Republic*, 33, 37–38.

13. Among important contributions, see Casanova, *Public Religions*; Charles Taylor, "Modes of Secularism"; Asad, *Formations of the Secular*; Casanova, "Secularization Revisited."

14. See Kantorowicz, *Kings' Two Bodies*. For a convenient first guide to the key historiography see Kahn, "Introduction."

15. Schmitt, *Political Theology*; Löwith, *Meaning in History*; Blumenberg, *Legitimacy of the Modern Age*. See as well D. Roberts, "Political Religion," 396–97.

16. Sandl, *Medialität und Ereignis*, 18; below, Postface.

17. See Sahlins, *Islands of History*; idem, *Historical Metaphors*.

18. Rivière, *Liturgies politiques*, 137. For a recent discussion of the concept, see D. Roberts, "Political Religion."

19. See Burgess, "Introduction: Religion."

20. Ferling, *Wilderness of Miseries*, 38, 49–51. A good recent German survey is Schild, "Burn Their Houses."

21. See, for the Middle Ages, Strickland, *War and Chivalry*.

22. See Hull, *Absolute Destruction*.

23. Browning, *Ordinary Men*.

24. See Lahire, *L'homme pluriel*, tr. *Plural Actor*, a potent critique of Pierre Bourdieu's determinism; Barth, *Process and Form*, 47–60; Levi, "Usages," 1333–35.

25. Aurell, *Chrétiens contre les croisades*. See before him P. A. Throop, *Criticism*, and Siberry, *Criticism*.

26. Kieser, *Nearest East*.

27. Housley, *Contesting*, 146–47.

28. *Disenchantment*, 125.

29. M. Bloch, *Apologie*, 85–89; Foucault, "Nietzsche."

30. See Buc, *Dangers*; Gregory, *Salvation*.

31. See the classic indictment of the Enlightenment in Talmon, *Origins*, 1–13; recently the counterindictment in Sternhel, *Anti-Enlightenment*, introduction. Some positions on the road from 1099 to 1942 cited in Elm, "Eroberung Jerusalems," 36–37.

32. Toscano, *Fanaticism*, passim, and Shorten, "Enlightenment." See, for the French Revolution, Mayer, *Furies*, 9, 17 (knowledge of ideologies do not allow to predict "a revolution's genesis, course, and outcome").

33. *Empire of Sacrifice*, 4, 26–29, 34–36 and passim. See below, Chapter 2 at n17 and Chapter 7 at nn4–8.

34. Keohane and Goldstein, "Ideas," 11–12; Graf, "Die Nation," 286; Weber, "Social Psychology," 280. See as well Rapoport, "Messianic Sanctions," 210.

35. Buc, "Vengeance," 473–86, historiography in footnotes 69–71, 83–84, 102, and now Rubenstein, *Armies*.

36. Crouzet, GdD; idem, NStB; idem, DesR. See in particular GdD 1.234–35, for a constructive criticism of Natalie Zemon Davis.

37. Very clear on this ill-defined age of peace is Reeves, *Influence*, 295–305, "The End of History."

38. Ambitious and stimulating suggestions on the many different sociopolitical outcomes of millennialism in Landes, *Heaven on Earth*. A reviewer for the Press proposed that other Christian fundamentals, Creation and Incarnation, should be explored in relation to violence: that the divine is enclosed in matter or the body can however both lead to an appreciation for physical life or on the need for the physical sword to protect the inner spiritual sword.

39. See R. Bloch, *Visionary Republic*, 33–42.

40. Harding, "Imagining the Last Days"; Albanese, *America*, 283–301, underlines the importance of millennialism in contemporary American religion.

41. With Richard Landes and Johannes Fried, and now Jay Rubenstein and Jean Flori, historians should take into account the erasure (or low survival chances) in the written record of eschatological prophecies or expectations that were invalidated by the later course of events.

42. See Headland, Harris, and Pike, eds., *Emics and Etics*.

43. Apt comment by Housley, *Religious Warfare*, 108.

44. See Bloch, *Apologie*, 188 with Le Goff, "Preface," 30; Veyne, *Comment on écrit*, chap. 9; tr. *Writing History*, chap. 9.

45. A classic example for medieval history is Geary, "Living"; see Althoff, *Spielregeln*.

46. Martin, *Violence*, 85, 95–96. See as well Šmahel, "*Pax externa*," on the complicated interplay of ideological and military pressures in relation to tolerance.

47. "Chanson de la Ligue," collected in Pierre de l'Estoile, *Belles figures*, 4.266–69; Crouzet, DesR, 429–34.

48. Marshall, *Meroz Cursed*, 22–23; cf. 9.

49. See CNN, November 6, 2001, "Bush Says It Is Time for action"; Heimert, *Religion and the American Mind*, passim.

50. Keteltas, *God Arising*, 30, cited by Hatch, *Sacred Cause*, 61.

51. Brantôme, *Des hommes*, 1.4.13 (Charles IX), in Buchon, ed., *Œuvres complètes*, 1.557. See also Strickland, *War and Chivalry*.

52. See, for the Rote Armee Fraktion (aka. the Baader-Meinhoff Gang), Matz, "Über gesellschaftliche und politische Bedingungen," 56, discussed below, Chapter 3, at nn193–97. Important is Graf, "Die Nation."

53. See Sageman, *Understanding Terror Networks*.

54. Bracher, *Schlüsselwörter*, 103–24.

55. See, e.g., Shaw, "Bandits."

56. See Gregor, "Fascism's Philosophy," 154, commenting on Panunzio, *Diritto, forza e violenza*.

57. Lukács, *History*, 240–41.

58. Fanon, *Wretched of the Earth*. I use the original French, *Damnés*; see Postface, at nn6–9.

59. Benjamin, "Critique of Violence."

60. Galtung, "Violence, Peace," esp. 168–69. And see below Chapter 3, at nn202–4.

61. N. Davis, "Rites of Violence."

62. Housley, "Eschatological Imperative." See Cohn, who, in *Pursuit*, 81–87, remarks how "in France messianic expectations centered on the Capetian dynasty."

63. For the contribution of official and university milieus to the genesis of the Bohemian reform, then revolution, see Marin, *L'archevêque*.

64. Cohn, *Pursuit* (3rd rev. ed.), 30, writes both that "even though official doctrine had any place for it, it [the apocalyptic tradition] persisted in the obscure underworld of popular religion" as a "tradition" and that at some moments people turned to "the Book of Revelation and the innumerable commentaries upon it," plus the Sibylline Oracles. See Housley, *Religious Warfare*, 101–11, on biblical texts.

65. See MacCulloch, *Reformation*, 108, with further references. Fine pages in Housley, *Religious Warfare*, 26–30, on universalism and exclusivism.

66. Inter alia, Wachtel, *Making a Nation*; Wucinic and Emmert, eds., *Kosovo: The Legacy*; Malcolm, *Kosovo*.

67. Nudelman, *John Brown's Body*.

68. See Buc, *Dangers*, 237–45. Jeffrey Burton Russell's oeuvre covers the centuries: *The Devil*; *Satan*; *Lucifer*; *Mephistopheles*.

69. See Girard, *I See Satan*, 43–45 and passim; more theologically, Caspary, *Politics and Exegesis*, 137–38.

70. René Girard's nonfalsifiable model of "mimetic" violence applies well to Christianity but perhaps less well to paganisms, insofar as mimesis will be more disturbing to a monotheism than to a polytheism.

71. See, among many studies by the same, Momigliano, "Freedom of Speech"; Stroumsa, *Barbarian Philosophy*. Good presentation of the Mexican gods' many faces in Ingham, "Human Sacrifice."

72. See Drake, "Lambs into Lions," 28–29.

73. Sizgorich, *Violence and Belief*. For hypocrisy fears, see as well Gaddis, *There Is No Crime*, 193–4 (a book recommended to me by Jay Rubenstein).

74. *Martyrdom of Pionius the Presbyter and His Companions* §14, ed. and tr. Musurillo, *Acts*, 154–5.

75. See below, Chapter 2, n82.

76. Augustine, *Contra epistulam Parmeniani* 1.9.15, ed. Petschenig, CSEL 51, 35.

77. Augustine, Sermon 2D (or 359B), §16–17, ed. Dolbeau, *Augustin d'Hippone, Vingt-six sermons*, 339. The reasoning was borrowed by Johannes Falkenberg, O.P., in his polemics against Poland-Lithuania, Johannes Falkenberg, *Veteres relegentes historias*, ed. Weise, *Traktate*, 204.

78. Cyprian, ep. 74.8, CSEL 3:2, 806:5, with Brisson, *Autonomisme*, 142.

79. *Acts of the Abitinian Martyrs* §22, ed. Maier, *Dossier*, 1.90. See Brisson, *Autonomisme*, 142.

80. Andreas of Strumi, *Vita Arialdi*, c. 10, 1057.

81. Gerson, "Discours au roi contre Jean Petit" (preached Sept. 4, 1413), ed. Glorieux, 7:2, 1027–28, cited by Contamine, *De Jeanne d'Arc*, 47.

82. Heimert, *Religion and the American Mind*, 491; see below, Chapter 4, for Raymond d'Aguilers.

83. "Die Aktion des 'Schwarzen Septembers' in München," in RAF, 159, also 175.

84. A useful compendium of sources, with analysis, on Jewish attitudes to violence is Bohrmann, *Flavius Josèphe*, 75–95.

85. Flavius Josephus, *Antiquities* 18.23.6, tr. Feldman, 9.21. The parallel passages are repertoried in Hengel, *Zealots*, 90, to wit, Josephus, *Jewish Wars* [henceforth *Bell.*]. 7.8.6.323–26, tr. Thackeray, 595–97; *Bell.* 7.10.1.411–19, tr. Thackeray, 3.620–22. For the first six books, I use the still incomplete critical edition of Josephus by André Pelletier, *Guerre des Juifs*, 3 vols. (Paris: 1975–1982).

86. Hengel, *Zealots*, 110–22.

87. *Bell.* 2.17.2–4.409, ed. Pelletier, 2.79. For the ambiguous meaning of "offerings for," which could cover "offerings to," see Price, *Rituals and Power*.

88. Horsley and Hanson, *Bandits, Prophets, and Messiahs*, dismiss too readily religious motivations in the revolt. While criticized for having lumped together diverse Jewish groups under a single Zealot movement, Hengel, *Zealots*, remains fundamental. See *Bell.* 2.258–65, ed. Pelletier, 2.54–55; *Antiquities* 20.8.6.167–72 and 20.8.10.185–88, tr. Feldman, 10.478–81 and 10.488–91, with Acts of the Apostles 21.38, suggesting that the *sicarii* were led by prophets who predicted apocalyptic miracles.

89. *The Scroll of the War of the Sons of Light Against the Sons of Darkness*, ed. Yadin, tr. Rabin and Rabin; *The Dead Sea Scrolls*, ed. Wise et al., 146–70; *Dead Sea Scrolls*, tr. García Martínez, 113ff.

90. *Charter of the Yahad*, col. 1.9–10; 9.16–17, 9.21–23, *Dead Sea Scrolls*, tr. García Martínez, 71; 93.

91. The comparison is by Appleby, "History," 499–500, 508.

92. *War Scroll*, col. 6:6, *Dead Sea Scrolls*, tr. García Martínez, 123. See the alternate translation in *Dead Sea Scrolls*, ed. Wise et al., 153: "The Kingship shall belong to the God of Israel, and by the holy ones of His people He shall act powerfully." "The Rule," col. 2:5–6, tr. Garcia Martinez, 73.

93. For the early Christian reading of this episode, see Caspary, *Politics and Exegesis*, 32–37.

94. Josephus, *Bell.* 7.10.1.417–19, tr. Thackeray, 3.621–23, slightly modified. See the early modern French translation, *Les sept livres de Flavius Iosephus*, fol. ccxxxv: "comme s'ils eussent receu le feu et les tormens non en corps garny d'esprit, mais en corps de beste brute." As to children, the translator (like Gilbert Genebrard, 313), uses "audace," "durté de leurs cueurs" or "[obstina]tion." *Histoire de Flavius Iosephe Sacrificateur Hebrieu*, tr. Genebrard, 313, translates "temerité outrecuidee [arrogant presumptuousness], ou de l'endurcissement opiniastre de leur volonté [headstrong hardening of their will]."

95. See below, Chapter 3.

96. Bruno of Segni, in Ps. 80:14–15, PL 164, 1016d-17a. On the theme of vengeance in the High Middle Ages, see S. Throop, *Crusading*.

97. Buc, "Vengeance"; earlier Elm, "Eroberung Jerusalems," esp. 46–53 (debated below, Chapter

7); and Bresc, "Historiens." Unlike Elm, 44–46, and following Kedar, "Jerusalem Massacre," I consider that the capture of Jerusalem was followed by systematic slaughter.

98. See below, Chapter 2, at nn8–14.

99. See also the important book by Whalen, *Dominion of God.*

100. But early Christian martyrdom arguably owes something to Roman notions of sacral self-destruction for victory (*devotio*); see Buc, *Dangers,* 124, 137; idem, "Martyre et ritualité," 75; earlier, Bowersock, *Martyrdom and Rome.*

101. See Landes, *Heaven on Earth,* 33–35, on activist millenarianism; Buc, "Martyre et ritualité"; Gaddis, *There Is No Crime,* 38–39 and passim.

102. State of the field by Drake, "Impact of Constantine."

103. See recently Gaddis, *There Is No Crime;* Drake, *Constantine and the Bishops;* Sizgorich, *Violence and Belief.*

104. Panorama of historiography in Kriegbaum, *Kirche der Traditoren,* 16–43.

105. For Augustine, see Brown, "Saint Augustine's Attitude"; idem, "Religious Coercion"; Gaddis, *There Is No Crime,* 151–250; and Schreiner, "'Duldsamkeit,'" 165–75.

106. Augustine, Ep. 93, to Vincentius, 5.1.9, CSEL 34, 2.453–54, or see the new edition of the letter in CCSL 31A, ed. Daur, 173: 187–209. The expression *legum terror* is in Ep. 93.5.18, CSEL 34, 2.462; CSEL 34, 180:415; it is also found in Ep. 187.7 §26, to Count Boniface, CSEL 57, 25:3.

107. Schreiner, "'Duldsamkeit,'" 177–80, with references to earlier historiography.

108. *Ovid's Fasti* 2.23, vv. 683–84, ed. Page et al., 106.

109. Christianity was not alone in its universalism; compare the so-called axial religions. The concept is owed to Jaspers, *Origin and Goal of History;* see Eisenstadt, ed., *Origins and Diversity.*

110. Ewig, "Zum christlichen Königsgedanken"; see also McCormick, *Eternal Victory;* Heim, *Théologie de la victoire.*

111. See the state-of-the-field article by Constable, "Historiography of the Crusades"; also Jean Flori, *Guerre sainte,* 19–27.

112. McCormick, "Liturgie et guerre."

113. Cf. inter alia Tyerman, *Invention,* 73, 74, 82ff.; Housley, *Contesting,* 57.

114. Tyerman, *Invention,* 82.

115. See Weinfurter, "Macht der Reformidee"; Remensnyder, "Purity, Pollution, and Peace."

116. I cite only the recent bibliography: the essays in Head and Landes, eds., *Peace of God;* Bull, *Knightly Piety;* Flori, "L'Église et la guerre sainte"; Cushing, *Reform;* Mastnak, *Crusading Peace,* with a good critique of Bull's denial of a linkage between the Peace of God and the crusade, 44–45; Barthélemy, "Peace of God."

117. Violante, *Pataria;* idem, "La pataria e la militia Dei"; Keller, "Pataria und Stadtverfassung"; Cowdrey, "The Papacy, the Patarenes"; Stock, *Implications of Literacy,* 1–240; Zumhagen, *Religiöse Konflikte;* Zey, "Im Zentrum des Streits."

118. Tellenbach, *Libertas;* Blumenthal, *Investiture Controversy;* Moore, "Family, Community, and Cult"; idem, *First European Revolution;* Robinson, *Authority and Resistance;* Cowdrey, *Pope Gregory VII;* Blumenthal, *Pope Gregory VII.*

119. Moore, "Family, Community, and Cult," 67–69; idem, *First European Revolution;* see as well Remensnyder, "Purity, Pollution, and Peace," 289–91.

120. Rousset, *Origines*, 194–96; Erdmann, *Origins*, 313–15, or. German, *Entstehung*, 311–13; see Mastnak, *Crusading Peace*, 50–51.

121. Fulcher of Chartres, *Historia* 1.4.6, ed. Hagenmeyer, 143.

122. The old Erdmann thesis has held well, notwithstanding amendments to its chronology by McCormick and others.

123. See Chapter 2 at nn110ff.

124. The classic study is Ladner, *Idea of Reform*.

125. See Matznak, *Crusading Peace*; Bird, "Reform or Crusade?"; eadem, "Heresy, Crusade, and Reform," which I have not been able to consult.

126. The most subtle analysis straddling late medieval and early modern holy war is Housley, *Religious Warfare*. See now Poumarède, *Pour en finir*, arguing for the superficiality of the crusading ideal in the early modern era (a thesis Denis Crouzet's œuvre puts into sharp question for the sixteenth century, insofar as crusade was deployed against heretics during the wars of religion).

127. See Constable, "Historiography."

128. For eschatology and 1095–1100, see especially the work of Jay Rubenstein, inter alia, "Godfrey of Bouillon"; and Gabriele, "Against the Enemies of Christ."

129. Bernheim, *Mittelalterliche Zeitanschauungen*, 74–75; Landes, "Sur les traces du Millennium"; Fried, *Aufstieg aus dem Untergang*. The data for the presence of apocalyptic expectations have not always been exploited with due caution, hierarchizing it according to evidentiary quality. See in particular Alphandéry and Dupront, *Chrétienté*, and Dupront, *Mythe de croisade* but also some moments in Landes's energetic production. Despite this, the critiques, in particular that of Gouguenheim, *Fausses terreurs*, fall short. See the review by Fried, "Endzeit."

130. I have relied here on Kaminsky, HHR; see also idem, "Chiliasm"; Šmahel, HR; and Housley, *Religious Warfare*, 31–61. Also useful are Heymann, *John Žižka*; and Fudge, *Magnificent Ride*. Some among Thomas A. Fudge's fine articles will soon be published as *Heresy and Hussites in Late Medieval Europe* (Aldershot: 2014). His "More Glory Than Blood" places together, as they should be, Hussite holy warfare and the First Crusade.

131. Jan Čapek, cited in Jan Příbram, *Život kněží Táborských*, as translated into German by Kalivoda, *Revolution und Ideologie*, 149, from the ed. by Macek, *Ktož jsú boží bojovníci*, 262–309, here 269.

132. Kaminsky, HHR, 321–22, 390–97.

133. See the discussion in Chapter 5.

134. See the survey by MacCulloch, *Reformation*.

135. Kantorowicz, *King's Two Bodies*.

136. Housley, *Religious Warfare*, 55–58, for the *Gesta*. See also the anonymous French sermon of 1302 concerning which Kantorowicz made so much, *King's Two Bodies*, 251–55.

137. Beaune, *Jeanne*, 267–68; Contamine, "Mourir pour la patrie," at 19–23, notably 22–23: The États du Dauphiné founded a daily mass "in perpetual memory of the courage and loyalty" of three hundred knights and squires fallen at the battle of Verneuil-Amperche (August 17, 1424). See below, Chapter 7, at n7.

138. Good conceptual orientation in Brendle and Schindling, "Religionskriege in der frühen Neuzeit."

139. Gregory, *Salvation*.

140. Brady, *German Histories*, 205–6.

141. See Stayer, *Anabaptists and the Sword*, who, furthermore, argues that the "flirtation" with violence was not so short lived. See also idem, *German Peasants' War*; and Rapoport, "Messianism and Terror," 203.

142. See the epilogue, at nn25ff.

143. See the discussion below, Chapter 5, at nn165–76.

144. Blickle, *Revolution of 1525*; Brady, *German Histories*, 185–206.

145. For Calvinist iconoclasm, see Eire, *War Against the Idols*.

146. See Crouzet, NStB.

147. Erlanger, *Massacre de la Saint-Barthélémy*, tr., *St. Bartholomew's Night*; Garrisson-Estèbe, *Saint-Barthélémy*; Crouzet, NStB. Wonderful elucidation of the on-the-ground forces that built up toward popular participation in the massacre by Diefendorf, *Beneath the Cross*.

148. Crouzet, DesR, 343–414.

149. Théodore de Bèze, *Du droit des magistrats*, ed. Kingdon.

150. See below, Chapter 1, at n76.

151. Narrative in Roelker, *One King, One Faith*, 331ff. For apostasy, see Benedict, *Rouen*, 125–49.

152. *Contre les fausses allegations*, 51 and 78. The sexual innuendo comes from Suetonius, *Vita divi Iulii* 68–69, Maximilian Ihm, ed., *De vita caesarorum libri VIII* (Stuttgart and Leipzig: 1908), 86–87. Recent analysis in Le Roux, *Régicide*.

153. *Tumbeau sur le trespas et assassinat*, collected by De l'Estoile, *Les belles figures*, 4.49–50 = fig. xxi.

154. Transcription in ibid., 4.46–47.

155. Crouzet, GdD, 179, citing the *Commentaires de Blaise de Monluc 1521–1576*, ed. Courteault, 1.474.

156. Greengrass, "Regicide, Martyrs," 185. Clément's martyr status was ferociously argued against by partisans of the two Henris, the dead king and Henri IV of Navarre. See below, Chapter 3, at nn14–17.

157. Jean Boucher (?), *Lettre missive de l'Evesque du Mans. Avec la réponse à icelle*, 37: "Have I not hated, Lord, those who hated You, and was I not dessicating myself in sadness against Your enemies? I hated them with perfect hatred, and held them as [my] enemies. O Lord put me to the test and know my heart; give me steadfastness and take knowledge of my ways. And above all see whether I am on the path of iniquity, to finally lead me into eternal life."

158. Boucher (?), *Responce du menu peuple*, Aiv (dated June 30, 1589).

159. See below, Chapter 6, at nn60–63.

160. El Kenz, *Bûchers du roi*, 154–55, 168ff.

161. *Commentaires et remarques chrestiennes sur l'edict d'Union*, 29 (follows the passage cited by Crouzet, GdD, 2.439).

162. *Lettre missive de l'Evesque du Mans. Avec la réponse à icelle*, 30–31.

163. Pryor and Burgess, eds., *England's War of Religion*, in particular, Burgess, "Introduction"; application in idem, "English Regicides," at 70–74.

164. See in general Baskerville, *Peace but a Sword*.

165. Notwithstanding the differences between Catholic and Protestant "rites of violence" posited by Davis, *Society and Culture*, refined on by Crouzet, GdD, and idem, DesR.

166. Johnson, *Ideology, Reason*, 15–16; "Publication de la croisade faite à Toulouse contre ceux de la nouvelle religion," Devic, Vaissette, et al., eds., *Histoire générale de Languedoc*, 12.889, with Crouzet, GdD 1.387.

167. Rare comment linking the sixteenth-century French ultra-Catholic Ligue to the Terror in Richet, "La monarchie au travail sur elle-même?" 35: "It matters not that the ideology changed; the underlying intellectual and emotive mechanisms—the dream of unanimity, which collided with reality and thus imposed Terror—remained the same." See now Van Kley, "Religious Origins." Comments on this strand of historiography in Higonnet, "Terror, Trauma," 126–27.

168. C. Becker, *The Heavenly City*, e.g., 29, 31, 130, 139, 142–51 (but was it only in the eighteenth century that utopia was projected onto earth?).

169. Lucas, "Presentation."

170. Baecque, *Corps de l'histoire*, citations at 360–61, 374. See as well Landes, *Heaven on Earth*, 260–61; Langlois, "La religion révolutionnaire," esp. 375; Billington, *Fire in the Minds of Men*, 20; also Langmuir, *History*, 308, on the remanence of Christian symbols "even in the religiosity of non-believers"; Graf, "Die Nation," 296–99.

171. Becker, *Heavenly City*, 29, 31, and passim. See the critique in Sternheel, *Anti-Enlightenment*, 34.

172. For Gramsci, see Portelli, *Gramsci*, 111–16, 248–49.

173. Tocqueville, *L'Ancien régime*, 56–57, 59.

174. Mathiez, *Contributions*, 40–41.

175. Quinet, *Le Christianisme*, 334. See Van Kley, "Christianity as Chrysalis."

176. In particular, Gauchet, *Désenchantement*. For the constitution as a new absolute, Schmale, *Entchristianisierung, Revolution und Verfassung*.

177. Doyle, *Oxford History of the French Revolution*.

178. The dynamic revolution-counterrevolution is analyzed in Mayer, *Furies*.

179. Giuglio, "'Terreur' et sa famille morphologique."

180. Surprisingly to many, inter alia Kessler, *Terreur*, 74–75, who finds the reversals "einigermassen befremdlich" (somewhat strange).

181. Clénet, *Colonnes infernales*; Gérard, "*Par principe d'humanité.*"

182. *Archives Parlementaires*, ed. Mavidal, Laurent, et al, 1.70.101b, 102a (August 1, 1793), cited by Kruse, *Erfindung*, 233.

183. *Archives Parlementaires*, ibid., 1.70.102a (August 1, 1793).

184. Marty, *Righteous Empire*; cp. Pahl, "Shifting Sacrifices."

185. Cited by Lepore, *Name of War*, 101.

186. Leach, *Flintlock and Tomahawk*, 190.

187. Mason, *A Brief History of the Pequot War*, 3. See Vaughan, *New England Frontier*, 143.

188. Vaughan, *New England Frontier*; Slotkin, *Regeneration Through Violence*; Salisbury, *Manitou and Providence*; Kupperman, *Settling with the Indians*; Jennings, *Invasion of America*.

189. For religion in the postrevolutionary era, see Wood, *Empire of Liberty*, 576–619. For the War of Independence and millennialism, see Hatch, *Sacred Cause of Liberty*, countered by Endy, "Just War, Holy War, and Millennialism," refusing to find among the majority a crusading zeal for an American New Israel, which appeared (so Endy) only later, and rather seeing prerevolution preachers drumming for a "just war" as opposed to a holy war. In this line is also Butler, *Awash in a Sea of Faith*, 195; idem,

"Enthusiasm Described," 320. See also Davidson, *Logic of Millennial Thought*, 213ff; Goff, "Religion and Revolution." Certainly, as with the French Revolution, Puritan or Puritan-like religious conceptions were one component among several, including common law, Whig political thought, Greco-Roman classical heritage, and Enlightenment reason; see Bailyn, *Ideological Origins*.

190. W. Gribbin, *Churches Militant*.

191. Foglesong, *American Mission*, 6 and passim.

192. Moorhead, *American Apocalypse*, 29 and passim.

193. Leach, *Flintlock*, 193–94.

194. Carwardine, *Evangelicals and Politics*, 22–55 and passim.

195. FitzHugh, "Disunion Within the Union," *DeBow's Review* 28, 1 (1860): 1–7, at 4, repr. in JB, 114. For FitzHugh, abolitionism was part of a general movement of "the reformation gone mad" (after Luther and Calvin, with the Puritans and Cromwell) that all conservatives should unite against.

196. See Albanese, *America*, 283–301.

197. See below, Chapter 6, for the Episcopal Church as one exception.

198. E.g., *Mary Chesnut's Civil War*, ed. C. Vann Woodward (New Haven, Conn.: 1981), 233, cited by Stout, AN, 85.

199. Stout, AN, 92–93, 408, 432–33, and passim. See earlier the pioneering study by Bercovitch, *American Jeremiad*.

200. Underhill, *Newes from America*, 42–43 (italics original); discussed by Cave, *Pequot War*, 84, 152. Slotkin, *Regeneration Through Violence*, 42.

201. Here siding with Cave, *Pequot War*, 2–3, 9–12, 168–74, with a useful discussion of modern historiography at 4–12. Cf. Katz, "Pequot War Reconsidered," esp. 220–21. See also Cave, "Canaanites in a Promised Land."

202. Norton, *In the Devil's Snare*, 180.

203. See Gentile, *Democrazia di Dio*.

204. E.g., Henry E. O'Keefe, "A Word on the Church and the New Possessions" (December 1898), if with caution and a hint that America might not be the very last world empire. Note, however, as shown by Kieser, *Nearest East*, how ideology back in New England offices and practice on the missionary ground could differ.

205. Fogleson, *American Mission*. See also Hinds and Windt, *Cold War as Rhetoric*. For World War I, Gamble, *War for Righteousness*; Ebel, *Faith in the Fight*; Mosse, *Fallen Soldiers*; A. Becker, *La guerre et la foi*; and the articles in Krumeich and Lehmann, eds., "Gott mit uns."

206. Gentile, *Le Religioni della politica*, tr. *Politics as Religion*.

207. For a recent, if polemical reiteration, see Burleigh, *Sacred Causes*. See as well H. Maier, "Political Religion."

208. Inter alia, Winkler, *Geschichte der RAF*; Tolmein, *Vom Deutschen Herbst zum 11. September*; Kraushaar, *Die RAF und der Linke Terrorismus*. Weinhauer, "Terrorismus in der Bundesrepublik," provides a good historiographic introduction with a compact narrative. Useful critique of RAF ideology in Rohrmoser and Fröhlich, "Ideologische Ursachen des Terrorismus."

209. Many in-depth comparative studies by Della Porta, including *Social Movements*; see her more recent "Politische Gewalt und Terrorismus"; see also the collected studies by Crenshaw, *Explaining Terrorism*.

210. Aust, *Baader-Meinhof Komplex*, abridged tr. *The Baader-Meinhof Complex*. The citations are from Burleigh's review, "*The Baader-Meinhof Complex*: Review."

CHAPTER I. THE AMERICAN WAY OF WAR THROUGH THE PREMODERN
LOOKING-GLASS

Epigraphs: "The United States a commissioned Missionary Nation," *American Theology Review* 1 (1859): 172, cit. by Moorhead, *AA*, 20; Jackson, dir., *The Return of the King*; Middletown WIHS FM 104.9, below, Chapter 2, at n51.

1. A critique that there was any such "way," in the singular, before the nineteenth century is found in Higginbotham, "Early American Way of War," 230–35, 272–73.

2. See Pahl, *Empire of Sacrifice*. Like the following, I owe this reference to one of the press's readers.

3. See Albanese, *America*, esp. 10–12, 15–16, 273–301.

4. Stephanson, *Manifest Destiny*, 86, also 53, 56, 63, 100; Lears, *Rebirth*. See also Linderman, *Mirror of War*; Johannsen, *To the Halls of the Montezumas*; Ebel, *Faith in the Fight*, chap. 1.

5. Schaff, *Bürgerkrieg*, 25, cited by Clebsch, "Christian Interpretations of the Civil War," 220; see Stout, *AN*, 250.

6. Stout, *AN*, 286–92.

7. "Whom God Honours," *The Presbyterian* 33, 3 (January 17 , 1863): 9.

8. Lears, *Rebirth*, 1–7, 204, 214–15 (citation).

9. See the historical-religious critique by Lawrence and Jewett, *Captain America*; Ebel, *Faith in the Fight*, 28–32.

10. Stephanson, *Manifest Destiny*, 53.

11. Reprinted in *Patriotic Addresses* (Boston: 1887), 328; cited by Stout, *AN*, 90.

12. "A National Fast Day Hymn," in *Banner of the Covenant* (September 21, 1861), cited and commented on by Stout, *AN*, 76.

13. Weinberg, *Manifest Destiny*, 17–18.

14. "Editorial Passing Comment," *Northwestern Christian Advocate* 46, 18 (May 4, 1898): 6.

15. See below, at n81.

16. Bercovich, *American Jeremiad*, 117; Anderson and Cayton, *Dominion of War*.

17. George W. Bush, "State of the Union Address" (January 20, 2004), and "The President's State of the Union Address" (January 29, 2002).

18. See, for the earliest period, Ferling, *Wilderness of Miseries*, 82; *Christian Advocate* (September 14, 1899): 9, cited by MacKenzie, *Robe and the Sword*, 107–8: "American imperialism," explained unapologetically the Methodist Reverend Matthias S. Kaufman, was a force for the "civilizing and christianizing of all continents . . . so that they may enjoy such liberties as make this republic great."

19. Foner, *Story of American Freedom*, 223–31, 252, citation of NSC 68, part four ("The Underlying Conflict in the Realm of Ideas and Values Between the U.S. Purpose and the Kremlin Design"), drafted by Paul Nitze, www.fas.org/irp/offdocs/nsc-hst/nsc-68.htm.

20. For American notions of freedom, see now principally Foner, *Story of American Freedom*, and

earlier Kammen, *Spheres of Liberty*, with the discussion in Ferguson, "Dialectic of Liberty," 27–28. My thanks for guidance in the field of America and its notions of liberty to my Stanford colleague Caroline Winterer.

21. Anderson and Cayton, *Dominion of War*.

22. Helmer, "The Stars and Stripes," 40, 43. See Ninde, *The Story of the American Hymn*.

23. Anon., "In Brief," *Northern Christian Advocate* 58, 14 (April 6, 1898): 8.

24. George W. Bush, "State of the Union Address" (January 20, 2004).

25. U.S. House of Representatives, Committee on Oversight and Government Reform (Harry Waxman, chair), "Misleading Informations from the Battlefield: The Tillman and Lynch Episodes" (July 14, 2008).

26. "Oration at Yale College," New Haven, July 26, 1865, 14, cited by Tuveson, RN, 205. Rich documentation and discussion for the Civil War in Stout, AN, e.g., 82–83, 92, 131, 201, 240–41, 340–41; see also Woodworth, *While God Is Marching On*.

27. Helmer, "The Stars and Stripes," 32–33.

28. Holmes, "Army Hymn," in Ninde, *Story of the American Hymn*, 202.

29. Foner, *Story of American Freedom*, 13.

30. Cited by MacKenzie, *Robe and the Sword*, 53, 59.

31. January 22, 2003. See Associated Press, "Rumsfeld Chides Europeans for Lack of 'Vision'."

32. *Western Christian Advocate* (March 9, 1898): 1, cited by MacKenzie, *Robe and the Sword*, 60.

33. "A Citizen," *Poughkeepsie Journal*, July 3, 1793, cited by Berens, *Providence & Patriotism*, 116.

34. Humphreys, *Poem on the Happiness of America*, 11, or *Miscellaneous Works of David Humphreys*, 30, discussed by Stephanson, *Manifest Destiny*, 19, and Weinberg, *Manifest Destiny*, 18.

35. Dwight, *Columbia*, in A Library of American Literature, ed. Stedman and Hutchinson, vol. 3, *Literature of the Revolutionary Period, 1765–1787*, 480, discussed by Weinberg, *Manifest Destiny*, 18.

36. O'Sullivan, "The Great Nation of Futurity," 427; Pahl, *Empire of Sacrifice*.

37. See Sheehan, *Where Have All the Soldiers Gone?*

38. Above, Introduction, at n195. See Stout, AN.

39. Stout, AN, 200, citing a letter, "Thought for Soldiers," in the *Richmond Daily Dispatch* (Sept. 27, 1862).

40. Stout, AN, 85, without reference (proclamation of a national fast for November 15, 1861).

41. Cited by Stout, AN, 409.

42. John Emerson Anderson, *Reminiscence*, 158, in Civil War Papers, Box I, Folder I, AAS, cited by Stout, AN, 340.

43. The classic reference is Erdmann, *Origins*, original German, *Entstehung des Kreuzzugsgedankens*.

44. See Tyerman, *Invention*, 73, 74, 82ff. Compare, for baptism in blood, the Civil War discourse in Stout, AN, 92 (citation).

45. *Pax in nomine domini*, Gaunt, Harvey, and Paterson, eds., *Marcabru*, 452, tr. 439; cf. tr. Goldin, *Lyrics*, 76.

46. Anon., *Gesta Francorum*, 9.24, ed. Hill, 58.

47. *The Presbyterian* 33, 24 (June 13, 1863): 94; ibidem, 33, 20 (May16, 1863): 77, 86 (cursing);

"Alarm," ibid., 33, 37 (July 4, 1863): 106. See, based on soldiers' letters, Woodworth, *While God Is Marching On.*

48. Anon., "In Brief," *Northern Christian Advocate* 58, 14 (April 6, 1898): 8.

49. Berens, *Providence and Patriotism*, 58–60, 122–23, citation at 59.

50. See Ozouf, "Régénération," in Furet and Ozouf, eds., *Dictionnaire critique*, 821–31; eadem, *L'homme régénéré.*

51. Billington, *Fire in the Minds of Men*, 20.

52. Cited by Blum, *Rousseau*, 280.

53. See Sepinwall, *Abbé Grégoire.*

54. Mosse, *Fallen Soldiers*, 32, 50, 75–76, and passim.

55. Heimert, *Religion and the American Mind.*

56. Stout, AN, 123, 174, citing, respectively, chaplain Horace James (letter to the Sabbath Society, June 21, 1862) and Israel E. Dwinell, *Hope for Our Country*, a sermon preached in Salem, October 19, 1862, 13.

57. Likely because its historical counterpart, the Church, *ecclesia*, was a corporate subject.

58. Vergil, *The Aeneid* 1.374–75, 4.313–15, tr. Fitzgerald, 13, 103.

59. Pseudo-Methodius, *Sermo*, and Tiburtine Sibyl, *Explanatio somnii*, both ed. Sackur, *Sibyllinische Texte*; Adso de Montier-en-Der, *De ortu et tempore antichristi*. For these scenarios, see most recently Gabriele, *Empire of Memory*; for how they played out interactively during the First Crusade, see Rubenstein, *Armies*, detailed on this point in idem, "Godfrey of Bouillon."

60. See now Potestà and Rizzi, eds., *L'anticristo*; Ebel, *Faith in the Fight*, 34–35.

61. For the universal conspiracy, see Chapter 2 below, at nn155–58, and Kamlah's classic *Apokalypse.*

62. Questioning the dichotomy is Coles, "Manifest Destiny Adapted."

63. See Kedar, *Crusade and Missions.* Chapter 7 below argues that it was specifically in the two pursuits of crusade and mission that the Christian could be a "co-helper of God," so an agent in History.

64. Staff, "Reflections after Desert Storm," *The Forerunner.* http://www.forerunner.com/forerunner/X0838_Refections_After_Des.html, April 6, 2010. This is an evolving document: the first time I accessed it, it was attributed to "Mark Shelby" and dated September 1991.

65. "Bible Belt Missionaries Set Out for a War for Souls in Iraq," *The Telegraph*, December 27, 2003. See the evidence collected in Trimondi and Trimondi, *Krieg der Religionen*, 143–44.

66. Ide, *Battle Echoes*, 306; see as well 299–302.

67. Below, Chapter 5, at nn73, 68. Beaune, *Jeanne d'Arc*, 245–46.

68. Reeves, *Influence*, 323–33, citation at 328 from Vatican MS. Reg. Latin 580, fol. 52r.

69. Milhou, "Chauve-souris," 69–71.

70. *Exhortatio ad proceres regni*, from Paris BNF Latin 4806, fol. 24vb, ed. Dümmler, 177.

71. A student at King's Academy, Amman, Jordan, in a question and answer session (2011) related universalism to these "coalitions." See as well Whalen, *Dominion of God*, for how Western Christians imagined a hierarchy of religious groups working ultimately for the good; Housley, "Holy Land," 234–41.

72. See France, *Victory in the East*, 17–21.

73. See Gabriele, *Empire of Memory*, here not fully convincing.

74. Van Laarhoven, "Chrétienté et croisade," 33–34; Fish, *Valley of Achor*, 18–19, cited by Stout, AN, 271.

75. Cottret, "1789–1791"; eadem, *Jansénismes*; Van Kley, *Religious Origins*, 213: The Jansenists' insistence "on 'unanimity' or 'unanimous consent'" was combined with the same's emphasis on "the inviolability of the individual or the small number's 'conscience'."

76. Marx, "Zur Kritik," 390; tr. "Towards a Critique," MacLellan, ed., 72–73, cited by Walicki, *Marxism*, 18. See Introduction, at n150.

77. See, e.g., Britt, "Curses Left and Right."

78. C. Gribben, *Writing the Rapture*, 140.

79. George W. Bush, "Remarks by the President at National Republican Congressional Committee Dinner," Free Library, March 13, 2008. Same theme in the 2003 State of the Union: "The liberty we prize is not America's gift to the world; it is God's gift to humanity." See "President Delivers State of the Union" (January 28, 2003). For George Bush's language and religious coding, see Lincoln, *Holy Terror*, 19–32; Denton-Borhaug, *U.S. War-Culture*, 64–68.

80. Tocqueville, *De la démocratie* 1.2.9, Schleifer and Lambert, eds., *Tocqueville, Œuvres*, 1: 339.

81. Tuveson, RN, 192; Tyng, "Preface," vi. "Generally" has here the strong meaning of "as a genus," not the weak meaning of "in general."

82. Mayhew, "What Great Cause We Have for Gladness and Rejoicing," 49, cited and explained by Hatch, *Sacred Cause*, 42. See generally ibid., 42–48.

83. Austin, "Downfall of the Mystical Babylon," in Austin et al., *The Millennium*, 392–93, discussed by Tuveson, RN, 117. See also in W. Gribbin, *Churches Militant*, 153, the Independence Day speech of the Connecticut Baptist Missionary Society, *Christian Secretary* (August 10, 1822).

84. Lamourette, *Instruction pastorale*, 9, 15–16, 18. For the role of Eastern Christians in scenarios of the End, see Whalen, *Dominion of God*, and Bresc, "Historiens."

85. Robespierre, "Discours à l'Assemblée Nationale" (April 1791), in *Œuvres*, 7.164. See Tallett, "Robespierre and Religion," 102.

86. Raymond d'Aguilers, *Liber*, 70 (my trans.; cf. Hill and Hill, 53). See full text below, Chapter 4, at n100, and also the discussion thereafter of social ideals, with Auffahrt, "Ritter und Arme," 39–55

87. Lamourette, *Instruction pastorale*, 17, 11–12.

88. For the frequent conjunction of tyranny and (Catholic) heresy in prerevolutionary colonial America, see Hatch, *Sacred Cause*, with a mild caveat (association acknowledged, but the latter more mentioned than the former) in R. H. Bloch, *Visionary Republic*, 42–45.

89. *Adversus simoniacos* 3.10, MGH Libelli de lite 1, 210, Szabó-Bechstein, "*Libertas ecclesiae*," 136.

90. Andreas of Strumi, *Vita sancti Iohannis Gualberti*, cap. 75, ed. Baethgen, 1099.

91. Rosenstock-Huessy, *Europäischen Revolutionen*; see also idem, *Out of Revolution*. As every so often with good titles, I owe this powerful thinker to Martial Staub's generous friendship. Gregory VII, Ep. 8.21, *Das Register*, ed. Caspar, 2.552:13–17.

92. See Szabó-Bechstein, "*Libertas ecclesiae*" and the discussion below, Chapter 6.

93. Field, *Liberty*, 25 (drawing on Cyprian of Carthage). See below, Chapter 6, at nn5–6.

94. *Washington Post*, "Full Text; Bush's Speech Aboard the *USS Abraham Lincoln*," May 1, 2003.

95. Pahl, *Empire of Sacrifice*; Denton-Borhaug, *U.S. War-Culture*, 56–89, 122–25.

96. Luther, *Wider die räuberischen und mörderischen Rotten*, in Luther, *Werke*, 18.357–61, here 360:28–32 (my translation); cf. tr. by Jacobs and Schultz, *Luther's Works*, ed. Lehmann, 46:53–54. See below, Chapter 5, at nn164–75.

97. *Discours veritable*, Biv verso. See the discussion Chapter 7, at nn33–47.

98. Robespierre, "Sur les tentatives d'assassinat contre des représentants du peuple" (May 25, 1794), in *Œuvres*, 10.471, my translation; see also translation with discussion in Blum, *Rousseau*, 246–47, underlining how the vow to kill and the call to be sacrificed were opposite sides of the same imperative.

99. Buc, "Vengeance," 463–64; below, Chapter 4, at n5.

100. See also Stroumsa, *Barbarian Philosophy*, chap. 2: "The Christian Hermeneutical Revolution and Its Double Helix."

101. *Western Christian Advocate* (March 9, 1898): 1, cited by MacKenzie, *Robe and the Sword*, 60.

102. Post, *Palingenesy*, 17, discussed by Moorhead, *AA*, 134.

103. Wood, *Empire of Liberty*, 546, for the "translation westward of knowledge" along with that of empire, Wood cites the bishop through Lewis P. Simpson, ed., *Federalist Literary Mind*, 34. Hatch, *Sacred Cause*, 149–56, here 156.

104. For America, see Moorhead, *AA*, x.

105. Robespierre, "Rapport sur les principes de morale politique," in *Œuvres*, 10.353.

106. Fukuyama, "The End of History?"

107. Sepúlveda, *Democrates Alter*, ed. Losada, 63; George W. Bush, "State of the Union" (January 28, 2003).

108. On Rev. 18.20, the "Blank Bible," ff. 895, 898, ed. Stein in the *Writings of Jonathan Edwards*, 24:2.1237, cited and explained by Stein, "Jonathan Edwards and the Cultures of Biblical Violence," 62.

109. See Heimert, *Religion*, 336–37.

110. George W. Bush, "State of the Union" (January 28, 2003). Paine, *Common Sense* (1776), ed. Foner, *Complete Writings*, 1.46, cited by Foner, *Story of American Freedom*, 16.

111. Paine, *Letter to the Abbé Raynal*, in *Complete Writings*, ed. Foner, 2.243. See below, Chapter 3, at nn.77–80; and Buc, *Dangers*, 136–37, with references to the doctrine of spiritual senses.

112. See Allen, "White-Jacket," 32–47.

113. Melville, *White-Jacket*, chap. 36, in *Writings of Herman Melville*, 5.150–51.

114. Merleau-Ponty, *Humanisme et terreur*, 30; tr. *Humanism and Terror*, 28.

CHAPTER 2. CHRISTIAN EXEGESIS AND VIOLENCE

I have reworked here several articles, including "Some Thoughts," "Exégèse et violence," and my booklet, *L'empreinte du Moyen Age*.

Epigraphs: Tertullian, *Against Marcion*, 5.4.14, CCSL 1, 675 ; Diderot, *Salon de 1762*, §42, in *Œuvres*, ed. Assézat and Tourneux, 10.185; Voltaire, *Essai sur les moeurs*, chap. vii, ed. Bernard et al., *Œuvres complètes*, 22.159–60.

1. Erdmann, *Origins*, or. German, *Entstehung*; for a critique of the chronology, see McCormick, "Liturgie et guerre," 236; and (replacing what seemed to other archaic "Germanic" bellicism in the

domain of biblical exemplarity) Keller, *"Machabeorum pugnae,"* 419–20, 422–23, 429. The classic survey by Bainton, *Christian Attitudes,* is still well worth the reading, although I take a darker view of early Christianity.

2. See, e.g., Heim, *Théologie de la victoire;* J. Russell, *Germanization;* Riley-Smith, "Crusading as an act of love," 190–92, repr. in Madden, ed., *The Crusades,* 48–50; Flori, "Une ou plusieurs première croisade," 18. But see now Gaddis, *There Is No Crime.*

3. See Kershaw, *Peaceful Kings.*

4. Schreiner, "Toleranz." See also the interesting considerations of Šmahel, *"Pax externa."*

5. Brandon, *Jesus and the Zealots;* see also Caspary, *Politics and Exegesis,* 31, 77–78.

6. See the refutation in Hengel, *Jésus et la violence,* reviewing Brandon and others (interesting also in that it documents polemics around liberation theology and German New Left exaltation).

7. Brandon, *Jesus and the Zealots,* 221–85. See the useful discussion of bellicism and irenicism in Stroumsa, "Early Christianity as Radical Religion" (I owe this reference to Brett Whalen).

8. A leader of the group, quoted in the *New York Times* (April 28, 1985), cited by Mendel, *Vision and Violence,* 278, said, "The spiritual underpinning for the group militarism's is contained in Matthew 10.34: 'Think not that I am come to send peace on earth; I come not to send peace, but a sword'."

9. Schiffman, *Reclaiming the Dead Sea Scrolls,* is one among the minority that rejects the connection between the scrolls (found near the Qumran settlement) and Qumran, and the connection between the Essenes and the scrolls (my thanks to Steven Weitzman for the reference). Whether these connections can be drawn does not make much difference for this book's arguments.

10. Brandon, *Jesus and the Zealots,* 60–69 and notes.

11. *Charter of the Community* 9.16–17, 9:21–23, in *Dead Sea Scrolls,* tr. García Martínez, 14.

12. Qumran *Thanksgiving Scroll* (Hymn 14), in *Dead Sea Scrolls,* ed. Wise et al., 189; cf. the translation by García Martínez, *Dead Sea Scrolls,* 342.

13. On the Essenes of Qumran, see Hengel, *Jésus,* 65–68.

14. Stayer, *Anabaptists and the Sword,* 285–86 and passim.

15. Eisenstadt, *Fundamentalism.*

16. See the tradition ranging from Louis, vicomte de Bonald's *Théorie du pouvoir politique et religieux* to the sociologist Swanson, *Religion and Regime,* with Buc, *Dangers,* 206–14.

17. Halfin, *Darkness to Light,* 59–62. Voegelin, *Politischen Religionen,* 32 = *Political Religions,* 32, sees political religions as perversions of the earlier *ecclesia.* The problem was "the [modern age] deification of the earthly ruling order, i.e., its world-immanent formulation and the simultaneous decapitation of the world-transcendent God."

18. See Gauchet, *Désenchantement;* tr., *Disenchantment.*

19. For such dialectics in Christian exegesis, see Buc, *L'ambiguïté du Livre,* 40–49: "le principe d'équilibre."

20. Joseph Cardinal Ratzinger with Vittorio Messori, "Liberation Theology," in *The Ratzinger Report,* 175; German, *Zur Lage des Glaubens,* 185.

21. An easy primer to the diversity in early Christian sects is still J. Kelly, *Early Christian Doctrines.*

22. See Caspary, *Politics and Exegesis;* Harnack, *Lehrbuch der Dogmengeschichte,* 1.226–43, tr. *History of Dogma,* 1.266–81.

23. See Daniélou, *From Shadows to Reality.*

24. De Lubac, *Medieval Exegesis*, vol. 1, *The Four Senses of Scripture*.

25. Chydenius, *Medieval Institutions and the Old Testament*.

26. Origen, *Homélies sur Josué*, ed. Jaubert, SC 71, 330, with Caspary, *Politics*, 19, and Harnack, *Milita Christi*, 48; tr. *Militia Christi*, 26–27.

27. Harnack, *Militia Christi*; see also Rosenwein, "Feudal War and Monastic Peace" (my thanks to Ed Peters for the reference). Rosenwein, however, views monastic liturgy as a kind of sublimation of forbidden fighting.

28. Caspary, *Politics*, 20–23. I use the 1582 Douay-Reims Vulgate English translation.

29. Jerome, *Commentary on Ephesians*, PL 26, cols. 545b–46b.

30. Smith, "Problem of the Philosophy of History," 4, analyzed by Tuveson, RN, 85. See the discussion in Chapter 7, at n199.

31. T. Davis, "Tradition of Puritan Typology." See also Noll, "Image of the United States," 45, 47, underlining the sincerity, continuing importance, and centrality of typology even beyond Jonathan Edwards, despite dissenting voices (including African American voices).

32. See Gratian, *Decretum*, dictum post C.23 q.4 c.15, ed. Friedberg, I.903–4.

33. Buc, *Dangers*, 137–39; idem, "Martyre et ritualité," 75–76.

34. Prudentius, *Psychomachy* vv. 719–25, ed. Lavarenne, *Psychomachie*, 73.

35. Hrabanus Maurus, in Macc. 3.12, PL 109, col. 1150a. For Hrabanus and Carolingian political thought, see De Jong, "The Empire as *ecclesia*"; eadem, "Exegesis for an Empress."

36. Caspary, *Politics*, 9, 125, 127–29, and for violence, 107–10.

37. See, for instance, Augustine, *Contra Adimantum* 17, CSEL 25:1, 167: "The most concise and most evident difference between the two Testaments is fear and love; the one pertains to the Old, the other to the New. Yet the most merciful dispensation of a single God has brought out and attached each of them to [each Testament]."

38. For the complicated history of interpretations of Revelation, see Kamlah, *Apokalypse und Geschichtstheologie*; Landes, inter alia, "*Millenarismus absconditus*"; idem, L'historiographie augustinienne"; idem, "Sur les traces du Millenium: la via negativa." Also Lobrichon, "L'Apocalypse des théologiens"; Lerner, inter alia, "Refreshment of the Saints"; idem, "Medieval Return to the Thousand-Year Sabbath"; Capp, "Transplanting the Holy Lands."

39. For millenarian violence, see Cohn, *Pursuit of the Millennium* (1957; rev. ed. Oxford: 1970), e.g., 75. Cf. the critique in Lerner, "Medieval Millenarianism and Violence."

40. Luther, *Ein Sendbrief von dem harten Büchlein wider die Bauern*, *Werke* 18.389. Hervé de Bourg-Dieu, *Commentaria in Epistolas divi Pauli*, in Rom. 13.4, PL 181, col. 777a. See Affeldt, *Weltliche Gewalt*, 142, 266–67.

41. *Expositio in Hieremiam*, 4.14 (in Hier. 19.7–9), CCSL 74, 184–85; see as well idem, *in Sophoniam* 1.9–10, *Commentarii in prophetas minores*, CCSL 76A, 667.

42. Augustine, Ep. 199 ad Hesychium, 9.26–27, CSEL 57, 266–67: The elements in Christ's tearful prophecies over Jerusalem concern either 70 C.E., or EndTime calamities with His wrathful final Advent, or the continuous advent of Christ in His body, that is, the Church. Matthew Henry follows Augustine's position, see on Matt. 24:4–31, *Matthew Henry's Commentary*, 1738; so does Jonathan Edwards, *Notes on the Apocalypse*, ed. Stein, *The Writings*, 5.150–51. See also, based on Augustine, Auerbach, "Figura," 70 (ternary temporality: the Law is figure; it is fulfilled in the Incarnation, which also

promises EndTimes; and EndTimes is the final fulfillment). I owe this reference to its fine usage by Gabriele, "Asleep at the Wheel," 52–53.

43. E.g., Hrabanus, in Matt. 24.20, CCCM 174A, 624–25, following Jerome, in Matt. 24.23, CCSL 77, 228:504–5; Haymo of Auxerre, in Is. 30.19 and 30.20, PL 116, col. 866d and 867c; in Mich. 4.4–7, PL 117, col. 154cd; in Soph. 3.15, PL 117, col. 209d, in Zach. 8.7, PL 117, col. 244a–b. Joachim of Fiore, *Expositio in Apocalypsim*, in Apoc.Rev. 20.4–7, fol. 211rb: the saints' millennial reign *et secundum partem incepit ab illo sabbato, quo requievit Dominus in sepulchro, et secundum plenitudinem sui, a ruina bestia et pseudoprophete*. For Joachim, see recently Potestà, *Il tempo dell'Apocalisse*.

44. Adams, *The necessity of the pouring out of the spirit*, 35 (sermon preached November 21, 1679, on the occasion of a general fast throughout the North American British colonies), cited by Bercovitch, *American Jeremiad*, 96 (emphasis in the original).

45. Wesley, *Explanatory Notes*, 1.203, on Luke 21.25 (Luke 21.24 announces 70 C.E.).

46. Bacon, *The Advancement of Learning*, ed. Kiernan, 71–72 (I normalize the English); Cooper, *Discourse on the Man of Sin*, 24–28, citations at 25–26.

47. Fuller discussion in Buc, "Vengeance," 461, 475–77.

48. Crabtree, *Christian Life*.

49. Linda Fahrlander, cited in Ernster, "Rediscovering Everyday Mothering," 134.

50. R. C. Sproul of Ligonier Ministries, Feb. 28, 2005, 10:00 a.m., WIHS FM 104.9, Middle-town, Conn.

51. Feb. 15, 2005, 4 p.m., WIHS FM 104.9. The song seems to be by Judy Belcher Rogers and is copyrighted 1990; see "Desert Storm," judylyrics.klsoaps.com/SU.html.

52. As explained by its author, Presbyterian minister George Duffield, Jr., on the eve of the Civil War, in Ninde, *Story of the American Hymn*, 220–22, here 221.

53. Appleby, *Ambivalence of the Sacred*, 11–12; Harnack, *Milita Christi*, 8; tr. *Militia Christi*, 32.

54. I owe the notion of miniaturization to Caspary, *Politics and Exegesis*, 117–18, with n16, and to his oral teaching. The duality vengeance-mercy is also at work in the last age, in the deviant model propounded by Joachim of Fiore, *Expositio in Apocalypsim* 14, fol. 176rb: "The first order will be more meek and sweeter in order to gather the harvest of the elect . . .; the other will be more ferocious and fiery to collect the wine-harvest of the reprobate." See Reeves, *Influence*, 143–44.

55. Willibald, *Vita Bonifacii* 11.35–12.38, in *Vitae sancti Bonifatii archiepiscopi Moguntini*, ed. Levison, 49–52. I follow here Buc, "Vengeance," 457–59.

56. Origen, *Contra Celsum* 8.73 (SC 150), 344–48; I paraphrase here Caspary, *Politics and Exegesis*, 128–29; cf. Field, *Liberty*, 48; and Bainton, *Christian Attitudes*, 84. Augustine, Ep. 189, to Count Boniface, CSEL 57, 134.

57. See as well Aelfric's Sermon on the Maccabees, in *Aelfric's Lives of the Saints*, ed. Skeat, 2.123–24, on the complementarity of the monks' spiritual warfare versus demons and the warriors' material warfare against visible enemies.

58. See below, Chapter 4, at nn29–30; Bainton, *Christian Attitudes*, 157–72.

59. Appleby, *The Ambivalence of the Sacred*, 11–13, 16, 30–31, 78–79.

60. Gaunt, Harvey, and Paterson, eds, *Marcabru*, 452, tr. 439; see tr. Goldin, *Lyrics*, 79. Hence the title of Mastnak's book, *Crusading Peace*. See also *Vos qui ameis de vraie amor*, ed. Bédier, *Les chansons de croisade*, 20.

61. Dante, *Paradiso*, 15.148, trans. and discussed by Kantorowicz, *King's Two Bodies*, 239.

62. *Ludus de Antichristo*, vv. 9–16, ed. Vollmann-Profe, 2.2.

63. *Ibid.*, vv. 39–42, ed. Vollmann-Profe, 2.4.

64. See Malegam, "No Peace for the Wicked," esp. 40–46; Bonnaud-Delamare, *L'idée de paix*, on the Augustinian notion of peace and its progeny in the Peace of God movement of the late tenth and eleventh centuries.

65. Sedulius Scottus, *Carmen* 2.12, ad Karolum regem, ed. Ludwig Traube, *MGH poetae aevi karolini*, vol. 3 (Berlin: 1896), 181:41–42.

66. Nicolas of Lyra, *Postilla* in Prov. 20.28, *in Biblia sacra*, 3.1694. He had many antecedents; see Anselm of Laon (?) on Matt. 5.7, PL 162, 1287c–d (*justitia sine misericordia crudelitas est; misericordia sine justitia dissolutio*). And posterity with Machiavelli, see Buc, "Pouvoir royal," 696–98; idem, *L'ambiguïté du Livre*, 46, 51–53.

67. Augustine, Ep. 140, *De gratia novi testamenti liber*, cap. 22.54, CSEL 44, 201. Robespierre, "Rapport sur les principes du gouvernement révolutionnaire" (December 25, 1793), in *Œuvres*, 10.275, 276–77 (citation). Cf. Walther, art. "Terror, Terrorismus," 345: "Robespierre defined Terreur as a militancy of the middle." Cf. Augustine, *De doctrina christiana* 3.10–11 (14–17), CCSL 32, 86–88.

68. Augustine, Sermo 279, PL 38, 1277: *Ubi terror, ibi salus . . . O saevitia misericors!* Jerome, *Commentarii in Esaiam* liber 6, in Isa. 13.17–18, CCSL 73, 233.

69. Augustine, *De Genesi ad litteram* 11.11, CSEL 28:3.1, 344.

70. Robespierre, "Second discours sur le jugement de Louis Capet" (December 28, 1792), in *Œuvres*, 9.184: "A sensitivity which would sacrifice innocence to crime is a cruel sensitivity; clemency which allies itself with tyranny is barbarous."

71. Saint-Just, "Sur les personnes incarcérées, rapport à la Convention au nom des Comités de Salut Public et de Sûreté Générale" (Feb. 26, 1794), in *Saint-Just: Discours et Rapports*, ed. Soboul, 139.

72. "Petition of the Section Guillaume Tell" (Dec. 27, 1793), ed. by Markov and Soboul, *Die Sansculotten von Paris*, 250; cited in Walther, "Terror, Terrorismus," 344.

73. Sigebert of Gembloux, *Leodicensium epistola adversus Paschalem papam* 12, ed. Sackur, MGH Libelli de lite 2, 463, with Malegam, *Sleep of Behemoth*, 252–53. See also the rejections of an exemplarity for the Maccabees in any dimension other than spiritual repertoried in Morton, "Defense of the Holy Land," 279.

74. This *pace* Bainton, *Christian Attitudes*, 118–21, and the inventory in Aurell, *Chrétiens contre les croisades*. See, in particular, Aurell's discussion of Isaac de l'Étoile and Walter Map, 98–111.

75. Lecler, *Histoire de la tolérance*; tr. *Toleration*. Castellion, *Traité des hérétiques*, ed. Olivet and Choisy, 167.

76. *Journal of George Fox*, ed. Penney, 2:12, cited by McLear, "New England and the Fifth Monarchy," 241n35.

77. Hodge, "The War," 158, analyzed by Stout, AN, 186. Such dissenting voices, if we trust Stout, were few.

78. Stout, AN, 260.

79. See Simonetta, "Pace e guerra"; Haines, "Attitudes and Impediments to Pacifism," 370; Stayer, *Anabaptists and the Sword*.

80. See Reinitz, "Separatist Background," 108, 111.

81. *On the Seven Deadly Sins*, 13 and 14, Arnold, ed., *Selected Works*, 3.136–38. For just war requirements, developed by Aquinas and others from Augustine, see F. H. Russell, *Just War*, and Brundage, *Medieval Canon Law*.

82. Kaminsky, HHR, 391–97; Housley, *Religious Warfare*, 170–74.

83. See above, at nn15–20.

84. Yuval, *Two Nations*.

85. *De bono patientiae* cap. 21, ed. Hartel, CSEL 3:1, 412:19–20, 25; see as well cap. 23, 414:18–23, 414:26–28. Cyprian concluded: let us remain patient within persecutions and martyrdoms "so that when that day of wrath and vengeance comes we be not punished with the impious and the sinners, but be honored with the just who fear God" (415:15–17).

86. Rothmann, "Von Verborgenheit der Schrift," ed. Stupperich, 352 ; idem, "Bericht von der Wrake," ed. Stupperich, 297. See Klaassen, *Living at the End*, 110, and on the passage to bellicism, Housley, *Religious Warfare*, 105–6.

87. Rothmann, "Von Verborgenheit der Schrift," ed. Stupperich, 352, 353.

88. *Policraticus* 8.23, ed. Webb, 2.403.

89. Ambrosius Spittelmaier, tr. Stayer, *Anabaptists and the Sword*, 155.

90. See the comments of Rapoport, "Messianic Sanctions," 203

91. Marginal note to a manuscript of the *Old Czech Chronicle*, sub anno 1419; ed. František Palacký, *Scriptores Rerum Bohemicarum*, 3:30, note, cited by Macek, *Hussitische revolutionäre Bewegung*, 67; I adapt the translation by Fudge, *The Crusade Against Heretics*, 29, with friendly help from Petr Maťa. See for the source and context, Šmahel, HR 2.1025, 2.1026n17.

92. Schiemer, tr. Stayer, *Anabaptists and the Sword*, 154.

93. "A vindication against the complaints of mr. Rogers, address'd to Edward Dandy, esq"; in *A collection of the state papers of John Thurloe, esq.*, 3:136–37, here 136 (dated in Lambeth, February 3, 1654).

94. Capp, *Fifth Monarchy Men*, 67, 151; idem, "Transplanting the Holy Lands"; also Hill, *Antichrist*, 115 (conversion of the Jews and "holy wars in the nations, beginning at France").

95. Capp, *Fifth Monarchy Men*; Housley, *Religious Warfare*, 103–9. See, in general, the articles by Landes (see above, n38), and Fried, *Aufstieg aus dem Untergang*.

96. Middletown evangelical Radio WIHS FM 104.9, Feb. 8, 2005, circa 11 a.m. Wars and natural disasters led to this interrogation, and every year one "wonders whether this is the year."

97. Ed. by Palacký, *Archiv český*, 6:41–42, tr. from Czech by Kaminsky, "Chiliasm," 49.

98. Ibid., tr. Kaminsky, "Chiliasm," 49.

99. Lieutenant-Colonel William Goffe, Putney debates (Oct. 29, 1647); see Chapter 7 below, at n.52.

100. See Hengel, *Jésus*, 68–69.

101. Lawrence, HH, 454–45. Another very similar list comes earlier, ibid., 414–45.

102. *Explanatio apocalypsis* 3.34, in Rev. 19.17–21, CCSL 121A, 499. Paschasius Radbertus, in Matt. 24.28, CCCM 56B, 1179, reported and rejected an opinion that the eagles were the Romans who destroyed Jerusalem.

103. Discussed by Stout, "Word and Order," 31; *Johnson's Wonder-Working Providence*, ed. Jameson, 25 and 60.

104. *Johnson's Wonder-Working Providence*, 164. And see below, Chapter 7, at nn138–44..

105. Guttiérrez, *Theology of Liberation*, 160–68, citation at 167.

106. Augustine, *Ep.* 138.2.14, CSEL 44:3, 139–40, or CCSL 31B, 284–85. Gratian, *Decretum*, C.23 q.1 c.2, ed. Friedberg, 1.890–91.

107. Lipton, *Images of Intolerance*. I am grateful to Professor Lipton for e-mail discussions about crusades in the *Bibles moralisées* and for her generous references to the places within this genre where crusaders appear. For plurality of spiritual meanings, see Caspary, *Politics and Exegesis*, e.g., 28, 32.

108. Gaddis, *There Is No Crime*, 267–68.

109. Gregory of Tours, *Ten Books of Histories* 2.37, ed. Krusch and Levison, 85.

110. *Gesta Francorum et aliorum Hierosolimitanorum* 6.17, ed. Hill, 37. See Lobrichon, *1099*, 97.

111. Roncetti, Scarpellini, and Tommasi, *Templari e Ospitalieri in Italia*. See Barber, *New Knighthood*, 205–8. Bernard, *Liber ad milites templi*, ed. Winkler, 1.214.

112. Maier, "Bible Moralisée and the Crusades," 218–22. Cf. Haussherr, "Zur Darstellung zeitgenössischer Wirklichkeit," at 213–14.

113. See Flori, "Une ou plusieurs première croisade," 20, underlining how the First Crusade was the "vengeance for Jesus against His enemies, Jews, Muslims, and heretics all at once."

114. Gilbert of Tournai, ed. and tr. Christoph Maier, *Crusade Propaganda*, 202–3.

115. Hrabanus Maurus, in 1 Macc. 5.33, PL 109, col. 1167c–d.

116. *Gesta Francorum* 6.17, ed. Hill, 37, cited above at n110.

117. Harnack, *Militia Christi*.

118. See below, at n190.

119. Gaddis, *There Is No Crime*; Drake, ed., *Violence in Late Antiquity*; Sizgorich, *Violence and Belief*.

120. Haymo, *Commentarium in Pauli epistolas*, PL 117, 732a–b (Biblical text underlined, as is customary in medieval exegetical manuscripts). For Haymo, see more recently Shimahara, "Représentation du pouvoir séculier."

121. Haymo, *Commentarium in Pauli epistolas*, PL 117, 732c–d.

122. Vogel and Elze, eds, *Pontifical romano-germanique*, 1.251.

123. Haymo, *Homilia iii, dominica vigesima prima post trinitatis*, PL 118, cols. 808d–9c.

124. Hincmar to Louis the Stammerer, PL 125, 989b.

125. *Cartulaire d'Afflighem*, n226, ed. De Marneffe, 306: *In nomine sancte et individua Trinitatis. Henricus dei gratia dux et marchio Lotharingie omnibus fidelibus in perpetuum. Quia teste Augustino de nulla re sic uincitur inimicus, quam cum misericordes sumus, iturus Ierusalem ut saracenos tam uisibiles quam inuisibiles possim superare.* I thank Carine Van Rhijn (Utrecht) for the transcription.

126. Arkin, "The Pentagon Unleashes a Holy Warrior." For Boykin, see Trimondi and Trimondi, *Krieg der Religionen*, 131–34.

127. See Department of Defense, Office of the Inspector General, Case H03L89967206, Aug. 5, 2004, 8 (see also 26 and Attachment 1 for further direct citations). I use quotation marks where the report itself uses them, denoting Boykin's own words; I stick otherwise close to the report, without quotation marks. Boykin's closing demand for prayers is consonant with Ephesians 6.18; see B. Johnson, *People's New Testament*, 2.205: "No one can wield the sword of the spirit rightly without constant prayer." The transcripts of the tapes, provided to me by William Arkin, verify the report; see the speech at the Good Shepherd Church, Sandy, Oregon, June 21, 2003, audiotape and videotape (slides, question, and spiritual army); speech at the Broken Arrow First Baptist Church, Oklahoma, June 30, 2002, videotape. The authenticity of Arkin's transcripts is in turn likely given their correspondence with

excerpts of one video showed on the NBC program. See NBC News clip 5115223939_s06, "War of Words: NBC News Investigates," dated Oct. 15, 2003 (mostly from a videotape filmed at Boring, Oregon, dated by NBC to June 21, 2003 [this date or place may be in error]).

128. For Bush beseeching God for a "spiritual shield," see Lincoln, *Holy Terrors*, 46 (and passim on American Protestant fundamentalist typology in reactions to the World Trade Center tragedy).

129. Case H03L89967206, Attachment 1, 1 and 2.

130. Johnson, *People's New Testament*, 2.205. Johnson (1833–1894) belonged to "the Disciples of Christ," a Presbyterian offshoot cross-bred with Baptism.

131. Department of Defense, Case H03L89967206, 8.

132. The controversies that whirled around his lectures forced the general to cover his tracks. Just one example: the Mozambique warlord's god whom Boykin had called a mere "idol" was not, he said in a CBS interview, Allah, but "his worship of money and power—idolatry"; see Richter, "General Apologizes." An exercise in indirection, his autobiography, Boykin, *Never Surrender*, papers over the statements attested to by the official Pentagon inquiry and the recordings.

133. White, "Apocalyptic Signs," in *Endtime*, ed. Griffin, 102, cited by Mendel, *Vision and Violence*, 271–72.

134. Keller, *"Machabeorum pugnae."* See also, for the longue durée, Schreiner, "Die Makkabäer"; De Jong, "The Empire as *ecclesia*."

135. Hrabanus, in 1 Macc. 2.6, PL 109, col. 1141b–d.

136. Hrabanus, in 1 Macc. 9.37, PL 109, col. 1184c–d.

137. Hrabanus, in 1 Macc. 5.30–35, PL 109, col. 1167b–c.

138. Hrabanus, in 1 Macc. 5.44, PL 109, col. 1169b–c.

139. Hrabanus, in 2 Macc. 8.12, PL 109, col. 1240c–d. See the variant, idem, in 1 Mac. 5.1, PL 109, col. 1163b–c, adding in idolaters. Both readings passed in the influential *Gloss*.

140. Hrabanus, in 1 Macc. 3.38, PL 109, col. 1152a.

141. Hrabanus, *Expositio in Matthaeum*, in Matt. 27.30, CCCM 174A, 742.

142. Hrabanus, in 2 Macc. 12.13–14, PL 109, col. 1247b–c.

143. Hrabanus, in 1 Macc. 15.38, PL 109, col. 1211b–c. Antichrist (and Satan) are, into this day, imagined as a tyrant, see, e.g., R. Bloch, *Visionary Republic*, 59–61, and La Haye's *Left Behind* and *Babylon Rising* series.

144. Hrabanus, in 1 Macc. 10.67–73, PL 109, col. 1190c–d.

145. Hrabanus, in 1 Macc. 3.27–30, PL 109, col. 1151c–d.

146. Hrabanus, in 1 Macc. 3.13, PL 109, col. 1150a–c.

147. Hrabanus, in 1 Macc. 4.41–45, PL 109, col. 1158d–9c..

148. *Roman de Judas Machabee*, Paris BNF Français 789, fol. 105r; see the rich study by McGrath, "Romance of the Maccabees," 234.

149. McGrath, "Romance," 150.

150. Discussed and analyzed in Cole, *Preaching of the Crusades*, 153–56, here 153.

151. Hrabanus, in Esther 8.12, PL 109, 664a–b.

152. Hrabanus, *Expositio in Matthaeum*, in Matt. 24.15, CCCM 174A, 622. Hrabanus follows almost verbatim Bede, in Mark. 13.14–16, CCSL 120, 598.

153. Eisenstadt, *Fundamentalism*, 90.

154. Lobrichon, "Courants spirituels"; and see above, introduction, at nn35 and 111–23; Savigny, "Il tema del millenio," 261–62, building on Hoffmann, ed., "Briefmuster des Vallicellianus B 63," 140–43, with Erdmann, "Endkaiserglaube und Kreuzzugsgedanke," 386–94.

155. Juergensmeyer, *Terror in the Mind of God*, 36, 153. For the *Protocols*, see Cohn, *Warrant for Genocide*.

156. Full discussion in Housley, "Crusades Against Christians."

157. Cowdrey, "Pope Gregory VII," 30, citing Gregory's *Registrum* 2.47, ed. Caspar, 1.187:30.

158. Gregory, *Registrum* 1.25 and 1.26, to Erlembald, ed. Caspar, 1.42 and 44 (see also 1.27, 44, calling on a bishop to help the same Erlembald and fight alongside the pope against "Simon Magus with the shield of faith and the helm of salvation"); *Epistolae Collectae* 12, Jaffé, 534, to the priest Liprand (1075); *Registrum* 3.15 and 4.7 (1076) to the knight Wifred, ed. Caspar, 1.276, 1.305. Cf. Vogel, *Gregor VII. und Heinrich IV.*, 15–17 and n26. Vogel repertories more such citations, e.g., *Registrum* 6.14, to Welf of Bavaria, ed. Caspar, 2.418–19.

159. Sigebert of Gembloux, *Leodicensium epistola adversus Paschalem papam*, MGH Libelli de Lite 2 (as n73 above), where Paschal II's letter to Count Robert of Flanders is excerpted, 451ff; Hehl, "Was ist eigentlich ein Kreuzzug," 321; Housley, "Crusades Against Christians," 77–78.

160. See Buc, "Krise des Reiches," 68–69; Housley, "Crusades Against Christians," 73–74.

161. Erdmann, *Origins*, 203; or German, *Entstehung*, 187.

162. See also Robinson, "'Political Allegory'," on the tendency of exegetes belonging to Gregory VII and Urban II's circles to read the Old Testament literally (but, one should add, a literal reading dyed through and through by the spiritual senses).

163. Remensnyder, "Purity, Pollution, and Peace," followed by Cushing, *Reform and the Papacy*, 40–41.

164. Mansi, 19.265e–8c.

165. Mansi, 19.741e–2c.

166. Frassetto, "Heretics and Jews," 57, citations from MS. Berlin D.S. Latin Phillipps 1664. For Adhémar, see Landes, *Relics, Apocalypse*.

167. Riley-Smith, *First Crusade*, 110–11; Schein, *Gateway*, 24–27.

168. Remigius of Auxerre, PL 131, col. 696d–697c.

169. Jean Boucher (?), *Lettre missive de l'Evesque du Mans. Avec la réponse à icelle*, 40.

170. Augustine, *Annotationes in Job liber unus*, 18, ed. Zycha (CSEL 28:2), 547: [Confortavit super eum sitiens] . . . *Ut vincant eum* [Antichristum] *esurientes et sitientes iustitiam.*

171. Bede, in Rev. 19.17–21, CCSL 121A, 499–503. The *Gloss* follows Bede, simplifying him in the direction of glee at vindicative violence: "The Birds, that is, all the saints took delight in the penalties [of the bad] and in the accomplishments of their brethren . . . so that you may delight in the torments of the impious, both of the great and of the small [in rank]."

172. Haymo, in Rev. 19.21, PL 117, col. 1180c–1b (viewing the contrast between divine punishments and their own fate, the saints rejoice all the more). Haymo, in Isa. 66.24, PL 116, col. 1086c–d, assumes less glee: the elect will be satisfied to see that the reprobates are set aside and lose the power that they had over innocents; or the reprobates will be so damned that the just will no longer desire nor call for vengeance as they now do (Rev. 6); or the just will be so sated that they shall rejoice for their own liberation and not for the reprobates' damnation.

173. Tertullian, *De spectaculis* 30.1–7, SC 332, 316–28.

174. Bruno of Segni, in Rev. 14.20, PL 165, col. 687b–c. See below, Chapter 7, at nn261ff., for the sublime. On Bruno, see North, "Polemic, Apathy."

175. Baldric, *Historia Jerosolimitana* 4.13, 100–101, on which already Chydenius, *Medieval Institutions*, 80–83. See as well Flori, *Pierre l'ermite*, 472–76, suggesting that the text may refract a sermon actually given; and Rubenstein, *Armies*, 284–85.

176. Hrabanus Maurus, in Matt. 11.14–15, CCCM 174, 329–30; idem, in Matt. 13.9, 379, citing Bede, in Mark. 4.9, CCSL 120, 481–82: "Whenever this short admonition is interjected, be it in the Gospel or in John's Revelation, it signals that what is being said is mystical, and has been placed here to be heard and learned for one's salvation. Ears to hear: the ears are those of the heart, and the interior senses are ears to obey and do what is being ordered." This was widely received, all the way to the *Gloss*. See also Haymo of Auxerre, in Rev. 2.7, PL 117, 967c.

177. Baldric, *Historia Jerosolimitana* 1.4, 14. For Urban and exegesis, see the fine article by Gabriele, "Last Carolingian Exegete." Albert of Aachen, *Historia Hierosolymitana* 6.27, ed. Edgington, 438, says that the "city of Jerusalem is the gate to the celestial fatherland."

178. Raymond, *Liber*, 150. Baldric, *Historia Jerosolimitana*, 102, said "up to the calves of those who walked [in the Temple]."

179. Bede, *Explanatio Apocalypsis*, in Rev. 14.20, CCSL 121A, 437. See the *Gloss*, 6.1516: "The blood, a physical punishment for sin, oozed. It is blood, not wine (which is placed in God's cellar). All the way to the bridles, that is, all the way to the very rulers of the unjust, to punish them, understand, [all the way] to the devils." Bede's explanation also passed into Hrabanus on Deut. 32.42, PL 108, col. 983d ("those who caused the sins will feel harm when retribution and penalty are doled out"). See Buc, "Vengeance," 483–84.

180. Robespierre, "Rapport sur les principes de morale politique," 10.357.

181. "Die Französische Revolution als allerchristliches Ereignis": Bloch, *Thomas Müntzer*, 82.

182. Ballanche, *Essai sur les institutions sociales*, 164, cited by Viallaneix, "Reformation et révolution," 360–61.

183. "Thoughts on French Affairs" (1791), 564; "Remarks on the Policy of the Allies," 601; see Mayer, *Furies*, 147.

184. See above, introduction, at nn172–75.

185. Introduction, at n175.

186. Viallaneix, "Reformation et révolution," 361, surmises that Michelet was drawing here on an originally Lutheran dyad.

187. See now Landes, *Heaven on Earth*, 250–87.

188. Speech to the Club des Jacobins (December 18, 1791), reproduced in the *Patriote Français* dated December 28, 1791, discussed in Kruse, *Erfindung des modernen Militarismus*, 114.

189. Letter, n.d., of the Société populaire de Censoir (Yonne), in *Archives Parlementaires* (June 16, 1794), ed. Mavidal et al., 1.91.654; the 2nd Regiment of Hussards (May 2, 1794), in ibid., 1.91.118.

190. Jerome, in Eph. 6, PL 26, 544.

191. See the texts cited in Kruse, *Erfindung des modernen Militarismus*, 257–63; Buc, "Some Thoughts," 25.

192. Robespierre, "Rapport sur les principes du gouvernement révolutionnaire" (December 25, 1793), in *Œuvres*, 10.278; see Kessler, *Terreur*, 89.

193. Saint-Just, "Sur les factions de l'étranger," Rapport présenté au nom du Comité de Salut Public à la Convention (March 13, 1794), ed. Soboul, *Saint-Just*, 160; M. Mulot, *Discours sur la liberté* (1789), 28, cited in Van der Heuvel, *Freiheitsbegriff*, 159.

194. E.g., Pope Innocent III, Ep. 167, to southern French bishops (1213), PL 213, 955c ("even though they bear different faces"); Saint-Just, "Sur les factions de l'étranger" (March 13, 1794), ed. Soboul, *Saint-Just*, 160, 164.

195. See Van Kley, *Religious Origins*, 213, on the Jansenist insistence both on unanimity and on minority.

196. Blum, *Rousseau*, 200, citing Robespierre, Letter-report of Sept. 1792, *Œuvres*, 5.17. See also Van der Heuvel, *Freiheitsbegriff*, 140–41.

197. Barère, "Bulletin des Victoires," cited by Van der Heuvel, *Terreur*, 21.

198. Robespierre, "Sur les crimes des rois coalisés contre la France" (May 26, 1794), in *Œuvres*, 10.476.

199. Brest, Nov. 10, 1793, *Aux officiers de la marine de la République*, in RACdSP, 2.368n3. This was a common pairing of material and moral warfare; see the texts adduced in Kruse, *Erfindung*, 257–63.

200. See Hampson, *From Regeneration to Terror*, 49–66; Ozouf, *L'homme régénéré*; De Baecque, *Le corps de l'Histoire* ; Sepinwall, *Abbé Grégoire*.

201. Saint-Just, "Discours à la Convention sur le jugement de Louis XVI" (September 13, 1792), ed. Soboul, *Saint-Just*, 62, 66.

202. Kruse, *Die Erfindung*; Guiomar, *Invention de la guerre totale*. See as well Blum, *Rousseau*, 263.

203. D. Bell, *First Total War*, 3.

204. See Tellenbach, *Libertas*.

205. Sieber-Lehmann, "Obscure but Powerful Pattern," 81–83.

206. *Register* 8.21, ed. Caspar, 2.552.

207. I refer to the second revised edition, *Die europäischen Revolutionen*. Robert Ian Moore, in the wake of Harold Berman, borrowed the title.

208. Tallett, *Robespierre and Religion*, 102–3.

CHAPTER 3. MADNESS, MARTYRDOM, AND TERROR {ALL NOTES IN THIS CHAPTER NOW 2 LESS THAN PREVIOUS.}

My thanks to Laura Smoller and Brad Bouley for trenchant medical advice, and to Jeff Miner for checking suicidal tendencies. Special thanks to Laura Smoller for comments and references in the field of History of Science.

Epigraph: Lévi-Strauss, "Introduction à l'œuvre de Marcel Mauss," here xviii (on sorcerers and the possessed), a profound discussion of psychopathology and society.

1. See below, and for the Salafist holy warriors and suicide bombers, Sageman, *Understanding Terror Networks*.

2. This chapter was finished when I came to read Toscano, *Fanaticism*, a stimulating critique that covers some of the same terrain and many of the same authors. My sole objection will be that he takes

too seriously the premodernity-Modernity divide; see *Fanaticism*, 28–29 (and Chapter 7 at nn14–17 below).

3. See also the article "Zèle" (zeal) in the *Encyclopédie* of Denis Diderot, 17.699, and (analyzed by Toscano, *Fanaticism*, 101–4) the one on "fanaticism" (6.393–401).

4. See the partial translation in Diefendorf, *The Saint Bartholomew's Day Massacre*, 152–54, from Gay, tr., Voltaire, *Philosophical Dictionary*, 267–69. I translate directly from the the French, *Dictionnaire philosophique*, ed. Naves and Benda, 196–97. This edition conveniently adds in its notes Voltaire's amplification in the *Questions sur l'Encyclopédie* of 1771; see here 535.

5. The Stoic position is presented in Cicero, *Tusculan Disputations* 3.5.10, ed. Fohlen, *Tusculanes*, 2.7: "So that wisdom may be the soul's health."

6. *Dictionnaire philosophique*, 197. The last two sentences are not in the 1769 edition republished in 1967 by Naves and Benda; they are, e.g., in the *Œuvres de Voltaire, avec notes*, ed. Beuchot, t. 33 = *Dictionnaire philosophique*, t. 4, (Paris: 1829), 38.

7. Fundamental on the English reaction, Heyd, *"Be sober and reasonable,"* and (I thank Brad Bouley for this reference) Porter, *Mind-Forg'd Manacles*, underlining the survival into the eighteenth century and even into the nineteenth of belief in possession among, especially, Methodists (66–81, 267–68).

8. See also Goldstein, "Enthusiasm or Imagination." The Devil remained, in the guise of the adjective "devilish," which came to be associated metaphorically to excesses. For the medieval saint-witch conundrum, see below, n98.

9. Kreiser, *Miracles, Convulsions*; Goldstein, "'Moral Contagion'."

10. See Maire, *Convulsionnaires de Saint-Médard*.

11. Pearl, *Crime of Crimes*, 48–51. For Marthe, see Berulle, *Traicté des energumenes*.

12. Pearl, *Crime of Crimes*.

13. So Goldstein, "Enthusiasm," 40; more detailed, Heyd, *"Be sober and reasonable."* Pinel assumed a correlation between exalted religion and clinical melancholy; see Goldstein, *Console and Classify*, 213.

14. Le Roux, *Régicide*, 11–34, 279–84; Crouzet, DesR, 434–45.

15. Ranke, *Französische Geschichte*, 225. There is a not always reliable translation by Garvey, *Civil Wars and Monarchy*, here 2.232.

16. Pasquier, "L'antimartyr de frere Jacques Clément, de l'Ordre des Jacobins," *Écrits politiques*, 179–246, here 218.

17. Boucher (?), *Lettre missive de l'Evesque du Mans. Avec la réponse à icelle*, 30. Chevallier, "Nouvelles lumières," on Dominican Michel Mergey's deposition, documents how Clément's convent considered him crazy (Chevallier, 61, from Paris AN U 533, 97–111): "One made fun of him, and one said he was a madman (*un folastre*)." Cf. Le Roux, *Régicide*, 12.

18. Zilboorg and Henry, *History of Medical Psychology*—my thanks to Brad Bouley for the reference.

19. Lucian, "How to Write History," 2–4. I use here the translation by Francklin, "Instructions", 389–90.

20. Cicero, *Tusculan Disputations* 3.5.11, ed. Fohlen, 2.8.

21. *Collectio Salernitana*, "Liber tercius, de egritudinibus cronicis," cap. 1, ed. De Renzi, 2.658,

reproducing the Hippocratic teachings («ambae fiunt ex uno et eodem humore . . . mania facit iracundos, melancholia facit timidos»).

22. Fritz, *Discours du fou*, 135, 137.

23. See Dodds, *Greeks and the Irrational*.

24. Audibert, *Études sur l'histoire du droit romain*, 1.41–42: "The various sorts of madmen bore the very names of the deities that tormented them," such as *Cerriti, furiosi, larvati, lymphati*, meaning, possessed by Ceres, the Furies, *larvae, lymphae*.

25. See ibid., 1.12n2, 1.19, 1.62ff.

26. Padel, *Whom Gods Destroy*, 47ff., 65–96.

27. Cicero, *De divinatione* 1.18.34 and 1.31.66, ed. Ax, *Cicero Scripta quae manserunt omnia*, 46.17 and 46.33, with Audibert, *Études*, 1.42.

28. Dio Cassius, *Roman History, Epitoma* 73.13.3–4, ed. and tr. Cary, 9.96–99.

29. See, e.g., Rapoport, "Fear and Trembling."

30. See Vidal-Naquet, "Du bon usage de la trahison;" Rajak, *Josephus*; Weitzman, *Surviving Sacrilege*.

31. Critical bibliography to the 1970s in Feldman, *Josephus and Modern Scholarship*.

32. See inter alia J. Price, *Jerusalem Under Siege*, 180–81.

33. See above, Introduction at nn88–89.

34. See Bohrmann, *Flavius Josèphe*, 137 at n294.

35. Tacitus, *Histories* 5.14, tr. Haddas et al., *The Annals and the Histories*, 569.

36. *Bell*. 2.259, ed. Pelletier, *Guerre des Juifs*, 2.54. An early modern French translation will suggest sixteenth-century reception, *Les sept livres de Flavius Iosephus* (1553), fols. lxiii–lxiv: "une maniere d'abuseurs, lesquelz souz espece de religion misrent en auant plusieurs novalitez, et telles, que maintz en deuindrent quasi insensez."

37. Renan, *Histoire des origines du Christianisme*, 4.227, cited by Vidal-Naquet, "Trahison," 96.

38. Ibid., 228.

39. The thesis of Bohrmann, *Flavius Josèphe*.

40. *Bell*. 5.i.34, E. tr. Thackeray, *Jewish Wars. Books IV–VII*, 211, slightly modified. Pelletier, *Guerre*, 3.113, translates: "à respirer la fureur (*aponoia*) que leur inspiraient les cadavres gisant à leurs pieds, ils n'en étaient que plus sauvages," which highlights the contagion of fury. See the early modern French translation by Genebrard, *Histoire de Flavius Iosephe* (1578), 213: "Et foulloient aux pieds les corps morts qui estoient amassez à grands tas, & batailloient dessus, & les voyans souz leurs pieds, prenoient plus furieuse hardiesse, & aiguisoient leurs cruautez & fureur."

41. Marcus Aurelius, *Meditations* 11.3, ed. Trannoy, 124; Epictetus, attributed in *Diatribai* 4.7.6, ed. Souilhé and Jagu, *Epictète*, 4.60. The proposed editorial amendment, *hupo aponoias*, is consistent with the common pairing of *mania* and *aponoia* but is essentially based on circular reasoning.

42. *Dementia*: *Acts of the Scillitan martyrs* §8, ed. Musurillo, 88:1. Exhortation to return to *sōphrosunē* from *aponoia*: *Pionus* §20:2–3, ed. Musurillo, 162:11–13. *Mōria*: e.g, *Conon* §4.7, ed. Musurillo, 190:2. *Mania*: e.g., *Agapē, Irenē and Chionē* §§3.2, 3.7, 5.1, ed. Musurillo, 282:29, 284:21, 286:30. On the other hand, Satan is powerless to change the martyr's mind (*logismos*) and make her sacrifice, ibid. §4.1, 286:1–3. *Aponoia*: e.g., *Agapē, Irenē and Chionē* §§4.3, 6.2, 286:13, 290:26–27, with the answer, "it is not *aponoia* but *theosebia* [piety toward God]."

43. *Convert!*, see *Apollonius* §§3, 7, ed. Musurillo 90:13, 92:10; *Pionus* §20.2, 162:10–11 (the proconsul continues asking "why have you lost your senses (*dia ti aponenoēsai*)." Pionus counters that he has not lost his senses; the magistrates insists that many have sacrificed and are now endowed with reason (*sōphrosunē*); *Polycarp* §§9.2, 11.1, 11.2, ed. Musurillo, 8:23, 10:11, 10:14.

44. See Field, *Liberty*, 19–20, for the equation of *constantia* and *parrēsia*. E.g., in the Donatist *Passio of Isaac and Maximianus* §5, ed. Maier, *Dossier*, 1.264: *diuturnam furoris insaniam aut christianae tolerantiae pertinaciam.* A little below, the hagiographer speaks of *perseuerentiae constantiam.*

45. *Acts of Marcellus* §4:2, tr. (slightly modified) by Musurillo, *Acts of the Christian Martyrs*, 252–53 (version M: *quo furore accensus es*) and 256–57 (version N: *Quem furorem passus es*).

46. Tertullian, *Apologeticus adversus gentes*, cap. 37.8–9, CCSL 1, 148–49; *Ad scapulam*, cap. 2, CCSL 2, 1128. For Cyprian, see below, at n50.

47. E.g., *The Martyrs of Lyons* §23, ed. Musurillo, 68:19, "Christ suffering in him;" ibid. §56, 80:3; or the Donatist *Maximian and Isaac* §5, Maier, *Dossier*, 1.264: "But Christ was present against them, who having vested himself in the limbs of his soldier hit back from within all the blows that the executioner, in fury, struck from without"; *Passion of Montanus and Lucius* §21.4, ed. Musurillo, 234:13–15: "It is another flesh that suffers when the soul is in heaven. The body does not feel this at all when the mind is entirely absorbed in [*sic Musurillo*, better: consecrated to] God."

48. *Acts of Phileas* §3, ed. Musurillo, 350–51.

49. Prudentius, *Peristephanon*, Hymn III (Eulalia), vv. 98–99, ed. Lavarenne, 26. See Brown, *Cult of the Saints*, 109 (using and citing Victricius of Rouen).

50. Cyprian, *Ad Demetrianum* §15, CCSL 3A, 43:285–44:296, here 43:285–88.

51. Prudentius, *Peristephanon*, Hymn III (Eulalia), vv. 100–111, ed. Lavarenne, 26–27.

52. It seems that the earliest (surviving) sources only mention "anger," *thumos* (e.g., *Martyrdom of Justin and companions* . . . , recension C §4, ed. Musurillo, 54:19). But the surviving sample is not significant enough to posit an evolution from mere anger to fuller madness.

53. *Passion of the Virgins of Thuburbo* §3, tr. Tilley, *Donatist Martyr Stories*, 20; Latin in Maier, *Dossier*, 1.98.

54. *Acts of Marian and James* §§2.4–5, 10.1, ed. Musurillo, 196:8–9 and 14, 208:1 (*rabies insanientis praesidis*); *Acts of Montanus and Lucius* §3.2, ed. Musurillo, 214:23 (*furens saevitia praesidis*). Cf. Baraz, *Medieval Cruelty*, 39–41. See already *The Martyrs of Lyons* §57, 80:6.

55. Josephus, *Jewish Antiquities*, 19.1, ed. Feldman, 212–14.

56. *Marian and James* §12.16–17, 210:16–17. See also §2:4, ed. Musurillo, 196:8–9: "the prefect's bloody and blind fury."

57. Audibert, *Études*, 1.19, citing among other legal pronouncements Justinian, *Institutes* 3.19.8: "A *furiosus* cannot conduct any [legal] business, since he does not understand what he is doing;" and Pomponius, *De reg. iuris* 40: "The *furiosus* does not have any will [at law]."

58. *Acts of the Abitinian Martyrs* §5, Maier, *Dossier*, 1.66, tr. mine; see Tilley, *Donatist Martyr Stories*, 31.

59. Gaddis, *There Is No Crime*, 53–54. See Tilley, tr., *Donatist Martyr Stories*; the Latin sources are collected, with a French translation, in Maier, *Dossier*.

60. See n58 above

61. Augustine, *Ep.* 185.8.28, CSEL 57, 27:10–11.

62. Augustine, *Contra Gaudentium* 1.26.29, CSEL 53, 227. See Ep. 185.2.8, CSEL 57, 8:3–10.

63. Cyprian, *De bono patientiae* 19, CSEL 3:1, 411:12–14. Cyprian, *Letter* 45.3, CSEL 3:2, 602:20–603:3 (cited below, n120), speaks of the *furor* of unrepentant heretics.

64. Augustine, Ep. 185.2.8, CSEL 57, 8:3–10 (*insanire*); See Ep. 185.2.11, 10:22 (*furor*); 3.11, 10:22 (*furor*); 3.12, 10:26–27 (*insanissima dominatio*); 3.14, 13:6 (*mortes voluntarias et furiosas*); 3.14, 21–22 (*insanorum mortes*); 8.32, 30:10 and 13 (*homines tanti furoris, homines desperati*); *Contra Gaudentium*, 1.26.29–27.30sq., CSEL 53, 228:14, 227:19, 228:22 (*furor, insania, dementia*). See, in particular, *Contra Gaudentium* 1.30.34, 233:5–6: *non est hoc consilium, sed furor, non est sapientia, sed amentia. Furentes* is often attached to the Donatists. On the Donatist side, see *A sermon on the Passion of Saints Donatus and Advocatus* §6 (*furias traditorum*) and 7 (*diaboli furor*), Maier, *Dossier*, 1.206 and 207, tr. Tilley, *Donatist Martyr Stories*, 56 and 57; *Maximian and Isaac* §5 (*insania*) and 6–7 (*furibundus, furere, furia*), Maier, *Dossier*, 1.264 and 265, tr. Tilley, *Donatist Martyr Stories* 66 and 67.

65. Augustine repeats this argument in *Contra Gaudentium* 1.27.30, CSEL 53, 229:11–21.

66. Augustine, Ep. 185.3.12, CSEL 57, 11:19–12:7. For the pigs, see Gorevich, *O Kritike Antropologii Zhivotnikh*, 3.123–26.

67. Ep. 185.1.7, CSEL 57, 6:17–18. The one slaps; the other ties up. Ep. 89.6, CSEL 34, 423:20–424:6, or CCSL 31A, 151:126–28, speaks of Donatist "lethargics" (i.e., melancholics) and "frenetics;" the former one should excite, the latter, restrain.

68. Ep. 185.3.14, CSEL 57, 13:1–24.

69. Ep. 185.3.14, CSEL 57, 13:1–5.

70. Ep. 185.8.32–33, CSEL 57, 29:10–30:16; paraphrased here is 30:12–16.

71. See below the discussion Chapter 7 at nn149–53. The citations are from *L'ami du peuple*, dated August 16, 1790, ed. De Cock and Goëtz, *Œuvres politiques, 1789–1793*, 2.1225, and ibid., dated August 3, 1790, *Œuvres politiques*, 2.1152.

72. Buc, *Dangers*, 136–38.

73. Prudentius, *Peristephanon*, Hymn II (Lawrence), vv. 166–67, ed. Lavarenne, 37.

74. Hymn II (Lawrence), vv. 57–64, 33–34.

75. Hymn X (Romanus), v. 395, 133; vv. 961ff., 152–53.

76. Cyprian, *De zelo et livore* 8, CSEL 3:3, 424:8–11.

77. Hymn III (Eulalia), vv. 100–102, ed. Lavarenne, 26.

78. Hymn II (Lawrence), vv. 182–84, ed. Lavarenne, 37; vv. 315–24, 41. See on these dynamics and on the function of ugliness (in this hymn, of the crippled poor), pointing to heavenly splendor but invisible to the blind pagans, Jauss, "Klassische und die christliche Rechtfertigung," 158.

79. Hymn II (Lawrence), vv. 372–92, ed. Lavarenne, 43.

80. "Its lily has a dual color and smell, but only the good can vest themselves with it: for it smells good, agreeable, and sweet to them, but not to bad men": Servin, *Recueil des poincts principaux*, 17.

81. Andreas of Strumi, *Vita sancti Arialdi* §17, ed. Baethgen, 1062:27–29.

82. Gregory the Great, *Moralia in Job* 5.45.78 (in Job 5.2), CSEL 143, 276–77. For a convenient panorama of early medieval "emotions," see Rosenwein, *Emotional Communities*; Dixon, *From Passions to Emotions*, provides a sophisticated narrative of partial secularization of the ancient and Christian understanding of Passions (my thanks to Ed Peters for the reference).

83. Maier, ed., *Crusade Propaganda*, 59, 131. See below, Chapter 6, at n63.

84. *Letter Concerning Enthusiasm,* 19; Hemmerich and Benda, eds., 330.

85. A good review of medieval theories of madness and its historiography can be found in the first chapter of Pfau, "Madness in the Realm." See, inter alia, Neaman, *Suggestion of the Devil;* Fritz, *Discours du fou,* esp. 117–52; Laharie, *Folie au Moyen Age.*

86. I depend here on Delaurenti, "Fascination," and eadem, *Puissance des mots,* 164–69. On medieval optics and theology, see recently Denery, *Seeing and Being Seen.*

87. Bacon, *Opus maius pars IV,* ed. Bridges, 1.141; for Bacon and the Crusades, see Mastnak, *Crusading Peace,* 196–208. For later explanations of plague contagion through the eyes, see Arrizabalaga, "Facing the Black Death," at 261.

88. See most recently Dickson, *Children's Crusade.*

89. The discussion earlier in the *Opus,* which mentions *opera stellificanda* and *opera astronomiae,* suggests that these objects were produced with the help of astronomical lore, the same science that allowed the identification of men with contagious complexions.

90. Bacon, *Opus maius pars IV,* 401–2. Laharie, *Folie,* 83–84, 86, categorizes the pastores' leader among likely psychopathological false prophets and false messiahs.

91. See Smoller, "Of Earthquakes," 167, 184.

92. The critical edition is Maggioni, *Legenda aurea.* See, inter alia, the chapters devoted to Sebastian (1.166), Vincent (1.175–76), Blasius (1.254), Agatha (1.259), Lawrence (2.759), Hippolytus (2.774–76), Hadrian (2.918), Caecilia (2.1184), and Catherine (2.1207 and 1210–11).

93. Munich, Alte Pinakothek, initially for the Dominican convent of San Marco in Florence. The two saints were doctors.

94. Catherine of Alexandria, *Legenda aurea* clxviii, ed. Maggioni, 2.1207.

95. *Traité de la domination de la raison,* 322, 324, 330.

96. Cp. Hrotsvith of Gandersheim's hagiography and martyrdom plays, in *Hrotsvithae Opera,* ed. Von Winterfeld, with Schütze-Pflugk, *Herrscher- und Märtyrer-Auffassung,* 16, 19–24.

97. Meyer-Kalkus, "Schöne Ungeheuer," 305–6. Cf. also Burschel, *Sterben und Unsterblichkeit.* Meyer-Kalkus, "Schöne Ungeheuer," 303–4, speaks of the "Stoic contraposition" of "violent affects" and "dominated affects" in the Christian death ecstasy.

98. Dinzelbacher, *Heilige oder Hexen?*; D. Walker, *Unclean Spirits;* Elliott, *Fallen Bodies;* eadem, "Seeing Double"; Cacciola, *Discerning Spirit,* backdating the beginnings of the issue to the very origins of female mysticism, so to ca. 1200.

99. Le Bon, *Révolution française,* 29; Gregory, *Salvation at Stake,* chap. 8, "The Conflict of Interpretations," 315–41; El Kenz, *Bûchers du Roi,* 161–65, 196–98. El Kenz draws on Bodin, *Démonomanie des sorciers,* 8–10, 26.

100. Le Hongre, *Sermon funebre.*

101. Crouzet, GdD, 2.544ff.; idem, DesR, 446–60. I have mined his sources.

102. Servin, *Recueil des poincts principaux,* 9.

103. Crouzet, GdD, 2.561. The citations are, via Crouzet, to the *Lettre missive aux parisiens,* 4, 5.

104. Crouzet, GdD, 2.541–74. See Servin, *Recueil des poincts principaux,* 27–31: Let reason rule; let the *thumos* or ire-prone fortitude serve reason and not lower passions.

105. *Panegyrique adressé au Roy,* 62.

106. *Lettre missive aux Parisiens,* 9.

107. *Panegyrique*, 68–69.

108. *Legenda aurea* xxxix, ed. Maggioni, 1.259.

109. *Panegyrique*, 69, 71; see Crouzet, DesR, 458–59.

110. Von Kerssenbroch, *Anabaptistici Furoris narratio*, ed. Detmer. *Furor* is a leitmotiv of this history, written in the 1570s by an eyewitness. There is an English translation by McKay, Hermann von Kerssenbrock, *Narrative of the Anabaptist Madness*. See as well Midelfort, "Madness and the Millennium."

111. Spanheim, "De origine" §11 = *Disputationum extraordinariarum Anti-Anabapisticarum*, 6.

112. Von Kerssenbroch, *Anabaptistici Furoris . . . narratio*, 2.677.

113. Ibid., 2.785 (dated February 9, 1535).

114. Spanheim, "De origine" §12 = *Disputationum extraordinariarum Anti-Anabapisticarum*, 7 (on Hubmaier, who did in the end confess he was inspired by Satan and his followers).

115. Corvinus, *De miserabili obsidione*, cited below, Chapter 7, at n194. See the rich pages in Gregory, *Salvation at Stake*, 323–41. For the positive, see Crouzet, DesR, 323.

116. Crouzet, DesR, 326, citing here Marcelin Cornet, O.F.M., *Discours Apologetique tres veritable*, 1.

117. Diderot, *Salon de 1761*, in *Œuvres complètes*, ed. Assézat and Tourneux, 10.105–56, at 123, cited by Dieckmann, "Das Abscheuliche und Schreckliche," 304. Dieckmann comments on Diderot's appreciation for (as was traditional) the sublime and dramatic in Christianity but also for "the tragic, terrifying, macabre, even cruel, the exaltation and the religious madness, the sinister coming together of heterogeneous sentiments" (303).

118. John Locke, *An Essay concerning human understanding*, 4.19 (introduced in the second edition, London, 1695, absent in the first edition of London, 1690, reprint Bristol: 2003). I cite the fifth edition of 1706, 4.19 §5 and 13 (reprint Bristol: 2003), 588, 592.

119. *Ami du peuple*, dated July 22, 1792, in *Œuvres politiques, 1789–1793*, ed. De Cock and Goëtz, 7.4150. For Cyprian and Gregory, see above, at n76 and n82.

120. Cyprian, Ep. 45.3, CSEL 3:2, 602:20–603:3: the Church tried to gather back the sheep "which the stubborn faction of some men and heretical temptations separates from Mother [Church]"; those who resisted this work did so either out of obstination or *furor*.

121. Marat, *Ami du peuple*, July 22, 1792, ed. De Cock and Goëtz, 2.4147 and 4148.

122. See Vovelle, *Religion et Révolution*, esp. 232–35.

123. See, e.g., "Millerism," in the first issue of the *American Journal of Insanity*. A commonplace since at least Voltaire's *Dictionnaire Philosophique* (as n5), where the contagion operates far less through "books" than through "assemblies and discourses."

124. "Monomania," a term invented by Jean-Etienne-Dominique Esquirol, circa 1810, was the nineteenth-century equivalent of the earlier "melancholy" but with its humoral connotations removed. See Goldstein, *Console and Classify*, 153–56; and Stauffer, *Black Hearts*, 42–43.

125. *Life and Letters of John Brown*, ed. Sanborn, 569 (also in Warch and Fanton, eds., *John Brown*, 78).

126. Bloch, *Heritage*, 97; *Erbschaft*, 4.104: "Nicht alle sind im selben Jetzt da." This insight is now common; see, e.g., Chakrabarty, *Provincializing Europe*.

127. See Toscano, *Fanaticism*, 105, 109, for the strands in the *Encyclopedia* and Rousseau favorable

to a constructive fanaticism or enthusiasm; and 120–24, for Kant (against fanaticism but for a constructive enthusiasm). See also the contrast in Montaigne, *Essais*, 1.56, ed. Villey, 321, between "zeal, which pertains to divine reason and justice and behaves in an orderly and moderate manner" and "anger" (or hatred and envy)—text discussed in El Kenz, "Civilisation des moeurs," 190.

128. Voltaire, *Essai sur les moeurs*, chap. vi:43–62, ed. Bernard et al., *Œuvres complètes*, 22.122–23.

129. Casaubon, *Treatise concerning enthusiasme*, ch. 6, 218. See Heyd, *"Be sober and reasonable,"* 70ff. For the original Messalians, see C. Stewart, *"Working the Earth."*

130. Casaubon, *Treatise*, chap. 3, 100–101, with Heyd, 90.

131. Casaubon, *Treatise*, chap. 3, 120–21.

132. Ibid., 82–83. See above, n119.

133. The author lists depressing public calamities, bad air or diet, and natural catastrophes.

134. Shaftesbury, *Letter Concerning Enthusiasm*, 15–16, ed. Hemmerich and Benda, 324. Citation and analysis in Heyd, *"Be sober and reasonable,"* 215–16.

135. See the entries for "aspect" in the *OED*.

136. Nye, *Origins*, 101; idem, "Introduction;" Barrows, *Distorting Mirrors*; and Van Ginneken, "The 1895 Debate."

137. Nye, *Origins*, 45–46.

138. Le Bon, *Crowd*, 18 (citation), 21.

139. Cited by Kedar, "Jerusalem Massacre," 15–76, here 42–48, at 45 for Hume. My thanks to Ed Peters for the reference to MacKay, *Extraordinary Popular Delusions*, here 2.25.

140. Le Bon, *Crowd*, 61.

141. Ibid., 14, 61, 65.

142. Nye, *Origins*, 46–47, 71.

143. Le Bon had read Numa-Denys Fustel de Coulanges and precisely the pages where the historian asserted that emperor worship maintained Rome; see *Crowd*, 61–62, and Buc, *Dangers*, 221–22.

144. On fideism, Gentile, *Religioni della politica*, Am. tr. *Politics as Religion*. Idem, *Culto del littorio*, Am. tr. *Sacralization of Politics*, on Le Bon's influence on Mussolini's "liturgy" and also his conclusion on "faith" and "cynicism," *Sacralization*, 161, *Culto*, 163, 313–14. Stern, "Adolf Hitler und Gustave Le Bon." Gentile shows that the Fascists were not instilling a faith for the propaganda of their message; they were, rather, instilling a myth in which the propagandists (e.g., G. Giuratti, G. Bottai, Tullio Cianetti, *Sacralization*, 149–43, It. *Culto*, 275–79) had themselves faith.

145. Toscano, *Fanaticism*, 20–42.

146. Le Bon, *Crowd*, 48, 53, 57.

147. Durkheim, *Formes élémentaires*, Am. tr. Fields, *Elementary Forms*; Nye, *Origins*, 101–9. See below, Postface, at nn3–5, for Sorel.

148. James, *Varieties of Religious Experience*, 11. See also ibidem, 14–22.

149. I rely in this paragraph on Goldstein, *Console and Classify*, 322f., 369–71. Laharie, *Folie*, 34–35, seems to take seriously Charcot and (influenced by him) Freud's understandings of demoniacs as hysterics or victims of their own projections. See Midelfort, "Charcot, Freud and the Demons."

150. *Procès-verbal*, citation at xv.

151. Szumowski, *Névroses et psychoses*, 8.

152. Ibid., 42–44, 44–50.

153. Ibid., 10, 34.

154. Little, "Function of the Jews," esp. 285–86, 282 (citation).

155. Little, *Religious Poverty*, 40–42, 51–60, citations at 54, 55. See the devastating review by Richard Trexler, "Review to Lester K. Little."

156. So my regretted colleague Gavin Langmuir in two books, *Toward a Definition of Antisemitism*, and *History, Religion and Antisemitism*. Regardless of the disagreement expressed here, I consider them fundamental thought pieces.

157. For Cohn's milieu and some of its present posterity, see Toscano, *Fanaticism*, 45–47, 65–68, 209–14. Cohn, *Pursuit of the Millennium* (1957), 312 (citation).

158. Cohn, *Pursuit of the Millennium* (1957), 309–14, citation at 309, with Landes, *Heaven on Earth*, 342

159. Zacour, "Children's Crusade," 328, 330; Riley-Smith, *First Crusade*, 34–35, 81–82. "Hysteria" is in the book's index, to which one may add "hysterical" on 104.

160. Ibid., 102.

161. Laharie, *Folie*, 83–84.

162. Bell, *Holy Anorexia*. I owe this reminder to Dominique Alibert. Norman Cohn lauded Bell's thesis in *New York Review of Books*, January 30, 1986.

163. Nash, *Red, White, and Black*, 85–86. See Cave, *Pequot War*.

164. For an incrimination of the individual pathology of the leader, see Waite, *Psychopathic God*; Binion, *Hitler Among the Germans*. See for Nazi group murders the historiography and critique in Browning, *Ordinary Men*, 165–67. And for critique of both individual and group psychohistory of Nazism, see Wehler, "Psychoanalysis and History," 531–32; earlier Mosse, *Crisis*, 300–301; recently the panorama in Paul, "Von Psychopathen."

165. Gérard, "Par principe d'humanité," 456–58, at 458. He surmises a "personal failure . . . a stain one wants to erase" (456), and comments, "All, it seems, are isolated males, who have broken away from their family, and who believe themselves to be surrounded by myriads of enemies."

166. Ibid. At 457, Gérard cites words of Saint-Just as an "avowal": "Love towards neighbor should not deceive us, insofar as its seems to be first and foremost based on self-hatred. 'I despise the dust of which I am made, and which now speaks to you,' admits Saint-Just." But listen to the rest of Saint-Just's words: "One may well persecute this dust and make it die, but I challenge anyone to wrest away from me this independent life that I gave myself for ages [to come] and in Heavens." Saint-Just was speaking of his own martyrdom and immortal posterity, in the mode of the classic Catholic *contemptus mundi*.

167. Sagan, *Citizens and Cannibals*, 239, 376–82.

168. Nye, *Origins*, 174, who led me to the works discussed in this paragraph. Many examples of such interpretations in Higonnet, "Terror, Trauma."

169. Clauzel, *Études humaines*, xxiii, xxv, 11.

170. Cabanès and Nass, *Névrose révolutionnaire*, 1.9–10, 1.16 (medieval "homicidal monomania"; see also 2.301), 2.316 (citation).

171. Ibid., 1.63–68, 1.216, 1.219, 2.300.

172. My thanks to Jeff Miner for this reference. Merari et al., "Personality Characteristics" (with

interviews and further analyses, 102–19); earlier, idem, "The Readiness to Kill and Die;" Lankford, "Suicide Terrorism;" and idem, "Do Suicide Terrorists." Discussion by Kix, "The Truth About Suicide Bombers"; also B. Gregory, *Salvation at Stake*, 100–110.

173. Cabanès and Nass, *Névrose révolutionnaire*, in particular, the chapters devoted to the Princess of Lamballe, to the "civic spankings," and to the *exaltées et illuminées*.

174. Le Bon, *Révolution française*, 66–67 (see the tr., *French Revolution*, 77).

175. George Sorel (as Nye, *Origins*, shows, 101–9) shared much with le Bon, with whom he corresponded.

176. Post, "Terrorist Psycho-Logic," 25–27. See the counterargument in Sageman, *Understanding Terror Networks*, 83–84. The Reich volume is a fine English-language collection arguing for terrorist irrationality (a thesis, however, balanced by an opening chapter owed to Martha Crenshaw).

177. Sageman, *Understanding Terror Networks*, 83.

178. Ibid., 89.

179. Becker, *Hitler's Children*. For anti-Semitism, see Colvin, *Ulrike Meinhof*, 10–11.

180. Becker, *Hitler's Children*, 41, also 42, 72, 157, 159 for hysteria; 90, for the comparison. For hysteria, see also Burleigh, cited above, Introduction, at n210.

181. Several psychological theories explaining the RAF and cognate groups' hostility toward Israel are referred to by Varon, *Bringing the War Home*, 70, 250–51. The RAF was the very last West European terror group to be exculpated from the presumption of madness, after the Italian Red Brigades; see Sageman, 130–33. Post used German studies of the 1970s; see Sageman, 84.

182. Colvin, "Ulrike Marie Meinhof," 84–86. Colvin, 90, commenting on the right-wing compilation of official documents, *Der Baader-Meinhof-Report*, 17, 33. See also Colvin, *Ulrike Meinhof*, 189–93; and Balz, *Von Terroristen*, 201–2.

183. See Della Porta, "Political Socialization." She has since revised her position.

184. See the survey in Varon, *Bringing the War Home*, 244–53 (notably the model proposed by Jörg Bopp). Varon's own hypothesis (249–50) is that the RAF members wanted to exculpate themselves from guilt but also redeem Germany as a whole. They also assumed the role of victims of Nazism (false equation of their prison, Stammheim, with Auschwitz, of abuse of RAF members with genocide), so claimed the Jewish mantle of martyrdom. Varon dismisses the notion that they were simply "Hitler's children"; rather, like the previous generation, they thought in radical binaries, with the attendant propensity to brutality and violence (250). Varon's suggestions are not antithetical with the considerations I develop in the paragraph that follows.

185. So Varon, *Bringing the War Home*, 252, concludes that, if there was a rebellion, it was against "the generation of their parents, not" against "their parents as such." This makes dubious a Freudian family romance explanation, where one falls in (neurotic) love with one's father's enemy.

186. Süllwold, "Stationen," 101–2.

187. Schmidtchen and Uehlinger, "Jugend und Staat."

188. "Das Konzept Stadtguerilla," in RAF, 28. Cf. Adorno et al., *The Authoritarian Personality*. The citation from (probably) Vesper, undated note relating to Ensslin's trial for arson (in Frankfurt, April 2–3, 1968) is from Koenen, *Vesper, Ensslin, Baader*, 180–81.

189. Sageman's critique, *Understanding Terror Networks*, 124–25.

190. See, e.g., De Lubac, *Postérité spirituelle*.

191. Sensitivity to this Christian dimension in Matz, "Über gesellschaftliche und politische Bedingungen."

192. Matz, "Über gesellschaftliche und politische Bedingungen," 82–84, at 83. See for the U.S. Weathermen's dualism, Varon, *Bringing the War Home*, 93, 204, 241.

193. Colvin, *Ulrike Meinhof*, 116–48.

194. Matz, "Über gesellschaftliche und politische Bedingungen," 89.

195. The formula comes from Revelation 2.9, characterizing the Jews who would not convert to Christianity (the True Israel) and (for this reason) lying in claiming to be true Jews. The best expression of this may be Donatist; see the Acts of the Abinitian Martyrs §22, tr. Tilley, *Donatist Martyr Stories*, 48. For Jerome and others, the synagogue of Satan contained the "princes of heretics": Commentariorum in Esaiam liber 7, in Isa. 22.3, CCSL 73, 299.

196. Ulrike Meinhof, *Konkret* 11 (1967), reprint in eadem, *Die Würde des Menschen*, 108.

197. "Die Aktion des 'Schwarzen September' in München. Zur Strategie des antiimperialistischen Kampfes" (Nov. 1972), in RAF, 151 and passim.

198. Ibid., 166.

199. Ensslin, *"Zieht den Trennungsstritch,"* 43. The same theme already appears in 1970, "Die Rote Armee aufbauen," in RAF, 24.

200. "Die Aktion des 'Schwarzen September'," in RAF, 165–66. For false freedom, see Marcuse, "Repressive Tolerance," here 106–9, with Kraushaar, "Herbert Marcuse," 198. Marcuse, "Repressive Tolerance," 120, speaks of "breaking the tyranny of public opinion."

201. Adorno developed the concept of *Verblendungszusammenhang* in a reflection on ancient madness. Discussion in Musolff, *Krieg gegen die Öffentlichkeit*, 159–60. On "system," see Stötzel and Wengeler, *Kontroverse Begriffe*, 363, 397.

202. "Über den bewaffneten Kampf in Westeuropa," in RAF, 86, 87.

203. Juergensmeyer, *Terror in the Mind of God*, 24–26, 36, 178 (for a citation from McVeigh's favorite novel, the apocalyptic *The Turner Diaries* by William Pierce, a.k.a. Andrew MacDonald: it was impossible to "destroy the System without hurting many thousands of innocent people—no way").

204. See Kupperman, *Settling with the Indians*, 78.

205. Müntzer, *Sermon to the Princes* (1524), a.k.a. "Auslegung des Unterschieds Daniel," ed. Frantz, *Thomas Müntzer. Schriften und Briefe*, 259:9–11, tr. Baylor, *Revelation and Revolution*, 111: "If you remove the mask from the world, then you will soon recognize it for what it is with a righteous judgement, John [Rev.] 7[.14]."

206. Crouzet, DesR, 174–84, 205–8; Robespierre, "Rapport sur les principes de morale politique," 10.361.

207. Augustine, Ep. 185.4.23, CSEL 57, 21; adopted by Gratian's *Decretum* C XXIII, q. iv, c. xliii, ed. Friedberg, 1.923.

208. See the recollections of Klein, *German Guerilla Terror*. Kraushaar, "A l'ombre de la Fraction Armée Rouge."

209. Becker, 17–18. The third edition of Becker, *Hitler's Children* (London: 1989), 250–57, elaborates on the theme of millenarian urges with comparisons to the Peasants' War and references to Norman Cohn—so strengthening in an incestuous way her hypotheses about madness.

210. Van der Knaap, "The New Executioners' Arrival," 286–87. Citation from Aust, *Baader-Meinhof Group*, 212–13; Varon, *Bringing the War Home*, 210, 244–45.

211. Baumann, "Tupamaros Westberlin," in *Wie alles anfing*; idem, "Shalom and Napalm," at 68–69, justifying the firebomb placed in Berlin's synagogue. The Palestinians were the "new Jews." Cf. Kloke, *Israel und die deutsche Linke*.

212. Kunzelmann, Letter "from Amman," in *Agit 883*, 55 (April 3, 1970): 11, cited by Kloke, *Israel und die deutsche Linke*, 166.

213. See below, Chapter 5, at nn132–34.

214. Meinhof, "Drei Freunde Israels," *Konkret* 7 (1967), repr. in *Die Würde des Menschen*, 100–103, commenting with great nuance on the 1967 Six-Day War, attributed sympathy toward Israel to a (respectable) feeling toward the victims of Nazism, to American interest in controlling access to oil, and to glee on the part of the German losers 1945 at seeing an anticommunist, anti-Soviet victory.

215. See above, Chapter 2.

216. Cf. J. Smith, "The Devil in Mr. Jones," 111–12, 120, a fine plaidoyer. I thank the anonymous reviewer for this reference.

CHAPTER 4. MARTYRDOM IN THE WEST: VENGEANCE, PURGE, SALVATION, AND HISTORY

My thanks to the Danish Center for the Study of Medieval Rituals (Copenhagen), in particular to its director, Professor Niels Holger Petersen, and to Dr. Mette Birkedal Bruun, who invited me to deliver there in 1997 the maiden version of this chapter. Gratitude here to Jochen Hellbeck, who allowed me to read after my Danish talk his then forthcoming article, "With Hegel to Salvation." Kiersten Jakobsen and Juri Lozovov checked the bolshevik Russian.

1. An example for the former, Buc, "Martyre et ritualité," reworked in Buc, *Dangers*, Chapter 4. An example for the latter, Juergensmeyer, *Terror in the Mind of God*; Pahl, *Empire of Sacrifice*.

2. See Buc, "Vengeance," 463–44.

3. Bruno of Segni, in Ps. 80.14–15, PL 164, 1016d–7a.

4. See Fögen, *Römische Rechtsgeschichten*, 21–22; Buc, "Vengeance," 463–64.

5. See Kamlah, *Christentum und Geschichtlichkeit*, e.g., 76, on the "eschatologically necessary" role of persecution: without it "the community of the saints cannot quite be thought of."

6. See below, Chapter 6, at nn47–48.

7. See below, Chapter 7, at nn3–12, with Mendel, *Vision and Violence*.

8. The expression in the subhead has biblical (Num. 35.33) and Puritan lineage and was used to argue for the punishment of Stuart royalists and justify the execution of Charles I. See Crawford, "Charles Stuart, That Man of Blood." For an attempt to read the Harpers Ferry raid as a "social drama" à la Victor Turner, see Joyner, "Guilty of Holiest Crime."

9. However, Brown denied this at his trial. See the journalistic report in *John Brown*, ed. Warch and Fanton [henceforth JB], 75, from *The Life, Trial and Execution of Captain John Brown* (New York: 1859; repr. Miami: 1969), 48.

10. For the impact and afterlife of Brown's execution, see Nudelman, *John Brown's Body*.

11. For the place of religion in the Civil War and its coming, see most recently Stout, *AN*, and Noll, *Civil War as a Theological Crisis*, with its discussion of historiography, esp. 9–14, 17–27.

12. See recently Nudelman, *John Brown's Body*. For an earlier era, Buc, "Martyre et ritualité" (or Buc, *Dangers*, Chapter 4).

13. The classic studies are Graus, *Volk, Herrscher und Heiliger*, and the pioneering thirty pages by Fichtenau, "Zum Reliquienwesen." See as well Geary, *Furta Sacra*, and the always stimulating, if functionalist, essay by Brown, *Cult of the Saints*.

14. E. Weiner and A. Weiner, *Martyr's Conviction*, 94–125.

15. I use "self-shaping" rhetorically, with full awareness of Brad Gregory's rejection of the notion of "self-fashioning" for an understanding of martyrdom (it is God and God-given exemplars that shape the martyr, not the martyr who makes himself or herself). See Gregory, *Salvation at Stake*, 132–33. Gregory would rather say that Brown understood himself to be the object of God's choices, not an autonomous, self-willed agent.

16. Brown et al., "A declaration of liberty by the representatives of the slave population of the United States of America" (1859), repr. in JB, 48, from Richard J. Hinton, *John Brown and His Men: With Some Account of the Roads They Traveled to Reach Harper's Ferry* (New York: 1894), 643; Apr. 8, 1858 letter to Sanborn, below n45.

17. As underlined for the sixteenth century's confessional cultures (with the exception of most Anabaptists), by Gregory, *Salvation at Stake*.

18. See Dugard, "International Terrorism."

19. Letter to Brown from N. S., dated New York, Nov. 25, 1859, Redpath, *Echoes*, 408; Wendell Phillips, "The Lesson of the Hour," Nov. 1, 1859, in ibid., 51.

20. Robespierre, "Second discours sur le jugement de Louis Capet" (Dec. 28, 1792), in *Œuvres*, 9.198–99 (my thanks for this reference to Keith Baker).

21. For my purposes, the best recent biography is DeCaro, *"Fire from the Midst of You."*

22. JB, 96, to Reverend McFarland (Nov. 23, 1859), from Sanborn, 598.

23. Brown did allow one exceptionally eager Southern Episcopalian priest to come to him, but with a caveat: "let him come, and I will pray for him, but he cannot pray for me," cited by DeCaro, *"Fire from the Midst of You"*, 274.

24. Brown to Reverend McFarland (Nov. 23, 1859), in JB, 96, from Sanborn, 588–89. Another version in a note to Mary Brown: "And I can say the words of our blessed Saviour: 'Father, forgive them; they know not what they do'," cited by DeCaro, *"Fire from the Midst of You"*, 277.

25. "Blank Bible," ff. 895, 898, on Rev. 18.20; see above, Chapter 1, n108.

26. Wesley, *Explanatory Notes*, 1.211.

27. *The New Testament of our Lord* (London, 1607), fol. 42r(b), facsimile in *The Geneva Bible*, ed. Sheppard. Admittedly, given the nineteenth-century Protestant primacy of "scripture sole," Brown is less likely to have been influenced in his use of scripture by a biblical commentary than would have been a medieval cleric or even layman. See Hatch, "Sola scriptura," esp. 64–76.

28. For Matthew Henry, *An Exposition*, 3.435b, Christ meant a conditional mercy: " 'Father, forgive them, not only these but all who shall repent, and believe in the Gospels;' and He did not intend that these should be forgiven upon any other terms." Fully irenic interpretations also circulated; see, e.g., the contemporary compilation Scott, *Comprehensive Commentary*, 4.587.

29. He was not the only one; see Stewart, *Holy Warriors*, 155–56, citing Steven S. Foster: "Every-man should act on his own convictions, whether he believes in using moral or physical force," his own usage of the former consisting in exhorting others to employ the latter.

30. JB, 90 (Nov. 1, 1859), from Sanborn, 582. The Quaker from Newport, R.I., dated her letter Oct. 27, 1859.

31. Brown, letter (Nov. 15, 1859) to Rev. H. L. Vaill, in JB, 93, from Sanborn, 590. For the medi-eval pericope of the swords, see Caspary, *Politics and Exegesis*.

32. JB, 97–98, to Reverend Dr. Heman Humphrey (Nov. 25, 1859), from Sanborn, 604.

33. Cited in Stayer, *German Peasants' War*, 82.

34. E.g., Reverend E. H. Sears, Sermon at Concord (Dec. 2, 1859), in Redpath, *Echoes*, 438. The preacher wished for God's anger not to express itself in war but in the bloodless conversion of the South: "Let the blood of all Thy martyrs for liberty . . . cry to Thee from the ground till the slave rises from his thralldom into the full glory of manhood. And when that day shall come, let it not be through the chaos of revolutions, nor by staining this fair earth with the blood of brothers, but let Thy spirit descend, and change the heart of the master, and melt off the fetters of the slave."

35. Redpath, *Echoes*, 397 (a friend in Syracuse, N.Y., Nov. 26).

36. Redpath, *Echoes*, 399–400 (from an Ohio clergyman, B. K. M., Cincinnati, Nov. 26); 408–9 (E. T., from New York, Nov. 26); 417 (from Lamont, Ottawa County, Michigan, Nov. 23); 423 (from Hudson, Ohio, Nov. 28).

37. Letter "from a Scottish Covenanter" (New Alexandria, Pa., Nov. 23), in Redpath, *Echoes*, 396: "You have been called before judges and governors, and 'it has been given you what to say and how to speak', and I pray that when you are called to witness a good confession before many witnesses, that there will be given you living words that will scathe and burn in the heart of this great and guilty na-tion, until their oppression of men and treason against God shall be clean purged out."

38. Ibid. A former Protestant missionary to Micronesia also referred to Dagon's temple: "Should a lock of your hair fall into my lap before the execution shall help you shake the pillars of the idol's temple, it would be valued" (New Haven, Conn., November 28), in Redpath, *Echoes*, 405. Wesley, *Explanatory Notes*, 2.861: The judge Samson "was by his office obliged to seek the destruction of these enemies and blasphemers of God, and oppressors of his people; which in these circumstances he could not effect without his own death." He was "a type of Christ, who by voluntarily undergoing death, destroyed the enemies of God and of his people." Cf. the very similar ideas in Matthew Henry, who seasons Old Testament vengeance with New Testament mercy while leaving the former valid, *Exposi-tion of the Old and New Testaments*, 1.616b: "That it was not from a principle of passion or personal revenge, but from a holy zeal for the glory of God and Israel, that he desired to do this, appears from God's accepting and answering the prayer. Samson died praying, so did our blessed Saviour; but Sam-son prayed for vengeance, Christ for forgiveness." That Samson was also a type of Christ (617a) points to the classic if paradoxical theological coinherence of vengeance and mercy.

39. Brown to Reverend L. H. Vaill (Nov. 15, 1859), JB, 94, from Sanborn, 590–91. See also the letter to Sanborn, Apr. 8, 1858, cited below, n45.

40. Redpath, *Echoes*, 391 (no name or date), 391 (emphasis original). Protestant commentaries on this passage did not wash off the theme of vengeance; see Matthew Henry, *An Exposition of the Old and New Testaments*, 3.1263b: "Even the spirits of just men made perfect retain a proper resentment of the

wrong they have sustained by their cruel enemies; and though they die in charity, praying as Christ did that God would forgive them, yet they are desirous that, for the honour of God, and Christ, and the Gospel, and for the terror and conviction of others, God will take a just revenge upon the sin of persecution, even while He pardons and saves their persecutors." Cf. Wesley, *Explanatory Notes*, 2.338: "Thou Holy and true—Both the holiness and the truth of God require Him to execute judgment and vengeance, dost Thou not judge and avenge our blood?—there is not impure affection in heaven. Therefore this desire of theirs is pure and suitable to the will of God."

41. This "How long, O Lord," could refer to a number of biblical passages, and not only Rev. 6.10. But most of these verses belong to same catena, the question being an interrogation about God's inaction and an eagerness for rectification of wrongs suffered.

42. Rev. Humphrey (a kinsman), Pittsfield, Mass., November 20, Sanborn, 602, 603.

43. Sanborn, 586. "Cheerful" points to the "cheerful countenance" of Prov. 15.13, characteristic of the elect. The expression recurs in the correspondence between Brown and his well-wishers.

44. Henry, *Exposition*, 3.1041b.

45. Letter to Frederick B. Sanborn (Apr. 8, 1858), in Sanborn, 445 (rev. ed. in JB, 38): "I expect to effect a mighty conquest, even though it be like the last victory of Samson. I felt for a number of years, in earlier life, a steady, strong desire to die; but since I saw any prospect of becoming a "reaper" in the great harvest, I have not only felt quite willing to live, but have enjoyed life much; and am now rather anxious to live for a few years more."

46. *An Exposition*, 3.1042: "This is the way to have the God of peace with us—to keep close to our duty to him."

47. Henry, on the other hand, called for patience vis-à-vis seeming "tares" in the Lord's field. See in Matt. 13.24–30, *An Exposition*, 3.104–5, esp. §6–7. He would have judged Brown "over-hasty and inconsiderate."

48. Sanborn, 620. The note gave its title to a useful narrative, Oates, *To Purge This Land with Blood*. See also Nudelman, *John Brown's Body*, 35.

49. Letter 57 (1524), ed. Frantz, *Thomas Müntzer*, 414:3–9, with Stayer, *Anabaptists and the Sword*, 84.

50. William Garrison, Dec. 2, 1859, speech, in *The Liberator* (Dec. 16, 1859), in Cain, ed., *William Lloyd Garrison*, 157. Stauffer, *The Black Hearts of Men*, 30–31 explains well how some radical abolitionists were willing to try a "merciful removal" of slavery but expected that they would have to accept "violence." In quotation marks, Gerrit Smith's words, mustering the traditional theological antithesis between mercy and justice, for which see above, Chapter 2, at nn54–72.

51. *Wendell Phillips on Civil Rights and Freedom*, ed. Filler, 113; from Redpath, *Echoes*, 66.

52. Ibidem.

53. Camus, *L'homme révolté*.

54. Narrative in Medvedev, *Let History Judge*, 327–83.

55. In English, People's Commissariat, *Report of Court Proceedings in the Case of the Anti-Soviet "Bloc of Rights and Trotskyites"* . . . *Moscow, March 2–13, 1938*, 712–13, available as well in a (slightly abridged) re-edition with commentary by Tucker and Cohen, eds., *Great Purge Trials*. Cf. the equally official Russian version, Narodnyĭ komissariat iustitsii SSSR, *Sudebnyĭ otchet po delu antisovetskogo "Pravo-Trotskistskogo bloka."*

56. See Hellbeck, *Revolution on My Mind*. Hellbeck's article, "With Hegel," brings together masterfully this culture and Bukharin's trial. There are dim premises to it in the short psychological analysis by A. Kriegel, *Grands procès*, 90–96.

57. For those techniques, see Kriegel, *Grands procès*, 67–117; and now Werth, *1936–1938, Les Procès de Moscou*, 163–83, on the combination between coercion and conviction. Hellbeck's approach, which I share, preserves conscious sincerity and diminishes coercive staging into Bukharin's death.

58. Gregory, *Salvation at Stake*.

59. Medvedev, *Let History Judge*, 381–83, discusses coercion, blackmail, and torture in the genesis of these confessions; opposes the line represented by Cohen; and considers that, unlike others, Bukharin was not physically broken but merely blackmailed. I found useful the discussion by Reinecke, "Das letzte Wort."

60. For these metaphors, see A. Weiner, "Introduction."

61. *Report*, 730.

62. Chernov: "By my honest work in the future I shall try to make up if even for a very small particle of these terrible crimes against the fatherland, against the great Soviet country" (*Report*, 725); Krestinsky also would accept a capital sentence but pleaded that "during these nine months I have undergone a radical change, and by sparing my life . . . [my judges can] give me the opportunity to expiate (*iskupit'*) my crimes in any way, even if only partially" (736, Russian: 649). Zubarov proposed: "if my life were preserved, I would, in practical work, justify not only in words, but also in deeds, the confidence of the Court" (737). Khodjayev asked for any way that might allow him "to obliterate (*snjat'*) at least some particle of my crimes and my profound guilt (*vina*)" and be of service to the country (748, Russian: 660); similarly Rakovsky: "I repent (*raskaivajus'*) deeply and sincerely, and I ask you to give me the opportunity to redeem even if an insignificant part of my guilt (*vina*), even by the most modest work, no matter under what circumstances" (764; Russian 674). Levin pleaded that he might expiate "at least a part of my crimes by honest work" (781); Bulanov asked for mercy because, simply, the trials are the successful "apotheosis of the counter-revolution" and so there is no need to kill (787); Pletnev would devote himself to "my Soviet country" (788); Kazakov would accept the decision but also was willing to "atone" (*zagladit*) by scientific labor for the USSR (790, Russian 699). Maximov-Dikovsky stated, "I am no longer an enemy. . . . I am not incorrigible" (791). Rykov (*Report*, 741) called on still secret conspirers to come forward, the sole way for them "to secure any sort of relief and disencumber themselves of the monstrous burden which has been revealed by the present trial"; Bessonov accepted death; so did Sharangovich and Zelensky.

63. *Report*, 721: "I will accept the most severe verdict—the supreme penalty—as deserved. I have only one wish: I wish to live through my last days or hours, no matter how few they may be, I wish to live through [them] and die not as an enemy taken prisoner by the Soviet government, but as a citizen of the U.S.S.R. who has committed the gravest treachery to the fatherland, whom the fatherland has gravely punished for this, but who repented."

64. *Report*, 757–58: "I do not want to die, still less do I want to die an enemy of the people, . . . I would like anywhere, in any place, to atone for the grave crimes which I have committed in company with these people."

65. *Report*, 751–52, Russian 663.

66. My translation based on the official German translation. See the official translation in *Report*, 778: "As a matter of fact, everything is clear. World History is a world court of judgement."

67. This shared disposition to surrender on the ground of Soviet success under Stalin was most bluntly expressed by Chernov, *Report*, 724: "The realization of this might of the Soviet power and Soviet state led me to down arms immediately after my arrest and give sincere and truthful testimony."

68. Bloch, "Bucharins Schlusswort," 363: "His consciousness was receptive to contrition and the recognition of what was right; it saw collectivization's successes, it noticed the powerful progress of socialist construction after initial setbacks; it grasped the proof of Stalin's conception on the basis of the most authentic Marxist criterion: that of Praxis."

69. Bloch, "Bucharins Schlusswort," 363–64. Amazingly, Bloch compares Bukharin and his confession to the fifteenth-century French patriot and sexual monster Gilles de Rais. He is led to this medieval parallel by the "Last Words" reference to "principles of medieval jurisprudence." Critiques had adduced medieval comparisons of their own—like Ivan the Terrible. Bloch countered that they should look for "surer parallels in faith, conversion, and reconversion (*Rückkehr*)."

70. I cite from the English *Humanism and Terror*, 29. Cf. Merleau-Ponty, *Humanisme et terreur*, 31; emphasis Merleau-Ponty.

71. Medvedev, *Let History Judge*, 365.

72. Getty, Naumov and Sher, *Road to Terror*, 556–60; see also Werth, *1936–1938*, 205–12.

73. Tucker, "Stalin, Bukharin, and History as Conspiracy," preface to Tucker and Cohen, *Great Purge Trials*, xlvii. In the same vein Medvedev, *Let History Judge*, 373.

74. Bukharin's "Last Words" referred to Dostoyevsky as well. And the "Political Testament" speaks of the new NKVD use of "medieval methods." Here as elsewhere I am in agreement with Walicki, *Marxism*, 454–67, as long as the formula "in agreement" does not obfuscate that Walicki anticipated my own musings. Cf. Medvedev, *Let History Judge*, 374.

75. Tucker, "Stalin, Bukharin," xlvi.

76. Translated in Larina, *This I Cannot Forget*, 345; another translation in Medvedev, *Let History Judge*, 366–67.

77. See " 'Ave, communisme'." See also Werth, *1936–1938*, 180–83.

78. Hellbeck, "With Hegel," 70–71, shows how Vyshinsky sought during the trial to deny the accused's claim to "humanity and thus to invalidate their claim to have rediscovered a place in its history."

79. More even, it formed the *koiné* of bolshevik self-shaping; see for example Zinaida Denizevskaia, analyzed by Hellbeck, *Revolution on My Mind*, 152, confronting the unlikeliness of some elements in the accusations levied against associates: "I am forcing myself to overlook petty details. One must not confuse the particulars with the general."

80. Hellbeck, *Revolution on my Mind*; Ivanov, from *Report*, 728–29 and 730, Russian, 642.

81. *Revelations from the Russian Archives*, ed. Koenker and Bachman, 109–10. Here Bukharin sounded very much like Ikramov (above, at n64). See Werth, *1936–1938*.

82. Rakovsky, *Report*, 763, attributed his failings to counterrevolutionary ideology, plus being "blinded by that passion, by that ambition for power." Ikramov's Russian, 665.

83. *Report*, 763; Russian, 673. Since at least Tertullian and Augustine, this satanic misunderstanding and blindness define heretical, false churches.

84. *Report*, 726.

85. Hellbeck, *Revolution on My Mind*; idem, "With Hegel," 60–69, 78–79.

86. A point well made by Walicki, *Marxism*, 463.

87. Larina, *This I Cannot Forget*, 345.

88. Translated in Larina, *This I Cannot Forget*, 343–4; cf. the Medvedev translation, *Let History Judge*, 366.

89. Lübbe, "Aufklärung und Terror," 45, citing the journal of the Cheka, *The Red Sword* (Aug. 18, 1919).

90. Maximilien Robespierre, "Rapport sur les principes de morale qui doivent guider la Convention nationale" (Feb. 5, 1794), in *Œuvres*, 10.357. See most recently Edelstein, "War and Terror."

91. Bérengaud, on Rev. 19.14, PL 17, col. 926b. My thanks to Guy Lobrichon for this text.

92. Ferrier, "La couronne refusée"; Riley-Smith, *First Crusade*, 101–7.

93. For a narrative, see France, *Victory in the East*. Flori, "Mort et martyre des guerriers vers 1100"; Morris, "Martyrs on the Field of Battle."

94. So the anonymous *Gesta Francorum*, ed. Hill, *Deeds of the Franks*, 17.

95. *Liber*, 45 (knight in shining armor); 133 (Saint George "the standard bearer of this army"); 70 (the saints want to to fight alongside us, in the flesh); 78 (all the deceased fight before Antioch), 82 (idem); tr. Hill and Hill, 28, 112, 53, 60, 63. A common belief among narrators of the First Crusade, see, e.g., the anonymous *Gesta Francorum*, ed. and tr. Hill, *Deeds of the Franks*, 69, and the letter of the Syrian patriarch of Jerusalem, ed. Hagenmeyer, *Die Kreuzzugsbriefe*, 147: [*sanctis diversibus*] *militibus Christi nos vere comitantibus.*

96. See Ferrier, "La couronne refusée"; Schein, *Gateway*, and earlier her "Die Kreuzzüge als volkstümlich-messianistische Bewegungen." Chiliast conceptions must be read between the lines of the document, as Ferrier, Flori, and Rubenstein show. Rubenstein, "How, or How Much," argues subtly for the presence of apocalyptic sentiments in northern France and Lotharingia during the earlier 1090s through an analysis of Guibert of Nogent, who is likely to have frowned upon them at the time of the Clermont call for the crusade.

97. See most recently France, "Two Types of Vision," and Rubenstein, *Armies*, 213–19, 252–62.

98. See Schein, "Die Kreuzzüge"; Kostick, *Social Structure*.

99. Ferrier, "La couronne refusée," a position accepted by Flori, *L'Islam*, 271 and passim. Raymond, *Liber*, 143 (clergy's position) and 152 (Raymund's refusal); tr. Hill and Hill, 121 and 129.

100. See Bresc, "Historiens," 736. Raymond, *Liber*, 70 (my translation; cf. Hill and Hill, 53). On this passage and its biblical echoes, see Buc, "Vengeance," 484–85. And cf. *La conquête de Jérusalem* 7.31, v. 7242, ed. Hippeau, 285: "There never was such a knight, nor will there ever be" (referring to Godfrey of Bouillon).

101. Robespierre, "Contre les continuateurs de Danton, d'Hébert et autres" (June 12, 1794), *Œuvres*, 10. 494.

102. Raymond, *Liber*, 86–87, tr. Hill and Hill (here modified), 68, continuing: "and it shall be seen in what manner God will save them. Truly, upon them shall be the same curse of God and His Mother as was placed on the falling Lucifer." Justice entails a public declaration of wealth and a proportional assistance to the poor. If they do not, "let the Count and the children of God" punish them (ibid., 69).

103. For the theology of the Passion seen from the *Blickwinkel* of animal anthropology, see Gorevich, *O Kritike Antropologii Zhivotnikh*, vol. 1, Chapter 3: "Corpus porcorum et porcus corporum." I thank Charlotte Visborg Andreasen for this reference.

104. Raymond, *Liber*, 113–15; tr. Hill and Hill, 94–95. See Rubenstein, "Godfrey of Bouillon," 68; idem, *Armies*, 252–55.

105. As did mutilated crucifixes; see Wipo, *Gesta Chuonradi*, 33, ed. Bresslau, 53, with Buc, "Vengeance," 466–67.

106. Compare Fulcher of Chartres, *Historia* 1.16.5, ed. Hagenmeyer, 227. For Fulcher, furthermore, purgation did not mean purge, *Historia* 1.16.3, 226.

107. See on this point Rubenstein; Flori, *Pierre l'ermite*, 176; idem, *L'Islam*, 272–80.

108. Ekkehard, *Chronicon*, recensio prima, an. 1099, in *Frutolfs und Ekkehards Chroniken*, ed. Schmale and Schmale-Ott, 148.

109. Ibid., 144. Pseudo-Methodius, ed. Sackur, *Sibyllinische Texte und Forschungen*, 94–95: "And through his lying miracles, tricks, and prodigies, Antichrist will even seduce the elect, if it can be done, as the Lord made plain [in the Gospels]."

110. Ekkehard, *Chronicon*, recensio prima, an. 1099, 148.

111. Ibid., 132: "In the days of Henry IV Roman [king] and of Alexius prince of Constantinople according to the Gospel prophecy there rose everywhere nation against nation and kingdom against kingdom [Matt. 24.7; Luke 21.10; Mark 18.8], and there were throughout many places great earthquakes and plagues, famines and fears inspired by the sky and great portents [Rev. 13.13], and since already (*iam*) the Gospel's trumpet sounded the advent of the Just Judge, behold! the whole Church scrutinized the whole world all around, which pointed to the prophesized portents."

112. Garnier de Saintes, Apr. 5, 1794, in Aulard, ed., *Société des Jacobins*, 6.47; cited by Van der Heuvel, *Freiheitsbegriff*, 166.

113. Augustine, sermon 111 (a.k.a. Lambot 18), ed. Lambot, *Revue Bénédictine* 57 (1947): 109–16, at 115.

114. Isidore, *Sententiarum*, 1.29.4–6, CCSL 111, 88. See below, Chapter 7, at n136, for more of this text. This theme, present in Gregory the Great's *Moralia in Job* 33.6.18, in Iob 40.18, CCSL 143B, 1683–84, was picked up by Burchard of Worms's *Decretum* 20.93, PL 140, 1052ab, and Ivo of Chartres, *Decretum* 17.103, PL 161, 1008c–1009a. See also Haymo, in Amos 7.4, PL 117, 118d–119a. Gregory, *Moralia* 14.23.27, in Iob 18.20, CCSL 143A, 713–14, states that the elect will not fall, but merely know great terrors.

115. See McGrath, "Romance of the Maccabees"; Buc, "Vengeance," 468–73, and above, Chapter 2 at n148.

116. Maier, ed., *Crusade Propaganda*, 86–87, translation slightly modified. For crusades and sermons, see as well Cole, *Preaching of the Crusades*; Bird, "Crusade and Conversion"; eadem, "Paris Masters."

117. Maier, ed., *Crusade Propaganda*, 90–91.

118. For the former, see below, Chapter 5, at nn30–60; for the latter, Barber, "Pastoureaux of 1320," with Nirenberg, *Communities of Violence*, 43–93.

119. This combination of election and purge is based on the same scriptural images as Jacques de Vitry's sermon. Syms, *Swords apology*, 10 (italics his). I expand here the citation in Capp, *Fifth Monarchy Men*, 37.

120. Aspinwall, *A brief description of the fifth monarchy*, 4, 6. Cited in Capp, *Fifth Monarchy Men*, 64. For Aspinwall, see McLear, "New England and the Fifth Monarchy," 250–53.

121. On Adhémar, see Brundage, "Adhémar"; Morris, "Policy and Visions." Interestingly, the *Gesta Francorum*, ed. Hill, 74, presents Adhémar as a "helper of the poor" who preached some redistribution to the richer crusaders. This may have enabled the radicals to whom the *Liber* gives a voice to trust in visions announcing his positive transit through fire. See Kostick, *Social Structure*, 133–34, and before him Rousset, *Origines*, 145.

122. Raymond, *Liber*, 72; tr. Hill and Hill, 54; ibid., 127; tr. 107.

123. Ibid., 84 (my translation); cf. tr. Hill and Hill, 66.

124. Ibid., 84–85; tr. Hill and Hill, 66–67.

125. As explained in another vision, *Liber*, 116–17; tr. Hill and Hill, 96–97. This is also why Peter Bartholomew was partly burnt in the ordeal by fire that he underwent to prove the lance's authenticity, *Liber*, 123 (my translation): "I delayed in the fire, he explained, because the Lord came to me in the middle of the flames and taking me by the hand said to me: Because you harbored doubts concerning the Lance's *inventio* even though blessed Andrew showed it to you, you will not go through the fire totally unharmed, but you will never see Hell."

126. Ibid., 85; trans. Hill and Hill, 67.

127. Ibid., 119, 145; tr. Hill and Hill, 99, 121–22. Paris BNF Latin 5132 contains this vision but diverges from this point onward from the tradition represented in the Hill edition. See France, "Text," 640. Again, my thanks to Jay Rubenstein for his guidance on this manuscript.

128. Raymond, *Liber*, 151; tr. Hill and Hill, 128. This detail is absent from the Paris BNF Latin 5132 version.

129. Riley-Smith, *First Crusaders*, 72–74; more discussion in Housley, *Contesting*, 41; see Flori, "Mort et martyre."

130. So Riley-Smith, *First Crusaders*, 72–74.

131. Raymond, *Liber*, 123–24. See Flori, *Pierre l'ermite*, 404.

132. The mechanism had been revealed by Peter Bartholomew, *Liber*, 96: "Thus fall all those who stand in disbelief vis-à-vis God's commandments or transgress them. But if they do penance concerning their misdeeds, and clamor to God, the Lord will put them back on their feet . . . and . . . God will take away and remove the sins of those who clamor to Him."

133. Raymond, *Liber*, 151: "This is the day of the purging of all paganism, of the confirmation of Christianity, and of the renewal of our faith." Cf. Peter Bartholomew's words before Antioch, *Liber*, 78: "Know for sure that those days have come, which the Lord promised to blessed Mary and His apostles, saying that He would raise up the reign of the Christians, and throw down and trample the reign of the pagans."

134. I owe this question, which had to be raised, to Mette Birkedal Bruun, and its answer to Gregory's book, *Salvation at Stake*.

135. Nudelman, *John Brown's Body*, 4, 9, 27–28. See as well Gregory, *Salvation*.

136. See Altman, "Two Types of Opposition," 2, 8.

137. Buc, *Dangers*, 137–38 (or "Martyre et ritualité," 75–76). Such is, indeed, the conclusion of Tertullian's *De Spectaculis*, cap. 30.1–5, SC 332, 320–22. See also the *Passio sanctorum Mariani et Iacobi* §12, ed. and tr. Musurillo, 210–11: "Now filled with the spirit of prophecy, with courage and confidence

[Marian] foretold that the blood of the just would soon be avenged, and as though he were speaking already from heaven's heights he threatened various temporal scourges, such as epidemics, enslavement, famine, earthquakes, and the torment of poisonous flies."

138. Compare Jacques de Vitry's apocalyptic image of fallen stars, above at n117, to the Civil War era *Presbyterian* 33, 7 (Feb. 14, 1863): 25, in its report that Bishop Simpson had predicted that God would "drive away the thick darkness" that had blotted out one-third of the stars" of the U.S. flag (the rebel states).

139. We do get individual conversions, see, e.g., the soldier Pudens in the *Passion of Perpetua and Felicitas* §21.1, 21.4, ed. Musurillo, 128, 130. And some strands of Christianity saw in the empire and its peace a providential, if heathen, matrix for the spread of the religion. See, inter alia, Frend, *Martyrdom and Persecution*.

140. E.g., *The Martyrdom of Apollonius* §7–9, ed. Musurillo, 92.

141. See, e.g., *Martyrdom of Saint Carpus*, ed. Musurillo, 23–24; "The Martyrs of Lyons," ibid., 68:7.

142. Prudentius, *Peristephanon*, Hymn II (Lawrence), vv. 1–4, ed. Lavarenne, 32. The prayer is at vv. 413–87 (44–46). Theodosius I's closing of the pagan shrines is prophesized at vv. 473–84 (46): "I foresee a prince to come." Thus, this hagiography verifies the second, inclusive or "gradational" pattern described by Altman, "Two Types," 8–9.

143. See above, at n106.

144. *Liber*, 37: "So that rustic men ignorant of God, having come to learn His knights' strength and their willingness to suffer, would either recover at some point from their ferocity or be led to God's Judgment and lack [there] any pardon." Cf. tr. Hill and Hill, 17.

145. For the scope of the purge, see Kedar, "Jerusalem Massacre."

146. My thanks to Luc Ferrier for having articulated during the Paris discussion Raymond's non-universalistic outlook.

147. See above, Chapter 1, at n78, and below, Chapter 5, at nn190–93.

CHAPTER 5. TWINS—NATIONAL HOLY WAR AND SECTARIAN TERROR

Epigraphs: Robespierre, "Rapport sur les principes de morale politique," *Œuvres*, 10.357; RAF, 30.

1. Lincoln, *Holy Terrors*, 19–32; Rapoport, "Introduction," xiv.

2. Brunner, *Land und Herrschaft*; tr. *Land and Lordship*.

3. "False Christians" could mean heretics; see Augustine, *De doctrina christiana* 2.35.53, CCSL 32, 69. But more often they constituted a subcategory in Satan's body next to pagans, heretics, and Jews, as in the text here cited, Primasius, *Commentarius in Apocalypsin*, 3.9, in Rev. 9.15–16, CCSL 92, 156:272–75.

4. See above, Chapter 2, at n68.

5. Below, Chapter 6.

6. There were pointed discussions around Samson—whether he had destroyed the Philistines in the suicidal collapse of Dagon's temple as a judge or as an inspired individual; see above, Chapter 4, at nn38–39.

7. Andreas of Strumi, *Vita sancti Arialdi* 19.56, ed. Baethgen, 1063–64; ibid. 10.23, 1056.

8. *Pax Sigiwini archiepiscopi coloniensis* §15, 605.

9. Goodman, *How Superior Powers Ought to Be Obeyed* § 13, 180–82, cited by Skinner, *Foundations*, 2.237.

10. Cf. N. Davis, "Rites of Violence."

11. See Kern, *Gottesgnadentum*, partial tr. as *Kingship and Law in the Middle Ages*; Tierney, *Foundations of the Conciliar Theory*; Skinner, *Foundations*; Kelley, "Kingship and Resistance"; Von Friedeburg, ed., *Widerstandsrecht*. The twelfth-century bases for later medieval resistance are addressed in Buc, *L'ambiguïté du Livre*, ch. 6.

12. Sepúlveda, *Democrates Alter*, ed. Losada, 61–62. Prov. 24.11, Ps. 71.12, Ambrose; compare Peter the Chanter, in Buc, *L'ambiguité*, 352–53; Rufinus, *Summa*, ed. Singer, on Gratian, *Decretum*, C. 23 q. 3 c.7, ed. Friedberg, 897–98, who cites Ambrose (cf. Buc, 361n1); Gratian, *Decretum*, C. 23 q. 3, *dictum post* c. 10 and c.11, ed. Friedberg, 1.898.

13. Kantorowicz, *The Kings' Two Bodies*, to be read with Boureau, *Le simple corps du roi*, for the notion of juridical fiction.

14. See as well Strayer, "France: The Holy Land." France was not exclusively precocious in promising martyrdom's rewards for the defense of the kingdom; see Norway (1164) and Castile (1166), in Housley, "Crusades Against Christians," 85.

15. Matthew Paris, *Chronica Majora*, vol. 6, *Addidamenta*, 155–62, here 156; tr. Jackson, *Seventh Crusade*, 86, slightly modified. Was Matthew Paris inspired by this letter in recounting the Master of the Temple's answer to a taunting Robert d'Artois right before the Mansurah Battle? See *Chronica Majora*, 5.150: "Insuperabiles essemus, si inseparabiles permanemus. Sed infeliciter dividimur, similes arenae sine calce, unde inepti ædificio spirituali et cæmento caritatis expertes, maceriæ depulsæ consimiles erimus profecto ruinosi." Cf. the sermon attributed to Bishop Adhémar by Robert the Monk, *Historia iherosolimitana* 7.10, 829–30.

16. Joinville, *Vie de saint Louis*, §207, ed. Monfrin, 100: "Biau Sire Diex, gardez moy ma gent!"

17. Compare Matthias of Janov's belief that frequent Communion would heal rifts in the mystical body of the Church (a position approved by the archbishop of Prague in 1391). Cf. Marin, *L'archevêque*, 495–98, and 496n1. See Riley-Smith, "Crusading as an Act of Love."

18. Richer of Senones, *Gesta Senoniensis ecclesie* 3.15, ed. Waitz, at 294, with Duby, *Dimanche de Bouvines*, 270–72; tr. *Legend of Bouvines*, 160–63.

19. For the reign of Philip the Fair, Louis' grandson, see Stayer, "France," 212. Cf. Hastings, *Construction of Nationhood*, 98: "the claim . . . that the French crown and kingdom were uniquely Catholic and Christian, derived, then, from a kind of focused universalism rather than from a straight claim that the French were the chosen of the Lord. But the result was the same." This thesis is developed by Housley, *Religious Warfare*, 26–30. See as well the fine discussion in Mastnak, *Crusading Peace*, 229–78.

20. Matthew Paris, *Chronica majora*, 5.23.

21. Letter to the duke of Burgundy (July 17, 1429), tr. Charles Taylor, *Jeanne d'Arc*, 95, from Quicherat, *Procès*, 5.126.

22. Cole, *Preaching of the Crusades*, 89–92, 127–28, noting, concerning Fulk of Neuilly, how the combination reform-crusade could veer to one pole at the expense of the other.

23. Aurell, "Eschatologie," 222–26.

24. Loeb, "Controverse de 1240"; Grayzel, *Church and the Jews*, 29–33; Rosenthal, "Talmud on Trial"; Nahon, "Les ordonnances de Saint Louis," 19, 28; Jordan, *Louis IX*, 84–85; idem, *French Monarchy*, 128–48; Le Goff, *Saint Louis*, 179–80, 793–814; Cohen, *Friars*.

25. Ordonnance de 1254, §32, ed. De Laurière, *Ordonnances des roys de France*, 1.75, with Brussel, *Nouvel examen* §2.39, 1.592–93.

26. Tr. Jackson, *Seventh Crusade*, 168, from Schaller, "Kuriale Briefsammlung," 212.

27. Ordonnance de 1254, ed. De Laurière, *Ordonnances des roys de France*, 1.65–75; see Le Goff, *Saint Louis*, 218–21; Jordan, *Louis IX*, ch. 6. Jordan, 127, states that, after 1250, "the remainder of his life was, in a certain sense, a long penance."

28. Matthew Paris, *Chronica Majora*, 5.102 *(Deo vindice)*, 5.170–72, cf. 5.23.

29. Tr. Jackson, *Seventh Crusade*, 177, from Jeanroy, "Le troubadour," 83.

30. Cohn, *Pursuit*, 81–87 (above, Introduction, n62); Barber, "Crusade of the Shepherds"; Dickson, "Advent." The old narrative by Röricht, "Pastorellen," has been superseded. A fine analysis of the shepherds that anticipates the direction here taken is Jackson, *The Seventh Crusade*, 179–81.

31. Matthew Paris, *Chronica Majora*, 5.253. See Barber, "Crusade of the Shepherds," 11.

32. See Le Goff, *Saint Louis*, 102–3.

33. *Chroniques de Saint-Denis*, excerpts in RHGF 21.115. See also Matthew Paris, *Chronica Majora* 5.246. *Chanson de Roland*, vv. 626, 633, ed. Bédier, 50.

34. Matthew Paris, *Chronica Majora*, 5.252.

35. Barber, "Crusade of the Shepherds," 10.

36. *Chronica universalis Mettensis*, MGH Scriptores 24, 522, tr. Jackson, *Seventh Crusade*, 189; for Bacon, see above, Chapter 3, at nn86–90.

37. Jean du Vignay (redacted 1250–85, possibly on the basis of a now lost Latin chronicle by Primat of Saint-Denis), in RHGF 23.8, tr. Jackson, *Seventh Crusade*, 182; cf. *Chronicon sancti Laudi Rotomagensis*, extracts in RHGF 23.395, tr. Jackson, 186. Le Goff, *Saint Louis*, 349, is uncertain whether there was an original by Primat.

38. For the Virgin of Peace, Offenstadt, *Faire la paix*, 119–23. For Mary, war, conquest, and consecration, see recently Remensnyder, "Marian Monarchy"; eadem, *Conquistadora*.

39. Anonymous canon of Laon, in RHGF 18.705. Malegam, *Sleep of Behemoth*, 240–43.

40. Geoffroy de Vigeois (finished in 1183), in Labbé, *Nova bibliotheca manuscriptorum*, 2.279–342. Excerpt from Labbé in RHGF 18.211ff, here 219. See Labbé, 290, for the dating.

41. See Fulcher of Chartres, *Historia* 1.8.3, ed. Hagenmeyer, 169, with a skeptic Riley-Smith, *First Crusade*, 81–82.

42. Matthew Paris, *Chronica Majora*, 5.248.

43. *Chroniques de Saint-Denis*, extracts in RHGF 21.115 («si commença à preéchier et à despecier mariages»).

44. Jean du Vignay, in RHGF 23.9, tr. Jackson, *Seventh Crusade*, 181–82. *Chronicon sancti Laudi Rotomagensis*, extracts in RHGF 23.396; *Actus pontificum Cenomannis in urbe degentium*, 500–501; Matthew Paris, *Chronica Majora*, 5.248. See Brundage, "Crusader's Wife"; and Kostick, *Social Structure*, 140, 271–80, with Raymond d'Aguilers, *Liber*, 96, tr. mine. For the twelfth century, Aurell, *Chrétiens*, 90–94.

45. Matthew Paris, *Chronica Majora*, 5.249.

46. Ibid., 4.612, 4.635.

47. Salimbene de Adam, *Cronica*, rev. ed. Scalia, CCCM 125–125A, 2.672; tr. Jackson, *Seventh Crusade*, 177, 192.

48. Dickson, "Advent," 263–65, who locates the anti-Staufen preaching in Capetian borderlands, Flanders, and Brabant, 257–58.

49. Tr. mine, from Jeanroy, "Le troubadour," 83.

50. See Jacques de Vitry, cited Chapter 4, at n116.

51. Letter of the Warden of the Franciscans of Paris to Adam Marsh, in *Annals of Burton*, ed. Luard, *Annales Monastici*, 291; *Chronica universalis Mettensis*, MGH Scriptores 24, 522, tr. Jackson, *Seventh Crusade*, 189.

52. *Chronicon sancti Laudi Rotomagensis*, extract in RHGF 23.396; similar is Jean du Vignay, in RHGF 23.9–10. In this source, as befits a royalist history, the citizens of Bourges exhibit a royalist reaction absent in the Norman chronicle: since the Jews were "in the king's protection" (*garde*), they attacked the shepherds "to avenge the insult done to the king in the Jews."

53. Alan of Lille, *Sermo de Cruce Domini*, ed. d'Alverny, 282–83. See also Bird, "Reform or Crusade."

54. Reeves, *Influence*, 307; Pseudo-Ioachim, *In Ieremiam Prophetam*, 123.

55. Barber, "Crusade of the Shepherds," 16; Jordan, *French Monarchy*, 148; Le Goff, *Saint Louis*, 804–7.

56. Loeb, "Bulles inédites"; rev. ed. and tr. in Grayzel, *Church and the Jews*, 274–81; Loeb, "Controverse de 1240," 3.39–57, at 50; also in Rosenthal, "The Talmud on Trial," 162 (I read "ipsis iudeis inimicantibus" not as Jewish targets of Jewish curses ("and all others and even Jewish enemies [of the Jews]") but as the complement to "et aliis omnibus" [*ipsis iudeis inimicantibus*]. Menache, "Tartars, Jews, Saracens"; Yuval, *Two Nations*, Chapter 6; M. Kriegel, "Reckonings," 24–25.

57. Grayzel, *Church and the Jews*, 275–79.

58. Jordan, *Louis IX*, 116: "Their actions . . . fall in line with traditional royal policies. The attacks on the Jews . . . were a continuation of the process begun by Louis IX." See also Jordan, *French Monarchy*, 147–48.

59. See Jordan, *Louis IX*, 61–62, 113 (citation), 84–87, 113–16.

60. So Jordan, *French Monarchy*, 147–48.

61. Vale, *Charles VII*, and esp. ch. 3 for Jeanne.

62. Alphandéry, *Chrétienté*, 487, and 6 (citation). See as well Beaune, *Jeanne d'Arc*, 127–28.

63. The *Journal du siège d'Orléans*, in *Procès de condamnation et de réhabilitation de Jeanne d'Arc*, ed. Quicherat, 4.129, 153, describes twice the banner; see also another banner, described in the trial proceedings, Tisset, 1.268–71. For a careful discussion, Contamine, "Remarques critiques."

64. Pasquerel, deposition at the rehabilitation, *Procès en nullité de la condamnation de Jeanne d'Arc*, ed. Duparc, 1.390; text highlighted by Beaune, *Jeanne*, 215.

65. Seibt, *Hussitica*, 100–101. See the discussion of universalism and revolution in Eisenstadt, *Fundamentalism*, 42, 92, and passim.

66. MS Prague University Library V G 3, fol. 5r, cited by Kaminsky, "The Prague Insurrection," 110 (translation his). Šmahel, "Idea of 'Nation'."

67. See David, "Universalist Aspirations," 194–95.

68. *Le Ditié de Jeanne d'Arc*, §41–43, ed. and tr. Kennedy and Varty, reproduced in Taylor, *Jeanne d'Arc*, 105. See Delaruelle, "L'antéchrist," 348–49, suggesting that one can speak of a "popular movement" encompassing Jeanne and her companions.

69. Housley, "*Pro deo et patria mori*," 232–25; Beaune, *Jeanne*, 256: "Wishing to prove that Jeanne's prophecies were true, the king's theologians could only leave aside a crusade that had [in the end] not taken place." Furthermore, why did the Rouen judges find incriminating that, as suggested in fourth private examination, Tisset, 1.142, tr. Taylor, *Jeanne d'Arc*, 186, she might have said (Latin): "Surrender this town [Paris] to Jesus" (*reddatis villam Iehu*) as opposed to "to the King of France." Note that the French version says, "Surrender the town, by Jesus (*Rendez la ville de par Jhesus*)." Why holy warfare would not feature centrally in the trial, far from it, is understandable. For ecclesiastical judges, being a witch was much more an issue than taking the French on a false crusade. There were polemics enough about "false crusades" because of the conflict between the Teutonic Knights and Poland-Lithuania.

70. Beaune, *Jeanne*, 234; Delaruelle, "L'Antéchrist," *Journal d'un Bourgeois*, §501, ed. Tuetey, 235, or ed. Beaune, 253–56; tr. Shirley, *Parisian Journal*, 230–33. According to the *Bourgeois*, a Dominican master of theology and inquisitor, in a 1231 sermon attacking the now-dead Jeanne, stated that Richard was Jeanne's confessor, §580, Tuetey, 271–72; Beaune, 300; tr. Shirley, 265.

71. Beaune, *Jeanne*, 245–47.

72. Vauchez, "La paix," 329–30.

73. "Lettre aux Anglais" (March 22, 1429), tr. in Taylor, *Jeanne d'Arc*, 76; Tisset, 1.222 (the better text). Cf. *Procès de condamnation et de réhabilitation*, ed. Quicherat, 5.95–98, at 98.

74. See Delaruelle, "Spiritualité de Jeanne," 369: "Jeanne n'admettant aucune compromission, veut une armée en état de grâce pour être digne de sa mission"; idem, "L'antéchrist," 348–49. Delaruelle is followed by Beaune, *Jeanne*, 248–55. The claims of the promoters of the revision of her trial, *Procès en nullité de la condamnation*, ed. Duparc, 1.113, are corroborated by other sources.

75. See Marin, *L'archevêque*, 457–508, noting that Jean Gerson, Chancellor of the Paris University, adopted the idea and pleaded for it in the 1410s, 506–7.

76. Once a week, says Chartier, *Chronique de Charles VII*, ed. De Viriville, 1.89, 1.122; twice a week, says her close associate, the Duc d'Alençon, *Procès en nullité de la condamnation*, ed. Duparc, 1.387. See the *Journal d'un Bourgeois de Paris* §547 and 580, ed. Tuetey, 260 and 271–72, ed. Beaune, 282 and 300, tr. Shirley, 254, 265 (for excessive frequency).

77. Lawrence, HH, 371.

78. See, e.g., Rubenstein, *Armies*, 153–54.

79. Jan Žižka's ordinance of 1423, arts. 11–12, tr. in Heymann, *John Žižka*, 496, or in Fudge, *Crusade Against Heretics*, 170. The original is in Toman, *Husitské valecnictvi*, appendix. For a discussion, Fudge, "'More Glory Than Blood'," 130.

80. Jean Chartier, *Chronique de Charles VII*, ed. De Viriville, 1.90, 122–23; Testimony of the Duke of Alençon (the nobleman closest to Jeanne), in *Procès en nullité de la condamnation*, ed. Duparc, 1.387; Pasquerel, in ibid., 1.393. See also Cousinot de Montreuil, *Chronique de la Pucelle*, ed. De Viriville, 283.

81. Brother Seguin, O.P., in *Procès en nullité de la condamnation*, ed. Duparc, 1.473; duke of Alençon, in ibid., 1.387.

82. Pasquerel, in ibid., 1.391. Idem, 1.393: She provided on the day after Ascension that no one was to go to battle without having first been confessed. See also Cousinot de Montreuil, *Chronique de la Pucelle*, 283.

83. Pasquerel, in *Procès en nullité de la condamnation*, ed. Duparc, 1.392–93.

84. Ibid., 1.339 (Andreas Bordez).

85. Tisset, 1.140 (very allusive).

86. Marguerite La Touroulde, in *Procès en nullité de la condamnation*, ed. Duparc, 1.378.

87. Pasquerel, in ibid., 1.396; Simon Beaucroix, squire and married cleric, ibid., 1.373.

88. Marguerite La Touroulde, in ibid., 1.378. Vale, *Charles VII*, 57.

89. See Delaruelle, "L'antéchrist," 340–47; rich research in Tanz, *Jeanne d'Arc*, 182–200.

90. Tr. in Franq, "Jean Gerson's Theological Treatise," here 63. See the ed. in Wayman, "The Chancellor and Jeanne d'Arc," here 300–301.

91. The Latin text is in Sickl, "Lettre de Jeanne d'Arc aux Hussites."

92. *Documenta Magistri Joannis Hus vitam*, ed. Palacký, 493–94, with Kaminsky's fine commentary, HHR, 929–33. See now also Jakoubek's "ad Bellum," edited in Soukup, "Dobývání hradu Skály," at 205–8.

93. *De quadam puella*, ed. Quicherat, 3.411–21, here 417–28.

94. Ibid., 419, 420. I follow here Fraioli, *Joan of Arc*.

95. See the evidence covered and analyzed in these terms in Michaud-Fréjaville, "L'effusion de sang." The "Lettre aux Anglais" in the trial version, Tisset, 1.221–22, with Krumeich, "Jeanne d'Arc a-t-elle menti?"

96. Fraioli, *Joan of Arc*—a core thesis of her book.

97. See the seventeenth and eighteenth articles of accusation, Tisset, 1.214–16.

98. *Opinio domini Pauli Pontani*, in Lanéry d'Arc, *Mémoires et consultations*, 35–54, here 36. Cf. Gratian, *Decretum*, C. 23, 1, 1, ed. Friedberg, 1.890. I discovered Krumeich, *Auf dem Weg zum Volkskrieg?* too late to take it into account here.

99. Lawrence, HH, 413–16, see also 454–55; Šmahel, HR, 2.1132–35.

100. *Journal du Bourgeois* §573, ed. Tuetey, 267, ed. Beaune, 293; tr. Shirley, 261.

101. Ibid., §577, ed. Tuetey, 268, ed. Beaune, 295; tr. Shirley, 262.

102. Ibid., §580, ed. Tuetey, 270–71, ed. Beaune, 298; tr. Shirley, 264, reporting the Dominican master's sermon.

103. Tisset, 1.14, tr. Taylor, *Jeanne d'Arc*, 135.

104. Tisset, 1.192.

105. Jeanne's abjuration in French, ibid., 2.389–90.

106. Michaud-Fréjaville, "L'effusion de sang," 332–33; see Tisset, 1.151, tr. Taylor, *Jeanne d'Arc*, 190.

107. *Journal d'un bourgeois* §519, ed. Tuetey, 245, ed. Beaune, 266, my translation; see the tr. Shirley, 240.

108. Jacques Gelu, *De puella aurelianensi Dissertatio*, in Lanéry d'Arc, *Mémoires*, 590–91, with Fraioli, *Joan of Arc*, 97–99.

109. Lanéry d'Arc, *Mémoires*, 173–74. Paul Pontanus, in ibidem, 40 and 61–62 (citing witness Brother Martin Ladvenu, O.P., Jeanne's confessor in Rouen), also asserts that the banner was there to

prevent Jeanne from killing. This was indeed her position at Rouen; see the first verdict, in Tisset, 1.269. Pontanus's reply asserts that she did not kill "and even forbade killing" (Lanéry d'Arc, *Mémoires*, 41).

110. See Beaune, *Jeanne*, 203–4, with, e.g., Duparc 1.366, 1.392, and 395–96. The Orléans and Paris witnesses for the rehabilitation underscore that she allowed the English, once defeated, to evacuate Orléans without being assaulted, e.g., Duparc 1.373.

111. Fraioli, *Joan of Arc*, 72–73, on Jeanne's use of Deuteronomy 20.10–14; see Beaune, *Jeanne*, 207. See Martin Berruier's opinion, ed. Lanéry d'Arc, *Mémoires*, 247, and Thomas Aquinas, *Summa Theologiae* I.II. q. 105, a. 3, reply to obj. 4, *Opera Omnia*, 7.270.

112. Lawrence, HH, 444 (see tr. by Fudge, 95, and in general Fudge, "'More Glory Than Blood'"); also Lawrence, HH., 425. Deuteronomy 13.12–15 provides that a city that God has granted to the Israelites should be burnt wholly and its population be slaughtered if it turned away from God. See Soukup, "Noblesse hussite," 155–56 (with reference to Czech historiography on the issue).

113. Perceval de Cagny, *Chroniques de Perceval de Cagny*, ed. Moranvillé. See Moranvillé's editorial comments on Perceval's trustworthiness, ibid., x–xii.

114. Ibid., 145. Perceval de Cagny's account of the storming of Jargeau suggests (if the sequence of events is proper) the killing of prisoners, ed. Moranvillé, 151. According to Chartier, *Chronique de Charles VII*, ed. De Viriville, 82–83, most of the English prisoners were killed "owing to some disagreements among some of the French" on the road to Orléans (no mention admittedly of Jeanne's agency one way or another); the *Journal du siège d'Orléans*, ed. Quicherat, 4.173, reports about the same: owing to a ransom dispute among the French.

115. Cf. Perceval de Cagny, *Chroniques*, ed. Moranvillé, 164–65 and 169–73; 205–6, 209.

116. For "false peace," see Malegam, *Sleep of Behemoth*, 4–12, and passim.

117. Vale, *Charles VII*, 47; *Procès de condamnation et de réhabilitation*, ed. Quicherat, 5.168–69, a summary of the dispatches sent to the people of Reims. Tisset, 1.192 (above, at n.104).

118. Tisset, 1.105. Cf. tr. Taylor, *Jeanne d'Arc*, 173. And see above, text at n97.

119. Letter to the people of Reims, *Procès de condamnation et de réhabilitation*, ed. Quicherat, 5.139–40; cf. tr. Taylor, *Jeanne d'Arc*, 118–19.

120. Molnár, "L'évolution de la théologie hussite."

121. Wagner, *Petr Chelčický*, 158.

122. See Chapter 2, at n59.

123. See in this sense Bainton, *Christian Attitudes*, 120; and Kaminsky, HHR, 321: pacifism "was a part of the general sectarian rejection of the established order's claim to be a Christian order; Taborite adventist violence preserved this rejection, indeed lifted it to a higher level, at which rejection of the established order implied not merely spiritual withdrawal, but physical withdrawal," and readiness to fight physically.

124. Especially when considering Hussite eschatology; see Kaminsky, "Nicholas of Pelhřimov's Tabor." Fine analysis in Fudge, "'More Glory Than Blood'."

125. See, however, the comments of Kalivoda, *Revolution und Ideologie*, 135f, doubting that one can establish a strict distinction between a pacifist chiliasm prior to February 1420 and a militant one after this date. Convenient master narrative in Lambert, *Medieval Heresy*, 306ff.

126. Kaminsky, HHR, 361–67; Heymann, *John Žižka*, 107–22.

127. Kaminsky, HHR, 320. See as well Fudge, "Crime, Punishment and Pacifism."

128. Appleby, "History in the Fundamentalist Imagination," 505.

129. Jakoubek of Stříbro, *Against Andrew of Brod*, ed. Hardt, 3.512, cited and commented on by Kaminsky, HHR, 123 n84. Also Fudge, "Crime, Punishment and Pacifism," 96–99, translating Mikuláš of Pelhřimov's speech at the Council of Basel.

130. See Malegam, "No Peace for the Wicked."

131. Jakoubek of Stříbro, *De quibusdam punctis*, transcribed in Kaminsky, HHR, 188 n140. See his discussion, 188–91.

132. *Ex libello accusatorio archiepiscopi Zbynconis—articuli ex partibus*, in Jan Sedlák, ed., *Studie a texty* 2.1 (Olomouc: 1915), 27. See the edition by, *Documenta*, ed. Palacký, 405. Marin, *L'archevêque*, 412.

133. In the English-speaking world, this passage was famously discussed by Walzer, *Exodus and Revolution*, 55–60. But see already Bloch, *Atheismus in Christentum* (1968), and *Geist der Utopie* (1918), a lineage pointed out by Momigliano, "Preliminary Indications," tr. in Momigliano, *Essays*, 88–100.

134. *Biblia sacra cum glosa ordinaria [et Nicolai Lyrani Postilla]*, 1.199vb.

135. See Loserth, *Hus und Wiclif*, 208; and Hus, *De ablatione bonorum temporalium*, 118v.

136. Hus, *De ablatione bonorum temporalium*, fol. 123r–v; Loserth, *Hus*, 207.

137. Jakoubek of Stříbro, *De quibusdam punctis*, transcribed in Kaminsky, HHR, 188, n140. See his translation there. Also Marin, *L'archevêque*, 403–15, on popular action.

138. *Apologia Magistri Jacobi de Misa contra Taboritas*, ed. Sedlák, 161. See Jakoubek of Stříbro, *Letter to a Priest or Priests, Refuting Adventist Prophecies*, ed. Kaminsky, HHR, 522; idem, "Noverint universi," ed. Kaminsky, HHR, 527.

139. "De bello," ed. Goll, *Quellen und Untersuchungen*, 2.56–57: A text listing nine conditions for just war but allowing divine inspiration ("either if God authorizes and orders to war, or a sovereign man orders it by his legitimate power") and resistance to evil rulers, evidently in the context of the German crusade against Bohemia. The duty to use the sword in Romans 13 is attributed implicitly to the *miles christi*.

140. Ed. Goll, 2.51–53; better in Kaminsky, HHR, 544–47. Kaminsky's fine discussion, HHR, 323–27, underlines "the masters' effort to limit the principle [of devolution] they had enunciated." See Šmahel, HR, 2.1044–47.

141. Goll, ed., *Quellen und Untersuchungen*, 2.57–59; better Kaminsky, HHR, 521–22.

142. Lawrence, HH, 391, 394–95

143. Lawrence, HH, 415.

144. Tr. Fudge, *Crusade Against Heretics*, 65–66, from Nejedlý, *Debry*, 909–10.

145. See Soukup, "Noblesse hussite," cit. at 156.

146. Letter of February 3,1421, in *Listář a listinář Oldřicha z Rožmberka*, ed. Rynešova and Pelikán, 1.33–43, tr. Fudge, *Crusade Against Heretics*, 102.

147. Letter of the Taborite leadership, Nov. 25, 1420, Stefan Scholz (Prague) has provided me the oldest text, in German (perhaps a translation from a now lost Czech original), *Eberhart Windeckes Denkwürdigkeiten zur Geschichte des Zeitalters Kaiser Sigmund*, ed. Wilhelm Altmann (Berlin: 1993), 148: *wir hassent ouch alle bösen Cristen*. Cf. Fudge, *Crusade Against Heretics*, 99–100.

148. Lawrence, HH, 427–78. See also Fudge, " 'More Glory Than Blood'."

149. "Extrait de la chronique de Michel le Syrien" (d. 1199/1200), in *Recueil des historiens des croisades, documents arméniens*, 1.329. This is the Armenian version; the passage is missing from the surviving Syrian, ed. and tr. Chabot, *Chronique de Michel le Syrien*, 3.184–85. Bresc, "Historiens," 728–29, 747–49, underlines how Syrian and Armenian Christians, at least initially circa 1098–1099, shared in the same eschatology as the Catholic crusaders. See Fudge, "'More Glory than Blood'," 135.

150. Ed. Hiestand, *Papsturkunden*, 92.

151. Cited by Kaminsky, "Nicholas," 151 n45, from MS Wien ÖNB 4520, f. 76r, in Rev. 7.9, s.v. *turbam magnam*.

152. Kaminsky, "Nicholas," 152–54.

153. Skinner, *Foundations*, 2.345–48.

154. See Crouzet, GdD, 1.754, discussing a lost treatise of 1563; ibid., 2.464–74; idem, DesR, 335–39; Skinner, *Foundations*, 221–28, 234–38.

155. Jean Boucher (?), *Lettre missive de l'Evesque du Mans. Avec la réponse à icelle*, 44–46.

156. Boucher (?), *Commentaires et remarques chrestiennes*, 28–29, with Crouzet, GdD, 2.439. *Responce du menu peuple*, Aiir and Aiv (dated June 30, 1589). See also Crouzet, GdD, 754, 781n181. On tyrannicide by a private person, Mousnier, *L'assassinat d'Henri IV*; tr., *Assassination of Henry IV*; and more recently the essays in Von Friedeburg, ed., *Murder and Monarchy*.

157. Rutherford, *Lex, Rex*, preface, §32–33, n.p. These excerpts in Woodhouse, *Puritanism and Liberty*, 199–200.

158. Knox, *Appellation of the Sentence*, in *Works*, ed. Laing, 4.461–520, at 4.504, cited by Skinner, *Foundations*, 2.237.

159. Goodwin, *Hybristodikai*, 40, 41, 43, 45–46, analyzed by Burgess, "English Regicides," 73; see Coffey, *John Goodwin*, 180–84. The continuity with the medieval tradition is visible in the clause, "[those] who have opportunity and means to perform it"; see Buc, *L'ambiguïté*, 380–98.

160. *Johnson's Wonder-Working Providence*, 165.

161. "Two Letters from the Agents of the Five Regiments" (October 28, 1647), ed. in Woodhouse, *Puritanism and Liberty*, 437; cf. the "Representation of the Army," a.k.a. "A Representation from his Excellencie Sr. Thomas Fairfax, And the Army under his command" (June 14, 1647), ed. in ibid., 403–9 at 404.

162. Burgess, "English Regicides," 69.

163. Coffey, *John Goodwin*, 183–84, citing Goodwin, *Hybristodikai*, 129, 78.

164. Engels, *Deutsche Bauernkrieg* §2, in *Karl Marx - Friedrich Engels - Werke*, 7.342–58, at 350; English tr. *The Peasant War in Germany*, 61. See Chapter 1, at n96.

165. Luther, *Wider die räuberischen und mörderischen Rotten*, in *Werke*, 18.360:28–32 (my translation).

166. Ibid., 18.359:30–34.

167. Ibid., 18.361:24–25.

168. By which Luther means, "this hour or soon"; cf. his earlier sense that the situation represented "a prelude to the Last Day, which cannot be distant" (ibid., 18.360:34–35).

169. Ibid., 18.360:8–11.

170. Ibid., 18.361:4–6 and 361:27–28. Luther had to wiggle out from his statement's implications that he had reintroduced salvation by works; see *Ein Sendbrief von dem harten Büchlein wider die Bauern*, in *Werke* 18.384–401.

171. Martin Luther, *Ein Sendbrief von dem harten Büchlein wider die Bauern*, in *Werke* 18.384–401, here 18.389:26–34; tr. from Jacobs and Schultz, in *Luther's Works*, ed. Lehmann, 46.70.

172. See above, Chapter 2 at n40 for a similar twelfth-century position (Hervé de Bourg-Dieu).

173. Figgis, *Studies*, 67; see also 71.

174. Troeltsch, *Social Teachings*, 2.563–76, esp. 2.565, 2.572.

175. Skinner, *Foundations*, 2.201–10.

176. See above, Chapter 1, n75.

177. Robespierre, "Second discours sur le jugement de Louis Capet" (December 28, 1792), in *Œuvres*, 9.198.

178. Van der Heuvel, «Terreur, Terroriste,» 103–4.

179. Danton (February 28, 1793), *Archives Parlementaires*, ed. Mavidal et al., 1.60.61.

180. Wahnich, "Économie émotive," esp. 902–3; developed in her book *La liberté ou la mort*; tr. *In Defense of the Terror*.

181. Nirenberg, "Le dilemme du souverain," 501–4; idem, "Massacre and Miracle?," Nirenberg's analysis inscribes itself in the same Giorgio Agamben-Carl Schmitt theoretical framework concerning sovereignty as does (in part) Wahnich's (n180).

182. *La juste et saincte défense de la ville de Lyon*, 205. On this text and Beza's position, I am guided by Crouzet, GdD, 1.586–88.

183. Letter to Jeanne d'Albret (May 23, 1562), in *Correspondance de Théodore de Bèze*, 4.91; Théodore de Bèze, *Histoire ecclésiastique*, 2.51, 2.59.

184. "Die Aktion des 'Schwarzen Septembers' in München," RAF, 151.

185. See Fetscher, Münkler, and Ludwig, "Ideologien der Terroristen," 67–69, 104–12.

186. "Über den bewaffneten Kampf in Westeuropa," in RAF, 86, 87–88.

187. Rohrmoser and Frölich, "Ideologische Ursachen," 296–303.

188. Matz, "Über gesellschaftliche und politische Bedingungen," 89. Above, Chapter 3, at nn191–94.

189. Speech at Good Shepherd Church, Sandy, Oregon, June 21, 2003, audiotape; ibid., Videotape; Boykin, speech at First Baptist Church, Broken Arrow, Oklahoma, June 30, 2002, transcription of audio recording by Arkin. Cp. Boykin, *Never Surrender*, 11. This is corroborated by the footage excerpted by NBC, NBC News clip 5115223939_s06, "War of Words: NBC News Investigates," dated October 15, 2003 (videotape filmed at Boring, Oregon, according to NBC also on June 21, 2003 [this date or place may be in error]).

190. Arkin transcripts from audiotape and videotape; speech at Good Shepherd Church, videotape.

191. Speech at Good Shepherd Church, audiotape.

192. Boykin, speech at First Baptist Church, audiotape. Cf. Boykin, *Never Surrender*, 139.

193. See Chapter 1, at nn77–78. See as well Lincoln, *Holy Terrors*, 33–50.

CHAPTER 6. LIBERTY AND COERCION

I expand here, vastly, on Buc, "Religion, Coercion, and Violence."

Epigraphs: Gregory VII to Altmann of Passau and William of Hirsau (1081), *Registrum* 9.3, ed. Caspar, 2.575, with Szabó-Bechstein, *"Libertas ecclesiae,"* 175, on which I draw a great deal; Désiré, *Plaisans et armonieux cantiques*, Aiir–v = 10r–v; Louis Antoine Léon de Saint-Just, "Sur les personnes incarcérées," Rapport à la Convention au nom des Comités de Salut Public et de Sûreté Générale (February 26, 1794), ed. Soboul, *Discours*, 142.

1. Robespierre, "Rapport sur les principes de morale politique," 10.357; Montesquieu, *Esprit des Lois* 6.8, in *Œuvres complètes*, 3.318.

2. "The Union, the Constitution, and Slavery," 543.

3. Gregory of Tours, *Ten Books of Histories*, Preface to Book V, ed. Krusch and Levison, 193–94. See above, Chapter 2, at n109.

4. See, e.g., the discussion by Skinner, "Paradoxes of Political Liberty."

5. Irenaeus, *Adversus haereses* 4.13.2, ed. Rousseau et al., SC 100, 528, with Field, *Liberty*, 7; Irenaeus, *Adversus haereses* 4.13.3, 532.

6. Tellenbach, *Libertas*.

7. Théodore de Bèze (1570), to Dudith, in *Correspondance*, 11.179. I use here the English rendition by Thomas Edwards, *Antapologia* (1644), partial ed. in Yule, *Puritans and Politics*, 320–41, here 326.

8. Cited by Gentiles, *Oliver Cromwell*, 116.

9. Dwight, *Discourse on Some Events*, 33, cited by Hatch, *Sacred Cause*, 169.

10. Tertullian, *Scorpiace* 5.4, CCSL 2, 1077.

11. Bohrmann, *Flavius Josèphe*, 136–37.

12. I depend for this paragraph on Szabó-Bechstein, *"Libertas ecclesiae,"* 7–17.

13. *American Quarterly Church Review* (April 1863): 106. For the Episcopalian position, see also "*The American Quarterly Review* and Our National Crisis," *ibidem* (April 1861): 153–63, esp. 154–55; "The Union, the Constitution, and Slavery," *ibidem* (January 1864): 541–75, esp. 544–45, 549, 555, 574.

14. Malegam, *Sleep of Behemoth*.

15. *Letters of John of Salisbury*, 2.726, and Becket's hagiography by Edward Grim, in *Materials*, 2.440; and by William FitzStephen, in *Materials*, 3.140. See Warren, *Henry II*, 478ff.

16. Tertullian, *De pudicitia* 14.4 and 14.9, CCSL 2, 1307.

17. See Szabó-Bechstein, *Libertas ecclesie*, passim.

18. This is not to deny the contribution of the English liberties tradition and of the Enlightenment to American liberty, for which see Bailyn, *Ideological Origins*, 55–85. See R. Bloch, *Visionary Republic*, 44–46, 61–62.

19. R. Bloch, *Visionary Republic*, 63–66.

20. *Curse of Meroz*, 24, 27, cited by Berens, *Providence*, 38; see in general 36–40.

21. *Itinerarium Perigrinorum* 1.61, ed. Mayer, 349.

22. See also Riley-Smith, *Crusades*, 4–7.

23. *Actes des comtes de Flandre*, ed. Vercauteren, n20, 62–63.

24. Ibid., n26, 77–82, at 81. See above, Chapter 2, at n75.

25. Lawrence, HH, 330, 348, 424.

26. *Urkundliche Beiträge*, ed. Palacký, n. 110, 1.112.

27. See in general for this issue of coercion Schreiner, "'Duldsamkeit'."

28. Useful recent panorama by H-J. Becker, "Die Stellung des kanonistischen Rechts."

29. Lactantius, *Divine institutes* (initial version, ca. 304–11) 5.19.11–13, SC 204, 232, with Field, *Liberty*, 78.

30. Firmicus Maternus, *De errore profanarum religionum* cap. 16.4, ed. Turcan, 112–13; see also caps. 6.9 and 28–29 (Bible), 12 and 150–54. It is unclear whether Firmicus calls merely for the banning of idolatrous sacrifices or for a blanket end to paganism.

31. See Drake, "Lambs into Lions"; *Henrici de Segusio Cardinalis Hostiensis Summa Aurea* 3.19, cols. 1141–42.

32. Tertullian, *Scorpiace* 2.1, CCSL 2, 1071. See Fields, *Liberty*, 14 (trans. his).

33. Augustine, Ep. 93.1.2, to Vincentius, CSEL 34:2, 447, or CCSL 31B, 168. See Chapter 3, at nn61–70.

34. Augustine, Sermo 279, PL 38, 1277, cited Chapter 2, at n68. Les représentants à Lyon [= Foucher, Albitte, Sébastien de Laporte, Collot d'Herbois], à la Convention Nationale (Dec. 12, 1793), RACdSP, 9.363: "La terreur, la salutaire terreur, est vraiment ici à l'ordre du jour."

35. Hugh of Saint-Cher, *Postilla*, in Deut. 20, 1.164ra.

36. The complexity of the legal tradition and practice is well presented in Jensen, "Gods War."

37. *Summa Theologiae* II.II. q. 29, a. 1, reply to obj. 1, *Opera Omnia*, 8.236.

38. Canons 10 and 11; see Given, *Inquisition*, 80; from Mansi, *Sacrorum conciliorum collectio*, 23.196.

39. See the discussion in Buc, "Religion, Coercion, and Violence," 162, along with the issue of coercion to undergo ordeals, 160–62; and also Althoff, "Der Privileg der *deditio*."

40. *Decretales Gregorii IX*, X.3.42.3, ed. Friedberg, *Corpus Iuris Canonici*, 2.646.

41. See Asad, "Medieval Heresy," 356: for Scholasticism, "belief or unbelief is an act of will, not a helpless mental condition." See also Fried, "Wille, Freiwilligkeit und Geständnis," a reference for which I am immensely grateful to Edward Peters.

42. Suárez, "Opus de virtute et statu religionis," 1.3.1.7, ed. André, 13.37. This interpretation seems early modern; it is absent in the *Gloss*, the Dominican *Postilla*, and Nicolas of Lyra.

43. Ibid., 2.1.1.1, 13.77–78; 2.2.1.7, 13.85. Suárez tweaks Aquinas, *Summa Theologiae* II.II. q. 84, a. 1–2 and II.II. q. 103, a. 1, *Opera Omnia*, 9.212–13 and 9.377. One can show honor to humans (as opposed to God) only by signs, so by words or deeds, which are external. See the discussions of this problem and of its outcomes in Stollberg-Rilinger, "Knien vor Gott—Knien vor dem Kaiser," in English as "Kneeling Before God—Kneeling Before the Emperor"; and Buc, *Dangers*, 161–72.

44. Spinoza, *Tractatus Theologico-Politicus* 18, ed. Elwes, 245; Hobbes, *Leviathan* 3.42, ed. Malcolm, 3.774–76.

45. Bernard Gui, *Practica Inquisitionis*, 217–18, tr. and commented by Given, *Inquisition*, 72.

46. Given, "Inquisitors of Languedoc"; idem, *Inquisition*, 74–75.

47. Ames, *Righteous Persecution*.

48. Hugh of Saint-Cher, *Postilla* in Isa. 66.15, 4.172rb. See also below, Chapter 7, at nn75–129, on the sublime.

49. Guibert, *Dei Gesta* 7.21, ed. Huygens, 304:991–1005.

50. Aquinas, *Summa Theologiae* I.II. q. 96, a. 5, *Opera Omnia*, 7.184; *Summa Theologiae* I.II. q. 95, a. 1, ibidem, 7.174; see Fried, "Wille, Freiwilligkeit und Geständnis," 395–96, 418–23.

51. See Introduction, n107. For the canon law developments, see Schreiner, " 'Duldsamkeit'," 177–80, with many leads to earlier historiography, and Cushing, *Papacy and Law*.

52. Cf. Brown, "Saint Augustine's Attitude," 109–10, noticing that Augustine argued from measures taken against pagans.

53. Augustine, Ep. 93.5.18, CSEL 34:2, 462, or CCSL 31A, 180.

54. Augustine, Ep. 93.1.3, CSEL 34:2, 448, or CCSL 31A, 169.

55. *Registrum* 1.27, 1.28 (October 13, 1073), ed. Caspar, 1.44–45, 45–46.

56. Andreas of Strumi, *Vita sancti Iohannis Gualberti* 75, ed. Baethgen, MGH SS 30:2, 1096.

57. Winand von Steeg, *De laude concilii Constanciensis*, in *Acta Concilii Constanciensis*, ed. Finke, 4.754 (Finke edited all there was to edit by Winand in the Vienna manuscript ÖNB 4971, fol. 51, a miscellanea on the reform councils; it is probably an excerpt from a longer work). I draw here on a seminar paper by my student Anja Brien (Wien).

58. See Crouzet, GdD 1.585, 1.599; idem, DesR, 205–6, 217.

59. Augustine, *Ennaratio* in Ps. 127.7–8, CCSL 40, 1872. For Calvin's version of this dialectic, see Crouzet, DesR, 148–54.

60. Valuable pages in Crouzet, DesR, 143–54, 310–13, 317–34, on which this paragraph draws.

61. *Responce du menu peuple*, Aiv(r); Jean Boucher (?), *Lettre missive de l'Evesque du Mans. Avec la réponse à icelle*, 34.

62. Boucher (?), *Lettre missive*, 30, 40. The author adds that one cannot quite preempt the Church's verdict and already say Jacques Clément is a martyr, but "the God of vengeances ordained this according to His pleasure" (56).

63. Eudes de Châteauroux, Sermo 1, ed. and tr. Maier, *Crusade Propaganda*, 131; and see 59.

64. Augustine, Ep. 140 ad Honoratum = *Liber de gratia novi testamenti*, ed. Goldbacher, CSEL 44, 155–234.

65. Augustine, Ep. 185.7.22, CSEL 57, 20–21. Augustine was adopted here by Gratian, *Decretum*, C.23, q.6 c.1, ed. Friedberg, 1.947, and during the Gregorian revolution by Ivo of Chartres, *Decretum* 10.59, PL 161, 707c.

66. The term *timor amicalis* (opposed to *timor servilis*) is already in Hrabanus, on Prov. 1.7, PL 111, col. 681b–c.

67. Peter Lombard, *Libri sententiarum* 3.34.4 §1, ed. Brady, 5.193.

68. Gratian, *Decretum*, C.23 q.6, d. ante c.1, ed. Friedberg, 1.949.

69. Augustine, Ep. 140 = *Liber de gratia*, c. 21.52 and c. 19.47–49, CSEL 44, 199 and 195–96. Gregory VII also employed this correspondence between Old Law—New Law, *timor—amor, servitus—libertas*; see Szabó-Bechstein, *"Libertas ecclesie,"* 151–55 and passim.

70. Peter Lombard, *Magna Glossatura* on Phil. 1.1 (*servi Jesu Christi*), PL 192, 223c.

71. Augustine, Ep. 185.2.10, CSEL 57, 9:22–23. See also Ep. 93.1.6, CSEL 34:2, 450, or CCSL 31A, 170–71.

72. MS Prague University Library V G 3, fol. 39r, cited and tr. by Kaminsky, "The Prague

Insurrection," 122, 125n75. In a slightly earlier sermon, Želivský had attacked those who like "kings and princes" did not "promote the common good"—adding in the margin *"iudices* [et] *iurati"* (122). See Šmahel, HR, 2.1000–1006.

73. Christiansen, *Northern Crusades,* 223–32. See Boockmann, *Johannes Falkenberg,* 234–37 for the pro-Teutonic polemicists.

74. Andreas Didaci de Escobar, "Revoco, casso, annulo," in Weise, *Traktate,* 408. Discussion in Kwiatkowski, *Deutsche Orden im Streit,* 16, and Miethke, "Heilige Heidenkrieg?" See Gratian, *Decretum* C.23 q.6 dictum post c.4, ed. Friedberg, 1.949–50, citing Augustine, *Ennaratio* in Ps. 127.7–8, CCSL 40, 1872–73: "As, owing to fear, they abstain from sin, there arises [in them] the custom to be just, and they begin to love what had been hard [to love]."

75. Falkenberg, *Veteres relegentes historias* (1416–17), Weise, *Traktate,* 172–228, here 191.

76. Augustine, through Gratian, *Decretum* C.23 q.5 c.33, ed. Friedberg, *Corpus Iuris Canonici,* 1.939–40.

77. "Revoco, casso, annulo," ed. Weise, *Traktate,* 408–9.

78. Ibid., 410. For the criterion *cadere in constantem,* see Fried, "Wille, Freiwilligkeit und Geständnis," 393–94.

79. Fried, "Wille, Freiwilligkeit und Geständnis," 423.

80. See Beinart, *Expulsion;* M. Kriegel, "Prise d'une décision."

81. Pierre d'Ailly, *Materia dominorum Prutenorum cum dominis Polonis* (1st half of 1417), Weise, *Traktate,* 269–70.

82. Falkenberg, *Veteres relegentes historias* (1416–1417), Weise, *Traktate,* 190.

83. Johannes Urbach, *Utrum fideles,* Weise, *Traktate,* 298–300.

84. Weinberg, *Manifest Destiny,* 109–13 and passim.

85. Ibid., 110.

86. James Buchanan, as reported in the *Congressional Globe,* 28th Cong., 1st sess. (March 12 1844), 372c, with Weinberg, *Manifest Destiny,* 128–29, and Binder, "James Buchanan," 80.

87. Brachlow, *Communion of Saints,* 265–66; Robinson, *Justification of Separation from the Church of England,* 298, cited in Brachlow, *Communion of Saints,* 265.

88. Brachlow, *Communion of Saints,* 230ff., 253; citation from Henry Barrow, *Reply to Dr. Some's A Godly Treatise,* in *Writings of Henry Barrow,* 158.

89. Barrow, *Reply,* 161.

90. Ibid., 160–61, with Brachlow, *Communion of Saints,* 253.

91. D. Little, *Religion, Order, and Law,* 125–26, citing Perkins, *Works,* vol. 2 (London: 1617), 412.

92. Augustine, Ep. 93.1.3, CSEL 34:2, 448, or CCSL 31A, 168–69.

93. See Chazan, *Daggers of Faith,* 38–48.

94. Little, *Religion, Order, and Law,* 95, 104.

95. Merleau-Ponty, *Humanisme et terreur,* 160–61; tr. *Humanism and Terror,* 149–50.

96. Bähr, "Furcht vor dem Leviathan."

97. "Über den bewaffneten Kampf in Westeuropa," in RAF, 100, with Balz, *Von Terroristen,* 61.

98. "Enlightened by violence, the people's consciousness rejects every pacification," Fanon, *Les damnés de la terre,* 91.

99. Rousseau, *Contrat Social* 1.7.8, tr. Gourevitch, *Social Contract,* 53. My thanks to Dan

Edelstein for the reference. Van der Heuvel, *Freiheitsbegriff*; G. Kelly, "Conceptual Sources of the Terror," 24–25, on the "important and effective continuity between the *terreurs salutaires* of the afterlife and the civic fright stirred up by the Jacobins." In this sense, see Hehl, "Terror als Herrschaftsmittel."

100. Carrier, "Au Comité de salut public" (November 12, 1793), in RACdSP, 8.381.

101. "Comité de salut public aux représentants à l'armée du Nord" (November 16, 1793), RACdSP, 8.458–59; Comité de salut public, signed Barère, Carnot, Billot-Varenne, to Le Bon (also November 16, 1793), in RACdSP, 8.458.

102. Robespierre, "Rapport sur les principes de morale politique," *Œuvres* 10.356.

103. Guibert, above, n49. Prudentius, *Peristephanon*, Hymn II (Lawrence), vv. 393–96, ed. Lavarenne, 4.48.

104. Crouzet, GdD 2.505, citing the *Pompe funèbre, faicte a Lyon au devot college des pénitens, aux obseques du Cardinal de Guise & de son frere* (Lyon: 1589), n.p.

105. Augustine, Ep. 89.7, CSEL 34, 424:23–25, or CCSL 31B, 152:146–48.

106. Cited by De Baecque, *Corps de l'Histoire*, 171–72. See as well Sepinwall, *Abbé Grégoire*, 71; Necheles, *Abbé Grégoire*, 14–16.

107. Doyle, *Oxford History of the French Revolution*.

108. Cobb, *Armées révolutionnaires*, 2.635–94.

109. For the dechristianization, see still Vovelle, *Religion et Révolution*, 183ff., n 243; idem, *1793. La Révolution contre l'Église*.

110. Malnou, "L'abbé J.-B. Lanot."

111. "Le représentant chargé de la levée en masse dans la Corrèze et la Haute-Vienne au Comité de Salut Public" (Brive, February 22, 1794), RAdCSP, 11.338–41.

112. Jeanbon Saint-André, "Le représentant à Brest et à Cherbourg au président de la Convention Nationale," speech to the locals submitted to the Convention for approval, RACdSP, 9.358n1 (Dec. 11–12, 1793).

113. Augustine, Ep. 93.1.3, CSEL 34:2, 448, or CCSL 31B, 168–69.

114. See the documentation in Flint, *Rise of Magic*.

115. Gregory I, instructions to Augustine of Canterbury, transmitted through Abbot Mellito, preserved in Bede, *Historia ecclesiastica gentis Anglorum* 1.30.2–3, SC 489, 246.

116. Gregory I, *Registrum epistularum* 5.7, CCSL 140–140A, 1.273. While Gregory I's words were not picked up—as far as I can see—by canon law, the same idea was propagated by Alcuin and others; see Lupoi, *Origins*, 270–71.

117. Augustine, Ep. 93.1.3; CSEL 34:2, 448, or CCSL 31B, 169.

118. Walzer, *Exodus and Revolution*.

119. See Crouzet, GdD, 2.436–37.

120. Quinet, *La Révolution* 13.1, "Le terrorisme français et le terrorisme hébraïque," 465–66.

121. Karl Marx, *Class Struggles in France*, in *Selected Works*, 1.193, cit. by Lukács, *History and Class Consciousness*, 315.

122. See Wood, *Empire of Liberty*, 582, 587–93.

123. See, e.g., Gentile, *Culto del Littorio*, tr. *The Sacralization of Politics*; idem, *Religioni della politica*, tr. *Politics as Religion*.

124. *Fi Sabil al-Ba'th* (Beiruth: 1959), 103, here trans. Makiya, *Republic of Fear*, 206. See also Makiya, 190–91.

125. Sayyid Qutb, *Milestones*, trans. International Islamic Federation of Student Organizations (Stuttgart: 1978), III, cited by Appleby, "History in the Fundamentalist Imagination," 508.

126. NSC 68, part four, section C. See above, Chapter 1, at n119.

127. Sepúlveda, *Democrates Alter*, ed. Losada, 62–63. Recent discussion in Michael Severnich, "Interkulturelle Kommunikation," 126–32; see as well Fernández-Armesto, *Before Columbus*, 231–36; Muldoon, *Popes, Lawyers and Infidels*; and P. Russell, "El descubrimiento de Canarias."

CHAPTER 7. THE SUBJECT OF HISTORY AND THE MAKING OF HISTORY

Epigraphs: *Chanson de Roland*, laisse 248, vv. 3366–68, ed. and Fr. tr. Bédier, *La chanson de Roland*, 254–55, cf. the tr. by Glyn Burgess, *The Song of Roland* (London: 1990), 136; Langhans and Teufel, eds., *Klau mich*, Bl. 4, Beweismittel-Ordner 4; Baumann, "Tupamaros Westberlin," in *Wie alles anfing*, 65, unreliable tr. *Terror or Love?*, 58.

1. De Baecque, *Corps de l'histoire*, 374. See, however, his position in *Gloire et l'effroi*, tr. *Glory and Terror*. Rich on revolutionary martyrdom are Dowd, *Pageant-Master*, and Pappenheim, *Erinnerung und Unsterblichkeit*.

2. Jourdan, "Robespierre and Revolutionary Heroism."

3. Knott, *Discourses of Martyrdom*, 156–58.

4. Koselleck, "Einleitung," 14, 11. See as well Mosse, *Fallen Soldiers*.

5. Camus, *L'homme révolté*, 207 and passim.

6. Voegelin, *Politischen Religionen*, 49; *Political Religions*, 57.

7. See above, Introduction, at n137. *Procès en nullité de la condamnation*, ed, Duparc, 1.397, with Beaune, *Jeanne*, 267–68, building on her own *Naissance de la Nation France*, 324–35; tr. *Birth of an Ideology*, 298–309.

8. See, inter alia, Haller, *Foxe's Book of Martyrs*; and Knott, *Discourses of Martyrdom*.

9. Kippenberg, *Discovering Religious History*, 2–3, building on Koselleck, *Kritik und Krise*, tr. *Critique and Crisis*. Hobbes, *Leviathan* 2.26, ed. Malcolm, 2.431. The connection to religion is found ibidem, 2.444–49.

10. Schmitt, *Political Theology*, esp. ch. 4.

11. See Rohrmoser and Fröhlich, "Ideologische Ursachen," 311–13.

12. See Crouzet, DesR.

13. On this, see Buc, *Dangers*, 239ff, and the older literature there cited. See recently Gaddis, *There Is No Crime*.

14. Toscano, *Fanaticism*, 28–29. See Badiou, *Le siècle*, 82.

15. "Die Aktion des 'Schwarzen Septembers' in München," in RAF, 151, 158. See Chapter 3 at nn197–99.

16. See on this point Caspary, *Politics and Exegesis*, 134–38.

17. D. Roberts, "'Political Religion'," 402–44, points out that a weakness of "political religion" as a concept bridging Christianity and twentieth-century totalitarianisms is that it assumes certainty in

the actors and a millennial endpoint to History, whereas Nazism and Bolshevism imagined an ongoing and fairly open-ended struggle.

18. See Landes, *Heaven on Earth*, 33–34.

19. To cite the whole movement in *The Holy Family* §6.2, *Marx-Engels Collected Works*, 4.92: "History does nothing, it 'possesses no immense wealth,' it 'wages no battles.' It is man, real, living man who does all that, who possesses and fights; 'history' is not, as it were, a person apart, using man as a means to achieve its own aims; history is nothing but the activity of man pursuing his aims." Idem, *Economic and Philosophic Manuscripts of 1844*, in *Collected Works*, 3.305: "The entire so-called history of the world is nothing but the creation of man through human labour."

20. Townshend, *Terrorism*, 37, 99–101, 99–100. The italics, which are mine, point to the hesitation.

21. See Gregory, *Salvation at Stake*.

22. *Passion of Montanus and Lucius*, §14, ed. Musurillo, 226–29, with Buc, *Dangers*, 135.

23. Eisenstadt, *Fundamentalism*, 116.

24. Van der Heuvel, "Terreur," 98.

25. Delaruelle, "Paix de Dieu et croisade," 69–70, with the *Chanson de la croisade albigeoise*, laisse 60, ed. Martin-Chabot, 1.148–51.

26. See Chapter 2 at n150.

27. See Riley-Smith, *The Crusades*, xxviii.

28. See below at note 104.

29. Tr. Kaminsky, HHR, 369, from *Archiv český* 3 (1844): 210–12, at 212; Latin rendition in Palacký, *Urkundliche Beiträge*, 1.35. See Kaminsky's discussion of the differences between the conservative version (here cited) and the radical version, HHR, 373–74 n. 32, with Šmahel, HR, 2.1074–75; recent discussion by Hruza, "'Audite'"; idem, "Hussitischen Manifesten," 135.

30. Tr. Kaminsky, HHR, 376, from Lawrence, HH, 397–99; Šmahel, HR, 2.1103–4. See, however, Kaminsky, HHR, 390.

31. *Archiv český* 3 (1844): 226–30, tr. Fudge, *Crusade Against Heretics*, 119–21

32. Many exemples in Offenstadt, *Faire la paix*, 63–68 and passim.

33. *Chanson de la Ligue* [n.p., 1593], in De l'Estoile, *Belles figures*, 4.266–69.

34. *Harangue sur les causes de la guerre*, 3–5.

35. *Tumbeau sur le trespas et assassinat*, in De l'Estoile, *Les belles figures*, 4.49–50 = fig. xxi. See above, Introduction, at nn153–54.

36. *Discours veritable de l'estrange et subite mort de Henry de Valois*, Biv–v*.

37. *Harangue sur les causes de la guerre*, 4–5, 6–7, detailing the worthy cause: "la conservation de l'honneur de Dieu, la maintenance de la foy de l'Eglise ancienne en son integrité, et l'extirpation des damnees heresies qui regnent pour le jourd'huy: la defense, protection, et entretenement de ce noble Royaume de France . . . et finalement le repos general et public de tous les bons et loyaux subjets et serviteurs de Dieu et du Roy."

38. *Juste et saincte défense de la ville de Lyon*, 201, 210. On this text, see Crouzet, GdD, 1.586–87.

39. Stayer, *Anabaptists and the Sword*, 126–27.

40. Origen, *Contra Celsum* 7.26, SC 150, 72–75, as explained by Caspary, *Politics and Exegesis*, 129–31.

41. Calvin, *Institutes* 4.20.15–17. See, e.g., the Puritan minister to Harvard College, Thomas Shepard, *Theses Sabbaticae* §1.38–42, 31–35.

42. Case, "Answer for the Messengers of the Nation," *Poems* (1778), 21, reprint in *Revolutionary Memorials*, 42, cited and analyzed in R. Bloch, *Visionary Republic*, 87.

43. See C. Gribben, *Writing the Rapture*, 157, 141, discussing Tim LaHaye and Jerry Jenkins, *Assassins* (Wheaton: 1999), 334 here cited.

44. But see the critique by Halfin, *From Darkness to Light*, 43ff., 53ff., 68, 78–79, 82.

45. Starting with Crouzet, GdD.

46. Joachim Opser S.J., sous-prieur du Collège de Clermont, lettre du 26 août 1572 à l'abbé de Saint-Gall, ed. Martin, "Deux lettres," 292. See Erlanger, *Massacre de la Saint-Barthélémy*, 262.

47. Sorbin, *Histoire*, 305; modernized French in Erlanger, *Le massacre*, 251. Pious dissimulation: Denis Crouzet, NStB, 605 n9.

48. "Sur l'association et prise d'arme," ed. Lacour, "*Cantiques*," 514; cf. Denis Crouzet, NStB, 172, and El Kenz, *Bûchers du roi*, 193.

49. See Heimert, *Religion*, 424–25.

50. Cook, *Monarchy*, 114–15.

51. *A Glimpse of Sions Glory*, 21 (cf. the edition in Woodhouse, *Puritanism and Liberty*, 237): the saints of Rev. 19 "triumphing with him" in white are "the army of Christ, that rather comes to triumph then [*sic*] for to fight. Christ fighteth and vanquisheth all these Enemies: and they come triumphing in white. All Teares shall be wiped away from the Church."

52. Lieutenant-Colonel William Goffe, Putney debates (October 29, 1647), *Clarke Papers*, ed. Firth, 1.282–83.

53. "*A vindication against the complaints of mr.* Rogers, *address'd to* Edward Dandy, *esq*", in *A collection of the state papers of John Thurloe, esq.*, 3.136–37, here 3.136 (dated from Lambeth, February 3, 1654). English modernized.

54. Cited and discussed in McLear, "New England and the Fifth Monarchy," 234.

55. *Sermon to the Princes* (1524), a.k.a. "Auslegung des Unterschieds Daniel," tr. Baylor, *Revelation and Revolution*, 112–13 and 111; *Thomas Müntzer*, ed. Frantz, 261:6–14, 259:4–6.

56. Rothmann, *Bericht von der Wrake* (1534), ed. Stupperich, 292.

57. Walzer, *Exodus and Revolution*, 10–11 and passim.

58. Beaune, *Jeanne*, passim.

59. Guillaume Aimeri, O.P., according to the deposition of Brother Seguin, O.P., in *Procès en nullité de la condamnation*, ed. Duparc, 1.472, tr. and discussed by Fraioli, *Joan of Arc*, 99. See also Cousinot de Montreuil, *Chronique de la Pucelle*, ed. De Viriville, 276.

60. Fraioli, *Joan of Arc*, 99–100, discussing Jacques Gelu, *De puella aurelianensi Dissertatio*, ed. Lanéry d'Arc, *Mémoires*, here 593.

61. See Buc, "Pouvoir royal," 707–8, and idem, "Book of Kings."

62. See here Rubenstein, *Armies*, 319.

63. Baldric, *Historia Jerosolimitana* 4.13, 101 (see above, Chapter 2, at nn175–77). Cf. Riley-Smith, "First Crusade and the Persecution of the Jews," 68.

64. Raymond, *Liber*, 157, reading with three manuscripts *adiutores*, plural, instead of *adiutorem*. Cf. tr. Hill and Hill, 134.

65. McGinn, *Visions of the End*. Gabriele, "Against the Enemies of Christ," 64, relates this observation to the Rhineland pogroms of 1096.

66. Ed. France, "Text," 653; with idem, "Unknown Account."

67. Bernard, *Liber de gratia et libero arbitrio* 13.45, ed. Winkler, 1.198:18–29.

68. James of Vitry, Sermo 2:26, ed. and tr. Maier, *Crusade Propaganda*, 116–17 (translation slightly modified). See also Gilbert of Tournai, ed. and tr. ibid., 186–87: "The Lord could have liberated Jerusalem, but He wanted to test His friends."

69. Peter of Blois, *Passio Raginaldi principis Antiochiae*, ed. Huygens, CCCM 194, 31–73, here 56. The translation of *actualiter* is warranted by contemporary usage; see John of Salisbury, *De septem septenis*, PL 199, 957b, where *actualiter* is identical to *in actu* and comprises *in operibus* (in deeds), as opposed to *in affectu* and *in intellectu*. See Markowski, "Peter of Blois"; Southern, "Peter of Blois."

70. *Turpini Historia*, cap. 17, ed. Castets, 27–34. Kedar, *Crusade and Mission*.

71. A cursory word search suggests that the expression was used for preaching (the edification of the celestial Jerusalem, in the initial Pauline meaning) and, by derivation, for the extension of God's city by the sword.

72. Henry de Marcy, *De perigrinante civitate Dei*, tractatus xiii, PL 204, 355b.

73. Ibid., xiii, PL 204, 359b–c. Karl Marx, "Speech at the Anniversary of the People's Paper, 14 April 1856," in *Marx-Engels Selected Works*, 1.500; see Exod. 12.7, 12.13.

74. See above, Chapter 5, at nn182–83.

75. France, "Text," 657. See Hartl, "Feindbild," 32–37.

76. Rubenstein, "Cannibals," with relevant historiography; idem, *Armies*, 240–42. I am also drawing here on the term paper written by my student Salman al-Rashid, "Cannibalism During the Crusades," itself building on my class lectures (spring 2008).

77. *Ademari Cabannensis Chronicon*, ed. Bourgain, Landes and Pons, CCCM 129:1, 174, with Rubenstein, "Cannibals," 541.

78. Fulcher, *Historia Hierosolymitana* 1.25, ed. Hagenmeyer, 267.

79. Raymond, *Liber*, 101 (my translation).

80. *Inbelles et pavidi recedentes a nobis*, identified to *apostasia*, Raymond, *Liber*, 35. See Rubenstein, "Cannibals," 535, 550 (with whom I disagree; Raymond was not trying to counter the stories about cannibalism propagated by deserters; rather, he was indicating that crusaders had deserted out of an inability to assume this deed); cp. the Hill and Hill tr., 15. The vision of the five wounds is in the *Liber*, 113–15, analyzed in Buc, "Martyrdom," 45–47, and above, Chapter 4, at nn103–6.

81. Guibert, *Gesta dei*, 7.23, ed. Huygens, 311, seems to draw on Raymond (see his *atrox fama* and *ad eorum terrorem*), and approvingly. See Rubenstein, "Cannibals," 540. I am not certain that Guibert's version constitutes a "tour de force in misdirection."

82. Raymond, *Liber*, 95–96, tr. Hill and Hill, 77.

83. Ibid., 100–101, tr. 81–82, with Flori, *Pierre l'Ermite*, 395; Rubenstein, *Armies*, 244–45; idem, "Godfrey of Bouillon," 67, speaking of a "divinely sanctioned mutiny." Cf. Riley-Smith, *First Crusade*, 89, for whom the count was merely "furious but, deprived of a base, had no option but to recommence the march to Jerusalem."

84. Schreckenberg, *Flavius-Josephus Tradition*, 190; Buc, "Vengeance," 460–62. In that article,

oddly, I failed to develop as announced at its n30 "les résonances de cette lecture lors de la croisade." I do so now, but see already Rubenstein, "Cannibals," 543–49.

85. *Jewish Wars*, 6.4.201–13, ed. Thackeray, 434–37.

86. Raymond, *Liber*, 78; Buc, "Vengeance," 463–64n36; Rubenstein, "Cannibals," 538, 544; idem, *Armies*, 241.

87. Prudentius, *Peristephanon*, Hymn II (Lawrence), vv. 372–392, ed. Lavarenne, 4.43; see above, Chapter 3, at n79.

88. See the discussion in Kedar, "Jerusalem Massacre."

89. Housley, *Contesting the Crusades*, 46.

90. France, *Victory in the East*, 356.

91. Elm, "Eroberung Jerusalems," 31–54, 46, 50, 51 (citation).

92. Kedar, "Jerusalem Massacre," 72. The paragraphs that follow owe a lot to Kedar's fine reconstruction of historiography's reception of the massacre from 1100 to the present.

93. Joachim Opser, "Deux lettres," ed. Martin, here 293, 291.

94. So the critique by Kedar, "Jerusalem Massacre," 67–72.

95. "Lapidibus obruentes," Albert of Aachen, *Historia Hierosolomitana* 6.23, 6.30, ed. Edgington, 432, 442.

96. The objections of David Hay have no place here; see Hay, "Gender Bias and Religious Intolerance," at 8–9 on Albert.

97. *Chanson d'Antioche* 262, vv. 6413–14, ed. Duparc-Quioc, 317–18; ed. Bernard Guidot, 706, based on the same manuscript. See also the recent edition based on a different manuscript by Nelson. tr. by Edgington and Sweetenham, 253–54. See also Christ's direct words of disapproval, 288, vv. 7142–45, ed. Guidot, 764; ed. Duparc-Quioc, 355; tr., 270.

98. Fulcher of Chartres, *Historia Hierosolymitana* 1.27.5, ed. Hagenmeyer, 257. See also Albert of Aachen, *Historia* 4.56, ed. Edgington, *Historia Ierosolimitana*, 336; Lobrichon, *1099*, 108–9; Caspary, *Politics and Exegesis*, 35–36.

99. See the evolving translation of *ashkenas* in Goitein, "Contemporary Letters," 172; idem, *A Mediterranean Society*, 5.612n84; and (spelling out the meaning of the word), idem, "Geniza Sources," at 312: "Ashkenaz was a general term for non-Mediterranean western Europeans, later confined to Germans and Germany." Heartfelt thanks on this to Mark Cohen. Also Kedar, "Jerusalem Massacre," 64; and now Jankrift, "Mein Freund, der Feind," 317–18. See Friedman, *Enounter*, 171.

100. Julian of Toledo, *Historia Wambae regis* §10, ed. Levison, 510. Wamba allegedly punished with castration soldiers who raped. See also Roberts, "Peace, Ritual and Sexual Violence."

101. Goiten, "Contemporary Letters," 171; Raymond, *Liber*, 150, tr. Hill and Hill, 127. See the manuscript G (Paris BNF Latin 5513) of Baldric, *Historia Jerosolimitana*, 103: "Many Jews were captured alive around the Temple, and transported, in the same way, the corpses. They were recognized [as Jews], and sold, and at Tancred's command they gave thirty [Jews] for one small gold coin (*nummus*), and mocked them (*deluxerunt*) them to the greatest extent. They took many of those that had been bought to Apulia, and some they drowned in the sea; others they beheaded." The imitation of the vengeance of the Savior's Titus and Vespasian is clear. On this manuscript, see N. Paul, "Crusade, Memory."

102. Albert of Aachen, *Historia Hierosolomitana* 6.23, ed. Edgington, 432; Aurell, *Chrétiens contre*

les croisades, 25–26. "Nimiam et cruentam cedem Saracenorum" (*Historia Hierosolomitana*, 430) does not mean "very great and cruel slaughter of Saracens," but just slaughter with blood (*cruor*); nor does "cedem nimia crudelitate" mean "a massacre with excessive cruelty," but rather "a massacre perpetrated with great cruelty," 6.25, 436. And even were *cruentus* to mean "cruel," this does not mean criticism; see below, at nn141–51. The third massacre appears only in Albert of Aachen, *Historia* 6.30–31, 440–43. The princes justify their decision on strategic ground (the Fatimid enemy would find in the Jerusalem's Muslim population an ally). But this argument is only developed to soothe an angry Tancred, in Albert's book a bad and foolish character (a *miles gloriosus*), who cannot quite understand why the Muslims who had taken refuge under his banner on the Temple's roof should have been slaughtered. The military considerations do not explain the slaughter of (evidently harmless) women and children, let alone the cruel manner in which it was performed.

103. Jacobsen, "Eroberung von Jerusalem," 343–45 and n33 for the 1087 Pisan campaign against Mahdia. This source is edited by Scalia, "Carme Pisano," and Cowdrey, "Mahdia Campaign."

104. *Fides cum ydololatria* = *Carmina Burana*, n46, ed. Hilka, 1:1.90, 92. Comments to this effect in Wentzlaff-Eggebert, *Kreuzzugsdichtung*, 55. The poem is commonly dated to the Second Crusade. See the fine discussion of ethos and historiography in Hartl, "Feindbild," 43–51.

105. *Fides cum ydololatria*, ed. Hilka, 90–91; Wentzlaff-Eggebert, *Kreuzzugsdichtung*, 52–57.

106. Jerome, *Commentariorum in Esaiam liber* 6, in Isa. 13.17–18, CCSL 73, 233.

107. Crouzet, NStB, 40–41 (several instances of slaughtered children and pregnant women; Huguenot sources). Agrippa d'Aubigné, "Les fers," vv. 1033–35, in *Les tragiques*, ed. Bailbé, 228, steers very close to Isaiah 13's words: "For, coerced, the father's eyes / were not allowed to cry over his son; speechless, the mother / watched the fruit of her belly and heart drag along."

108. *Briefe Friedrichs des Frommen*, ed. Kluckhon, 2:1, 485–88, at 486–87 (n672). See Crouzet, NStB, 54–55, from a modern French translation.

109. Tudebode, *Historia de Hierosolymitano itinere*, ed. Hill and Hill 142.

110. See the related words in the anonymous *Gesta Francorum*, ed. Hill, 92. They had a now lost common source; see Rubenstein, "What Is the *Gesta Francorum*?"; Flori, *Chroniqueurs et propagandistes*, summarizing idem, "De l'anonyme Normand."

111. Kedar, "Massacre," 68.

112. Raymond, *Liber*, 150. Cf. tr. Hill and Hill, 127–28.

113. For the Augustinian theory of the three kinds of sight presented in the *De Genesi ad litteram*, see Schmitt, "La culture de l'*imago*," 5, with Augustine, *De Genesi as literam libri duodecim* 12.6–36, CSEL 28:1, 386–433. Fine explanation and elaboration in Lewis, *Reading Images*, 6–14.

114. Michaud, *Histoire des Croisades*, 1:443–44n1, discussed by Kedar, "Jerusalem Massacre," 49–51.

115. Bruno of Segni, on Isa. 14.20, PL 165, col. 687b. Quintilian, *De Institutione oratoria* 8.6.67 and 76, ed. Cousin, 5.123 and 125; Seneca, *De beneficiis*, 7.23.2 and 1, ed. Préchac, 2.100–101.

116. *In Iohannis Evangelium tractatus* 124.8, CCSL 36, 668: "Even though credence in the reality [depicted] is not in question, oftentimes words seem to overshoot what is credible, which . . . is done when something that is clear is either amplified or diminished, while still not erring away from the track of the reality to be signified, because the words go beyond the reality that is pointed to, in such a way that it is apparent that the speaker does not have a desire to deceive."

117. Isidore, *Etymologiae* 1.37, ed. Lindsay, 1.72, picked up the notion from Augustine or a common source.

118. Alcuin, PL 100, col. 1007c; Pseudo-Bede, PL 92, cols. 936d–38a.

119. *Biblia sacra cum glossa ordinaria et Nicolas de Lyra*, vol. 5, col. 1340.

120. In 2 Macc. 5.3, PL 109, cols. 1232b–33a, on the signs of conflict seen in the sky, placed in parallel with the signs Josephus reported in his *Jewish Wars*, 6.5.3, ed. Thackeray, 3.458–67, commenting: "prodigiosus apparuit visus et fidem pene excedens, quod vere falsum putaretur, nisi occul(t)orum fidem confirmasset." For Maccabean exemplarity, see Buc, "Vengeance," 469–73, 481–82, building on earlier historiography.

121. Raymond, *Liber*, 151.

122. Michaud, *Histoire*, 1.444. Lobrichon, *1099*, 130.

123. Raymond, *Liber*, 65; tr. Hill and Hill, 48; 125, tr. 105, as noticed by Lobrichon, *1099*, 91–92.

124. Raymond, *Liber*, 109; cf. tr. Hill and Hill, 88–89; see Riley-Smith, *First Crusade*, 117–18. For the beauty of the martyr's body already in the second century, see Brown, *Body and Society*, 72–73.

125. Heimert, *Religion and the American Mind*, 336–43.

126. *Vie de Saint Louis*, ed. Monfrin, §§148, 158–59, 646, 72–73, 76–79, 320–21. See Le Goff, *Saint Louis*, 477–78.

127. Gaunt, Harvey, and Paterson, eds., *Marcabru: A Critical Edition*, 438; tr. Goldin, *Lyrics*, 79.

128. This is Flori's position, *Pierre l'Ermite*, 419–22; also Lobrichon, *1099*, 123–33.

129. See also Kedar, "Jerusalem Massacre," 71–72.

130. Elm, "Die Eroberung Jerusalems," 52–53 (*violence et le sacré* in French, a reference to René Girard's œuvre).

131. Coleman, "Fatal Charades."

132. *On the Spectacles* 5(6), 14(12), 20(17), 27(24), 33(29/30); I use Coleman's recent translation and commentary; Martial, *Liber Spectaculorum*, 62, 126, 156, 195, 244 (slightly modified). For *sanctus* and *sacer*, see Sauter, *Der römische Kaiserkult*; for *credere* and *fides*, see Scheid and Linder, "Quand croire c'est faire," with bibliography.

133. Dumézil, *Idées romaines*, 48–59, at 51–52. Deviations from the mythological plot, just as conformity to it, underscored the power of the emperor; see Coleman, "Fatal Charades," 69; eadem, "Launching into History," 74.

134. See Flori, *Pierre l'Ermite*, 466.

135. Aelred, Sermo 30.20–21, ed. Raciti, *Sermones I–LXXXIV*, CCCM 2A, 248.

136. Isidore, *Sententiarum libri tres*, 1.29.4–6, CCSL 111, 88. See above, Chapter 4, at n114.

137. Prudentius, *Peristephanon*, Hymn II (Lawrence), vv. 372–92, ed. Lavarenne, 43, discussed Chapter 3, at nn79–81, and above, n87.

138. Bradford, *Of Plymouth Plantation, 1620–1647* §2.28, ed. Morison, 296.

139. Mason, *Brief History of the Pequot War*, 8.

140. Heimert, *Religion and the American Mind*, 337–38, citing Finley, *The Curse of Meroz*, 20, and David Avery, *The Lord is to be Praised*, 8.

141. Kupperman, *Settling with the Indians*, 175, followed by Simmons, "Cultural Bias," 67–68.

142. Underhill, *Newes from America*, 39–40.

143. Calvin, Sermo LXXXVII on Deut. 13, no. 3 (1555), in *Opera*, 27.251; Commentary on Deuteronomy, *Opera*, 24.360.

144. Underhill, *Newes from America*, 2.

145. Calvin, on Psalm 137.9 [136.9 Vulgate], in *Commentaires de Jehan Calvin*, 2.526–27.

146. Marshall, *Meroz Cursed*, 11–12, preached to the commons on Feb. 23, 1642. See Hill, *English Bible*, 88–89, citing Jeffs, ed., *Fast Sermons to Parliament*, 2.208–9.

147. Discussion in Kahn, *Wayward Contracts*, 123–27.

148. Wahnich, "Économie émotive de la Terreur," at 907–8.

149. "Les représentants à Lyon à la Convention nationale" (Dec. 12, 1793), RACdSP, 9.363.

150. *Ami du peuple*, dated Aug. 3, 1790, in *Œuvres politiques*, ed. De Cock and Goëtz, 2.1152. See Van Heuvel, "Terreur, Terroriste," 103.

151. Duranton, "Humanité," 37–38.

152. *Ami du peuple* dated July 8, 1792, 7.4099–4100, opposing "a hundred criminal heads" to the already lost "100,000 innocent heads, the flower of its [France's] children."

153. De Baecque, "Trajectory of a Wound," 167 (translation and analysis), or idem, *Glory and Terror*, 134–35. Alas, the text is not, as footnoted, in *Archives Parlementaires*, ed. Mavidal et al., 1.91, 663.

154. Fulcher, *Historia* 1.20.2, ed. Hagenmeyer, 247; Raymond, *Liber*, 78; tr. Hill and Hill, 60.

155. De Baecque, *Glory*, 122, 137–40.

156. See Markus, *Saeculum*, and Hanning, *Vision of History*, esp. 20–43.

157. See, among many, Müller-Mertens, "Frankenreich oder Nicht-Frankenreich?"

158. Splendid examples are (still hardly studied) Ralph the Black's commentaries on the four books of Kings and the two books of Chronicles; see Buc, "Exégèse et pensée politique."

159. See Whalen, *Dominion of God*.

160. See Mendel, *Vision and Violence*, 141–45; Assmann, "Recht und Gerechtigkeit"; Baker, "Inventing the French Revolution." Guy Lobrichon, conversation of Sept. 16, 2007, reminds me that Henri de Lubac pointed to the genealogy linking Joachim of Fiore to Georg Friedrich Hegel. See De Lubac, *La postérité spirituelle*.

161. For illustrations of Titus and Vespasian's "Vengeance of the Savior," see Lewis, *Reading Images*, 218, 220.

162. See Buc, "Vengeance de Dieu"; Bresc, "Historiens."

163. Flori, *Pierre l'Ermite*, 420, considers that, already by 1100/1005, the eyewitness chroniclers, including Raymond d'Aguilers, saw in the 1099 conquest the realization of prophecies announcing the purification of Jerusalem, and no longer of the prophecies of EndTimes. Lobrichon, *1099*, 108, 130–32, is, in my estimate, closer to the truth. See as well Rubenstein, *Armies*, 310–11, 313–14, and his forthcoming "Crusade and Apocalypse: Making History at the End of Times."

164. Edgington, "Religious Ideas," 142–43; contra, Flori, *Pierre l'Ermite*, 56–63.

165. See Edgington, "Religious Ideas"; Kleber, "Pélerinage, vengeance, conquête"; Flori, "Une ou plusieurs 'première croisade'?" 18–20; Riley-Smith, "First Crusade and the Persecution of the Jews," 69–70.

166. *Chanson d'Antioche*, viii–xiii, ed. Duparc-Quioc, 1.26–29; ed. Guidot, 196–204; tr. Edgington and Sweetenham, 106–8. See Riley-Smith, *First Crusade*, 55–56. By the mid-thirteenth century, the dialogue between Jesus and the good thief could be related to crusading hopes; see Gilbert de Tournai,

sermon 3.20, ed. and tr. Maier, *Crusade Propaganda*, 208 (tr. slightly modified): "The cross is in fact the key to heaven, that opened the gates of paradise, which had been closed for 5000 years, to the crusader and the good thief who was crucified [with Christ]. At that time . . . God gave the greatest hope to crusaders when, even though the cherubs guarded paradise with the sword of flame, the thief entered paradise."

167. Haymo, in Isa. 63.3, PL 116, col. 1054c–d; to be read with in Isa. 2.12, PL 116, col. 733d–4a.

168. See Bernheim, *Mittelalterliche Zeitanschauungen*, 74–75, and my comments in "Vengeance," 474n70.

169. *Chanson d'Antioche*, xiii, vv. 245–49, ed. Duparc-Quioc, 29; ed. Guidot, 206: "Dont fu vengiés Nos Sire et encore sera. Ki lui ira vengier bon loier en avra : / En paradis celestre corone portera."

170. Ibid., iv, vv. 98–100, ed. Duparc-Quioc, 23; ed. Guidot, 192.

171. Ibid., iv, v. 99, ed. Duparc-Quioc, 23; ed. Guidot, 192.

172. Albert of Aachen, 6.6, ed. Edgington, 410; *Chanson d'Antioche*, ix, vv. 179–80, ed. Duparc-Quioc, 26; ed. Guidot, 199.

173. Rubenstein, "Godfrey of Bouillon," 65–66. To Rubenstein's already full proof of the existence of a belief, still in 1108, that with the crusade Christendom had entered the Final Times, one can add the words of Gilon de Paris, who ends his poem with wishes that Godfrey, elected king on the eighth day since the fall of the city, might live into the eighth age. Gilo, *Historia Vie Hierosolimitane* ix, vv. 371–72, ed. Grocock and Siberry, 250: "vir regno dignus, cum rege beato, vivat in octava." See Grocock, "L'aventure épique," 18.

174. For this, see Flori, *L'Islam*, esp. 280ff.

175. Gerhoh of Reichersberg, *In Psalmum 33*, ed. van der Eynde et al., vol. 2:1, 257–63. My thanks to Professor B. Whalen for this reference.

176. Alexander Minorita, *Expositio in Apocalypsim*, ed. Wachtel. See Schmolinsky, *Apokalypsenkommentar des Alexander Minorita*, 105ff; and Krey, "Nicholas of Lyra and Paul of Burgos," 105–6.

177. Pierre Aureol, *Compendium sensus litteralis*, ed. Seeboeck.

178. See *Nicholas of Lyra's Apocalypse Commentary*, tr. Krey; Krey, "Apocalypse Commentary of 1329."

179. Flori, *Pierre l'ermite*, 466.

180. "C'est la complainte d'Outremer," vv. 12–24, in *Rutebeuf*, ed. Zink, 2.313–23, here 314.

181. Ekkehard of Aura, *Chronica* version 1, ed. Schmale and Schmale-Ott, 158–60. I discussed these passages' meanings and translation with Jay Rubenstein in February 2013 and with Elisabeth Mégier in April–May 2013.

182. Guibert, *Gesta dei*, 7.21, ed. Huygens, 302:942–45.

183. Rubenstein, "Crusade and Apocalypse: Making History at the End of Times." For the earlier tradition, see Mégier, "Senso letterale dell'Apocalisse."

184. Guibert, *Gesta dei*, 303:972–74.

185. Guibert, *Contra iudaizantem et iudeos*, ed. Huygens, CCCM 171, 374; Rubenstein, *Guibert of Nogent*, 116.

186. They are named in the "Nouvelle complainte d'Outremer," v. 335, ed. Zink, *Rutebeuf*, 2.425–45, at 442, which also calls to "start anew a new history." In the "Complainte," v. 151 and vv. 158–59, ibidem, 322, are named Godfrey, Engleger (Angeliers), Tancred, and Baldwin.

187. *Ad Heinricum IV. imperatorem*, 1.15, ed. Seyffert, 144. For Benzo of Alba, see primarily Erdmann, "Endkaiserglaube", and Dasberg, *Untersuchungen*, plus now the fine pages in Gabriele, *Empire of Memory*, 113–15, and the even richer elaborations in Potestà, *L'ultimo messia*, 98–101.

188. *Ad Heinricum imperatorem* 1.17, ed. Seyffert, 148: *Caesar* [Heinricus], *hymago mea*.

189. Ibid.,, ed. Seyffert, 152. Garrison, "The Franks as the New Israel."

190. The *Chanson d'Antioche* compares favorably its heroes to antecedents, the Carolingian knights of Roncesvalles. And the martyrs of Charlemagne's wars in Spain are transmuted into white-bearded fighters who struggle alongside the crusaders before Antioch, *Chanson* cccxxi vv. 8091–8121, ed. Duparc-Quioc, 399–400 (with Duparc-Quioc's commentary ad v. 8091), ed. Guidot, 838; tr., 291. See Kleber, "Pélerinage, vengeance, conquête," 766–67, underlining that the first crusaders "suffer" more than Carolingian heroes; *Chanson* cccxxxvii vv. 8612–16, ed. Duparc-Quioc, 424; ed. Guidot, 876–78; tr. 303

191. See most recently Gabriele, "Otto III, Charlemagne."

192. Gabriele, *Empire of Memory*, 127 and passim. We came to this conclusion independently, but Gabriele published it first.

193. See Landes, "Lest the Millennium Be Fulfilled"; Brandes, "Tempora periculosa sunt."

194. Corvinus, *De miserabili Monasteriensium anabaptistarum obsidione*, C2r (or *Flugschriften*, ed. Köhler, vol. 2, pamphlet n579): "adeoque certum sit, Satanam iis quos irretitos tenet laqueis suis, fere robur addere ac constantiam."

195. Rothmann, "Von Verborgenheit der Schrift," ed. Stupperich, 352; see Chapter 2, at nn85–87.

196. Corvinus, *Gesprech oder disputatio Antonii Corvini und Johannis Rymei meit Johan von Leida*, A2v (or *Flugschriften*, ed. Köhler, vol. 2, pamphlet n636). See Stayer, *Anabaptists and the Sword*, 278.

197. Corvinus, *Gesprech*, F4v.

198. "Laws of Progress," *Presbyterian Quarterly Review* 2 (1853): 416ff., cited by Tuveson, *Redeemer Nation*, 78; *Presbyterian Quarterly Review* 5 (1857): 608, cited by Tuveson, 65. See also AA, 52–53, 147.

199. Smith, "Problem of the Philosophy of History," 4, with the analysis in Tuveson, RN, 85. See above, Chapter 2, n30.

EPILOGUE: NO FUTURE TO THAT PAST?

1. Massively documented by Gentile, *Le Religioni della politica*, tr. *Politics as Religion*.

2. Cited by Ivianski, "Moral Issue," 232. On this milieu, see Pomper, *Russian Revolutionary Intelligentsia*.

3. Sorel, *Réflexions sur la violence*, 21, 127, 120 (citation), 90 (citation). For Sorel and myth, see Stanley, *Sociology*, 235–37.

4. See Crouzet, NStB, 605n29.

5. Stanley, *Sociology*, 245–46.

6. Perinbam, *Holy Violence*; Fanon, *Damnés*, preface by Jean-Paul Sartre, dated November 1961; tr. *Wretched*. See Arendt, *On Violence*, for the traditions informing Sorel, Fanon, and Sartre.

7. Robespierre, "Sur les tentatives d'assassinat contre des représentants du peuple" (May 25, 1794), in *Œuvres*, 10.471. See Blum, *Rousseau*, 199, 246–47; Sartre, in Fanon, *Damnés*, 29, 31, 29, 30

8. Fanon, *Damnés*, 128 (my translation; see *Wretched*, 132–33).

9. Ibid., 134 (see *Wretched*, 139): There must be limits to destructive martyrdom, to this "almost pathological dream-state, in which . . . my blood calls for the blood of the other, in which my death through its mere inertia calls for the death of the other." For Durkheim's neo-Catholicism, see Buc, *Dangers*, 223–26. See as well Bhabha, "Foreword: Framing Fanon," here ix–x.

10. Yehoshafat Harkabi, *Fedayeen Action and Arab Strategy*, Adelphi Papers 53 (London: 1968), cited by Laqueur, *Terrorism Reader*, 149–52. The source Harkabi analyzes seems to be a pamphlet titled "The Revolution and Violence, the Road to Victory."

11. Ensslin, *"Zieht den Trennungsstritch,"* 13; Bhabha, "Introduction," xxviii–xxx.

12. MacCormack, "Loca sancta"; Housley, "Holy Land or Holy Lands"; idem, *Religious Warfare*, 26–32, with references to key sources and bibliography. See Jonathan Z. Smith's prolific discussions of the religious category space, starting with his "Earth and Gods."

13. Ekkehard, *Chronica*, Recensio prima, sub an. 1099, ed. Schmale and Schmale-Ott, 132. For Jerusalem prior to the Crusades, see still Konrad, "Himmlische und irdische Jerusalem," and most recently Bruun, "Bernard of Clairvaux," 257–64, with further references.

14. Konrad, "Himmlische und irdische Jerusalem," 528; with *Alcuini epistola* 198, ed. Dümmler, MGH Epp. 4 (Berlin: 1895), 327. See also Auffarth, "Himmlisches und irdisches Jerusalem."

15. Arnulf, *Liber gestorum recentium* 3.22, ed. Zey, 201.

16. Lewis, *Reading Images*, 201, 221–24. See, for the immediate aftermath of the First Crusade, Hehl, "Was ist eigentlich ein Kreuzzug," 319–21, building on Housley, "Jerusalem," 36–38.

17. Šmahel, HR, 2.735–52; Mengel, "From Venice to Jerusalem"; Matthias of Janov, *Narracio de Milicio*, ed. Kybal, 361–62.

18. Kaminsky, HHR, 10; Matthias of Janov, ed. Kybal, 361.

19. Tr. Fudge, *Crusade Against Heretics*, 65–66; idem, *Magnificent Ride*, 187–88; Housley, *Religious Warfare*, 31–22.

20. Šmahel, HH, 2.1083; Housley, "Holy Land," 240–41.

21. Jan Příbram, *Contra articulos picardorum* (1420) = "Isti articuli sunt Picardorum et aliorum eos sequencium dampnati et reprobati per fideles Bohemorum." I amplify the partial transcription in Kaminsky, HHR, 180n118, from Vienna ÖNB Handschrift 4749, ff. 37r–92r, here f. 71v–72r: "Quod autem scribentes et docentes vocaverunt eam Babilon . salvo timore Christi recte mentiti sunt . cum sit Jerusalem . super quam invocatum est nomen fortissimum dei . ita ut quadraginta principes et gens de tot regnis colectam innumere multitudinis fidelibus lacrimis . devotisque orationibus superavit et viriliter stans . et resistens . usque in finem effugavit et in alio bello miraculoso xviii* octodecim barones una cum multitudine hostium interfecit et fortissimum castrum regni Wissegradense debellavit . . . Unde si ab operibus iudicari habet . ipsa fuit dei famula."

22. *Victoire obtenue par Monseigneur le Duc de Mayenne*, Biiv; Crouzet, GdD, 2.380–81.

23. Crouzet, GdD, 2.367–68, citation from the *Coppie d'une ancienne Resolution traduitte de latin en François, trouvée en la grande salle de la Théologie, du college du Cardinal lemoyne, par M. François Vatable, lecteur en Hebreux* (Paris: 1589).

24. Weinstein, *Savonarola and Florence*, esp. 142–47, 157–58, 294–95, 309–11, 318–20, 325; Housley, *Religious Warfare*, 30–31, 80–83.

25. *Anonymous Account* (1422x24) = *Anonymus de origine Taboritarum et de morte Wenceslai IV*, ed.

Höfler, *Geschichtschreiber*, 1.529 and 532, with Kaminsky, "Prague Insurrection," 117 (translation his); Šmahel, HR, 2.1002–5. Generally, Housley, *Religious Warfare*, 105–9.

26. Jakoubek of Stříbro, *Letter to John of Jičín*, ed. Kaminsky, HHR, 544. See Šmahel, HH, 2.1042–46; Kalivoda, *Revolution und Ideologie*, 125.

27. Max Weber, "Politik als Beruf," ed. Mommsen and Schluchter, *Max Weber Gesamtausgabe*, 1.240; tr. Lassmann and Speirs, "Profession and Vocation of Politics," in *Max Weber, Political Writings*, here 361. See Crouzet, DesR, 19–42, to whose discussion of eschatology in Weber I am indebted.

28. Chapter 2, at nn89–97.

29. *Anonymus de origine Taboritarum*, ed. Höfler, 529 (*hypocritica patientia*).

30. See the stimulating thoughts in Kaminsky, "Nicholas of Pelhřimov's Tabor."

31. Introduction, at n180.

32. The propensity to think eschatologically (that humankind's time on earth could be limited, as opposed to unbounded) has been reheightened in the second half of the twentieth century, with the prospect of atomic war and of ecological catastrophes. See, for a recent discussion, Zwierlein, "Grenzen der Versicherbarkeit," 448–49.

33. See Introduction, at n27.

Select Bibliography

SOURCES (PUBLISHED)

Note that, in an essay like this, the boundary between primary and secondary sources is not always absolute.

Actes des comtes de Flandre, 1071–1128, ed. Ferdinand Vercauteren. Brussels: 1938.

The Acts of the Christian Martyrs, ed. Herbert Musurillo. Oxford: 1971.

Actus pontificum Cenomannis in urbe degentium, ed. Gustave Busson and Ambroise Ledru. Archives Historiques du Maine 2 (1901).

Adams, William. *The necessity of the pouring out of the spirit from on high upon a sinning apostatizing people.* Boston: John Foster: 1679.

Adémar de Chabannes. *Chronicon*, ed. Pascale Bourgain, Richard Landes, and George Pons. *Ademari Cabannensis Chronicon.* CCCM 129:1. Turnhout: 1999.

Adorno, Theodor et al. *The Authoritarian Personality.* New York: 1950.

Adso de Montier-en-Der. *De ortu et tempore antichristi*, ed. Daniel Verhelst. CCCM 129. Turnhout: 1999.

Aelfric of Eynsham. *Aelfric's Lives of the Saints being a set of sermons on Saints' Days formerly observed by the English Church*, ed. Walter W. Skeat. 4 vols. London: 1881–1900.

Aelred of Rielvaux. *Sermones I–LXXXIV*, ed. Gaetano Raciti. CCCM 2A. Turnhout: 1990.

Ailly, Pierre d'. *Materia dominorum Prutenorum cum dominis Polonis quantum ad ea, que iuris sunt naturalis vel divini*, ed. Weise, *Traktate*, 269–70.

Alan of Lille. *Sermo de Cruce Domini*, ed. Marie-Thérèse d'Alverny. *Alain de Lille: Textes inédits*, 279–83. Paris: 1965.

"Alarm." *The Presbyterian* 33, 37 (July 4, 1863): 106.

Albert of Aachen. *Historia Hierosolimitana. Historia Ierosolimitana: History of the Journey to Jerusalem*, ed. Susan B. Edgington. Oxford: 2007.

Alexander Minorita. *Expositio in Apocalypsim*, ed. Alois Wachtel. MGH Quellen zur Geistesgeschichte des Mittelalters 1. Weimar: 1955.

Andreas of Strumi. *Vita sancti Arialdi*, ed. Friedrich Baethgen. MGH SS 30:2, 1047–75. Leipzig: 1934.

———. *Vita sancti Iohannis Gualberti*, ed. Friedrich Baethgen. MGH SS 30:2, 1104–10. Leipzig: 1934.

Annals of Burton, ed. Henry Richard Luard. Annales Monastici. Rerum Britannicarum medii aevi scriptores 36. Vol. 1. London: 1864.

Anonymus de origine Taboritarum et de morte Wenceslai IV, ed. Konstantin Höfler. *Geschichtschreiber der husitischen Bewegung in Böhmen.* Vol. 1, 528–36. Vienna: 1856.

Archiv český čili staré písemné památky české i moravské, ed. František Palacký et al. 40 vols. Prague: 1844–2004.

Archives curieuse de l'histoire de France, depuis Louis XI jusqu'à Louis XVIII, ed. Louis Cimber and Félix Danjou. Paris: 1834–1837.

Archives Parlementaires de 1787 à 1860, première série, 1787–1799, ed. Jules Mavidal, Émile Laurent, et al. 101 vols. Paris, 1867–2005.

Arnulf of Milan. *Liber gestorum recentium*, ed. Claudia Zey. MGH Scriptores rerum germanicarum 67. Hannover: 1994.

Aspinwall, William. *A brief description of the fifth monarchy or kingdome that shortly is to come into the world.* London: M. Simmons, 1653.

Aubigné, Agrippa d'. *Les tragiques*, ed. Jacques Bailbé. Paris: 1968.

Augustine. *Annotationes in Job liber unus*, ed. Joseph Zycha. CSEL 28:2. Vienna: 1895.

———. *Collection antique de sermons de Saint Augustin*, ed. Cyrille Lambot. *Revue Bénédictine* 57 (1947): 89–108.

———. *Contra Adimantum*, ed. Joseph Zycha. CSEL 25:1. Vienna: 1891.

———. *De doctrina christiana*, ed. Joseph Martin. CCSL 32. Turnhout: 1962.

———. *De Genesi ad litteram libri duodecim*, ed. Josef Zycha. CSEL 28:3. Vienna: 1894.

———. *Enarratio in Psalmos*, ed. Emilius Dekkers and Johannes Fraipont. CCSL 38–40. Turnhout: 1956–1966.

———. *Epistulae*, ed. Alois Goldbacher. CSEL 34:1–2, 44:3, 57. Prague-Vienna-Leipzig: 1895–1911.

———. *Epistulae*, ed. Klaus-Detlev Daur. CCSL 31A–B. Turnhout: 2005–2009.

———. *Epistulae*, tr. Wilfrid Parsons. *Saint Augustine: Letters.* Fathers of the Church 18. New York: 1951–56.

———. *In Iohannis Evangelium tractatus*, ed. Radbod Willems. CCSL 36. Turnhout: 1954.

———. *Psalmus contra partem Donati, Contra epistulam Parmeniani, De baptismo*, ed. Michael Petschenig. CSEL 51. Vienna: 1908.

———. *Scripta contra Donatistas*, ed. Michael Petschenig. CSEL 53. Vienna-Leipzig: 1910.

———. "Le sermon CXI de saint Augustin," ed. Cyrille Lambot. *Revue Bénédictine* 57 (1947): 109–116.

———. *Sermones*, ed. François Dolbeau. *Augustin d'Hippone, Vingt-six sermons au peuple d'Afrique.* Études Augustiniennes, Antiquité 147. Paris: 1996.

Auriol, Pierre. *Compendium sensus litteralis totius scripturae divinae*, ed. Philibert Seeboeck. Quaracchi: 1896.

Austin, David. "The Downfall of the Mystical Babylon." In Austin et al., *The Millennium, or the thousand years of prosperity, promised to the Church of God, in the Old Testament and in the New, Shortly to commence . . . .* Elizabethstown: 1794.

"'Ave, communisme, Morituri te salutant!' Nikolai Bucharins 'Letzte Wort'," ed. editorial staff [of *UTOPIE kreativ*], *UTOPIE kreativ* 89 (1998): 63–82.

Avery, David. *The Lord is to be Praised for the Triumphs of His Power.* Norwich: 1778.

Der Baader-Meinhof-Report: Dokumente—Analysen—Zusammenhänge: Aus den Akten des Bundeskriminalamts, der 'Sonderkommission Bonn' und dem Bundesamt für Verfassungsschutz. Mainz: 1972.

Bacon, Francis. *The Advancement of Learning*, ed. Michael Kiernan. Oxford: 2000.

Bacon, Roger. *The Opus Majus of Roger Bacon*, ed. Henry Bridges. Vol. 1. London: 1900.

Baldric of Dol. *Historia Jerosolimitana*. In *Recueil des historiens des Croisades, historiens occidentaux*. Vol. 4, 10–110. Paris: 1879.

Ballanche, Pierre-Simon. *Essai sur les institutions sociales*. Paris: 1818.

Barrow, Henry. *Writings of Henry Barrow, 1587–1590*, ed. Leland H. Carlson. London: 1962.

Bartoš, František Michálek. *Manifesty města Prahy z doby husitské: Les manifestes de la ville de Prague de l'epoque des guerres hussites*. Prague: 1932.

Baumann, Bommi [Michael]. *Wie alles anfing*, 67–69. Munich: 1980. Tr. *Terror or Love?* New York: 1979.

Bede the Venerable. *Explanatio apocalypsis*, ed. Roger Gryson. CCSL 121A. Turnhout: 2001.

———. *Historia ecclesiastica gentis Anglorum*, ed. Michael Lapidge et al. SC 489. Paris: 2005.

———. *In Lucae evangelium exposition; in Marci evangelium expositio*, ed. David Hurst. CCCM 120. Turnhout: 1960.

Beecher, Henry Ward. "Sermon." Repr. in *Patriotic Adresses*, 328. Boston: 1887.

Benzo of Alba. *Ad Heinricum IV: imperatorem*, ed. Hans Seyffert. *Sieben Bücher an Heinrich IV*. MGH Scriptores rerum germanicarum in usum scholarum separatim editi 65. Hannover: 1996.

Bernard of Clairvaux. *Liber ad milites templi de laude novae militia*, ed. Gerhard B. Winkler. *Bernhard von Clairvaux, Sämtliche Werke*, vol. 1, 267–326. Innsbruck: 1990.

———. *Liber de gratia et libero arbitrio*, ed. Gerhard B. Winkler. *Bernhard von Clairvaux, Sämtliche Werke*, vol. 1, 153–225. Innsbruck: 1990.

Berulle, Pierre. *Traicté des energumenes; suivy d'un Discours sur la possession de Marthe Brossier*. Troyes: 1599.

Bèze, Théodore de. *Correspondance de Théodore de Bèze*, ed. Hippolyte Aubert et al. Vol. 4. Geneva: 1965.

———. *Correspondance de Théodore de Bèze*, ed. Hippolyte Aubert et al. Vol. 11. Geneva: 1970.

———. *Du droit des magistrats*, ed. Robert Kingdon. Geneva: 1970.

———. *Histoire ecclésiastique des églises réformées au Royaume de France*, ed. Guillaume Baum and Édouard Cunitz. 3 vols. Paris: 1883–1889.

Biblia sacra cum glossa ordinaria et Nicolas de Lyra. 6 vols. Venice: 1603.

Biblia sacra cum glosa ordinaria [et Nicolai Lyrani Postilla]. 7 vols. Venice: 1638.

Bodin, Jean. *De la Démonomanie des sorciers*. Paris: 1580. Repr. Paris: 1979.

Bonald, Louis, vicomte de. *Théorie du pouvoir politique et religieux*. Constance: 1796.

Boucher, Jean (?). *Commentaires et remarques chrestiennes sur l'edict d'Union de l'an 1588: Où est escrit le devoir d'un vray Catholique contre les Polytiques de nostre temps . . .* Paris: 1590.

——— (?). *Lettre missive de l'Evesque du Mans: Avec la réponse à icelle . . . asçavoir si l'acte de Frere Jacques Clement Jacobin doit estre approuvé en conscience*. Lyon: 1589. Orléans: 1590.

——— (?). *Responce du menu peuple a la declaration de Henry . . . semee ces jours passez par les politiques de Paris*. s.l.: 1589.

Boykin, William G. *Never Surrender: A Soldier's Journey to the Crossroads of Faith and Freedom*. New York: 2008.

Bradford, William. *Of Plymouth Plantation, 1620–1647*, ed. Samuel Eliot Morison. New York: 1953.

Brantôme, Pierre de Bourdeille, abbé séculier de. *Des hommes*, ed. Jean-Alexandre-Charles Buchon. In *Œuvres complètes de Brantôme*. Vol. 1. Paris: 1848.

Brown, John. *The Life and Letters of John Brown, liberator of Kansas, and Martyr of Virginia*, ed. F. B. Sanborn. Boston: 1891.

Brussel, Nicolas. *Nouvel examen de l'usage général des fiefs en France, Pendant les onzième, douzième, treizième & quatorzième siécles* [*sic*]. Vol. 1. Repr. Paris: 1750.

Burke, Edmund. *Remarks on the Policy of the Allies*. In *The Works of the Right Hon. Edmund Burke*, 1: 588–606. London: 1834.

———. *Thoughts on French Affairs*. In *The Works of the Right Hon. Edmund Burke*, Vol. 1, 563–80. London: 1834.

Bushnell, Horace. *Oration at Yale College, 26 July 1865*. New Haven, Conn.: 1865.

Cagny, Perceval de. *Chroniques de Perceval de Cagny*, ed. Henri Moranvillé. Paris: 1902.

Calvin, Jean. *Commentaires de Jehan Calvin sur le Livre des Pseaumes*. 2 vols. Paris: 1859.

———. *The Institutes of the Christian Religion*, tr. Henry Beveridge. Edinburgh: 1846.

———. *Ioannis Calvini Opera quae supersunt omnia*. 59 vols. = Corpus Reformatorum 29–89. Brunswick, then Berlin: 1863–1900

Cantiques d'un huguenot sur les règnes de Henri II et François II (. . .) 1560–1562, ed. Louis Lacour. *Bulletin de la Société de l'Histoire du Protestantisme Français* 5 (1857): 382–98, 507–22.

Carmina Burana, ed. Alfons Hilka. 2 vols. Heidelberg: 1930.

Cartulaire d'Afflighem, ed. Edouard de Marneffe. Louvain: 1894.

Casaubon, Méric. *A Treatise concerning enthusiasm*. London: 1655.

Case, Wheeler. "An Answer for the Messengers of the Nation." Repr. in *Revolutionary Memorials: Embracing Poems by the Rev. Wheeler Case, Published in 1778*, 40–47. New York: 1852.

Cassius Dio. *Roman History, Epitoma*, ed. and tr. Ernest Cary. 9 vols. Cambridge, Mass.: 1955–69.

Castellion, Sébastien. *Traité des hérétiques*, ed. Albert Olivet and Eugène Choisy. Geneva: 1913.

La chanson d'Antioche, ed. Jan A. Nelson. Tuscaloosa: 2003.

La chanson d'Antioche, ed. Suzanne Duparc-Quioc. 2 vols. Paris: 1976.

La chanson d'Antioche: Chanson de geste du dernier quart du XIIe siècle, ed. Bernard Guidot. Paris: 2011.

The Chanson d'Antioche: An Old French Account of the First Crusade, tr. Susan B. Edgington and Carol Sweetenham. Farnham: 2011.

Chanson de la croisade albigeoise, ed. Eugène Martin-Chabot. 3 vols. Paris: 1931–61.

La chanson de Roland publiée d'après le manuscrit d'Oxford, ed. Joseph Bédier. Paris: 1922.

Les chansons de croisade, ed. Joseph Bédier. Paris: 1909.

Chartier, Jean. *Chronique de Charles VII*, ed. Auguste Vallet de Viriville. Vol. 1. Paris: 1858.

Christine de Pizan. *Le Ditié de Jeanne d'Arc*, ed. and tr. Angus Kennedy and Kenneth Varty. Oxford: 1977.

Chronica universalis Mettensis, ed. Georg Waitz, MGH Scriptores 24, 502–26. Hannover: 1879.

Chronicon sancti Laudi Rotomagensis, in RHGF 23, 395–97. Paris: 1894.

Chroniques de Saint-Denis, in RHGF 21, 103–23. Paris: 1855.

Cicero. *De divinatione*, ed. Wilhelm Ax. *Cicero Scripta quae manserunt Omnia*. Vol. 46, 1–129. Leipzig: 1938. Repr. Stuttgart: 1969.

———. *Tusculanes*, ed. Georges Fohlen. 2 vols. Paris: 1968.

Clarke, William. *The Clarke Papers, Selections from the Papers of William Clarke*, ed. Charles Harding Firth. 4 vols. London: 1891–1901.

Collectio Salernitana, ed. Salvatore de Renzi et al. 2 vols. Naples: 1852–58.

Commentaires et remarques chrestiennes sur l'edict d'Union de l'an 1588: Où est escrit le devoir d'un vray Catholique contre les Polytiques de nostre temps . . . Paris: 1590. Paris BNF Réserve des Imprimés Lb34.502.

La conquête de Jérusalem, ed. Célestin Hippeau. Repr. Geneva: 1969.

Contre les fausses allegations que les plus qu'Achitofels, Conseillers Cabinalistes, proposent pour excuser Henry le meurtrier de l'assassinat par luy perfidement commis en la personne du tresillustre Duc de Guise. Lyon: 1589.

Cook, John. *Monarchy*. Waterford: 1651.

Cooper, Samuel. *A Discourse on the Man of Sin, delivered in the Chapel of Harvard College . . . September 1, 1773.* Boston: 1774.

Coppie d'une ancienne Resolution traduitte de latin en François, trouvée en la grande salle de la Théologie, du college du Cardinal lemoyne, par M. François Vatable, lecteur en Hebreux. Paris: 1589.

Cornet, Marcelin. *Discours Apologetique tres veritable, des causes qui ont contrainct les habitans de S. Malo, de s'emparer du Chasteau de leur ville, avec une bresve histoire de la prise d'iceluy, advenuë le 12. de Mars, 1590.* s.l.: 1590.

Corvinus, Antonius. *Acta: Handlungen: Legation und schriffte . . . in der Münsterschen sache geschehen.* Wittemberg: 1536.

———. *De miserabili Monasteriensium anabaptistarum obsidione, excidio, memorabilibus rebus tempore obsidionis in urbe gestis. Regis, Knipperdollingi ac Rrechtingi confessione et exitu.* Wittemberg: 1536.

"Cuba and Humanity." *Northern Christian Advocate* (allegedly March 23, 1898): 8.

Cyprian of Carthage. *Ad Demetrianum*, ed. Manlio Simoneti. *Sancti Cypriani Episcopi Opera pars 2*, 35–51. CCSL 3A. Turnhout: 1976.

———. *Sancti Thasci Caecili Cypriani Opera Omnia*, ed. Wilhelm Hartel. CSEL 3:1–3. Vienna: 1868–1871.

The Dead Sea Scrolls, tr. Florentino Garcia Martinez. Leiden: 1994.

The Dead Sea Scrolls: A New Translation, ed. Martin O. Wise et al. Rev. ed. San Francisco: 2005.

Désiré, Artus. *Plaisans et armonieux cantiques de devotion.* Paris: 1561.

Didaci de Escobar, Andreas. *Revoco, casso, annulo*, ed. Weise, *Traktate*, 391–413.

Diderot, Denis. *Œuvres complètes de Diderot*, ed. Jules Assézat and Maurice Tourneux. Paris: 1875–77. Repr. Neudeln: 1966.

Diderot, Denis, et al. *Encyclopédie, ou dictionnaire raisonné des sciences, des arts et des métiers.* 17 vols. Paris: 1751–65.

Discours veritable de l'estrange et subite mort de Henry de Valois, advenuë par permission divine, luy estant a S. Clou, ayant assiegé la Ville de Paris, le Mardy 1. jour d'Aoust, 1589. Par un Religieux de l'ordre des Jacobins. Troyes: s.d. [1589].

Documenta Magistri Joannis Hus vitam, doctrinam, causam in Constantiniensi Concilio actam et controversias de religione in Bohemia annis 1403–1418 motas illustranti, ed. František Palacký. Prague: 1869. Rev. ed. Osnabrück: 1966.

Donatist Martyr Stories: The Church in Conflict in Roman North Africa, ed. and tr. Maureen A. Tilley. Liverpool: 1996.

Le dossier du Donatisme, ed. Jean-Louis Maier. 2 vols. Berlin: 1987–1989.

Dwight, Timothy. *Columbia*, ed. Edmund Clarence Stedman and Ellen McKay Hutchinson. In *A Library of American Literature*. Vol. 3. *Literature of the Revolutionary Period, 1765–1787*, 480–81. New York: 1888.

———. *A Discourse on Some Events of the Last Century*. New Haven, Conn.: 1801.

Ekkehard. *Chronicon, recensio prima*, ed. Franz-Josef Schmale and Irene Schmale-Ott. *Frutolfs und Ekkehards Chroniken und die anonyme Kaiserchronik*, 124–205. Ausgewählte Quellen zur deutschen Geschichte des Mittelalters 14. Darmstadt: 1972.

Ensslin, Gudrun. *„Zieht den Trennungsstrich, jede Minute": Briefe an ihre Schwester Christiane und ihren Bruder Gottfried aus dem Gefängnis 1972–1973*. Hamburg: 2005.

Epictetus. *Diatribai*, ed. Joseph Souilhé and Amand Jagu. *Epictète, Entretiens*. 4 vols. Paris: 1943–1991.

Edwards, Jonathan. *Blank Bible*, ed. Stephen J. Stein. *Writings of Jonathan Edwards*. Vol. 24: 1–2. New Haven, Conn.: 2006.

———. *Notes on the Apocalypse*, ed. Stephen J. Stein. *The Writings of Jonathan Edwards*, vol. 5. New Haven, Conn.: 1977.

Edwards, Thomas. *Antapologia, or a full answer to the Apologetical Narration of Mr Goodwin, Mr Nye, Mr Sympson, Mr Burroughs, Mr Bridge, Members of the Assembly of Divines*, ed. George Yule. *Puritans and Politics: The Religious Legislation of the Long Parliament 1640–1647*, 320–41. Appleford: 1981.

Engels, Friedrich. *Der Deutsche Bauernkrieg*. Repr. in Karl Marx and Engels. *Werke*, vol. 7, 327–413. Berlin: 1961. Tr. *The Peasant War in Germany*. New York: 1926.

Ernster, Barb. "Rediscovering Everyday Mothering." *National Catholic Register* (May 14–20, 2006): 134–35.

Estoile, Pierre de l'. *Les belles figures et drolleries de la Ligue = Mémoires-Journaux, 1574–1611*, vol. 4, ed. Gustave Brunet et al. Paris: 1877. Enlarged ed. Paris: 1982.

Exhortatio ad proceres regni, ed. Ernst Dümmler. *Gedichte aus dem elften Jahrhundert*, 175–85. Neues Archiv der Gesellschaft für ältere deutsche Geschichtskunde 1:1. Hannover: 1876.

Falkenberg, Johannes, O.P. *Veteres relegentes historias*, ed. Weise, *Traktate*, 172–228.

Finley, Samuel. *The Curse of Meroz, or, the Danger of Neutrality, in the Cause of GOD, and our Country*. Philadelphia: 1757.

Firmicus Maternus. *De errore profanarum religionum*, ed. Robert Turcan. *L'erreur des religions païennes*. Paris: 1982.

Fish, Henry Clay. *The Valley of Achor, a Door of Hope*. New York: 1863.

Flavius Josephus. *Antiquities*, tr. Louis Feldman. 9 vols. Cambridge, Mass., and London: 1930–1965.

———. *Guerre des Juifs*, tr. André Pelletier. 3 vols. Paris: 1975–1982.

———. *Histoire de Flavius Iosephe Sacrificateur Hebrieu*, tr. Gilbert Genebrard. Paris: 1578.

———. *Jewish Wars*, tr. H. St. J. Thackeray. 3 vols. Cambridge, Mass.: 1928.

———. *Les sept livres de Flavius Iosephus de la guerre et de la captivité des Iuifz*. Paris: 1553.

Floyd, L. C., Rev. "God's Hand at the Battle in Manila." *Northern Christian Advocate* 59, 22 (June 1, 1898): 4.

Flugschriften des späteren 16. Jahrhunderts [microfiches], ed. Hans-Joachim Köhler. Leiden: 1990–.

Fox, George. *The Journal of George Fox*, ed. Norman Penney. Vol. 2. Cambridge: 1911.

Frederick III of Simmern, the Pious. *Briefe Friedrichs des Frommen, Kurfürsten von der Pfalz, mit verwandten Schriftstücken*, ed. August Kluckhon. Vol. 2: 1. Braunschweig: 1870.

Fudge, Thomas A. *The Crusade Against Heretics in Bohemia, 1418–1437*. Aldershot: 2002.

Fulcher of Chartres. *Historia Hierosolymitana*, ed. Heinrich Hagenmeyer. *Fulcheri Carnotensis Historia Hierosolymitana (1095–1127): Mit Erläuterungen und einem Anhange*. Heidelberg: 1913.

Garrison, William Lloyd. *William Lloyd Garrison and the Fight Against Slavery: Selections from "The Liberator,"* ed. William E. Cain. Boston: 1995.

Gelu, Jacques. *De puella aurelianensi Dissertatio*, ed. Pierre Lanéry d'Arc. *Mémoires et consultations en faveur de Jeanne d'Arc par les juges du procès de réhabilitation*, 565–600. Paris: 1889.

The Geneva Bible, ed. Gerald T. Sheppard. New York: 1989.

Geneva Study Bible: The New Testament of our Lord. London: 1607.

Geoffroy de Vigeois. *Chronicon*, ed. Philippe Labbé. *Nova bibliotheca manuscriptorum*. T. 2, 279–342. Paris: 1657.

Gerhoh of Reichersberg. *In Psalmum 33*, ed. Damien van der Eynde et al. *Gerhohi praepositi Reichersbergensis opera inedita*. Vol. 2:1, 257–63. Rome: 1956.

Gerson, Jean. *Discours au roi contre Jean Petit*, ed. Palémon Glorieux. *Œuvres complètes*. Vol. 7:2, 1005–30. Paris: 1968.

Gesta Francorum et aliorum Hierosolimitanorum, ed. Rosalind T. Hill. *The Deeds of the Franks and the Other Pilgrims to Jerusalem*. Rev. ed. Oxford: 1972.

Gilo of Paris. *Historia vie Hierosolimitane*, ed. Chris W. Grocock and J. Elizabeth Siberry. Oxford: 1997.

Ginés de Sepúlveda, Juan. *Democrates Alter*, ed. Angel Losada. *Democrates secundo o De las justas causas de la guerra contra los indios*. Madrid: 1951. Rev. ed. Madrid: 1984.

A Glimpse of Sions Glory or, the Churches Beautie specified. London, William Larnar: 1641.

Goldin, Frederick. *Lyrics of the Troubadours and the Trouvères: An Anthology and a History*. Garden City, N.Y.: 1973.

Goll, Jaroslav, ed. *Quellen und Untersuchungen zur Geschichte der böhmischen Brüder*. 2 vols. Prague: 1878–1882.

Goodman, Christopher. *How Superior Powers ought to be Obeyed of their Subjects, and wherein they may lawfully by God's Word be Disobeyed and Resisted*. Geneva: 1558.

Goodwin, John. *Hybristodikai: The Obstructours of Justice*. London: 1649.

Gratian. *Decretum*, ed. Emil Friedberg. *Corpus Iuris Canonici*. 2 vols. Leipzig: 1879–1881.

The Great Purge Trials, ed. Robert C. Tucker and Stephen Cohen. New York: 1965.

Gregory of Tours. *Libri Historiarum decem: Ten Books of Histories*, ed. Bruno Krusch and Wilhelm Levison. MGH SS rerum Merowingicarum 1:1. Hannover: 1951.

Gregory the Great. *Moralia in Job*, ed. Marc Adriaen. CSEL 143. Turnhout: 1979

———. *Registrum epistularum*, ed. Dag Norberg. 2 vols. CCSL 140–140A. Turnhout: 1982.

Gregory VII. *Registrum epistularum*, ed. Erich Caspar. *Das Register Gregors VII*. 2 vols. MGH Epp. selectae 2. Berlin: 1920–1923. Repr. Berlin: 1955.

Gui, Bernard. *Practica Inquisitionis heretice pravitatis*, ed. Célestin Douais. Paris: 1886.

Guibert de Nogent. *Contra iudaizantem et iudeos*, ed. R[obert] B[urchard] C[onstantijn] Huygens. CCCM 171. Turnhout: 2000.

———. *Gesta dei per Francos*, ed. R[obert] B[urchard] C[onstantijn] Huygens. CCCM 127A. Turnhout: 1996.

Hagenmeyer, Heinrich, ed. *Die Kreuzzugsbriefe aus den Jahren 1088–1100*. Innsbruck: 1901.

Harangue sur les causes de la guerre entreprise contre les Rebelles & seditieux du Royaume de France. Enuoyee à Monseigneur le Duc de Guyse, et à toute la Noblesse Catholique de France, ce 4. d'Octobre 1587. Par un Evesque de l'Eglise Catholique, Apostolique et Romaine. Paris and Troyes: 1587.

Helmer, Charles D. "The Stars and Stripes." In *The true and the false, An oration by Charles Tray, esq.. also The Stars and Stripes, A poem by Rev. Charles D. Helmer; pronounced before the Phi Beta Kappa Society. Yale College, July 30, 1862*. New Haven, Conn.: 1862.

Henry, Matthew. *An Exposition of the Old and New Testaments . . . by Matthew Henry*. 3 vols. New York: 1833.

———. *Matthew Henry's Commentary on the Whole Bible*. Peabody: 1991. Repr. 2006.

Hiestand, Rudolf, ed. *Papsturkunden für Kirchen im Heiligen Lande*. Abhandlungen der Akademie der Wissenschaften in Göttingen, Phil.-hist. Klasse, 3. F., 136. Göttingen: 1985.

Hill, Christopher. *Antichrist in Seventeenth-Century England*. Oxford: 1971.

Hobbes, Thomas. *Leviathan*, ed. Noel Malcolm. 3 vols. = Clarendon Edition of the Works of Thomas Hobbes. Vols. 3–5. Oxford: 2012.

Hodge, Charles. "The War." *Biblical Repertory and Princeton Review* 35, 1 (January 1863): 140–69.

Hoffmann, Hartmut, ed. "Die Briefmuster des Vallicellianus B 63 aus der Zeit Paschalis II." *Deutsches Archiv* 19 (1963): 130–48.

Hostiensis. *Henrici de Segusio Cardinalis Hostiensis Summa Aurea*. Venice: 1574.

Hrabanus Maurus. *Expositio in Matthaeum*, ed. Bengt Löfstedt. CCCM 174A. Turnhout: 2000.

Hrotsvith of Gandersheim. *Hrotsvithae Opera*, ed. Paul von Winterfeld. MGH scriptores rer. germ. in u. s. 34. Berlin: 1902.

Hugh of Saint-Cher, *Postilla* = *Opera omnia in universum vetus et novum testamentum*. 8 vols. Venice: 1703.

Humbert of Moyenmoutier. *Adversus simoniacos*, ed. Friedrich Thaner. MGH Libelli de lite. Vol. 1, 95–235.

Humphreys, David. *A poem on the happiness of America, addressed to the citizens of the United States*. Repr. New York: 1871.

———. *Miscellaneous Works of David Humphreys*. New York: 1804.

Hus, Jan. "De ablatione bonorum temporalium a clericis determinatio." In *Historia et monumenta Johannis Hus atque Hieronymi Pragensis confessorum Christi*, fol. 117v–125. Nurenberg: 1558.

———. *Ex libello accusatorio archiepiscopi Zbynconis—articuli ex partibus*, ed. Jan Sedlák. *Studie a texty k náboženským dějinám*. Vol. 2:1, 25–27. Olomouc: 1915.

Ide, George B. *Battle Echoes: or, lessons from the war*. Boston: 1866.

"In Brief." *Northern Christian Advocate* 58, 14 (April 6, 1898): 8.

Irenaeus. *Adversus haereses*, ed. Adelin Rousseau et al. SC 100. Paris: 1965.

Isidore of Seville. *Etymologiae*, ed. W[allace] M[artin] Lindsay, *Isidori Hispalensis Episcopi Etymologiarvm sive originvm libri XX*. 2 vols. Oxford: 1911.

————. *Sententiarum libri tres*, ed. Pierre Cazier. CCSL III. Turnhout: 1998.

Das Itinerarium Perigrinorum: eine zeitgenössische englische Chronik zum dritten Kreuzzug in ursprünglicher Gestalt, ed. Hans Eberhard Mayer. Schriften der MGH 18. Stuttgart: 1962.

Jackson, Peter. *The Seventh Crusade, 1244–1254: Sources and Documents*. Aldershot: 2007.

Jakoubek of Stříbro. *Against Andrew of Brod*, ed. Hermann von der Hardt, *Rerum concilii oecumenici constantiensis*, 3:335–933. Frankfurt: 1698.

————. *Apologia Magistri Jacobi de Misa contra Taboritas*, ed. Jan Sedlák. *Studie a texty k náboženským dějinám*. Vol. 2:1, 161–64. Olomuc: 1915.

Jean du Vignay. *Chronique de Primat*, in RHGF 23, 1–106. Paris: 1894.

Jeanne d'Arc. «Lettre de Jeanne d'Arc aux Hussites,» ed. Theodor Sickl. *Bibliothèque de l'Ecole des Chartes* 22 (1861): 81–83.

Jeffs, Robin, ed. *Fast Sermons to Parliament*. 34 vols. London: 1970–71.

Jenkins, Jerry. *Assassins*. Wheaton, Ill.: 1999.

Jerome. *Commentarii in Esaiam*, ed. Markus Adriaen. CCSL 73. Turnhout: 1963.

————. *Commentarii in prophetas minores*, ed. Marcus Adriaen. 2 vols. CCSL 76–76A. Turnhout: 1964–1969.

————. *Commentariorum in Matheum Libri IV*, ed. David Hurst et al. CCSL 77. Turnhout: 1969.

————. *Expositio in Hieremiam*, ed. Sigfried Reiter. CCSL 74. Turnhout: 1960.

Joachim of Fiore. *Expositio in Apocalypsim*. Venice: 1527. Repr. Frankfurt: 1964.

John of Salisbury, *Letters of John of Salisbury*, ed. Harold Edgeworth Butler, William James Millor, and Christopher N. L. Brooke. Oxford: 1955–1979.

————. *Policraticus*, ed. Clement C. J. Webb. *Johannes Saresberiensis episcopi Carnotensis Policraticus sive de Nugis curialium*. 2 vols. Oxford: 1909.

Johnson, Barton Warren. *People's New Testament*. 2 vols. Saint Louis/Nashville: 1889–1891.

Johnson, Edward. *Johnson's Wonder-Working Providence, 1628–1651*, ed. J. Franklin Jameson. New York: 1910.

Joinville, Jean de. *Vie de saint Louis*, ed. Jacques Monfrin. Paris: 1995.

Journal d'un Bourgeois de Paris, 1405–1449, ed. Alexandre Tuetey. Paris: 1881. Tr. Janet Shirley. *A Parisian Journal, 1405–1449*. Oxford: 1968.

Julian of Toledo. *Historia Wambae regis*, ed. Wilhelm Levison. MGH SS rerum Merowingicarum 5, 486–535. Hannover: 1910.

La juste et saincte défense de la ville de Lyon. Lyon: 1563. Repr. in *Archives curieuses de l'histoire de France*, ed. Louis Cimber and Félix Danjou. 1st s. 4, 195–214. Paris: 1835.

Kalivoda, Robert. *Revolution und Ideologie des Hussitismus*. Cologne: 1976.

Kerssenbroch, Hermann von. *Kessenbrochs Wiedertäufergeschichte*, ed. Heinrich Detmer. 2 vols. Geschichtsquellen des Bisthums Münster 5. Münster: 1899–1900. tr. Christopher McKay, *Narrative of the Anabaptist Madness: The Overthrow of Münster, the Famous Metropolis of Westphalia*. Leiden: 2007.

Keteltas, Abraham. *God Arising and Pleading His People's Cause*. Newburyport, Mass.: 1777.

Knox, John. *The Works of John Knox*, ed. David Laing. 6 vols. Edinburgh: 1846–1855.

Lactantius. *Divine institutes*, ed. Pierre Monat. SC 204. Paris: 1973.

Lamourette, Antoine-Adrien. *Instruction pastorale de M. l'évêque du département de Rhône et Loire au Clergé et aux Fidèles de son diocese*. Lyon: 1791.

Langhans, Rainer and Fritz Teufel, eds. *Klau mich.* Frankfurt-am-Main: 1968.

Laurière, Eusèbe de. *Ordonnances des roys de France de la troisième race.* Vol. 1. Paris: 1723.

Larina, Anna. *This I Cannot Forget: The Memoirs of Nikolai Bukharin's Widow.* Tr. New York: 1993.

"Laws of Progress." *Presbyterian Quarterly Review* 2 (1853): 416ff.

Legenda aurea, ed. Giovanni Paolo Maggioni. 2 vols. Florence: 1998.

Le Hongre, Jacques, O.P. *Sermon funebre proclame par frere Jaques [sic] le Hongre . . . en l'Eglise Cathedrale de nostre Dame de Paris le xx. Mars 1562.* Paris: 1563.

Lettre missive aux Parisiens d'un gentilhomme serviteur du Roy, n'agueres sorti de prison, representant le danger & peril qui menace leur ville, s'ils ne recognoissent promptement leurs fautes, & ne reçoivent sa Majesté, comme ils sont obligez par le commandement de Dieu. n.p.: 1591. Paris BNF Réserve des Imprimés Lb35 396.

Listář a listinář Oldřicha z Rožmberka, 1418–1462, ed. Blažena Rynešova and Josef Pelikán. 4 vols. Prague: 1929–1954.

Locke, John. *An Essay concerning human understanding.* London: 1690; 2nd ed. London: 1695; 5th ed. London: 1706. Repr. Bristol: 2003.

Loeb, Isidore. "Bulles inédites des papes." *Revue des Études Juives* 1 (1880): 294–98. Rev. ed. and tr. in *The Church and the Jews in the Thirteenth Century,* ed. Solomon Grayzel. 2nd ed. New York: 1966.

Lucian of Samosata. *How to Write History,* ed. Austin Morris Harmon, tr. K. Kilburn. *Lucian* [*Works*]. Vol. 6, 1–73. Cambridge, Mass: 1959.

———. *Instuctions for Writing History,* tr. Thomas Francklin. *The Works of Lucian, From the Greek.* Vol. 1, 389–412. London: 1780.

———. *The Way to Write History,* tr. Henry Watson Fowler and Francis George Fowler. *The Works of Lucian of Samosata, Complete with Exceptions Specified in the Preface,* 109–36. Oxford: 1905.

Ludus de Antichristo, ed. Gisela Vollmann-Profe. 2 vols. Göppingen: 1981.

Luther, Martin. "Ein Sendbrief von dem harten Büchlein wider die Bauern." In idem, *Werke,* vol. 18, 384–401. Weimar: 1908. Tr. *Luther's Works,* ed. Hartmut Lehmann. tr. Charles M. Jacobs and Robert C. Schultz. Vol. 46. Philadelphia: 1967.

———. "Wider die räuberischen und mörderischen Rotten der Bauern." In idem, *Werke.* Vol. 18, 357–61. Weimar: 1908. Tr. *Luther's Works,* ed. Hartmut Lehmann. tr. Charles M. Jacobs and Robert C. Schultz. Vol. 46. Philadelphia: 1967.

Macek, Josef. *Ktož jsú boží bojovníci.* Prague: 1951.

Maier, Christoph T., ed. *Crusade Propaganda and Ideology: Model Sermons for the Preaching of the Cross.* Cambridge: 2000.

Marat, Jean-Paul. *Œuvres politiques, 1789–1793,* ed. Jacques De Cock and Charlotte Goëtz. 10 vols. Brussels: 1989–1995.

Marcabru. *Marcabru: A Critical Edition,* ed. Simon Gaunt, Ruth Harvey, and Linda Paterson. Cambridge: 2000.

Marcus Aurelius. *Meditations,* ed. Amédée Trannoy. Paris: 1925.

Markov, Walter and Albert Soboul. *Die Sansculotten von Paris: Zur Geschichte der Volksbewegung, 1793– 1794.* Berlin: 1957.

Marshall, Stephen. *Meroz Cursed, or, A sermon preached to the honourable House of Commons, at their late solemn fast, Febr. 23, 1641.* London: 1641, vere 1642.

Martial. *On the Spectacles*, ed. and tr. Kathleen M. Coleman. *M. Valerii Martialis Liber Spectaculorum*. Oxford: 2006.

Marx, Karl. "Economic and Philosophic Manuscripts of 1844." In *Karl Marx—Frederick Engels, Collected Works*. Vol. 3, 229–348. London: 1975.

———. "The Holy Family." In *Karl Marx-Frederick Engels, Collected Works*. Vol. 4, 5–211. London: 1975.

———. "Zur Kritik der Hegelschen Rechtsphilosophie." In Marx and Friedrich Engels. *Werke*, vol. 1, 378–91. Berlin: 1976. Tr. "Towards a Critique of Hegel's Philosophy of Right." In *Marx: Selected Writings*, ed. David MacLellan, 71–82. New York: 1985.

Mason, John. *A Brief History of the Pequot War*. Boston: 1736.

Materials for the History of Thomas Becket, ed. James C. Robertson. 7 vols. London: 1875–1885.

Matthew Paris. *Matthaei Parisiensis monachi sancti Albanensis Chronica majora*, ed. Henry Richard Luard. 7 vols. Rerum Britannicarum medii ævi scriptores 57. London: 1872–1883.

Matthias of Janov. *Narracio de Milico*, ed. Vlastimil Kybal. *Matthiae de Janov dicti Magister Parisiensis Regule veteris et novi testament*. Vol. 3, 358–67. Prague and Innsbruck: 1911.

———. *Vita venerabilis presbyteri Milicii, praelati iecclesiae Pragensis*, ed. J. Emler. Fontes Rerum Bohemicarum. Vol. 1, 431–6. Prague: 1873.

Mayhew, Jonathan. "What great Cause we have for Gladness and Rejoicing." In idem. *Two Discourses Delivered October 25th, 1759*. Boston: 1759.

Meinhof, Ulrike. *Die Würde des Menschen ist antastbar: Aufsätze und Polemiken*. Berlin: 1980.

Melville, Herman. "White-Jacket, or The World in a Man-of-War." In *The Writings of Herman Melville*, vol. 5. Evanston, Ill.: 1970.

Mémoires et consultations en faveur de Jeanne d'Arc par les juges du procès de rehabilitation, ed. Pierre Lanéry d'Arc. Paris 1889.

Michael the Syrian. *Chronicon*, ed. and tr. Jean-Baptiste Chabot. *Chronique de Michel le Syrien, patriarche jacobite d'Antioche, 1166–1199*. 4 vols. Paris: 1899–1910. Repr. Bruxelles: 1962.

———. *Extrait de la chronique de Michel le Syrien*, ed. Edouard Dulaurier. *Recueil des historiens des croisades, documents arméniens*, vol. 1, 305–409. Paris: 1869.

"Millerism." *American Journal of Insanity* 1, 3 (1845): 249–53.

Monluc, Blaise de. *Commentaires de Blaise de Monluc 1521–1576*, ed. Paul Courteault. 2 vols. Paris: 1911–1913. Rev. ed. Paris: 1964.

Montreuil, Cousinot de. *Chronique de la Pucelle*, ed. Auguste Vallet de Viriville. Paris: 1859.

Montaigne, Michel de. *Essais*, ed. Pierre Villey. Paris: 1988.

Montesquieu. *L'Esprit des Lois*. In Montesquieu. *Œuvres complètes*. Vol. 2. Paris: 1979.

Moray, B. de, and Armand Bénet. *Procès-verbal fait pour délivrer une fille possédée par le malin esprit à Louviers. Publié . . . par Armand Bénet . . . précédé d'une introduction par B. de Moray*. Paris: 1883.

Mulot, M. *Discours sur la liberté, prononcé à l'occasion de la cérémonie de la bénédiction des drapeaux du district de Saint-Nicolas du Chardonnet dans l'église paroissiale de ce nom, le mercredi 2 septembre 1789*. Paris: 1789.

Müntzer, Thomas. *Revelation and Revolution: Basic Writings of Thomas Müntzer*, ed. and tr. Michael G. Baylor. Bethlehem, Pa.: 1993.

————. *Thomas Müntzer: Schriften und Briefe*, ed. Günther Frantz. Quellen und Forschungen zur Reformationsgeschichte 33. Gütersloh: 1968.

Nejedlý, Zdeněk. *Dějiny husitského zpěvu za válek husitských* [The history of song during the Hussite War]. Prague: 1913.

Nicolas of Lyra. *Nicholas of Lyra's Apocalypse Commentary*, tr. Philip D. Krey. Kalamazoo, Mich.: 1997.

————. *Postilla in Biblia sacra cum Glossa ordinaria*. 6 vols. Antwerp: 1617.

Old Czech Chronicle, ed. František Palacký. Scriptores Rerum Bohemicarum. Vol. 3, 1–466. Prague: 1829.

O'Keefe, Henry E. "A word on the Church and the New Possessions." *Catholic World* 78 (December 1898): 319–22.

Opser de Wyl, Joachim. *Deux lettres de couvent à couvent écrites de Paris, pendant le massacre de la Saint-Barthélemy (le jour même et le surlendemain 25 et 26 août) par Joachim Opser de Wyl*, ed. Henri Martin. *Bulletin de la Société de l'Histoire du Protestantisme Français* 8 (1852): 284–94.

Origen. *Contra Celsum*, ed. Marcel Borret. *Contre Celse*. 4 vols. SC 132, 136, 147, 150. Paris: 1967–69.

————. *Homélies sur Josué*, ed. Annie Jaubert. SC 71. Paris: 1960.

O'Sullivan, John. "The Great Nation of Futurity." *United States Democratic Review* 6, 23 (November 1839): 426–30.

Ovid. *Fasti*, ed. T. E. Page et al. London: 1959.

Paine, Thomas. "Common Sense." (1776) In *Complete Writings of Thomas Paine*, ed. Philip S. Foner. Vol. 1, 1–46. New York: 1945.

————. "Letter to the Abbé Raynal." In *Complete Writings of Thomas Paine*, ed. Philip S. Foner. Vol. 2, 211–63. New York: 1945.

Le Panegyrique adressé au Roy de la part de ses bons subjects de sa ville de Paris. Contenant un discours des vertus du Roy, et des tyrannies de la ligue, de la precellence de la Liberté Françoise souz la legitime royauté, de la difference des comportements du peuple, des conspirateurs, des innocents et de la clemence du Roy ouverte aux liguez. n.p.: 1590.

Paschasius Radbertus. *Expositio in Mattheo*, ed. Beda Paulus. 2 vols. CCCM 56–56B. Turnhout: 1984.

Pasquier, Estienne. *Écrits politiques*, ed. Dorothy Thickett. Geneva: 1966.

Pax Sigiwini archiepiscopi coloniensis, ed. Ludwig Weiland. MGH Constitutiones. Vol. 1, 602–5. Hannover: 1893.

People's Commissariat of Justice of the U.S.S.R. *Report of court proceedings in the case of the anti-Soviet "bloc of Rights and Trotskyites" . . . Moscow, March 2–13, 1938 . . .* Moscow: 1938. Russian: Narodnyĭ komissariat iustitsii SSSR. *Sudebnyĭ otchet po delu antisovetskogo "Pravo-Trotskistskogo bloka": rassmotrennomu Voennoĭ kollegieĭ Verkhovnogo Suda Soiuza SSR 2–13 marta 1938 g. po obvineniiu Bukharina N.I. . . .* Moscow: 1938.

Peter of Blois. *Passio Raginaldi principis Antiochiae*, ed. R[obert] B[urchard] C[onstantijn] Huygens. CCCM 194, 31–73. Turnhout: 2002.

Petrus Lombardus. *Libri sententiarum*, ed. Ignatius Brady. *Spicilegium Bonaventurianum*. Vols. 4–5. Grottaferrata: 1971–81.

Phillips, Wendell. *Wendell Phillips on Civil Rights and Freedom*, ed. Louis Filler. 2nd ed. Lanham, Md.: 1982.

Le pontifical romano-germanique du dixième siècle, ed. Cyrille Vogel and Reinhard Elze. Vol. 1. Vatican: 1963.

Post, Truman M. *Palingenesy: National Regeneration*. Saint Louis: 1864.

Přibram, Jan. *Život kněží táborských*, ed. Josef Macek. *Ktož jsú boží bojovníci*, 262–309. Prague: 1951.

Primasius. *Commentarius in Apocalypsin*, ed. Arthur White Adams. CCSL 92. Turnhout: 1985.

Procès de condamnation et de réhabilitation de Jeanne d'Arc, dite la Pucelle, ed. Jules Quicherat. 5 vols. Paris: 1841–1849.

Procès en nullité de la condamnation de Jeanne d'Arc, ed. Pierre Duparc. 5 vols. Paris: 1977–1989.

Prudentius. *Peristephanon: Le livre des couronnes*, ed. Maurice Lavarenne = idem, *Œuvres*. Vol. 4. Paris: 1963.

———. *Psychomachie*, ed. Maurice Lavarenne. Paris: 1948.

Pseudo-Ioachim. *Abbatis Ioachim Divina prorsus in Ieremiam Prophetam Interpretatio*. Cologne: Lodovicum Alectorium, 1577.

Quintilian. *De Institutione oratoria*, ed. Jean Cousin. *Quintillien, Institution Oratoire*. 7 vols. Paris: 1975–1980.

Qutb, Sayyid. *Milestones*, tr. International Islamic Federation of Student Organizations. Stuttgart: 1978.

Ranke, Leopold von. *Französische Geschichte (1852–61)*. 2 vols. Rev. ed. Willy Andreas. Wiesbaden and Berlin: 1957.

Redpath, James, ed. *Echoes of Harper's Ferry*. Boston: 1860.

Renan, Ernest. *Histoire des origines du Christianisme*. Vol. 4, *L'Antéchrist*. Paris: 1873.

Responce du menu peuple a la declaration de Henry, par la grace de Dieu, autant Roy de France que de Polongne, semee ces jours passez par les politiques de Paris. s.l.: 1589.

Revelations from the Russian Archives, ed. Diane P. Koenker and Ronald D. Bachman. Washington, D.C.: 1997.

Richer of Senones. *Gesta Senoniensis ecclesie*, ed. Georg Waitz. MGH Scriptores 25, 249–345. Hannover: 1880.

Richter, Paul. "General Apologizes for Remarks on Islam, Says He's 'No Zealot'." *Los Angeles Times* (October 18, 2003): A11.

Robert the Monk. *Historia Iherosolimitiana*. In *Recueil des historiens des croisades, historiens occidentaux*. Vol. 3, 717–882. Paris: 1866.

Robespierre, Maximilien de. *Œuvres de Maximilien Robespierre*, ed. Marc Bouloiseau, Jean Dautry, Georges Lefebvre, Albert Soboul et al. 11 vols. Rev. ed. Ivry: 2000.

Robinson, James. *Justification of separation from the Church of England*. Amsterdam: 1610.

Rothmann, Bernhard. *Die Schriften Bernhard Rothmanns*, ed. Robert Stupperich. Münster: 1970.

Rousseau, Jean-Jacques. *The Social Contract and Other Later Political Writings*, ed. and tr. Victor Gourevich. Cambridge: 1997.

Rufinus. *Summa*, ed. Heinrich Singer. *Die Summa decretorum des magister Rufinus*. Paderborn: 1902.

Rutebeuf. *Rutebeuf, Œuvres complètes*, ed. Michel Zink. 2 vols. Paris: 1989–90.

Rutherford, Samuel. *Lex, Rex: The Law and the Prince: A Dispute for the Just Prerogative of King and People*. London: 1644.

Sackur, Ernst. *Sibyllinische Texte und Forschungen: Pseudo-Methodius, Adso, und die tiburtinische Sibylle*. Halle: 1898.

Saint-Just, Louis Antoine de. *Discours*, ed. Albert Soboul. *Saint-Just: Discours et Rapports*. Paris: 1988.

Salimbene de Adam. *Cronica*, rev. ed. Giuseppe Scalia. CCCM 125–125A. 2 vols. Turnhout: 1998–1999.

Scalia, Giuseppe. "Il carme Pisano sull' impresa contro i Saraceni del 1087." In *Studi di Filologia Romanza: Scritti in onore di Silvio Pellegrini*, 1–63. Padua: 1971.

Scott, Thomas, Rev. *The comprehensive commentary on the Holy Bible; containing . . . Matthew Henry's Commentary, condensed, but retaining the most useful thoughts; the practical observations of Rev. Thomas Scott, D.D. with extensive . . . notes selected from Scott, Doddridge, Gill, Adam Clarke, Patrick, Poole, Lowth, Burder, Harmer, Calmet, Stuart, Robinson, Bush, Rosenmueller, Bloomfield, and many other writers on the Scriptures . . .* 5 vols. Brattleboro, Mass.: 1838.

The Scroll of the War of the Sons of Light Against the Sons of Darkness, ed. Yigael Yadin, tr. Batya Rabin and Chaim Rabin. Oxford: 1962.

Seneca. *De beneficiis*, ed. François Préchac. *Sénèque: Des bienfaits*. 2 vols. Paris: 1961.

Servin, Louis. *Recueil des poincts principaux de la harangue faicte a l'ouverture du Parlement apres le iour Sainct Martin, 1589. Par M. L. Seruain Advocat du Roy.* Tours: 1589.

Shaftesbury, Anthony Ashley-Cooper, Third Earl of. *Anthony Ashley Cooper, Third Earl of Shaftesbury, Standard Edition*, ed. Gerd Hemmerich and Wolfram Benda. 11 vols. Stuttgart: 1981–2008.

———. *A Letter Concerning Enthusiasm, to My Lord ******. London: 1708.

Shepard, Thomas. *Theses Sabbaticae*. London: 1655.

Sigebert of Gembloux. *Leodicensium epistola adversus Paschalem papam*, ed. Ernst Sackur. MGH Libelli de lite 2, 449–64. Rev. ed. Berlin: 1955.

Smith, Henry Boynton. "The Problem of the Philosophy of History." Phi Beta Kappa address at Yale College, 27 July, 1853. Philadelphia: 1854.

La société des Jacobins. Recueil de documents pour l'histoire du Club des Jacobins de Paris, 5 Apr. 1794, ed. François-Alphonse Aulard. Vol. 6. Paris: 1897.

The Song of Roland, ed. Glyn Burgess. London: 1990.

Sorbin, Arnaud. *Histoire contenant un abregé de la vie, mœurs et vertus du roi très-chrétien et débonnaire Charles IX*. Paris: 1674.

Spanheim, Friedrich. *De origine, progressu, sectis, nominibus, et dogmatibus Anabaptistarum = Disputationum extraordinariarum Anti-Anabapisticarum, pars 1 . Disputationum Theologicarum Miscellanearum Pars Prima*. Geneva, Pierre Chouët: 1652.

Spinoza, Baruch. *Tractatus Theologico-Politicus*, ed. R. H. M. Elwes. Tr. *A Theologico-Political Treatise*. New York: 1951.

Suárez, Francisco. *Opus de virtute et statu religionis*, ed. Michel André. *Opera Omnia*. Vol. 13. Paris: 1859.

Syms, Christofer. *The Swords apology and necessity in the act of Reformation*. London: 1644.

Tacitus. *The Annals and the Histories*, tr. Moses Haddas et al. Rev. ed. New York: 2003.

Tertullian. *Opera*, ed. Eligius Dekkers, Alois Gerlo et al. 2 vols. CCSL 1–2. Turnhout: 1954, 1986.

———. *Scorpiace*, ed. August Reifferscheid and Georg Wissowa. Rev. Radbod Willems. CCSL 2. Turnhout: 1954.

———. *Les spectacles*, ed. Marie Turcan. SC 332. Paris

Thomas Aquinas. *Summa Theologiae*. Rome: 1888–1906 = *Sancti Thomae de Aquino Opera Omnia*. Vols. 4–12.

Thurloe, John, esq. *A collection of the state papers of John Thurloe, esq.* 7 vols. London: 1742.

Tiburtine Sibyl. *Explanatio somnii,* ed. Ernst Sackur. *Sibyllinische Texte und Forschungen: Pseudo-Methodius, Adso, und die tiburtinische Sibylle.* Halle: 1898.

Tocqueville, Alexis de. *L'Ancien régime et la revolution.* Rev. ed. Paris: 1960.

———. *De la démocratie en Amérique,* ed. James T. Schleifer and Jean-Claude Lambert. Paris: 1986.

Tudebode, Petrus. *Historia de Hierosolymitano itinere,* ed. John Hugh Hill and Laurita L. Hill. Documents relatifs à l'histoire des croisades 12. Paris: 1977.

Turpini Historia Karoli Magni et Rotholandi, ed. Ferdinand Castets. Paris: 1880.

Tyng, S[tephen] H[igginson]. "Preface [to Hollis Read]." In Hollis Read, *The Coming Crisis of the World: or, The Great Battle and Golden Age,* v–viii. Columbus, Ohio: 1861.

Underhill, John. *Newes from America; or, a new and experimentall discoverie of New England . . .* London: 1638.

"The Union, the Constitution, and Slavery." *American Quarterly Church Review* (January 1864): 541–75.

Urbach, Johannes. *Utrum fideles,* ed. Weise, *Traktate,* 298–300.

Urkundliche Beiträge zur Geschichte des Hussitenkrieges vom Jahre 1419 an, ed. František Palacký. 2 vols. Prague: 1873.

Vergil. *The Aeneid,* tr. Robert Fitzgerald. New York: 1990.

La victoire obtenue par Monseigneur le Duc de Mayenne . . . Troyes: 1589. Paris BNF Réserve des Imprimés La25.24.

Voltaire. *Dictionnaire philosophique.* t. 4. Paris: 1829, ed. Adrien-Jean-Quentin Beuchot = *Œuvres de Voltaire, avec notes, préfaces, avertissemens, remarques historiques et littéraires.* 72 t. in 59 vols. Paris: 1829–1840. Tome 33.

———. *Dictionnaire philosophique,* ed. Raymond Naves and Julien Benda. Paris: 1967.

———. *Essai sur les mœurs et l'esprit des nations,* ed. Bruno Bernard et al. *Les œuvres complètes de Voltaire,* vol. 22. Oxford: 2009.

———. *Philosophical Dictionary,* tr. Peter Gay. New York: 1962.

———. *Questions sur l'Encyclopédie.* Geneva: 1771.

Wesley, John. *Explanatory Notes Upon the New Testament.* 2 vols. 3rd American ed. New York: 1812.

"Whom God honours." *The Presbyterian* 33, 3 (January 17, 1863): 9.

Willibald. *Vitae sancti Bonifatii archiepiscopi Moguntini,* ed. Wilhelm Levison. MGH Sriptores rer. germ. in u. s. 57. Hannover: 1905.

Winand von Steeg. *De laude concilii Constanciensis,* ed. Heinrich Finke. *Acta Concilii Constanciensis,* 4: 753–55. Münster: 1928.

Wipo. *Gesta Chuonradi,* ed. Harry Bresslau. SS rer. Germ. 61. Hanover: 1915. Repr. 1977.

Woodhouse, A[rthur] S[utherland] P[igott]. *Puritanism and Liberty, being the Army Debates (1647–9) from the Clarke Manuscripts with supplementary documents.* Chicago: 1951. 3rd ed. London: 1986.

Wyclif, John. *On the seven deadly sins,* ed. Thomas Arnold. *Selected Works of John Wyclif.* Vol. 3, 119–67. Oxford: 1871.

MANUSCRIPTS CONSULTED

Paris BNF Ms. français 789. Anonymous. *Roman de Judas Machabee.*
Paris BNF Ms. français 21306.
Paris BNF Ms. Latin 4806. Anonymous. *Exhortatio ad proceres regni.*
Paris BNF Ms. Latin 5132. Raymond d'Aguilers. *Historia Francorum qui ceperunt Iherusalem.*
Paris BNF Latin 5513. Baldric, *Historia Jerosolimitana* (version G).
Vienna ÖNB 4749, fols. 37r-92r. Jan of Příbram. *Contra articulos picardorum* = "Isti articuli sunt Picardorum . . . damnati et reprobati."
Vienna ÖNB 4971, fol. 51. Winand von Steeg. *De laude concilii Constanciensis.*

ONLINE SOURCES

Associated Press. "Rumsfeld Chides Europeans for Lack of 'Vision'," January 22, 2003, *Fox News* (June 11, 2003). http://www.foxnews.com/story/2003/06/11/rumsfeld-chides-europeans-for-lack-vision/.
"Bible Belt Missionaries Set Out for a War for Souls in Iraq." *The Telegraph*, December 27, 2003. http://www.telegraph.co.uk/news/worldnews/northamerica/usa/1450296/Bible-Belt-missionaries-set-out-on-a-war-for-souls-in-Iraq.html.
Burleigh, Michael. "The Baader-Meinhof Complex: Review." *The Telegraph*, December 8, 2008. http://www.telegraph.co.uk/culture/books/non_fictionreviews/3702548/The-Baader-Meinhof-Complex-by-Stefan-Aust-review.html.
Bush, George W. "Bush Says It Is Time for Action." CNN.com/U.S. (November 6, 2001).
"Remarks by the President at National Republican Congressional Committee Dinner." *Free Library* (Mar. 13, 2008). http://www.thefreelibrary.com/Remarks by the President at National Republican Congressional . . . -a0176620768. Initially published by *Business Wire.*
———. "Speech Aboard the USS *Abraham Lincoln*." *Washington Post*, May 1, 2003.
———. "State of the Union." January 29, 2002. http://georgewbush-whitehouse.archives.gov/news/releases/2002/01/20020129-11.html.
———. "State of the Union." January 28, 2003. http://georgewbush-whitehouse.archives.gov/news/releases/2003/01/20030128-19.html.
———. "State of the Union." January 20, 2004. http://georgewbush-whitehouse.archives.gov/news/releases/2004/01/20040120-7.html.
Cottret, Monique. "1789–1791: Triomphe ou échec de la minorité janséniste?" *Rives Mediterranéennes* 14 (2003).
Department of Defense, Office of the Inspector General. Case H03L89967206, August 5, 2004. "Alleged Improprieties Related to Public Speaking: Lieutenant-General William G. Boykin, U.S. Army Deputy Under-Secretary of Defense for Intelligence."
Kix, Paul. "The Truth About Suicide Bombers." *Boston Globe*, December 5, 2010.
Marx, Karl, and Friedrich Engels. *Collected Works.* 50 vols. London: 1975–2005. http://marxists.org/archive/marx/works/cw/index.htm
———. *Selected Works.* 3 vols. Moscow: 1969. http://marxists.org/archive/marx/works/sw/index.htm.

Nitze, Paul. National Security Council 68. www.fas.org/irp/offdocs/nsc-hst/nsc-68.htm.

"Reflections After Desert Storm." *The Forerunner*, December 22, 2007.

U.S. House of Representatives, Committee on Oversight and Government Reform (Harry Waxman, chair). "Misleading Information from the Battlefield: The Tillman and Lynch Episodes," July 14, 2008. http://oversight-archive.waxman.house.gov/documents/20080714111050.pdf.

OTHER

Boykin, William G., Lieutenant-General. Speech at the First Baptist Broken Arrow Church. City, Broken Arrow, Oklahoma. June 30, 2002. Videotape.

———. Speech at the Good Shepherd Church. Sandy, Oregon. June 21, 2003. Audiotape and videotape.

Fra Angelico. *The Martyrdom of Cosmas and Damian*. Munich. Alte Pinakothek.

Jackson, Peter, dir. *The Lord of the Rings III: The Return of the King*. New Line Cinema: 2003.

Middletown Evangelical radio WIHS FM 104.9, February 8, 2005, circa 11:00.

Sproul, R. C. "Sermon." February 28, 2005, 10:00. WIHS FM 104.9 Middletown, Conn.

Rogers, Judy Belcher. *Desert Storm*. http://judylyrics.klsoaps.com/SU.html.

SECONDARY WORKS

Affeldt, Werner. *Die weltliche Gewalt in der Paulus-Exegese*. Götingen: 1969.

Albanese, Catherine L. *America: Religions and Religion*. 5th ed. Belmont, Calif.: 2012.

Allen, Priscilla. "White-Jacket: Melville and the Man-of-War Microcosm." *American Quarterly* 25, 1 (1973): 32–47.

Alphandéry, Paul and Alphonse Dupront. *La chrétienté et l'idée de croisade*. Paris: 1954–1959. Rev. ed. 1995.

Althoff, Gerd. "Das Privileg der *deditio*." Repr. in idem, *Spielregeln der Politik im Mittelalter: Kommunikation in Frieden und Fehde*, 99–125. Darmstadt: 1997.

———. *Spielregeln der Politik in Mittelalter: Kommunikation in Frieden und Fehde*. Darmstadt: 1997.

Altman, Charles F. "Two Types of Opposition and the Structure of Latin Saints' Lives." *Medievalia et Humanistica* n.s. 6 (1975): 1–11.

Ames, Christine Caldwell. *Righteous Persecution: Inquisition, Dominicans and Christianity in the Middle Ages*. Philadelphia: 2009.

Anderson, Fred and Andrew Cayton. *The Dominion of War: Empire and Liberty in North America, 1500–2000*. New York: 2005.

Appleby, R. Scott. *The Ambivalence of the Sacred: Religion, Violence, and Reconciliation*. Oxford: 2000.

———. "History in the Fundamentalist Imagination." *Journal of American History* 89, 2 (2012): 498–511.

Arendt, Hannah. *On Violence*. New York: 1969, 1970.

Arkin, William. "The Pentagon Unleashes a Holy Warrior: A Christian Extremist in a High Defense Post Can Only Set Back the U.S. Approach to the Muslim World." *Los Angeles Times* (October 17, 2003): B17.

Arrizabalaga, Jon. "Facing the Black Death: Perceptions and Reactions of University Medical Practitioners." In *Practical Medicine from Salerno to the Black Death*, ed. Luis Garcia-Ballester, 237–88. Cambridge: 1994.

Asad, Talal. *Formations of the Secular: Christianity, Islam, Modernity.* Stanford: 2003.

———. "Medieval Heresy: An Anthropological View." *Social History* 11, 3 (1986): 345–62.

Assmann, Jan. *Die mosaische Unterscheidung oder der Preis des Monotheismus.* Munich: 2003. Tr. *The Price of Monotheism.* Stanford, Calif.: 2010.

———. "Recht und Gerechtigkeit als Generatoren von Geschichte." In *Die Weltgeschichte—das Weltgericht?* ed. Rüdiger Bubner and Walter Mesch, 296–311. Stuttgart: 2000.

Audibert, Adrien. *Études sur l'histoire du droit romain.* Vol. 1. *La folie et la prodigalité.* Paris: 1892.

Auerbach, Erich. "Figura." Repr. in idem. *Gesammelte Aufsätze zur romanischen Philologie,* 55–92. Bern and Munich: 1967.

Auffarth, Christoph. "Himmlisches und irdisches Jerusalem: Ein Religionswissenschaftlicher Versuch zur 'Kreuzzugseschatologie'." *Zeitschrift für Religionswissenschaft* 1 (1993): 25–49, 91–118.

———. "Ritter und Arme auf dem Ersten Kreuzzug: Zum Problem Herrschaft und Religion ausgehend von Raymond von Aguilers." *Saeculum* 40 (1989): 39–55.

Aurell, Martin. *Des chrétiens contre les croisades, XIIe–XIIIe siècle.* Paris: 2013.

———. "Eschatologie, spiritualité et politique dans la confédération catalano-aragonaise (1282–1412)." In *Fin du monde et signes des temps: Visionnaires et prophètes en France méridionale (fin XIIIe–début XVe siècle),* ed. Marie-Humbert Vicaire = *Cahiers de Fanjeaux* 27, 191–235. Toulouse: 1992.

Aust, Stephen. *Der Baader-Meinhof Komplex.* 3rd ed. Hamburg: 2008. Abridged tr. *The Baader-Meinhof Complex.* London: 2008.

Badiou, Alain. *Le siècle.* Paris: 2005.

Baecque, Antoine de. *Le corps de l'histoire: Métaphores et politique (1770–1800).* Paris: 1993.

———. *La gloire et l'effroi: Sept morts sous la Terreur.* Paris: 1997. Tr. *Glory and Terror.* London: 2001.

———. "The Trajectory of a Wound: From Corruption to Regeneration; The Brave Locksmith Geoffroy, Herald of the Great Terror." In *The French Revolution and the Creation of Modern Political Culture,* ed. Keith M. Baker. Vol. 4. *The Terror,* 157–75. Oxford: 1994.

Bähr, Andreas. "Die Furcht vor dem Leviathan: Furcht und Liebe in der politischen Theorie des Thomas Hobbes." *Saeculum* 61, 1 (2011): 73–97.

Bailyn, Bernard. *The Ideological Origins of the American Revolution.* Cambridge, Mass.: 1967.

Bainton, Roland H. *Christian Attitudes Toward War and Peace: A Historical Survey and Critical Re-Evaluation.* New York: 1960.

Baker, Keith Michael. "Inventing the French Revolution." In *Inventing the French Revolution: Essays on French Political Culture in the Eighteenth Century,* ed. idem, 203–23 and 345–49. Cambridge: 1990.

Balz, Hanno. *Von Terroristen, Sympathisanten und dem starken Staat: Die öffentlichen Debatte über die RAF in den 70er Jahren.* Frankfurt: 2008.

Baraz, Daniel. *Medieval Cruelty: Changing Perceptions, Late Antiquity to the Early Modern Period.* Ithaca, N.Y.: 2003.

Barber, Malcolm. "The Crusade of the Shepherds in 1251." In *Proceedings of the Tenth Annual Meeting of the Western Society for French History, 1982*, ed. Hohn F. Sweets, 1–23. Lawrence, Kan.: 1984.

———. *The New Knighthood*. Cambridge: 1994.

———. "The Pastoureaux of 1320." *Journal of Ecclesiastical History* 32 (1981): 143–66.

Barrows, Susanna. *Distorting Mirrors: Visions of the Crowd in Late Nineteenth-Century France*. New Haven, Conn.: 1981.

Barth, Fredrik. *Process and Form in Social Life = Selected Essays of Fredrik Barth*, vol. 1, 47–60. London: 1981.

Barthélemy, Dominique. "The Peace of God and the Bishops at War in the Gallic Lands from the Late Tenth to the Early Twelfth Century." *Anglo-Norman Studies* 32 (2009): 1–23.

Baskerville, Stephen. *Peace but a Sword: The Political Theology of the English Revolution*. London: 1993.

Beaune, Colette. *Jeanne d'Arc*. Paris: 2004.

———. *Naissance de la nation France*. Paris: 1985. Tr. *The Birth of an Ideology*. Berkeley, Calif.: 1991.

Becker, Annette. *La guerre et la foi: De la mort à la mémoire, 1914–1930*. Paris: 1994.

Becker, Carl L. *The Heavenly City of the Eighteenth-Century Philosophers*. New Haven, Conn.: 1932.

Becker, Hans-Jürgen. "Die Stellung des kanonistischen Rechts zu den Andersgläubigen: Heiden, Juden und Ketzer." In *Wechselseitige Wahrnehmung der Religionen im Spätmittelalter und in der Frühen Neuzeit*, ed. Ludger Grenzman et al, 101–23. Berlin: 2009.

Becker, Jillian. *Hitler's Children: The Story of the Baader-Meinhof Terrorist Gang*. Philadelphia: 1977.

Beinart, Haim. *The Expulsion of the Jews from Spain*. Jerusalem: 1994. Tr. Oxford: 2002.

Bell, David. *The First Total War: Napoleon's Europe and the Birth of Warfare as We Know It*. Boston: 2007.

Bell, Rudolph. *Holy Anorexia*. Chicago: 1985.

Benedict, Philip. *Rouen During the Wars of Religion*. Cambridge: 1981.

Benjamin, Walter. "Critique of Violence." Tr. Peter Demetz. In Walter Benjamin, *Reflections*, 277–300. New York: 1978. Orig. *Archiv für Sozialwissenschaft und Sozialpolitik* 47 (1920–1921): 809–32.

Bercovich, Sacvan. *The American Jeremiad*. Madison, Wis.: 1978.

Berens, John F. *Providence and Patriotism in Early America, 1640–1815*. Charlottesville, Va.: 1978.

Bernheim, Ernst. *Mittelalterliche Zeitanschauungen in ihrem Einfluss auf Politik und Geschichtsschreibung*, Vol. 1: *Die Zeitanschauungen: Die Augustinischen Ideen—Antichrist und Friedenfürst—Regnum und Sacerdotium*. Tübingen: 1918.

Bhabha, Homi K. "Foreword: Framing Fanon." To Franz Fanon, *Wretched of the Earth*, vii-xli. New York: 2004.

Billington, James H. *Fire in the Minds of Men: Origins of the Revolutionary Faith*. New York: 1980.

Binder, Frederick Moore. "James Buchanan: Jacksonian Expansionist." *The Historian* 55, 1 (1992): 69–84.

Binion, Rudolph. *Hitler Among the Germans*. New York: 1976.

Bird, Jessalynn. "Crusade and Conversion After the Fourth Lateran Council (1215): Oliver of Paderborn's and James of Vitry's Missions to Muslims Reconsidered." *Essays in Medieval Studies* 21 (2005): 23–47.

———. "Heresy, Crusade, and Reform in the Circle of Peter the Chanter, c. 1187–c. 1240." D.Phil. thesis Oxford, 2001.

———. "Paris Masters and the Justification of the Albigensian Crusade." *Crusades* 6 (2007): 117–55.

———. "Reform or Crusade? Anti-Usury and Crusade Preaching During the Pontificate of Innocent III." In *Pope Innocent III and His World*, ed. John Moore, 165–85. London: 1999.

Blickle, Peter. *The Revolution of 1525: The German Peasants' War from a New Perspective*. Tr. Baltimore: 1985.

Bloch, Ernst. *Atheismus im Christentum: Zur Religion des Exodus und des Reichs*. Frankfurt: 1968.

———. "Bucharins Schlusswort." *Die neue Weltbühne* (May 5, 1938): 558–63. Repr. in *Viele Kammern im Welthaus*, ed. Friedrich Dieckmann and Jürgen Teller, 360–67. Frankfurt: 1994.

———. *Erbschaft dieser Zeit = Gesamtausgabe der Werke*. Vol. 4. Zürich: 1935. Tr. *Heritage of Our Times*. Oxford: 1991.

———. *Geist der Utopie*. Munich: 1918.

———. *Thomas Müntzer als Theologe der Revolution*. Munich: 1927. Rev. ed. Berlin: 1960.

Bloch, Marc. *Apologie pour l'histoire ou le métier d'historien*. Preface by Jacques Le Goff. Paris: 1993.

Bloch, Ruth H. *Visionary Republic: Millennial Themes in American Thought, 1756–1800*. Cambridge: 1985.

Blum, Carol. *Rousseau and the Republic of Virtue: The Language of Politics in the French Revolution*. Ithaca, N.Y.: 1986.

Blumenberg, Hans. *The Legitimacy of the Modern Age*. Tr. Cambridge, Mass: 1985.

Blumenthal, Uta-Renate. *The Investiture Controversy*. Tr. Philadelphia: 1988.

———. *Pope Gregory VII, 1073–1085*. Ger. orig. Darmstadt: 2001.

Bohrmann, Monette. *Flavius Josèphe, les Zélotes et Yavné: Pour une relecture de la "Guerre des Juifs."* Berne: 1989.

Bonnaud-Delamare, Roger. *L'idée de paix à l'époque carolingienne*. Paris: 1939.

Bonner, Michael. *Jihad in Islamic History: Doctrines and Practices*. Princeton, N.J.: 2008.

Boockmann, Hermann. *Johannes Falkenberg: Der deutschen Orden und die polnische Politik: Untersuchungen zur politischen Theorie des späteren Mittelalters: Mit einem Anhang: Die Satira des Johannes Falkenberg*. Göttingen: 1985.

Bossy, John. *Christianity in the West, 1400–1700*. Oxford: 1985.

Boureau, Alain. *Le simple corps du roi: L'impossible sacralité des souverains français, XVe–XVIIe siècles*. Paris: 1988.

Bowersock, Glenn. *Martyrdom and Rome*. Cambridge: 1995.

Bracher, Karl-Dietrich. *Schlüsselwörter in der Geschichte: Mit einer Betrachtung zum Totalitarismusproblem*. Düsseldorf: 1978.

Brachlow, Stephen. *The Communion of Saints: Radical Puritan and Separatist Ideology, 1570–1625*. Oxford: 1989.

Brady, Thomas A. *German Histories in the Age of Reformations, 1400–1650*. Cambridge: 2009.

Brandes, Wilhelm. "*Tempora periculosa sunt*. Eschatologisches im Vorfeld der Kaiserkrönung Karls des Großen." In *Das Frankfurter Konzil von 794: Kristallisationspunkt karolingischer Kultur*, ed. Rainer Berndt. Vol. 1, 49–79. Mainz: 1997.

Brandon, S. G. F. *Jesus and the Zealots: A Study of the Political Factor in Primitive Christianity*. Manchester: 1967.

Brekus, Catherine A. and W. Clark Gilpin, eds. *American Christianities: A History of Dominance and Diversity*. Chapel Hill, N.C.: 2011.

Brendle, Franz and Anton Schindling. "Religionskriege in der frühen Neuzeit. Begriff, Wahrnehmung, Wirkmächtigkeit." In *Religionskriege im Alten Reich und in Alteuropa*, ed. Brendle and Schindling, 15–52. Münster: 2006.

Bresc, Henri. "Les historiens de la croisade: Guerre sainte, justice et paix." *Mélanges de l'École Française de Rome* 115, 2 (2003): 727–53.

Brisson, Jean-Paul. *Autonomisme et christianisme dans l'Afrique romaine de Septime Sévère à l'invasion vandale*. Paris: 1958.

Britt, Brian M. "Curses Left and Right: Hate Speech and the Biblical Tradition." *Journal of the American Academy of Religion* 78, 3 (2010): 633–61.

Brown, Peter. *Body and Society: Men, Women and Sexual Renunciation in Early Christianity*. New York: 1988.

———. *The Cult of the Saints: Its Rise and Function in Late Antiquity*. Chicago: 1981.

———. "Religious Coercion in the Later Roman Empire: The Case of North Africa." *History* 48 (1963): 283–305.

———. "Saint Augustine's Attitude to Religious Coercion." *Journal of Roman Studies* 54 (1964): 107–16.

Browning, Christopher R. *Ordinary Men: Reserve Police Battalion 101 and the Final Solution in Poland*. Rev. amplified ed. New York: 1998.

Brundage, James. "Adhémar of Puy: The Bishop and His Critics." *Speculum* 34, 2 (1959): 201–12.

———. "The Crusader's Wife: A Canonistic Quandary." Repr. in idem, *The Crusades, Holy War and Canon Law*. Aldershot: 1991.

———. *Medieval Canon Law and the Crusader*. London: 1969.

Brunner, Otto. *Land und Herrschaft: Grundfragen der territorialen Verfassungsgeschichte Südostdeutschlands im Mittelalter*. Baden: 1938. Tr. H. Howard Kaminsky and James van Horn Melton, *Land and Lordship: Structures of Governance in Medieval Austria*. Philadelphia: 1992.

Bruun, Mette Birkedal. "Bernard of Clairvaux and the Landscape of Salvation." In *A Companion to Bernard of Clairvaux*, ed. eadem, 249–78. Leiden: 2011.

Buc, Philippe. *L'ambiguïté du Livre: Prince, pouvoir et peuple dans les commentaires de la Bible*. Paris: 1994.

———. "The Book of Kings: Nicholas of Lyra's Mirror of Princes." In *Nicholas of Lyra: The Senses of Scripture*, ed. Philip D. W. Krey and Lesley Smith, 83–109. Leiden: 2000.

———. *The Dangers of Ritual: Between Early Medieval Texts and Social Scientific Theory*. Princeton, N.J.: 2001.

———. *L'empreinte du Moyen Age: La guerre sainte*. Avignon: 2012.

———. "Exégèse et pensée politique: Radulphus Niger (vers 1190) et Nicolas de Lyre (vers 1330)." In *Représentation, pouvoir et royauté à la fin du Moyen Age*, ed. Joël Blanchard, 145–64. Paris: 1995.

———. "Exégèse et violence dans la tradition occidentale." *Annali di Storia Moderna e Contemporanea* 16 (2010): 131–44.

———. "Die Krise des Reiches unter Heinrich IV., mit und ohne Spielregeln." In *Spielregeln der Mächtigen: Mittelalterliche Politik zwischen Gewohnheit und Konvention*, ed. Claudia Garnier and Hermann Kamp, 43–75. Darmstadt: 2010.

———. "Martyre et ritualité dans l'antiquité tardive: Horizons de l'écriture médiévale des rituels." *Annales, Histoire, Sciences Sociales* 52, 1 (1997): 63–92.

————. "Pouvoir royal et commentaires de la Bible (1150–1350)." *Annales, Histoire, Sciences Sociales* 44, 3 (1989): 691–713.

————. "Religion, Coercion and Violence in Medieval Ritual." In *State, Power and Violence*, vol. 2: *Rituals of Power and Consent*, ed. Bernd Schneidmüller, 157–70. Wiesbaden: 2010.

————. "Religion, violence, pouvoir, vers 1050–vers 1500: doute et contrainte." Forthcoming in *Formes de convivència a la baixa edat mitjana*, ed. Flocel Sabaté Curull. Lleida/Lerida: 2015.

————. "Some Thoughts on the Christian Theology of Violence, Medieval and Modern, from the Middle Ages to the French Revolution." *Rivista di Storia dell Cristianesimo* 5, 1 (2008): 9–28.

————. "La vengeance de Dieu: De l'exégèse patristique à la réforme ecclésiastique et à la première croisade." In *La vengeance, 400–1200*, ed. Dominique Barthélemy, François Bougard, and Régine Le Jean, 451–86. Collection de l'École Française de Rome 357. Rome: 2006.

Bull, Marcus. *Knightly Piety and the Lay Response to the First Crusade: The Limousin and Gascony, c. 970–c.1130*. Oxford: 1993.

Burgess, Glenn. "The English Regicides and the Legitimation of Political Violence." In *Terror: From Tyrannicide to Terrorism*, ed. Michael T. Davis and Brett Bowden, 56–76. St. Lucia, Queensland: 2008.

————. "Introduction: Religion and the Historiography of the English Civil War." In *England's War of Religion, Revisited*, ed. Charles Pryor and idem, 1–25. Farnham: 2011.

Burleigh, Michael. *Sacred Causes: Religion and Politics from the European Dictators to Al-Quaeda*. New York: 2006.

Burschel, Peter. *Sterben und Unsterblichkeit: Zur Kultur des Martyriums in der frühen Neuzeit*. Munich: 2004.

Butler, Jon. *Awash in a Sea of Faith. Christianizing the American People*. Cambridge, Mass.: 1990.

————. "Enthusiasm Described and Decried: The Great Awakening as Interpretive Fiction." *Journal of American History* 69 (1982): 305–25.

Cabanès, Augustin and Lucien Nass. *La névrose révolutionnaire*. 2nd ed. 2 vols. Paris: 1924.

Cacciola, Nancy. *Discerning Spirits: Divine and Demonic Possession in the Middle Ages*. Ithaca, N.Y.: 2003.

Camus, Albert. *L'homme révolté*. 1951. 2nd ed. Paris: 1958

Capp, Bernard S. *The Fifth Monarchy Men: A Study in Seventeenth-Century English Millenarianism*. Totowa, N.J.: 1971.

————. "Transplanting the Holy Lands: Diggers, Fifth Monarchists, and the New Israel." In *The Holy Land, Holy Lands, and Christian History*, ed. Robert N. Swanson, 288–98. Studies in Church History 36. Woodbridge: 2000.

Carrasco, Davíd. *City of Sacrifice: The Aztec Empire and the Role of Violence in Civilization*. Boston: 1999.

Carwardine, Richard W. *Evangelicals and Politics in Antebellum America*. New Haven: 1993.

Casanova, José. *Public Religions in the Modern World*. Chicago: 1994.

————. "Secularization Revisited: A Reply to Talal Asad." In *Powers of the Secular Modern: Talal Asad and his Interlocutors*, ed. David Scott and Charles Hirschkind, eds., 12–30. Stanford: 2006.

Caspary, Gerard. *Politics and Exegesis: Origen and the Two Swords*. Berkeley, Calif.: 1979.

Cave, Alfred A. "Canaanites in a Promised Land: The American Indian and the Providential Theory of Empire." *American Indian Quarterly* 12, 4 (1988): 277–97.

————. *The Pequot War*. Amherst, Mass.: 1996.

Chakrabarty, Dipesh. *Provincializing Europe: Postcolonial Thought and Historical Thought*. Rev. ed. Princeton, N.J.: 2007.

Chazan, Robert. *Daggers of Faith: Thirteenth-Century Christian Missionizing and Jewish Response*. Berkeley, Calif.: 1989.

Chevallier, Pierre. "Nouvelles lumières sur le fait de Jacques Clément assassin de Henri III." *Annuaire-Bulletin de la Société de l'Histoire de France* (1988): 39–66.

Chilton, Bruce. *Abraham's Curse: The Roots of Violence in Judaism, Christianity and Islam*. New York: 2008.

Christiansen, Eric. *The Northern Crusades: The Baltic and the Catholic Frontier, 1100–1525*. London: 1989.

Christie, Niall. "Religious Campaign or War of Conquest? Muslim Views of the Motives of the First Crusade." In *Noble Ideals and Bloody Realities: Warfare in the Middle Ages*, ed. idem and Maya Yazigi, 57–72. Leiden: 2006.

Chydenius, Johannes. *Medieval Institutions and the Old Testament*. Helsinki: 1965.

Clauzel, Raymond. *Études humaines: Fanatiques*. Vol. 1, *Maximilien Robespierre*. Paris: 1912.

Clebsch, William A. "Christian Interpretations of the Civil War." *Church History* 30 (1961): 212–22.

Clendinnen, Inga. *Aztecs: An Interpretation*. Cambridge: 1991.

Clénet, Louis-Marie. *Les colonnes infernales*. Paris: 1993.

Cobb, Richard. *Les armées révolutionnaires, instrument de la Terreur dans les départements, Avril 1793–Floréal An II*. 2 vols. Paris: 1961–1963.

Coffey, John. *John Goodwin and the Puritan Revolution: Religion and Intellectual Change in Seventeenth-Century England*. Woodbridge: 2006.

Cohen, Jeremy. *The Friars and the Jews: The Evolution of Medieval Anti-Judaism*. Ithaca, N.Y.: 1982.

Cohn, Norman. "Review to Rudolph Bell, *Holy Anorexia*." *New York Review of Books*, January 30, 1986.

————. *The Pursuit of the Millennium: Revolutionary Messianism in Medieval and Reformation Europe and Its Bearing on Modern Totalitarian Movements*. 1st ed. Fairlawn, N.J.: 1957; 2nd ed. New York: 1961; 3rd rev. ed. Oxford: 1970.

————. *Warrant for Genocide: The Myth of the Jewish World-Conspiracy and the Protocols of the Elders of Zion*. London: 1967.

Cole, Penny J. *The Preaching of the Crusades to the Holy Land, 1095–1270*. Cambridge, Mass.: 1990.

Coleman, Kathleen M. "Fatal Charades: Roman Executions Staged as Mythological Reenactments." *Journal of Roman Studies* 80 (1990): 44–73.

————. "Launching into History: Aquatic Displays in the Early Empire." *Journal of Roman Studies* 83 (1993): 48–74.

Coles, Roberta L. "Manifest Destiny Adapted for 1990s War Discourse: Mission and Destiny Intertwined." *Sociology of Religion* 63, 4 (2002): 403–26.

Colvin, Sarah. "Ulrike Marie Meinhof as Woman and Terrorist: Cultural Discourses of Violence and Virtue." In *Baader-Meinhof Returns: History and Cultural Memory of German Left-Wing Terrorism*, ed. Gerrit-Jan Berendse and Ingo Cornils, 83–101. German Monitor 70. Amsterdam: 2008.

————. *Ulrike Meinhof and German Terrorism: Language, Violence and Identity*. Woodbridge: 2009.

Conrad, Geoffrey W. and Arthur A. Demarest. *Religion and Empire: The Dynamics of Aztec and Inca Expansionism*. Cambridge: 1984.

Constable, Giles. "The Historiography of the Crusades." In *The Crusades from the Perspective of Byzantium and the Muslim World*, ed. Angeliki Laiou and Roy Mottahedeh, 1–22. Washington, D.C.: 2001.

Contamine, Philippe. *De Jeanne d'Arc aux guerres d'Italie: Figures, images et problèmes du XVe siècle*. Orléans: 1994.

———. "Mourir pour la patrie, Xe–XXe siècle." In *Les lieux de mémoire*, Part 2, *La Nation*, vol. 3, ed. Pierre Nora, 11–43. Paris: 1986.

———. "Remarques critiques sur les étendards de Jeanne d'Arc." *Francia* 39, 1 (2007): 187–200.

Cook, David. *Understanding Jihad*. Berkeley, Calif.: 2005.

Cottret, Monique. *Jansénismes et Lumières*. Paris: 1998.

Cowdrey, H. E. J. *Pope Gregory VII, 1073–1085*. Oxford: 1997.

———. "Pope Gregory VII and the Bearing of Arms." Repr. in idem, *The Crusades and Latin Monasticism, 11th–12th Centuries*, 21–35. Aldershot: 1999.

———. "The Mahdia Campaign of 1087." Repr. in idem, *Popes, Monks, and Crusaders*. London: 1984.

———. "The Papacy, the Patarenes and the Church of Milan." *History* 51 (1966): 25–48. Repr. in idem, *Popes, Monks and Crusaders*. London: 1984.

Crabtree, Harriett. *The Christian Life: The Traditional Metaphors and Contemporary Theology*. Minneapolis: 1991.

Crawford, Patricia. "Charles Stuart, That Man of Blood." *Journal of British Studies* 16, 2 (1977): 41–61.

Crenshaw, Martha. *Explaining Terrorism: Causes, Processes and Consequences*. London: 2011.

Cushing, Kathleen G..*Papacy and Law in the Gregorian Revolution. The Canonistic Work of Anselm of Lucca*. Oxford: 1998.

———. *Reform and the Papacy in the Eleventh Century: Spirituality and Social Change*. Manchester: 2005.

Daniélou, Jean. *From Shadows to Reality: Studies in the Biblical Typology of the Fathers*. Tr. London: 1960.

Dasberg, Lea. *Untersuchungen über die Entwerung des Judaismus im 11. Jahrhundert*. Paris: 1965.

David, Zdeněk V. "Universalist Aspirations of the Utraquist Church." *Bohemian Reformation and Religious Practice* 7 (2006): 194–212.

Davidson, James West. *The Logic of Millennial Thought: Eighteenth-Century New England*. New Haven, Conn.: 1977.

Davis, Natalie Zemon. "Rites of Violence: Religious Riot in Sixteenth-Century France." *Past & Present* 59 (1973): 53–91.

———. *Society and Culture in Early Modern France*. Stanford, Calif.: 1976.

Davis, Thomas M. "The Tradition of Puritan Typology." In *Typology and Early American Literature*, ed. Sacvan Bercovitch, 11–45. Amherst, Mass.: 1972.

Dawkins, Richard. *The God Delusion*. New York: 2006.

DeCaro, Jr., Louis A. *"Fire from the Midst of You": A Religious Life of John Brown*. New York: 2002.

Delaruelle, Étienne. "L'antéchrist chez S. Vincent Ferrier, S. Bernardin de Sienne et autour de Jeanne d'Arc." In *L'attesa dell'età nuova nella spiritualità della fine del medioevo*, 39–64. Todi: 1962. Repr. in idem, *La piété populaire au Moyen Age*, 329–54. Turin: 1975.

———. "Paix de Dieu et croisade dans la Chrétienté du XIIe siècle." In *Paix de Dieu et guerre sainte en Languedoc au XIIIe siècle*, 51–71. Cahiers de Fanjeaux 4. Toulouse: 1969.

———. "La spiritualité de Jeanne d'Arc." *Bulletin de Littérature Ecclésiastique* 65 (1964): 17–33, 81–98. Repr. in idem, *La piété populaire au Moyen Age*, 355–88. Turin: 1975.

Delaurenti, Béatrice. "La fascination et l'action à distance: questions médiévales (1230–1370)." *Médiévales* 50 (2006): 137–54.

———. *La puissance des mots, «virtus verborum»: Débats doctrinaux sur le pouvoir des incantations au Moyen Age.* Paris: 2007.

Della Porta, Donatella. "Political Socialization in Left-Wing Underground Organizations: Biographies of Italian and German Militants." *International Social Movement Research* 4 (1992): 259–90.

———. "Politische Gewalt und Terrorismus: Eine vergleichende und soziologische Perspektive." In *Terrorismus in der Bundesrepublik: Medien, Staat und Subkulturen in den 1970er Jahren*, ed. Klaus Weinhauer, Jörg Requate, and Heinz-Gerhard Haupt, 33–58. Frankfurt: 2006.

———. *Social Movements, Political Violence and the State: A Comparative Analysis of Italy and Germany.* Cambridge: 1995.

Denery, Dallas G. *Seeing and Being Seen in the Later Medieval World: Optics, Theology and Religious Life.* Cambridge: 2005.

Denton-Borhaug, Kelly. *U.S. War-Culture: Sacrifice and Salvation.* Sheffield: 2011.

Dickson, Gary. "The Advent of the Pastores (1251)." *Revue Belge de Philologie et d'Histoire* 66 (1988): 249–67. Repr. in idem, *Religious Enthusiasm in the Medieval West*. Aldershot: 2000.

———. *The Children's Crusade: Medieval History, Modern Mythistory.* Basingstoke: 2007.

Dieckmann, Herbert. "Das Abscheuliche und Schreckliche in der Kunsttheorie des 18. Jahrhunderts." In *Die nicht mehr Schönen Künste: Grenzphänomene des Aesthetischen*, ed. Hans-Robert Jauss, 271–317. Poetik und Hermeneutik 3. Munich: 1968.

Diefendorf, Barbara B. *Beneath the Cross: Catholics and Huguenots in Sixteenth-Century Paris.* Oxford: 1991.

———. *The Saint Bartholomew's Day Massacre.* Boston: 2009.

Dinzelbacher, Peter. *Heilige oder Hexen? Schicksale auffälliger Frauen in Mittelalter und Frühneuzeit.* Zürich: 1999.

Dixon, Thomas. *From Passions to Emotions: The Creation of a Secular Psychological Category.* Cambridge: 2006.

Dodds, Eric Robertson. *The Greeks and the Irrational.* Berkeley, Calif.: 1951.

Dowd, David Loyd. *Pageant-Master of the Republic: Jacques-Louis David and the French Revolution.* University of Nebraska Studies n.s 3. Lincoln: 1948.

Doyle, William. *Oxford History of the French Revolution.* Rev. ed. Oxford: 2002.

Drake, H[arold] A[llen]. *Constantine and the Bishops: The Politics of Intolerance.* Baltimore: 2000.

———. "The Impact of Constantine on Christianity." In *The Cambridge Companion to the Age of Constantine*, ed. Noel Lenski, 111–36. Cambridge: 2006.

———. "Lambs into Lions: Explaining Early Christian Intolerance." *Past & Present* 153 (November 1996): 3–36.

———, ed. *Violence in Late Antiquity: Perceptions and Practices.* Aldershot: 2006.

Duby, George. *Le dimanche de Bouvines.* Paris: 1973. Tr. *The Legend of Bouvines: War, Religion and Culture in the Middle Ages.* Berkeley, Calif.: 1990.

Dugard, John. "International Terrorism and the Just War. " In *The Morality of Terrorism: Religious and Secular Justifications, ed.* David C. Rapoport and Yonah Alexander, 77–98. New York: 1989.

Dumézil, Georges. *Idées romaines*. Paris: 1969.

Dupront, Alphonse. *Le mythe de croisade*. Rev. ed. Paris: 1997.

Duranton, Henri. "Humanité." In *Handbuch politisch-sozialer Grundbegriffe in Frankreich 1680–1820*, vols. 19–20, ed. Rolf Reichardt et al. Munich: 2000.

Durkheim, Émile. *Les formes élémentaires de la vie religieuse*. Paris: 1912. Tr. Karen Fields, *The Elementary Forms of the Religious Life*. New York: 1995.

Ebel, Jonathan H. *Faith in the Fight: Religion and the American Soldier in the Great War*. Princeton, N.J.: 2010.

Edelstein, Dan. "War and Terror: The Law of Nations from Grotius to the French Revolution." *French Historical Studies* 31, 2 (2008): 229–62.

Edgington, Susan B. "Religious Ideas in the Chanson d'Antioche." In *The Holy Land, Holy Lands, and Christian History*, ed. R. N. Swanson, 142–53. Studies in Church History 26. Woodbridge: 2000.

Eire, Carlos M. N. *War Against the Idols: The Reformation of Worship from Erasmus to Calvin*. Cambridge: 1986.

Eisenstadt, Schmuel N. *Fundamentalism, Sectarianism, and Revolution: The Jacobin Dimension of Modernity*. Cambridge: 1999.

———, ed. *The Origins and Diversity of Axial Age Civilizations*. Albany, N.Y.: 1986.

El Kenz, David. "La civilisation des mœurs et les guerres de Religion: Un seuil de tolérance aux massacres?" In idem, *Le massacre, objet d'histoire*, 182–97. Paris: 2005.

———. *Les bûchers du roi: La culture protestante des martyrs (1523–1572)*. Paris: 1997.

Elliott, Dyan. *Fallen Bodies: Pollution, Sexuality and Demonology in the Middle Ages*. Philadelphia: 1999.

———. "Seeing Double: Jean Gerson, Joan of Arc and the Discernment of Spirits." *AHR* 107, 1 (2002): 26–54.

Elm, Kaspar. "Die Eroberung Jerusalems im Jahre 1099: Ihre Darstellung, Beurteilung und Deutung in den Quellen zur Geschichte des Ersten Kreuzzugs." In *Jerusalem im Hoch- und Spätmittelalter: Konflikte und Konfliktbewältigung—Vorstellungen und Vergegenwärtigungen*, ed. Dieter Bauer et al., 31–54. Frankfurt-am-Main: 2001.

Endy, Melvin B. "Just War, Holy War, and Millenialism in Revolutionary America." *William and Mary Quarterly* 3rd ser. 42, 1 (1985): 3–25.

Erdmann, Carl. "Endkaiserglaube und Kreuzzugsgedanke im 11. Jahrhundert." *Zeitschrift für Kirchengeschichte* ser. 3, 51, 2 (1932): 384–414.

———. *Die Entstehung des Kreuzzugsgedankens*. Stuttgart: 1935. Tr. *The Origins of the Idea of Crusade*. Princeton, N.J.: 1977.

Erlanger, Philippe. *Le massacre de la saint-Barthélémy: 24 août 1572*. Paris: 1960. Tr. *St. Bartholomew's Night*. New York: 1962.

Ewig, Eugen. "Zum christlichen Königsgedanken im Frühmittelalter." Repr. in idem, *Spätantikes und fränkisches Gallien*, 1:3–71. Munich: 1976.

Fanon, Frantz. *Les damnés de la terre*. Paris: 1961. Rev. ed. Paris: 2002. Tr. *The Wretched of the Earth*. New York: 2004.

Feldman, Louis H. *Josephus and Modern Scholarship (1937–1980)*. Berlin: 1984.

Ferguson, Robert A. "The Dialectic of Liberty: Law and Religion in Anglo-American Culture." *Modern Intellectual History* 1, 1 (2004): 27–54.

Ferling, John E. *A Wilderness of Miseries: War and Warriors in Early America*. Westport, Conn.: 1980.

Fernández-Armesto, Felipe. *Before Columbus: Exploration and Colonisation from the Mediterranean to the Atlantic, 1229–1492*. Houndsmills: 1987.

Ferrier, Luc. "La couronne refusée de Godefroy de Bouillon: Eschatologie et humilation de la majesté aux premiers temps du royaume latin de Jérusalem." In *Le concile de Clermont de 1095 et l'appel à la croisade: Actes du Colloque . . . de Clermont-Ferrand (23–25 juin 1995)*, 245–65. Collection de l'École Française de Rome 236. Rome: 1997.

Fetscher, Iring, Herfried Münkler, and Hannelore Ludwig. "Ideologien der Terroristen in der Bundesrepublik Deutschland." In *Ideologien und Strategien*, ed. Fetscher, Günter Rohrmoser et al. = Bundesministerium des Innern. Analysen zum Terrorismus 1, 15–271. Opladen: 1981.

Field, Lester L. *Liberty, Dominion and the Two Swords*. Notre Dame, Ind.: 1998.

Figgis, John Neville. *Studies of Political Thought from Gerson to Grotius, 1414–1625*. Cambridge: 1907.

Flint, Valerie. *The Rise of Magic in Early Medieval Europe*. Princeton, N.J.: 1991.

Flori, Jean. *Chroniqueurs et propagandistes: Introduction critique aux sources de la première croisade*. Genève: 2010.

———. "De l'anonyme Normand à Tudebode et aux Gesta Francorum." *Revue d'histoire ecclésiastique* 102, 3–4 (2007): 717–46.

———. "L'Église et la guerre sainte, de la paix de Dieu à la croisade." Repr. in idem, *Croisade et chevalerie, XIe–XIIe siècles*, 3–20. Bruxelles: 1998.

———. *La guerre sainte: La formation de l'idée de croisade dans l'Occident chrétien*. Paris: 2001.

———. *L'Islam et la fin des temps: Interprétation prophétique des invasions musulmanes dans la chrétienté medieval*. Paris: 2007.

———. "Mort et martyre des guerriers vers 1100: L'exemple de la première croisade." *Cahiers de Civilisation Médiévale* 35, 2 (1991): 121–39.

———. *Pierre l'ermite et la première croisade*. Paris: 1999.

———. "Une ou plusieurs 'premières croisades'? Le message d'Urbain II et les plus anciens pogroms d'Occident." *Revue Historique* 285, 1 (1991): 3–27.

Fögen, Marie-Theres. *Römische Rechtsgeschichten: Über Ursprung und Evolution eines sozialen Systems*. Veröffentlichungen des Max-Planck-Instituts für Geschichte 172. Göttingen: 2002,

Fogleson, David S. *The American Mission and the „Evil Empire."* Cambridge: 2007.

Foner, Eric. *The Story of American Freedom*. New York: 1998.

Foucault, Michel. "Nietzsche, la généalogie, l'histoire." In *Hommage à Jean Hippolyte*, ed. Suzanne Bachelard, 145–72. Paris: 1971. Repr. in *Dits et Écrits* 21: 36–56. Paris: 1994.

Fraioli, Deborah. *Joan of Arc: The Early Debate*. Woodbridge: 2000.

France, John. "The Text of the Account of the Capture of Jerusalem in the Ripoll Manuscript, Bibliothèque Nationale (Latin) 5132." *English Historical Review* 103, 3 (1988): 640–57.

———. "Two Types of Vision on the First Crusade: Stephen of Valence and Peter Bartholomew." *Crusades* 5 (2006): 1–20.

———. "An Unknown Account of the Capture of Jerusalem." *English Historical Review* 87 (1972): 771–83.

———. *Victory in the East: A Military History of the First Crusade*. Cambridge: 1997.

Franq, H. G. "Jean Gerson's Theological Treatise and Other Memoirs in Defense of Joan of Arc." *Revue de l'Université d'Ottawa* 41 (1971): 58–80.

Frassetto, Michael. "Heretics and Jews in the Early Eleventh Century: The Writings of Radulfus Glaber and Ademar of Chabannes." In idem, *Christian Attitudes Toward the Jews in the Middle Ages: A Casebook*, 43–59. New York: 2007.

Frend, W. C. *Martyrdom and Persecution in the Early Church: A Study of Conflict from the Maccabees to Donatus*. Oxford: 1965.

Fried, Johannes. *Aufstieg aus dem Untergang: Apokalyptisches Denken und die Entstehung der modernen Naturwissenschaft im Mittelalter*. Munich: 2001.

———. "Die Endzeit fest im Griff der Positivismus? " *Historische Zeitschrift* 275, 2 (2002): 281–322.

———. "Wille, Freiwilligkeit und Geständnis um 1300: Zur Beurteilung des letzten Templergrossmeister Jacques de Molay." *Historisches Jahrbuch* 105, 2 (1985): 388–425.

Friedeburg, Robert von, ed. *Murder and Monarchy: Regicide in European History, 1300–1800*. Houndsmill: 2004.

———, ed. *Widerstandsrecht in der frühen Neuzeit*. Berlin: 2008.

Friedman, Yvonne. *Encounter Between Enemies*. Leiden: 2002.

Fritz, Jean-Marie. *Le discours du fou au Moyen Age*. Paris: 1992.

Fudge, Thomas A. "Crime, Punishment and Pacifism in the Thought of Bishop Mikuláš of Pelhřimov." *Bohemian Reformation and Religious Practice* 3 (2000): 69–103.

———. *Heresy and Hussites in Late Medieval Europe*. Aldershot: 2014.

———. *The Magnificent Ride: The First Reformation in Hussite Bohemia*. Aldershot: 1998.

———. " 'More Glory Than Blood': Murder and Martyrdom in the Hussite Crusades." *Bohemian Reformation and Religious Practice* 5, 1 (2005): 117–37.

Fukuyama, Francis. "The End of History?" *National Interest* (Summer 1989): 3–18.

Gabriele, Matthew. "Against the Enemies of Christ: The Role of Count Emicho in the Anti-Jewish Violence of the First Crusade." In *Christian Attitudes Towards the Jews in the Middle Ages: A Casebook*, ed. Michael Frassetto, 61–82. New York: 2007.

———. "Asleep at the Wheel? Messianism, Apocalypticism and Charlemagne's Passivity in the Oxford Chanson de Roland." *Nottingham Medieval Studies* 67 (2003): 46–72.

———. *Empire of Memory: The Legend of Charlemagne, the Franks, and Jerusalem Before the First Crusade*. Oxford: 2011.

———. "The Last Carolingian Exegete: Pope Urban II, the Weight of Tradition, and Christian Reconquest." *Church History* 81, 4 (2012): 776–814.

———. "Otto III, Charlemagne, and Pentecost A.D. 1000: A Reconsideration Using Diplomatic Evidence." In *The Year 1000: Religious and Social Response to the Turning of the First Millennium*, ed. Michael Frassetto, 111–32. New York: 2002.

Gaddis, Michael. *There Is No Crime for Those Who Have Christ: Religious Violence in the Christian Roman Empire*. Berkeley, Calif.: 2005.

Galtung, Johan. "Violence, Peace, and Peace Research." *Journal of Peace Research* 6, 3 (1969): 167–91.

Gamble, Richard M. *The War for Righteousness: Progressive Christianity, the Great War, and the Rise of the Messianic Nation*. Wilmington, Del.: 2003.

Garrison, Mary. "The Franks as the New Israel." In *The Uses of the Past in Early Medieval Europe*, ed. Yitzhak Hen and Matthew Innes, 114–61. Cambridge: 2000.

Garrisson-Estèbe, Janine. *La Saint-Barthélemy, 1572.* Brussels: 1987.

Garvey, M. A. *Civil Wars and Monarchy in France in the Sixteenth and Seventeenth Centuries.* 2 vols. London: 1852.

Gat, Azar. *War in Human Civilization.* Oxford: 2006.

Gauchet, Marcel. *Le désenchantement du monde: Une histoire politique de la religion.* Paris: 1985. Tr. *The Disenchantment of the World: A Political History of Religion.* Princeton, N.J.: 1997.

Geary, Patrick J. "Living with Conflicts in Stateless France: A Typology of Conflict-Management Mechanisms, 1050–1200." Repr. in idem, *Living with the Dead in the Middle Ages,* 125–60. Ithaca, N.Y.: 1994.

Gentile, Emilio. *Il culto del littorio: La sacralizzazione della politica nell'Italia fascista.* Rome: 1993. Tr. *The Sacralization of Politics in Fascist Italy.* Cambridge, Mass.: 1996.

———. *La democrazia di Dio: La religione americana nell'era dell'impero e del terrore.* Milan: 2006.

———. *Le religioni della politica: Fra democrazie e totalitarismi.* Rome: 2001. Tr. *Politics as Religion.* Princeton, N.J.: 2006.

Gentiles, Ian. *Oliver Cromwell: God's Warrior and the English Revolution.* Houndsmill: 2011.

Gérard, Alain. *"Par principe d'humanité . . .": La Terreur et la Vendée.* Paris: 1999.

Getty, J. Arch, Oleg V. Naumov, and Benjamin Sher. *The Road to Terror: Stalin and the Self-Destruction of the Bolsheviks, 1932–1939.* New Haven, Conn.: 1999.

Gillespie, Susan. "Blaming Moteuczoma: Anthropomorphizing the Aztec Conquest." In *Invasion and Transformation: Perspectives on the Conquest of Mexico,* ed. Rebecca P. Brienen and Margaret Jackson, 25–55. Boulder, Colo.: 2008.

Ginneken, Jaap van. "The 1895 Debate on the Origins of Crowd Psychology." *Journal of the History of the Behavioral Sciences* 21 (1985): 375–82.

Girard, René. *I See Satan Fall like Lightning.* Tr. J. G. Williams. Maryknoll, N.Y.: 2001.

———. *Violence and the Sacred.* Tr. Baltimore: 1977.

Giuglio, Michèle. " 'Terreur' et sa famille morphologique de 1793 à 1796." In *Néologie et lexicologie: Hommage à Louis Guilbert,* ed. Rosine Adda, 124–41. Paris: 1976.

Given, James. *Inquisition and Medieval Society: Power, Discipline, and Resistance in Languedoc.* Ithaca, N.Y.: 1997.

———. "The Inquisitors of Languedoc and the Medieval Technology of Power." *American Historical Review* 94, 2 (1989): 336–59.

Goff, Philip. "Religion and Revolution: Historiographic Turns Since Alan Heimert's *Religion and the American Mind.*" *Church History* 67, 4 (1998): 695–721.

Goitein, Shelomo Dov. "Contemporary Letters on the Capture of Jerusalem by the Crusaders." *Journal of Jewish Studies* 3, 4 (1952): 162–77.

———. "Geniza Sources for the Crusades Period: A Survey." In *Outremer: Studies in the History of the Crusading Kingdom of Jerusalem Presented to Joshua Prawer,* ed. Benjamin Kedar et al., 306–22. Jerusalem: 1982.

———. *A Mediterranean Society: The Jewish Communities of the Arab World as Portrayed by the Documents of the Cairo Geniza.* Vol. 5. Cambridge: 1988.

Goldstein, Jan Ellen. *Console and Classify: The French Psychiatric Profession in the Nineteenth Century.* Cambridge: 1987.

———. "Enthusiasm or Imagination? Eighteenth-Century Smear Words in Comparative National Context." *Huntington Quarterly* 60 (1997): 29–49.

———. "'Moral Contagion': A Professional Ideology of Medicine and Psychiatry in Eighteenth-Century France." In *Professions and the French State, 1700–1900*, ed. Gerald Geison, 181–222. Philadelphia: 1984.

Gorevich, Igor. *O Kritike Antropologii Zhivotnikh*. Vol. 1, *Prichasheniye i Shashlik*. Kabul-Kishinev: 1987.

———. *O Kritike Antropologii Zhivotnikh*. Vol. 3. *O Kentavrah i Rusalkah: Raznovidnosti i Granitsy*. Kabul-Kishinev: 1987.

Gouguenheim, Sylvain. *Les fausses terreurs de l'an mil: Attente de la fin des temps ou approfondissement de la Foi?* Paris: 1999.

Graf, Friedrich Wilhelm. "Die Nation—von Gott ,erfunden'? Kritische Randnotizen zum Theologiebedarf der historischen Nationalismusforschung." In *„Gott mit uns": Nation, Religion und Gewalt im 19. und frühen 20. Jahrhundert*, ed. Gerd Krumeich and Hartmut Lehmann, 285–317. Veröffentlichungen des Max-Planck-Instituts für Geschichte 162. Göttingen: 2000.

Grayzel, Solomon. *The Church and the Jews in the Thirteenth Century*. 2nd ed. New York: 1966.

Greengrass, Mark. "Regicide, Martyrs and Monarchical Authority in France in the Wars of Religion." In *Murder and Monarchy: Regicide in European History, 1300–1800*, ed. Robert von Friedeburg, 176–92. Houndsmill: 2004.

Gregor, A. James. "Fascism's Philosophy of Violence and the Concept of Terror." In Rapoport and Alexander, *Morality of Terrorism*, 152–68.

Gregory, Brad S. *Salvation at Stake: Christian Martyrdom in Early Modern Europe*. Cambridge, Mass.: 1999.

Gribben, Crawford. *Writing the Rapture: Prophecy Fiction in Evangelical America*. Oxford: 2009.

Gribbin, William. *The Churches Militant, the War of 1812 and American Religion*. New Haven, Conn.: 1973.

Grocok, Chris W. "L'aventure épique: Le traitement poétique de la première Croisade par Gilon de Paris et son continuateur." In *Autour de la première Croisade*, ed. Michel Balard, 17–28. Paris: 1996.

Guiomar, Jean-Yves. *L'invention de la guerre totale*. Paris: 2004.

Guttiérrez, Gustavo. *A Theology of Liberation: History, Politics, and Salvation*. Tr. Maryknoll, N.Y.: 1973.

Haines, Keith. "Attitudes and Impediments to Pacifism in Medieval Europe." *Journal of Medieval History* 7 (1981): 369–88.

Halfin, Igal. *From Darkness to Light: Class, Consciousness, and Salvation in Revolutionary Russia*. Pittsburgh: 2000.

Haller, William. *Foxe's Book of Martyrs and the Elect Nation*. London: 1963.

Hampson, Norman. "From Regeneration to Terror: The Ideology of the French Revolution." In *Terrorism, Ideology, and Revolution*, ed. Noel O'Sullivan, 49–66. Brighton: 1986.

Hanning, Robert W. *The Vision of History in Early Britain, from Gildas to Geoffrey of Monmouth*. New York: 1966.

Harding, Susan. "Imagining the Last Days: The Politics of Apocalyptic Language." *Bulletin of the American Academy of Arts and Sciences* 48, 3 (1994): 14–44.

Harnack, Adolf von. *Lehrbuch der Dogmengeschichte*. 2 vols. Rev. ed., Freiburg-im-Breisgau: 1888–1890. Tr. *History of Dogma*. 2 vols. Boston: 1901.

————. *Milita Christi: Die christliche Religion und der Soldatenstand in den ersten drei Jahrhunderten.* Tübingen: 1905. Tr. *Militia Christi: The Christian Religion and the Military in the First Three Centuries.* Minneapolis: 1981.

Hartl, Ingrid. "Das Feindbild in der Kreuzzugslyrik." MA Diplomarbeit Deutsche Philologie, Vienna, 2005.

Hassig, Ross. "Aztec and Spanish Conquest in Mesoamerica." In *War in the Tribal Zone: Expanding States and Indigenous Warfare,* ed. R. Brian Ferguson and Neil L. Whitehead, 83–102. Santa Fe, N.M.: 1992.

————. *Time, History and Belief in Aztec and Colonial Mexico.* Austin, Tx.: 2001.

Hastings, Adrian. *Construction of Nationhood: Ethnicity, Religion and Nationalism.* Cambridge: 1997.

Hatch, Nathan O. *The Sacred Cause of Liberty: Republican Thought and the Millennium in Revolutionary New England.* New Haven, Conn.: 1977.

————. "Sola scriptura and novus ordo sec[u]lorum." In *The Bible in America: Essays in Cultural History,* ed. idem and Mark A. Noll, 59–78. Oxford: 1982.

Haussherr, Reiner. "Zur Darstellung zeitgenössischer Wirklichkeit und Geschichte in der Bible Moralisée und in Illustrationen von Geschichtsschreibung im 13. Jahrhundert." In *Il medio oriente e l'occidente nell'arte del XIII secolo,* ed. Hans Belting. 2: 211–17. Bologna: 1982.

Hay, David. "Gender Bias and Religious Intolerance in Accounts of the 'Massacres' of the First Crusade." In *Tolerance and Intolerance: Social Conflict in the Age of the Crusades,* ed. Michael Gervers and James M. Powell, 3–10. Syracuse, N.Y.: 2001.

Head, Thomas and Richard Landes, eds. *The Peace of God: Social Violence and Religious Response in France Around the Year 1000.* Ithaca, N.Y.: 1992.

Headland, Thomas, Marvin Harris, and Kenneth Pike, eds. *Emics and Etics: The Insider/Outsider Debate.* London: 1990.

Hehl, Ernst-Dieter. "Terror als Herrschaftsmittel des früh- und hochmittelalterlichen Königs." *Das Mittelalter* 12 (2007): 11–23.

————. "Was ist eigentlich ein Kreuzzug?" *Historische Zeitschrift* 259 (1994): 297–336.

Heim, François. *La théologie de la victoire de Constantin à Théodose.* Paris: 1992.

Heimert, Alan. *Religion and the American Mind, from the Great Awakening to the Revolution.* Cambridge, Mass.: 1966.

Hellbeck, Jochen. *Revolution on My Mind: Writing a Diary Under Stalin.* Cambridge, Mass.: 2006.

————. "With Hegel to Salvation: Bukharin's Other Trial." *Representations* 107 (2009): 56–90.

Hengel, Martin. *Jésus et la violence révolutionnaire.* Paris: 1973.

————. *The Zealots: Investigations into the Jewish Freedom Movement in the Period from Herod I until 70 A.D.* Tr. Edinburgh: 1989.

Heuvel, Gerd van der. *Der Freiheitsbegriff der Französischen Revolution.* Schriftenreihe der Historischen Kommission bei der Bayerischen Akademie der Wissenschaften 31. Göttingen: 1988.

————. "Terreur, Terroriste, Terrorisme." In *Handbuch politisch-sozialer Grundbegriffe in Frankreich 1680–1820,* vol. 3, ed. Rolf Reichardt and Eberhard Schmitt. Munich: 1985.

Heyd, Michael. *"Be sober and reasonable": The Critique of Enthusiasm in the Seventeenth and Early Eighteenth Centuries.* Leiden: 1995.

Heymann, Frederick. *John Žižka and the Hussite Revolution.* Princeton, N.J.: 1955.

Higginbotham, Don. "The Early American Way of War." *William & Mary Quarterly* 44, 2 (1987): 230–73.

Higonnet, Patrice. "Terror, Trauma and the 'Young Marx' Explanation of Jacobin Politics." *Past & Present* 191 (2006): 121–64.

Hill, Christopher. *The English Bible and the Seventeenth-Century Revolution.* London: 1992.

Hillenbrand, Carole. *The Crusades: Islamic Perspectives.* Edinburgh: 1999.

Hinds, Lynn Boyd and Theodore Otto Windt. *The Cold War as Rhetoric: The Beginnings, 1945–1950.* New York: 1991.

Holzem, Andreas. "Gott und Gewalt. Kriegslehren des Christentums und die Typologie des Religionskriege." In *Formen des Kriegs: Von der Antike bis zur Gegenwart,* eds. Dietrich Beyrau, Michael Hochgeschwender, and Dieter Langewiesche, 374–413. Krieg in der Geschichte 37. Paderborn: 2007.

Horsley, Richard A. and John S. Hanson. *Bandits, Prophets, and Messiahs: Popular Movements in the Time of Jesus.* Minneapolis: 1985.

Housley, Norman. *Contesting the Crusades.* Oxford: 2006.

———. "Crusades Against Christians: Their Origins and Early Development, c. 1000–1216." Repr. in *The Crusades: The Essential Readings,* ed. Thomas E. Madden, 71–97. Malden, Mass.: 2002.

———. "The Eschatological Imperative: Messianism and Holy War in Europe, 1260–1556." In *Towards the Millennium: Messianic Expectations from the Bible to Waco,* ed. Peter Schäfer and Mark R. Cohen, 123–50. Leiden: 1998. Repr. in Housley, *Crusading and Warfare in Medieval and Renaissance Europe.* Aldershot: 2001.

———. "Holy Land or Holy Lands? Palestine and the Catholic West in the Late Middle Ages and Renaissance." In *The Holy Land, Holy Lands, and Christian History,* ed. Robert N. Swanson, 228–49. Studies in Church *History* 36. Woodbridge: 2000.

———. "Jerusalem and the development of the Crusade Idea, 1099–1128." In *The Horns of Hattin,* ed. Benjamin Z. Kedar, 27–40. Jerusalem: 1992.

———. "Pro deo et patria mori: Sanctified Patriotism in Europe, 1400–1600." In *War and Competition Between States,* ed. Philippe Contamine, 221–48. Oxford: 2000.

———. *Religious Warfare in Europe, 1400–1536.* Oxford: 2002.

Hruza, Karel. "'Audite et cum speciali diligencia attendite verba litere huius': Hussitische Manifeste: Objekt—Methode—Definition." In *Text-Schrift-Codex: Quellenkundliche Arbeiten aus dem Institut für Österreichischen Geschichtsforschung,* ed. Christoph Egger and Herwig Weigl, 345–84. MIÖG Ergänzungband 35. Wien: 2000.

———. "Die hussitischen Manifeste vom April 1420." *Deutsches Archiv für Erforschung des Mittelalters* 53 (1997): 119–77.

Hull, Isabel W. *Absolute Destruction: Military Culture and the Practices of War in Imperial Germany.* Ithaca, N.Y.: 2005.

Ingham, John M., "Human Sacrifice at Tenochtitlan." *Comparative Studies in Society and History* 26, 3 (1984): 379–400.

Ivianski, Zeev. "The Moral Issue: Some Aspects of Individual Terror." In Rapoport and Alexander, *Morality of Terrorism,* 229–66.

Jacobsen, Peter Christian. "Die Eroberung von Jerusalem in der mittellateinischen Dichtung." In

Jerusalem im Hoch- und Spätmittelalter: Konflikte und Konfliktbewältigung—Vorstellungen und Vergegenwärtigungen, ed. Dieter Bauer et al., 335–65. Frankfurt-am-Main: 2001.

James, William. *Varieties of Religious Experience: A Study in Human Nature.* New York: 1902. Rev. ed. London: 2002.

Jankrift, Kay Peter. "Mein Feund, der Feind: Individuellen Begegnungen zwischen 'Franken,' Muslimen und Juden im Alltag der levantinischen Kreuzfahrerstaaten." *Questiones Medii Aevi Novae* 17 (2012): 315–33.

Jaspers, Karl. *The Origin and Goal of History.* London: 1953.

Jauss, Hans-Robert. "Die klassische und die christliche Rechtfertigung des Hässlichen in Mittelalterlicher Literatur." In *Die nicht mehr Schönen Künste: Grenzphänomene des Aesthetischen*, ed. idem, 143–68. Poetik und Hermeneutik 3. Munich: 1968.

Jeanroy, Alfred. "Le troubadour Austorc d'Aurillac et son sirventés sur la septième Croisade." *Romanische Forschungen* 23 (1907): 81–87.

Jennings, Francis. *The Invasion of America: Indians, Colonialism, and the Cant of Conquest.* Chapel Hill, N.C.: 1975.

Johannsen, Robert W. *To the Halls of the Montezumas: The Mexican War in the American Imagination.* New York: 1985.

Johnson, James Turner. *Ideology, Reason, and the Limitation of War: Religious and Secular Concepts, 1200–1740.* Princeton, N.J.: 1975.

Jong, Mayke de. "The Empire as *ecclesia*: Hrabanus Maurus and Biblical Historia for Rulers." In *The Uses of the Past in the Early Middle Ages*, ed. Yitzhak Hen and Matthew Innes, 191–226. Cambridge: 2000.

———. "Exegesis for an Empress." In *Medieval Transformations: Texts, Power and Gifts in Context*, ed. eadem and Esther Cohen, 69–100. Leiden: 2001.

Jordan, William Chester. *The French Monarchy and the Jews: From Philip Augustus to the Last Capetians.* Philadelphia: 1989.

———. *Louis IX and the Challenge of the Crusade: A Study in Rulership.* Princeton, N.J.: 1979.

Jourdan, Alphonse. "Robespierre and Revolutionary Heroism." In *Robespierre*, ed. Colin Haydon and William Doyle, 54–74. Cambridge: 1999.

Joyner, Charles. "'Guilty of Holiest Crime': The Passion of John Brown." In *His Soul Goes Marching on: Responses to John Brown and the Harpers Ferry Raid*, ed. Paul Finkeman, 296–334. Charlottesville: 1995.

Juergensmeyer, Mark. *Terror in the Mind of God: The Global Rise of Religious Violence.* 3rd ed. Berkeley, Calif.: 2003.

Kahn, Victoria. "Introduction." *Representations* 105 (2009): 1–11.

———. *Wayward Contracts: The Crisis of Political Obligation in England, 1640–1674.* Princeton, N.J.: 2004.

Kaminsky, H. Howard. "Chiliasm and the Hussite Revolution." *Church History* 26, 1 (1957): 43–71.

———. "Nicholas of Pelhřimov's Tabor: An Adventure into the Eschaton." In *Eschatologie und Hussitismus*, ed. Alexander Patschovsky and František Šmahel, 139–69. Historica, series nova, supplementum 1. Prague: 1996.

———. "The Prague Insurrection of 30 July 1419." *Medievalia et Humanistica* 17 (1966): 106–26.

Kamlah, Wilhelm. *Apokalypse und Geschichtstheologie: Die mittelalterliche Auslegung der Apocalypse vor Joachim von Fiore.* Berlin: 1935.

———. *Christentum und Geschichtlichkeit:Untersuchungen zur Entstehung des Christentums und zu Augustins "Bürgerschaft Gottes."* Stuttgart: 1951.

Kammen, Michael. *Spheres of Liberty: Changing Perceptions of Liberty in American Culture.* Madison, Wis.: 1986.

Kantorowicz, Ernst. *The King's Two Bodies: A Study in Medieval Political Theology.* Princeton, N.J.: 1957.

Katz, Steven T. "The Pequot War Reconsidered." *New England Quarterly* 64, 2 (1991): 206–24.

Kedar, Benjamin. *Crusade and Missions: European Approaches Toward the Muslims.* Princeton, N.J.: 1984.

———. "The Jerusalem Massacre of 1099 in the Historiography of the Crusades." *Crusades* 3 (2004): 15–75.

Keller, Hagen. "*Machabeorum pugnae*: Zum Stellenwert eines biblischen Vorbilds in Widukinds Deutung der ottonischen Königsherrschaft." In *Iconologia sacra: Mythos, Bildkunst und Dichtung in der Religions- und Sozialgeschichte Alteuropas: Festschrift für Karl Hauck zum 75. Geburtstag,* ed. idem and Nikolaus Staubach, 417–37. Arbeiten zur Frühmittelalterforschung 23. Berlin: 1994.

———. "Pataria und Stadtverfassung, Stadtgemeinde und Reform." In *Investiturstreit und Reichsverfassung,* ed. Josef Fleckenstein, 321–50. Sigmaringen: 1973.

Kelley, Donald R. "Kingship and Resistance." In *The Origins of Modern Freedom in the West,* ed. Richard W. Davis, 234–68. Stanford, Calif.: 1995.

Kelly, George Amstrong. "Conceptual Sources of the Terror." *Eighteenth-Century Studies* 14, 1 (1980): 18–36.

Kelly, Jay Norman Davidson. *Early Christian Doctrines.* 5th ed. London: 1977.

Keohane, Robert and Judith Goldstein. "Ideas and Foreign Policy: An Analytical Framework." In *Ideas and Foreign Policy: Beliefs, Institutions and Political Change,* ed. isdem, 3–30. Ithaca, N.Y.: 1993.

Kern, Fritz. *Gottesgnadentum und Widerstandsrecht im früheren Mittelalter.* 4th ed. Darmstadt: 1967. Partial tr. *Kingship and Law in the Middle Ages.* Oxford: 1939.

Kershaw, Paul J. E. *Peaceful Kings: Peace, Power and the Early Medieval Political Imagination.* Oxford: 2011.

Kessler, Helmut. *Terreur: Ideologie und Nomenklatur der revolutionären Gewaltanwendung von 1770 bis 1794.* Munich: 1973.

Kieser, Hans-Lukas. *Nearest East: American Millennialism and Mission to the Middle East.* Philadelphia: 2010.

Kippenberg, Hans J. *Discovering Religious History in the Modern Age.* Princeton, N.J.: 2002.

Klaassen, Walter. *Living at the End of the Ages: Apocalypic Expectations in the Radical Reformation.* Lanham, Md.: 1992.

Kleber, Hermann. "Pélerinage, vengeance, conquête: La conception de la première croisade dans le cycle de Graindor de Douai." In *Au carrefour des routes d'Europe: La chanson de geste = Xe congrès . . . Renscesvals (1985),* ed. Jean Subrenat, 2: 757–75. Aix-en-Provence: 1987.

Klein, Hans-Joachim. *German Guerilla: Terror, Reaction, and Resistance.* Sanday and Minneapolis: 1981.

Kloke, Martin W. *Israel und die deutsche Linke. Zur Geschichte eines schwierigen Verhältnisses.* 2nd. ed. Frankfurt: 1994.

Knott, John R. *Discourses of Martyrdom in English Literature, 1563–1694.* Cambridge: 1993.

Koenen, Gerd. *Vesper, Ensslin, Baader: Urszenen des deutschen Terrorismus.* 2nd ed. Frankfurt-am-Main: 2005.

Konrad, Robert. "Das himmlische und das irdische Jerusalem im mittelalterlichen Denken: Mystische Vorstellung und geschichtliche Wirkung." In *Speculum Historiale: Geschichte im Spiegel von Geschichtsschreibung und Geschichtsdeutung, Festschrift Johannes Spörl,* ed. Clemens Bauer, Laetitia Boehm, and Max Müller, 523–40. Munich: 1965.

Koselleck, Reinhart. "Einleitung." In *Der politische Totenkult: Kriegerdenkmäler in der Moderne,* ed. idem and Michael Jeismann, 9–20. Munich: 1994.

——. *Kritik und Krise: Ein Beitrag zur Pathogenese der bürgerlichen Welt.* Freiburg: 1959. Tr. *Critique and Crisis: Enlightenment and the Pathogenesis of Modern Society.* Cambridge, Mass.: 1988.

Kostick, Conor. *The Social Structure of the First Crusade.* Leiden: 2008.

Krakau, Knud. "Response [to John H. Moorhead]." In *Many Are Chosen: Divine Election and Western Nationalism,* ed. William Hutchison and Hartmut Lehmann, 166–72. Harrisburg, Pa.: 1994.

Kraushaar, Wolfgang. "A l'ombre de la Fraction Armée Rouge, genèse des 'Cellules Révolutionnaires'." In *Terrorismes: L'Italie et l'Allemagne à l'épreuve des «années de plomb» (1970–1980): Réalités et représentations du terrorisme,* ed. Gius Gariulo and Otmar Seul, 105–21. Paris: 2008.

——. "Herbert Marcuse und das lebensweltliche Apriori der Revolte." In *Frankfurter Schule und Studentenbewegung,* ed. idem, 3: 195–203. Hamburg: 1993.

——. *Die RAF und der Linke Terrorismus.* 2 vols. Hamburg: 2006.

Kreiser, Robert. *Miracles, Convulsions and Ecclesiastical Politics in Early Eighteenth-Century Paris.* Princeton, N.J.: 1978.

Krey, Philip D. "The Apocalypse Commentary of 1329: Problems in Church History." In *Nicholas of Lyra: The Senses of Scripture,* ed. idem and Lesley Smith, 267–88. Leiden: 2000.

——. "Nicholas of Lyra and Paul of Burgos on Islam." In *Medieval Christian Perceptions of Islam,* ed. John V. Tolan, 153–74. London: 2000.

Kriegbaum, Bernhard. *Kirche der Traditoren oder Kirche der Martyrer? Die Vorgeschichte des Donatismus.* Innsbruck: 1986.

Kriegel, Annie. *Les grands procès dans les systèmes communists.* Paris: 1972.

Kriegel, Maurice. "La prise d'une décision: L'expulsion des juifs d'Espagne en 1492." *Revue Historique* 260 (1978): 49–90.

——. "The Reckonings of Nahmanides and Arnold of Villanova: On the Early Contacts Between Christian Millenarianism and Jewish Messianism." *Jewish History* 26 (2012): 17–40.

Krumeich, Gerd. "Auf dem Weg zum Volkskrieg? Jeanne d'Arc als «chef de guerre.»" In *Soldatinnen: Gewalt und Geschlecht im Krieg vom Mittelalter bis heute,* ed. Klaus Latzel, Franka Maubach, and Silke Satjukow, 113–28. Krieg in der Geschichte 60. Paderborn: 2010..

——. "Jeanne d'Arc a-t-elle menti? La 'Lettre aux Anglais' et les dénégations de la Pucelle: Un détail du Procès." *Écrire l'Histoire* 3 (Printemps 2009): 17–22.

Krumeich, Gerd, and Hartmut Lehmann, eds. *"Gott mit uns": Nation, Religion und Gewalt im 19. und frühen 20. Jahrhundert.* Veröffentlichungen des Max-Planck-Instituts für Geschichte 162. Göttingen: 2000.

Kruse, Wolfgang. *Die Erfindung des modernen Militarismus: Krieg, Militär und bürgerliche Gesellschaft im politischen Diskurs der Französichen Revolution 1789–1799.* Munich: 2003.

Kupperman, Karen Ordahl. *Settling with the Indians: The Meeting of English and Indian Cultures in America, 1580–1640*. Totowa, N.J.: 1980.

Kwiatkowski, Stefan. *Der Deutsche Orden im Streit mit Polen-Litauen*. Beiträge zur Friedensethik 32. Stuttgart: 2000.

Laarhoven, Jan van. "Chrétienté et croisade." *Cristianesimo nella storia* 6, 1 (1985): 27–43.

Lambert, Malcolm D. *Medieval Heresy: Popular Movements from the Gregorian Reform to the Reformation*. 3rd ed. Oxford: 2002.

Ladner, Gerhart B. *The Idea of Reform: Its Impact on Christian Thought and Action in the Age of the Fathers*. Rev. ed. New York: 1967.

Laharie, Muriel. *La folie au Moyen Age, XIe–XIIIe siècles*. Paris: 1991.

Lahire, Bernard. *L'homme pluriel: Les ressorts de l'action*. Paris: 1998. Tr. *The Plural Actor*. Cambridge: 2011.

Landes, Richard. *Heaven on Earth: The Varieties of the Millennial Experience*. Oxford: 2011.

——. "Lest the Millenium Be Fulfilled: Apocalyptic Expectations and the Pattern of Western Chronography, 100–800 CE." In *The Use and Abuse of Eschatology in the Middle Ages*, ed. Werner Verbeke et al., 137–211. Louvain: 1988.

——. "Millenarismus absconditus: L'historiographie augustinienne et l'An Mil." *Le Moyen Age* 98 (1993): 355–77.

——. *Relics, Apocalypse, and the Deceits of History: Ademar of Chabannes, 989–1034*. Cambridge, Mass.: 1995.

——. "Sur les traces du Millennium: La via negativa." *Le Moyen Age* 99 (1993): 5–26.

Langlois, Claude. "La religion révolutionnaire." In *Pratiques religieuses, mentalités et spiritualités dans l'Europe révolutionnaire, 1770–1820*, ed. Bernard Plongeron et al., 369–78. Turnhout: 1988.

Langmuir, Gavin I. *History, Religion and Antisemitism*. Berkeley, Calif.: 1990.

——. *Toward a Definition of Antisemitism*. Berkeley, Calif.: 1990.

Lankford, Adam. "Do Suicide Terrorists Exhibit Clinically Suicidal Risk Factors? A Review of Initial Evidence and Call for Future Research." *Aggression and Violent Behavior* 15 (2010): 334–40.

——. "Suicide Terrorism as a Socially Approved Form of Suicide." *Crisis: The Journal of Crisis Intervention and Suicide Prevention* 31, 6 (2010): 287–89.

Laqueur, Walter. *The Terrorism Reader: A Historical Anthology*. New York: 1978.

Lawrence, John Shelton and Robert Jewett. *Captain America and the Crusade Against Evil: The Dilemma of Zealous Nationalism*. Grand Rapids: 2003.

Leach, Douglas. *Flintlock and Tomahawk: New England in King Philip's War*. New York: 1958.

Lears, Jackson. *Rebirth of a Nation: The Making of Modern America, 1877–1920*. New York: 2009.

Le Bon, Gustave. *The Crowd: A Study of the Popular Mind*. Tr. Dunwoody, Ga.: 1968.

——. *La Révolution française et la psychologie des revolutions*. Paris: 1912. Tr. *The French Revolution and the Psychology of Revolutions*. New York: 1913.

Lecler, Joseph. *Histoire de la tolérance au siècle de la Réforme*. 2 vols. Paris: 1955. Tr. *Toleration and the Reformation*. London: 1960.

Lefort, Claude. "Introduction." In Edgar Quinet, *La revolution*. Paris: 1869. Rev. ed. Paris: 1986.

Le Goff, Jacques. "Préface." In Marc Bloch, *Apologie pour l'histoire ou le métier d'historien*. Paris: 1993.

——. *Saint Louis*. Paris: 1998.

Lepore, Jill. *The Name of War. Philip's War and the Origins of American Identity*. New York: 1998

Lerner, Robert A. "Medieval Millenarianism and Violence." In *Pace e guerra nel basso Medioevo*, 37–52. Atti dei convegni dell'Accademia tudertina e del Centro di studi sulla spiritualita medievale 40. Spoleto: 2004.

————."The Medieval Return to the Thousand-Year Sabbath." In *The Apocalypse in the Middle Ages*, ed. Richard K. Emmerson and Bernard McGinn, 51–71. Ithaca, N.Y.: 1992.

————. "Refreshment of the Saints: The Time After Antichrist as a Station for Earthly Progress in Medieval Thought." *Traditio* 32 (1976): 97–144.

Le Roux, Nicolas. *Un régicide au nom de Dieu: L'assassinat d'Henri III, 1er août 1589*. Paris: 2006.

Levi, Giovanni. "Les usages de la biographie." *Annales* E.S.C. 44, 6 (1989): 1325–36.

Lévi-Strauss, Claude. "Introduction à l'œuvre de Marcel Mauss." In Marcel Mauss, *Sociologie et anthropologie par Marcel Mauss précédé d'une Introduction à l'œuvre de Marcel Mauss par Claude Lévy-Strauss*, ix–lii. Paris: 1950.

Lewis, Suzanne. *Reading Images: Narrative Discourse and Reception in the Thirteenth-Century Illuminated Apocalypse*. Cambridge: 1995.

Lincoln, Bruce. *Holy Terrors: Thinking About Religion After September 11*. Chicago: 2003.

Linderman, Gerald. *The Mirror of War: American Society and the Spanish-American War*. Ann Arbor, Mich.: 1974.

Lipton, Sara. *Images of Intolerance: The Representation of Jews and Judaism in the Bible Moralisée*. Berkeley, Calif.: 1999.

Little, David. *Religion, Order, and Law*. Chicago: 1969.

Little, Lester K. "The Function of the Jews in the Commercial Revolution." In *Povertà e ricchezza nella spiritualità dei secoli XI e XII*, 273–87. Atti dei convegni del Centro di studi sulla spiritualita' medievale 8. Todi: 1969.

————. *Religious Poverty and the Profit Economy in Medieval Europe*. Ithaca, N.Y.: 1978.

Lobrichon, Guy. "L'Apocalypse des théologiens." Thèse de Doctorat du troisième cycle. *Histoire du futur: Lectures de l'Apocalypse au Moyen-Age (XIe–XIIe siècles)*. Paris: forthcoming.

————. "Les courants spirituels dans la Chrétienté occidentale à l'aube du Concile de Plaisance." In *Il concilio di Piacenza e le cruciate*, ed. Pierre Racine, 51–62. Piacenza: 1996.

————. *1099. Jérusalem conquise*. Paris: 1998.

Loeb, Isidore. "La controverse de 1240 sur le Talmud." *Revue des Études Juives* 1 (1880): 247–60; 2 (1881): 248–70; 3 (1881): 39–57.

Loserth, Johann. *Hus und Wiclif: Zur Genesis der husitischen Lehre*. Prague: 1884.

Löwith, Karl. *Meaning in History: The Theological Implications of the Theology of History*. Tr. Chicago: 1957.

Lubac, Henri de. *Medieval Exegesis*. Vol. 1, *The Four Senses of Scripture*. Paris: 1959. Tr. Grand Rapids, Mich.: 1998.

————. *La postérité spirituelle de Joachim de Fiore*. 2 vols. Paris: 1979–81.

Lübbe, Hermann. "Aufklärung und Terror. Geschichtsmetaphysische Voraussetzungen totalitärer Demokratie." In *„Vergangene Zukunft": Revolution und Künste 1789 bis 1989*, ed. Erhard Schütz and Klaus Siebenhaar, 34–47. Bonn: 1992.

Lucas, Colin. "'Presentation' to Mona Ozouf and François Furet." In *The French Revolution and the*

Creation of Modern Political Culture. Vol. 3. *The Transformation of the Political Culture, 1789–1848,* ed. Mona Ozouf and François Furet, 343–50. Ann Arbor, Mich.: 1989.

Lukács, György. *History and Class Consciousness: Studies in Marxist Dialectics.* Tr. Cambridge, Mass.: 1971. 2nd ed. Tr. London: 1978.

Lupoi, Maurizio. *The Origins of the European Legal Order.* Tr. Cambridge: 2000.

MacCormack, Sabine. "Loca sancta: The Organization of Sacred Topography in Late Antiquity." In *The Blessings of Pilgrimage,* ed. Robert Ousterhout, 7–40. Urbana, Ill.: 1990.

MacCulloch, Diarmaid. *Reformation: Europe's House Divided, 1490–1700.* London: 2003.

Macek, Josef. *Die hussitische revolutionäre Bewegung.* Ger. tr. Berlin: 1956.

MacKay, Charles. *Extraordinary Popular Delusions and the Madness of Crowds.* 3 vols. London: 1841.

MacKenzie, Kenneth. *The Robe and the Sword: The Methodist Church and the Rise of American Imperialism.* Washington, D.C.: 1961.

Maier, Christoph T. "The Bible Moralisée and the Crusades." In *The Experience of Crusading,* vol. 1, *Western Approaches,* ed. Marcus Bull and Norman Housley, 209–22. Cambridge: 2003.

Maier, Hans. "Political Religion: A Concept and Its Limitations." *Totalitarian Movements and Political Religions* 8, 1 (2007): 5–16.

Maire, Catherine-Laurence. *Les convulsionnaires de Saint-Médard: Miracles, convulsions et prophéties à Paris au XVIIIe siècle.* Paris: 1985.

Makiya, Kanan. *Republic of Fear: The Politics of Modern Iraq.* Rev. ed. Berkeley, Calif.: 1998.

Malcolm, Noel. *Kosovo: A Short History.* London: 1998.

Malegam, Jehangir Yezdi. "No Peace for the Wicked: Conflicting Visions of Peacemaking in an Eleventh-Century Monastic Narrative." *Viator: Medieval and Renaissance Studies* 39, 1 (2008): 23–49.

———. *The Sleep of Behomoth: Disputing Peace and Violence in Medieval Europe, 1000–1200.* Ithaca, N.Y.: 2013.

Malnou, François. "L'abbé J.-B. Lanot, curé d'Ussac." *Bulletin de la Société des Lettres, Sciences et Arts de la Corrèze* 93, 2 (1990): 37–46.

Marcuse, Herbert. "Repressive Tolerance." In *A Critique of Pure Tolerance,* ed. Robert Paul Wolff, Barrington Moore, and idem, 93–137. Rev. ed. Boston: 1969.

Marin, Olivier. *L'archevêque, le maître et le dévôt: Genèses du mouvement réformateur pragois, années 1360–1419.* Paris: 2005.

Markowski, Michael. "Peter of Blois and the Conception of the Third Crusade." In *Outremer: Studies in the History of the Crusading Kingdom of Jerusalem Presented to Joshua Prawer,* ed. Benjamin Z. Kedar, Hans Eberhard Mayer, and R. C. Smail, 261–69. Jerusalem: 1982.

Markus, Robert A. *Saeculum: History and Society in the Thought of Saint Augustine.* Rev. ed. Cambridge: 1970.

Martin, Jean-Clément. *Violence et révolution: Essai sur la naissance d'un mythe national.* Paris: 2006.

Marty, Martin E. *Righteous Empire: The Protestant Experience in America.* New York: 1970.

Mastnak, Tomaž. *Crusading Peace: Christendom, the Muslim World, and Western Political Order.* Berkeley, Calif.: 2002.

Mathiez, Albert. *Contributions à l'histoire religieuse de la Révolution française.* Paris: 1907.

Matz, Ulrich. "Über gesellschaftliche und politische Bedingungen des deutschen Terrorismus." In

Gewalt und Legitimität, ed. idem and Gerhard Schmidtchen, 15–103. Analysen zum Terrorismus 4:1. Opladen: 1983.

Mayer, Arno J. *The Furies: Violence and Terror in the French and Russian Revolutions*. Princeton, N.J.: 2000.

McCormick, Michael. *Eternal Victory: Triumphal Rulership in Late Antiquity, Byzantium, and the Medieval West*. Cambridge: 1986.

———. "Liturgie et guerre des Carolingiens à la première croisade." In *'Militia Christi' e Crociata nei secoli XI–XIII, Atti della undecima Settimana internazionale di studio, Mendola, 28/08–1/09 1989*, 211–40. Miscellanea del Centro di studi medioevali 30. Milan: 1992.

McGinn, Bernard. *Visions of the End: Apocalyptic Traditions in the Middle Ages*. New York: 1979.

McGrath, Robert Leon. "The Romance of the Maccabees in Mediaeval Art and Literature." Ph.D. dissertation, PrincetonUniversity, 1963.

McLear, J[ames] F. "New England an the Fifth Monarchy: The Quest for the Millennium in Early American Puritanism." *William & Mary Quarterly* 3rd ser. 32, 2 (1975): 223–60.

Medvedev, Roy. *Let History Judge: The Origins and Consequences of Stalinism*. Rev. ed. New York: 1989.

Mégier, Elisabeth. "Il senso letterale dell'Apocalisse: negazione e affermazione, in alcuni commentari latini del Medioevo monastico, da Beda il Venerabile a Ruperto di Deutz." In *L'Apocalisse nel Medio Evo: Atti del convegno internazionale dell'Università degli studi di Milano e della Società Internazionale per lo Studio del Medioevo Latino, Gargnano sul Garda, 18–20 maggio 2009*, ed. Rossana E. Guglielmetti, 133–79. Florence: 2011.

Menache, Sylvia. "Tartars, Jews, Saracens and the Jewish-Mongol 'Plot' of 1241." *History* 81 (1996): 319–42.

Mendel, Arthur P. *Vision and Violence*. Ann Arbor, Mich.: 1992.

Mengel, David C. "From Venice to Jerusalem and Beyond: Milíč of Kroměříž and the Topography of Prostitution in Medieval Prague." *Speculum* 79, 2 (2004): 407–42.

Merari, Ariel. "The Readiness to Kill and Die: Suicidal Terrorism in the Middle East." In *Origins of Terrorism: Psychologies, Ideologies, Theologies, States of Mind*, ed. Walter Reich, 192–206. Cambridge: 1990.

Merari, Ariel et al. "Personality Characteristics of 'Self Martyrs': 'Suicide Bombers' and Organizers of Suicide Attacks." *Terrorism amd Political Violence* 22, 1 (2010): 87–101.

Merleau-Ponty, Maurice. *Humanisme et terreur: Essai sur le problème communiste*. Paris: 1947. Tr. *Humanism and Terror: An Essay on the Communist Problem*. Boston: 1969.

Meyer-Kalkus, Reinhard. "‚Schöne Ungeheuer' und ‚Menschliche Geschosse': Gotthold Ephraim Lessing, Walter Benjamin und Ernst Jünger über Märtyrer und Märtyrerdramen." In *Martyrdom in Literature: Visions of Death and Meaningful Suffering in Europe and the Middle East from Antiquity to Modernity*, ed. Friederike Pannewick, 301–27. Wiesbaden: 2004.

Michaud, Joseph François. *Histoire des Croisades*. 5 vols. 4th ed. Paris: 1825–28.

Michaud-Fréjaville, Françoise. "L'effusion de sang dans les procès et les traités concernant Jeanne d'Arc (1430–1456)." In *Le sang au Moyen Age*, ed. Marcel Faure, 331–40. Cahiers du CRISIMA 4. Montpellier: 1999.

Midelfort, H. C. Erik. "Charcot, Freud and the Demons." In *Werewolves, Witches, and Wandering*

Spirits: Traditional Belief and Folklore in Early Modern Europe, ed. Kathryn A. Edwards, 199–215. Kirksville, Mo.: 2002.

———. "Madness and the Millennium of Münster, 1534–1535." In *Fearful Hope*, ed. Christopher Kleinhenz and Fannie J. Lemoine, 115–34. Madison, Wis.: 1999.

Miethke, Jürgen. "Heiliger Heidenkrieg? Theoretische Kontroversen zwischen Deutschem Orden und dem Königreich Polen vor und auf dem Konstanzer Konzil." In *Heilige Kriege: Religiöse Begründungen militärischer Gewaltanwendung. Judentum, Christentum und Islam im Vergleich*, ed. Klaus Schreiner and Elisabeth Müller-Luckner, 109–25. Munich: 2008.

Milhou, Alain. "La chauve-souris, le nouveau David, et le roi caché (trois images de l'empereur des derniers temps dans la péninsule ibérique: XIIIe–XVIIe s)." *Mélanges de la Casa de Velásquez* 18, 1 (1982): 61–78.

Molnár, Amedeo. "L'évolution de la théologie hussite." *Revue d'Histoire et de Philosophie Religieuse* 43 (1963): 133–71.

Momigliano, Arnaldo. "Freedom of Speech and Religious Tolerance in the Ancient World." In *Anthropology and the Greeks*, ed. Susan Humphreys, 179–93. London: 1978.

———. "Preliminary Indications on the Apocalypse and Exodus from the Jewish Tradition." Italian orig. in idem, *Pagine ebraice*. Turin: 1987. Tr. in idem, *Essays on Ancient and Modern Judaism*, 88–100. Chicago: 1994.

Moore, Robert Ian. "Family, Community and Cult on the Eve of the Gregorian Reform." *Transactions of the Royal Historical Society* 5th ser. 30 (1980): 49–69.

———. *The First European Revolution, c. 970–1215*. Oxford: 2000.

Morris, Colin. "Martyrs on the Field of Battle Before and During the First Crusade." In *Martyrs and Martyrologies*, ed. Diana Wood, 93–104. Studies in Church History 30. Oxford: 1993.

———. "Policy and Visions: The Case of the Holy Lance at Antioch." In *War and Government in the Middle Ages: Essays in Honour of J. O. Prestwich*, ed. John Gillingham and J. C. Holt, 33–45. Totowa, N.J.: 1984.

Morton, Nicholas. "The Defense of the Holy Land and the Memory of the Maccabees." *Journal of Medieval History* 36, 3 (2010): 275–93.

Mosse, George L. *The Crisis of German Ideology: Intellectual Origins of the Third Reich*. New York: 1964.

———. *Fallen Soldiers: Reshaping the Memory of the World Wars*. Oxford: 1990.

Mousnier, Roland. *L'assassinat d'Henri IV. 14 mai 1610*. Paris: 1964. Tr. *The Assassination of Henry IV: The Problem of the Tyrannicide and the Consolidation of the French Monarchy in the Early Seventeenth Century*. New York: 1973.

Müller-Mertens, Eckhard. "Frankenreich oder Nicht-Frankenreich? Überlegungen zum Reich der Ottonen anhand des Herrschertitels und der politischen Struktur des Reiches." In *Beiträge zur mittelalterlichen Reichs- und Nationsbildung in Deutschland und in Frankreich*, ed. Lothar Gall, 45–52. Historische Zeitschrift Beihefte 244. Munich: 1997.

Muldoon, James. *Popes, Lawyers and Infidels*. Liverpool: 1979.

Musolff, Andreas. *Krieg gegen die Öffentlichkeit. Terrorismus und politischer Sprachgebrauch*. Opladen: 1996.

Nahon, Gérard. "Les ordonnances de Saint Louis sur les juifs." *Nouveaux Cahiers* 23 (1970): 18–35.

Nash, Gary. *Red, White, and Black: The People of Early America*. Englewood Cliffs, N.J.: 1974.

Neaman, Judith S. *Suggestion of the Devil: The Origins of Madness.* New York: 1975.

Necheles, Ruth F. *The Abbé Grégoire, 1787–1831: The Odyssey of an Egalitarian.* Westport, Conn.: 1971

Ninde, Edward S. *The Story of the American Hymn.* New York: 1921.

Nirenberg, David. *Communities of Violence.* Princeton, N.J.: 1996.

———. "Le dilemme du souverain: génocide et justice à Valence, 1391." In *Un Moyen Age pour aujourd'hui: Mélanges offerts à Claude Gauvard,* ed. Julie Claustre, Oliver Mattéoni, and Nicolas Offenstadt, 494–508. Paris: 2010.

———. "Massacre and Miracle in Valencia, 1391." In *La corona catalanoaragonesa, l'Islam i el món mediterrani: Estudis d'història medieval en homenatge a la doctora Maria Teresa Ferrer i Mallol,* ed. Josefina Mutgé, Roser Salicrú i Llich, and Carles Vela Aulesa, 515–26. Barcelona: 2013.

Noll, Mark. A. *The Civil War as a Theological Crisis.* Chapel Hill: 2006.

———. "The Image of the United States as a Biblical Nation, 1176–1865." In *The Bible in America: Essays in Cultural History,* ed. Nathan O. Hatch and idem, 39–58. Oxford: 1982.

North, William. "Polemic, Apathy, and Authorial Initiative in Gregorian Rome: The Curious Case of Bruno of Segni." *Haskins Society Journal* 10 (2001): 115–29.

Norton, Mary Beth. *In the Devil's Snare: The Salem Witchcraft Crisis of 1692.* New York: 2002.

Nudelman, Franny. *John Brown's Body: Slavery, Violence, and the Culture of War.* Chapel Hill, N.C.: 2004.

Nye, Robert A. "Introduction: Gustave LeBon's *Psychology of Revolution*: History, Social Science, and Politics in Nineteenth and Early Twentieth Century France." In Gustave Le Bon, *The French Revolution and the Psychology of Revolution,* v–xlix. Tr. New Brunswick and London: 1980.

———. *The Origins of Crowd Psychology: Gustave Le Bon and the Crisis of Mass Democracy in the Third Republic.* London: 1975.

Oates, Stephen B. *To Purge This Land with Blood: A Biography of John Brown.* 2nd ed. Amherst, Mass.: 1984.

Offenstadt, Nicolas. *Faire la paix au Moyen Age: Discours et gestes de la paix pendant la guerre de cent ans.* Paris: 2007.

Ozouf, Mona. *L'homme régénéré: Essais sur la Révolution française.* Paris: 1989.

———. "Régénération." In *Dictionnaire critique de la Révolution française,* ed. François Furet and eadem, 821–31. Paris: 1988.

Padel, Ruth. *Whom Gods Destroy: Elements of Greek and Tragic Madness.* Princeton, N.J.: 1995.

Pahl, Jon. *Empire of Sacrifice: The Religious Origins of American Violence.* New York: 2010.

———. "Shifting Sacrifices: Christians, War, and Peace in America." In *American Christianities: A History of Dominance and Diversity,* ed. Catherine A. Brekus and W. Clark Gilpin, 445–65. Chapel Hill, N.C.: 2011.

Panunzio, Sergio. *Diritto, forza e violenza: Lineamenti di una teoria della violenza.* Bologna: 1921.

Pappenheim, Martin. *Erinnerung und Unsterblichkeit: Semantische Studien zum Totenkult in Frankreich.* Stuttgart: 1992.

Paul, Gerhard. "Von Psychopathen, Technokraten des Terrors und ganz gewöhnlichen Deutschen: Die Täter der Shoah im Spiegel der Forschung." In idem, *Die Täter der Shoah: Fanatische Nationalsozialisten oder ganz normale Deutsche?,* 13–80. Göttingen: 2002.

Paul, Nicholas L. "Crusade, Memory and Regional Politics in Twelfth-Century Amboise." *Journal of Medieval History* 31, 2 (2005): 127–41.

Pearl, Jonathan L. *The Crime of Crimes: Demonology and Politics in France 1560–1620*. Waterloo [Canada]: 1999.

Perinbam, B. Marie. *Holy Violence: The Revolutionary Thought of Frantz Fanon*. Washington, D.C.: 1982.

Pfau, Aleksandra Nicole. "Madness in the Realm: Narratives of Mental Illness in Late Medieval France." Ph.D. dissertation. University of Michigan, 2008.

Pomper, Philip. *The Russian Revolutionary Intelligentsia*. New York: 1970. 2nd ed. Arlington Heights, Ill.: 1993.

Portelli, Hughes. *Gramsci et la question religieuse*. Paris: 1974.

Porter, Roy. *Mind-Forg'd Manacles: A History of Madness in England from the Restoration to the Regency*. London: 1987.

Post, Jerrold M. "Terrorist Psycho-Logic: Terrorist Behavior as a Product of Psychological Forces." In *Origins of Terrorism: Psychologies, Ideologies, Theologies, States of Mind*, ed. Walter Reich, 25–40. Cambridge: 1990.

Potestà, Gian Luca. *Il tempo dell'Apocalisse: Vita di Gioacchino da Fiore*. Rome: 2004.

———. *L'ultimo messia: Profezia e sovranità nel Medioevo*. Milan: 2014.

Potestà, Gian Luca and Marco Rizzi, eds. *L'anticristo*. Vol. 1, *I nemico di tempi finali*. Milan: 2005. Vol. 2, *Il Figlio della perdizione: Testi dal IV al XII seculo*. Milan: 2012.

Poumarède, Géraud. *Pour en finir avec la croisade: Mythes et réalités de la guerre contre les Turcs aux XVIe et XVIIe siècles*. Paris: 2004.

Price, Jonathan J. *Jerusalem Under Siege: The Collapse of the Jewish State 66–70 C.E.* Leiden: 1992.

Price, Simon. *Rituals and Power: The Roman Imperial Cult in Asia Minor*. Cambridge: 1984.

Pryor, Charles and Glenn Burgess, eds. *England's War of Religion, Revisited*. Farnham: 2011.

Quinet, Edgar. *Le Christianisme et la Révolution française*. Paris: 1845.

———. *La revolution*. Rev. ed. Paris: 1986.

Rajak, Tessa. *Josephus: The Historian and His Society*. 2nd ed. London: 2002.

Rapoport, David C. "Fear and Trembling in Three Religious Traditions." *American Political Science Review* 78, 3 (1984): 658–77.

———. "Introduction." In Rapoport and Alexander, *Morality of Terrorism*, 1–7. 2nd ed. New York: 1989.

———. "Messianism and Terror." *Center Magazine* 19 (1986): 30–39.

———. "Messianic Sanctions for Terror." *Comparative Politics* 20, 2 (1988): 195–213.

Rapoport, David C. and Yonah Alexander, eds. *The Morality of Terrorism: Religious and Secular Justifications*. 2nd ed. New York: 1989.

Ratzinger, Joseph, with Vittorio Messori. *The Ratzinger Report: An Exclusive Interview on the State of the Church*. Tr. San Francisco: 1986. Orig. *Zur Lage des Glaubens: Ein Gespräch mit Vittorio Messori*. Munich: 1985.

Reeves, Marjorie. *The Influence of Prophecy in the Later Middle Ages: A Study in Joachimism*. Oxford: 1969.

Reinecke, Stefan. "Das letzte Wort des Angeklagten Bucharin." In *Das letzte Wort des Angeklagten in der Strafsache des antisowjetischen „Blocks der Rechten und Trotzkisten": Verhandelt vor dem Militärkollegium der Obersten Gerichtshofes der UdSSR in der Abendsitzung des 12. März 1938*, 39–78. Hamburg: 1996.

Reinitz, Richard. "The Separatist Background of Roger William's Argument for Religious Tolera-tion." In *Typology and Early American Literature*, ed. Sacvan Bercovitch, 107–37. Amherst, Mass.: 1972.

Remensnyder, Amy G. *La Conquistadora: The Virgin Mary at Peace and at War in the Old World and the New*. Oxford: 2014.

———. "Marian Monarchy in Thirteenth-Century Castile." In *The Experience of Power in Medieval Europe, 950–1350*, ed. Robert Berkhofer, Alan Cooper and Adam Kosto, 253–70. Aldershot: 2005.

———. "Purity, Pollution, and Peace: An Aspect of Social Reform Between the Late Tenth Century and 1076." In *The Peace of God: Social Violence and Religious Response in France Around the Year 1000*, ed. Thomas Head and Richard Landes, 280–307. Ithaca, N.Y.: 1992.

Richet, Denis. "La monarchie au travail sur elle-même?" In *The French Revolution and the Creation of Modern Political Culture*, vol. 1, *The Political Culture of the Old Regime*, ed. Keith Michael Baker, 25–39. Oxford: 1987.

Riley-Smith, Jonathan. *The Crusades: A Short History*. New Haven, Conn.: 1987.

———. "Crusading as an Act of Love." *History* 65 (1980): 177–92. Repr. in *The Crusades: The Essential Readings*, ed. Thomas F. Madden, 31–50. Oxford: 2002.

———. *The First Crusade and the Idea of Crusading*. Philadelphia: 1986.

———. "The First Crusade and the Persecution of the Jews." In *Persecution and Toleration*, ed. W. J. Sheils. *Studies in Church History* 21 (1984): 51–72.

———. *The First Crusaders, 1095–1131*. Rev. ed. Cambridge: 1998.

Rivière, Claude. *Les liturgies politiques*. Paris: 1988.

Roberts, David D. " 'Political Religion' and the Totalitarian Departures of Inter-War Europe: On the Uses and Disadvantages of an Analytical Category." *Contemporary European History* 18, 4 (2009): 381–414.

Roberts, Penny. "Peace, Ritual and Sexual Violence During the Wars of Religion." *Past & Present* 214, supplement 7 (2012): 75–99.

Robinson, Ian S. *Authority and Resistance in the Investiture Contest*. Manchester: 1978.

———. " 'Political Allegory' in the Biblical Exegesis of Bruno de Segni." *Recherches de Théologie Anci-enne et Médiévale* 50, 1 (1983): 69–98.

Roelker, Nancy. *One King, One Faith: The Parlement de Paris and the Religious Reformations of the Six-teenth Century*. Berkeley, Calif.: 1996.

Rohrmoser, Günter and Jörg Fröhlich. "Ideologische Ursachen des Terrorismus." In *Ideologien und Strategien*, ed. Iring Fetscher, et al., 277–339. Bundesministerium des Innern. Arbeiten zum Ter-rorismus 1. Opladen: 1981.

Roncetti, Mario, Pietro Scarpellini, and Francesco Tommasi. *Templari e Ospitalieri in Italia: La chiesa di San Bevignate a Perugia*. Milan: 1987.

Röricht, Reinhold. "Die Pastorellen (1251)." *Zeitschrift für Kirchengeschichte* 6 (1884): 290–96.

Rosenstock-Huessy, Eugen. *Die europäischen Revolutionen und der Charakter der Nationen*. 2nd rev. ed. Stuttgart: 1951.

———. *Out of Revolution: Autobiography of Western Man*. New York: 1938.

Rosenthal, Judah M. "The Talmud on Trial." *Jewish Quarterly Review* 47 (1956–1957): 58–76, 145–69.

Rosenwein, Barbara. *Emotional Communities in the Early Middle Ages*. Ithaca, N.Y.: 2006.

Rosenwein, Barbara. "Feudal War and Monastic Peace: Cluniac Liturgy as Ritual Aggression." *Viator* 2 (1971): 128–57.

Rousset, Paul. *Les origines et les caractères de la première croisade.* Neuchâtel: 1945.

Rubenstein, Jay. *Armies of Heaven: The First Crusade and the Quest for Apocalypse.* New York: 2011.

———. "Cannibals and Crusaders." *French Historical Studies* 31, 4 (2008): 525–52.

———. "Crusade and Apocalypse: Making History at the End of Times." Manuscript, under review with *Questiones Medii Aevi Novae.*

———. "Godfrey of Bouillon vs. Raymond of Saint-Gilles: How Carolingian Kingship Trumped Millenarianism at the End of the First Crusade." In *The Legend of Charlemagne in the Middle Ages: Power, Faith, and Crusade,* ed. Matthew Gabriele and Jace Stuckey, 59–75. New York: 2008.

———. *Guibert of Nogent: Portarit of a Medieval Mind.* New York: 2002.

———. "How, or How Much, to Reevaluate Peter the Hermit." In *The Medieval Crusade,* ed. Susan J. Ridyard, 53–70. Woodbridge: 2004.

———. "What Is the Gesta Francorum and Who Was Peter Tudebode?" *Revue Mabillon* n.s. 16 (2005): 179–204.

Russell, Fredrick H. *The Just War in the Middle Ages.* Cambridge: 1975.

Russell, James C. *The Germanization of Medieval Christianity: A Sociohistorical Approach.* Oxford: 1996.

Russell, Jeffrey Burton. *The Devil: Perceptions of Evil from Antiquity to Primitive Chrisitianity.* Ithaca, N.Y.: 1977.

———. *Lucifer: The Devil in the Middle Ages.* Ithaca, N.Y.: 1984.

———. *Mephistopheles: The Devil in the Modern Age.* Ithaca, N.Y.: 1986.

———. *Satan: The Early Christian Tradition.* Ithaca, N.Y.: 1981.

Russell, P. E. "El descubrimiento de Canarias y el debate medieval acerca de los derechos de los príncipes y pueblos paganos." *Revista de historia canaria* 36 (1978): 9–32.

Sagan, Eli. *Citizens and Cannibals: The French Revolution, the Struggle for Modernity, and the Origins of Ideological Terror.* Lanham, Md.: 2001.

Sageman, Marc. *Understanding Terror Networks.* Philadelphia: 2004.

Sahlins, Marshall. *Historical Metaphors and Mythical Realities: Structure in the Early History of the Sandwich Islands Kingdom.* Ann Arbor, Mich.: 1981.

———. *Islands of History.* Chicago: 1985.

Salisbury, Neal. *Manitou and Providence: Indians, Europeans and the Making of New England.* Oxford: 1982.

Sandl, *Medialität und Ereignis: Eine Zeitgeschichte der Reformation.* Zürich: 2011.

Sauter, Franz. *Der römische Kaiserkult bei Martial und Statius.* Tübinger Beiträge zur Altertumswissenschaft 21. Stuttgart: 1934.

Savigny, Rafaele. "Il tema del millenio in alcuni commentari altomedievali latini." *Annali di storia dell' esegesi* 15, 1 (1998): 231–73.

Schaff, Phillip. *Der Bürgerkrieg und das christliche Leben in Nordamerika.* 3rd ed. Berlin: 1866.

Schaller, Hans-Martin. "Eine kuriale Briefsammlung des 13. Jahrhunderts mit unbekannten Briefen Friedrich II." *Deutsches Archiv* 18 (1962): 171–213.

Scheid, John and Marc Linder. "Quand croire c'est faire. Le problème de la croyance dans la Rome ancienne." *Archives de Sciences Sociales des Religions* 81, 1 (1993): 47–62.

Schein, Sylvia. *Gateway to the Heavenly City: Crusade, Jerusalem and the Catholic West (1099–1187)*. Aldershot: 2005.

———. "Die Kreuzzüge als volkstümlich-messianistische Bewegungen." *Deutsches Archiv* 47 (1991): 119–38.

Schiffman, Lawrence H. *Reclaiming the Dead Sea Scrolls: The History of Judaism, the Background of Christianity, the Lost Library of Qumran*. Philadelphia: 1995.

Schild, Georg. "'Burn Their Houses and Cut Down Their Corn': Englische Kolonisierungskriege in Virginia und Neu-England, 1607–1646." In *Formen des Krieges: Von der Antike bis zur Gegenwart*, ed. Dietrich Beyrau, Michael Hochgeschwender, and Dieter Langewiesche, 243–68. Krieg in der Geschichte 37. Paderborn: 2007.

Schmale, Wolfgang. *Entchristianisierung, Revolution und Verfassung: Zur Mentalitätsgeschichte der Verfassung in Frankreich, 1715–1794*. Berlin: 1988.

Schmidtchen, Gerhard and Hans-Martin Uehlinger. "Jugend und Staat: Übergänge von der Bürger-Aktivität zur Illegalität: Eine empirische Untersuchung zur Sozialpsychologie der Demokratie." In *Gewalt und Legitimität*, ed. Ulrich Matz, Gerhard Schmidtchen and Hans-Martin Uehlinger 105–437. Analysen zum Terrorismus 4:1. Opladen: 1983.

Schmitt, Carl. *Political Theology: Four Chapters on the Concept of Sovereignty*. Tr. Chicago: 1985, 2006.

Schmitt, Jean-Claude. "La culture de *l'imago*." *Annales, Histoire, Sciences Sociales* 51, 1 (1996): 3–36.

Schmolinsky, Sabine. *Der Apokalypsenkommentar des Alexander Minorita: Zur frühen Rezeption Joachims von Fiore in Deutschland*. MGH Studien und Texte 3. Hannover: 1991.

Schreckenberg, Hans. *Die Flavius-Josephus Tradition in Antike und Mittelalter*. Leiden: 1972.

Schreiner, Klaus. ",Duldsamkeit' (tolerantia) oder ,Schrecken' (terror)." In *Religiöse Devianz: Untersuchungen zu sozialen, rechtlichen und theologischen Reaktionen auf religiöse Abweichung im westlichen und östlichen Mittelalter*, ed. Dieter Simon, 159–210. Frankfurt-am-Main: 1990.

———. "Die Makkabäer. Jüdische Märtyrer und Kriegshelden im liturgischen und historischen Gedächtnis der abendländischen Christenheit." In idem, *Märtyrer, Schlachtenhelfer, Friedenstifter: Krieg und Frieden im Spiegel mittelalterlicher und frühneuzeitlicher Heiligenverehrung*, 1–53. Opladen: 2000.

———. "Toleranz." In *Geschichtliche Grundbegriffe*, ed. Otto Brunner, Werner Conze, and Reinhart Koselleck, 6: 445–605. Stuttgart: 1990.

Seibt, Ferdinand. *Hussitica: Zur Struktur einer Revolution*. Cologne: 1965.

Selch Jensen, Carsten. "Gods War: War and Christianisation on the Baltic Frontier in the Early 13th Century." *Quaestiones Medii Aevi Novae* 16 (2011): 123–47.

Sepinwall, Alyssa. *The Abbé Grégoire and the French Revolution: The Making of Modern Universalism*. Berkeley, Calif.: 2005.

Severnich, Michael. "Interkulturelle Kommunikation und christliche Mission in der frühen Neuzeit." In *Wechselseitige Wahrnehmung der Religionen im Spätmittelalter und in der Frühen Neuzeit*, ed. Ludger Grenzman et al., 125–41. Berlin: 2009.

Shaw, Brent. "Bandits in the Roman Empire." *Past & Present* 105 (1984): 3–52.

Sheehan, James. *Where Have All the Soldiers Gone? The Transformation of Modern Europe*. New York: 2008.

Shimahara, Sumi. "La représentation du pouvoir séculier chez Haymon d'Auxerre." In *The Multiple Meaning of Scripture*, ed. Ineke van't Spijkers, 77–99. Leiden: 2009.

Shorten, Richard. "The Enlightenment, Communism and Political Religion: Reflections on a Misleading Trajectory." *Journal of Political Ideologies* 8, 1 (2003): 13–37.

Siberry, Elizabeth. *Criticism of Crusading, 1095–1274*. Oxford: 1985.

Sieber-Lehmann, Claudius. "An Obscure but Powerful Pattern: Crusading, Nationalism and the Swiss Confederation in the Late Middle Ages." In *Crusading in the Fifteenth Century: Message and Impact*, ed. Norman Housley, 81–93. Basingstoke: 2004.

Simmons, William. "Cultural Bias in the New England Puritans' Perception of Indians." *Williams and Mary Quarterly* 3rd ser. 38, 1 (1981): 56–72.

Simonetta, Stefano. "Pace e guerra nel movimento wycliffitta." In *Pace e guerra nel basso medioevo*, 79–111. Atti dei convegni dell'Accademia tudertina e del Centro di studi sulla spiritualita' medievale 40. Spoleto: 2004.

Sizgorich, Thomas. *Violence and Belief in Late Antiquity: Militant Devotion in Christianity and Islam*. Philadelphia: 2009.

Skinner, Quentin. *The Foundations of Modern Political Theory*. 2 vols. Cambridge: 1978.

———. "The Paradoxes of Political Liberty." In *The Tanner Lectures in Human Values*, ed. Sterling M. McMurrin, 193–221. Cambridge, Mass.: 1986.

Slotkin, Richard. *Regeneration Through Violence: The Mythology of the American Frontier*. Middletown, Conn.: 1973.

Šmahel, František. "The Idea of 'Nation' in Hussite Bohemia." *Historica* 7 (1969): 143–247; 8 (1969): 93–197.

———. "*Pax externa et interna*: Vom Heiligen Krieg zur erzwungenen Toleranz im hussitischen Böhmen (1419–1485)." In *Toleranz im Mittelalter*, ed. Alexander Patschovsky and Harald Zimmermann, 221–73. Vorträge und Forschungen 45. Sigmaringen: 1998.

Smith, Caroline. *Crusading in the Age of Joinville*. Aldershot: 2006.

Smith, Jonathan Z. "The Devil in Mr. Jones." In *Imagining Religion: From Babylon to Jonestown*, ed. idem, 102–20. Chicago: 1982.

———. "Earth and Gods." In *Map Is Not Territory: Studies in the History of Religion*, ed. idem, 104–28. Studies in Judaism in Late Antiquity 23. Leiden: 1978.

Smoller, Laura A. "Of Earthquakes, Hail, Frogs, and Geography: Plague and the Investigation of the Apocalypse in the Later Middle Ages." In *Last Things: Death and the Apocalypse in the Middle Ages*, ed. Paul Freedman and Caroline W. Bynum, 157–87. Philadelphia: 2000.

Sorel, Georges. *Réflexions sur la violence*. Rev. ed. Paris: 1950.

Soukup, Pavel. "Dobývání hradu Skály v roce 1413 a husitská *teorie* války: Ke spisku Jakoubka ze Stříbra o duchovním *boji.*" *Mediaevalia Historica Bohemica* 9 (2003): 175–210.

———. "La noblesse hussite, entre chevalerie et guerre sainte." In *La noblesse et la croisade à la fin du Moyen Age*, ed. Martin Nejedlý and Jaroslav Svátek, 147–62. Toulouse: 2009.

Soustelle, Jacques. *La vie quotidienne des Aztèques à la veille de la conquête espagnole*. Paris: 1955.

Southern, Richard W. "Peter of Blois and the Third Crusade." In *Studies in Medieval History Presented to R. H. C. Davis*, ed. Henry Mayr-Harting and R. I. Moore, 207–18. London: 1985.

Stanley, John. *The Sociology of Virtue: The Political and Social Theories of George Sorel*. Berkeley, Calif.: 1981.

Stauffer, John. *The Black Hearts of Men: Radical Abolitionists and the Transformation of Race*. Cambridge, Mass.: 2002.

Stayer, James M. *Anabaptists and the Sword*. 2nd rev. ed. Eugene, Ore.: 1976.

———. *The German Peasants' War and Anabaptist Community of Goods*. Montreal: 1991.

Stein, Stephen J. "Jonathan Edwards and the Cultures of Biblical Violence." In *Jonathan Edwards at 300: Essays on the Tercentenary of His Birth*, ed. Harry S. Stout et al., 54–64. Lanham: 2005.

Stephanson, Anders. *Manifest Destiny: American Expansion and the Empire of Right*. New York: 1995.

Stephenson, Paul. "Religious Services for Byzantine Soldiers and the Possibility of Martyrdom, c. 400–c. 1000." In *Just War, Holy Wars and Jihads: Christian, Jewish and Muslim Encounters and Exchanges*, ed. Sohail H. Hasmi, 25–46. Oxford: 2012.

Stern, Alfred. "Adolf Hitler und Gustave Le Bon: Der Meister der Massenbewegung und sein Lehrer." *Geschichte in Wissenschaft und Unterricht* 6 (1955): 362–68.

Sternhel, Zeev. *The Anti-Enlightenment Tradition*. New Haven, Conn.: 2010.

Stewart, Columba. *"Working the Earth of the Heart": The Messalian Controversy in History, Texts, and Language to AD 431*. Oxford: 1991.

Stewart, James Brewer. *Holy Warriors: The Abolitionists and American Slavery*. New York: 1976.

Stock, Brian. *The Implications of Literacy*. Princeton, N.J.: 1983.

Stollberg-Rilinger, Barbara. "Knien vor Gott—Knien vor dem Kaiser: Zum Ritualwandel im Konfessionskonflikt." In *Zeichen- Rituale-Werte*, ed. Gerd Althof, 501–33. Symbolische Kommunikation und gesellschaftliche Wertesysteme 3. Münster: 2004. Tr. "Kneeling Before God—Kneeling Before the Emperor." In *Resonances: Historical Essays on Continuity and Change*, ed. Nils Holger Petersen et al., 149–72. Turnhout: 2011.

Stötzel, Georg and Martin Wengeler, *Kontroverse Begriffe: Geschichte des öffentlichen Sprachgebrauchs in der Bundesrepublik Deutschland*. Berlin: 1995.

Stout, Harry S. "Word and Order in Colonial New England." In *The Bible in America: Essays in Cultural History*, ed. Nathan O. Hatch and Mark A. Noll, 19–38. Oxford: 1982.

Strayer, Joseph R. "France: The Holy Land, the Chosen People, and the Most Christian King." In *Action and Conviction in Early Modern Europe: Essays in Memory of E. H. Harbison*, ed. Theodore K. Rabb and Jerrold E. Seigel, 3–16. Princeton, N.J.: 1969. Repr. in idem, *Medieval Statecraft and the Perspectives of History: Essays*, 300–314. Princeton, N.J.: 1971.

Strickland, Matthew. *War and Chivalry: The Conduct and Perception of War in England and Normandy, 1066–1217*. Cambridge: 1996.

Stroumsa, Guy Gedaliahu. *Barbarian Philosophy: The Religious Revolution of Early Christianity*. Tübingen: 1999.

———. "Early Christianity as Radical Religion: Context and Implications." *Israel Oriental Studies* 14 (1994): 173–93.

———. "Mystical Jerusalems." In *Jerusalem: Its Sanctity and Centrality to Judaism, Christianity, and Islam*, ed. Lee I. Levine, 15–40. New York: 1999.

Süllwold, Lieselotte. "Stationen in der Entwicklung von Terroristen: Psychologische Aspekte biographischer Daten." In *Lebenslaufanalysen*, ed. Herbert Jäger, Gerhard Schmidtchen, and eadem, 79–116. Analysen zum Terrorismus 2. Opladen: 1981.

Swanson, Guy E. *Religion and regime: A Sociological Analysis of the Reformation*. Ann Arbor, Mich.: 1967.

Szabó-Bechstein, Brigitte. *"Libertas ecclesiae": Ein Schlüsselbegriff des Investiturstreits*. Studi Gregoriani 12. Rome: 1985.

Szumowski, Wladyslaw. *Névroses et psychoses au Moyen Age et au début des temps modernes.* Paris: 1939.

Tallett, Frank. "Robespierre and Religion." In *Robespierre,* ed. Colin Haydon and William Doyle, 92–108. Cambridge: 1999.

Talmon, Jacob L. *The Origins of Totalitarian Democracy.* London: 1952.

Tanz, Sabine. *Jeanne d'Arc: Spätmittelalterliche Mentalität im Spiegel eines Weltbildes.* Forschungen zur Mittelalterlichen Geschichte 33. Weimar: 1991.

Taylor, Charles. "Modes of Secularism." In *Secularism and Its Critics,* ed. Rajeev Bhargava, 31–53. Delhi-New York: 1998.

Taylor, Craig. *Jeanne d'Arc: La pucelle.* Manchester: 2006.

Tellenbach, Gerd. *Libertas: Kirche und Weltordnung im Zeitalter des Investiturstreites.* Leipzig: 1936. Partial tr. R[alph] F[rancis] Bennett, *Church, State, and Christian Society.* Oxford: 1940. Rev. ed. Toronto: 1991.

Throop, Palmer A. *Criticism of the Crusades: A Study of Public Opinion and Crusade Propaganda.* Amsterdam: 1940.

Throop, Susanna A. *Crusading as an Act of Vengeance, 1095–1216.* Farnham: 2011.

Tierney, Brian. *Foundations of the Conciliar Theory: The Contribution of the Medieval Canonists from Gratian to the Great Schism.* Rev. ed. Leiden: 1998.

Tolmein, Oliver. *Vom Deutschen Herbst zum 11. September: Die RAF, der Terrorismus und der Staat.* Hamburg: 2002.

Toman, Hugo. *Husitské valecnictvi.* Prague: 1898.

Toscano, Alberto. *Fanaticism: On the Uses of an Idea.* London: 2010.

Townshend, Charles. *Terrorism: A Very Short Introduction.* Oxford: 2002.

Treadgold, Warren. "Byzantium, the Reluctant Warrior." In *Noble Ideals and Bloody Realities: Warfare in the Middle Ages,* ed. Niall Christie and Maya Yazigi, 209–33. Leiden: 2006.

Trexler, Richard. "Review to Lester K. Little, *Religious Poverty and the Profit Economy in Medieval Europe.*" *Speculum* 55, 4 (1980): 809–12.

Trimondi, Victor and Victoria Trimondi. *Krieg der Religionen: Politik, Glaube und Terror im Zeichen der Apokalypse.* Munich: 2006.

Troeltsch, Ernst. *The Social Teachings of the Christian Churches,* tr. Olive Wyan. 2 vols. London: 1931.

Tucker, Robert C. "Stalin, Bukharin, and History as Conspiracy." In *The Great Purge Trials,* ed. Tucker and Stephen Cohen, ix–xlviii. New York: 1965.

Tyerman, Christopher. *The Invention of the Crusades.* Basingstoke: 1998.

Vale, Malcolm. *Charles VII.* Berkeley, Calif.: 1973.

Van der Knaap, Ewout. "The New Executioners' Arrival: German Left-Wing Terrorism and the Memory of the Holocaust. " In *Baader-Meinhof Returns,* ed. Gerrit-Jan Berendse and Ingo Cornils, 285–99. Amsterdam and New York: 2008.

Van Kley, Dale. "Christianity as Chrysalis and Casualty of Modernity: The Problem of Dechristianization in the French Revolution." *American Historical Review* 108, 4 (2003): 1081–1104.

———. *The Religious Origins of the French Revolution: From Calvin to the Civil Constitution of the Clergy, 1560–1791.* New Haven, Conn.: 1996.

———. "The Religious Origins of the French Revolution, 1560–1791." In *From Deficit to Deluge: The*

Origins of the French Revolution, ed. Thomas E. Kaiser and idem, 104–38, 288–94. Stanford, Calif.: 2011.

Varon, Jeremy. *Bringing the War Home: The Weather Underground, the Red Army Faction, and Revolutionary Violence in the Sixties and Seventies.* Berkeley, Calif.: 2004.

Vauchez, André. "La paix dans les mouvements religieux populaires." In *Pace e guerra nel basso medioevo*, 313–33. Atti dei convegni dell'Accademia tudertina e del Centro di studi sulla spiritualita' medievale 40. Spoleto: 2004.

Vaughan, Alden T. *New England Frontier: Puritans and Indians, 1620–1675.* Boston: 1965. 3rd ed. Norman, Okla.: 1995.

Veyne, Paul *Comment on écrit l'Histoire.* Paris: 1971. Tr., *Writing History: Essays on Epistemology.* Manchester: 1984.

Viallaneix, Paul. "Réformation et révolution." In *The French Revolution and the Creation of Modern Political Culture*, vol. 3, *The Transformation of Political Culture, 1789–1848*, ed. François Furet and Mona Ozouf, 359–74. Oxford: 1989.

Vidal-Naquet, Pierre. "Du bon usage de la trahison." Preface to *Flavius Josèphe: La guerre des Juifs*, tr. Pierre Savinel, 8–115. Paris: 1977.

Violante, Cinzo. "La pataria e la militia Dei nelle fonti e nella realtà." In *"Militia Christi" e Crociata nei secoli XI-XIII, Atti della undecima Settimana internazionale di studio, Mendola, 28/08–1/09 1989*, 103–28. Miscellanea del Centro di Studi Medioevali 30. Milan: 1992.

———. *La pataria milanese e la riforma ecclesiastica, Le premesse (1045–1057).* Rome: 1955.

Voegelin, Eric. *Die politischen Religionen.* Stockholm: 1939. Tr. *The Political Religions.* Lewiston, N.Y.: 1985.

Vogel, Jürgen. *Gregor VII. und Heinrich IV. nach Canossa: Zeugnisse ihres Selbstverständnisses.* Berlin: 1983.

Vovelle, Michel. *La Révolution contre l'Église: De la raison à l'Etre Suprême.* Brussels: 1988. Rev. ed. Paris: 2001.

———. *Religion et Révolution: La déchristianisation de l'an II.* Paris: 1976.

Wachtel, Andrew. *Making a Nation, Breaking a Nation: Literature and Cultural Politics in Yugoslavia.* Stanford, Calif.: 1998.

Wagner, Murray L. *Petr Chelčický: A Radical Separatist in Hussite Bohemia.* Scottsdale, Ariz.: 1983.

Wahnich, Sophie. "De l'économie émotive de la Terreur." *Annales, Histoire, Siences Sociales* 57, 4 (2002): 889–913.

———. *La liberté ou la mort: Essai sur la Terreur et le terrorisme.* Paris: 2003. Tr. *In Defence of the Terror: Liberty or Death in the French Revolution.* London: 2012.

Waite, Robert. *The Psychopathic God: Adolf Hitler.* New York: 1977.

Walicki, Andrzej. *Marxism and the Leap to the Kingdom of Freedom: The Rise and Fall of the Communist Utopia.* Stanford, Calif.: 1995.

Walker, Daniel Pickering. *Unclean Spirits: Possession in France and England in the Late Sixteenth and Early Seventeenth Centuries.* Philadelphia: 1981.

Walker, Phillip L. "A Bioarchaeological Perspective on the History of Violence." *Annual Review of Anthropology* 30 (2001): 573–96.

Walther, Rudolf. "Terror, Terrorismus." In *Geschichtliche Grundbegriffe: Historisches Lexikon zur politisch-sozialen Sprache in Deutschland*, ed. Otto Brunner, Werner Conze, and Reinhard Koselleck, 6: 323–444. Stuttgart: 2004.

Walzer, Michael. *Exodus and Revolution*. New York: 1985.

Warren, W[ilfred] L[ewis]. *Henry II*. Berkeley, Calif.: 1973.

Wayman, Dorothy G. "The Chancellor and Jeanne d'Arc." *Franciscan Studies* 17 (1957): 273–305.

Weber, Max. *The Disenchantment of the World: A Political History of Religion*. Tr. Princeton, N.J.: 1997.

———. "Politik als Beruf." In *Max Weber Gesamtausgabe*, ed. Wolfgang J. Mommsen and Wolfgang Schluchter. Vol. 1, 113–252. Tübingen: 1992. Tr. Peter Lassmann and Ronald Speirs, "The Profession and Vocation of Politics." In *Max Weber, Political Writings*, 309–69. Cambridge: 1994.

———. "The Social Psychology of World Religions." In *From Max Weber: Essays in Sociology*, ed. H. H. Gerth and C. Wright Mills, 267–302. New York: 1946.

Wehler, Hans-Ulrich. "Psychoanalysis and History." *Social Research* 47, 3 (1980): 519–36.

Weinberg, Albert K. *Manifest Destiny: A Study of Expansionist Nationalism in American History*. Baltimore: 1935. Repr. New York: 1979.

Weiner, Amir. "Introduction." In *Landscaping the Human Garden: Twentieth-Century Population Management in Comparative Perspective*, ed. idem, 1–18. Stanford, Calif.: 2003.

Weiner, Eugene and Anita Weiner. *The Martyr's Conviction: A Sociological Analysis*. Atlanta: 1990.

Weinfurter, Stefan. "Die Macht der Reformidee: Ihre Wirkkraft in Ritualen, Politik und Moral der spätsalischen Zeit." In *Ordnungsvorstellungen und Frömmigkeitspraxis im Hoch- und Spätmittelalter*, ed. Jörg Rogge, 13–39. Korb: 2008.

Weinhauer, Klaus. "Terrorismus in der Bundesrepublik der Siebzigerjahre: Aspekte einer Sozial- und Kulturgeschichte der Inneren Sicherheit." *Archiv für Sozialgeschichte* 44 (2004): 219–42.

Weinstein, Daniel. *Savonarola and Florence: Prophecy and Patriotism in the Renaissance*. Princeton, N.J.: 1970.

Weitzman, Stephen. *Surviving Sacrilege: Cultural Persistence in Jewish Antiquity*. Cambridge, Mass.: 2005.

Wentzlaff-Eggebert, Friedrich-Wilhelm. *Kreuzzugsdichtung des Mittelalters: Studien zu ihrer geschichtlichen und dichterischen Wirklichkeit*. Berlin: 1960.

Werth, Nicolas. *1936–1938, Les Procès de Moscou*. Rev. ed. Paris: 2006.

Whalen, Brett Edward. *Dominion of God: Christendom and Apocalypse in the Middle Ages*. Cambridge, Mass.: 2009.

White, Richard. *The Middle Ground: Indians, Empires and Republics in the Great Lake Region, 1650–1815*. Cambridge: 1991. Rev. ed. Cambridge: 2011.

Winkler, Willi. *Die Geschichte der RAF*. Berlin: 2007.

Wood, Gordon. *Empire of Liberty: A History of the Early American Republic, 1789–1915*. Oxford: 2009.

Woodworth, Steven E. *While God Is Marching On: The Religious World of Civil War Soldiers*. Lawrence, Kan.: 2001.

Wucinic, Wayne and Thomas Emmert, eds. *Kosovo: The Legacy of a Medieval Battle*. Minneapolis: 1991.

Yuval, Israel Jacob. *Two Nations in Your Womb: Perceptions of Jews and Christians in the Middle Ages*. Tr. Berkeley, Calif.: 2006.

Zacour, Norman P. "The Children's Crusade." In *A History of the Crusades*, ed. Kenneth M. Setton. Vol. 2, 325–42. Madison, Wis.: 1969.

Zey, Claudia. "Im Zentrum des Streits: Mailand und die oberitalienischen Kommunen zwischen regnum und sacerdotium." In *Vom Umbruch zur Erneuerung? Das beginnende 12. Jahrhundert: Positionen der Forschung*, ed. Nicola Karthaus, Jörg Jarnut, and Matthias Wemhof, 595–611. Munich: 2006.

Zilboorg, Gregory and George W. Henry. *A History of Medical Psychology*. New York: 1941.

Zumhagen, Olaf. *Religiöse Konflikte und kommunale Entwicklung: Mailand, Cremona, Piacenza und Florenz zur Zeit der Pataria*. Cologne: 2002.

Zwierlein, Cornell. "Grenzen der Versicherbarkeit als Epochenindikatoren? Von der europäischen Sattelzeit zur Globalisierung des 19. Jahrhunderts." *Geschichte und Gesellschaft* 38 (2012): 423–52.

Index

abolitionism, nineteenth-century American, 41–43, 308n195; Brown and, 15, 42–43, 64, 132–33, 154–61, 175; as madness, 132; pacifists' approval of radicals' use of force, 79, 157–58, 336n29; Quakers, 79, 158; rhetoric of pollution and purification, 51. *See also* Brown, John

Acts of Marian and James, 121

Adalbert of Acqui, 225

Adams, William, 76

Adhémar de Chabannes, 101, 262

Adhémar, Bishop of Le Puy, 168, 172–73, 176, 247, 342n121

Adorno, Theodor, 141, 148, 333n201

Aelred of Rielvaux, 274

'Aflaq, Michel, 240

agency, divine/human, 247, 253–61; colonial America, 253, 256; early modern Wars of Religion, 253–57; English Civil War, 255–56; evangelical American Christianity, 253; First Crusade chroniclers, 258–61, 271–72; French Wars of Religion, 254–55; Jeanne d'Arc, 257–58; Münster Anabaptists, 256

Ailly, Pierre d', 230

Alamany, Fray Joan, 55

Alan of Lille, 186

Albert of Aachen, 266–67, 362–63n102

Albigensian Crusade, 221

Alcuin, 270, 291

Alexander II, Pope, 59

Alexander Minorita, 281–82

Alexander the Great, 96

Alexius, Byzantine emperor, 282

Allenby, Edmund, 54

Alphandéry, Paul, 187–88

America, colonial, 10, 40–41, 76–77; and Devil/Satan, 16–17, 40, 42; and devolution of duty to resist, 205–6; Fort Mystic massacre (1637) and Pequot War, 42, 89, 141, 205–6, 275–76; and liberty, 218; and Native religion, 40, 149; notion of regeneration, 46; notions of human/divine agency, 253, 256; postrevolutionary era, 40, 307n189; Puritans' holy warfare, 5, 35–36, 40, 141, 275–76; witchcraft scare, 40, 42. *See also* American Revolution/ War for Independence

America, nineteenth-century: Episcopal Church, 216–17; images of fanatical madness, 132–33; "manifest destiny" and expansionism, 50, 65, 231; Protestant belief in history moved forward by conflict, 287. *See also* abolitionism, nineteenth-century American; American Civil War

American Civil War, 41–43; and Episcopal Church, 216–17; and evangelical culture, 41–42; as holy war, 40–42; militaristic two swords imagery, 77; notion of regeneration, 46, 47; and notion of temporal movement from Old World to New, 62; pacifists' opposition, 83; and Protestant belief in History moved forward by conflict, 287; rhetoric of pollution and purification, 46, 51–52; as war about purification of the moral self, 46, 51–52; as war for "freedom" (liberty), 57; as war generating martyrdom/martyrs' consecrating blood, 49; as world's war, 47, 53, 54. *See also* abolitionism, nineteenth-century American; Brown, John

American Review, 231

American Revolution/War for Independence: as fulfillment of eschatological prophecies, 89; as merciful war, 50; and notion of temporal movement from Old World to New, 49; as war about purification of the moral self, 52; as war for "freedom" (liberty), 48; as world's war, 47, 53

American wars, 45–66; anxieties over contagion/ contamination, 231; connections between war, empire, and liberty, 48–49, 50–51, 57, 66; and

Acknowledgments

Many factors came into the making of this book. Geographically, it was produced between America and Europe. This takes some explaining in the credits. First, my colleagues at the Stanford University Department of History allowed me pursuits hardly imaginable in many other places. Alongside them, sharp, select students honed my thought. In Vienna, where I am now, some no less sharp students have kept morale and the mind afloat, in particular those who took part on my seminars on the massacres of 1099 in Jerusalem.

For I landed in Vienna. Inspired, not to say visionary, decisions by Stanford University's leadership convinced me that the wind of freedom, famous through the local motto, *Die Luft der Freiheit weht*, blew at my home institution with such an intensity that I could not help but be diverted off course to Old Europe. Here I can mourn my sins, and regret, like Nikolai Bukharin (see Chapter 4), to have misread history's trajectory. And, like that famous Roman magistrate, ponder, *Quid est veritas?* As to Stanford, this book is dedicated to two men who disappeared tragically from my horizons: Provost Condoleezza Rice's worthy successor John Etchemendy, and Google board member and University president John Hennessy. How not to be totally impressed by a man who uttered "extraordinary" or "amazing" every other sentence in the Faculty Senate, and whose enterprising spirit favored at Google much data-gathering, now thanks to the NSA in good, freedom-loving hands? Or by his second-in-command, whose enthusiastic concern for physical immortality kept all of us in his Stanford flock in good health? It is with a smile that I recall his shepherding employees and colleagues along Stanford's sun-drenched paths. May the Lord of Hosts reward them as they deserve, alongside the holy warrior George W. Bush.

Besides debts to the irresistible wings of change, I have to acknowledge also debts to friends and colleagues. I want to thank in particular my research assistants Kiersten Cray Jakobsen (Stanford) and Katharina Hausmann (Köln) respectively for Bolshevik Russian and for help on the RAF. My assistant in in

Vienna, Alexandra Kaar, both kept me sane in a new environment and spared me the drudgery of compiling the bibliography from the endnotes. Juri Lozowoj took a last look at the Russian semantic fields undergirding Chapter 4. Guy Lobrichon listened to my ideas and forgot, characteristically, to remind me that some of the best ones came from him. Next to them my thanks go, alphabetically, to Dominique Alibert, Salman Al-Rashid, Gerd Althoff, Charlotte Visborg Andreasen, William Arkin, Keith Baker, Brad Bouley, Alain Boureau, Claudia Brosseder, Chris Clark, Mark Cohen, Charly Coleman, David Como, Denis Crouzet, Abedelkebir Ismaili el-Alaoui, Luc Ferrier, Jean Flori, Robert von Friedeburg, Anna Jagosova, Mayke de Jong, M. Cecilia Gaposchkin, Igor Gorevich, Brad Gregory, Sven Rune Havsteen, Jochen Hellbeck, Carsten Selch Jensen, Colin Jones, H. Howard Kaminsky, Sara Lipton, Jehangir Malegam, Petr Maťa, Elisabeth Mégier, Jeff Miner, Mette Birkedal Nielsen, Nils Holger Petersen, Barbara Pitkin, Gian Luca Potestà, Jack Rakove, Amy Remensnyder, Carine van Rhijn, Alex Robbins, Aron Rodrigue, Aram Roston, Stefan Scholz, Sumi Shimahara, Laura Smoller, Brent Sockness, Pavel Soukup, Martial Staub, Barbara Stollberg-Rilinger, Laura Stokes, Caroline Winterer, Björn Weiler, Amir Weiner, Steven Weitzman, Brett Whalen, and Richard White. Jay Rubenstein, Pavlina Richterova, and Wolfgang Schmale read the whole manuscript. May they be thanked for this labor. Ed Peters adjudicated and commented for the University of Pennsylvania Press. His remarks have also been precious. So has been the good cheer and quiet intelligence of the series editor, Jerry Singerman. A second anonymous reader, whose fundamental Girardian positions cannot be reconciled with mine, also provided suggestions and energetic rejoinders. While I would never convert to her (or his) church, I am quite grateful.

Institutions should also be thanked. First of all the ACLS, which financed a research year at Yale during academic year 2005–2006. There, I was hosted, generously, by the Whitney Humanities Center and its director, the regretted María Rosa Menocal. The Department of History at Stanford, which allowed me to take this leave, and the then Dean of Humanities and Sciences, Sharon Long, secured additional financing. Thanks also to Dean Theune-Vogt and the Faculty of Historical Studies at the University of Vienna for financial aid toward printing. Intellectually, I benefited from audiences at the Whitney in New Haven, and at the Universities of Heidelberg, Münster, and Wien, Paris IV Sorbonne, the EHESS Paris, the universities of Avignon, Utrecht, and Rotterdam, and det Teologiske Fakultet Københavns Universitet. I shall not forget the first institution of all, the Garden of Eden.

My thanks to Brepols Publishers, who allowed me to rework into Chapter 4 my "Martyrdom in the West: Vengeance, Purge, Salvation, and History," published in *Resonances: Historical Essays on Continuity and Change*, ed. Nils Holger Petersen, Andreas Bücker, and Eyolf Oestrem (Turnhout: 2011), 21–56. I have freely drawn on earlier publications: "La Vengeance de Dieu: de l'exégèse patristique à la réforme ecclésiastique et à la première croisade," in *La Vengeance, 400–1200*, ed. Dominique Barthélemy, François Bougard, and Régine Le Jean (Rome: Collection de l'École Française de Rome 357, 2006), 451–86; "Some Thoughts on the Christian Theology of Violence, Medieval and Modern, from the Middle Ages to the French Revolution," *Rivista di Storia del Cristianesimo* 5 (2008): 9–28; "Religion, Coercion and Violence in Medieval Rituals," in *State, Power, and Violence*, vol. 2, *Rituals of Power and Consent*, ed. Bernd Scheidmüller (Wiesbaden: Harrassowitz, 2010), 157–70; "Exégèse et violence dans la tradition occidentale," *Annali di Storia Moderna e Contemporanea* 16 (2010): 131–44; *L'empreinte du Moyen Age: La guerre sainte* (Avignon: EUA, 2012).

Given my intellectual trajectory, this book is dedicated to the memory of Gerard Caspary, a man who escaped the July 1942 Grande Rafle, a man who taught me much. Alas, he did not live to see these pages' completion. Yet I like to think that he would have read them; penned comments all over them; grunted (he did grunt when happy); smiled; and begun a long conversation with something like "this is not quite right, Philippe." To him I owe more than can ever be returned.

Fra Ørkenen

CPSIA information can be obtained
at www.ICGtesting.com
Printed in the USA
BVOW03s2005020817

490581BV00002BA/3/P